Slavery
in Africa

SLAVERY IN AFRICA

Historical and Anthropological Perspectives

edited by
Suzanne Miers and Igor Kopytoff

The University of Wisconsin Press

Published 1977
The University of Wisconsin Press
Box 1379, Madison, Wisconsin 53701
The University of Wisconsin Press, Ltd.
70 Great Russell Street, London

First printing

Printed in the United States of America

For LC CIP information see the colophon

ISBN 0-299-07330-0

Contributors

Ralph A. Austen
History
University of Chicago

Stephen Baier
History
Boston University

Bernd Baldus
Sociology
University of Toronto

Roberta Ann Dunbar
History
University of North
Carolina at Chapel Hill

John J. Grace
History
Jos University
Jos, Nigeria

Gerald W. Hartwig
History
Duke University

Svend E. Holsoe
Anthropology
University of Delaware

Allen Isaacman
History
University of Minnesota

Barbara Isaacman
Sociologist
Minneapolis, Minnesota

Martin A. Klein
History
University of Toronto

Igor Kopytoff
Anthropology
University of Pennsylvania

Paul E. Lovejoy
History
York University

Carol P. MacCormack
Anthropology
Cambridge University

Wyatt MacGaffey
Anthropology
Haverford College

Suzanne Miers
History
Ohio University

Joseph C. Miller
History
University of Virginia

K. Nwachukwu-Ogedengbe
History
Institute of Continuing Education
Warri, Nigeria

Thomas Tlou
History
University of Botswana
Lesotho and Swaziland
(Gaborone, Botswana)

Victor C. Uchendu
Anthropology
University of Illinois

James H. Vaughan
Anthropology
Indiana University

Contents

Igor Kopytoff and Suzanne Miers

Slavery and Freedom: Western Concepts and African Realities, **3**. Rights-in-Persons in African Societies, **7**. Implications for the Definition of 'Slavery,' **11**. The Acquisition of 'Slaves' in Africa, **12**. The Outsider and His Marginality, **14**. Dimensions of Marginality in Relation to Mobility, **18**. Conditions and Constraints in the Institutionalization of Marginality, **21**. The Humanity of the Outsider, **21**. The 'Slavery'-to-Kinship Continuum, **22**. The Outsider and the Acquisitor's Kin Group, **24**. Abolition of Marginality through Dissociation: Redemption and Manumission, **26**. Affective Marginality and Worldly Success, **27**. Incorporation of the First Generation into the Kin Group, **29**. First-Generation Males in the Kin Group, **29**. First-Generation Females in the Kin Group, **30**. The Incorporation of the Second Generation, **32**. The Position of 'Slave' Offspring in the Kin Group, **34**. Incorporation into the Society as a Whole: The Role of the Acquisitor, **39**. The Structure of Marginalities and the Existence of 'Slave' Strata, **40**. Treatment and Resistance: Some Problems of Comparative Study, **49**. Versatility and Variation in the Use of Acquired Persons, **55**. Numbers and Concentrations of 'Slaves,' **59**. The Dynamics of African 'Slavery,' **61**. The Problem of the Origins of African 'Slavery,' **66**. The Impact of the Overseas Trade and of Abolition, **69**. Addendum: A Plea on Terminology, **76**. References, **78**.

Maps

Preface

This work has been nearly a decade in the making. It springs from two different sources. It was conceived when one of us, Suzanne Miers, searching for material on African slavery to incorporate in a work on the slave trade, found a dearth of data that would allow comparison between different African societies and would permit broad generalization. Meanwhile, the other of us, Igor Kopytoff, struck by the clearly unsatisfactory existing generalizations about African slavery scattered through the literature and the lack of general theory on slavery in the social sciences, was seeking to organize a conference on the subject. The need to fill these strange lacunae on so important a subject was confirmed by each of us separately in the seminars we held on African slavery—one of us at the University of Wisconsin, at Madison, and Ohio University; and the other at Bryn Mawr College.

When we finally met, in 1971, through the efforts of George Brookes, we found we had between us an array of prospective contributors from history, anthropology, and sociology, enabling us to tap oral as well as archival and literary sources and to cover many different kinds of societies with a wide geographical distribution.

The final selection of contributions was, we must confess, less precisely representative of the range of societies and areas than we originally wanted. Some scholars, approached because they had worked among particular peoples, had insufficient information on the subject, while others could not meet our deadlines and withdrew. The resulting spread and sample, if not ideal, is surely wide-ranging enough to open discussion on this long-neglected topic, as well as informative and suggestive enough to give rise to the broad generalizations in our Introduction. The fact that our contributors belong to various disciplines is particularly gratifying as it enables the reader to appreciate differences in approach to a similar topic. Ralph A. Austen, Stephen Baier, Roberta Ann Dunbar, John J.

Grace, Gerald W. Hartwig, Allen Isaacman, Martin A. Klein, Paul E. Lovejoy, Joseph C. Miller, K. Nwachukwu-Ogedengbe, and Thomas Tlou are historians. Svend E. Holsoe, Carol P. MacCormack, Wyatt MacGaffey, Victor C. Uchendu, and James H. Vaughan are anthropologists. Barbara Isaacman and Bernd Baldus are sociologists. One of the editors, Suzanne Miers, is a historian and the other, Igor Kopytoff, is an anthropologist.

To give the book unity we issued a comprehensive guide with some broad theoretical musings and a list of the topics contributors were to attempt to cover. Each of them, however, was asked to follow his research interests and this, we think, produced articles far more interesting, varied, and suggestive than would have emerged from a mechanical adherence to a rigid set of questions. Their spontaneity brought up issues, perspectives, and ideas that would not have emerged otherwise and our Introduction is, as a result, all the more comprehensive as well as indicative of the need for further and fuller exploration of the subject.

All was done in a rather old-fashioned way—no grant supported our efforts, no conferences were held, and we struggled with difficulties of time and space. One or the other of us and many of our contributors were often in Africa. The editing of chapters and the revisions by the authors had to be fitted into other research and busy teaching schedules. We managed to organize one panel at the African Studies Association meetings in 1972; otherwise, discussion with the contributors as a group had to be conducted by mail. We owe a particular debt to our authors, who resisted the temptation and often considerable pressure to publish their chapters elsewhere and who had often to update their materials in the face of new research. This work has been a joint venture requiring patience and forbearance from contributors and publisher alike. We discussed our Introduction in settings ranging from a flat in London to a medieval farmhouse in southern France, in the icy halls of which we contemplated slavery in tropical Africa. As editors, we owe a special debt to Barbara Klamon Kopytoff, whose comments, questions, and comparative perspective from the Caribbean sharpened many issues raised in the Introduction. For their particularly helpful comments on the Introduction we must also thank Ralph A. Austen, Bernd Baldus, Ronald Cohen, Philip D. Curtin, Stanley L. Engerman, Eugene D. Genovese, Gerald W. Hartwig, Martin A. Klein, and James H. Vaughan.

Since we began this book, interest in slavery, African and other, has risen dramatically. Research is being done on it in various societies, ancient and modern. The subject is being examined from a comparative perspective, and the study of New World slavery has grown into a major intellectual enterprise. For Africa specifically, the historical survey by

Allan G. B. Fisher and Humphrey J. Fisher, *Slavery and Muslim Society in Africa,* came out in 1970; and, as our volume was being completed and put together, Claude Meillassoux's *L'esclavage en Afrique précoloniale* (1975), containing original articles by anthropologists, made a major contribution to the understanding of African slavery. Everything points to a continuing growth of interest in the subject. We hope this book will serve to enliven the discussion among scholars by giving facts and a framework that will spur further research on a topic still to be explored not only in the context of African history and anthropology but also in comparison with similar institutions elsewhere in the world.

Suzanne Miers
London, England

Igor Kopytoff
Palm, Pennsylvania

August 1976

Introduction

Part I

1

African 'Slavery' as an Institution of Marginality

Igor Kopytoff and Suzanne Miers

SLAVERY AND FREEDOM: WESTERN CONCEPTS AND AFRICAN REALITIES

Any discussion of African 'slavery' in English is necessarily bedeviled by the fact that the word conjures up definite images in the Western mind. Anglo-Americans in particular tend to visualize slavery as they believe it was practiced on the plantations of the southern United States and the British Caribbean. This image may not be historically accurate but it was widely publicized in the literature and debates of the great nineteenth-century campaigns against slavery and the slave trade, and it has come to be widely accepted as the true picture of the normal form of slavery. Only comparatively recently have scholars begun to reveal the range of institutions in the Western Hemisphere that have been called slavery—revelations which show that the reality was far more complex than the stereotype.

The slave of the common Western image is first and foremost a commodity, to be bought and sold and inherited. He is a chattel, totally in the possession of another person who uses him for private ends. He has no control over his destiny, no choice of occupation or employer, no rights to property or marriage, and no control over the fate of his children. He can be inherited, moved, or sold without regard to his feelings, and may be ill-treated, sometimes even killed, with impunity. Furthermore, his progeny inherit his status. Slaves as a group form a "class" apart, at the very bottom of the social ladder, although they may in fact be more secure and

3

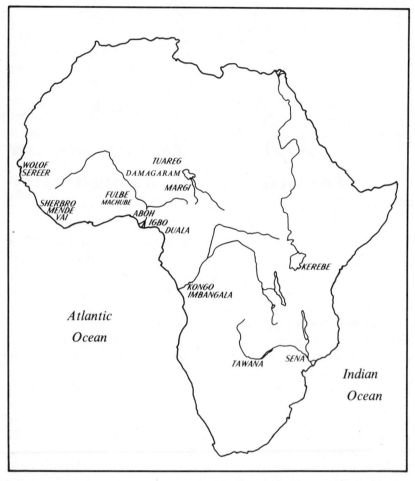

Cartographic Laboratory UW-Madison

Map 1. The Societies Discussed in This Volume

better provided for than some of the free. To Westerners, therefore, slaves constitute a social "stratum" and slavery is seen, like class and caste, as a form of "social stratification."

In this image, the antithesis of slavery is 'freedom,' in the sense that this term has also come to assume in the West. A 'free' man cannot be bought, sold, inherited, or physically ill-treated by another private individual. Theoretically, at least, he can choose his occupation, employer, and style of life. He can own and dispose of property, marry if and whom he wishes, and control his children until they in turn become free adults. In contrast to freedom, therefore, slavery means economic, social, and political deprivation, legal impotence and oppression, all this as part of a system of social stratification. Given this grim picture, it is assumed that all slaves must be unhappy, since their autonomy is so severely restricted. If they do not appear unhappy, then their autonomy is either not so limited or for some reason they do not feel that it is. These images of slavery and freedom are, to be sure, stereotypes—and modern ones at that (for the history of their development, see Davis 1966). They nevertheless have provided a frame of reference, a yardstick against which institutions in non-Western societies have been identified, named, measured, and compared.

It should be emphasized, as Victor Uchendu (Ch. 4) points out in his analysis of Igbo 'slavery,' that this modern Western stereotype of slavery covered in fact a "bundle" of traits, consisting of a number of elements— and these need not necessarily all occur together. For instance, a father, as in ancient Rome, could have rights over his children extending to life and death without their being considered slaves. Equally, a wife in Victorian England lost control of her property to her husband upon marriage but was still a 'free' woman. An indentured servant in the New World owed his labor to his master for a period of time but was still able to control much of his social life and to own property.

It was the total bundle of traits, however, forming the Western model of 'slavery,' that many Western observers and scholars had in mind when they considered African traditional societies. Consequently they soon found themselves in a dilemma. There clearly were persons in these societies who had been bought or captured (just as slaves in the West had been) and subsequently incorporated on a basis different from those born into them. They should therefore have been slaves, but there the similarity with the Western model often ended. Many of them seemed to live and work just as their so-called masters did, and Europeans, and often other Africans, could not tell them apart. Many were not even considered salable—and were therefore not chattels. In fact, sometimes 'free' people were sold and 'slaves' were not, or both could be sold. Some 'slaves' became rich and powerful and even bought people for themselves. Others were put to economic use—sometimes working on their masters' estates— but they did not form a distinct stratum or class apart. Many seemed not unhappy with their lot. In fact, they would sometimes turn down offers of freedom or escape. In all these cases, some but not all of the vital charac- teristics of the Western model of slavery were missing.

A common response was to call African 'slavery' "benign" because it did not correspond to the Western model. But this was simply to apply Western concepts of 'slavery' and 'freedom' to institutions in other cul- tural and historical contexts and, perhaps worse, to treat the African phenomenon as a deviation from the Western one—the latter being seen as the true norm. This begs the important question as to which is the norm in comparative historical and cultural perspective.

A second important problem to be borne in mind is the modern Westerner's essential squeamishness about the entire subject—a squeamishness partly born from his sense of guilt over the Atlantic slave trade and the subsequent treatment of its victims and their descendants in parts of the Western hemisphere. This squeamishness has affected, often perhaps unconsciously, much of the treatment of slavery by Western scholars.

Scholars have in fact tended to avoid the issue of African 'slavery' or to present it as almost entirely benign. The reasons for this await thorough study. Meillassoux (1975:14) points to the hesitation of anthropologists to dwell upon institutions such as slavery or human sacrifice for fear of contributing to the unfavorable stereotypes held by the wider public about cultures that anthropologists were committed to defend. He notes, by contrast, that anthropologists who are Africans treat African 'slavery' in a far more matter-of-fact way than do Westerners. We would like to suggest some additional reasons for the hesitations of Western scholars.

When anthropologists encountered 'slavery' in the field, it was already a moribund institution, greatly eroded by colonial control. It looked benign, it was benign, and informants presented it as benign because (as explained later in this chapter) the continuing relations with former 'slaves' had often been retranslated into a kinship idiom and often depended on a social myth of benignity. At the same time, early British functionalist anthropology (which dominated African anthropology) had an antihistorical bias. This made the anthropologist focus on the present reality around him, though he implicitly equated it with "traditional" Africa. This antihistoricism also discouraged reconstructions of the past and a historical use of oral tradition, while a measure of disciplinary arrogance questioned the reliability of anthropologically unsophisticated early travelers, whose picture of 'slavery' was less benign. What local historical background anthropologists usually obtained came from local administrative records, and these often had their own built-in distortions. As Manning (n.d.), for instance, suggests, the benign picture of internal African 'slavery' was cultivated by early colonial administrators as a way of avoiding the political problems of suppressing it or as an excuse for not suppressing it.[1]

1. Whatever the relative weight of these various factors, it remains true that slavery has received scarcely any theoretical attention in anthropology, where, until recently, most of the Africanist work was concentrated. Siegal's (1945) relatively lengthy general theoretical treatment stands out as a pioneering exception. With the recent renewal of interest in slavery, the vacuum in theoretical treatment is, as a result, often filled by going back to such dated analyses as that by Nieboer (1900), written at a time when there were scarcely any African data available.

Historians have equally only recently turned their attention to African internal 'slavery,' partly because African history itself has only become an important field of study in the last twenty-five years and first priority was naturally given to the reconstruction of basic events. Moreover, Western historians had some of the same hesitations as the anthropologists, upon whom indeed they largely relied for their cultural information. Only now is African social and economic history receiving the attention it deserves and consequently more and more research is being done on African 'slavery.'

It is not our aim to compare African 'slavery' with recent Western or indeed any other form of 'slavery.' Nor is our aim to find a definition that might fit all—a fruitless exercise in semantics. Rather, it is to present to the reader a series of studies examining the various African institutions that have been referred to as 'slavery' or seen as closely related phenomena, and to provide a framework within which these institutions can be understood and the full range of variations be clearly seen.

RIGHTS-IN-PERSONS IN AFRICAN SOCIETIES

At the heart of any discussion of 'slavery' in Africa—and indeed anywhere —lie the rights that one person or group exercises over another—what anthropologists call "rights-in-persons." Such rights, usually mutual but seldom equal, exist in almost all social relationships. Thus, children have the right to support and protection from their parents, who have the right to demand obedience from them; a husband in many Western societies could until recently expect domestic services from his wife in return for material support from him, and they had exclusive rights to each other's sexual activity, adultery on either side being grounds for divorce. Such rights need not be reciprocal: in many other societies, including most African ones, the husband is legally injured by his wife's adultery but she does not have exclusive sexual rights over him. Such rights-in-persons may cover not just a person's services but his entire person—thus, the father in ancient Rome could kill or sell his children.

When the question of rights-in-persons is considered in relation to African cultures, it becomes clear, first, that such rights tend to be explicitly recognized and precisely defined in law; second, that they are the subject of complex transactions; and, finally, that the position of the so-called 'slave' can only be understood in the general cultural context of these rights. It is therefore necessary at this point to discuss them in some detail.

Transactions[2] in rights-in-persons are an integral part of African systems of kinship and marriage. Through the payment of bridewealth,

2. The very useful term "transactions," as applied to formal transfers of rights-in-persons in the realm of kinship, has been used by Goodenough (1970) in examining "adoption" in Oceania.

the husband, and behind him his corporate kin group, acquire certain rights in his wife from her kin group; these usually include some rights in the children in addition to domestic services and sexual rights. In a matrilineal society, the right to claim the children as members of one's kin group is not transferred to the husband and they therefore belong to their mother's kin group. On the other hand, in a patrilineal society the husband acquires this right, and the children therefore belong to his group. Hence, in a patrilineal society, "brideprice," here called bridewealth, in fact includes a "childprice" (Jeffreys 1951). There can be variations in these transactions even in the same society. For example, among the Goba of Zambia (Lancaster 1971), children belong to their father's group only if the bridewealth is paid in cattle; otherwise they belong to their mother's lineage. Here, no kin group is consistently patrilineal or matrilineal; rather, it consists of members belonging to it sometimes through their fathers and sometimes through their mothers, depending on the marriage contract. Similarly, among the Ijo (Ijaw) of the Niger Delta, a man acquires control over his children if he pays a "big dowry," whereas payment of a "little dowry" enables his wife's lineage to retain her children. Significantly, however, the husband in the latter case may later acquire control over his children by additional payments for each child (Talbot 1932:189; Williamson 1962; Leis 1972:17-18).

The complexity and precision of transactions in rights-in-persons may be illustrated by a glance at the matrilineal Suku of Zaïre (see Kopytoff 1964). Here, marriage transactions involve, beside the bride and groom, three corporate groups: the groom's matrilineage, the bride's, and her father's. The prospective husband and his matrilineage hand the agreed bridewealth over to the bride's kin group and to her father; the father is entitled to two thirds of the amount in compensation for having safely raised his daughter. Through this transaction, the father surrenders to his daughter's lineage all claim to any share of bridewealth should she marry again, and he surrenders to the groom control over sexual access to his daughter; hitherto, it was he who collected fines from men caught making love to her. The groom also acquires the right to his bride's domestic labor and she moves to his village and begins to cultivate a field for him. He is now responsible for supplying her with a roof, utensils, meat, and clothes. He has not as yet, however, the right of sexual access to her. This he only acquires after he has presented her lineage elders—usually her mother's brother—with a goat and after this goat has been ritually sacrificed by her kin group.

The payment of bridewealth gives the husband the right to expect sons born of the marriage to live with him all his life and to collect two thirds of the bridewealth paid for his daughters. His children, however, will all belong to their mother's matrilineage, owing their primary allegiance to it and holding all property in trust for it. Should the marriage end in divorce, the bride's lineage must return to the husband the amount he paid in bride-wealth, minus half for every daughter and a quarter for every son (thus, if there are several children, the husband gets nothing at all back). These deductions for the children are made because the husband will later profit from them: the sons will live with him, help him, and give him game, and the daughters will enrich him with part of the bridewealth that they will fetch when they grow up. However, at the time of the divorce, the husband may choose to demand the complete reimbursement of everything he had paid; but if he does this, he loses all his rights in his children. These rights will be transferred to their matrilineage. Thus, as a result of a transfer of wealth, the matrilineage now holds the totality of rights in the offspring and has the complete power to dispose of them as it wishes.

It must be stressed that these transactions are made, and the rights are held, by kin groups acting as corporate bodies and transcending the individuals who belong to them, just as Western corporations transcend their owners and management. Thus, when the husband dies, his various rights are inherited by his lineage. In many parts of Africa, such rights-in-peope may belong to political offices. When a chief dies, his successor usually becomes the legal husband, father, and uncle to the surviving wives, children, nephews, and nieces of all previous incumbents of his office, inheriting all their rights. Equally, other forms of corporations may hold rights-in-persons. An unusual instance is found among the Lele of Zaïre (Douglas 1963); here, all the men of an age-set of a village could jointly acquire a woman who then became the honored and pampered "village wife," producing children whose "father" was deemed to be the village as a whole. It was also possible in some societies, such as the Fon kingdom of Dahomey (Herskovits 1938) or the Igbo (Uchendu 1965), for a woman to acquire the rights of a husband over another woman. By this device, a childless wealthy woman could found a lineage of her own, since the children of her "wife," sired by an approved mate, belonged to the lineage of their female "father."

It is clear from these examples that rights-in-persons and intricate transactions in these rights occur between individuals and offices and also, and indeed more commonly, between corporate groups. Further-more, these rights can be manipulated to increase the number of people in one's kin group, to gather dependents and supporters, and to build up wealth and power (see, for example, Schneider 1968 and Tardits 1970). Westerners tend to regard these transactions with some ambivalence. Although few today would go as far as the League of Nations in 1926 and define bridewealth and transfers of children of the type just described as "slavery," nevertheless there are logical extensions of this system that seem to the Westerner highly suspect, and these were in fact outlawed by colonial governments (see United Nations 1956).

For instance, a lineage in need of money, or forced to pay compensation for a homicide or some other crime, or unable to feed all its members in time of famine, might transfer all of its rights in a person to another lineage in return for goods or money. The individual, usually a child, would now be totally at the disposal of the recipient lineage, to which he would "belong," and which could do with him as it wished, just as it could with those born into the group. Alternatively, the transfer of such rights could be temporary. This is usually called "pawning" in the literature and was extremely widespread. In exchange for a loan, a kin group would transfer to its creditor a pawn—often a girl—who could be redeemed later. If the debt was never paid, the pawn remained permanently and totally transferred to the creditors. The pawn was not a hostage to insure good behavior but an object of equivalent value to the loan, and the whole transaction was a pecuniary one. Joseph Miller (Ch. 8), describing this system among the matrilineal Imbangala, shows that creditors acquired certain rights in the pawn for the duration of the pawn's residence. If a female pawn married, for instance, the creditor lineage received the bride-wealth. It also held the important right of affiliating her children, although her own lineage enjoyed the privilege of "buying" them back if it wished to have them as members.

Crucial to an understanding of rights-in-persons in Africa is an appreciation of the position of the individual in his kin group. Members of such corporate groups may be said to "belong" to them in the double sense of the word in English—that is, they are members of the group and also part of its wealth, to be disposed of in its best interests. In order to distinguish between these two concepts, henceforward "belonging to" will be used to denote that the individual is part of the wealth of his corporate group, while "belonging in" will refer to his position as a member of the group. In theory, the best interests of the group as a whole override the personal interests of each of its members, whatever the member's age. Elders, however, have a higher position in the lineage hierarchy and a greater participation in its administration than the younger members. The children and younger adults are the most easily disposed of in times of crisis, and are also the most likely to find a buyer, but older people may also be sacrificed in the best interests of the group—thus old men convicted of witchcraft may be executed to eliminate a danger in its midst.

Several points may now be stressed. Concepts of rights-in-persons, various and complex, and transactions in them are widespread in Africa and constitute some of the basic elements of which kinship systems are constructed. While all social systems in the world can be analyzed in terms of such rights, Africa stands out *par excellence* in the legal precision, the multiplicity of detail and variation, and the degree of cultural explicitness in the handling of such rights. They are a formal part of African concepts of kinship relations—and not merely an analytical artifact created by outside observers examining these relations. The transactability of such rights as discrete and separate items is also remarkable. Moreover, transfers of such rights are normally made in exchange for goods and money, and the transfers may cover total rights-in-a-person. Therefore, such phenomena as kinship, adoption, the acquisition of wives and children are all inextricably bound up with exchanges that involve precise equivalences in goods and money.

IMPLICATIONS FOR THE DEFINITION OF 'SLAVERY'

The foregoing has obvious implications for the terminology of 'slavery' —a matter that is discussed in the Addendum to this chapter. It also has implications for any definition of 'slavery.' Westerners considering 'slavery' in African societies must discard their own concepts of ownership, property, and the purchasing of people. For, as we have seen, African lineages "own" their members and these members constitute lineage wealth. Hence, to define "slavery" as "the legal institutionalization of persons as property" (Tuden and Plotnicov 1970:12) is not very helpful. Property is best defined cross-culturally as "a set of rights over an object." Consequently, to say that what makes a person a 'slave' is the fact that he is "property" is to say, in effect: "A slave is a person over whom certain (unspecified) rights are exercised." This does not tell us what rights are involved nor how they differ from the rights of a kin group over its ordinary members.

An indication of Western implicit views of what constitutes 'slavery' can be gauged in attitudes to adoption. Consider, for example, the reaction that would greet the idea that parents should be allowed to give their children out for adoption in exchange for money. Though this would change nothing in the present relationship of adopted children to their adoptive parents, many people would see it as being "like slavery" because the transaction is a "sale"; and a relatively brisk adoption system of this kind might be called a "slave traffic in children." Kinship rights, most Westerners feel, cannot be acquired by purchase. Indeed, one thing that would threaten to nullify an adoption is a payment to the parent. Before deciding whether the analogy with 'slavery' holds, however, some people would want to know something about the treatment of adopted children. This, in effect, shifts the concern away from the manner in which the children are acquired to what happens to them afterward. If it turns out that the adoptive parents can, in turn, "resell" the children, or hire them out as laborers, or kill them, few Westerners would hesitate to call this "slavery." But should they then be told that all this can also be legally done with one's own children, some might again decide to call it "adoption" after all. Such a decision would, in effect, ignore the method of acquisition and the subsequent treatment *per se* and concentrate on the adoptee's status in the context of other statuses in the society. The uncertainties of decision we have described are similar to the dilemmas facing a Western observer who sees, in an African society, that a kin group acquires people by purchase, then finds out that it treats them like its own members, and finally discovers that this equal treatment means that acquired person and member can be sold, killed, or pawned.

Neither the criterion of property nor that of salability can be useful, then, in separating 'slavery' from simple "kinship" in African societies, in which rights in wives, children, and kin-group members are usually acquired through transactions involving material transfers and in which kin groups "own" and may dispose of their blood members in ways that Westerners consider appropriate to "property." These rights and transactions are an integral part of the traditional social organization of African societies. As such, they comprehend phenomena for which no Westerner would use the term slavery. Yet a few of these transactions, *were they to take place in the Westerner's society,* would clearly partake of the bundle of traits by which he would identify slavery in the West. Hence, we must discard Western concepts as we try to understand what it is that Western observers have, for various reasons, called 'slavery' in Africa. The position of the 'slave' must be examined in the context of the society to which he belongs—comparing his position not to the 'free' in the West but to the other members of his own society.

THE ACQUISITION OF 'SLAVES' IN AFRICA

'Slaves' were acquired in many ways in Africa, some more personally wrenching than others. Among the more benign ways was the buying of Margi orphans who would otherwise have died, or the picking up, both by the Fulani (Fulbe) of Borgou and by the royal clan of BuKerebe, of infants considered supernaturally dangerous and abandoned by their parents to die, and who were brought up by their rescuers to render them lifelong service. Similarly, children and even sometimes adults were bartered for grain in times of famine to save the rest of the group—a common phenomenon discussed in the chapters on the Margi, Sena and Kerebe. Strangers also would voluntarily place themselves in positions of dependence when forced to leave their own people because of quarrels, threats, hunger, hope of a better life, or because they had committed some crime.

Other transfers involved more compulsion. Many unredeemed hostages and pawns, for instance, ended up in servitude. Compensation for homicide and other crimes was commonly paid in people—usually children from the offending kin group and not the actual transgressor. Criminals, especially incorrigibles (but also some falsely accused), were sold out of the society, or, as among the Margi, were moved into a special social category. Sometimes persons were simply tricked into 'slavery,' as among the Vai; or were victims of kidnapping, casual or well organized, usually of children or young women.

A kidnap victim was more readily bought far from his home, where he could not be claimed by kinsmen or find his way back. Such long-distance trading required some degree of organization and specialization, and the transfers were no longer simple bilateral transactions but involved middlemen and entrepreneurs. With brisk demand, the entrepreneurial scale might expand, and the transactions themselves were increasingly impersonal and far less humane than, for example, the transfer of persons for debts between local kin groups. Even more impersonal was the capture and disposal of prisoners of war or the tribute in human beings often demanded by rulers, because such transfers involved military and trading entrepreneurship on a large scale.

The acquisition of persons through capture in wars and raids was widespread and its scale reflected the dimensions of political and economic development—bigger states and greater development naturally giving rise to increased demand for people to serve as social and political retainers and as a source of labor. Thus the Sena, Kerebe, Aboh, Margi, Vai, and Igbo, even in earlier times, when their economies were relatively sluggish, still captured and kidnapped, but haphazardly and occasionally. Polities organized on a greater scale, such as Damagaram, the Wolof and Sereer kingdoms, and that of the Tuareg, acting as agents for savanna kingdoms, made raiding and the capture of prisoners into a regular enterprise and fed the victims into a complex trading network. By contrast, some large and well-organized trading polities, such as that of the Imbangala, acquired numbers of 'slaves' by purchase from smaller polities, without themselves resorting to extensive warfare. Increases in regional trade allowed small polities to participate in economic networks far wider than their own political spheres. Sometimes the result was (as with some Igbo groups) to increase the scale of capturing 'slaves' for sale. More often, the limited military capabilities of the smaller polities made greater involvement in the trade a more attractive response, leading them to increase their acquisition of 'slaves' by purchase. Thus, the Kerebe and the Sena in the nineteenth century bought more 'slaves' in exchange for products. Others, finding themselves in the position of middlemen on the major trade routes, like the Igbo and the Aboh, or minor routes, like the Kongo of Mbanza Manteke, could skim off those they needed for themselves while the majority went past them.

The acquisition of people, then, was a process ranging from voluntary or peaceful personal transactions between neighboring groups to bilateral compulsory transfers and, with increasing degrees of coercion and organization, to the large-scale entrepreneurship of raiding and war. What is striking in all this is the overwhelming impression that here was a supplier's market. Strangers seeking patrons were welcomed; orphans or abandoned children were wanted; captives, unless dangerous or unmanageable, were eagerly sought. Kidnappers found a ready market for their victims.

Uses of acquired persons were many and varied. They provided extra wives and children to expand a kin group, labor to till the fields, retainers in the compound, soldiers for warfare, paddlers for trading canoes and war canoes, trading agents, servants and officials at court, and even victims for human sacrifice. Political and social power rested with those who could command a large number of kinsmen and dependents, whether clients, followers, or 'slaves.' Throughout most of Africa there is indisputable evidence that people were an important and much-wanted resource. Their versatility, mobility, and capacity to support and reproduce themselves made them important assets at all levels and in all types of societies. Thus, Wyatt MacGaffey (Ch. 9) describes the ideally successful Kongo lineage as one in which a continuous series of commercial transactions brought ever-increasing numbers of people into the group. A Sherbro proverb quoted by Carol MacCormack (Ch. 7)—"You cannot sit alone and be a chief"—expresses a sentiment widely shared throughout Africa.

In sum, African societies were receptive to all opportunities for bringing outsiders into their midst as dependents and retainers. This readiness and willingness to absorb people is a fact that will come up many times in the pages that follow.

THE OUTSIDER AND HIS MARGINALITY

When people were transferred from one group to another there was usually an element of compulsion, sometimes by relatives and sometimes by force of arms. Either way, the individual was wrenched from his own people, losing his social personality, his identity and status. He suffered a traumatic and sometimes violent withdrawal from kin, neighbors, and community, and often from familiar customs and language. The change was usually drastic and total—on a different order from the transfers effected as a normal part of the workings of systems of kinship and marriage already discussed. In all the various examples of 'slavery' given here, the 'slaves' have one thing in common: all are strangers in a new setting, be it a new kin group, community, region, or even country. The degree of trauma experienced clearly varied with the harshness of the change and the age of the victim. We have in fact scarcely any material on the psychological aspects of this experience and such material is probably almost unrecoverable now. It is, however, the structural and institutional aspects of their incorporation into the receiving group that we shall focus upon here.

The condition of the person detached from his native group in this way is analogous to the situation of one who is in the midst of what anthropologists, following van Gennep (1908), have called *rites de passage*, rituals of transition. Such rituals are widespread and accompany normal changes of status, such as the graduation from adolescence into adulthood. The person is expelled from his old social niche and put into a temporary limbo—van Gennep called it *marge*, margin. He is then in a state of marginality—quite literally on the margins of society, indeed of all societies, for he has lost his old social identity and not yet acquired a new one. He is, structurally speaking, simply not a person—an ambiguous being without name, position, or status (hence, ritually, his nonexistence is often symbolized by his "playing dead").

The captive outsider, and indeed to some extent any outsider, is initially in this position vis-à-vis his new society. He is not a person in it—nor to it. In Simmel's definition of the perfect stranger, "the relation to him is a non-relation" (1923/1950:407), unless, that is, there is a universalistic doctrine with a concept of a transcendent human family. If the intention is simply to resell such a captive stranger, he can remain in this marginal state and thus be literally an object or commodity. It is scarcely surprising that most reports emphasize that the "trade slave"—the one bought or captured for barter—was the worst treated of all. Victor Uchendu (Ch. 4) sums up his position among the Igbo as "no more than trade goods," and this was doubtless typical.

The outsider who is to be retained, however, cannot be left in this limbo; he must somehow be incorporated. This problem of the slave as a resident "stranger"—raised by Henri Lévy-Bruhl (1934) as the jural key to Roman slavery—is common to all slave systems. All too often, the widespread emphasis on the disabilities of slavery makes the analysis of it one-sided by concentrating attention on how slaves are *excluded* from the host society. But the problem for the host society is really that of *including* the stranger while continuing to treat him as a stranger. As Miller (pers. comm.) put it, the problem is "how to append someone who does not belong to the local social system, who when included still remains less than fully an insider." Every society must somehow tackle this problem which, from the sociological perspective, we might call the "institutionalization of marginality"—the term suggested by James Vaughan (Ch. 2 and elsewhere).[3] In his analysis of the Margi, Vaughan points out that 'slavery' involves "both marginality and integration, contradictory principles"— hence his concept of "limbic institution." Furthermore, as we shall see, the outsider's marginality is not just a marginality to the host society as a whole but also to all and every person, group, position, and institution in it. Each of these marginalities must be dealt with and each of them may be dealt with differently.

James Vaughan shows that the Margi saw the *mafa*'s marginality to society as a whole to be the ineradicable essence of *mafakur* ('slavery'). Outsiders who had been acquired, and Margi who had been condemned to be outsiders as punishment, remained marginal to the whole society. This did not prevent them from living ordinary lives. The key, Vaughan emphasizes, lay not in "what mafa do" but "what they are." The Margi case is significant because it shows that marginality-to-society may be institutionalized to continue over the generations, even though other marginalities, such as those of kinship, for example, may lapse. Discussions of African 'slavery' often dwell on the successful integration of the 'slave' into the kin group and thereby tend to assume that this must also mean integration into the society as a whole. But the two marginalities are different and the marginality-to-society has its own distinct significance. It institutionalizes a generalized social identity of 'slave', which may continue even when, after abolition, there are no more specific masters left. This marginality-to-society was probably quite widespread in Africa. It was found, in addition to the Margi, at least among the Aboh, Tuareg, Vai, Fulani, Duala, and Tawana (Batawana). In the last three cases, it

3. Vaughan first introduced the idea of approaching African 'slavery' through the notion of marginality and suggested the term "institutionalization of marginality" at the session on African slavery at the November 1972 meetings in Philadelphia of the African Studies Association. Our view of the acquired person as a "nonperson" who must be "rehumanized" in the host society closely parallels the views of Meillassoux and several contributors to his volume on African precolonial slavery (1975), notably J. Bazin, C. Perrot, M.-H. Piault, and E. Terray, whose ethnographic analyses are particularly revealing of this process and its implications. The notion of the slave as a permanent marginal "stranger" occurs in classical scholarship (for example, Lévy-Bruhl 1934) and is discussed by Finley (1968).

Van Gennep himself (1908/1960:39) refers very briefly to the transfer of slaves between masters as a ritual of transition. This view suggests that their incorporation should involve rituals. The material from some of our contributors (for example, Nwachukwu-Ogedengbe on the Aboh and Miller on the Imbangala) indicates as much. The outstanding modern contribution following van Gennep's insights is by Victor Turner (1964, 1969), who has examined the ritual and symbolic processes surrounding "interstructural situations," such as marginality. It may prove fruitful to apply Turner's ideas to slavery, if sufficiently detailed data can be found.

was also clearly reinforced by ideas about the ethnic superiority of the host society.

For the stranger's marginality to be reduced and institutionalized, new bonds must be created, in the integrative sense of "bonding" him to the new society as well as in the more onerous sense of "bondage" to it. His state, of necessity, falls somewhere between two extremes. He is moving away from the condition of the trade slave—the complete outsider—and he would like to assume, but cannot, the condition of the complete insider, of the man born into the society as a full-fledged citizen. But the insider in most traditional societies of Africa was not an autonomous individual. His full citizenship derived from belonging to a kin group, usually corporate, which was the fundamental social, legal, political, and ritual protective unit.

This contrasts with the modern Western ideology of 'freedom' (though not exactly with Western sociological reality). For in the Western conception, the antithesis of "slavery" is 'freedom,' and 'freedom' means autonomy and a lack of social bonds. However, as Simmel (1908/1950: 274) points out, unless a society has developed laws that specifically protect personal autonomy, such 'freedom' must depend more on having the power to protect oneself than on actual autonomy; without such laws, autonomy cannot be a social value. In most African societies, 'freedom' lay not in a withdrawal into a meaningless and dangerous autonomy but in attachment to a kin group, to a patron, to power—an attachment that occurred within a well-defined hierarchical framework. It was in this direction that the acquired outsider had to move if he was to reduce his initial marginality. Here, the antithesis of 'slavery' is not 'freedom' qua autonomy but rather "belonging." Significantly, the Giriama of the Kenya coast, when asked to name the opposite of *mtumwa* ('slave'), invariably replied "Mgiriama," meaning simply a Giriama (Miers fieldnotes). Among the Suku of Zaïre, a man who had quarreled with his lineage and set up his own compound with his wife and children in isolation in the countryside was compared to a *muhika*, the term for outsiders acquired by a lineage. His condition, which to a Westerner represents the height of freedom and autonomy, was considered to be analogous to that of a muhika because he had ceased to belong in, and to, a group, and thus lacked the protection enjoyed by those who really "belonged." By the same logic, the Suku, who had a king, would taunt their neighbors the Mbala, who had none, by singing that the Mbala "are the *bahika* because they have no king"—because, that is, they did not belong to and were not protected by a superior power. Here again, the greater apparent autonomy of the Mbala, living in independent villages, was irrelevant.

The process of reduction of marginality is well illustrated by Ralph Austen's (Ch. 12) description of the Duala. Here, members of the first generation of 'slaves' were called *bakom*, a term applied to all alien ethnic groups—that is, to all outsiders, whether or not they lived in Duala territory. The marginality of the bakom in Douala was institutionalized and unalterable. However, the second generation, the *miyabedi*, were in a more ambiguous position. As children of bakom, they were still outsiders and were so perceived, but since they were born locally, their marginality was reduced. They no longer "belonged" to any master, yet their status was depressed. The Germans called them "half-free." But since they had no masters and no restrictions on their movements, their disability lay in the impossibility of their acquiring full Dualahood. Instead of half-free, "half-belonging" or "half-stranger" would seem to describe their position better. Significantly, their final 'freeing,' or incorporation, in modern times has taken place by means of a cult that in the past was used as an instrument to exclude them from full Dualahood.

The fact that the Duala applied the same term to the first generation of acquired strangers as to 'free' aliens was logical because what mattered was their common social distance from Dualahood—that is, their relative marginality and not their relative 'freedom.' Had the classification been concerned with 'freedom,' it would have lumped together the 'free' Duala and the 'free' alien in contrast to the 'slave.' Similarly, we find this principle of relative marginality among the Kerebe who classified free immigrant clients with 'slaves,' and the Aboh, who used the term *ndichie* to include both.

For our purpose, we shall focus upon the extreme point in this continuum of marginality: on the outsider who has involuntarily crossed the boundary of the society and is forcibly retained within it, or within a single society, one who has lost his own kin ties and has come to be under the full authority of another kin group in which he is a kind of resident alien. He is distinct from the voluntary immigrant—the alien who can choose to remain a permanent resident stranger, able to leave when he wishes. We shall call this involuntary outsider the *acquired outsider* or *acquired stranger*. The peculiarity of his condition lies in that while he is unable to leave and must have his marginality resolved, it is his acquisitors who have the power to define how his marginality is to be institutionalized. It is in this that his lack of 'freedom' resides, and not necessarily in the particular institutional arrangements that follow and that may be humane or harsh, rigidly fixed or socially mobile, covering every aspect of his life or only part of it.

DIMENSIONS OF MARGINALITY IN RELATION TO MOBILITY

The institutionalization of the outsider's marginality provides him with a position in the host society. In time, this position may change, and his descendants may have a different position. These changes in degrees of marginality have to do with what has been called "social mobility." The phrase "social mobility of slaves" has been used, however, to refer to several kinds of changes, and these differences are of great importance to our discussion. It will therefore be useful to clarify them here.

The acquired outsider moves from total marginality toward greater and greater *incorporation*[4] into the institutions of the host society. The reduction of his marginality occurs along at least three dimensions that may be usefully distinguished: the dimension of formal status, the dimension of informal affect, and the dimension of worldly achievement and success. His movement into the society along each of these different dimensions of marginality represents different kinds of social mobility and involves different processes of incorporation.

The acquired outsider's *status mobility* reflects the process of his *formal incorporation* into the new society. This means changes in his institutionalized marginality in terms of formal (usually legal) rights, duties, and privileges. For example, when the total outsider—the nonperson—becomes someone's 'slave,' he moves into a definite status with defined rights and obligations. If, in a few years, he acquires the recognized right not to be resold, his status has changed further. If his offspring are recognized as 'free' and become incorporated as full members of the acquisitor lineage, this represents intergenerational status mobility.

His *affective mobility* leads to a reduction in his *affective marginality* and to his greater *affective incorporation.* This change is in the sphere of emotion and sentiment rather than formal and legal codes. It has to do with the esteem and affection in which he is held and the way he is treated. An acquired outsider, for example, may be warmly accepted by his acquisitor lineage and come to be held in high regard, yet his formal rights may remain entirely unchanged. He may, for example, still be legally liable to be resold, even though his masters would never consider doing it.

His *worldly success mobility* means changes toward a better style of life, more political influence, and even control over greater wealth, all of which reduce the marginality of his everyday existence and indicate success in

---

4. We use the term "incorporation" here in one of its ordinary dictionary meanings of making an object or person a part of a larger body. This essentially nontechnical usage may be compared with other recent uses in the literature: Cohen and Middleton (1970:9-17), while using the term broadly enough to cover our meaning, are mainly concerned with the processes by which boundaries between previously separate groups (for example, "tribes") are reduced to produce new corporate entities (such as "nations"); and Smith (1974:187ff.) develops the concept of "incorporation" to examine processes by which a corporate entity comes into being (in much the same sense that firms become "incorporated" when they come into being in the business world).

the business of living. Needless to say, this may occur with or without any change in either his formal status or his affective incorporation.

Affective mobility and mobility in worldly success can obviously exhibit many and subtle gradations. One's progress in these dimensions is usually gradual. By contrast, formal statuses are clear-cut and discrete, and have definite rights and obligations associated with them. Thus, changes in them tend to be not a slide but a jump, even if a small one, from one constellation of precise rights to another. It should also be emphasized that mobility in any one of these three dimensions operates independently from mobility in each of the others. When one speaks of the social mobility of a 'slave,' it is best to specify which dimension is involved.

The status mobility of 'slaves' should not be regarded as being primarily a matter of movement out of the 'slave' status. There was seldom in African societies a single, all-embracing status of 'slave' (such as existed in the early modern Anglo-American world). Rather, a series of different statuses existed for acquired persons and their descendants, all of which or only some of which may be called 'slavery.' Much of the social mobility of acquired persons took place within this series, and great personal success could be achieved without ever taking the final step into the category of full-fledged citizen or complete insider.

Changes in the three dimensions—those of legal status, affective marginality, and worldly success—may occur to a single person in his lifetime. This represents his *lifetime mobility*, and it should be clearly distinguished from the changes that his offspring or descendants will experience, that is, from *intergenerational mobility*. The rather obvious distinction must be kept in mind because such statements as "The slave becomes integrated in the lineage in several generations" have sometimes been taken as showing the flexible or benign nature of a 'slave' system. It should be remembered that intergenerational flexibility can coexist with rigid statuses into which each particular generation may be frozen.

Finally, we may note the fallacy of interpreting the existence of a range of 'slave' statuses as showing great mobility. In the same society, acquired persons may be found in a wide range of positions, from agricultural laborers to high state officials. This need not mean that the state official began at the bottom and worked his way up, or that persons acquired by farmers have the slightest chance of becoming state ministers, as has sometimes been interpreted. All it may mean is that the acquired strangers were from the beginning marginal to quite different institutions—the peasant household in one case and the palace in the other.

All these distinct forms of mobility and varieties of status must be borne in mind when considering such phenomena as mobility, redemption, manumission, integration, and inheritance of 'slave' status.

CONDITIONS AND CONSTRAINTS IN THE
INSTITUTIONALIZATION OF MARGINALITY

Although the outsider comes into the new society as it were as a non-person, he can only remain as such to his acquisitors so long as their interaction is minimal, as when, for instance, he is kept in a barracoon, awaiting sale to a passing ship or caravan. The moment he actually enters the new society to stay, interaction with him begins, and with it the process of his social placement. This process takes place under a set of simultaneous conditions and constraints, some general and some specifically characteristic of Africa.

First, the outsider is a human being with volition, and not an inert object.

Second, his placement in the new society will be greatly affected by the position of his acquisitor, who may be regarded as his sponsor in the new setting. In Africa, the sponsor himself is deeply enmeshed in his own kin group and the relation of the outsider to that kin group will be of special importance.

Third, the outsider is acquired for a purpose—to be put to some use. In principle, human beings are an extremely versatile resource, capable of being used in an almost infinite variety of ways. Any particular society is constrained, however, in how it uses him by a number of cultural, social, economic, and political factors—and sometimes even by sheer limits of inventiveness. The question of use, then, is never purely an economic matter, but is governed by the total social and political economy of each society.

THE HUMANITY OF THE OUTSIDER

The acquired stranger is a person with a will of his own, and even the most one-sided relationship will have some human consequences. For instance, harshness will provoke recalcitrance or rebellion and these will require additional controls. If such controls are too difficult or too expensive to be imposed, the constraint on the relationship is obvious. The human factor permits *quasi* brotherhood with the outsider—but it also prevents complete brotherhood because he brings with him a "baggage" of past experiences, with memories of his former status, culture, language, and so forth. Because of this, there is often a preference for acquiring children, who can be molded into the society, or young women, who can fit into the usually well-developed niche of stranger-wife—this when the outsider is to be used within the family, as among the Kerebe or Sena. But if the outsiders are to be used in other occupations in which contact is less intimate—as, for example, in villages of 'slave' cultivators—this preference is less marked. It is precisely where the use of strangers is most familial, and the conditions of 'slavery' most benign, that we are apt to find that young women and children captured in wars or raids are kept (being easy to incorporate) whereas the men are killed or held for ransom.

Such patterns emphasize that the use to which acquired persons may be put is constricted by the niches that exist in the structure of the host society. These niches may be influenced by quite minor variations in the social and even the kinship systems. Thus, Svend Holsoe (Ch. 11) indicates that the early Vai, lacking as yet the outlet of the Atlantic slave trade, kept only those Vai captives who were already 'slaves'; those who had been 'free' were either killed or offered for ransom. We would suggest that this was not unrelated to the Vai kinship system, which was rigidly and exclusively patrilineal; Vai lineages had no place to offer to a 'free' outsider who had no local lineage connections and who, being unused to servitude, would prove difficult to handle if enslaved. By contrast, the nearby and culturally quite similar Sherbro had more flexible, nonunilineal kin groups that could easily absorb strangers. And indeed, as Carol MacCormack (Ch. 7) indicates, when the Sherbro captured or bought a 'free' alien, they adopted him and sometimes used such adoptions to form alliances with the kin group of the captive.

The human factor therefore can have different consequences: in one case it allows adoption, in another it leads to killing. It is an additional element in the calculus of use for the acquired outsider. It does not, as has sometimes been claimed, result in an inherent contradiction in 'slavery' between the "humanity" of the 'slave' and his use as property. For, as we have seen, these can coexist in ordinary kinship relations. Hence, we find it difficult to accept Tuden and Plotnicov's (1970:12) contention that the property-person contradiction "ultimately" makes slavery untenable as an institution (a statement that is, by its nature, ultimately impossible to disprove in any case). Ronald Cohen's view seems more realistic, that "the capacity to create servile institutions that engender exploitation, cruelty, and oppression is part of the human condition" (Cohen 1971:165). The analysis presented here, which sees the 'slave' as initially a nonperson, suggests that the basic problem in 'slavery' is not the impossibility of dehumanizing a person into property, for the newly acquired alien is already a mere object. Rather, the central problem of 'slavery' is the "rehumanization" of the nonperson in a new social setting.

THE 'SLAVERY'-TO-KINSHIP CONTINUUM

Kinship relations and the kin group are dominant elements in most African social systems, and kinship usually provides both the idiom and the metaphor for social and political relations. It is therefore not surprising that the institutionalization and reduction of the outsiders' marginality in Africa should involve kinship. Furthermore, as we have stressed, the realm of kinship and marriage in Africa is characterized by the acquisition of various rights-in-persons, including rights to the whole person, in exchange for wealth. The realm of African kinship, therefore, contains precisely one of the important features by which Westerners identify the realm of 'slavery.' Thus, the two realms are very often inter-twined in a way that modern Westerners may find striking: African 'slaves' may often look to Westerners like relatives of the masters, and relatives may sometimes look like 'slaves.' In fact, a person is sometimes both. In the recent past in the West, the intermingling of the two realms was most often an unconvincing metaphor ("Colonel Wright treats his slaves like his own children"). In Africa, metaphor and reality may be much closer and often merge. 'Slaves' could also be wives, sons, brothers, or fathers to the 'free,' and this without great strains on the relationships. But there is a danger of misinterpreting this easy mingling of the two realms. One should not assume that there is never a metaphor in African situations. As we shall see, when a 'slave' is referred to as a "son," one should not interpret this to mean that he is treated as one.

The intermingling of the two realms can result in ambiguities that lend themselves to manipulation, for relationships of 'slavery' can be redefined into those of kinship, and vice versa. For example, when a patrilineage is torn by quarrels, with descendants of one of the wives of the founder pitted against those of another, one of these lineage-branches may claim that the other branch is in fact 'slave,' and that the goods given for their ancestress were in fact not for bridewealth but for purchase. Similarly, a 'slave' branch of a matrilineage may, in time, claim that their ancestress was in fact a relative brought in because she was orphaned. Thomas Tlou (Ch. 14) provides another example of such redefinitions. He states that the Yei claim that they gave some of their children to the Tawana for adoption, but the Tawana transformed the adoption into "serfdom." Whatever the historical truth, the accusation is culturally plausible. Wyatt MacGaffey (Ch. 9) similarly shows the political uses to which the kinship-'slavery' ambiguities are put among the Kongo. Here, lineage branches, competing for political recognition, resort to mutual accusations of 'slavery' precisely because such accusations are both so plausible and so impossible to prove or disprove.

In Africa, then, the kinsman, the adopted, the dependent, the client, and the 'slave' abutted on one another and could merge into one another in the same way that tenants, serfs, and slaves did in medieval Europe (Bloch 1947). This should not be misunderstood to mean that a 'slave' in Africa was always a quasi kinsman and never a chattel. Far from it. In some African societies there were acquired outsiders, sometimes with their descendants, whose marginality was so little reduced that their position was like that of chattels. What we wish to stress, however, is that this chattellike position nevertheless lay on a continuum of marginality whose progressive reduction led in the direction of quasi kinship and, finally, kinship. The overlap and intermingling between the realm of 'slavery' and that of kinship occurred only in this latter portion of the continuum and it is here that the redefinitions of relationships we have described took place. What gives African 'slavery' its particular stamp, in contrast to many other slave systems, is the existence of this 'slavery'-to-kinship continuum.

THE OUTSIDER AND THE ACQUISITOR'S KIN GROUP

In his movement from being a total outsider toward becoming an insider, the acquired person's relationship with his acquisitor's kin group is crucial. His placement by the group into some permanent relationship is the first step by which his marginality begins to be reduced.

It has already been pointed out that Africans "belong to" as well as "belong in" a kin group. For real members of the kin group, their position in its hierarchy reflects a balance between their authority as members and their vulnerability as wealth. The scales are tipped against the recently acquired outsider who almost entirely belongs to rather than in the group. As time goes on, however, the balance often begins to swing, so that he belongs in it to a greater extent. This process is usually vaguely referred to as his "integration" into the group. But what is striking is that all the cases presented here show that he never completely reached the status of a real member of the group. Even among the Sena, where he could participate in the ancestral cult—a good indication of reduction of marginality—the Isaacmans state that, nevertheless, other things being equal, he was more likely to be sold in time of trouble than was a real member. Among the Kerebe, where "integration" also proceeded relatively fast, Gerald Hartwig finds that he still had a lower status than true kinsmen. In other societies, the line was not only even more rigid but was maintained over the generations, the core members with their real blood ties being distinct from the descendants of the acquired strangers. In some cases, such as among the Vai and Fulani, the 'slave' and his descendants overwhelmingly belonged to, and scarcely at all in, the kin group.

Consequently terms such as "adoption" and "integration" should only be used with much care. For example, ceremonies introducing the newly acquired stranger to the ancestors should not be hastily interpreted, without careful investigation into their meaning, as representing adoption. Such ceremonies among the Aboh were a presentation to the ancestors at their shrine of the newly acquired wealth of the lineage; actual adoption was accomplished by a different ceremony. The Imbangala also ritually took the *abika* into the kin group, but they clearly remained in an inferior status. Given the shadings of what "belonging to" kin groups can mean, "adoption" should perhaps only be used where the newcomer legally becomes the duplicate of a born kin-group member.

As with adoption, so with other family analogies and metaphors. One should keep in mind that Africans often use the kinship idiom to indicate hierarchy, rather than sentiment, in nonkinship relations. Thus, subordinate chiefs may be referred to as the "children" of the ruler; the relative prestige among related rulers may be indicated by one being known as the "older brother" of another; and a kingdom that is an offshoot of another one may be called its "child." Similarly, a diviner refers to another diviner who trained him as his "father," and a cult house that was set up under the direction of another is its "child." Hence, if the acquired outsider calls the acquisitor "father," this should not be taken to mean literally that he is in exactly the same position as his sons. To arrive at the reality, we must first know the position of a real son and how it changes at different stages in his life. Quite consistently, the metaphor "child" in fact signifies that the acquired outsider is a legal minor. To call him a "legal minor" is preferable to saying that he is "like a child," because "child" carries to Westerners emotional connotations of nurture that are culturally very specific. At the same time, it may also carry equally inappropriate connotations of a relationship of condescension. As James Vaughan (Ch. 2) points out, among the Margi the fact that the mafa was a legal minor does not at all mean that he was treated like a child. He was a minor because he did not have certain rights enjoyed by most Margi, but in every other respect he was treated as an adult. Moreover, legal majority in many African societies is not attained until middle age, when one succeeds to a position of familial authority. It is often also a relative matter, for one's elders continue to be "more adult" and to exercise some authority over one. Conversely, an old man may be a "child" to the successor to his father's kinship position. Thus, the metaphorical use of kin terms may be deceptive and should not, above all, be taken at their Western face value. The actual difference between the outsider and his new "kinsmen" is a matter for careful ethnographic investigation.

The difference may only become apparent by studying a man's life cycle: discussing the Tawana, Thomas Tlou stresses the fact that *batlhanka* were juniors through their entire lives; and John Grace (Ch. 16) describes Mende 'slaves' as being, socially, "minors who would never grow up"—a status common elsewhere. As a legal minor, the outsider did not get the authority and power within the group that went with fully belonging in it. What influence he developed in the group he held not by right but through personal skill. Although 'slaves' could become rich and

successful, they could also be "pushed down" at the whim of the masters
—a point that Nwachukwu-Ogedengbe stresses in discussing the Aboh
and that is also made by several other contributors. Whether, and how often, this was done in practice is, of course, a different question, but the difference between 'slave' and 'free' partly hinged precisely on such legal possibilities. In effect, this meant that there was a lack of balance between the
mutual obligations of the kin group and its acquired member. If the kin
group ignored its obligations to a true member, he was free to leave—this,
indeed, was the common reason for the widespread pattern of kin-group
segmentation in Africa. The acquired person, by contrast, did not have
the legal right to opt out of the relationship. A quasi kinsman, he was
also a captive kinsman.

ABOLITION OF MARGINALITY THROUGH DISSOCIATION: REDEMPTION AND MANUMISSION

One way of dealing with the marginality of the acquired stranger was to
abolish it through manumission or redemption. Like other solutions, these
were related to the type of social structure and the theory behind his
incorporation. Manumission means a withdrawal from the master and his
kin group, and it may or may not also mean withdrawal from the host
society and sometimes a return to one's own. The manumitted stranger
regains, structurally speaking, his initial condition of a "nonperson" who
must now find a new niche for himself. Thus, manumission always raises
new problems of marginality. This may occur even when the manumitted
person returns to his own natal group, as shown by a Kongo practice
described by Wyatt MacGaffey (Ch. 9). When a Kongo 'slave' was
redeemed by being bought back by his own natal lineage, he did not
automatically regain his former status in it but became its 'slave.'

Initially, the manumitted stranger is a 'free' nonperson in search of new
legal ties, but he is also one with established local connections, which can
help him fashion a new social identity. Among the Sherbro, for instance,
Carol MacCormack (Ch. 7) reports that the 'slave' who wished to redeem
himself could not legally do so since he was not allowed to own property.
He therefore handed over his secretly accumulated funds to a local
resident from his own area of origin, who then officially redeemed him.
Significantly, he thereby immediately acquired new ties by becoming the
fictive redeemer's client. Among the Tuareg, Baier and Lovejoy (Ch. 15)
show that the 'slaves' went through successive physical withdrawals from
their desert-based masters. But their movement was not toward abstract
'freedom' but rather toward a marginality in the host Hausa society—a
marginality resolved by incorporation into quasi-ethnic groups in the
savanna. In some societies, the ties to the old master were merely

redefined. This could be a matter of law, implying incomplete manumission. Thus, by Muslim law (Brunschvig 1960:30), the freed slave and his descendants became, in perpetuity, the clients of their former master, as they also did in the late Roman Empire (Bloch 1947:216).

A manumitted 'slave' may also choose to remain with his former master if, by leaving, he is exposed to unbearable problems with new marginalities; one of the risks run by a freeman on the loose is new enslavement by someone else. We should expect, then, that patterns of manumission should have some relationship to the society in question. Thus, manumission followed by dissociation from the master, while the manumitted person remains in the host society, should be most pronounced in the more complex societies, which offer a variety of new niches for the manumitted. Indeed, such manumission was found most clearly in such societies as the Wolof, Hausa, and Tuareg-in-the-savanna. By contrast, in the less complex societies few niches exist outside the kin-group structure. Unless the manumitted 'slave' rejoins his own natal kin group, he can best improve his condition by closer incorporation and deeper entrenchment in the master's kin group. Advancement through dissociation from the masters could be risked only by exceptionally forceful men, sure of a following of their own, such as Azaka, who founded his own lineage among the Aboh, but even he could not acquire the rights of full citizenship. Among the Duala, where the locally born offspring of acquired persons were automatically free of their parents' masters, those whose parents had belonged to the same master formed a quasi kin group. Similarly, former 'slaves' of the Tuareg defined their quasi-ethnic groups in the savanna by reference to the particular tribe of their erstwhile desert masters.[5]

AFFECTIVE MARGINALITY AND WORLDLY SUCCESS

We have seen that status mobility—change in the legal position of 'slaves'—was rare in the first generation, that there was usually some threshold that they could not cross. Their worldly success mobility, on the other hand, was sometimes very impressive.

One of the great advantages of acquiring a stranger as a human resource lay precisely in the fact that he was kinless and therefore more or less completely under the control of, and dependent upon, his acquisitors. He had no competing loyalties, no outside obligations or protectors; at the same time, he could not compete for power, resources, or wealth with his

5. It is interesting to note that in the New World, Maroons (escaped slaves) in Surinam, in their independent societies in the interior, sometimes organized themselves into lineages in which membership was defined with reference to the former master and plantation from which they had escaped (see Price 1974:49-51; Köbben 1967).

masters. Hence, in Africa as elsewhere, he was often relied upon for delicate positions requiring trust, descretion, and complete loyalty. 'Slaves,' therefore, served as ministers of state and counselors, as soldiers and commanders, as governors of provinces, as trading agents, and, in the case of women, as favored wives.

The male 'slave' in particular could have, in the more complex societies, a wide range of occupations open to him and was often given positions of power over 'free' people. Purchased as a child, he could become a member of an elite and solidary corps of quasi-military administrators, such as the Wolof *tyeddo,* who were not unlike the Turkish Janissaries or Egyptian Mamluks.

Hausa 'slave' courtiers in Damagram could hold positions that gave them control over villages of 'slave' cultivators. Aboh canoemen could trade their way to wealth and own their own 'slaves.' Tuareg captives could become successful savanna merchants. But, as with all success stories, these illustrate principles rather than statistics. For most Hausa 'slaves,' success really lay in merging over the generations with their 'free' peasant neighbors; and, as is shown for the Aboh and Sherbro and is true for most societies, success was achieved entirely by the sufferance of the masters. In some societies, such as the Borgou Fulani, the Vai, the Mende, and the Tawana, even relatively humble worldly success was denied to the acquired outsider.

What is of more interest than the spectacular success story, however, is the variation in affective marginality within the same legal status. Success is this sphere varied widely according to such things as a person's attractiveness, length of residence, age at acquisition, willing service, social skill, kinship bonds, personal ties, and so forth. Success developed, nevertheless, in the context of particular institutions and some of these could be more encouraging than others. Thus, the chance of affective mobility was greater if the acquired outsider lived in his master's household rather than in a 'slave' village on his estate, or if he worked side by side with him as a farmer rather than being one of fifty paddlers in a trading canoe.

Whether the acquired persons were male or female had also much to do with their affective mobility. The variation was much greater among men, since their social roles and occupations tended to span a wider range, involved different degrees of intimacy with their masters, and responded to a large number of factors. Women were more limited in their roles—not least because their sexuality and reproductive capacity gave them such special social value. An acquired woman's way of life tended to be determined at the outset by the position of her mate, be he lineage elder, 'slave,' or ruler, and thereafter she could achieve little worldly success on her own. At the same time, women's roles in Africa were more narrowly defined than those of men and were less varied and stratified. In most cases, an acquired woman's position was never far from that of an ordinary wife who was also usually brought in from outside. They shared the same social world, separate from men, and generally the same daily activities and work. The difference was that the acquired woman had no kinsmen to protect her; she could not break her bonds and had no kin group to go back to, no kin group to return the bridewealth if her marriage was unhappy. This very lack of outside ties, however, could sometimes work to reduce her affective marginality more than that of the 'free' wife in the domestic and sentimental spheres.

INCORPORATION OF THE FIRST GENERATION INTO THE KIN GROUP

In societies whose social structures were so largely governed by formal systems of rights-in-persons, the role of acquired persons as genitors was of particular importance to the host kin group. An acquired woman was a potential mate and mother, and the main problem for the acquisitors was the conditions under which she was to be given out to men. Conversely, acquired men had to be furnished with women, also under defined conditions. We shall examine the social structural contexts of these problems in the next two sections.

FIRST-GENERATION MALES IN THE KIN GROUP

In certain broad respects, the position of the acquired male in the kin group differs in matrilineal and patrilineal societies. In a matrilineal society, no man, be he 'slave' or 'free,' produces children to be affiliated to his own kin group; they belong to his wife's kin. The acquired male may be provided with a mate from within the master lineage or from outside it, but his status does not affect that of his children. There was as a result, a tendency in matrilineal societies to be relatively unconcerned about "unequal" marriages with male 'slaves.' Indeed, there was some advantage in having the offspring of the matrilineage's women fathered by its own 'slaves,' for these children ('free' because of their mothers' status) had no loyalties outside their lineage, as they would have had if their fathers had been 'free.' By becoming the father of full-fledged 'free' lineage members, the acquired outsider reduced his own affective marginality. Among the matrilineal Imbangala and Kongo, and the ambilineal Sherbro, such a 'slave' even had a recognized legal status different from other acquired outsiders. But no matter how great his success and acceptance within the kin group, he was unlikely to pose a political threat.

In a matrilineage, a political faction is apt to be composed of brothers by the same mother and their sisters with their children; a first-generation acquired man cannot form such a faction.

In a patrilineal society, the position of a 'free' male is more complex. He normally acquires control over his children by virtue of his bridewealth payments. The same rules apply to a slave for whom his master has acquired a wife by paying bridewealth. However, unlike the 'free' male, who can found a lineage segment of his own, such a 'slave' usually cannot found a new segment, for his offspring are in the complete control of his master. This expression of the status of the 'slave' as a legal minor represents a serious disability in Africa, where founding a kin group and thereby becoming a remembered ancestor is a strongly desired form of self-fulfillment. If a master married his male 'slave' to a 'free' woman by paying bridewealth for her, the children became the master's 'slaves' or low-status members of his lineage. However, 'free' women would be reluctant to marry 'slaves' and consign their children to this lowly status. This explains the willingness of Duala women to become concubines but not wives of male 'slaves;' since no bridewealth was paid in concubinage, the children became full-fledged members of their mother's patrilineage. The most common wife for an acquired male, however, was another 'slave,' usually owned by the same master, who thereby also acquired the offspring. If the 'slave' wife belonged to another master, the children also belonged to her master and his lineage.

In sum, then, the first generation of acquired males usually lived out their lives as legal minors in the host kin group, their inferior position being demonstrated in a realm of particular importance in Africa—that of control over their progeny. In contrast to their inferior legal status, however, their personal influence and esteem in the kin group could be considerable, as could sometimes be their worldly success.

FIRST-GENERATION FEMALES IN THE KIN GROUP

As we have noted, the acquired woman has a special value as a potential mother—a producer of human resources—and her position in the host kin group to a large extent hinges on this fact.

In a matrilineal society, like the 'free' (full-fledged) women members of the kin group, she produces children for the group. Structurally, her position is thus analogous to the sisters and mother of her male acquisitor —and not to the wives (who, in a matrilineal society, do not produce children for the husband's group). The men of matrilineal groups are generally sensitive to the risk of losing control over their sisters' children, since the sisters usually live with their husbands, often some distance away. With a 'slave' woman, this risk is doubled because of her tenuous ties to her acquisitor. But unlike the case of her master's sisters, there is no incest bar against marrying her. Hence, she can produce children for the group *in situ*. Women acquired by a matrilineage thus tend to be married off either to related lineages, to close relatives (for example, the master's sons), or, preferably, to men of the acquisitor lineage itself.

An acquired woman as a wife has another great advantage over 'free' wives—she has no kinsmen and her children, unlike theirs, have no outside ties, no conflicting loyalties, and are wholly in the control of their lineage and their father, who is also their surrogate uncle. Thus, a man often preferred to have a 'slave' wife and children, who could provide a nucleus of exclusive supporters for him, and this, as Joseph Miller (Ch. 8) shows for the Imbangala, had important implications for lineage politics.

Having 'slave' wives allowed the men of a matrilineage to get around one of the problems kin groups face in a matrilineal society—namely, their dependence for the group's growth on reproduction by the men's sisters, whose number is fixed. In patrilineal societies, by contrast, a kin group can rapidly increase when its men marry many wives. For a matrilineage, the 'slave' wives become acquired, surrogate sisters whose numbers can be increased by purchase. Thus, the 'slave' wife has a chance for considerable affective integration into her new home, and, in time, structural integration, for she can become the ancestress of a new 'slave' matrilineal branch of the master lineage. A 'slave' wife does not compete with the 'free' wives but rather with her master's sisters, who produce the true heirs—the blood-members of the lineage.

Let us now turn to the acquired woman's position in patrilineal societies. By acquiring her, the kin group obtains rights over her fertility and her children. It can retain these rights in several ways. It can simply give sexual rights in her to a man from another lineage. This arrangement would have to be local, for otherwise control of the children might lapse. It was usually considered a kind of concubinage rather than a marriage and it was undesirable from the point of view of a husband who wished to build up his own patrilineage. Hence, it was often practiced by temporary male residents—strangers interested in a mate but not in starting a local descent group. Such concubinage was also often practiced by 'slave' couples when the man and woman belonged to different masters. Among the Fulani and Tawana, for instance, who had a relatively chattellike 'slavery,' this was a means of reproducing their chattel, since the owner of the mother retained her children.

Alternatively, the patrilineal kin group might wish simply to marry the acquired girl off in the normal way and receive bridewealth for her. But it would do this only if the bridewealth was higher than the price of outright sale. Moreover, in the case of a marriage with bridewealth, the group incurred the obligation to return the bridewealth and take the woman back if the marriage failed. Given its lack of sentimental ties to the acquired woman, the group would probably be unwilling to take this risk, while the prospective husband would be equally unwilling to take the risk, in case of divorce, of claiming back his payment from people who were indifferent to the fate of the woman. Thus, if a patrilineal kin group wished not to keep an acquired woman, it would find it far simpler to sell her outright than to give her out in marriage.

The commonest fate for a 'slave' girl was to marry her master, or another member of his patrilineage, or a male 'slave' of the patrilineage. The added attraction here was that she had no kin to protect her or take her back in time of trouble. This would tend to result in her greater affective integration but, since Africans usually see it as demeaning for a woman not to have been properly acquired with bridewealth, her prestige probably suffered. In some societies, such as the Aboh and Tawana, such marriages were considered tantamount to concubinage. In patrilineal societies, wives are often ranked by precedence and seniority, and such a concubine or wife would have low status. This can be important, as will be seen, in a patrilineal compound in which each woman competes to promote the interests of her children.

In conclusion it may be noted that, as we have seen with male 'slaves,' so with female 'slaves' an important way of reducing their marginality to the acquisitor kin group was for them to become a kind of blood-relative through their children when these were, by existing rules, full-fledged members of the kin group. Thus, among the Mende, the Wolof, the Tawana, and the Hausa, a 'slave' mother properly married to a 'free' man gave birth to 'free' children—and thereby became 'free' herself.

THE INCORPORATION OF THE SECOND GENERATION

The question of what happens to the second generation of 'slaves' is often phrased as How, if at all, is 'slave' status inherited? We shall phrase it in keeping with the frame of reference adopted here and in the form of several questions: How is the marginality of the second generation dealt with? Does it remain as in the first generation? Is it reduced or eliminated? And by what rules?

'Slaves' of the second generation were in a different position from that of their parents. Born on the soil of the society (often a matter of ritual significance in Africa), knowing no other language or culture, having no outside ties, or exotic knowledge, or hankering for a lost past—the offspring of acquired 'slaves' were not strangers except by origin and were accepted on a different footing from their parents. (For the same reason, outsiders acquired in childhood were also sometimes treated in the same way as second-generation 'slaves'.) Also, second-generation 'slaves' were not kinless but had some local kinship ties. Sometimes, one of their parents was 'free' and this, in some societies, eliminated outright their legal marginality. In most societies, however, their marginality continued, but was redefined with reference to several variables.

The position of the second generation is least ambiguous in matrilineal societies. In this respect, the Imbangala and the Kongo are typical: the children of a 'free' woman of the lineage were 'free' members of it, regardless of who their father was; and if the mother was a 'slave' of the lineage, so were her children. Eventually, the progeny of a 'slave' woman tended to form a 'slave' branch within the main matrilineage.

In patrilineal societies, the placement of the child of the acquired outsider varies more widely. Among those examined here only the Margi, the Sena, and the Hausa followed their normal descent rule in that the legitimate child of a 'free' man was 'free'—regardless of the status of the mother. Most patrilineal societies, however, made some distinction between the various children of a 'free' man, based on the status of their mother—this in contrast to matrilineal societies, where the status of the child of a 'free' woman did not vary with the father's status. The difference is related once again to the different workings of the two kinds of kin groups. As previously stated, full members of a matrilineage can only be produced by its womenfolk; since their numbers are finite, lineage growth cannot be accelerated. The problem here is to insure that these women produce enough blood members for the lineage to maintain itself; the status of their male genitor is of minor, if any, importance. By contrast, the way a matrilineage can rapidly expand in numbers is by acquiring 'slave' women, who (regardless of who their husbands are) will produce offspring for it and become ancestresses of matrilineal branches within it. Since these branches could in time compete with the master matrilineage for authority and resources, they were usually kept as distinct 'slave' branches, their origins remembered and their potential threat controlled.

In patrilineal societies, on the other hand, it is the men who produce the new members of their lineages through wives taken in from outside. Given polygyny, numbers can be rapidly increased by bringing in more wives, and a rich and successful man can easily fulfill the dream of creating many descendants in a single lifetime. This poses a problem, however, for his descendants and his kin group, since it means that he is surrounded by clusters of wives and children, all potentially competing for inheritance and position within the group. In this competition, the status of his various wives (or concubines) provides a ready principle for differentiating among the numerous lines of offspring and ordering their access to the group's resources. When such material resources are minimal, as among the Sena, or when the compound itself is the main corporate property-holding unit, as among the Hausa, or when both these factors are combined, as among the Margi, there is less need for differentiation among offspring and therefore the mother's status need not be taken into account. On the other hand, in patrilineal societies with greater resources, and with large corporate property-owing groups, the differentiation is made. Among the Tawana, for instance, the 'free' children of the father (from proper marriages in which bridewealth was paid, the woman herself being either 'free' or the 'slave' of another master) were differentiated from the children of an acquired concubine. The Aboh carried this principle a step further; they claimed that the child of a 'slave' woman could never be 'free' because it was impossible to pay real bridewealth for her as she had no relations to receive it. Another interesting variant of the principle operated among the Duala. Here, the child of a 'free' man by a 'slave' woman had the lower status of what we might call "half-citizen"—like the offspring of two 'slaves.' However, the child of a 'free' woman, fathered in concubinage with a 'slave' or a "half-citizen," was a full citizen and 'free' member of the woman's patrilineage—because no bridewealth had been paid and therefore the right to the woman's fertility had not been given up by her patrilineage. Finally, of the patrilineal societies described here, the Vai and Fulani also differentiated the 'free' children by 'free' wives from those of an acquired 'slave' wife.

From the foregoing, the question of the elimination of marginality in the offspring of acquired strangers leads to some clear conclusions. There were some societies in which the 'free' status of the parent of the sex upon which the descent system was based automatically eliminated the child's marginality. In others, the child of a "mixed marriage" could not overcome the disadvantage of one 'slave' parent. And, finally, in no society was marginality eliminated for the children of two acquired persons; even among the absorptive Sena, the marginality lingered on in subtle differences in such things as discrimination in the assignment of land and a certain disdain in their treatment. In sum, in every society described here, there were people who were legally inferior because either one or both of their parents were acquired outsiders. Furthermore, except among the Sena and Kerebe and sometimes the Hausa, the rules for their descendants were such that this body of persons perpetuated itself in the following generations.

THE POSITION OF 'SLAVE' OFFSPRING IN THE KIN GROUP

If the children of acquired strangers were, in most societies, differentiated from the blood members of the kin group, their legal position was still an advance on that of their parents. They were rarely chattels in the same sense. It was often considered wrong or at least unseemly to sell them, except in the same circumstances in which real members of the group were sold. They might also be called by different terms from their first-generation 'slave' parents, terms reflecting shadings in marginality, as among the Duala and Imbangala.

In examining the position of the offspring of 'slaves,' a distinction that is not always clearly made must constantly be kept in mind. The offspring's position involves not only the question of whether he becomes 'free' or not (and in what degree), which is a question of status, but also what kin group he belongs in and to, which is a question of affiliation. For example, in some patrilineal societies, in a marriage between a 'free' man and a 'slave' woman, the offspring may be affiliated with the 'slave' woman's owner (who may or may not be the husband himself). This, however, is quite distinct from the rules that determine the offspring's status in the owner's kin group. There may, for example, be a rule by which the offspring is a full-fledged member of the group if his father is a 'free' member of the group; otherwise the offspring is affiliated with the kin group as its 'slave.'

As has already been seen, one of the great advantages of the acquired person as a human resource is that he is kinless and therefore completely under the control of his acquisitors, with no competing loyalties, outside obligations, or protectors—"kinlessness" indeed being sometimes considered to be an essential feature of slavery (Bohannan 1963:179). This advantage, however, was threatened in the second generation, whose members had local kin of some sort. Some societies saw to it that such ties were minimized: the Mende, Vai, Fulani, Tawana, and, to a lesser extent, the Wolof and Sereer all had a relatively chattellike form of 'slavery' in which the children of a 'slave' woman belonged to her master and not to their father (unless the father was the master himself). Such rules for the offspring of "mixed marriages" forced most descendants of acquired 'slaves' into a marriage and family system that differed from that of the 'free.'

The threat to the master's control was greatest when 'slaves' married 'free' people. This established ties for their offspring, which led to a dilution of the absolute control the acquisitor lineage had over the children by giving them 'free' kinsmen, who might attract some of their loyalty or offer them protection. The surest way to prevent this was for the acquisitors to marry their 'slaves' within their own kin group. Evidence that such marriages were preferred is plentiful. Many of the chapters here mention marriages of an acquired woman with the master or members of his household or lineage, with his clients, dependents, or other 'slaves.' Through such careful transactions, maximum rights over the offspring could be assured.

In this respect, the matrilineal Imbangala illustrate a practice widespread in Central Africa. When an Imbangala man acquired a 'slave' woman, he and his lineage acquired lineage rights to her offspring; but there were certain rights that belonged to the children's father. If, however, the acquisitor himself married the 'slave' woman, he had double rights over her children—those of lineage and those of fatherhood—and full ritual powers, as well as special ties of sentiment. Such children were preferable to other 'slave' children, and in some respects to his children by 'free' wives, who belonged to their mother's lineage. They were also sometimes preferable to his sister's children—the 'free' members of his lineage —who, although under his authority, had other ties and ambitions in the kin group as well as links with other lineages through their fathers.

On the other hand, when acquired 'slaves' married 'free' people outside the master's kin group, the offspring ended up with another set of 'free' kinsmen. They did not usually belong in or to this group, but they nevertheless had links with it, rights and privileges in it, and could expect some protection from it. Among the Kongo, for example, where such ties were traced through the grandparents, a person was under the jurisdiction and protection of no less than three kin groups in addition to his own matrilineage. This meant that a 'slave' could have powerful connections outside his acquisitor group. For instance, in a matrilineal society, one could be a 'slave' through a 'slave' mother in one's own lineage and yet be the son of a chief, with special privileges in the chiefly lineage. Similarly, in the rare patrilineal society in which 'free' women married 'slave' men, their offspring might have powerful connections through their mother. The relative rarity of such marriages in patrilineal societies partly explains the tendency in these societies—as opposed to matrilineal ones—to have rather sharp status differences between the 'free' and those born as 'slaves,' who only rarely acquired important kin ties outside their master's lineage that might enhance their standing.

The net result of such mixed marriages was that the rights in the acquired stranger, which originally belonged as a single bundle to the acquisitor and his kinsmen, became broken up and reallocated in the case of his offspring among more people and more kin groups. It is thus hardly surprising that in many societies the acquisitors, seeking to maintain their control and to minimize friction with other interested lineages, applied different rules of descent to 'slaves' and their progeny. They might also, like the Tawana, discourage all unions between 'slave' and 'free' or, like the Mende, redeem the 'slaves' of other lineages before their marriages.

The same problems arose when two 'slaves' belonging to different lineages married. In such cases normal descent rules were often not applied. Among the patrilineal Hausa, the offspring were considered to belong to both kin groups. More commonly they belonged to the mother's owner, as they did among the Mende, Vai, Fulani, Tawana, and Wolof and Sereer. Some Mende were so afraid that their 'slaves' would develop family ties and loyalties among themselves that they discouraged all permanent 'slave' unions and even separated children from parents—but this was an extreme case. As has been seen, the usual method of retaining control over the descendants of acquired persons was to marry them within the acquisitor kin group.

Such manipulation of marriages to maximize control over 'slave' offspring brings 'slavery' into close coordination with the kinship system, with its many similar principles of rights-in-persons. In fact, the two become increasingly and easily intertwined and overlapping, and as the 'slaves' become also relatives, their affective marginality is greatly reduced.

This, though, brings its own problems. The 'slaves' of second and later generations become deeply embedded in the structure of the master lineage, as they become more and more related by blood ties, and begin to act as quasi blood members of the kin group. This brings about two kinds of contradictions and a dialectic that may defeat the very ends being sought. First, we have seen that one great advantage of 'slaves' was that they, like insiders, could produce children for the group, yet no incest bar prevented them from marrying into the group like outsiders. This balance could be destroyed if 'slaves' became like real members of the kin group. Second, a similar balance had to be kept in their political position in the kin group, for as their affective marginality threatened to vanish, they might begin to compete for the group's authority and resources.

Thus, in societies dominated by corporate kin groups, whose political power depended upon their numbers, one wanted 'slaves' to be "in" the group to assure their loyalty—but not so far in that they became unmarriageable kinsmen and competitors. This posed a dilemma and left the 'slave'-kinsman in an ambiguous position. Thus, the Isaacmans found outright disagreement among Sena informants as to whether the children of acquired persons were still 'slaves' or not. In societies where greater wealth and power were at stake, the problem was more serious than one of classification. 'Slave' relatives became involved in internal lineage politics. In disputes within a lineage, the normal claims and counterclaims as to which was the senior and which the junior branch would be bolstered by new "ammunition"—accusations and counteraccusations of 'slave' origin.

These "politics of 'slavery' " occur openly or sub rosa in many contemporary African societies and are well illustrated in MacGaffey's chapter on
the Kongo.

In the framework of the Anglo-American model, the position of the
African 'slave' is often inconsistent and sometimes paradoxical. This
comes out in the attitudes expressed by Africans toward the 'slave.' On the
one hand, 'slaves' can occupy very important and prestigious positions.
On the other hand, they are almost universally looked down upon and the
term itself may be used to insult them. The two strands in the attitude are
exemplified in Cohen's (1970:162) description of the position of 'slave'
noble lineages in Bornu: "Other nobles sometimes pass slurring remarks
about the slave origins of such people, but in general they have a high
status in the society as a whole." The paradox here is not greater than that
of bastardy—also an institution of marginality—in past centuries in
Europe. A noble line was formally recognized to be descended from a
bastard, its origins being forever marked on the escutcheon, and it was
more prestigious to be the bastard son of a duke than the legitimate son of
a merchant. Yet the term itself was still a term of abuse. This paradox of
sentiments arose from the structural ambiguity of a bastard; he was flesh
and blood physically yet a stranger legally. The structural ambiguity in the
position of the African 'slave' is the reverse. It lay in his *not* being of the
same "real blood" even while being legally part of the kin group.[6] This
incomplete, yet fixed, belonging "in" the kin group was a potential
feature of almost all systems of African 'slavery,' and it came most clearly
to the fore in the familial use of 'slaves,' particularly in societies where kin
groups were the dominant sociopolitical units. Here, "who is" and "who
isn't" a slave are even now sensitive questions, important yet shunned in
public discussions, a confidential matter neither to be openly mentioned
nor forgotten. To bring up the fact, even though the fact was normally
accepted, in contexts where solidarity was the prevailing mood, was the
height of bad manners; and to bring it up in the midst of a quarrel was an
insult.

The structural factors that made 'slavery' a confidential lineage matter
operated most strongly in societies whose political structure consisted of

6. Mary Douglas (1966) has put forth the thesis that objects and beings that cannot be
fitted into the dominant cognitive categories in a culture are seen as awesome or dangerous.
Given the structural ambiguity in the position of the African 'slave,' this suggests a very
interesting line of investigation into the more esoteric aspects of the ambiguity of 'slaves,'
particularly those who are deeply but incompletely incorporated into a kin group. For
example, if they are perceived as being in some sense "dangerous," then their careful treatment by the kin group is not only a matter of political calculation, as we stress, but must also
contain placatory ritual and magical elements. This hypothesis finds support among the
Kabi and Mawri groups of the Hausa: Piault (1975:345ff.) provides rich and striking data on
the way 'slaves' were endowed with mystical dangers and ritually placated.

autonomous and relatively scattered kin groups. By contrast, in societies with large, organized settlements and overarching political institutions, questions of 'slavery' became a matter of communal interest, as among the Aboh and Duala.[7] Both had a concept of citizenship that comprised an exclusive core of insiders related by blood, for whom alone were reserved certain central political institutions, such as councils and secret societies. Here, even though the affective marginality of 'slave' offspring might be reduced to a minimum within their lineage, their marginality to the civil core of the society at large remained, keeping alive in turn the distinctions in the lineage that might otherwise have vanished. Here, who was a 'slave' and who was not was a matter of public knowledge, thus making internal lineage 'slave' politics more difficult.

We would stress, then, that the process of incorporating the descendants of 'slaves' lacked neither tension nor contradictions. Incorporation was not necessarily more simple in societies where political life centered around autonomous kin groups than it was in those with state systems, as Meillassoux (1971:20-21) suggests when he contrasts the process of absorption in the West African forest societies with those of the savanna. He argues that in the forest, integration was smoother because 'slaves' were reproducers of people rather than producers of goods or services, and there was, therefore, less possibility of exploiting them economically. It cannot, however, be assumed that there must inherently be less exploitation or fewer contradictions in societies in which people are a less specialized resource than in those in which they are an economic, productive one. Where people are wealth and power, competition takes the form of competition over people—a process that need not lack dialectical tensions. Indeed, the humanity of the acquired outsider and his descendants makes such competition more complex. Tensions over power, prestige, and position can breed as many contradictions as those over physical resources and may be less easy to resolve precisely because they involve many intangibles. As MacGaffey's description of "the politics of 'slavery'" among the Kongo indicates, disputes over prestige, devoid of any material prize, can in fact be endless.

INCORPORATION INTO THE SOCIETY AS A WHOLE: THE ROLE OF THE ACQUISITOR

The outsider's initial point of contact with his new society is through his acquisitor. It is the acquisitor and his kin group that provide the *point of entry* into the community as a whole. In effect, the master sponsors the

7. The contrast we are making here between scattered, autonomous kin groups and those living in compact settlements has been made by Robin Horton (1971); this creates distinctions that are structurally more subtle than the more common one between "segmentary" or "acephalous" societies on the one hand, and "state" or "complex" societies on the other.

outsider's placement in the social structure and the master's position
determines through what gates the outsider may enter it. The outsider's
subsequent status and style of life are a function of this point of entry.
Obviously, if he is bought by a ruler, he may find his way into a palace and
a military or administrative career; if he is bought by a merchant, he may
end up as a trading agent, and a farmer will put him to work on the land.
Western travelers were often amazed to find that ministers were 'slaves,'
often with 'slaves' of their own.

Yet this phenomenon was unusual only in later Western experience.
Important positions in the Muslim world were often filled by slaves; and in
ancient Rome the emperor's slaves, set over freemen, commanded ships of
the imperial fleet (Jones 1956:186). These apparent anomalies have sometimes been taken, rather illogically, as proof that slavery was benign in
these societies: the chapters on the Wolof and Sereer and on Damagaram
show that such a conclusion is unwarranted. The high positions of some
slaves have also been interpreted as indicating the overall social mobility
of slaves; but this fails to distinguish between mobility within the society
and the point of entry into it. In modern Western slavery, the same kind of
seeming anomaly could exist. The great-grandfather of the Russian poet
Pushkin was an African slave acquired in France by Peter the Great, who
ordered his marriage into a Russian noble family—a clear instance of the
influence of sponsorship on social placement. In the New World, however,
almost all slaves entered the society as the chattels of private persons,
acquired for economic ends, and further formal limitations on their
mobility were often imposed by society at large on the basis of race.

Clearly, the greater the differentiation of status in the host society, the
greater the number of gates through which an acquired outsider can enter
it and the greater the variety of uses to which he can be put and of
positions he can occupy. We shall return to this when considering the
range of occupations of 'slaves' and their descendants in Africa. Suffice it
here simply to contrast a society like the Sena with one like the Wolof. The
Sena, with an extremely limited hierarchy and range of occupations, had
really only one gate for the outsider. Entering the acquiring lineage with a
lowly status, he became a farmer—like everyone else, including members
of chiefly lineages. In contrast, Wolof society offered numerous points of
entry, and 'slaves' became laborers on the peanut fields of rich masters, or
worked side by side with poor ones, or became tyeddo retainers of
individual chiefs or of lineages, thus joining an aristocratic military elite.

THE STRUCTURE OF MARGINALITIES AND THE
EXISTENCE OF 'SLAVE' STRATA

Initially, the acquired outsider is marginal to all of the host society—to
his acquisitor and his kinsmen, and to all groups, persons, and insti-

tutions in it. We have examined so far the ways in which the structure of
the kin group affects the manner in which the outsider's marginality to it
is institutionalized. But this process is not isolated. It takes place simultaneously with the institutionalization of the outsider's marginality to
society at large. One should expect that there will be some connection
between these two processes and an interplay between them, resulting in a
particular structure of marginalities in each society. We shall examine this
question in this section.

Let us take again a simple example from the Suku of Zaïre. This society
is composed of corporate, autonomous matrilineages, and a person's
relation to other institutions is derived from his lineage membership. As
soon as the outsider was incorporated into a kin group, albeit in an
inferior status, his marginality to the society at large was automatically
resolved. He was accepted as a member of his acquisitor's lineage and his
inferior status in it was regarded as purely an internal matter for his kin
group. This was all the easier as most acquired persons came from nearby
peoples who were culturally and linguistically akin to the Suku.

For contrast, let us turn to the Margi. Here, the mafa ('slaves') were
defined as being marginal to society as a whole; in other respects, they
lived much like everyone else. To simplify drastically: among the Suku,
the outsider's marginality was to his kin group and was not the business of
the society, whereas among the Margi, it was the society's concern but did
not much affect the individual's way of life and was an abstract concept.

These contrasting models raise the issue of "social stratification." In
the visual idiom of social scientists, Suku society may be seen as divided
vertically into lineages, the horizontal status differences within each
lineage being irrelevant to society as a whole. Among the Margi, by contrast, the primary division was horizontal, with the mafa forming a bottom
stratum. The question arises as to whether this is an apt metaphor. As
Martin Klein points out in discussing Wolof and Sereer stratification,
Westerners tend to see social categories as unequal strata. The historical
reasons for this have been suggestively argued by Dumont in *Homo Hierarchicus* (1970)—namely, that to modern Westerners the very existence of
social categories implies a denial of "equality" and, therefore, becomes a
matter of its conceptual opposite, "inequality." But are the Margi mafa a
"horizontal bottom stratum"? Are they "unequal" by being deprived in a
fundamental aspect of life? Their deprivation consists of being marginal
to Marginess and it stops there. In the visual metaphor, their marginality
can be regarded as placing them on the side of the society rather than at the
bottom. As we shall see in other cases, 'slaves' as a group are often marginal
to society precisely in this "side" manner and need not be a bottom stratum
or indeed a stratum at all; and stratification can exist among the 'slaves'
as a direct extension of the stratification in the society at large.

Other societies show greater interplay than the Suku and Margi between marginality to the kin group and marginality to society at large. Among the late-nineteenth-century Kongo, described by MacGaffey (Ch. 9), 'slavery' was also essentially a lineage affair. But the division within the lineage was somewhat harder; 'slaves' formed distinct matrilineal branches within the acquisitor matrilineage and sometimes competed with the 'free' branches. However, 'slavery' in the leading lineages in the community was of some public interest. These leading lineages, which had founded the community, controlled tracts of land, and later lineages that used the land owed them a largely symbolic deference. The deference was not, however, given to the 'slave' branches of these leading lineages, and their claim to such deference represented attempts to usurp a 'free' status within the lineage. Since the usurpation needed recognition by other lineages in the community, 'slavery' became a public matter. Miller (Ch. 8) shows that this spillover of internal lineage distinctions into the society at large was even more pronounced among the Imbangala, who constituted a large kingdom. Here, 'slaves' as retainers were a vital resource in the active political struggles within and among lineages, struggles that involved the public political institutions of the kingdom.

Among the patrilineal Sena and Kerebe, in the earlier periods, as the outsider and his descendants became absorbed into their host kin groups, they also lost their marginality to the society at large. In this they fit the Suku model. But we also glimpse among them the other principle, the one that dominated the Margi model. The Isaacmans mention that the Sena consciously preferred to acquire children because they could the better shape them culturally; and Hartwig states that the Kerebe, who do not circumcise, sought out uncircumcised children for similar reasons of better assimilation. Both concerns show a consciousness of cultural marginality and of symbols of ethnicity—the stuff out of which can be fashioned concepts of marginality to society as a whole.

The Aboh, living in a close community, with a king and central governing institutions that transcended lineages, defined full citizens, the *umudei*, as those descended from the original founders of the state. Nwachukwu-Ogedengbe's analysis shows that whatever the position of the outsider and his descendants in his lineage, their marginality to the society remained and barred them from the central political institutions of the polity. In the political sphere, we may thus speak of two horizontal strata: the umudei (the citizens) and the ndichie (both clients and slaves). In spheres other than public politics, however, a man's position in his lineage was more important than the stratum to which he belonged. A similar pattern prevailed among the Igbo, described by Victor Uchendu.

The Vai and the Sherbro reveal more obvious strata. Both refused to incorporate acquired outsiders into their kin groups, although the Sherbro made a few exceptions. Slaves unambiguously belonged to, but not in, their kin groups. In keeping with this, they were also despised and suffered serious disabilities, forming a recognizable stratum in society at large. There were also degrees of marginality among 'slaves.' The household 'slaves,' living with their masters and interacting with them in daily life, were less separated as a stratum than the tenant-farmer 'slaves,' who were settled in villages apart and had only an impersonal and distant relationship with their owners.

A question often associated with depressed strata can now be considered—the question of revolts. In general, we may posit that the more a group resembles a stratum, the more likely it is to be conscious of itself; this in turn can lead to solidarity and consequently to the possibility of concerted action. The relevant distinction here is the one Marx saw between objective class and conscious class; the relevant dynamic is that of the transformation of one into the other, of "class in itself" into "class for itself."

In this respect, the differences between the Vai and the Sherbro—differences we have mentioned in another connection—are of special interest. The rigidly patrilineal Vai maintained an uncrossable boundary between 'slave' and 'free,' and their lineage system of small, local patrilineal segments, with inheritance of 'slaves' within them, resulted in an unambiguous allocation of 'slaves' to masters. By contrast, among the Sherbro the nonunilineal descent group was large and its members were widely scattered. In any particular locality, its membership tended to shift and was sometimes ambiguous. The outsider here began as the clear property of his acquisitor. But the 'slave' descendants, particularly those farming apart on the kin group's lands, did not always so clearly belong to a particular person or group within the large kin group, though they did belong to the descent group as a whole and, specifically, to its locally resident members. Sometimes they were attached to the chieftaincy, but chieftaincy was elective and was not fixed in a specific descent line. As a result, some descendants of 'slaves' enjoyed a certain flexibility in being able to attach themselves to important members of the master descent group; others were assigned and reassigned to such members. The result was a system of corporate rights vested in the master kin group over the descendants of the 'slaves' as a group. Purely as a structure, this is reminiscent of Spartan helotry, where the Spartans as a group held sway over a conquered population and the state had the right to assign individual helots to individual Spartans. With the Sherbro, the scale was smaller and the rights belonged to kin groups and not the state. Also, Sherbro 'slaves' could sometimes move among different masters, establishing a form of client relationship within the confines of the kin group and thus escaping the domination of one lifelong master. There was thus less rigidity in Sherbro 'slavery' than there was among the Vai, whose 'slaves' formed a clear stratum, strictly defined, divided into small groups, each bound to the inescapable direct and personal control of specific masters, whether in households or on estates. Significantly, Svend Holsoe mentions revolts of Vai 'slaves,' while Carol MacCormack speaks only of individual escapes among the Sherbro, where 'slaves' had more freedom to shape satisfactory vertical relations that crosscut those necessary for the emergence of stratum consciousness.

The scattering of acquired persons among widely dispersed small households, as among the Fulani, also was not conducive to the development of stratum consciousness. The *machube,* attached to small mobile camps and given the most onerous tasks, were regarded as completely marginal to Fulani society because of their alien ethnic origins. They may thus be seen as clearly forming a stratum, but one that was crosscut by strong, discrete vertical bonds, existential and mythical, to their individual masters. Bernd Baldus (Ch. 17) raises some crucial questions as to the psychological and ideological reasons why the machube accept even now their servile status—questions to which we shall return. Significantly, Baldus does report a revolt among them, but this was in colonial times when outside factors were at play. On the face of it, the structure of machube marginalities led to ambiguities: they were in a situation conducive to the development of a stratum, but geographical scattering helped prevent the emergence of stratum consciousness.

Among the Duala, in contrast, geography played the opposite role. Here, the acquired 'slaves,' like all outsiders, were marginal to Dualahood and could not be incorporated into a kin group. Moreover, they were excluded from the more prestigious occupations of trading and fishing, were relegated to agriculture, and were segregated in their own quarter of the town. Thus the conditions for the existence of a stratum were there, and it was formally institutionalized. What reduction of marginality occurred in the following generations was only partial: they became "half-strangers." They did not belong to anyone, but were still strictly excluded from the central political structures of the society and were still residentially segregated, having to live in the same areas as the acquired 'slaves.' Even while their position hardened into that of permanent semialiens, marginal to society as a whole, the potentially integrative ties to specific kin groups were loosened. They formed an incipient stratum, with weakened crosscutting vertical bonds to their masters. These semi-aliens formed their own social, and even political, local structures. In sum, the Duala system created an imported and ever-expanding underclass, living apart with the full 'slaves.' Yet the Duala lacked such mechanisms of control as the arbitrary terrorism by which Sparta kept its helots from revolting and the Post-Reconstruction South restrained its emancipated slaves. It is hardly surprising that both the threat and the reality of slave revolts were a fact of Duala life.

The Tawana exemplify an interesting way of mitigating the threat of the formation of a self-conscious stratum—not by crosscutting vertical bonds, as among the Sherbro; nor, as among the Fulani, by scattering the stratum geographically. As Thomas Tlou shows, the Tawana bowed to geography by attenuating the disabilities of subordination in proportion to their ability to exert effective physical control over the subordinate. In the Tawana home area, acquired strangers belonged to specific masters and were given the most onerous tasks. Their marginality was accentuated by the strong ethnic self-consiousness of the Tawana and by their exclusion from Tawana political structures. They could not form their own wards nor appeal to the courts. There were, however, relatively few outsiders in the Tawana area proper. As one moved away from this area, the Tawana could no longer exert the same control and the strangers became clients; while on the far fringes, economic relations took the form of trade. What was a small stratum of slaves within Tawana settlements was dispersed outside them into large but increasingly autonomous communities with fewer disabilities and ever greater political, social, and cultural independence. A self-conscious, solidary stratum did not emerge, since onerous controls lessened and autonomy increased with geographical distance. This arose as an adaptation to the increased difficulties of remote control.

Among the Tuareg, Stephen Baier and Paul Lovejoy (Ch. 15) describe a similar pattern as an adaptation to the cycles of drought in the Sahara. In the core area of Tuareg operations, the desert, acquired outsiders were used as servants, herders, and farmers, and belonged either to individuals, to tribal "sections," or to offices. Those in areas beyond direct control, however, particularly the herders, were more like clients. Still farther away, in the savanna, some were settled on agricultural estates administered by resident agents and seem to have occupied a position somewhere between that of tenant farmers and serfs; others, who were artisans and traders, were clients—former 'slaves' who now simply owed hospitality to their former masters. This was carried a step further along the way to independence in the case of those artisans and traders fully established in Hausaland. These formed quasi-ethnic groups and owed at most merely symbolic hospitality to their erstwhile Tuareg masters. The theme was the same as with the Tawana, but the structure of the marginalities was more complex. It provided the Tuareg with a geographical continuum of human resources upon which they could fall back as they withdrew from the desert in the face of drought, and it enabled the 'slaves' to move into these various slots as the desert resources shrank. However, as these Tuareg 'slaves' moved physically away from the Tuareg core area and went deeper into the savanna, so they moved into the more complex economy and society of the Hausa. Here again they were marginal, even though 'free," and to establish a niche they had to adopt a quasi-ethnic corporate identity—defined, ironically, as that of former Tuareg 'slaves.' In other words, their new marginality in Hausa society was resolved by rooting the new identity in their former marginality in the desert society. This gave substance to the continuation of their clientship to the Tuareg (largely symbolic though it had become) and it provided them with continued access to the resources of the desert-savanna economic system.

It is apparent from the foregoing that as the complexity of the society increases and the use of 'slaves' becomes more varied, so there is greater variation in their social position—legal and otherwise. It becomes increasingly difficult to find a single pattern that will cover them all. The Hausa-Kanuri state of Damagaram, described by Roberta Ann Dunbar (Ch. 6), and the Wolof and Sereer, discussed by Martin Klein (Ch. 13), represent further variations in complexity. In fact, each of them encompasses, in a single society, all the different kinds of institutionalized marginalities that have appeared in other societies. The career of the 'slave' of a Hausa or Wolof peasant, for instance, is similar to that of the acquired outsider of the Sena or Kerebe. The 'slave' of a Wolof merchant is very like the trading agent or canoeman of an important Aboh. The numerous 'slave' retainers of the sultan of Damagaram correspond to those of the Imbangala king. And the corporate control of persons by Imbangala lineages or Sherbro kin groups is similar in its principles and political functions to that of politically important Wolof matrilineages.

This variety in types of servitude among the Wolof and Sereer and in Damagaram introduces in a new form the question posed earlier in relation to the Margi: When should acquired outsiders be seen as forming a bottom stratum in a society? Acquired persons in these societies occupy positions at all levels of power and a few participate in the administration of the government. 'Slaves' may thus more appropriately be said to be not at the bottom of society but at its side, as were Margi mafa. But in the complex societies this occurs because of their multiplicity of functions, whereas with the Margi it was because of their singular simplicity of functions.

In the complex societies, some 'slaves,' but only some, may form a stratum. Thus, certain persons acquired by the sultan of Damagaram held political office, ruling over estates of 'slave' cultivators. Their marginality was not thereby abolished; on the contrary, their worldly success was possible precisely because they were marginal to society, having no outside connections and being entirely dependent on their masters, which made them into reliable officials. They were not, however, a stratum. On the other hand, at the bottom of society were the peasants and their 'slaves,' who labored side by side with their owners and were eventually assimilated by them. These peasant masters and their 'slaves' formed together a stratum in the larger society. Similarly, the tyeddo—the military and administrative elite 'slaves' of the Wolof and Sereer—were a stratum, composed of outsiders; they were also a self-conscious stratum, aware of the bases of their power and the threats to it, as shown in their opposition to Islam and their readiness to engage in "stratum warfare." As Klein puts it, the Wolof and Sereer were divided into the mass of people and the elite, and the latter included the 'slave' tyeddo.

In sum, then, it seems clear that the placement of the acquired outsider in society at large is related to his marginality in regard to his acquisitor and his acquisitor's kin group. Indeed, in some cases, as among the Kerebe, the kin group is the sole sponsor of the outsider's position in society and whether he is a 'slave' or not is considered an internal matter, irrelevant to society as a whole. In such more homogeneous societies, the institutionalization of marginality is also more uniform. By contrast, in the more complex societies, with hierarchies of position and power, the points of entry or gates by which the outsider enters the community are more varied and may, as in Damagaram, span the social scale from peasant to sultan. Here marginality to the acquisitor is institutionalized in a number of ways; it is different, for instance, for a wife, a trading agent, or an estate serf, and it may overlap closely, slightly, or not at all with the sphere of kinship. In the more complex societies, the acquired outsiders can also be put to a greater variety of uses, with the result that there is a great proliferation of niches, positions, statuses, and styles of life for them. Western observers who lump them all together as 'slaves' might then conclude that they have mobility, basing their conclusion on the ethnocentric assumption that such persons always enter society at the bottom of the scale, and this conclusion might reinforce their view that such 'slavery' is benign.

In many instances, however, society at large does not define the marginality of the acquired outsider exclusively by reference to his acquisitor. His alien ethnic origin may be seen as an important factor. It can be of only slight importance, as among the Kerebe, Aboh, or Sena; but sometimes it is a crucial factor, as among the Tawana, Duala, and pastoral Fulani. The use of differences in ethnicity and physique as criteria for status distinctions in African societies requires more study (see, for example, Burnham 1972, on the Fulani of Adamawa). In the meantime, one might venture to hypothesize that such distinctions are most pronounced when differences in physique and culture are found in a parochial rather than a cosmopolitan setting.

Finally, a few remarks on 'slave' revolts. These appear to have been relatively rare in Africa, although further research into this question is needed. For such revolts to take place, a large number of 'slaves' must come to form a self-conscious stratum. Separate settlements of 'slaves' would favor such stratum-consciousness, as would a relatively sudden influx of large numbers of recently acquired trade 'slaves,' who would be used as productive labor or for further trading, and whose marginality would remain very high. More commonly, even when there was a stratum, as among the Vai and Duala and in Zanzibar and on the Swahili coast (Akinola 1972; Cooper 1974:304-5), revolts were absent or only sporadic. Among the Borgou Fulani, there was a stratum, but 'slaves' were too scattered and so imbued with a sense of inferiority and gratitude, because of their rescue in infancy by the Fulani, that little consciousness of common interest, identity, and grievance could emerge. Elsewhere, as among the Kerebe, the nineteenth-century Kongo, and the Imbangala, slaves were recognized as a category but not as a stratum, since their status rested within their lineages and this determined their standing in society as a whole. In the more complex societies—precisely those which had a political and economic basis for oppression—the use of 'slaves' was so varied that they were dispersed throughout the social structure, and 'slave' as a discrete category had little existential reality. This is in striking contrast to the New World, where political and economic complexity led to a narrower specialization in the use of slaves, which was conducive to the formation of a discrete stratum. This problem calls for extensive historical and comparative investigation. At present, one can only speculate as to the directions the various 'slave' systems in Africa might have taken had the colonial occupation not intervened, an issue that Roberta Ann Dunbar raises in connection with Damagaram.

One should avoid the error of assuming that 'slaves' were always a category with an identity of interests and that, where they had no such common bond, it was because it was undermined by other loyalties. In fact, these other loyalties could be—by any objective criteria—more important than any common bond based on 'slavery.' For instance, hard realism made a sultan's 'slave' retainer see his interests as different from those of his fellow captives on his master's farms. Equally inescapable logic made a Kongo 'slave' see that his future depended upon the manipulation of the lineage structure and not on abstract "stratum interests." To suggest that people "should" necessarily share an identity of interests because they belong to a slave class or stratum is to commit the fallacy of misplaced concreteness. An analytical class or category, no matter how theoretically interesting to the outside observer, should not be assumed to have a social reality that it cannot have in the concrete historical conditions of the society in question.

TREATMENT AND RESISTANCE: SOME PROBLEMS OF COMPARATIVE STUDY

The question of the treatment of 'slaves' is of particular importance in Western perceptions. We have therefore taken pains to distinguish between "status mobility" and "affective" and "worldly success mobility" —a distinction between the legal position of the 'slave' and the way people actually treat him as well as how he lives. This distinction is important because the modern Western view of the relationship between status and behavior has often been applied to 'slavery' in general, and this has clouded the perceptions and interpretations in a way that must be understood by the historian and the social scientist. The issue has a bearing on such vital questions as reactions to enslavement, the role of coercion, the incidence of flight and rebellion, the meaning of docility—all of which have been relevant to some ideologically tinged problems of interpreting non-Western 'slavery' and, by implicit contrast, Western slavery as well.

In the Western experience, the distinction between legal status and outward behavior has become more and more blurred in the past century and a half, as formal status differences between people have been crumbling under the impact of egalitarian ideology and practice and of the ever increasing complexity and multiplicity of social structures in the West. The idea that a noble as a noble and a peasant as a peasant (or a woman as a woman) should enjoy different rights with legal sanction is contrary to modern ideas of a common and uniform citizenship and of universal human rights. Differences of status persist, to be sure, but less and less as a legal matter; hence they must often be discovered by complicated and arguable indices devised by sociologists. In fact, these informal status differences are almost synonymous with differences in worldly success, and Westerners assume, not unreasonably for their own societies, that outward success or misery is a direct clue to status. Conversely, a low status, such as that of 'slave,' is assumed to carry with it relative poverty, deprivations of all kinds, and ill-treatment.

This association of the 'slave' status with a deprived way of life has been reinforced by the picture of plantation slavery, as practiced in the Anglo-American world and as painted during the abolitionist debates of the nineteenth century. The indelible impression was created that a slave was necessarily miserable and badly treated. Moreover, in the highly specialized New World plantation economy, the emphasis was on labor—

how slaves worked, what work they did, and how hard they worked, all in contrast to free laborers. The image of the slave as laboring under harsh conditions, exploited, ill-treated and confined to the bottom of the social scale, has come to dominate the Western conception of the essence of slavery.[8]

Such, then, was the yardstick against which Westerners measured an institution in other societies to determine whether or not it was "really" slavery. Crucial to the judgment were such questions as the individual's worldly success, treatment, type of work, living conditions, and the differences between the lives of the 'slaves' and those of the rest of the community. The assumption was that no man could "really" be a 'slave' if he was not obviously deprived in a material sense. When such deprivation was not visible, the Western observer might never notice differences in status *per se* and never inquire into the legal differences between the acquired stranger and his acquisitor.

Our contributors repeatedly mention the unreliability of such observers, particularly of travelers, both early and late. Martin Klein states that Europeans could not tell the difference between the various statuses among the Wolof and Sereer. Roberta Ann Dunbar points out that important status distinctions among the Hausa were "camouflaged" to European eyes. Thomas Tlou shows that Europeans confused Tawana clients with batlhanka and that their reports emphasized good or bad treatment depending on whether or not they wished to abolish 'slavery.' Nwachukwu-Ogedengbe states that European witnesses in nineteenth-century Aboh were not only unreliable on treatment and on categories of 'slaves,' but even when they recorded wide variations in treatment, they still wrote as though 'slavery' must have been a uniform institution about which it should have been easy to generalize. Gerald Hartwig writes that when Europeans found the condition of the 'slave' to be better than it was in the Western stereotype, they proceeded to give an idealized description of the local institution. Moreover, such problems of perception were not exclusively European. Stephen Baier and Paul Lovejoy point out that the Hausa could not accurately distinguish between the various statuses among the Tuareg, and Gerald Hartwig states that among the Kerebe the everyday life of acquired strangers was such that Kerebe themselves could not tell the difference between 'slave' and 'free' in clans other than their own.

Given the evident unreliability of perceptions by European and sometimes by African observers, historical sources have to be very carefully

---

8. Thus, Genovese (1969) has shown the misinterpretations that the confusion of "treatment" with other elements has led to in analyses of New World slavery.

interpreted when they are examined for references to 'slavery' in African societies. A lack of such references also calls for careful inquiry and precise definition. Thus, we must treat with caution Rodney's (1966; 1970: 262-63) argument that "slavery" and other "institutions of social oppression" (both undefined) were absent on the upper Guinea coast and perhaps in other areas of West Africa because there are no references to them in the early Portuguese records. One must surely hesitate to draw conclusions from what Portuguese visitors of the fifteenth and sixteenth centuries *failed* to report. Nonexistence is but one possible reason among many for their failure to describe the complex institutions that go under that vague umbrella term of "slavery" in Africa.

Having discussed the unreliable nature of past perceptions of 'slavery' in Africa, we now come to the question of the actual treatment of 'slaves.' The data show very wide variation in the treatment of 'slaves,' just as they show wide variations in their use. As Nwachukwu-Ogedengbe emphasizes, there may be great variation in treatment within a single category of 'slave' in a single society. One would expect that, in general, treatment would reflect some balance between the degree of their marginality and the kind of use to which they were put. Certainly the worst treated were those captured or bought for sale, whose position combined the greatest marginality with use only as a commodity. In this position of greatest marginality, instrumental needs dominated treatment: male captives were sometimes killed if they could not be ransomed or easily sold, and it was new outsiders who were often used for sacrifice. At the other end of the scale, the best treatment occurred with the least marginal persons, such as the descendants of 'slaves,' who functioned as quasi kinsmen.

The situation of most acquired outsiders usually fell between these extremes and was fraught with contradictions and ambiguities that were often unresolved. Treatment might depend on personality. Some were liked more than others; the lazy were more likely to be sold; the faithful might be kept when a real lineage member was sold. The disobedient were more likely to be sacrificed. The personal element came most often into play when the outsider served in a small household rather than on a large estate. Sometimes, however, distance had an advantage. On Hausa estates, 'slave' sharecroppers were likely to merge with other tenants, but house 'slaves' remained apart from the 'free.' Among the Sherbro, a 'slave' on a farm could secretly accumulate money for redemption more easily than one living under his master's eye.

In interpreting treatment, concentration on either the legal position of the 'slave' by itself, or his actual treatment by itself, can be misleading. Thomas Tlou and Nwachukwu-Ogedengbe emphasize that a mere recitation of the "rights" of slaves—such as one often gets from informants in the field—ignores such crucial questions as how these rights were enforced and by whom; and if by the master alone, could the slave appeal? All too often, slaves are described as "children" of their owners. This stresses the familial side of the relationship but ignores, as we have already said, the fact that this meant that they were permanent, legal minors without rights of appeal to outside authorities. Thus, among the Aboh, Tawana, Sherbro, and Kerebe, we are specifically told that 'slaves' had no access to courts that were open to the 'free.' However, in those societies where lineages were essentially sovereign units, neither 'slave' nor 'free' could appeal to outside courts or authorities, so that this fact by itself cannot be taken to show deprivation. Also, a 'slave' in a small-scale society did not have very far to go to take refuge with another kin group and get beyond the reach of his masters. In this instance, knowledge of the formal legal position alone throws no light on the actual way the rules were applied and whether they could be applied at all. The discussions of the Aboh, Hausa, Kerebe, Tawana, and Sena also stress the fact that the formal rules were likely to be applied more strictly, more intransigently, and more capriciously where 'slaves' were concerned.

If too great a concentration on legal rules has its dangers, so does too heavy a reliance on "what really happened." For example, among the Tuareg, in periods of adequate rainfall, differences in the way of life among the different kinds of servile dependents were scarcely apparent; but the legal distinctions were there and became very real when, with drought, access to vital resources depended upon position in the legal hierarchy. Those at the bottom were considered expendable and were forced to seek their livelihood elsewhere. Similarly, among the Sena, whose 'slavery' was among the most benign, it was in times of famine, when people had to be sold off, that the normally invisible differences in marginalities became apparent and important.

In assessing treatment and disabilities, we must distinguish between what Fortes (1969:95-98) has called the different "domains" of the social structure. For example, in the domain of kinship and familial relations, there may scarcely be any perceptible differences between 'slaves' and real kinsmen, but this does not mean that there are no pronounced differences in the domain of politics or religion. The 'slave' may be excluded from certain rituals or from powerful secret societies, or barred from certain public offices. Equally, special ritual and administrative positions may be reserved for 'slaves' and carry considerable prestige even while publicly stamping the incumbent as a 'slave.' The stigma may sometimes outweigh the prestige, as in the case reported by James Vaughan when a Margi 'slave' asserted his personal dignity by refusing to take a prestigious position in the king's entourage.

Resistance, flight, and rebellion give some indication of treatment. The conditions prerequisite to rebellion and their relative rarity in Africa have already been discussed. The more usual form of resistance was, of course, escape. This was simpler, usually less dangerous, and often hard to prevent. For one thing, the geographical area over which the master and his lineage, or even a state, had effective jurisdiction was usually quite small (when contrasted, for instance, with European spheres of colonial control in the Caribbean or with the southern United States). Masters were only too aware of this problem and took precautions when possible. Thus, chiefly Sherbro kin groups returned one another's fugitives, and the Tuareg used 'slaves' in desert-savanna trading corridors far from the 'slaves'' homeland. Masters were also selective at the outset: women and children from remote areas were preferred and adult men often had no buyers. In general, captives of war and victims of kidnapping were sold off as soon as possible to distant regions or, as among the Vai and Sherbro, into the overseas trade, or used for sacrifice locally, as among the Duala. Children were widely preferred because they could be easily acculturated, an advantage recognized by the Sena and Kerebe. Also, children were more likely to accept their servile position, a point that Carol MacCormack makes when discussing the conscious training of acquired children for their subordinate role in Sherbro homes. We have, however, all too little material on this important question of methods of socialization into servility in Africa; since the material must come from oral sources, it will all too likely soon be lost forever.

In spite of all precautions, however, escapes did occur. There is evidence of escape both from small-scale societies like that of the Giriama (Miers fieldnotes) and some described here, and from large-scale societies. This is particularly true where there were large numbers of recently acquired, first-generation 'slaves,' or 'slaves' used as agricultural labor on large estates, or both—in brief, where there were large numbers of highly marginal 'slaves,' as in parts of the Western Sudan (Klein, pers. comm.; Miers 1975:164) and on the Swahili coast (Cooper 1973:95-96; 1974: 301ff., 323ff.; Miers 1975:99). It is apparent that, benign as many forms of African 'slavery' may have seemed to Westerners, there were always some 'slaves' who were dissatisfied with their lot and sought escape from it. The question that requires study, of course, is not the simplistic one of whether African 'slavery' in general was benign or not, or whether African 'slaves' in general sought to escape or not. Such questions are based on a false premise. They assume that these complex and extremely varied systems can be treated as a single institution—"African 'slavery.'" The relevant questions are those that accept the reality of a wide range of responses by 'slaves' to their condition, and move on to ask about the variables that account for this range and for the statistical prevalence of some reactions over others in specific places and periods.

The issue of the acceptance of, and socialization into, the role of 'slave' is dealt with by Bernd Baldus (Ch. 17) in describing the Fulani machube in the framework of the Marxian notion of "false consciousness" and with a Gramscian concern about the processes that support it. Here, in one of the clearest cases of chattellike slavery, we find the "oppressed" willingly accepting their oppression and the social myths that support it. They insist that to be machube is purely an internal matter within their master's compound and relevant only in regard to their relationship with him. They thus dwell only on their marginality to their acquisitor and not to Fulani society as a whole. This allows them to identify with and assume the trappings of the Fulani in their dealings with the other peoples of Borgou, to the amusement of the latter, who are well aware that the Fulani regard them as outsiders.

As Baldus indicates, the problem of interpretation hinges on assumptions about human nature that usually remain implicit. Thus, the prevalent "liberal" model of human nature, which is largely dominant in social science, assumes that man is a freedom-loving and autonomy-seeking being, pursuing his natural rights and rebelling when he is thwarted. Consequently, if he does not resist what appears to be oppression, then he is either suppressed by force or, contrary to appearances, not in fact oppressed. This model—which is also "vulgar Marxist"— accommodates any and all variations in behavior; when men do not resist, this is attributed to factors external to human nature, such as the lack of alternative choices: there is nowhere to run, or the risks of escape or revolt outweigh the benefits, or immediate repression is likely, and so on. These explanations preserve intact the basic assumption about human nature, and lead to premature closure on very complex issues of human motivation.

The "false-consciousness" approach, by contrast, raises many more interesting questions. Where the "liberal" model would concentrate on instances of revolt, the "false-consciousness" model would examine the absence of revolts as well as their occurrence to determine the conditions for both. It also raises questions about the relation between consciousness and social setting and their bearing on action, rather than assuming a human nature that consists of inflexible yearnings expressed in an infinitely flexible utilitarian calculus. But the approach also poses some difficulties. Whereas the "liberal" model assumes an a priori knowledge of human nature—largely as set out in the eighteenth-century European Enlightenment—and finds puzzles in unexpected reactions, the "false-consciousness" model assumes an a priori knowledge of social reality and of the "appropriate" consciousness of it, and then puzzles over people's failure to act according to them.

The question of treatment, it is clear, carries with it a host of implications and raises questions that are central to further serious work on African 'slavery,' beginning with the recognition of the immense variations in institutions covered by this name. Until recently, 'slavery' was seen as relatively uniform throughout the continent, and relatively benign, and its nature was clarified by contrasting it with New World slavery. But the picture of the latter, it now appears, has not been without its own stereotypes. The dominant image of the brutal and brutalizing plantation has given way to a far more complex reality (see Fogel and Engerman 1974; Genovese 1975; Gutman 1975; Walton 1975), which in turn raises a host of new questions. Similarly, the clear impossibility of maintaining a uniformly benign picture of African 'slavery' should lead to the asking of complex questions that should put the analysis of African 'slavery' into the same realm of discussion as other systems of servitude.

VERSATILITY AND VARIATION IN THE USE OF ACQUIRED PERSONS

Unlike novelists, who explore the varied and subtle uses to which human beings are constantly put by each other, most social scientists seem to think that people are worth acquiring and controlling only or mainly for the labor or the wealth that they bring—a measure of the extent to which the crassly economic assumptions about human motivation that flourished in the nineteenth century are still with us. There is also a more subtle version of this assumption: that where wealth is difficult to store or accumulate, control over people is a convenient alternative. Slavery, however, flourished in societies where the accumulation of wealth in material form presented no difficulties. The essential point we wish to stress here is that people can be acquired and controlled for a great many different purposes, and many of these are not economic. A quick survey of the uses of acquired outsiders in Africa will serve to show their versatility and flexibility.

In the realm of kinship, they were used as wives, concubines, children for the childless, and producers of more people. In productive activities, they were herdsmen, farmers, and canoemen, and they were often skilled artisans. For instance, Roberta Ann Dunbar's list for Damagaram mentions them as spinners, weavers, butchers, masons, builders, salt producers, cloth dyers, roofers, and tanners. Acquired persons served as domestics, messengers, trading agents, retailers, and experts in literacy, as retainers at the courts of rulers and high officials, as officers of state, bureaucrats, and warriors and military commanders, whose duties included the capture of others. Some were used in ritual sacrifices, or killed to accompany a dead chief or master to the afterworld; and among the Duala, in one instance they became a source of heads for a vainglorious but inept chief who had failed to get enough heads in battle.

Acquired persons were valuable as economic, social, and political capital, as a type of wealth that could be easily converted from one use to another and that had the incomparable advantage of being also self-supporting and self-reproducing. They could serve as pawns and as a means of paying fines or legal compensation. They could be held in reserve and bartered in time of scarcity, or, as among the Tuareg, they could serve as hosts during famines. Finally, they were the currency of political transactions—tribute to chiefs, gifts among rulers, or rewards to subordinates.

Obviously, not every society used them in all these capacities. The range of possible uses varied with the overall complexity of the society—that is, its total social and political economy, and not merely its productive-labor economy. The Sena and Kerebe show the limits imposed on the use of 'slaves' by a predominantly subsistence economy and a relatively unstratified social structure. The Sena society had no niches for trading agents, full-time bureaucrats, or artisans in large-scale enterprises; nor could they afford such exuberant and conspicuous consumption of human capital as even the Duala or Aboh, let along big kingdoms like Dahomey. The Sena primarily wanted 'slaves' as social and not labor units, and the precariousness of their subsistence meant that too many people might at times be a liability. The essential impossibility of extracting any surplus value from labor did not, however, eliminate the exchange value of human beings against grain in times of shortage. The Kerebe, with a secure subsistence base, could acquire many more outsiders than the Sena, and in the nineteenth century large numbers were used as farmers, retainers, and political gifts. Neither the Kerebe nor the Sena, however, could mount large-scale tenant-farming operations or organize gang labor, since they lacked the technical means of social and political control that such systems require.

That use is not governed purely by labor needs is shown by the Kongo of Mbanza Manteke. With a modest subsistence agricultural base, they engaged in fierce competition for prestige and position as valuables in themselves—a situation familiar enough to academics; this created a separate motive for increasing one's dependents, including 'slaves.' The Tawana furnish a further illustration of the importance of nonlabor factors in patterning forms of 'slavery.' The Tawana economic level, taken by itself, would suggest a relatively benign and assimilative form of 'slavery,' similar to that of the Sena or Kerebe. Yet we find that Tawana 'slaves' were kept from easy integration with their masters by ethnic considerations—as were the machube of the Fulani whose rather simple productive economy coexisted with a very onerous and chattellike 'slavery.'

The Tuareg case shows that the use of acquired persons also need not be entirely governed by the limitations of the host society itself. The niches open to them in the Tuareg-dominated desert were limited but they could move periodically, with their masters' encouragement, into the far greater range of niches in the savanna. Here, the boundaries of the Tuareg political community were narrower than those of their economic sphere.

The greater the complexity of the economic, social, and political setting, then, the wider the range of uses for acquired outsiders. Complexity itself may, however, be specialized and confined to only some spheres of the social structure. Thus the Aboh are not more complex in purely sociopolitical terms than the Kerebe, but their position on the trade route to the coast led to an expansion of the trading sector; 'slaves' were used in this sector in large numbers as trading agents and canoemen, whereas they were not used in the political system. By contrast, the Imbangala, also located on a trade route, and needing 'slaves' for some of the same purposes, in addition used them extensively in the sociopolitical sphere as lineage branches, lineages, officials, and rulers sought to increase their dependents in keen competition with one another.

In relating sociopolitical complexity to complexity of use, one must remember that it is the range of uses that expands. Hence, however complex the society, 'slaves' may still be used in it as they are in simpler communities. There is nothing to prevent the use of some 'slaves' as chattels on agricultural estates or in a workshop even while others are simultaneously closely integrated into kin groups and still others serve as aristocratic warriors or bureaucrats. Industrial 'slavery' need not, after all, preclude familial 'slavery'; increased complexity merely creates more specialized types of servitude. On the other hand, where there is little role differentiation, a person tends to function simultaneously in many spheres that, in a complex society, are separate. Thus, in the more homogeneous and structurally simpler societies, 'slaves' are used in less specialized ways. But this does not mean, as it has sometimes been interpreted to mean, that they are necessarily used in more benign—social, rather than economic—ways. Among the Giriama, an egalitarian people on the Kenya coast whose economy in the nineteenth century was similar to that of the Sena, more dependents meant both greater social prestige and greater wealth, for they produced an agricultural surplus that could be traded with neighboring peoples, particularly for goats, which could in turn be used to acquire more wives and thus further increase the size of the group (Miers fieldnotes). A 'slave' could thus be both a quasi kinsman and a

productive unit of wealth at one and the same time, as indeed real
kinsmen also were. Even the Sena, with their social use of acquired
strangers, also used them economically—as a reserve for obtaining grain
in times of famine. By contrast, in a society where roles are more
specialized, quasi kinsmen would be less likely to be simultaneously units
of economic exchange, partly because other 'slaves' would be serving that
specialized function.

We should expect that the manner in which 'slaves' are used is governed
by some measure of efficiency. For example, Bloch (1947) has shown that,
in the late Roman Empire and in early medieval Europe, the decline of
large markets for agricultural produce led to a change of method in the
exploitation of slaves: plantationlike use of gang labor gave way to sharecropping by slaves. And Jones (1956:199) suggests that, on the whole,
gang-labor slavery in ancient Rome and Greece was economically viable
only when slave "prices stood at rock bottom" and labor could be continuously employed. Such relationships between overall economic conditions
and forms of 'slavery' in Africa remain to be explored, both comparatively
and historically. The task is complicated, for a wide range of different
uses makes relative and comparative "costs" difficult to estimate. How,
for instance, does one compare the relative profitability of use as a retainer
with use as agricultural laborer or artisan? Nevertheless, interesting possibilities emerge once we stop looking at 'slavery' simply as a labor system.
For example, when the most efficient method of labor exploitation is not
through 'slavery' but through other methods (such as farm tenancy or
seasonally hired labor), this does not preclude the use of 'slaves' in other
capacities (as household servants, retainers, warriors, administrators,
concubines, eunuchs, etc.). In brief, a primary productive sphere in which
there is no slavery need not preclude—and may indeed finance—the use of
'slaves' in other spheres.

Finally, one problem must be faced when we conclude that the more
complex the society, the wider the range of uses for slaves. Although this
seems to have been true in Africa and in the ancient Mediterranean area,
there is an exception—the New World. It is true that recent research is
bringing to light a wider variety of uses for slaves here than the old stereotype suggests; they were used, for example, in crafts, factories, and mines,
as overseers and even as soldiers, as well as being employed as field hands
and domestics. However, in the New World, and particularly in the Anglo-
American territories, there was a cultural insistence on the slaves' racial
marginality to society as a whole, which closed to them a whole range of
higher occupations. There was also a political economy in which the
primary use for them was as units of labor in a specialized and partial
economic system appended to a much larger one. Furthermore, since

government was far less personal than in Africa, and kin groups were not the basic social units, the incentive for and possibility of using them for social and political purposes in the same way as they were used in Africa was lacking. Finally, a highly monetized economy, with banking, credit, and storage facilities, provided varied and flexible forms of capital accumulation and investment, and a cosmopolitan society served by worldwide trade made available many forms of conspicuous consumption. To return to a point made early in this analysis, the Anglo-American New World type of slavery, far from being a norm, was in fact a rather unusual historical creation.

NUMBERS AND CONCENTRATIONS OF 'SLAVES'

With such a variety of uses for acquired persons in Africa, one would expect to find them used in great numbers. When one considers numbers, however, the problem posed by African 'slavery' is not merely one of counting but the more interesting conceptual one of how and whom to count, and why.

The problem of whom to count hinges on what the term 'slave' means and whether it can mean very much in quantitative comparisons with other continents and, indeed, within Africa itself. The worst possible solution, of course, is to take whatever it is that individual Western observers, lay and academic, have decided to call 'slave' in each of the respective societies observed and proceed to compare quantities on that basis.

The need to be clear as to what a count means is illustrated by the example of Damagaram. There, the assimilation of 'slaves' by peasants was continuous, and this resulted in a constant demand for new 'slaves.' Damagaram would have had less need for new 'slaves' had there been less assimilation of 'slave' descendants. Does this make Damagaram a " 'slave society"—usually defined as one whose total economy depends on 'slavery'? If one does not count assimilated 'slave' descendants, then it probably was not; yet it did depend on fresh imports of 'slaves'—and that, paradoxically, precisely because its assimilation of 'slaves' to the 'free' prevented it from becoming a 'slave' society. In brief, is the significant count here, for comparison, the number of existing 'slaves,' or the number of the 'slaves' and their descendants, or the numbers being imported yearly? The decision for Damagaram would not be the same as for another society with a different dynamic of 'slavery.'

The question of numbers is also related to the difference between physical (biological) reproduction and social reproduction, the latter being the reproduction by a local 'slave' population of people who continue to be classified as 'slaves.' Where, as in the New World, the 'slave' population consists of relatively discrete and identifiable reproductive units, its natural attrition or increase can be assessed and the significance of either can be discussed (as, for example, in Curtin 1968, and Fogel and Engerman 1974). In Africa, however, the social reproduction rate may diverge widely from the physical reproduction rate. Depending on the specific rules in each society about the offspring of 'slaves,' a 'slave' population could as a category reproduce itself very rapidly or (when most of the offspring became 'free') very slowly. This makes comparisons between societies difficult. One society may have high imports and few 'slaves' while in another the position may be reversed—yet the two may have populations with exactly the same birth and death rates.

With these difficulties in mind, we shall try to discuss the question of numbers in terms broad enough to be realistic.

In small-scale and relatively undifferentiated societies, the proportion of 'slaves' appears on the whole to have been lower than in the larger and more complex ones. Among the Margi, for instance, Vaughan estimates that mafa were only 1 or 2 percent of the population. The Sena, where assimilation and hence attrition was high, had a 'slave' population of perhaps 10 percent. In contrast, among the Kongo of Mbanza Manteke, where the memory of 'slave' origins was preserved and 'slave' status was perpetuated in self-reproducing 'slave' branches of lineages, the proportion was much higher—perhaps half the population was 'slave,' though the society was relatively uncomplex.

When small-scale societies become part of an important trading network, the number of 'slaves' may rise significantly and their distribution may become uneven, reflecting differential commercial success among lineages and individuals. Among both the Giriama and the Kamba of Kenya, for instance, 'slavery' seems to have been most important among those groups who participated most actively in trade with the Swahili (Miers fieldnotes). Moreover, political power was often used to acquire wealth in people. Thus, Hartwig states that among the Kerebe, the ruler and persons of importance controlled most of the servile population by the end of the nineteenth century, where earlier the fewer 'slaves' were more widely held. Similarly, among the Aboh, Nwachukwu-Ogedengbe estimates that 'slaves' and their recognized descendants probably composed about half the population, heavily concentrated in the hands of the ruler, his relatives, and a few important families and lineages. Miller gives no precise figures for the Imbangala, but indicates a considerable inflow and retention of 'slaves' in the later nineteenth century, when the overseas outlets vanished.

Among the more complex societies, Klein refers to estimates that about one third of the Wolof and Sereer population included 'slaves' of all categories, from the elite tyeddo to the servile peasant. These figures compare with other estimates for the Sudan. Smith (1959:242) estimates half the Hausa population to have been 'slaves' and Meillassoux (1971:22) speaks of 30 to 60 percent for the Western Sudan as a whole.

In these complex societies, the difficulty in counting lies not, as in simpler homogeneous communities, in the difficulty of distinguishing 'slaves' from kinsmen, but in the obverse—in the heterogeneity of the society and of the functions in it of acquired outsiders, who range from chattels to warriors and from farmers to bureaucrats. Such a diversity of units and functions makes "the relative number of 'slaves' in a society" as meaningless a comparative notion as that of "the relative number of 'transport units' in a society" when the term "transport unit" indiscriminately comprehends carts, jet planes, wheelbarrows, horses, automobiles, and people carrying loads on their backs.

To conclude the consideration of numbers, one point emerges clearly: over the past centuries African institutions—including households, kin groups large and small, offices, and whole societies—have been strikingly absorptive of outsiders. The circulation of outsiders, by means ranging from single transfer to large-scale capture and sale, has been great, but their fate and that of their descendants has varied so much that static quantitative data can only yield superficial and usually meaningless comparisons.

THE DYNAMICS OF AFRICAN 'SLAVERY'

Our conclusion on quantitative comparisons suggests that instead of counting 'slaves' under static conditions in each society, a processual approach to the problem may prove more enlightening. In this approach, we first examine each society for patterns of historical shifts in the ways and frequencies with which acquired outsiders are used; we then proceed to compare the societies in terms of such dynamics in order to discern some common pattern. Viewed in this way, the material presented here reveals a generalized pattern of entrepreneurship in the use of acquired persons, and with it, a readiness to respond to new opportunities of use.

We may begin with the Sena. The Isaacmans point out that the acquisition of outsiders occurred in a setting of openly available land, shifting agriculture, small agricultural surplus, and periodic famine. This imposed a situation in which, in good times, one sought to increase one's kin-group membership, in bad times to reduce it, and at all times to have a human reserve to call upon to exchange for grain when needed. The system of acquired outsiders was quite directly integrated with the kinship system: one built up one's reserve of people by giving grain for them, by acquiring wives to produce children, and by accepting strangers. There was nothing in the system, we should stress, that hinged on exogenous factors such as long-distance trade, or the introduction of stratification from outside, or the impact of alien ideas.

We have already noted that in societies where acquired persons were sought primarily as quasi members of kin groups, there was a marked preference for the more pliable children and for women as reproducers of children, rather than for men. This was often expressed directly in exchange rates. Women were frequently worth double what men were, and when legal compensation for homicide, for example, was paid in people, the same rate applied. Women and children rather than men, were also the preferred units of compensation. The reasons were partly economic. While the Sena preferred children because they were easier to assimilate, they were also aware that children had ahead of them long years of productive labor, and, in the case of girls, a long reproductive period.

Whereas the Sena exemplify a relatively stable situation in which human resources are converted into production and vice versa, in an almost cyclical fashion, the Kerebe offer an example of a long-term reorganization in response to new opportunities. In the nineteenth century, with the rise in trade, the Kerebe found a greater outlet for their millet; at the same time their population shrank owing to the introduction of new diseases. The Kerebe reaction was twofold—to acquire more outsiders and to use more of them (although by no means all) as units of productive labor in agriculture rather than as quasi relatives. Here, we have a response to new opportunities that took the form of shifting proportionately more acquired persons to one use, whereas before another use had been dominant. This response, be it noted, occurred in the context of a general expansion of regional economic activity, of which the long-distance eastern African 'slave' trade was a part; but the peripheral contact of the Kerebe with the 'slave' trade was not as suppliers of people but rather as recipients. Internally, their responses to economic opportunities led to a change in the *frequencies* of 'slave' transactions and not in their *nature*. As they sought more servile agricultural laborers, the proportion of 'slaves' used primarily as social units began to wane as the number of chattellike outsiders, acquired by outright purchase for immediate use as economic units, increased. There was also an increase in the use of acquired outsiders as artisans, as personal retainers, and as the currency of political patronage.

Whereas the Kerebe offer an example of a relatively short-term entrepreneurial response to new opportunities, the Vai, with a longer documented history, have had a series of such adjustments—such responsiveness being, as Svend Holsoe (Ch. 11) shows, a central thread in their history over the past four hundred years. They began as exporters of ivory, gold, and a few 'slaves.' With the suppression of the Atlantic slave trade early in the nineteenth century, they became well organized and specialized exporters for the illicit slave trade and importers of food. With the end of the Atlantic slave trade, they converted 'slaves' from salable commodities into productive labor units, using them on domestic plantations in the production and transport of palm oil, coffee, and piassava for export. The Duala made a similar series of adaptations, continuing to do so into the twentieth century. Ralph Austen provides precise data on how these shifts were reflected in exchange rates that fluctuated depending on the balance between domestic and foreign demand for men, women, and children, and on the demand for 'slaves' as labor units, social units, reproducers of people, or salable export commodities.

The Imbangala case is instructive in reminding us that entrepreneurship should not be understood only in purely economic terms. We are, in effect, dealing here with responses in what can appropriately be called a total political economy. With the cutting off of the overseas export slave trade as a major outlet, the Imbangala intensified their use of acquired outsiders for internal purposes. Instead of being mainly used as salable commodities, they were now primarily wanted as retainers and dependents —units of social and political power in the struggles involving king, chiefs, lineages, lineage sections, and ambitious individuals.

In Senegambia, the reshuffling of uses and the changes in frequencies of one use over another were particularly complex. The Wolof and Sereer responded in quick succession to a series of new situations: French military pressures, the fragmentation of the traditional political systems, the rise in Islamization, the decline of outlets to the Atlantic slave trade, the appearance of new opportunities in the export peanut trade, and the ever-present possibilities of the internal 'slave' trade. The shifting opportunities here embraced almost the entire range of possible uses of persons: as salable commodities, cultivators, dependents, elite administrators, armed retainers, 'slave' raiders, and convertible capital. Wolof and Sereer history emphasizes the importance to be given to the inherent versatility of human beings as a resource when considering the dynamics of 'slavery.' It is this versatility that allows for a calculus of use and of response to opportunities far more comprehensive than would be possible if 'slaves' were considered merely as labor units.

Rising opportunities for new uses and a readiness to respond to them lead to yet another kind of opportunity—that for middleman and entrepreneur. For a middleman, the gain lies not simply in exchanging for use but in engaging in a series of exchanges for profit. By contrast to a rise in mere bilateral exchanges, this leads to a rise in trafficking and the

creation, in effect, of a new occupation. This role of middleman was sometimes the major new opportunity for a society. The Aboh, Duala, and Vai
are representative of numerous peoples near the coast whose entrepreneurship very largely found its expression in such a role. In the larger
societies and the larger regional economic systems, however, trafficking in
people must always have been but a minor part of the total entrepreneurial
activity.

We should therefore consider such trafficking in 'slaves' as a systemic
emergent—something inherent in the system which arises whenever the
intensification of a total system of exchange reaches a point when the
specialized niche of full-time middleman becomes available and is exploited by entrepreneurs. Trafficking as an occupation would rise and
wane and rise again according to whether the exchange system was brisk
or sluggish. Nor should we focus exclusively on trafficking in people, for it
is far more likely that people would be but one commodity among many,
and that the entrepreneurs would maximize their activity over the whole
range of commodities available for trafficking.

The African responsiveness to opportunities in using and trading
human beings is clearly associated with a strikingly high demand for
people, expressed in a general, high circulation of people among social
groups—a circulation not simply of acquired persons but of women,
adoptees, clients, and relatives. The high demand is related to a view of
people as a resource adaptable to a multitude of uses, most of which are
social and political and not merely economic. The resulting configuration
is a particular kind of consumer society—one in which social groups have
a driving urge to take in new persons, much in the same way that modern
consumer societies have a built-in and almost infinite urge to absorb
more consumer goods. This absorptiveness of people was often an integral part of social and political competition: each person, or office, or
kin group, or political entity wanted more people because its competitors
might get more of them.

Such a situation means that, other things being equal, satiation of
demand cannot be quickly achieved—hence the very high percentage of
'slaves' in societies where descendants of acquired persons are classified in
a way that makes it easy to count them. When people are used in a great
number of different capacities, and not simply as productive labor, the
calculation of "how much is enough" becomes extremely complex. As
long as one uses acquired persons only to grow products for sale, "enough"
is controlled by clear external factors, such as price of the product, price
of the laborer, and the number of laborers that one's productive capacity
(based on land and capital) will permit. But when one is after dependents
and retainers, and the measure of "enough" is how many dependents and

retainers are under one's competitors' control, one becomes involved in what is essentially a hopelessly inflationary game of numbers. The spiral of rising demand cannot, obviously, be infinite, and if the model we are proposing here is at all relevant, we need research into factors that inhibited the rising spiral. On the basis of our discussion of the problem of 'slavery' in societies dominated by corporate, autonomous kin groups, we would suggest here that the potential threat of having too many quasi relatives—the threat of being swept by "the politics of 'slavery'"—may have been one such inhibiting factor in the spiral of demand in these societies. The more complex societies, on the other hand, may have had far more varied inhibiting mechanisms, and some of them perhaps had none; it is possible that in some societies the exponential growth of the 'slave' population was stopped not by systemic factors but by such accidental historical events as wars, the breakup of polities, and, finally, colonial occupation.

The above argues for an understanding of African 'slavery' in terms of a heavy domestic demand for people, which is only partially a demand for units of labor and to a very great extent a demand for social and political units.[9] This noneconomic emphasis in terms of use has, however, an interesting consequence for the method of acquiring persons. Once again, it is useful to make a contrast with types of slavery emphasizing labor use. If persons are bought as labor units, they can clearly compete with hired labor, for the acquisitor can calculate when to prefer one over the other in given circumstances. But if one is seeking quasi relatives, dependents, and loyal followers, one in effect seeks whole persons rather than particular services. One can hire the specific services of a cultivator or servant or even warrior, but it is scarcely possible to hire a relative or a dependent. One can only obtain them through marriage, beget them, adopt them, or, failing that, capture them or buy them; and in a situation of high demand, buying would seem to be a particularly adaptive approach to the problem. What this suggests is that the presence of a highly "social" type of 'slavery' does not at all preclude acquiring 'slaves' by the same methods that one acquires commodities—indeed, the two are highly compatible.

This suggests further that the transition from social to chattel 'slavery' is to be understood not in the sphere of acquisition but in the sphere of

9. This obviously does not preclude, in many areas, an extensive demand for people as production units. That such a demand probably existed is persuasively argued on economic grounds by A. G. Hopkins (1973:21-27). What we are stressing here is that African societies were so organized that there was a high demand for acquired people in many nonproductive and noneconomic roles. Hence we do not need to appeal to an economic raison d'être for the existence of African 'slavery,' though economic factors are clearly relevant to an understanding of the economic use of African 'slaves'—as, indeed, military factors are to their use as military manpower, and so on for other uses.

subsequent use. The question of transition that must be posed is this: "How easy or how difficult is it to begin using as commodities and as labor units persons that one has been acquiring till now as commodities but using as dependents?" Such transitions in fact occurred among the Sena and the Kerebe without great difficulties and almost imperceptibly. And in terms of our discussion of the acquired 'slave' as always being initially a kind of marginal nonperson, the ease of these transitions to chattellike use is understandable. In sum, while we should not be blind to the more dramatic aspects of the dynamics of 'slave' systems, we should also recognize that many changes can come about not through radical alterations of the system but through what might be called "permutations" of it.

THE PROBLEM OF THE ORIGINS OF AFRICAN 'SLAVERY'

Anthropologists no longer look for the "origins" of social institutions, as if, like pottery types, they develop in one area and then diffuse to others. Questions such as "Did African 'slavery' originate on that continent, and if so, when and where? Or did it come from outside?" are both unanswerable and meaningless. 'Slavery' in Africa is simply one part of a continuum of relations, which at one end are part of the realm of kinship and at the other involve using persons as chattels. 'Slavery' is a combination of elements, which if differently combined—an ingredient added here or subtracted there—might become adoption, marriage, parentage, obligations to kinsmen, clientship, and so forth. As the various elements are reshuffled under changing conditions, institutions we choose to call 'slavery' can arise, disappear, and reappear, now in benign form, now as chattel servitude, and sometimes in both forms practiced side by side. It is possible to trace, as some of the studies described here do, the specific conditions that gave rise to particular combinations of these elements, but it is not possible to discuss the "origins" of 'slavery' as such. For 'slavery' is neither a single idea invented in some particular place from which it spread nor is it a single, clear-cut institution. It is simply an English word, a label, that we feel reasonably comfortable in applying to certain combinations of elements and feel we should not apply to other somewhat different combinations.

From this perspective, we find it impossible to join in discussions and arguments about the "origins" of African 'slavery' such as those of Walter Rodney (1966) and John Fage (1969). In their discussion, the nature of 'slavery' is nowhere defined and is simply taken for granted. Our discussion in this chapter, on the other hand, makes it clear that once the problem of definition is tackled, the main question being debated— whether African 'slavery' emerged in response to European or Arab or Sudanese stimuli—comes to be beside the point. We can only repeat that the emergence of the various institutions termed 'slavery' must have occurred under a multitude of different conditions. To see such institutions in Africa as necessarily developing only in response to outside stimuli is to deprive the African past of internal economic dynamism, inventiveness, entrepreneurship, and, above all, of its fundamental cultural concepts of rights-in-persons. We simply cannot accept that the servile end of the kinship-to-'slavery' continuum sprang forth only under the impetus of extra-continental, and never internal, demand for people.

In this connection, a perspective beyond Africa is useful. For in every large cultural area of the world, other "bundles" containing some traits that lead us to call them 'slavery' have emerged, disappeared, and reemerged. This is hardly surprising, as there is nothing unusual or particularly inventive about acquiring people by means other than marrying or begetting them and more or less forcibly putting them to various uses. In the perspective of human history, it is not this that requires explanation but the various forms that such processes have taken. Moreover, it is the absence of such institutions rather than their presence that is unusual, and it is the claim that acquisition and use of people are absent that must bear the burden of proof.

Our analysis also makes it impossible to accept the suggestion by Claude Meillassoux (1971:23) that a slave is "necessarily the product of an act of violent capture" and that, therefore, "warriors or bandits are of necessity found at the origin of his economic and social existence." Our view is less dramatic and more domestic. We see the roots of these servile institutions in the need for wives and children, the wish to enlarge one's kin group, and the desire to have clients, dependents, servants, and retainers. Outsiders can fill these wants. War and brigandage can be one method of acquiring outsiders, but they are no more the mainspring of such rights-in-persons than they are of other forms of wealth. And as methods of acquisition, they could scarcely precede methods based on what Adam Smith saw as the human "propensity to truck and barter."

Finally, we must examine a set of related theories of the origins of servile institutions. In 1900, in a comparative ethnological study, Nieboer, following earlier authors,[10] postulated that where there is a shortage of labor and a surplus of land suitable for labor-intensive farming, slavery is likely to emerge; because freemen will wish to work their own land rather

10. Philip D. Curtin points out, in a personal communication: "Nieboer picked up the idea from the classical economists, and it ultimately goes back at least to Adam Smith. It was most commonly discussed, however, in the 1830's and 1840's by the 'Colonial Reformers' headed by E. Gibbon Wakefield and finds especially detailed treatment in Herman Merivale, *Lectures on Colonization and Colonies.* The fact is that Nieboer repeated the idea without proper credit to its source."

than hire themselves out for wages, coerced labor becomes necessary. Where, on the other hand, the population is dense, land is scarce, and agriculture is capital intensive, hired labor is both available and preferable. In this economic argument, Nieboer assumes that slaves are primarily acquired as tillers of soil. The Russian historian Kliuchevsky (1906), using similar economic variables, explained the emergence of a different kind of labor coercion—serfdom in sixteenth- and seventeenth-century Russia. Kliuchevsky adds, however, the political factor as an important variable. The administration of Russia depended on the tsar's officials, who were given the right to collect rents and to demand military service from the peasants under them. As the state expanded, new territories became open for settlement and attracted the peasants away. Its administrative system threatened, the government attached the peasants to the land as serfs. The thesis points to the often critical dimension of the role of government—that is, of political factors—in distorting the working of purely economic forces and in determining the shape of the institution that emerges. Domar (1970) agrees with Nieboer that surplus land makes bound labor desirable and he adds further examples to Kliuchevsky's of the various devices used to coerce labor and prevent it from flowing into independent activity. Thus, the later Roman Empire, like sixteenth-century Russia, bound the peasants to the land by law. On the other hand, Domar points out that political factors can sometimes make this impossible. Neither the English government after the Black Death of the fourteenth century nor the northern United States in the nineteenth century could have contemplated such a solution when faced with a similar outflow of independent labor.

In sum, then, Nieboer puts forward a basic premise about the economic conditions under which coerced labor might be expected to take root, whereas Kliuchevsky and, more formally, Domar indicate that political and other factors may lead to other solutions of the problem of labor shortage and unused land. Finally, Domar points out that solutions can linger on after the conditions that gave rise to them have disappeared.

What is the bearing of these theories on the African data? On the face of it, one may claim that the presence of 'slavery' in Africa can thus be accounted for by the existence of surplus land and labor-intensive agriculture. However, the sparsely settled Sena, who fulfill those conditions best, have the most "social" and the least labor-oriented form of 'slavery,' while the Aboh, Igbo, Duala, and Vai, with effectively less open land, have a more "economic" use for 'slaves.' The problem with these theories is, essentially, their unstated assumptions that slavery has to do primarily with labor, and that labor has to do with agriculture.

As we have seen, control over people is sought for many more reasons than that they are units of labor, in farming or elsewhere. Shortage of labor is but one kind of shortage of personnel that people may seek to remedy. As the Wolof, Hausa, Imbangala, and Duala show clearly, half the search in a society may be concerned with finding persons to fill purely social and political needs. Thus, calculation of the relative efficiencies in using 'slave' or 'free' persons depends on what one uses them for. In the above theories, the calculation is assumed to be only between bound labor and the hired services of the free. But as we have previously noted, when one seeks dependents and retainers, one wants whole persons and not their partial services. This is a need that hired labor cannot fill. In the broadest terms, then, we would suggest that a necessary (but far from sufficient) condition for the emergence of 'slavery' is that in which one prefers to acquire men and women to be used and controlled as total persons, rather than merely to use their specific services. [11]

As to the argument that free people will move into surplus land whenever it is available, the African data suggest that sociopolitical problems of insecurity may prevent people from moving in the direction of an independent farming existence and push them toward serflike dependence. Thus, political considerations may override economic ones not only at the level of government but also in individual decisions.

The existence of African 'slavery' cannot be understood, then, in terms of the economics of the classic triad of labor, land, and capital. In the economy of living, the economics of material production is but one of a multitude of concerns, and the management of resources involves human beings as social and political resources. Hence, the roots of institutions concerned with the acquisition and use of human beings must be sought in the total social and political economy of a society.

THE IMPACT OF THE OVERSEAS TRADE AND OF ABOLITION

Although we are not concerned here with the Atlantic, trans-Saharan, and eastern African 'slave' trade, our analysis does suggest some pointers for the investigation of the impact of exogenous factors on African internal 'slavery.'

11. This proposition represents a significant alteration of the suggestion by Keith Hopkins (1967:175), who condenses the problem of the emergence of slavery in classical antiquity into the question of what it is that "determined the choice of buying men's bodies rather than occasionally hiring their labor as it was required . . . ." But Hopkins sees slavery as a species of the "genus" of "dependent labor," a definition that, in our view, discourages theoretical explorations of nonproductive and noneconomic factors.

Our entire discussion has been concerned with making clear distinctions among the different aspects of 'slavery.' There is the phenomenon of transacting in persons—both in specific rights-in-persons and in total rights-in-persons. There are the phenomena of exchange systems in which rights-in-persons, persons, and commodities are interchangeable. This is distinct from the great variety of uses to which persons are put. There is also the aspect of the individual's formal status and informal condition. There is the matter of bilateral transactions for use and serial transactions for profit. There is the responsiveness to new uses for acquired persons and the responsiveness to entrepreneurial opportunities. And there is, finally, the pace of transactions in the system—whether the exchange system is sluggish or rapid—and the sheer volume of the flow of goods and persons, these being independent of the nature and kind of the transactions themselves.

All these elements are in principle independent of one another. Some of them may change while others remain the same. For example, an increase in the frequency of a certain pattern of acquiring persons should not be confused either with the origin of the pattern itself or with the origin of the idea of acquiring people. With an increase in the general volume of trade, manpower needs in a society may rise, and more outsiders may be acquired to be canoemen or porters; the frequency of acquiring total rights-in-persons may rise relative to the frequency of acquiring partial rights, and some types of acquisition may become more frequent than others. But what has changed here is the configuration of the system of using people, and not the principles and types of transactions. It would be erroneous to attribute the origins of 'slavery' in this society to the impact of the trade without specifying very carefully whether one is talking about the new configuration of old elements or about the emergence of the elements themselves. Similarly, the custom of acquiring outsiders is a separate issue from the question of how they are put to use and in what proportions; the first may remain the same while the second may change, or one may resort to new methods of acquisition (for example, turning from peaceful purchase to capture) but continue to use people in the same way. Or one may exploit acquired outsiders more harshly yet make their redemption easier—a point made by Genovese (1969:203) in commenting on "the danger of confusing the extent to which a slave society is closed with the extent to which it deals severely with its slaves on a day-to-day basis."

In examining the historical impact of exogenous factors on the system of using acquired persons, it is therefore important to determine precisely which particular elements of the configuration have been affected and how. One cannot speak of the "rise of 'slavery' " without explaining which elements one means, and whether the nature of transactions has changed or just their frequency, whether entirely new elements have appeared or old elements have simply increased or decreased.

This is not to say that these elements do not affect one another. For example, greater possibilities of use tend to encourage the acquisition of more persons. Greater rewards in some spheres of activity will tend to shift their use in that direction. A rise in the number of transactions will open up new niches for middlemen. The importance of such systemic relations should not be minimized, for it means that changes in some elements can bring profound transformations to the total configuration. For example, when the existence of an overseas outlet for selling people leads to the rise of entrepreneurship in this field, the transformation is indeed profound. But not all elements of the new configuration should be attributed to the existence of this outlet, nor should one assume a priori that similar shifts in the configuration never occurred before.

Such questions, historically, must remain moot for lack of data. But from a systemic point of view, assumptions about unprecedented changes require careful scrutiny. It will be remembered, for example, that the Sena system of acquiring persons rested on purely local and scarcely unique factors: the wish to expand kin groups, the availability of land, the threat of famines, the desire for a manpower reserve, the exchange of people for grain. Similarly, the early Kerebe system of acquiring strangers had to do with raiding and the agricultural advantages of their area. The later Kerebe shift—toward acquiring more persons and using them increasingly as units of labor to grow more grain in exchange for goods—also does not depend on factors inconceivable before the nineteenth century. The Imbangala involvement in supplying the overseas 'slave' trade on the coast brought shifts in frequencies of transactions and in configurations of a kind that had a profound political effect on the area; but there is no reason to regard their use of acquired people for bolstering one's political position as an idea inherently inconceivable before the sixteenth century. To think otherwise is to see central Africa as a backwater, culturally and economically, in which "nothing happened" for a thousand years before A.D. 1500.

As with the impact of the overseas slave trade, so with the impact of the abolition of that trade early in the nineteenth century: both changes must be considered in the total setting of available choices, of changes in frequencies of transactions, and of entrepreneurial responses to new opportunities and uses of people. The material in this volume illustrates reshufflings in methods of procurement, of use, of disposal of acquired persons. And in many cases, there was ample time for such readjustments, since the internal trade in people often continued for a half-century or more after the external trade had been abolished. The pattern of adjustment and readjustment shown in the studies described here is well in keeping with the overall pattern of entrepreneurial responsiveness shown by Manning (1969) to be one of the keys to the understanding of the political history of the West African coast.

African entrepreneurial responsiveness, however, could not have been limited to external stimuli alone, given that a widespread demand for persons was, as we have seen, an outstanding feature of African social systems. The almost exclusive concentration, until recently, on Africans as suppliers in the Atlantic slave trade is understandable from the perspective of the New World, the Middle East, and North Africa; and our understanding of the slave trade can be enhanced by an economic model, such as that offered by Gemery and Hogendorn (1974), in which Africa figures in the role of supplier to the outside world. But this concentration, when transferred into Africa itself, highlights the Africans' role as gatherers rather than as users of people. The result is to overstress one element—the African use of people as a salable commodity—over the multitude of competing internal uses. Given the possible volume of the internal African demand for people, it may be more rewarding to begin considering the external trade as an appendage to the internal "market"—which conforms with Curtin's (1975) conclusions about Senegambia. Future investigation must deal with the intricate interrelationship of two sets of markets, that were linked by the Atlantic trade. For example, Curtin (1975:175-77) points out that the larger imports of males than females into the New World owed much to the retention of the females in the internal African market—this in contrast to previous attempts to explain the disparity in terms of preferences in the New World Market.

The emphasis on the African as "supplier" rather than "user" of people has also contributed to making the effects of the abolition of African internal 'slavery' in the twentieth century something of a puzzle. Patrick Manning (n.d.) has raised this question in the context of the history of European ideas about African 'slavery.' How is it, he asks, that an institution considered to be so central to the functioning of so many African societies in the nineteenth century should have passed out of the picture so easily? We have a few studies of the process of abolition and its consequences (for example: Smith 1954; McLoughlin 1962; Igbafe 1975; Grace 1975 and Ch. 16) but with a few notable exceptions (such as McLoughlin 1962) we generally lack detailed studies of the postabolition functioning of former servile institutions in African societies. It must be remembered, moreover, that the colonial powers were often slow to tackle the question and sometimes tried to soften the impact of their measures (Miers 1975:299ff.), and that the abolition of slavery was only one of a great number of changes attendant on the colonial occupation. We may, nevertheless, make some speculative points here, suggested by the preceding sociological and cultural analysis of these institutions.

Many of the factors shaping the reactions to abolition in Africa are the same as those that in the past probably often inhibited slaves from escaping: there was nowhere to run; they were usually incorporated into the local society more strongly than they were likely to be in a new place; their position was often that of quasi kinsmen or indeed actual kinsmen; and their common aspiration was, quite realistically, to move further into the host society rather than to move out of it in search of 'freedom.' The official abolition of 'slavery' by the colonial power would not by itself have changed these conditions. As John Grace (Ch. 16) concludes his study of emancipation among the Mende (who had a comparatively harsh form of 'slavery'): "only a small proportion of emancipated slaves left their homes; most of them just 'sat down' with their former masters." Igbafe (1975) reaches similar conclusions about the effects of emancipation in Benin. We would expect, then, that abolition would result not in a wholesale flight of 'slaves,' not in a mass breakup of relationships, but rather in their complex readjustment. Those who were truly chafing under the burden of dependency and oppression certainly left early on, their departure facilitated in some areas by the disturbance attendant on the colonial conquest (Miers 1975:300-301). They were probably mainly first-generation 'slaves.' Some went to missions, or to cities if wage labor was available. Some returned to the area of their origin, if they knew where it was and had reason to expect to be welcomed. Some set up their own enclaves and communities in the midst of their former masters; this was most likely in areas where the 'slaves' had been treated as marginal to society as a whole and constituted an emergent stratum. These sudden desertions in the early years of abolition seemed threatening to many masters, and sometimes large-scale owners were even ruined.

The question, however, is how profound an effect these events had on the social organization and ongoing life in the society. The actual percentage of those who left is important, and it varied in different societies. But one must be careful in evaluating reports in the documents that "thousands of slaves" left their masters for missions, cities, or plantations. If the percentage of 'slaves' in the population was as high as 50 and not less than 10 percent, the figures would have to be in the hundreds of thousands before one could speak of widespread social upheaval. This seems to have been the case in parts of the Western Sudan, but in most areas there were few desertions.[12] When we examine abolition at the level of the kin group, the effects would scarcely have been more pronounced than the effects of occasional epidemics that, in the past, could carry off a third of one's dependents or of raids that could carry off most of them. Where 'slaves' constituted a separate lineage branch, their withdrawal to become an autonomous lineage would have been in no way different from the normal and recurrent splitting up of a lineage.

Thus, the loss of persons following abolition was not a new experience, given the structure of African kin groups. As in the past, after such events they would begin to gather dependents again, no longer through purchase or capture but through the many other available means of acquisition. At the same time, the new political conditions of colonial Africa removed a powerful incentive for collecting very large numbers of followers. The result, then, was a reshuffling of persons within a structure that continued to operate as before.

One suspects that, overall, the majority of the 'slaves' remained where they were. In most areas, the paucity of new economic niches into which they could move was matched by the paucity of new social niches available to them. The major change would lie in the redefinition of relationships, either into a form of clientship or in the more desirable direction of moving further into the kin group and becoming more like kinsmen. This does not mean assimilation or adoption. Former 'slaves' in most modern African communities are recognized as such. But the sense of delicacy about their position has increased.

We discussed at some length the intricate balance, in autonomous descent groups, between the acceptance of 'slaves' as quasi relatives and their continuing marginality. This held particularly true in societies where such autonomous kin groups were the dominant social and political

12. For example, Martin Klein (pers. comm.) estimates that the figure for fleeing 'slaves' during the early years of colonial rule in former French West Africa may be shown to be as high as 500,000 people, single cantons losing as many as 10,000. Though an impressive figure when taken by itself, 500,000 represents about 1 in 10 out of the total 'slave' population of the area (assuming the entire population to have been about 10,000,000, half of it 'slave'). Thus, when interpreting "massive flights," one must not forget the 4,500,000 'slaves' who did not flee. Also, if fleeing was very high in some cantons and localities, this means that, statistically, in most cantons the nonfleeing proportion has to be even higher than 90 percent. (If one wished to look at the figures purely in terms of personnel turnover, a 10 percent rate of desertion, spread over several years, is well within the range found in any business enterprise, some enterprises and areas having greater turnover than others.) All this suggests that localities and areas of massive flights, exceptional as they are in the West African as well as continental perspective, bear special historical investigation to isolate the special factors operating in them. We have suggested here that the presence of large numbers of first-generation 'slaves' would be one such factor.

units. In modern Africa, this pattern has become more general. Since national governments have monopolized political power and refused to give legal sanction to 'slavery,' a kin group has no more significant coercive powers over its former 'slaves' than over its own members. Both remain in the kin group to a large extent at their pleasure and their satisfaction; they all now belong "in" it and scarcely at all "to" it. Leaving the group is relatively easy, mystical sanctions aside. On the one hand, however, the group continues to want to maintain its power by retaining members, but on the other hand, the core members do not want fully to share their control of its corporate resources with marginal 'slave' members. The result is extreme delicacy in the treatment of former 'slaves' and what we might call a "sociological pampering" of their past and present status in discussion, so that their affective marginality is thereby further reduced and sometimes publicly (though seldom, in fact, completely) abolished. This has an obvious bearing on present-day informants who gingerly give rather softened descriptions of the treatment and rights of 'slaves' in the past—what Nwachukwu-Ogedengbe (Ch. 5) refers to as their "tendency to romanticize the master-slave relationship." The old question of "who is" and "who isn't" tends nowadays to be more completely a matter of concern only to the kin group. It bursts out into the open only when the group is in fact splitting, with "the politics of 'slavery'" coming to the surface as the former 'slave' branch breaks off to become an autonomous kin group in its own right.

A somewhat different restructuring is apt to have taken place in societies where 'slaves' were less integrated into the kin group, belonging "to" rather than "in" it, and where they constituted either a potential or actual stratum. Here, abolition has tended to result in greater dissociation from the former masters: 'slave' families have become autonomous but essentially powerless units, lacking a wide kin base; or they have formed independent 'ex-slave' communities; or they have attached themselves to new social groupings (such as the reform-Muslim Mouride communities in Senegambia), which conferred on them a completely new identity. Another solution has been the redefinition of their position, from involuntary 'slave' into voluntary client, retainer, household servant, or poor quasi relative to the former masters.

Abolition has, in general, removed the obligation to have a "vertical" tie to the master. This has given greater prominence to the "horizontal" dimension of the social identity of the former 'slave,' thereby reinforcing the perception of 'slaves' as a stratum whose members are identified by descent—or, to use an idiom more appropriate to African values, by lack of depth in descent. At their extreme, such new structures, characteristic of societies that were traditionally more rather than less complex, create clearly recognizable and recognized social strata of 'ex-slaves.' To be a "former 'slave,'" even though without any recognized master, has in itself become a new status, even if one that is seldom publicly attributed to specific persons.

We would suggest, then, that the abolition of internal 'slavery' in Africa should be examined from the same perspective as other changes affecting 'slavery' have been examined in this essay and in several of the studies that follow. This means looking at the data in terms of shifts within existing patterns, changes of emphasis in the use of dependents, variations in methods of obtaining them, and redefinitions of old relationships and reinterpretations of new ones in the framework of the old—in brief, examining the 'slave' systems in terms of what we have called "permutations" of it as well as alterations in it. Thus, the Isaacmans, writing of the Sena, and Martin Klein of the Wolof and Sereer, mention the functional continuity between 'slavery' and the new pattern by which immigrant workers come in and become clientlike dependents, sometimes staying on to become permanent, voluntary marginals whose incorporation proceeds through various steps. The pattern is scarcely new, and it appears as a traditional pattern among the Sherbro, Aboh, and Kerebe in the very early periods of their history. New problems, that is, do not exclude old solutions any more than old problems exclude new solutions.

Such "permutations" of the system involved the total range of needs and considerations—social, political, and economic. The importance of the noneconomic uses of acquired outsiders is thus crucial to understanding the relatively undramatic consequences of abolition. For, on the whole, Africans continued to seek to enlarge their households and kin groups, to increase the circle of relatives, to acquire more wives and children, more clients and dependents, adjusting their numbers, as in the past, to current circumstances. Outsiders continued to be "acquired," even if one method (among many) of acquiring them had lapsed, even if one kind of dependent and quasi relative (among many) was no more to be had, and even if some uses of dependents (among many) had disappeared. Abolition did not deal a shattering blow to the organizing principles of the social system or to the fundamental African conceptions of the value of enlarging one's circle of relatives and dependents.

ADDENDUM: A PLEA ON TERMINOLOGY

In scholarship, few pursuits are more sterile than the pursuit of "correct" terminology and few declarations are more impotent than those proclaiming new obligatory definitions. Like living languages, scholarly vocabularies are subject to their own mysterious dynamics. We shall not therefore even attempt here to suggest the abolition of old terms, the adoption of new ones, and the construction of elaborate typologies. But as in living language so in scholarship, precision and lack of ambiguity are necessary, and it is in this spirit that we make this plea on terminology.

For all our efforts and endless resort to euphemisms, we have been unable, in this essay, to avoid the use of the term *slavery*, even as we insisted that its Western semantic field caused much of the misinterpretation of African data. To assuage our misgivings, we put the term in single quotation marks. But ours was an exercise in analysis, in which we had to talk about the very thing that we wished to dismantle as a "thing." In more descriptive studies, dealing with specific societies, the problem can be avoided: one can use the local term and describe what it means—and let the reader decide whether he wishes to translate the term in his own mind as "slavery." The danger is that he often will do precisely that, by implicitly resorting to the Western semantic bundle of traits that we have analyzed, and will proceed to fall into all the conceptual traps that the applications of this bundle to other cultures carries. The other solution is to fear the word less but to be diligent with qualifiers that can narrow down the meaning of whatever kind of 'slavery' one is talking about to its proper context and thus rob the term of some of its misleading ambiguities.

Some qualifiers can suggest the structural context. Miller (Ch. 8), for instance, uses the term *lineage slavery* to indicate the institutional setting in which slavery operated. Other such contexts might be indicated by *office slavery, state slavery, palace slavery, individual slavery*, and so on. When one wishes to emphasize function, several precise terms suggest themselves: *plantation, sharecropping, agricultural, industrial, craft, retainer, bureaucratic, military*. We suggest that when slaves are quasi relatives, the term *familial* or *adoptive slavery* be used. Slaves used as servants might be called *household slaves*. This is less ambiguous than *domestic slaves*—a term sometimes used by the British to denote slaves born in the master's household. Moreover, *domestic slavery* in British literature often means slavery as practiced in Africa by Africans. This might better be called *African internal slavery*.

Since we are not proposing a typology, we do not feel that these terms should be mutually exclusive, arrange themselves on particular dimensions, or fill all the empty spaces of large matrices. We are simply suggesting that the use of a specific adjective indicates the aspect of 'slavery' being focused upon while frankly leaving its other dimensions open and undefined. For example, the term *agricultural slavery* indicates a particular use of 'slaves,' but also explicitly leaves open questions about such matters as mode of acquisition, treatment, type of ownership, and so forth. If there is anything this essay has achieved, it is, we hope, the realization that these various aspects are logically discrete and that their interrelationships are to be examined and not assumed.

Finally, we would suggest the time-honored use of foreign and archaic terms that do not carry potentially misleading connotations. Moreover, foreign terms will often capture the essence of an institution better than current English terms. In this essay, for example, we have found some structural analogies to *helotry;* it is conceivable that some systems of 'slavery' may be appropriately described by this term. We should explore African terminologies, and could also draw on those of Rome, medieval Europe, Polynesia, and others. In brief, in searching for new concepts we can begin to act on the safe assumption that Providence did not create the English language to be the one and ideal meta-language for describing social phenomena in all their complex variations around the world.

REFERENCES

UNPUBLISHED SOURCES
Cooper, F. 1974. Plantation slavery on the east coast of Africa in the nineteenth century. Ph.D. dissertation, Yale Univ.
Manning, P. Undated. The "conventional wisdom" of African slavery. Typescript.
Miers, S. 1972-74. Fieldnotes collected in Kenya.

PUBLISHED SOURCES
Akinola, G. A. 1972. Slavery and slave revolts in the sultanate of Zanzibar in the nineteenth century. *J. hist. Soc. Niger.* 6:215-28.
Bloch, M. 1947. Comment et pourquoi finit l'esclavage antique. *Annales* 2:30-44, 161-70.
Bohannan, P. 1963. *Social anthropology.* New York.
Brunschvig, R. 1960. 'Abd. *The encyclopedia of Islam.* 1:24-40. Leiden and London.
Burnham, P. 1972. Racial classification and identity in the Meiganga region: North Cameroon. In *Race and social difference: selected readings,* ed. P. Baxter and B. Sansom. Harmondsworth, Eng.
Cohen, R. 1970. Incorporation in Bornou. In *From tribe to nation in Africa: studies in incorporation processes,* ed. R.Cohen and J. Middleton. Scranton, Pa.
———. 1971. Servility in social evolution. In *Migration and anthropology.* Proceedings of the American Ethnological Society. Seattle.
Cohen, R., and Middleton, J. 1970. Introduction. In *From tribe to nation in Africa: studies in incorporation processes,* ed. R. Cohen and J. Middleton. Scranton, Pa.
Cooper, F. 1973. The treatment of slaves on the Kenya coast in the nineteenth century. *Kenya hist. Rev.* 2:87-107.

Curtin, P. D. 1968. Epidemiology and the slave trade. *Polit. Sci. Q.* 83:190-216.

———. 1975. *Economic change in precolonial Africa: Senegambia in the era of the slave trade.* Madison.

Davis, D. B. 1966. *The problem of slavery in Western culture.* Ithaca, N.Y.

Domar, E. D. 1970. The causes of slavery or serfdom: a hypothesis. *J. econ. Hist.* 30:18-32.

Douglas, M. 1963. *The Lele of the Kasai.* London.

———. 1966. *Purity and danger: an analysis of concepts of pollution and taboo.* London.

Dumont, L. 1970. *Homo hierarchicus: the caste system and its implications.* London.

Fage, J. D. 1969. Slavery and the slave trade in the context of West African history. *J. Afr. Hist.* 10:393-404.

Finley, M. I. 1968. Slavery. *International encyclopedia of the social sciences.* 14: 307-13. New York.

Fogel, R. W., and Engerman, S. L. 1974. *Time on the cross.* 2 vols. Boston.

Fortes, M. 1969. *Kinship and the social order.* Chicago.

Gemery, H. A., and Hogendorn, J. S. 1974. The Atlantic slave trade: a tentative economic model. *J. Afr. Hist.* 15:223-46.

Gennep, A. van. 1908. *Les rites de passage.* Paris. Eng. tr. by M. B. Vizedom and G. L.Caffee, *The rites of passage.* 1960. Chicago.

Genovese, E. D. 1969. The treatment of slaves in different countires: problems in the application of the comparative method. In *Slavery in the New World: a reader in comparative history,* ed. L. Foner and E. D. Genovese. Englewood Cliffs, N.J.

———. 1974. *Roll, Jordan, roll.* New York.

Goodenough, W. H. 1970. Transactions in parenthood. In *Adoption in eastern Oceania,* ed. V. Carroll. Honolulu.

Grace, J. J. 1975. *Domestic slavery in West Africa.* London.

Gutman, H. G. 1975. *Slavery and the numbers game: a critique of Time on the cross.* Urbana.

Herskovits, M. J. 1938. *Dahomey: an ancient West African kingdom.* 2 vols. New York.

Hopkins, A. G. 1973. *An economic history of West Africa.* London.

Hopkins, K. 1967. Slavery in classical antiquity. In *Caste and race: comparative approaches,* ed. A. de Reuck and Julie Knight. London.

Horton, R. 1971. Stateless societies in the history of West Africa. In *History of West Africa,* ed. J. F. A. Ajayi and M. Crowder. Vol. 1. London.

Igbafe, P. A. 1975. Slavery and emancipation in Benin, 1897-1945. *J. Afr. Hist.* 16:409-43.

Jeffreys, M. D. W. 1951. Lobolo is child-price. *Afr. Stud.* 10:145-84.

Jones, A. H. M. 1956. Slavery in the Ancient World. *Econ. Hist. Rev.* 2d ser. 9:185-99.

Kliuchevsky, V. 1906. *Kurs russkoi istorii.* Eng. tr. by C. J. Hogarth, *A history of Russia.* 1960. New York.

Köbben, A. J. F. 1967. Unity and disunity: Cottica Djuka society as a kinship system. *Bijdr. Taal-, Land-, Volkenkunde* 123:10-52.

Kopytoff, I. 1964. Family and lineage among the Suku of the Congo. In *The family estate in Africa*, ed. R. F. Gray and P. H. Gulliver. London.

Lancaster, C. 1971. The economics of social organization in an ethnic border zone: the Goba (northern Shona) of the Zambezi Valley. *Ethnology* 10: 445-65.

Leis, P. 1972. *Enculturation and socialization in an Ijaw village*. New York.

Lévy-Bruhl, H. 1934. Théorie de l'esclavage. In *Quelques problèmes du très ancien droit romain*, by H. Lévy-Bruhl. Paris.

McLoughlin, P. F. M. 1962. Economic development and the heritage of slavery in the Sudan Republic. *Africa* 32:355-91.

Manning, P. 1969. Slaves, palm oil, and political power on the West African coast. *Afr. hist. stud.* 2:279-88.

Meillassoux, C. 1971. Introduction. In *The development of indigenous trade and markets in West Africa*, ed. C. Meillassoux. London.

———, ed. 1975. *L'esclavage en Afrique précoloniale*. Paris.

Miers, S. 1975. *Britain and the ending of the slave trade*. London.

Nieboer, H. J. 1900. *Slavery as an industrial system: ethnological researches*. The Hague.

Piault, M.-H. 1975. Captifs du pouvoir et pouvoir des captifs. In *L'esclavage en Afrique précoloniale*, ed. C. Meillassoux. Paris.

Price, R. 1974. *Saramaka social structure: analysis of a Maroon society in Surinam*. Caribbean Monograph Series 12, Institute of Caribbean Studies. Rio Piedras, Puerto Rico.

Rodney, W. 1966. African slavery and other forms of social oppression on the upper Guinea coast in the context of the Atlantic slave trade. *J. Afr. Hist.* 7: 431-43.

———. 1970. *A history of the upper Guinea coast, 1545-1800*. Oxford.

Schneider, H. K. 1968. People as wealth in Turu society. *SWest. J. Anthrop.* 24:375-95.

Siegal, B. J. 1945. Some methodological considerations for a comparative study of slavery. *Am. Anthrop.* 47:357-92.

Simmel, G. 1908/1950. Superordination and subordination. In *The sociology of Georg Simmel*, ed. K. H. Wolff. New York, 1950. Originally published in 1908.

———. 1923/1950. The stranger. In *The sociology of Georg Simmel*, ed K. H. Wolff. New York, 1950. Originally published in 1923.

Smith, M. G. 1954. Slavery and emancipation in two societies. *Social econ. Stud.* 3:239-90.

———. 1959. The Hausa system of social status. *Africa* 29:239-52.

———. 1960. *Government in Zazzau*, London.

———. 1974. *Corporations and society*. London.

Southall, A. W. 1970. Stratification in Africa. In *Essays in comparative social stratification*, ed. L. Plotnicov and A. Tuden. Pittsburgh.

Talbot, P. A. 1932. *Tribes of the Niger Delta*. London.

Tardits, C. 1970. Femmes à crédit. In *Echanges et communications: mélanges offerts à Cl. Lévi-Strauss*, ed. J. Pouillon and P. Maranda. Paris.

Tuden, A., and Plotnicov, L. 1970. Introduction. In *Social stratification in Africa,* ed. A. Tuden and L. Plotnicov. New York.

Turner, V. 1964. Betwixt and between: the liminal period in rites de passage. In *Symposium on new approaches to the study of religion.* Proceedings of the American Ethnological Society. Seattle. Also in V. Turner, *The forest of symbols.* 1967. Ithaca, N.Y.

_____. 1969. *The ritual process.* Chicago.

Walton, G. M., ed. 1975. A symposium on Time on the cross. *Explors. econ. Hist.* Vol. 12, Fall issue.

Williamson, K. 1962. Changes in the marriage system of the Okrika Ijo. *Africa* 31:53-60.

Uchendu, V. C. 1965. *The Igbo of southeastern Nigeria.* New York.

United Nations, Economic and Social Council. 1956. U.N. Conference of Plenipotentiaries on a supplementary convention on the abolition of slavery, the slave trade, and institutions and practices similar to slavery. Document E, Conf. 24/20.

The Slave as Institutionalized Outsider

Part II

2

Mafakur: A Limbic Institution of the Margi

(Nigeria)

James H. Vaughan

The Mandara Mountains, a relatively low and rugged chain, form part of the nothern border between Nigeria and Cameroon. They are densely populated with numerous ethnic groups and subgroups whose conventional "tribal" names often reflect the administration's search for order rather than their ethnic identity. In most cases, loyalties are intensely provincial, even where a wider social identity is recognized. This situation, understandable where topography restricts travel and communication, has led to a noticeable lack of uniformity in history, custom, and language. The differences may not be great by the ethnologist's standards, but they make generalization hazardous, particularly as little research has been done in the area and there are few complete studies of Mandara societies. This study necessarily, therefore, concentrates upon an institution of one society—the Margi of Nigeria. A broader interpretation of the institution will be suggested, however, using some comparative data, though a less speculative interpretation must await more comparative work.

The Margi live today in the states of Gongola and Bornu. Census data are unreliable, but they number at least a hundred thousand and possibly even two hundred thousand. Their legendary home is in the mountains

85

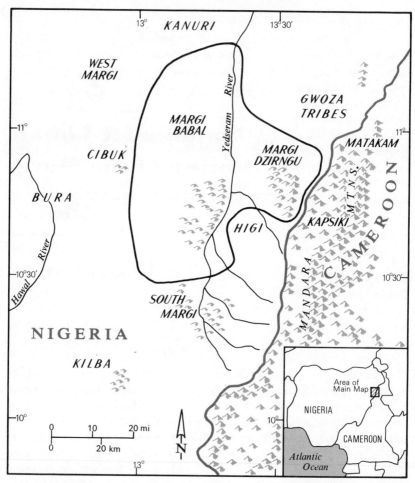

Map 2. Margiland

Cartographic Laboratory UW-Madison

where many still live and population is most dense. Others have spread toward and into the adjacent Chad Basin, seemingly because of general population pressures originating in the northern Cameroon highlands. This sporadic, unplanned, movement has been going on for a very long time.

Until this century, Margi ventured into the Chad Basin only with the greatest caution and probably only under extreme pressure for land, and they tended to settle on or near the inselbergs which rise abruptly from the grasslands of the basin. These outcroppings certainly offered a topography familiar to these mountaineers, but fear of attack is the more probable reason for their settlement pattern. There was considerable intervillage warfare, and raids on Margi and other "pagans" by the militant Fulani of the Adamawa Emirate occurred throughout the nineteenth and the first quarter of the twentieth centuries.

The contemporary Margi have come from diverse ethnic strains of varying historical depth. Oral traditions suggest that this coalescence began between 500 and 300 years ago and has continued into this century. Consequently, there is no unifying historical tradition, only the individual and contrasting histories of numerous clans. This historical and cultural diversity, however, has not prevented interaction among them. Historical legends, undeveloped and vague, tend to focus upon local and postmigration events, and, in general, Margi, unlike many West Africans, do not place much importance on past history. Although two clans or two villages may differ historically and culturally, if each calls itself Margi, both accept the identification. While ethnic origins are of little concern, ethnic identity *is* important, for it facilitates alliances of mutual benefit. Uniformity of behavior is not expected among subgroups, although within any one of these some consistency is normal. Consequently, a Margi from a distant area may find acceptance in a new village and a remarkable tolerance for his customs, but a non-Margi will live in cultural isolation.

Margi recognize four somewhat indistinct regional subgroups; this chapter deals only with the easternmost of them, the Margi Dzirngu, or Margi near the mountains. They live either in compact mountain villages, farming terraced slopes, or strung along the foot of the mountain, farming the valley floor. Their farms are fertile and they are able to subsist adequately on the products of their own labor. There are numerous small weekly markets at which specialties can be bought and surpluses sold. These are important social events but have little economic significance.

They are organized into patrilineal clans, each clan having its own traditions and name. Clans are very imperfectly localized. Though the Margi are patrilocal (i.e., sons live where their fathers live), clan members do become dispersed in time. The traditional political organization consisted of several dynastic centers linking groups of villages into mutually autonomous "divine kingdoms." The secular power of a king was typically weaker the more remote the village; and some villages were, for all practical purposes, not firmly in the control of any center, although each would have had ritual ties to a dynasty. Improved communications, and the attention of colonial and national regimes, have in many cases strengthened the central control of some of these kingdoms; in other cases, the government has broken uncooperative kingdoms. The colonial regime also created new autonomous political units out of some outlying semi-independent villages.

The data given here were gathered primarily in a kingdom with an old and strong dynastic tradition. At the time of the study, it had a population of approximately 10,000 and occupied 110 square miles. Because of their smallness, such kingdoms are officially designated "village" administrations and their kings are termed "village heads." Though in the case of the newly created administrative units this may be a reasonable nomenclature, it seems demeaning when applied to old kingdoms.

MAFA: STATUS AND RECRUITMENT

Margi vocabulary recognizes several social categories of varying importance. For example, the distinction between commoner (*talaka*) and royalty (*mcilili*) is of minor significance and one might never know the terms existed; on the other hand, that between caste (*ngkyagu*) and noncaste (*mbilim*) is of great importance. (Vaughan 1970). The designation *mafa* is also of considerable importance, though lacking the ideological sanctions associated with caste. The term has been translated as "slave" and *mafakur* as "slavery" since the middle of the nineteenth century, when Heinrich Barth traveled through the area collecting vocabulary (see Benton 1912) and noting customs. Whether this is an apt translation is, of course, a major concern of this discussion and a topic to which I will return. It should be noted, however, that this translation was accepted by both the colonial and national administrations and mafakur is technically outlawed. But Margiland is remote, and the forces of change had been little felt in 1959 and 1960, when I collected these data, and the institution was then alive. In fact, I was not aware that any local person knew it was illegal until many months had passed and the events noted below took place. No one was secretive about mafakur; I knew a dozen or more mafa, all of whom accepted their status without complaint or objection. This was in contrast to antiwitchcraft, for example, which, although practiced, was known to be illegal and was kept secret from higher government officials. Except where noted, the conditions described here existed in 1959-60 and the mafa referred to are persons known to me.

The question of the origin of mafakur must be left open, there being no conclusive historical or comparative data and no Margi legends about it. It is simply assumed to be one of the basic principles of society. Since mafa do not constitute kin-groupings, they lack migration legends of their own, although individuals know something of their family history. The institution must therefore be approached in terms of its function within the society in recent times, and whatever raison d'être it may originally have had must be set aside for the time being.

The status of mafa is hereditary in the male line and manumission is not a traditional concept. In addition to birth there were three other methods of recruitment: capture in war, punishment for certain crimes, and barter or purchase. No specific instance of capture is known after about 1875. After that date Margi were so often on the defensive in their continuing war with the Adamawa Emirate and the Fulani of Madagali that traditional intervillage raiding seems to have markedly declined. Capture of Margi by some Fulani, however, was common through the first quarter of this century, thereby keeping the notion of capture current. Mafakur as a form of punishment was extremely rare and I could discover only vague references to it. No contemporary mafa was the descendant of such a criminal and it may be that this punishment was more threatened than practiced. Bartering for existing mafa was common between Margi and other ethnic groups, and there are also records of freemen being bartered into mafakur.

Traditions of mafakur by capture and by punishment abound in the legendary culture of the "old days"; so much so that one is challenged to explain why more descendants of these victims are not found today. Although traditions may be exaggerated, the explanation is undoubtedly due to the difficulty the mafa had in acquiring spouses and supporting families and in the peculiar characteristics of these two types of mafakur.

Desire for mafa is said to have been one of the most common reasons for warfare. Captives—men, women, and children—became the mafa of their captors. Several adjustments followed, however. Some were ransomed by their families; others escaped and returned home. It is unlikely that a warrior could bring back more than one mafa. It is also conceivable that warrior might find it impractical and inconvenient to keep many mafa and would trade them to wealthy men of the kingdom or give them to the king as an act of good will. The standard of trade for a mafa was a distinctive wrist dagger called a *jangum* (Vaughan 1973), although more practical exchanges were frequent. It is said that captive mafa who accepted their role were better treated and more successful than those who were made mafa as punishment.

Women were the principal captives; not only were they easier to capture than men but there were more desired, being more likely to accept their new status, which differed little from that of a wife acquired without benefit of bridewealth. It is said their new relationships usually became so normal that they would return to their homes for visits. It should be remembered that since patrilocality is the customary rule of maritial residence, and since there is a tendency toward kin-based communities, few women expect to live in their natal hamlets. Apart from the loss of potential or actual bridewealth, the physical displacement of a woman would not be a socially disruptive event. Families expect their daughters to move away and husbands are accustomed to fragile marriages in a society with a divorce rate about nine times that of the United States.

To a considerable extent, all wives share the statuses of their husbands, and so it is for mafa wives. A captive wife would share the status of her captor, who very likely would be a person of wealth and prestige. Furthermore, women who are mafa suffer no noticeable loss of prestige or desirability. I knew two much-admired women who were mafa and married to men of importance, one the king and the other a young man of recognized promise, while one of the most attractive girls in the royal village, much sought after by young men, was a mafa. Moreover, a mafa female does not command smaller bridewealth and, in one instance of which I knew, a mafa father held out for an unusually high amount because his daughter was reputed to be a hard worker and many men desired her as a wife.

This is not the place to go into Margi domestic relations, but it may be pointed out that while wives work hard, they enjoy considerable freedom, have their own farms, and accumulate wealth. A captive wife would not, initially, enjoy independence. Notably, her right to divorce was restricted. Even should she be permitted to divorce her husband because of flagrant and publicly recognized abuse, she would be retained by his brothers or sons. On the other hand, as nearly as can be reconstructed today, the domestic chores of a captive differed little from those of any other wife, and in time she could have full domestic rights. Today, noncaptive mafa wives certainly have the same status and rights as other wives.

A major distinction between male and female mafa in this patrilineal society is that, lineally speaking, a female mafa is a dead end. She cannot produce more mafa unless she marries a male mafa. She is spared the emotional stress of inflicting her status upon her children and this undoubtedly accounts for the better adjustment attributed to female mafa. The preference for female captives and the nonheritability of their status also accounts for the apparent discrepancy between statements about the large numbers of mafa captives and the scarcity of their descendants today. Assuming most captives were women, they did not leave mafa descendants.

Free men universally abhor the idea of being mafa. It is seen as a loss of control over one's condition and destiny—a very important theme in Margi culture. Since mafakur is heritable, the idea that one's sons would be mafa is also intolerable to Margi men. Partly a matter of pride, this is also a consequence of the lineal orientation imposed by their clan system. All men say that they would go to any length to avoid capture in war, and it seems unlikely that many men were ever successfully captured or retained.

As punishment, mafakur was less avoidable but probably very rare. Traditional law suggests that it could be resorted to freely, but concrete cases are lacking. Such severe punishments were only inflicted by the king. Most of his judicial duties involved arbitration, but for certain serious offenses mafakur could be adjudged. The crime mentioned most frequently was premeditated murder (*thlikul*), and there is a tradition that in ancient times thefts of guinea corn, roselle, or chickens also might be punished by mafakur. Guinea corn is the staple crop, for which roselle seeds were substituted in time of famine, and chicken was probably the only meat eaten consistently by Margi of former times. Whether this punishment was ever administered for such thefts seems doubtful, but the tradition emphasizes the power of the king and reflects a past when things were less plentiful.

A person who was made a mafa as a result of a crime belonged to the king. Although no one today can remember such a person, his position must have been very difficult. Breaches of the law are common and generally carry no stigma, but the crimes for which mafakur was imposed were likely to be severely condemned. Since mafa status is heritable, there was no relief from and no end to the punishment of a male offender, which also extended to his descendants. Under the circumstances, however, it seems very unlikely that he would have been able to marry and lead an ordinary life. Normally, a master is expected to treat his mafa like a dependent and to provide him with bridewealth for at least one wife, but a king was not obligated to provide bridewealth for a criminal mafa. For a man who might already have a family, the situation is unclear. Some say that the family members, too, became mafa, but this seems unlikely, as he would probably not have been able to hold on to his wives, who were always free to initiate divorce, and his children would undoubtedly have been taken care of by his brothers.

The function of those who became mafa by capture or punishment was not primarily related to the subsistence or production economy. Mafakur by capture served largely as a wife-recruiting and ransom-collecting institution. It was an adjunct to warfare and thus a part of the boundary-maintaining functions of the kingdom. In contrast, criminal mafakur was essentially a legal institution, roughly analogous to life imprisonment in other societies. To be sure, economic services were given by both types of mafa, particularly the rare male captive, but neither type was recruited to fulfill production ends nor, given their apparent numbers, could they ever have made a vital or even substantial contribution to the economy.

The remaining category of mafa comprised the purchased mafa. These were characteristically men, who could found a line of mafa and were usually acquired with an eye to their potential as workers. All mafa I knew were persons bartered into mafakur or descendants of such mafa. A purchased mafa could conceivably have been a captive or criminal, but this was unlikely, for no one would normally purchase a mafa unless it were known that he would accept his status and would not flee. Such stability was unlikely in the case of captive mafa, who could always escape to their own people. It was also improbable that anyone would want to purchase a criminal mafa or that a king would sell him. The stability of the purchased mafa arose from the legality and acceptability of a purchase or barter transaction and from the fact that the contract was agreed to by the mafa's family or community. The mafa himself therefore accepted the legitimacy of his position. Unless a purchaser were satisfied with the good faith of the mafa and his family, he would not enter into the transaction. Such acquiescence in the mafa's position was not present in the other two types of mafakur.

Orphans were one source for mafakur of this type. Although there were numerous parent surrogates in large families, sometimes in a small family no one was able to take care of another child. Nursing infants, for example, would present an immediate problem and they were occasionally bartered to other families better able to care for them. In such cases, the alternative was clearly death for the child and in no reported instance was the act motivated by the desire for economic gain. Giving up a child might be humiliating for persons of wealth or prestige and they would agree to it only in the most extreme cases, but for many others it was an acceptable alternative.

Under conditions of severe deprivation, such as a famine, villages have been known to sell one or more of their members into mafakur in exchange for food (see Kirk-Greene 1958:66 n.1). Although sale for this reason is infrequent, the only instance of purchase that I encountered firsthand was of this type. A very old mafa, Birma D., told me that he was born a Higi, in a village near Kamale, approximately fifteen miles farther into the mountains. When a severe famine struck his village, he and his father were traded to a Margi for a now-forgotten number of head baskets of guinea corn. This was probably during the famous Mandara famine of 1899-1904, which followed a locust plague. He obviously accepted the legality and the morality of his status; being well aware that he and his father had saved his village, he seemed to take pride in this. When it was suggested that he might run away, he found the idea dishonorable both to himself and his former village. In exasperation at the suggestion, he remarked, "But where could I run?"

THREE EXAMPLES OF MAFA

The stories of D. and two other mafa, W. and K., enable us to see how mafa were recruited and also how mafakur functions today. The three represent strikingly different mafa.

D. did not remain with his purchaser but moved to the royal village when, as a young man, he was bought by the senior wife of the king. It should be noted that women could legally own mafa, that some of them could afford them, and that they had need of them. D. was subsequently inherited by her son, who succeeded his father as king. D. eventually acceded to the office of *birma*, an important political post reserved in this and some other Margi kingdoms for a mafa. The birma is primarily an acolyte to the king, but he is also one of but three persons entitled to adjudicate disputes in the ruler's absence and to act as an official legal adviser. He may also acquire considerable informal power as a result of his close contact and influence with the king.

Although D. became much revered, he apparently never became powerful; despite the importance and opportunities of his office, his personal life was unsuccessful. He never became head of a large established household. One wife, a single daughter, and eventually a few grandchildren were the extent of his family. To have no son is particularly regretted by Margi men and the grave of such a man is like that of a boy, for neither has perpetuated his line.

In old age, D. lived alone in a very dilapidated house across the open square from the king's compound. His possessions were meager and he bore himself without pride or dignity. On the other hand, he truly lacked for nothing important and might have been able to have more than he had. The king and virtually everyone in the royal village and many others outside showed him genuine affection. His extreme age, his links with the past, and his exotic status made him something of a legendary character, and he was treated with more respect than his impoverished, impotent condition might have suggested.

His funeral revealed much of the depth of feeling for him. An old man's death is not mourned as a tragedy; instead, his funeral is a festive occasion at which his grandchildren celebrate the passing of a good and full life. The scarcity of descendants was not permitted to detract from D.'s funeral, for all of the villagers called him "grandfather" in deference to his age and ties with an almost legendary past. A prosperous and admired young man specifically dressed and acted as his grandson, and the oldest brother of the king acted as his son. The funeral, which took place in the square, was attended by the entire community and by many from his daughter's village. The chief mourners, who exhorted others to sing and dance, were three surviving sons of the famous king whose wife had originally purchased D., all distinguished and honored men in the kingdom. Even the king attended and saluted the body as it was carried to its grave, although it was said a king should not attend funerals, and he went to no other one during my residence, not even that of his classificatory brother. So many people took roles as descendants of D. that the king was moved to joke about his numerous progeny. A distinctive ritual in the funeral revealed one final note to D.'s life and shed additional light on the status of mafakur: he had been a warrior of note and killed a man in a raid on a distant kingdom early in this century. Further investigation revealed that such loyalty was not uncommon.

The story of W., the second mafa, presents a striking contrast. W. was one of the important men of the royal village; his father, a mafa, had been the birma before D., and W. may have profited from his father's achievement. His father's father, though unrelated to D., was also a Higi who had been bartered into mafakur. The details of the transaction had been forgotten. W. had only one wife, a deaf mute, which probably made her relatively unattractive as a spouse and suggests that, as a young man, W. had been handicapped in attracting wives. The marriage turned out to be very successful in Margi terms. They had ten living children, nine of whom were girls, and although Margi are predisposed to want sons who will further their line, daughters mean bridewealth, which is a more immediate reward. Furthermore, the daughters of W. were extremely accomplished, talented, and hardworking. One was married to a wealthy young man who was a favorite of the king, another to the king himself and was the woman previously mentioned as having been so much sought after that she fetched a very high bridewealth, while a third was one of the most popular local girls, a leader among them, and the village's best female singer. W. profited both materially and in prestige from the size and quality of his family. (One local male humorist also pointed out the advantages of having a mute wife.)

His greatest prestige came, however, from his long and intimate association with the king. By coincidence, they had grown up as neighbors and friends, and they still lived close together and met daily. There were men of greater wealth in more senior positions who had the ear of the king, but few had greater influence than W. Although his position was entirely unofficial, it lent him a dignity and respect matched only by the most important men of the kingdom. He dressed well and owned a warrior's shield which he displayed on ceremonial occasions. As D. grew older and more infirm, W. assumed more and more ceremonial importance in the kingdom, having learned much from his father, the former birma. Sometimes he replaced D. when the latter was ill, and he became the authority on political rituals.

It was, therefore, a great surprise to everyone when, following D.'s death, W. refused the office of birma when it was offered to him by the makarama, the king's first minister. Most assuredly the offer was made with the king's knowledge and consent, but because it came through an intermediary it was possible for W. to refuse. His reason astounded us all; it was phrased in terms of a reaction against the status of mafa. He said that his "eyes had been opened" and that he would not take the position; by which he meant that times had changed, that being a mafa was demeaning and he wanted no part of it.

The situation, however, requires closer analysis, for less than a month after his refusal, W. was again assisting the king in important ceremonies. He never indicated to me, either before he refused the position or after, that he was ashamed or even dissatisfied with being mafa. In fact, he was my principal informant on mafakur, was completely open in discussing it, and seemed perfectly adjusted to it. I had had no idea that he even knew that times had changed with respect to "slavery." I believe the logic of his action lay in the contrast between the role of birma with its peculiar relationship to the king, on the one hand, and the personal relationship that had grown up between him and the king, on the other. The birma had ritual and political duties but he was also expected to be the king's personal servant. Old D. frequently had been seen cleaning the square and doing other menial tasks, and I believe it was this against which W. rebelled, sensing that his personal position was above these aspects of the office of birma, and realizing that the role would also require him to be a servant to a man who was his friend. In this, his refusal was entirely understandable.

His rejection of the office, however, did not alter his relation with the king, who, by having the makarama make the offer, made refusal possible. As we have observed, less than a month later W. was virtually acting as the birma, apparently at the request of the king, who claimed that the new birma, K., did not know enough. It was also possible that the king did not really like K., though he was the next logical candidate, and there was no other mafa about who knew enough to handle the office. Finally, when the king and the birma were to travel back to an ancient village on the mountain, the king took W. instead of K., probably because he preferred to make the journey with a friend.

K., the third mafa, lacked the stature and wisdom of W. He was ten to fifteen years younger than W., who was his father's younger brother. When I first met K., he had recently been deserted by his wife and lived with a daughter of about fifteen. He lived in meager circumstances in an abandoned compound and, having no land of his own to farm, he helped W. Although his poverty may have stemmed, in part, from his being a mafa, it should be remembered that free Margi are also sometimes poor and dependent. Even poor men are expected to behave with dignity and pride and to command respect, but K. was servile and obsequious, completely unlike W. It was the general consensus that K.'s demeanor was more typical of mafa, whereas W., who was both dignified and respected, was exceptional.

K. was involved in a humiliating incident, typical of his fortune. After becoming birma, he lured away the wife of a man from a neighboring village. She wanted to marry him, but her husband wanted her back and refused the bridewealth settlement that K. was willing to work out. K. refused to send the woman back, and her husband reported the incident formally to the king, both as K.'s master and the appropriate legal authority. It was unusual for a husband to want a wife back under such circumstances but legal precedent was clearly on the husband's side and, although the king would have been happy to accommodate K., he had to tell him that the wife must return to her husband. It was generally felt that K. should have known that he had no right to the woman and should have returned her without bringing his master, the king, into the case. Everyone was embarrassed by K.'s behavior.

As a final example of K.'s plight, his dispute with the makarama, the king's first minister, may be cited. This occurred after K. had been appointed birma and may reflect an exploration of the limits of his new status but, if so, the volatile makarama was not an apt choice for an adversary. The two got into a public argument over money and the makarama, a jovial but proud and aggressive man, soundly beat K., who was much smaller. Again, it was a humiliating event for K., so much so that his daughter, a charming girl betrothed to a son of the king, was inconsolable over his public embarrassment. Although he was not cowed by his defeat, word of the fight passed quickly through the village and his prestige suffered further. Some thought it was this that had led the king to ask W.'s help during the subsequent ceremonies.

THE PROBLEM OF "OWNERSHIP"

The question of the "ownership" of mafa in general, and these three individuals and their families in particular, is a convoluted topic. Ownership is today outlawed, but even so it is clear that the traditional practice was not everything we understand by the term. The information is least ambiguous for D., who was owned by right of purchase and worked as a member of his masters' households throughout his life. His responsibilities decreased as he got older, particularly as he became infirm. His ritual duties to the king may have lessened some of his labor obligations, but it is clear that throughout his life he was a laborer and servant. At the same time, it should be noted that his obligations were little more than those of any dependent in a compound. The question of his ownership is clear only until he was installed as birma. Then he apparently ceased to belong to any individual and became a permanent adjunct of the office of king, serving subsequent rulers and considered to belong to them although the succession did not follow the rule of inheritance. In all other cases, however, mafa are heritable and, indeed, D. passed to the first king by the normal rules of inheritance.

It seems probable that the ownership of D. was clearer simply because he was a first-generation mafa, whereas W. or K., both of whom were also of Higi descent, were born mafa. It was said that they were mafa of the king: but he could show no clear title to them and they were not his personal property. When the king married the daughter of W. and his son married the daughter of K., bridewealth was paid to the fathers. I received no satisfactory answers to my questions about this seemingly anomaly. It appears that the marriages involved the king as individual, while the proprietorship of the mafa was invested only in his office. In point of fact, "ownership" of W. or K. was not an issue of any importance and attempts to clarify it led inevitably to contradictions.

Once K. became birma, the statement that he was mafa of the king did take on significance. He was henceforth as D. had been, a personal servant of the king, a position in which he took pride. He worked in the royal fields, cleaned the square, did other minor public works in the village, and looked after the king's house. In return he received sustenance and security, eating well and never having to fear scarcity. Had his marriage been successful, his wife might have been able to aid him considerably. Her responsibilities to the king would have been nil so long as K. was fit, and she would have farmed his land and been provided with land of her own either by her husband or, if necessary, by his master the king. Assuming that she would have shared her produce with K., he might have been able to accumulate some resources. Circumstances, or perhaps his ineptitude, conspired against him, however.

W.'s ownership was the most anomalous of all. Basically, it should have been the same as K.'s, but whereas the appointment to birma clarified K.'s position, W.'s not only remained ambiguous but was confused by his refusal to take the office. Had he truly been owned by the king, as was said, it is doubtful whether he could or would have refused. Like the other mafa we have discussed, W. perhaps had difficulty attracting wives because of his status, but, we have seen, it did not handicap him in other respects. At the time I knew him, W. was a substantial farmer who owned his land. Certainly, no one interfered in his affairs. It is doubtful that even the king himself would have done so, since he did not try to compel W. to become birma, although he obviously would have liked him to take the position.

All this was glossed over by the circumstances of emancipation. It was said that no one would attempt to force W. to do this or that because it was no longer possible. Yet it would seem that this was a rationalization, for W. was virtually a free man because of his achieved status in the community and not because he had been freed by the national government. It is, of course, impossible to say whether his achievement could have happened under former conditions. Certainly, modern developments had given to his new status a legitimacy that would previously have been missing. W. did not see his personal accomplishments as unusual. He claimed that his father had been a prosperous man, but Margi frequently exaggerate the accomplishments of their forebears and, frankly, it is difficult to imagine a mafa with W.'s independence early in this century, at the very time when D. and his father were sold into mafakur. W. stands out as a fascinating exception to the rules of Margi society.

Although Margi have a concept of ownership and a man may be the owner of property, he is the "master" (*mthlagu*) of a mafa. This term connotes reciprocal obligations as well as status differences. The status of a mafa is very much like that of a minor child except in the matter of inheritance. One's behavior toward a mafa is generally what would be expected toward a dependent, with all the mutual responsibilities implicit in that relationship. On the other hand, the mafa is not treated or thought of as a minor; he is recognized as a capable adult with adult responsibilities and problems. A mafa who committed a crime would be treated as any other individual, although it might be difficult to fine him. In former times, if the crime indicated a failure of his master—assuming one to be clearly recognized—then the master might be fined. For example, if a mafa stole food or property because he was in need himself, his master might well be fined on the logic that he should have taken better care of his mafa. No one remembered an instance of this actually happening, and in general mafa enjoy good reputations as law-abiding persons.

One striking practice has tended to obscure the rights of a master over his mafa. When a king died, one or more mafa were killed and buried with him. This happened as recently as 1906. The eldest son of the king who died then not only tends a shrine to his father but a mafa shrine as well. The wife who cooked for a king was also put to death. The folk logic for both sacrifices is the same: these were people to serve the king in the afterworld. In fact, except at the death of a king, no man has the legal right to kill or abuse unduly a mafa—or a wife.

In general, it seems that although a new mafa may initially be regarded as a personal possession, with the passage of time and in succeeding generations the issue of specific title may become confused. Even in cases where the title is clear, the responsibility between mafa and master is mutual. A master is obliged to support and protect his mafa and is enjoined from demanding more than can normally be expected of another person. Title to all forms of property is closely associated with need and ability to use. In a practical sense, no man may own more than he may reasonably use or have need of. Thus the community—with the king as its collective representative—is the ultimate proprietor of all property. It is in this somewhat amorphous way that mafa ultimately belong to the king.

Although the concept of ownership is essential to the Western notion of slavery, to Margi the question of ownership is secondary to the fact that there are mafa in society. The status exists without regard to specific ties of ownership. In short, title, which seems so important to the Western notion of slavery, is not essential to a definition of mafakur.

THE MEANING OF MAFAKUR

Although there is little to indicate that the actual functioning of the institution has been unduly restricted by recent developments, the mafa population has declined. Recruitment—other than by birth—has undoubtedly been curtailed. After 1875, Fulani incursions became so serious that intra-Margi warfare seems almost to have vanished, and since the 1920s virtually all forms of warfare have ceased. Famines have also been effectively eliminated in recent years. Consequently, even though externally imposed norms are easily circumvented, it is unlikely that any freeman has become a mafa in the last thirty or forty years.

Knowledgeable old men estimate that there might have been as many as a hundred mafa—men, women, and children—in a kingdom in the "old days," but individual memories suggest that there have been no more than fifty at any time in this century. Even the most generous estimates would not put mafa at more than 1 or 2 percent of the population. Remembering that they are only used as farm and domestic labor and that Margi are basically subsistence farmers, we can conclude that it is unlikely that they constituted a labor force of any importance to the economy, although their higher numbers in the royal village undoubtedly meant that they were more important there.

As an aside, it should be noted that the importance of demographic data to an understanding of slavelike institutions is critical. It is of little consequence to talk of an institution's functions without knowing something of numbers and distribution of personnel.

CONCLUSIONS

I would like to suggest that we might find it more profitable to view the institution of mafakur not in terms of what it does, but in terms of how it fits into the structure of the society at large and the role it plays in Margi social dynamics. I am suggesting that it will be more profitable to focus less on what mafa do and more on what they are. By seeking the principles of social organization by which this institution articulates with the other institutions of society, focus is shifted from mafakur per se to mafakur in Margi society.

Contemporary Margi society is, in theory, a closed system, recognizing birth as the only method of recruitment. Yet, as we have noted, all Margi are in one way or another immigrants, and the incorporation of relatively self-sufficient migrant groups through acculturation and eventual assimilation has been characteristic of their history. Their social charter recognizes the diversity of clan origins and it is tolerant of remarkably diverse clan customs so long as they occur within the group calling itself Margi. They are sensitive to a unifying "Marginess"—largely consensual—that distinguishes them from the numerous other societies around them. Matakam, Higi, Fulani, and others are perceived as outsiders and strangers not so much because they behave in incomprehensible ways, but because they are not and do not wish to be Margi. Thus Margi might be hostile and rude to itinerant Bura, a society with a culture very much like their own, but open and friendly to my family because we lived and identified with them.

The boundaries of this closed system were, however, on occasion breached, as we have noted. In the past, the aggressive and warlike Margi took prisoners like trophies, to add to their polygynous households, and sometimes made profitable exchanges of consumables for aliens. The institution of mafakur enabled such persons to be accepted and integrated into Margi society with a minimum of social disruption. Thus the institution bestows a rational—even utilitarian—place upon the anomaly of the permanently resident alien, by giving him an institutional marginality.

The outstanding general characteristic of mafakur is that all mafa, without regard to political position, private influence, or wealth, hold in common a status that in structural terms is fundamentally and irrevocably intermediate with regard to membership in Margi society. But it is equally apparent that, despite their marginal status, their roles are fully integrated into society. The birma, whose office is reserved for a mafa, is the classic and perhaps symbolic demonstration of this, for he is a crucial and integral part of the political system.

The institution, then, reveals both marginality and integration, contradictory principles. This is achieved by formalizing—literally institutionalizing—the marginality. The resulting institution can be called a "limbic" institution, for its members exist in the hem of society, in a limbo, neither enfranchised Margi nor true aliens. The limbic function of mafakur, in conjunction with the society's need to maintain its social boundaries, makes its persistence in the face of indistinct rules of ownership and questionable economic value more understandable.

It is this limbic quality of the institution that makes it singularly appropriate as the ultimate punishment in the legal system. The miscreant was stripped of his rights in a peculiarly humiliating way. He remained in the society: a part of it, yet apart from it. He was not expelled, for that would be less humiliating and conceivably leave the way open for his return. Nor was it the labor required of mafa that represented the punishment, for they work no harder than others. Rather, it was the loss of identity and normality that was so objectionable to the proud Margi.

Having admitted candidly that questions of the origins of mafakur seem unanswerable, given the lack of data, I shall nevertheless introduce a speculative discussion suggesting origins consistent with the interpretation of mafakur as a limbic institution. In his pioneering work on the societies of northern Nigeria, C. K. Meek encountered several groups known as Fali in the Mandaras north of Mubi. Two things struck him: they revealed a high degree of heterogeneity and were certainly not a part of a large society some fifty or more miles to the south-southeast, also known as the Fali. These groups are still frequently designated as the "Fali of Mubi," although Murdock classified one part of them as Gude and the other as Margi (1959:92-93). Missionaries have reported to me that indeed one of the groups calls itself Margi and there is a firm tradition of Margi having migrated into the area. Meek concluded: " . . . the word Fali may have come to be used as a general term for any immigrants irrespective of their tribe. It was possibly a term of contempt meaning 'slaves', for among the Nzangi the word for 'slave' is 'fali' " (1931, 2:300-301). Charles Kraft (n.d.) has also recorded "fali" to mean "slave" for the Ngwaghi, a Margi-Bura group. In this context, it is important to recall that the word slave is derived from Slav, reflecting the fact that Slavic peoples were captured and made bondsmen in the Middle Ages.

The possibility of a similar derivation for mafa exists. The society immediately east of the Margi is customarily known as the Matakam. Podlewski, however, refers to it as Mafa (1961:76 n.2), and Lembezat says that the Matakam are subdivided into two groups, one of which is called Mafa (1961:7). To be fair, it must be pointed out that Margi have no tradition of mafa having originated from the Matakam, though they generally view Matakam as their inferiors. Several other Mandara groups refer to "slaves" by the term "mava" or "mavan." Most of these are more distant from the Matakam than the Margi, and the shift from f to v may represent simply a linguistic change. The attractiveness of this highly speculative suggestion is that it relates the intermediate position of immigrants in society to the status of mafa and is consistent with my description of mafakur as a limbic institution.

In the course of this discussion I have indicated that there are major problems and risks of distortion in conceptualizing the mafa as property or in interpreting mafakur as primarily an economic institution. Yet both concepts, in varying degrees, are important to the Western meaning of slavery. I have suggested that an understanding of mafakur requires a recognition of its limbic functions; no definitions of slavery place importance upon this characteristic. Consequently, the term seems an inappropriate translation of mafakur. However, an analysis that stays too close to its data may lack broader applicability, and it may be that at a higher level of abstraction mafakur and "slavery" can be classified together. But my analysis of mafakur indicates that the economic aspects of the institution should not be overemphasized. More importantly, the limbic quality of mafakur—especially considering the derivation of the word "slavery"—suggests dynamics of social identity and marginality unrecognized in the usual definition of the concept, which may have a wider relevance than the conventional use of the term "slavery" would indicate.

GLOSSARY

birma: an important political post reserved for a *mafa*.
fali: "slave" or "slaves" in some Mandara languages, but not in Margi.
jangum: a wrist dagger, a standard of value in exchange for a *mafa*.
mafa: a limbic person, sometimes translated as slave or slaves.
mafakur: institutional marginality, sometimes translated as slavery.
makarama: the king's first minister.
mbilim: noncaste.
mcilili: royalty.
mthlagu: master.
ngkyagu: caste.
talaka: commoner.
thlikul: premeditated murder.

REFERENCES

Benton, P. A. 1912. *Notes on some languages of the western Sudan.* London.
Kirk-Greene, A. H. M. 1958. *Adamawa: past and present.* Oxford.
Kraft, C. H. Undated [ca. 1959]. Untitled: a word list of Margi and related languages. Handwritten.
Lembezat, B. 1961. *Les populations païennes du Nord-Cameroun et de l'Adamawa.* Paris.
Meek, C. K. 1931. *Tribal studies in northern Nigeria.* 2 vols. London.
Murdock, G. P. 1959. *Africa: its peoples and their culture history.* New York.
Podlewski, A. M. 1961. Enquête sur l'émigration des Mafa hors du pays Matakam. *Rech. Etud. cameroun.* 5:73-95.
Vaughan, J. H. 1970. Caste systems in the western Sudan. In *Social stratification in Africa,* ed. A. Tuden and L. Plotnicov. New York.
———. 1973. Ngkagu as artists in Marghi society. In *The traditional artist in African societies,* ed. W. L. d'Azevedo. Bloomington, Ind.

Variations in the Uses of Slaves

Part III

3

Slavery and Social Stratification among the Sena of Mozambique

A Study of the Kaporo System

Barbara Isaacman and Allen Isaacman

Anthropologists and historians have traditionally employed the term "domestic slavery" as a convenient rubric to include a wide range of deprived-status positions. So global an approach overlooks the profound differences among African slave systems. It neither focuses on the underlying patterns that define the respective institutions nor does it explain cross-cultural variation. Detailed case studies and systematic typologies are needed to remedy this situation. This chapter examines the organization and operation of the *kaporo* (pl. *akaporo*) system among the Sena of the lower Zambesi Valley and places it within their larger system of social stratification.[1]

The shallow time depth of the oral traditions and the superficial and distorted descriptions of slavery in the early Portuguese accounts require us to limit our discussion to the nineteenth century, although the

1. We wish to express our gratitude to Paul Lovejoy, Stuart Wagner, and Jan Vansina for their valuable criticism of an earlier draft of this article. Research for this study was carried out under a generous grant provided by the Foreign Area Fellowship Program.

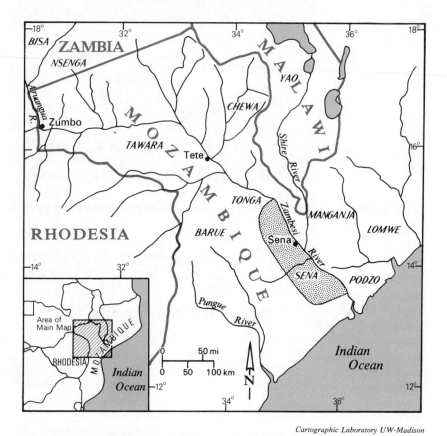

Cartographic Laboratory UW-Madison
Map 3. Peoples of the Zambesi Region, ca. 1750-1850

antecedents of the kaporo system date back at least two hundred years.[2] Dealing explicitly with the nineteenth century also avoids the pitfalls of "the ethnographic present," which have marred so many discussions of African social history. Moreover, the oral data must be subject to careful scrutiny. Because the majority of the akaporo were foreigners and the bulk of the testimonies came from Sena elders, many of whose ancestors owned akaporo, a built-in bias reinforces the tendency to depict this institution in a highly idealized form. As Joseph C. Miller suggests in Chapter 8 of this volume, such a study therefore represents as much an examination of the

2. According to all our Sena informants, the kaporo system historically had been an integral part of their social organization. Miranda's account, written in the eighteenth century, suggests that the system was operating during this period. See A.N.T.T., Ministério do Reino, Maço 604: António Pinto de Miranda, "Memória sobre a Costa de Africa," pp. 54-59, ca. 1760.

Sena notion of "slavery" as a description of the actual operation of the kaporo system.

SENA SOCIETY

Sena polities were small in scale and relatively undifferentiated.[3]   Most Sena chieftaincies rarely exceeded two hundred households. The localized three-generation extended family with a patrilineal segment as its core constituted the basic social unit. This corporate patrilineal segment served as the principle reference group for the individual; it determined his descent and residence, acted in all legal matters, and provided a wide range of economic and social services (interviews: Camalizene; Cado). Several such contiguous lineage segments formed, in turn, the core of a Sena village.

Within Sena society, the major stratifying variables were the control over the allocation of land and the ability to mobilize human resources. Land by itself had no intrinsic value. It was only significant as a means of attracting and supporting a large following. Thus, through the fiction of first arrival, the royal lineage in each chieftaincy, led by the *mambo* (pl. *amambo*), maintained its prerogative to allocate land to the village headmen, or *afumu* (sing. *mfumu*), who, in turn, redistributed it to their subordinates (interviews: Chibante; Cado; Tito).

Although the agricultural yield was relatively low, the size of the surplus that a lineage segment could accumulate varied in direct proportion to the number of its economically productive members. By exchanging this surplus for some nonperishable status item, a particular lineage could enhance its relative position. In general, Sena families used their excess agricultural produce as bridewealth, or *chuma,* as an incentive to attract strangers, and to buy akaporo. Each transaction improved the relative position of the group, since more dependents led to greater wealth, which in turn increased the possibility of obtaining additional dependents.

THE ACQUISITION OF AKAPORO

The Sena acquired akaporo in various ways: by trading with neighboring ethnic groups, through voluntary enslavement and pawning, and by kidnapping. Of these, trade provided the largest and most regular source of akaporo.

Most akaporo were bought from the Manganja, who lived on the northern bank of the Zambesi River (see Map 3), although smaller numbers of Lomwe, Podzo, and Chewa were purchased as well as a few

---

3. For a detailed discussion of the social characteristics of simple horticultural societies, see Lenski (1966:117-41).

Barue, Tonga, and Tawara. The general direction of the trade, which antedated the period under examination, reflected both the relative prosperity that the Sena enjoyed *vis-à-vis* their northern neighbors and their access to highly desired cloth (interviews: Camalizene; Pomba; Zimbaue; Tito; Gogodo; Nhanticole; Renço and Pangacha; Jasere and Gunda; Chave and Sinto).

A brief overview of Sena commercial relations with the Manganja suggests the nature and scale of this institutionalized trading system. Periodically, an individual Sena man or a small group of related merchants traveled to designated villages north of the Zambesi where their local counterparts had gathered a group of slaves. These ventures generally occurred toward the end of the dry season, when supply and price factors were most favorable to the buyers. Throughout the nineteenth century, the Manganja suffered from seasonal famines as well as the more pronounced economic dislocations caused by civil strife, the Matequenha conquest, and Yao slave raiding.[4] Economic hardship compelled many people to sell their slaves and even members of their own families. In return, they received sorghum, corn, and other grains as well as Sena cloth, which was in great demand as a substitute for their coarse bark cloth and animal skins (interviews: Camalizene; Gogodo; Nhanticole; Pomba; Tito; Vicente; Zimbaue; Renço and Pangacha; Jasere and Gunda).

There was no fixed price for akaporo, and protracted negotiations preceded each agreement. The average price per slave seems to have been several bushels of grain plus three to six meters of cloth (interviews: António; Gogodo; Jasere and Gunda; Tito; Zimbaue; Chave and Sinto). This varied, however, according to the degree to which food was locally available, the quality of the cloth, and the desirability of the akaporo. Some informants contended that their ancestors paid more for females because of their ability to procreate (interviews: Gogodo; Pomba; Zimbaue). Others claimed that males were worth more since their work capacity was greater (interviews: Nhanticole; Tito). Since Sena traders did not generally resell their slaves, the differing explanations may simply reflect the distinct productive needs of particular lineage segments. Whatever the sex, young people were more expensive because of both their potential productivity and the ease with which they could be integrated into the kin group.

Before his departure, the Sena trader presented the local headman with a small gift and gave each slave a piece of cloth and some food to secure

4. For a summary of aspects of Manganja history during this period, see Isaacman 1972: 134-38). Matthew Schoffeleers is currently engaged in a detailed analysis of Manganja society.

his or her loyalty. As an added precaution, the trading party left only after dark so that the captives would not know the route back to their homes (interview: Zimbaue).

Disparities in the levels of agricultural production within Sena society also underlay the practice of voluntary enslavement. During a serious famine or drought, it was common for a man to seek to attach himself or his dependents to a wealthy person in exchange for food, clothing, and security (interviews: Chibante; Domingos; Pomba). As Gamitto noted in the 1830s: "In this part of Africa famines are frequent and make terrible depradations [sic]; they are experienced in some lands more than in others, and people from the affected lands flood into those areas where food is to be found. They buy it with anything they possess, including their own freedom, making themselves the slaves of those who give them sustenance" (Gamitto 1960, 2:145-46). These general comments are confirmed by another observer who resided among the Sena for many years. Most slaves, he noted, "came to be captive from the time of famines, pestilence and locust, because their urgent needs obliged them to come and offer themselves as captives."[5] According to both oral traditions and nineteenth-century written accounts, desperate individuals destroyed an item of some worth which belonged to a wealthier neighbor; this symbolic act, known as "breaking the *mitete,*" invariably resulted in enslavement (interview: Pomba).[6]

Pawning, by which a man gave the services of his son for a specified period of time in return for food and clothing, was a variation of voluntary enslavement. Failure to repay the debt resulted in the permanent loss of the youth. This arrangement was highly desirable to the lender; he was not only assured a supply of labor in return for his investment but also had the possibility of increasing the size of his lineage at a minimal cost.[7]

The Sena also obtained slaves, especially women and children, through robbery or wars. Informants acknowledged the existence of a class of thieves, known as *mupanga,* who specialized in stealing young children. These thefts generally occurred during the harvest when most adults were working in the fields and the grass was high, enabling the mupanga to approach a village undetected (interviews: António; Chave and Sinto; Renço and Pangacha). Although there is no evidence that the Sena

5. A.N.T.T., Ministério do Reino, Maço 604: Miranda, pp. 54-59, ca. 1760 (our translation). Although his account was written in the preceding century, all the evidence suggests that the situation he described recurred with frequency during the period under examination.

6. Gamitto (1859:398) described how the neighboring Portuguese recognized this practice in order to acquire slaves for their *prazos,* legally defined as crown estates.

7. Interviews: António; Pomba; Tesoura. A.N.T.T., Ministério do Reino, Maço 604: Miranda, p. 58, ca. 1760. Gamitto (1859:370).

engaged in slave raiding, their disputes with neighboring chieftaincies over land and water rights, over thievery, and over sexual improprieties occasionally led to clashes and the enslavement of younger members of the defeated community (interviews: Costa; Domingos; Chave and Sinto).

SOCIAL STATUS OF AKAPORO

Despite the numerous opportunities to acquire akaporo, only the most affluent members of Sena society—successful farmers, a few traders, senior members of the royal family, and local village headmen—could afford them. Even among this elite, however, few had more than four or five slaves, and a man was considered exceptionally well off and quite powerful if he owned eight or ten (interviews: Camalizene; Domingos; Pomba; Zimbaue; Jasere and Gunda). The inability to acquire a greater following indicates the limits of capital accumulation, even at the upper levels of Sena society.

The multiple patterns of recruitment did not generate separate systems of slavery, as they did in some African societies. Whether purchased, stolen, or captured, slaves were grouped together with those who had voluntarily given up their freedom to form one rather ambiguous social category. Moreover, the absence of pejorative stereotypes implies that akaporo enjoyed a status which was not dramatically inferior to that of the free Sena. In this sense, the kaporo system simply reflected the relatively undifferentiated nature of the larger society.

From the outset, the position of young akaporo was defined in kinship terms. Upon arrival in their new home, they received the *mutupu,* or clan name, of their patron. This symbolic act created fictitious familial links in the absence of a blood relationship. The akaporo addressed their patron as *baba,* or "father," used the appropriate kin terms for other adopted relatives, and paid homage to the local ancestor spirits at periodic religious ceremonies (interviews: Gogodo; Pomba; Tesoura; Zimbaue; Penga, Chambe, and Guede; Renço and Pangacha). Rowley (1867:47), writing in the 1860s, observed that "within the natives there is no such distance as master and slave . . . [since the owner is] recognized and called father and those who are subject to him are spoken of and regarded as his children."

Akaporo spent their early years like other Sena children. Young akaporo resided in the compound of their patron, who took complete responsibility for their upbringing and protection. Their tasks, which included guarding livestock, collecting firewood, and working in the fields during the harvest, were shared by all others of their age. They were consciously raised as Sena by their adopted grandparents, who served as the principal socializing agents. The intimate relationship that developed not only fostered the characteristic alliance of alternate generations but prepared the akaporo for puberty school, *gowere*, where they formally learned the traditions, beliefs, and values of Sena society and what was expected of them as adults (interviews: Gogodo; Pomba; Tesoura; Zimbaue).

Akaporo married shortly after this *rite de passage*. Generally they wed a member of the patron's family or another kaporo attached to the lineage. These unions were similar to preferential marriages in which chuma did not have to be paid. On occasion, akaporo married outside the lineage. In the cases of the male kaporo, his patron assumed a major role in the premarital negotiations and provided the necessary bridewealth. Conversely, the patron received the bridewealth when one of his female akaporo married into another lineage. The new couple followed the customary rules of initial patrilocality and built their home among the male's adopted relatives, who provided them with a small field to plant and appropriate foodstuffs. Their children enjoyed an intimate relationship with the baba, who acted as an adopted grandfather, just as he had served as adopted father to the kaporo (interviews: Antonio; Pangacha; Tesoura).

Marriage was the principal mechanism for incorporating recently acquired adult akaporo into the lineage segment. Patrons often married their female akaporo or betrothed them to their sons or junior brothers. Similarly, male akaporo became the husbands of female members of the lineage segment. As in the case of akaporo raised since childhood, they and their spouses followed the prescribed residence rules and were considered part of the lineage. The only obvious difference was in the slower rate of acculturation among the older akaporo.

Such marriage between akaporo and free Sena were a form of institutionalized manumission. They provided akaporo with real and extensive kinship affiliations that completed their integration and legitimized their new position within the larger society (interviews: António; Pangacha; Pomba; Tesoura; Tito). For their offspring, a biological link existed, which assured them a perpetual position within the lineage structure.

In practice, the social position of these manumitted akaporo remained somewhat ambiguous. Some were assigned less desirable tasks, allocated plots and hut sites of poorer quality, and treated condescendingly by junior kinsmen. In crisis, they were more likely to be sold than were their freeborn relatives. This inferiority created some tensions and was the principal reason for migration away from the village of their adopted family after marriage. The majority who remained, however, could draw solace from the knowledge that their children would not suffer such indignities (interviews: Gogodo; Pomba; Jasere and Gunda).

While akaporo were automatically manumitted when they married free members of Sena society, there was no consensus on the status of two akaporo who married each other. The lack of agreement may either reflect a certain amount of confusion on the part of the elders or, more likely, a structural ambiguity. Most informants believed the couple to be free (interviews: Nhanticole; Pangacha; Pomba; Penga, Chambe, and Guede), while a minority held that it was only their children who acquired full status within the lineage (interviews: António; Tesoura). In either case, this situation occurred infrequently, and the patron only enjoyed the right to the services of the person he had acquired and not to those of his off-spring. Most akaporo, therefore, endured their low status for a relatively short period of time and in the most extreme instance manumission was deferred only one generation.

Even before their manumission, akaporo and free Sena played similar economic roles. Both the sex division of labor, which governed the alloca-tion of jobs, and the availablility of free land reduced the likelihood of economic discrimination. Male akaporo cleared their own lands and helped their wives during the harvest. Like free, able-bodied lineage members, they also worked in the plots of the elders of the lineage, especially during the harvest. The game and fish they caught during the dry season belonged to them, although they were expected to share their catch with other lineage members. Female akaporo, like free women, performed most of the domestic chores and planted and harvested the crops. There is some evidence that they also drew water and cooked and cleaned for their patron, but this seems to have varied from one Sena family to another. In short, akaporo engaged in the same undifferentiated tasks as natural-born Sena, though the allocation of less desirable plots and residual domestic responsibilities indicated their relatively lower position within the lineage, a position which often continued even after the their manumission (interviews: Gogodo; Pomba; Jasere and Gunda).

As a legitimate member of the kin group, a kaporo was also eligible to inherit wealth. Among the Sena, the inheritance passed to either a junior brother or the senior son of the deceased. If the principal adult heirs had died or resettled in a distant region, a senior kaporo in the deceased's household could administer the estate. He inherited, in addition to the wealth, his patron's wives and children as part of his new responsibility as guardian of the family. He also enjoyed an increase in status since he was automatically manumitted and recognized as the lineage head (interviews: António; Gogodo; Nhanticole; Tesoura; Zimbaue).

The refusal of the Sena to sell their akaporo to Portuguese slave dealers provides the clearest expression of the strong familial ties that bound the akaporo to their lineages. Throughout much of the nineteenth century the

Portuguese were frustrated in their attempts to purchase large numbers of slaves from the Sena to meet overseas demands in Brazil, the Caribbean, and the islands of Príncipe and Réunion (interviews: Domingos; Pomba; Chave and Sinto; see also Isaacman 1972:85-94). Instead, slave dealers were forced to travel to the homelands of the Manganja and the more distant Chewa and Nsenga to acquire captives.[8] Others resorted to violence to compel the Sena to part with their akaporo. "But when the demand is great, or the chiefs and others refuse to sell those people over whom they have power—and though sorely tempted by their necessities they do frequently refuse to sell their people . . . —the slavers then take up bribes, such as guns and gunpowder; they stir up strife between village and village, and between tribe and tribe" (Rowley 1867:48).

Although there were undoubtedly individuals who willingly sold akaporo, this only occurred with regularity during a serious crisis such as a famine or a drought. Only under circumstances when the entire lineage segment was threatened did the akaporo's low status and lack of blood-relationship make them expendable. Nevertheless, most informants agreed that such options were exercised only reluctantly and when no other alternative existed. In the absence of akaporo, lineage elders had to part with other relatives (interviews: António; Chibante; Domingos; Pomba; Tesoura).

KAPORO IN THE CONTEXT OF SENA SOCIETY

The relative lack of discrimination, the ease and rapidity of integration, and the subsequent acquisition of nearly equal status suggest that the term kaporo referred to a transitional position that corresponds more precisely to the concept of "adopted dependency" than to that of "domestic slavery." In order to understand the operation of the institution, however, it is necessary to examine it within the context of the larger system of stratification and to isolate the interrelated economic, social, and political factors that explain its function in Sena society. Although Sena society was relatively undifferentiated, three social categories can nevertheless be distinguished, each differentially related to the two stratifying factors—the control over the allocation of land and the ability to mobilize human resources. The small political elite, the large group of free agriculturalists, and the akaporo constituted the three principal strata in Sena society.

The Sena political elite used landownership to explain and legitimize its preeminent position. Through the manipulation of traditions, the

8. For a discussion of the Portuguese slave-trading activities and the responses of different Zambesian peoples, see Isaacman (1972:85-94).

land chiefs, amambo, asserted that their ancestors had been the first inhabitants of the area (interviews: Cado; Chibante; Ganunga). By virtue of this descent, each mambo inherited secular and religious responsibilities to safeguard the ancestral land and the sole right to alienate territory within his polity. As the owner of the land and guardian of its inhabitants, the mambo performed a wide range of activities to maintain the health and well-being of the polity. He served as the principal link between the people and the royal ancestors, or *mizimu*. Throughout the course of the year he periodically propitiated the mizimu to gain their assistance and guidance and he personally directed the religious ceremonies designed to insure both abundant rainfall and the continued fertility of the land. In the secular sphere he resolved all serious litigation, appointed all subordinate officials, served as the final judicial authority, and directed the militia in times of emergency (interviews: Cado; Camalizene; Chibante; Ganunga; Tesoura; Chave and Sinto).

The amambo initially distributed grants of land to both junior kinsmen and strangers willing to acknowledge their authority. These subordinates, known as afumu, then allocated parcels to their kinsmen and followers. To reaffirm the mambo's ownership of the land, all the members of the chieftaincy paid an annual tax, or *mutsonkho*. The mambo also received a number of symbolic gifts, of which the most important were the larger tusk of any dead elephant and prescribed parts of other animals killed in his territory (interviews: Cado; Camalizene; Chibante; Ganunga).

Succession to the position of mambo was restricted to candidates who belonged, by descent, to the founding lineage of the chieftaincy; but within this category, achievement criteria were of some importance. A senior son or junior brother could be bypassed in favor of a more qualified younger sibling or distant relative. The Sena also acknowledged the right of the chiefly family to overthrow a mambo who was either inept or who suffered a physical disability that indicated his loss of the sacredness that the *amambo* were believed to possess.

Below the mambo in the political hierarchy were the afumu, or village headmen. The mambo allocated land and designated limited administrative and judicial authority to these subordinate officials. They resolved minor disputes, transmitted and enforced the dictates of the land chief, collected the mutsonkho, and sat on the mambo's council. In return for these services, they received the rights to settle their people on the land and to retain a portion of the collected taxes (interviews: Tito; Penga, Chambe, and Guede).

Entry into this local political elite was slightly more open than at the higher level. Although many afumu were junior kinsmen of the mambo, it was very common to appoint the senior member of a prominent local lineage to this position. Such a practice prevented the growth of a narrow political elite of "royal" blood. The periodic establishment of new villages in response to demographic pressures and internal conflicts ensured a continued availability of new elite positions. When a mfumu died, a qualified successor was chosen from among the members of his family.

The free agriculturalists constituted the largest single stratum in Sena society. The principal determinants of status were seniority and sex. Seniority was an important organizing principle at all levels. The elders served both as the lineage heads and as the mfumu's unofficial council of advisors. The members of the extended family were ranked according to their seniority, and one's specific position within this ranking system determined his rights and responsibilities *vis-à-vis* the other members. This was most graphically illustrated when a member of the lineage died. All his wealth and dependents were inherited by the deceased's senior brother in his capacity as guardian of the localized patrilineal segment.

Differences in wealth created some distinctions within villages. Social distance, however, remained relatively small, given the low level of production. The cultivation of grains, primarily sorghum and corn, rarely yielded a substantial surplus, and seasonal famines periodically afflicted the poor.[9] The perishable nature of agricultural commodities further reduced capital accumulation, which, in turn, inhibited the development of full-time occupational specialization. A few itinerant traders, or *musambadzi*, and weavers were the principal exceptions.[10] In both cases, the scale of their operations was small; most confined their activities to the dry season when the manpower needs of the agricultural sector were minimal. With the exception of the commerce in akaporo, goods and services generally circulated through networks of kinship, affinity, and clientage without reliance on external trade.

Although wealth was only one criterion of an individual's social status, it was the single most important determinant of the relative position of Sena lineages. Individual wealth was translated into increased lineage status through the acquisition of akaporo, the incorporation of strangers, and the arrangement of marriage alliances.

Affluent members of Sena society enjoyed a distinct advantage in attracting strangers to their lineage. According to traditions, the arrival of aliens fleeing from wars, litigations, or famines occurred with great regularity (interviews: Camalizene; Penga, Chambe, and Guede). Gamitto (1960, 1:101) observed that when an individual violated the law, "be it

9. Interviews: Cado; Camalizene. A.H.M., Códice 2-443, F.E. 7, fol. 56: José Gomes Barbosa to Joaquim de Azevedo Alpoim, July 30, 1855: Thorton (1864:196).

10. Interview: Chave and Sinto. A.H.U., Moçambique, Cx. 19: António Manoel de Mello de Castro to Martinho de Mello e Castro, May 7, 1783.

adultery, theft, or anything else, his remedy is flight for with such a crime there is no form of process. If he is seized he is killed and his whole family enslaved." Foreigners attached themselves to wealthy Sena families who could offer them some economic security and a nexus of kinship ties. The full incorporation of strangers into Sena society was formalized through marital unions in which the requisite bridewealth was either waived or substantially reduced. The new couple received a plot of land and a supply of food to carry them through the first harvest. Poorer Sena could not offer such inducements, since they needed the bridewealth which they received for their women to secure wives for the male members of their lineage.

Wealthy individuals and lineages also used their surplus to negotiate a wide network of marital alliances. Bridewealth, or chuma, consisting of grain and cloth, transferred the woman's fertility to the patrilineage and economic and sexual rights over her to the husband. Barrenness was a principal cause of divorce, and the returned chuma was used to obtain fertile partners to increase the size of the lineage (interviews: António; Pangacha; see also Lopes 1907:362).

While the Sena lineages placed a high priority on the acquisition of new members, the ideal pattern of continuously converting wealth into people was limited by certain environmental constraints. The more important of these, directly impinging on the size of the lineage, were (1) the availability of usable land, within easy access of the village, that could be cultivated by the newcomers, and (2) a relatively long period of plentiful harvests and freedom from natural disasters.

Despite the availability of land, the practices of shifting agriculture and observing a long fallow period meant that only about one-fifth of the total arable acreage could be farmed at any one time.[11] This extensive utilization of the land limited the capacity of Sena lineages to absorb strangers and raised the possibility that a substantial influx would strain their limited resources. The likelihood of such an occurrence was relatively small, however, since the surplus that could be converted into dependents was never very large and demographic pressures could be somewhat neutralized by fission within lineages. Nevertheless, a theoretical point existed at which an increase in the number of lineage members was no longer advantageous.

A more serious difficulty with increased size arose during periods of prolonged regional famines and droughts. At such times, larger groups were obviously very vulnerable. During seasonal famines and others of short duration, the consumption requirements could be met by circulating

11. For an excellent account of the traditional agricultural system, see A.H.U., Moçambique, Cx. 17: António Manoel de Mello de Castro to José Vasconcellos Almeida, June 18, 1780.

akaporo within Sena society. But this internal mechanism lapsed during a protracted famine, when the people were forced to sell dependents and even relatives to the Portuguese slave traders (interviews: Chibante; Domingos; Pomba; see also Rowley 1867:47; Gamitto 1859:398).

Because the surplus produced by any one dependent was relatively small and the number of akaporo was also limited, narrow economic considerations do not seem to have been the sole incentive for increasing the size of the lineage. The principal motivation for acquiring dependents was to enhance the social and political position of the patrilineage. Additional members increased its power, prestige, and reproductive capacity, and enabled it to arrange a wider network of alliances through marriages. Since social status was largely determined by the number of followers attached to each lineage, both the receptivity to strangers and the relatively rapid incorporation of akaporo were logical.

Increased social status was not an end in itself. It was pursued as a means of attaining political power, which tended to be the most salient stratifying element in precolonial African societies. According to Fallers (1966:147):

In traditional Africa goods and services, both as symbols and as facilities, circulate primarily in terms of political relations, for it is only the polity that dominates stratification. Persons and groups strive to control the symbols and facilities that are the expressions of authority and the means of strengthening and extending it. A good case could be made that, at least in eastern, central and southern Africa, the most important facilities are people . . . and in the production of goods and services in this part of Africa, the most problematic factor is usually human labor.

The size of the lineage segment and, to a lesser extent, the range of marriage alliances had a direct bearing on its relative position within the village structure. A large following enabled the lineage to mobilize a disproportionate number of people in times of internal conflict. The absence of a standing army meant that larger lineage segments also played a more prominent role in the defense of the village. The ability to cope with such crises enhanced its prestige, as reflected in the important position that the elder of such a lineage enjoyed on the mfumu's advisory council.

Internal lineage tensions and demographic pressures were often resolved by the hiving off of localized groups and the formation of new villages. In such a situation the senior member of the largest lineage segment would gain recognition as the new mfumu (interviews: António; Ganunga; Tito). Acquisition of a mfumu position enabled the lineage to control the allocation of land and to acquire a new source of wealth from collecting the tax (mutsonkho). Both of these enabled it to attract additional followers. Over time, an enlarged membership would add to the lineage's status and power within the larger polity and could result in a more important role on the mambo's council of elders.

In the most extreme situation a powerful mfumu, after consulting the senior ancestor spirits, might secede from the local polity and organize a new chieftaincy on lands that were uninhabited.[12] The relatively small scale of Sena chieftaincies and the lack of formalized relationships among them facilitated these centrifugal tendencies. Without a well-developed bureaucratic system and a military arm to enforce the dictates of the mambo, local afumu enjoyed not only a large amount of power in comparison to their counterparts within state systems but also the option of secession.

CONCLUSION

Lisbon abolished the kaporo system in the beginning of the twentieth century to counter charges that its nationals were involved in slave trading and that the government was actively fostering a system of forced labor.[13] Nevertheless, many Sena continued to use akaporo as a means of increasing the size of their lineage segments (Lopes 1907:353). This practice seems to have persisted for at least a generation, indicating the important and unchanging role it played in Sena society. Even today the absorption of strangers, which satisfies the same essential function, continues. Many of the forced laborers who came from distant lands to build roads, lay tracks, and work on plantations were ultimately incorporated into the local population (interviews: Camalizene; Chibante).

The kaporo system of deprived status is of a type common to other parts of precolonial Africa. Allowing for some differences in detail, the neighboring Tonga and Tawara possessed comparable systems, as did the Ila of Zambia, to name only a few.[14] The evidence from these central African cases indicates that societies which were small in scale, with a low level of economic production, a relatively undifferentiated social system, and an undeveloped political superstructure often contained similar institutions of slavery.

12. Before moving to new lands, the mfumu and his principal advisors visited the prospective site and left a handful of grain in the center of the location for a twenty-four-hour period. If the grain scattered it meant that the mizimu approved the site and the migration could proceed.

13. For a discussion of forced labor, see Duffy (1967).

14. This conclusion is based on oral data we collected among the Tonga, Tawara, and Chewa of Makanga in 1968. The material is part of the Isaacman Collection, African Studies Association oral data archives, Indiana University. For an interesting discussion of Ila slavery, see Tuden (1970).

GLOSSARY

baba: father.
chuma: bridewealth.
gowere: puberty school.
kaporo (pl. *akaporo*): a slave or adopted dependent.
mambo (pl. *amambo*): land chief.
mfumu (pl. *afumu*): village headman.
(breaking of the) *mitete*: a symbolic act, which (if committed) results in slavery.
mizimu: royal ancestors.
mupanga: Sena thieves who stole children, primarily from the Manganja.
musambadzi: traders.
mutsonkho: a tax paid to the mambo.
mutupu: clan name.
prazos: legally defined as crown estates.

REFERENCES

ORAL SOURCES
A copy of these tapes is deposited in the Isaacman Collection at the African Studies Association, Center for African Oral Data, housed in the Archives of Traditional Music, Indiana University, Bloomington, Indiana.

Sena
Jasse Camalizene, interview on August 6, 1968. T.T. 8(1); E.T. 5(1).
Mozesse Domingos, interview on August 6, 1968. T.T. 8(1); E.T. 5(1).
Mortar Nhacalazi, interview on August 7, 1968. T.T. 9(1); E.T. 5(2).
Gonçalves Chibante, interview on August 8, 1968. T.T. 9(2); E.T. 5(2).
Botão Ganunga, interview on August 8, 1968. T.T. 8(2); T.T. 9(1); E.T. 6(1).
Gimo Tito, interview on August 9, 1968. T.T. 8(2); E.T. 5(1); E.T. 5(2).

Chemba
Renço Cado, interview on August 13, 1968. T.T. 9(1); T.T. 9(2); E.T. 6(1).
Tomás Chave and Oliveira Sinto, joint interview on August 14, 1968. T.T. 9(2); E.T. 6(2).
Lole Nhanticole, interview on August 26, 1968. T.T. 10(1); T.T. 10(2); E.T. 7(1).
Sete Catondo, interview on August 26, 1968. Untaped.

Caya
João Pomba, interview on August 31, 1968. T.T. 10(1); E.T. 7(2).
Aleixo Jasere and José Gunda, joint interview on September 1, 1968. T.T. 10(1); E.T. 8(1).
Tomás Zimbaue, interview on September 2, 1968. T.T. 10(2); E.T. 8(1).
Dauce Angolete Gogodo, interview on September 3, 1968. T.T. 10(2); E.T. 8(2).

Gente Renço and Quembo Pangacha, interview on September 4, 1968. T.T. 10(2); T.T. 11(1); E.T. 8(1).

D. Anna Mascalenha Costa, interview on September 9, 1968. Untaped.

Cheringoma

José António, interview on September 7, 1968. T.T. 12(1); E.T. 8(2).

Chale Penga, Tomás Chambe, and Jamusse Guede, joint interview on September 7, 1968. T.T. 12(1); E.T. 8(2).

Andisseni Tesoura, interview on September 8, 1968. T.T. 12(2); E.T. 9(1).

Alface Pangacha, interview on September 9, 1968. T.T. 11(2); T.T. 12(1).

UNPUBLISHED SOURCES

A.H.M.: Arquivo Histórico de Moçambique, Maputo.

    Códice 2-443, F.E. 7, fol. 56: José Gomes Barbosa to Joaquim de Azevedo Alpoim, July 30, 1855.

A.H.U.: Arquivo Histórico Ultramarino, Lisbon.

    Moçambique, Caixa 17: António Manoel de Castro to José Vasconcellos Almeida, June 18, 1780.

    Moçambique, Caixa 19: António Manoel de Mello de Castro to Martinho de Mello e Castro, May 7, 1783.

A.N.T.T.: Arquivo Nacional da Torre do Tombo, Lisbon.

    Ministério do Reino, Maço 604: António Pinto de Miranda, "Memória sobre a Costa de África," ca. 1760.

PUBLISHED SOURCES

Duffy, J. 1967. *A question of slavery.* Oxford.

Fallers, L.A. 1966. Social stratification and economic processes in Africa. In *Class, status, and power,* ed. R. Bendix and S. M. Lipset. 2d ed. New York.

Gamitto, A. C. P. 1859. Escravatura na África oriental. *Arch. Pittoresco* 2: 369-73, 397-400.

————. 1960. *King Kazembe.* Tr. by Ian Cunnison. 2 vols. Lisbon.

Isaacman, A. F. 1972. *Mozambique: the Africanization of a European institution, the Zambesi prazos, 1750-1902.* Madison.

Lenski, G. 1966. *Power and privilege: a theory of social stratification.* New York.

Lopes, M. M. 1907. Usages and customs of the natives of Sena. *Jl R. Afr. Soc.* 6:350-65.

Rowley, H. 1867. *The story of the universities mission to central Africa.* London.

Thorton, R. 1864. Notes on the Zambesi and the Shire. *Jl R. geogr. Soc.* 34: 196-99.

Tuden, A. 1970. Slavery and social stratification among the Ila of central Africa. In *Social stratification in Africa,* ed. A. Tuden and L. Plotnicov. New York.

4

Slaves and Slavery in Igboland, Nigeria

Victor C. Uchendu

Western conceptualizations of slavery tend to have one important common feature: slaves are treated legally as if they were a "single commodity," their status involving a single transaction. A sample of definitions of slavery by Western writers will make the point. For Ingram, "the essential character of slavery may be regarded as lying in the fact that the master was owner of the person of the slave, though the rights arising from such ownership might be variously limited" (1895:262). Nieboer, who views slavery as an industrial system, defines a slave as "a man who is the property or possession of another man and [who is] forced to work for him: [while] slavery is the fact that one man is the property or possession of another" (1900:8-9). On the other hand, Westermarck views "the compulsory nature of the slave's relation to his master" as the chief characteristic of slavery (1906, 1:671). In Bohannan's view, slavery is a servile relationship which is "not derived from either contractual or kinship obligations." Slaves, therefore, "are essentially kinless people; kinlessness is an essential of slavery wherever it is found and whatever else may accompany or mark it" (1963:179-80).

The system of slavery practiced in Igboland up to the nineteenth century provides ethnographic support for a different thesis—namely, that there is a bundle of "commodity rights" in a person, and these rights are capable of different combinations in a market transaction. Each of these combinations of "commodity rights," however culturally defined, may be differently institutionalized by society and consequently result in varying status

121

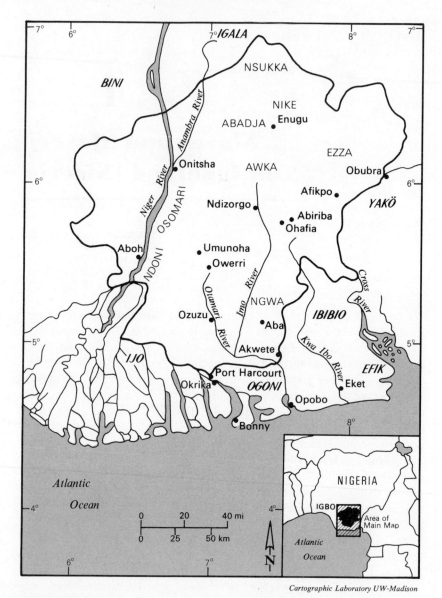

Map 4. Igbo Country

Cartographic Laboratory UW-Madison

disabilities in a given social structure. Slavery, therefore, constitutes a continuum of status disabilities and the disabilities vary with the number of "commodity rights" in a person that are acquired. Viewed in this way, it becomes clear that what Western society recognizes, at least legally, as slavery is the acquisition of all the "commodity rights" in a person, and this allows Westerners to treat slaves as if they embodied a single commodity rather than a bundle of commodities. The contrast between the extreme form of plantation slavery in the United States and the treatment of slaves in South America (Elkins 1959) seems to reflect this kind of distinction, a distinction that becomes even more apparent when one considers African systems of slavery.

THE ETHNOGRAPHIC AREA

Behind the surf-beaten eastern Nigerian coastline lie about 30,000 square miles of deltaic swamps, virgin and secondary forests, and high savanna. In this area are found a number of ethnic groups—the Ijo, the Ndoni, the Ogoni, the Igbo,[1] the Ibibio, and the Yakö. The Igbo-speaking people, whose traditions of slavery we will examine in this chapter, are numerically the dominant ethnic group in this region. Geographically, the area falls into two broad ecological zones: the delta, with a specialized fishing economy; and the hinterland, of which Igboland is a part, which produces much of the foodstuffs consumed in the area. Since neither the delta nor the hinterland was self-sufficient economically, a highly developed system of distributive trade grew up in the region, a factor that helps to account for its high cultural homogeneity. Salt and smoke-dried fish from the delta were traded for yams, cocoyams, palm oil, and plantains from the hinterland. In the precolonial period, as in modern times, migrant labor supplemented trade, and the Igbo country was a particularly important area of out-migration. Skilled craftsmen and artisans (such as medicine men, priests, blacksmiths, carvers, and teeth filers) and unskilled labor (such as agricultural workers and housebuilders) and, in the eighteenth and nineteenth centuries, slaves were all-important in this traffic (Jones 1963:13-16).

THE SOCIOPOLITICAL ORGANIZATION OF THE IGBO

Although there were, and still are, some regional variations, the Igbo exhibited many similarities in their kinship and political structures (Uchendu 1965). The most enduring kinship unit, which had important social as well as political functions, was the patrilineage. The unit of political action was the village, a corporate group of patrilineages of common descent, inhabiting a common territory. Village government was republican in temper. A general meeting of all freeborn adults decided

1. The mother-tongue rendering of the word; Ibo is the anglicized version.

major issues, though the elders and important household heads tended
to have greatest authority. Age, descent in the male line, wealth, and
ability were important criteria for leadership. Political position without
ability was accorded recognition but not much respect (Green 1947:124).
Contrary to widespread misconception, the Igbo achieved a level of
political integration higher than the village. The village polity was
integrated with the village-group, a larger and more authoritative political
unit.

Supporting the authority of the elders and the whole political system
were tutelary deities and oracles (*Igwe, Ozuzu, Agbara*), which functioned
as the final court of appeal; and the Earth deity and other natural and
fertility spirits, which enforced compliance to laws and maintained the
moral tone of the village. Age-grade associations served to restrain the
powers of the elders by giving the youth active participation in the political
processes.

Rank in society was measured by the multiple criteria of age, wealth,
and ability. Prestige was achieved by those who could convert their wealth
into less tangible symbols by buying "positions" in exclusive clubs and
secret societies. For the many who did not command wealth, prestige was
attainable in other fields: the "man-killer" society or the "leopard-killer"
society was open to young men who distinguished themselves by killing an
enemy or potential enemy of the village—a stray headhunter or a leopard,
for instance. Social position was reflected by the possession of wealth and
by other objective indicators, such as the number of slaves (*ohu*—in some
dialects, *oru*) and the number of wives. Command over the loyalty of a
large number of people—children, wives, kinsmen, friends, in-laws, and
slaves—was a measure of social position. The support of a large following
also meant economic and political power. One needed economic power to
maintain an effective political control, and in a labor-intensive agricultural system it is a large labor force that sustains economic power.
Economically, labor could be deployed for farming and trading; and
politically, the men could be mobilized for war and plunder. Many people
aspired to these goals, but only a few achieved them. Slaves in particular
were owned by only a few people. Their number was limited by the
economic realities of the time. Although the Igbo were a slave-owning
society, slavery was never the basis of the social system, notwithstanding
the fact that slaves formed an important part of it. This has important
implications for defining the role of slaves and their social mobility in Igbo
society.

METHODS OF RECRUITING SLAVES

There were six principal methods of recruiting slaves. Four of these—
capture, kidnapping, purchase, and political intrigue—gave the victim no

choice in his fate. Two other methods—pawning and dedication to the service of deities—allowed the slave some choice of master. According to Igbo elders, "the distance between the status of *diala* (free) and of *ohu* (slave) is a very short one." This saying becomes more meaningful when we consider capture as a method of recruiting slaves. Although warfare was not a prominent feature of Igbo society, there is good evidence that when slavery became a profitable business, as a result of the demand for slaves in the New World, the incidence of warfare and slave raids increased. Before then, there had been intervillage raids for slaves, but there is no evidence that political conquest or domination was an important goal, and village solidarity, a characteristic feature of Igbo society, seems to have been sustained by these conflicts. As far as Igbo informants can now tell, the tradition before the eighteenth century had been to capture men and women but to spare the children. In the eighteenth and nineteenth centuries, however, there arose special mercenaries, recruited from particular regions of Igboland, who were hired to loot and capture slaves. The *Abam* and the *Ekumeku* were such mercenaries.

Kidnapping, as distinct from capture in war, was a more individual operation. Its targets were usually unprotected strangers and children. It gave rise to a specialized "man-stealing" profession, which continued in Nigeria long after the end of the slave trade. Newspaper reports in Nigeria indicate that this activity, although not common now, is not yet ended. The usual technique is to steal children on market days when parents and other adults are away. The children are usually gagged, slipped into a big wicker basket, and carried off on a bicycle.

Rights in slaves were often acquired through outright purchase. This was a business transaction usually preceded by a ritual that separated the slave-to-be from his kinsmen. Before a person was sold in this way, his agnates and his mother's agnates had to agree to it, and the usual reasons for such sales were "delinquency or abnormality, e.g. incorrigible boys, persistent debtors and abnormal children" (Forde and Jones 1962:23).

Prices paid for slaves varied according to supply and demand, as well as age and sex. In intra-Igbo slave dealings, young girls commanded the highest price. Despite regional variations, knowledgeable Igbo elders regard one-and-a-half times the average bridewealth to have been the standard price for a slave girl; for boys, the price was two-thirds the price for girls. The reason for the lower price was that boys were more likely to run away to freedom than girls; furthermore, they had limited exchange value in the domestic slavery that prevailed. Payment was made in such items as cloth, gunpowder, guns, and machetes. Talbot gave the money equivalents of the trade commodities paid for a slave in the 1880s as follows: seven pieces of cloth, worth 35 shillings; one keg of gunpowder, 5 shillings; a gun, 15 shillings; a machete, one shilling; for a total of 56 shillings. By the early decades of this century, a slave among the Ekoi cost between 150 and 200 shillings—the equivalent of one cow or thirty pieces of cloth (Talbot 1912:327).

Important too in the acquisition of slaves was political intrigue expressed through the medium of oracles. Among the Igbo, important oracles such as the *Ibinokpabi*, the Ozuzu, the Agbara, and the Kamalu, who acted as the final court of appeal in judicial matters, sentenced their victims to be sold into slavery. Guided by a well-informed intelligence service, these oracles were able to feel the pulse of local opinion and rendered judgment accordingly. It was in this way that the Igbo political system shifted the burden of making a difficult but necessary decision from the human to the spiritual domain (Uchendu 1965:100; Ottenberg 1958:295-317).

Serving a deity was another method of enslavement. Cases are reported by informants of children who foiled their parents' attempt to sell them into slavery by taking refuge at the shrines of local deities. By electing to be servitors of these deities, they and their descendants became cult-slaves, or *osu*, for life.

Slaves were sometimes obtained through the institution of the pawning of persons. A pawn, strictly speaking, is not a slave, although the term "debtor-slaves" has sometimes been used for pawns. The distinction between the two is conveyed in Igbo by referring to pawns as *nvunvu ego*, as opposed to ohu. Unlike those sold into slavery or dedicated to the service of a deity, pawns did not lose their lineage affiliation. Masters had no right of life and death over their pawns, whose services during the period of pawnship constituted a return on the master's outlay. The death of the pawn left the debt unsettled. Pawning was engaged in as the last resort to meet a pressing indebtedness or to raise much-needed money. Thus, a man in need of money for bridewealth payments or for an initiation fee into a title society, an exclusive membership club, could pledge his children or a younger brother or sister as security for a loan, or he could pledge himself. The connection of pawnship with slavery lay in the fact that failure to repay the debt resulted in the pawn becoming a full-fledged slave of the creditor. Also, "a girl who was pawned might become the wife of a member of her master's household, the difference between the marriage payment and the amount of the loan being adjusted" (Forde and Jones 1962:24). In some parts of Igbo country, girls were pawned in the idiom of marriage, a practice that is not yet dead; the neighboring Yakö and the Okrika communities still provide their Igbo clients with the best markets for marriage pawns.

In summary, recruitment into slavery was achieved through many channels, the principal ones being capture in war, kidnapping by professional "man-stealers," outright purchase, political intrigues through the oracles, voluntary dedication to certain deities, and pawning.

THE ROLE OF SLAVES

Any evaluation of the role of slaves in society must take into consideration the economic base of the society, the number of slaves in relation to freemen, and the specific duties that distinguish freemen from slaves. In traditional Igbo society, economic activities primarily served subsistence needs, and only secondarily did they serve prestige needs. Farming and fishing, the traditional occupations, were not regarded as "business." Slaves fulfilled domestic labor needs, including farming and fishing. In domestic activities, no operation was strictly reserved for slaves. Not all households could afford to keep slaves, and some families sold some of their own members or put them into "debt-slavery." It is generally agreed that slaves were "worked harder" than free members of the household. "He works me like a slave" is a popular complaint of laborers against demanding employers.

Generally speaking, slaves had to fit into the role structure of the society. Sex, age, and the length of residence in the household were important factors in shaping the roles of slaves. As children, slaves followed the roles appropriate for freeborn children of the household: fetching water and wood, and if they were girls, cooking and trading. On the farms, they did such work as was required of freeborn children of their age and sex. Adult male slaves performed men's tasks on the farm, collected palm nuts, and repaired houses—tasks that they shared with other adult men of the household.

Slaves owed complete obedience to the master. Their relationship with him governed the relationships with other members of the household and with the wider community. Thus the slave of a powerful master would be ranked higher than one whose master was poor. Slaves were considered to be the adopted children of their owners. For domestic convenience, they were "adopted" into the matricentric units of the polygynous household, irrespective of their age or sex. The matricentric units became the working, cooking, and eating units for the affiliated slaves until the males married and established independent domestic units and the females were married out or taken as wives by their master. The quality of the slave-master relationship was sometimes determined by the influence of the slave's "adopted mother" (i.e., the master's wife) over her husband. In a polygynous household, this created rivalry and jealousy, an extension of typical sibling rivalry to the slave members of the household. The lot of the slaves seems to have been better if they were adopted by wealthy "mothers" who had no children in their domestic units. Because husbands had to depend on their wealthy wives for occasional loans and favors, and since they had to treat them with special favor if they had no male children, the bargaining position of such wives on behalf of their affiliated slave dependents can easily be imagined.

Although slaves were generally well treated, they still had their social disabilities. In this respect, we must make a distinction between the folk theory of these disabilities and the socioeconomic realities of slave life. There is a general agreement among the Igbo that slaves could not officiate at the shrine of the earth goddess, apparently in recognition of the fact that they were strangers to the community; but some slaves were needed for specialized ritual roles. According to folk theory, slaves could not be admitted to certain secret societies and exclusive clubs, but these associations cost a lot of money and, with the exception of second-burial rites, were the chief single cause of pawning. From the point of view of the slave, his exclusion from these societies was a hypothetical matter, since he could not have afforded the membership fee. It is revealing that elderly informants admit that if a slave had been able to afford the membership fee, he would no longer have been considered a slave!

Theoretically, slaves had certain rights. Since they could not enforce these rights, it is more accurate to say that they were granted certain privileges. It was the duty of the master to feed and clothe his slaves. He was bound, by a code of honor enforced by his social position, to provide them with wives. As a general rule, slaves were given an opportunity to earn an independent income to support their families. A slave worked for himself or hired himself out to his master or to other employers one day out of each four-day week. Payment was made in kind (food crops, access to farming land on usufructuary basis) or in cash. If payment was made in cash, the prevailing wage was usually paid.

THE SOCIAL MOBILITY OF SLAVES

In spite of its apparent clarity, the dichotomy between slaves and freemen is weak for many reasons. It treats each category as a homogeneous status group, when in fact there is much differentiation within that group; and, by creating an illusory antithesis, it oversimplifies the ranking of slaves.

Social mobility among slaves in Igboland was gradual, but it did occur. A folk distinction with important ranking implications is the one between "old," "new," and "transit" slaves. "Old" slaves were those who had a long residence in the household and had fully reconciled themselves to their status, preferring to work themselves free through the accepted channels. "New" slaves were those whose fate in the household was not certain and who had yet to pass many "tests" before their residence in the household was established. It was from this group that slaves could be drawn for sacrifices and, in the event of the master's death, some would be killed "to accompany the master's spirit"—a fate, it must be pointed out, which was not restricted to slaves. Slaves-in-transit had no attachment to the master's household and were no more than trade goods. This kind of slave was found among big slave dealers, drawn from the village and city-states—an innovation associated with the response to the demand for slaves in the New World.

Given the corporate character of the Igbo lineage, the effective social mobility of slaves depended on the degree of their incorporation into the lineage system. Freeborn and slaves "were both equally the property of these [lineages] and, in cases of necessity, both could be sold to meet [certain] financial commitments" (Jones 1963:58). But a slave was a stranger to this corporate unit, belonging to it by virtue of purchase. In the course of time, long residence made him more a member of the unit. A slave born into the group, however, had a stronger claim to membership than one who was brought in by purchase. A differentiation of slaves by rank became institutionalized, high-ranking slaves being those born in the master's household and low-ranking slaves being "bought slaves." Within the rank of "bought" slaves, there was a further distinction of "old" and "new" slaves. Through this process of social incorporation, "a slave became the companion of his master and [was] put in a position demanding great trustworthiness" (Basden 1921:109).

THE NATURE OF MANUMISSION

The transition from the status of a slave to that of a freeman was a slow one. It was easier for some categories of slaves than for others, and for one class of slaves freedom was theoretically out of the question. Slaves in the three categories, which were differently institutionalized, followed different paths to freedom.

First, there were the "bought slaves," who were, to adopt Bohannan's word, a people who had been "unkinned" (1963:180). For them, manumission meant a process of "re-lineagization," i.e., their incorporation into the master's lineage. This took more than a lifetime to achieve and could require many generations. Several steps were followed in the lineage incorporation process. A child slave might be attached to the household of one of his master's wives, where he strengthened its labor force and therefore gained his subsistence. Approaching adulthood, he was allowed to earn an independent income by hiring himself out one day in the four-day week. He could invest his income in livestock and take their increase (Uchendu 1964:89-94). This acquisition of wealth, which is recognized by the Igbo as an important index of social status, seemed to complete the process. In the case of women, marriage quickened the process of manumission provided that it was a union between slave woman and her master or another freeman. On the other hand, marriages between slaves tended to perpetuate a slave lineage, with all the attached stigma.

For another category of servile persons, that of pawns (nvunvu ego), the period of servitude depended on the time it took their primary "owners", the debtors, to redeem them. For girls, marriage often terminated their pawn status. An interesting feature of the Igbo rank system was that a person who became a pawn in his effort to raise a bridewealth payment was considered to rank higher than a free but unmarried man.

Osu were the cult-slaves. They either volunteered for the role to avoid being sold into slavery or were dedicated by their master, who could be an individual or a lineage. This type of slavery was peculiar to the central Igbo communities of Orlu, Okigwi, and Owerri. The osu were a people much hated and feared, and they constituted one of the most embarrassing features of Igbo social structure (Leith-Ross 1937:206-20; Green 1947:23-24, 49-51; Uchendu 1965:89-90). Meek describes them as persons who had been "bought and dedicated to the service of the owner's cult or the descendants of such a person" (1950:203). Their main public duty was to offer certain types of sacrifices on behalf of their masters and to tend the shrines of their deity.

Unlike the "bought slaves" and pawns, the osu were not exploited economically. Like other free Igbo, they farmed on their own account and held property as of right; but their social, cultural, and economic achievements were undervalued by society. They were excluded from the mainstream of Igbo institutions. In the hierarchy of servile status, they ranked the lowest, their often impressive wealth notwithstanding. For them, social mobility was almost impossible. They formed a compartmentalized, parallel, noncomplementary social structure apart from the free Igbo society and they had different sets of social institutions. They were not to intermarry with other freemen or slaves. Any such intermarriage would make their spouses and their descendants osu. The principle link between the osu and other members of the community, whether slave or free, was a ritual one, the osu functioning as a special kind of priest. Paradoxically, although the Igbo society accorded priests a high social status, the osu were condemned to the lowest status, performing ritual activities considered to be beneath freemen. If the osu suffered social disabilities, however, their status preserved them from being resold into slavery as well as from economic exploitation. For their part, they sometimes used their ritual position to exact from the community a levy that amounted to blackmail (Green 1947:51).

Finally, though it was by no means common in this area, a class of slaves was deployed as militia. This occurred especially in the northeastern Igbo area, where slave communities developed from such military camps

(Horton 1954:311-36). The northern Igbo community of Nike was unique among Igbo in the amount of legal and social disabilities it imposed on "bought slaves." They were in a frontier region where the need for defense and for cheap farm labor created a demand for slaves. Powerful families planted their slaves in satellite villages, which were located in the distant farmlands. This resulted in two resident farming communities—*ani uno*, the parent village where free Igbo (*diala* or *amadi*) lived with a few household slaves, and *ani agu*, the satellite village where most slaves were located to defend the parent villages and to do farming. Over time, the satellite villages developed into slave communities which were subject to the political and economic control of the descendants of their masters. It required the administrative intervention of the British colonial government in this century for the slaves in this area to regain their economic, legal, and religious rights. It appeared that the slave villages served as "advance warning systems" to the better-organized, stronger master villages, which were located away from the frontier.

CONCLUSION

We have said that Igbo society was not based on slavery, though slaves were kept and they served certain social and economic functions. The internal traffic in slaves was one of the factors that resulted in the cultural homogeneity of eastern Nigeria as a whole. There is good evidence that a large part of the population of the delta area consisted of slaves, most of them derived from Igbo areas (Dike 1956).

Social differentiation based on wealth is a characteristic feature of the structure of Igbo society. Slaves contributed their labor to farming and fishing, which in turn enabled the master to gain more wealth, and the master's corporate group to achieve prestige and fame. Many capable slaves are known to have risen to positions of power and influence. Slaves also functioned as a special class of low-status priests. And slaves were used, in some cases, as a special military force. The rights of a master over a slave varied. With "bought slaves," he had a total right over the slaves— a right of life and death. A master's right over a pawn, sometimes called a "debtor-slave," was limited to domestic use of his labor, other rights being retained by the debtor lineage. In the case of osu, cult-slaves, the slave retained rights over his life and economic powers while providing his owner—an individual family or social group—with ritual services.

The fact that varying combinations of property rights in a single person could be differently institutionalized for transaction purposes poses a fundamental question about the traditional definition of "slaves." Is a slave a single commodity or a bundle of commodities? The Igbo data presented here indicate that the latter is the relevant definition.

GLOSSARY

Agbara: an oracle.
amadi: a free person.
ani agu: a satellite slave village.
ani uno: a village controlling the satellite slave village.
diala: a free person.
Ibinokpabi: an oracle.
Igwe: an oracle.
Kamalu: an oracle.
nvunvu ego: debtor-slave, or pawns.
ohu (*oru,* in some dialects): slave, slaves.
osu: cult-slaves.
Ozuzu: an oracle.

REFERENCES

Basden, G. T. 1921. *Among the Ibos of Nigeria.* London.
_____. 1938. *Niger Ibos.* London.
Bohannan, P. 1963. *Social anthropology.* New York.
Dike, K. O. 1956. *Trade and politics in the Niger Delta, 1830-1885: an intro-duction to the economic and political history of Nigeria.* Oxford.
Elkins, S. M. 1959. *Slavery: a problem in American institutional and intellectual life.* Chicago.
Forde, D., and Jones, G. I. 1962. *The Ibo and Ibibio-speaking peoples of south-eastern Nigeria.* London.
Green, M. M. 1947. *Ibo village affairs.* London.
Horton, W. R. G. 1954. The Ohu system of slavery in a northern Ibo village-group. *Africa* 26:311-16.
Ingram, J. K. 1895. *A history of slavery and serfdom.* London.
Jones, G. I. 1963. *The trading states of the Oil Rivers: a study of political develop-ment in eastern Nigeria.* London.
Leith-Ross, S. 1937. Notes on the Osu system among the Ibo of Owerri Province, Nigeria. *Africa* 10:206-20.
Meek, C. K. 1950. *Law and authority in a Nigerian tribe.* London.
Nieboer, H. J. 1900. *Slavery as an industrial system: ethnological researches.* The Hague.
Ottenberg, S. 1958. Ibo oracles and inter-group relations. *SWest. J. Anthrop.* 14: 295-317.
Talbot, P. A. 1912. *In the shadow of the bush.* London.
Uchendu, V. C. 1964. Livestock tenancy among Igbo of southeastern Nigeria. *Afr. Stud.* 23:89-94.
_____. 1965. *The Igbo of southeast Nigeria.* New York.
Westermarck, E. 1906. *The origin and development of the moral ideas.* Vol. 1. London.

5

Slavery in
Nineteenth-Century Aboh

(Nigeria)

K. Nwachukwu-Ogedengbe

The comparative analysis of slave systems has to a great extent been impeded by the lack of universally applicable analytical categories. The bulk of the historical source material on slavery in the non-Western world comes from European missionaries, explorers, and traders, whose notions of slavery have been colored by Western models. According to one authority, slavery in Western societies is generally understood to imply "the existence of a slave-owning class whose income and political authority is derived from ownership of *all* the factors of production and a social system whose political and economic organization could not be maintained without the existence of a population of human chattel" (Klein 1969:88). While it is sometimes unavoidable, the application of models derived from one culture to societies formed by quite different historical and cultural factors may be grossly misleading. Certainly, the European emphasis on the economic role and chattel characteristic of slavery has not been entirely useful in the task of isolating the variety of institutions lumped indiscriminately together under the term "slavery." In this chapter,[1] an

1. Some of the data on which this chapter is based derive from fieldwork conducted in Nigeria during 1969 and 1970 and supported by the Ford Foundation and the African Studies Program of the University of Wisconsin, Madison. Grateful appreciation is extended to these institutions.

133

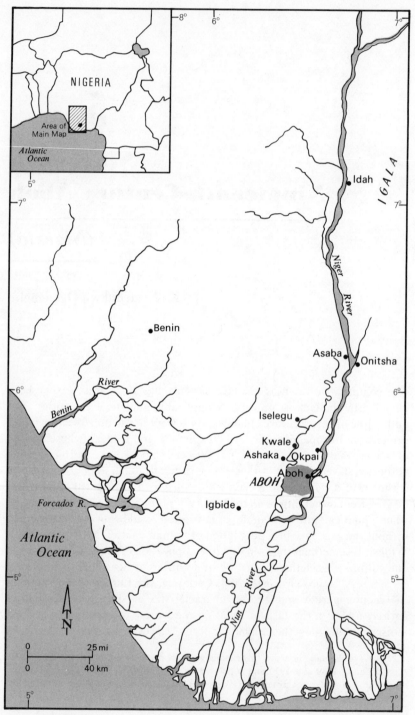

Map 5. The Lower Niger

attempt is made to describe the social structure of the kingdom of Aboh, emphasizing the recruitment of slaves and their role in the economic organization as well as their relationship to the other classes or groups in the society during the nineteenth century, more specifically the period from 1830 to 1900. It must be stressed, however, that although the legal status of slavery has long been abolished, the relationship between the "free" and the "nonfree" (i.e., the descendants of slaves) is still, to a considerable extent, governed by forces that operated in the period when slavery was both customary and legal.

The Aboh are an Igbo-speaking people of about 10,000 situated on the western bank of the lower Niger River, some 130 miles from the Atlantic coast, in Nigeria. Although the main occupations of the Aboh people are farming and fishing, it was as merchants that they became famous in the centuries preceding the imposition of British rule. The strategic location of the town of Aboh at a point where the Niger divides into its major outlets (the Nun and the Forcados), combined with a well-organized centralized administration, enabled the Aboh to exercise a great deal of control over much of the trade of the entire lower Niger. Aboh merchants were largely responsible for carrying European goods as well as the products of the coastal peoples to the great markets of the confluence. They were also responsible for distributing goods to the markets in the neighborhood of Aboh as well as bringing down slaves, palm oil, ivory, and other produce for shipment to the coast.

Territorially, the town of Aboh was divided into four wards, *ebo*. Social relationships within the ward were in the main based upon kin ties, the members claiming descent from a common ancestor. The basic socioeconomic group was, however, the compound (*ogbe*) consisting of agnatic relatives, their wives and children, as well as a number of clients and slaves. Land and other economic resources were held in trust for the compound by the elder, *okpala*, who was also the political and ritual head. Commercial activities, more particularly long-distance trade, were also centered on the compound, whose leader was usually the patron and master of the majority of the clients and slaves.

Unlike many Igbo groups, the Aboh developed a centralized political system under the authority of a ruler—the *obi*—and a hierarchy of palace and town chiefs. The obi was also the highest priest, offering annual sacrifices on behalf of the community. He was usually selected from among candidates from each of the four maximal lineages, centered on the four wards. In practice, the candidacy was restricted to the *umudei*, the upper stratum of Aboh society.

The population of Aboh was divided into three status groups: nobles or "sons of the soil" (umudei), who exercised dominant political authority;

clients (*ndichie ukwu*); and slaves (*ndichie nta*). According to Aboh traditions, the umudei are patrilineal descendants of Esumei, who migrated from Benin to the region of Aboh, where he eventually succeeded in founding a kingdom.

NDICHIE UKWU, OR CLIENTS

The origin of the group of clients is shrouded in obscurity. Aboh traditions assert that the term ndichie ukwu (higher ndichie) initially applied to free persons who immigrated into Aboh from the neighboring communities. Some were perhaps criminals who sought refuge in Aboh and others were immigrant merchants and skilled craftsmen. A considerable number of this group were, however, kinsmen of women whom Aboh men had taken as wives from surrounding communities. It was a common practice for women, particularly those of the higher social strata, to be accompanied to their matrimonial homes by their relatives. Such persons were invariably absorbed into the household of the woman's husband. Although the Aboh imply that the ndichie ukwu stratum is a later accretion, thus seeking to validate their status as first settlers, it may be safely assumed that a considerable number of these people are descendants of the Akarai, an Igbo-speaking people from whom the Aboh took the country.

At this point it may be observed that among Igbo-speaking peoples as a whole, the use of the term ndichie for clients and slaves is unique to the Aboh. Elsewhere in Igboland, ndichie is a title of reverence, reserved for clan elders and senior titleholders.[2] It therefore seems likely that ndichie originally referred to the elder and titled men of the original inhabitants whom the Aboh conquered and presumably absorbed.

According to Aboh traditions, an alien immigrant who had been a free person in his home community was required to attach himself to someone in the umudei category, usually a prominent lineage head, as a dependent, a process described as *onwa ku se,* "to attach oneself to a guardian." Such an individual was provided with living quarters in his patron's compound and was entitled to such resources as land and fishing lakes that the head of the compound held in trust for the group. As the client's economic status improved, at a rate that depended on the status of his patron, he could expect to build his own house on land allocated to him. The client also relied upon his patron's connections and even material assistance in obtaining a wife. In this regard, it may be pointed out that clientage presented no definite barrier to intermarriage with women of the umudei class, who are known as *akpe.*

2. At Onitsha, for example, ndichie means chiefs, and is collectively used to designate some sixty chiefs with whom the obi (king) of Onitsha governed the kingdom.

In return, the client was expected to work his patron's farm once in the Aboh week of four days (or *olie*). Most men of substance in Aboh were long-distance traders. They were usually at the head of trading corporations, the success of which depended, to a large extent, on the number of men under their control. Of the latter, some manned the giant canoes while others served as the patron's armed retainers. The client was also expected to make regular gifts of choice yams, especially at harvest times, as well as fish and game to his patron as a practical demonstration of his fealty, as did all members of the patron's group.

In theory, a client retained membership in his ancestral kin group and was free to visit his village. Presumably he was at liberty to terminate his association with his patron and go somewhere else to live. In practice, however, he acquired membership in his patron's lineage. His children and those of his patron were raised together with little or no distinction. He practiced his craft or traded under the protection of his patron and had as much opportunity for economic advancement as anyone in the society. Some probably returned to their ancestral homes, but most clients and their descendants remained in Aboh, fully integrated into the total society and indistinguishable from the rest of the population.

In spite of the incorporation of the client into his patron's family and his integration into the society, there was a clear social and ritual differentiation between the ndichie ukwu and the umudei, and the distinction was even more pronounced in the area of politics, there being no equal access to power. Members of the client class are to this day restricted to certain titles designated *nzele ndichie ukwu* (ndichie ukwu titles), and while some of these are of very high rank—e.g., the office of *iyasele,* "prime minister" —the majority are clearly of inferior status to umudei titles. And even with iyasele, custom required that only sons of umudei mothers and ndichie ukwu fathers could hold the office.

NDICHIE NTA, OR SLAVES

The main written sources on slavery in Aboh come from the nineteenth century, when the institution of slavery in the areas of the interior attracted the notice of British expeditions to the Niger. Modern research by Dike (1959:21-35), Jones (1963:24-48), Lloyd (1963), and Horton (1969) has shown the close relationship between the pattern of slavery and the economic development of the delta city-states. In particular, these studies link the institution of slavery in these states to the economic revolution brought about by the Atlantic trade. Put simply, the growing trade in slaves and other tropical commodities created manpower problems for the sparsely populated fishing and salt-producing villages of the coast. One solution hit upon by the more successful traders was to incorporate some of the slaves purchased in the interior into the descent group to form what has generally been described as canoe houses. The canoe house was in essence the traditional descent group adapted to the needs of an increasingly commercialized society. It was not only a close-knit trading corporation under the effective leadership of a house-head or chief, it was as well a military unit characterized by its ability to equip and man a war canoe. The war canoes protected the trade of their respective groups and were also used in the defense of the community against enemies (Jones 1963:55-57; Horton 1969:46-51). Similar forces were at work in the interior. At Aboh, the ogbe, under the leadership of the okpala, was gradually transformed into a trading corporation as trade became the dominant economic activity of the kingdom. In order to meet the demand for trade-hands and fighting men, enterprising compound heads actively recruited slaves who were incorporated into the households. It is thus clear that slavery in Aboh had a critical economic dimension that is perhaps absent in some of the cases in this volume.

Alagoa (1970) has argued with notable skill that the Atlantic trade was not as crucial in the development of the institutions of the delta states as Dike and others would have us believe. According to him, the change from fishing village to city-state was set in motion by preexisting patterns of trade between the coastal Ijo and the communities of the interior. The full validation of this thesis depends, however, on unavailable or at best tenuous data. Although trade and exchange predated the arrival of Europeans on these shores, the fact seems incontestable that the greater volume of trade of the European era left a peculiar character on the political and social institutions of the societies affected by it, be these on the coast or in the interior. As Alagoa himself concedes, "the great influence exerted by the overseas trade in the internal development of these states is beyond doubt." Quantitative and qualitative changes noticeable during the era of European trade (the phenomenal expansion of canoe houses is a case in point) would lead to the conclusion that developments during this period were so profound as to be unlike anything known in the region before.

The recruitment of slaves took several forms. Quite a few slaves were captured in wars between the Aboh and their neighbors. Others were seized in unorganized and individual slave-raiding expeditions. Wars between the Aboh and their neighbors were a common occurrence in the nineteenth century. A few of these are documented by European visitors, and almost every one commented on the warlike character of the Aboh. We know, for example, that the Aboh conquered Asaba with devastating results in 1831, carrying away some two hundred captives. In 1841, Obi Ossai of Aboh told Captain Trotter that although he did not make war indiscriminately, it was customary for him to take as many captives as he could in the event of war with neighboring chiefs (P.R.O., Trotter 1843). Raids were undertaken specifically to obtain slaves, but it cannot be said that the wars were fought with the same motive. Since documented cases clearly attest to diplomatic and economic undercurrents, it is clear that slaves were only a by-product of wars fought for many different objectives. At the same time, the insatiable demand for slaves along the coast increased the frequency and intensity of these wars.

Slaves were often the victims of uncoordinated activities by individual entrepreneurs. Thus, individuals or small bands kidnapped lone travelers, farmers, and children. Olaudah Equiano, a west bank Igbo, captured in 1756 and taken to the New World, has left us this vivid account of his capture by bands whose activities were paralleled in the Aboh area: "one day, when all our people were gone out to their works . . . and only I and my dear sister were left to mind the house, two men and a woman got over our walls, and in a moment seized us both; and without giving us time to cry out, or make resistance, they stopped our mouths and ran off with us into the nearest wood" (Jones, 1967:85). Kidnapping of this kind was systematically carried out in the Aboh area as late as the 1920s. In 1928, the district officer for what is now Ndokwa Division reported the existence of "gangs of men whose profession is to entice girls into canoes when markets are being held and then take them by night to Ijaw country for sale" (N.N.A., Kwale District 1928).

The majority of slaves were, however, acquired by purchase from neighboring markets, notably Ashaka, Iselegu, and Okpai on the Niger River, and from markets as far north as Idah in the Igala country. From the preponderance of Hausa-Fulani names in the records (e.g., Mousa, Ali, Aminah), it would appear that the bulk of the slaves in this category came from the Niger-Benue markets, which were well supplied in the nineteenth century by the constant warfare and organized raids in the Hausa-Fulani emirates. The slaves were purchased for cowrie shells and such highly desirable European goods as guns, beads, cloth, and spirits. The value fluctuated a great deal, but when Dr. Baikie visited Idah in 1854, he discovered that a young male slave was valued at about 50,000 cowries or approximately sixty to eighty shillings (Baikie 1856:275).

As a social category, Aboh slaves were known as ndichie nta (lesser ndichie). However, the generic term for such persons was osu. This term more generally implies a servant who is not remunerated for his labor and over whom his master exercises complete control. Its main defining feature is perhaps unquestioned obedience to the wishes of another. (It must be emphasized here that the term osû in Aboh usage has the same connotation as ohu elsewhere in Igboland, and has no affiliation whatsoever with the well-known *osŭ* system, or "cult slavery," which was practiced in certain parts of Igboland east of the river Niger. See Leith-Ross 1937; and Chapter 4 of this volume.)

Since a person from whom one may demand and receive such unquestioned loyalty, as well as unpaid labor, could not be obtained from within the patrilineages of "free" Aboh (claiming descent from Esumei), an important characteristic of the *osu* was the fact of his or her purchase or captivity from outside the community. It follows, therefore, that an osu, slave, was invariably a stranger recruited into the community for use as his owner saw fit. He was somebody who had become separated from his natural kin. This distinction is of crucial importance, for while an umudei —i.e., a "free" Aboh—might conceiveably offer his services to another person under conditions that are hardly distinguishable from those of slaves, he could not be called osu. It follows therefore that the Aboh osu has also to be seen in ethnic and cultural terms, since only strangers could belong to this group. A slave is sometimes designated by the not-too-polite term *onye igbo,* or simply *igbo,* which means no more than "an Igbo" or someone from Igbo country. The term may have originated from the fact that some slaves were obtained from among Igbo-speaking groups across the Niger. On the other hand, it may have been copied from the Igala, with whom the Aboh had extensive trade connections and whose name for a slave is *onigbo.* Nineteenth-century records also show that slave owners often used the Pidgin "nigger" in everyday reference to their slaves when talking to outsiders.

It must, however, be stressed that slaves were not designated by these terms in day-to-day life. The terms osu and igbo are today regarded by the Aboh people as words of singular indignity and are seldom used to describe a person except in the most private conversations. Indeed, stereotypes concerning slaves are most difficult to elicit from the Aboh, who show great reluctance in discussing the ancestry of slaves who, they claim, are members of the lineage. The records show that a slave was more commonly addressed by his given name (e.g., Ali, Aminah, Mousa) or by nicknames such as Blue Beard or Downcast.

Data on the magnitude of slavery in Aboh are very sketchy. Judging, however, from European accounts of the nineteenth century, as well as contemporary traditions, slavery was without doubt extensively practiced in Aboh. In 1841 Simon Jonas, an Igbo slave who had been liberated by the British naval squadron and educated in Sierra Leone, accompanied the Henry Trotter expedition to the Niger River as an interpreter. The objectives of the expedition were to promote legitimate trade through the conclusion of anti-slave-trade treaties with the rulers of the interior and to promote Christianity and agriculture. Simon Jonas, who spent one month at Aboh as part of this missionary enterprise, estimated that "the number of slaves is greater than the number of free people" (P.R.O., Trotter 1843). The population of Aboh was at that time estimated at about 7,000. It is not known, however, if Jonas' estimate referred only to first-generation slaves or to all persons of slave ancestry. Jonas most likely meant the latter, but whatever the case, it is apparent that slaves and their descendants constituted a sizable proportion of the population of Aboh. European records of the nineteenth century contain estimates of the number of slaves held by some of the more wealthy Aboh chiefs, and these appear to strengthen the above estimate. Thus, Obi Ossai (who died in 1844) had about 300, his eldest son, Chukwumah, had about 100, and Aje, a younger and more enterprising son, was said to be master of some 200 slaves. Neither was slave holding restricted to men. A woman whom Macgregor Laird visited in 1831 was reported to be the mistress of over two hundred whom she employed in trading and agricultural tasks.

The acquisition of slaves was surrounded by elaborate rituals. On acquiring a slave, an individual offered sacrifice to a special shrine, *inyama,* and his *ikenga,* or "god of fortune," symbolized by the right arm. The sacrifice and feasting that accompanied the acquisition of a slave clearly indicates the importance that the Aboh people attached to slavery. In fact, we are told (Crowther and Taylor 1859:438-39) that individuals accumulated slaves to show how well off they were, for a man's worth was often estimated by the number of his slaves. The same purpose, however, was served by the acquisition of wives and the birth of many children. The larger one's household and the more numerous one's relatives, wives, children, clients, and slaves, the higher was one's prestige.

A newly acquired slave was usually assigned by his or her master to one of the master's wives. Such slaves, together with other clients and children, formed a subhousehold within the master's compound. The wife took the role of mother to the slaves and ensured that they received adequate food and clothing. According to traditions, the slaves were given proper care, the foster mother seldom drawing distinctions between them and her own children. When older slaves were assigned as guardians to newly acquired slaves, however, new slaves were said to have fared less well. Moreover, the picture presented in the traditions contradicts that of the Reverend Samuel Crowther and the Reverend J. Taylor (1859:431)—both Africans—who observed that "with the exception of some very little boys, very few of them get any meals at their master's expense . . . ." There is no doubt that Aboh traditions have idealized the lot of these domestic slaves. With perhaps the exception of smaller households, where masters developed close bonds with their slaves, the majority led a precarious existence with what little food and clothing they were personally able to procure. The high incidence of theft among slaves during the nineteenth century leads one to conclude that their basic needs were not adequately met.

It may be noted that the majority of slaves retained by the Aboh tended to be children. The reasons are not hard to find. Most victims of kidnapping and raids were children and women. Besides, European traders preferred men and women of working age (between fifteen and thirty-five years), who could be put to work on the plantations immediately upon arrival in the New World. Aboh merchants therefore disposed of the adults, retaining the "unmarketable" children as domestic slaves. The time and expense, if any, expended in raising them was worthwhile since acculturation was more easily accomplished than was possible with adults. Moreover, children from such distant lands as the Hausa-Fulani country were less likely to run away. Finally, children who were deemed to be too young for the New World plantations could be put to work on farms with productive results.

THE ECONOMIC BASIS OF SLAVERY

As has already been mentioned, the main feature of the Aboh economy was trade. From the establishment of the kingdom sometime in the seventeenth century until the successful penetration of the Niger by Europeans in the 1830s, the town of Aboh was perhaps the busiest port in the lower Niger Valley. Its merchants were involved in a complex network of trade, distributing European goods and coastal products in the interior, and collecting slaves and palm oil for export overseas. Such extensive trading operations consumed a great deal of labor, the bulk of which was provided by slaves. They were used mainly as crew in the large trading canoes, some of which held up to seventy persons. The Reverend Samuel Crowther observed that Aboh slaves did little else between trips to the markets of the confluence. "It is very difficult," he wrote, "to get them to work especially in handling the hoe or any agricultural implements, they priding themselves as being the sailors of the great waters." The armed retinues of the chiefs consisted essentially of slaves. They protected the trading canoes from pirates and engaged in such raids and wars as their masters might direct. These personal troops were placed at the disposal of the obi in the event of a general war, and the more important chiefs were usually able to equip three war canoes with men and arms. Slaves of proven ability were sometimes put in charge of trading expeditions while many acted as commercial agents for their masters.

In warfare, manning canoes, and trading, the differences between the roles of slaves and freemen were of degree only. Captain William Allen, who visited Aboh first in 1831 and again in 1841, observed that all the commercial and agricultural labor was performed by slaves. The truth, however, was that while slaves may have been assigned the most onerous tasks, there were no clear-cut distinctions with regard to the allocation of work. Even the most influential chiefs led their own trading missions, and the evidence also reveals that they took great pride in personally leading their troops into battle. There was perhaps greater similarity of roles in situations where a master had but a few slaves. In such cases, master and slave lived and worked under conditions that were virtually identical and the absence of guardians and overseers led not only to a closer personal bond between master and slave but to better treatment.

TREATMENT OF SLAVES

The discussion of the treatment of slaves is bedeviled by the paucity of evidence. Such ambiguous statements as "slaves are humanely treated" or "slaves are treated harshly," which one frequently reads in the literature, tell us very little about the everyday relations between slaves and freemen. Most accounts abound in inconsistencies. To take one example, William Cole, who lived for a year or so in Aboh during the late 1850s, tells us that slavery in Aboh was "in many cases a blessing and not a bane," adding that the slaves were not as oppressively treated as the "unpitied English artisans." Yet, as we shall see, Cole records several incidents that clearly contradict the above sentiment. Such reports show that observers rarely appreciated the very wide variation in the treatment meted out to slaves, nor did they realize that there were different categories of slaves. A generalized opinion on the lot of the aggregate of slaves is thus not likely to tell us how a particular master might have treated a particular slave.

Oral traditions are of little help in this regard for, as already noted, there is a tendency to romanticize the master-slave relationship. Informants boldly assert that slaves were absorbed into the kinship system and could neither be identified nor referred to in nonkinship terminologies. Again, documented evidence belies this claim. To take a minor example, Aboh tradition asserts that a slave was obliged to work for his master once in the Igbo week of four days; the rest of the week was devoted to his own farm and household. But one wonders how any slave was able to hold his master strictly to this rule. It is unlikely that there was any mechanism for ensuring that this and any other rights he might be entitled to were respected, especially since the majority of slaves served in the trading and war canoes, which might be away for several weeks at a time.

Tradition asserts that a master was under an obligation to procure a wife for his male slave. This was perhaps easy if his master owned a suitable female slave, but where it was necessary to seek beyond the household, the master's prestige and material assistance had to be put at the disposal of the slave. Here again, there exists no evidence that the slave could enforce his rights. As a matter of fact, documented evidence from Onuabo, near Aboh, shows that the slave had little say in the matter. In 1928, an Isoko from Igbide, who had been kidnapped and enslaved at Onuabo, told the district officer that his only complaint against his master was the latter's failure to provide him with a wife (N.N.A., Kwale District 1928). It would seem that masters were under pressure to provide wives for their slaves not so much because society willed it but from purely practical considerations. The slave and his descendants belonged to the household of his master, and since value was placed on large households, this objective was best served by providing the male slave with a wife.

A good starting point from which to consider the status of slaves is the pattern of authority exercised by the master over his slave. As previously indicated the main defining feature of the osu in Aboh is his complete subordination to the authority of his master. The question here is whether the apparent integration of the slave into the kinship structure in any way mitigated this conception of the slave. In other words, was the pattern of authority the same for the slave as for true kinsmen? The answer to this question is not a simple one. The treatment of slaves varied among masters, and such factors as the number of slaves in a household, and the tasks to which they were put, greatly affected master-slave relationships. Unfortunately, most of our evidence comes from the larger households where slaves were militarily and economically valuable. But even allowing for this bias, evidence of day-to-day events in master-slave relationships indicates that masters exercised complete authority over the lives of their slaves in ways they would not inflict upon true kinsmen. The slaves do not appear to have been protected by the ordinary rules governing relations between freemen. For instance, in the matter of disciplinary action, custom no doubt deplored cruel punishments and individuals might criticize a slave owner in private for inflicting an unusual punishment on an offending slave. Nevertheless, a master was both accuser and judge in such cases. Unlike a freeman, the slave was not summoned before the lineage heads or, in major cases, the council of chiefs. From the master's personal court and from sanctions that were often of the harshest kind, there was no appeal. A few examples will serve to illustrate this point.

In 1859, Nwadei Okeyea, a wealthy Aboh chief, had entrusted one of his slaves with a canoe. When it was found to be missing, Okeyea put the slave in chains until such a time as the canoe could be found. Cole (1862: 92-93) reported that the slave "lay upon a heap of excrement and other refuse; his legs fettered to a huge block of lumber." In another case, Chief Aje's slave was alleged to have committed adultery with his master's wife. From Cole's account (1862:127-29), the slave was an individual of some substance who held a position of trust in Aje's household. The fact that he had risen to such heights suggests that he was not a newly acquired slave. Yet Aje had the slave's vital organs and ears cut out and his body pierced through with stakes and exhibited at the beach to serve as a deterrent to others. In another case of adultery, the suspect was reported to have committed suicide before the facts became known to his master.

For minor offenses, slaves were usually whipped or placed in blocks and those who persisted in, say, attempting to escape, might be sold. But the punishment could be harsher, as the following incidents amply illustrate. A slave whose labor Cole had hired from his master was apprehended for petty theft. When the matter was reported to his master, he promptly sent the slave to Cole with orders that he be executed (Cole 1862:137-38). Another slave, who had stolen twelve bags of salt from his master's store, was reportedly "gagged and tied up in the most inhuman manner . . . his body covered with lacerations . . . ." He was finally drowned in the Niger (Cole 1862:195).

While these examples do not show that the lot of the typical slave was torture and execution, they point clearly to an assimilation of inter-personal rights to the norm of property rights. The chattel characteristics of Aboh slaves are given ample demonstration in the use of slaves in funerals. It was, for instance, customary for a large number of slaves (the figure is usually put at forty) to be buried with an Aboh king. However, according to Simon Jonas the slaves used on such occasions "were specially purchased . . . domestic slaves never being so treated" (P.R.O., Trotter 1843). As with some of the customary rights already discussed, it is not certain that slaves were really able to enforce this custom, if custom it was. Thus, Cole (1862:147-48) reports the execution of a number of slaves in circumstances which suggest that they were domestic slaves: "A large crowd had gathered to celebrate the demise of one Tschukuma who had departed this life with years and bullocks. *It had been his desire to be followed to heaven when defunct by ten of his most faithful and willing slaves* and this was proclaimed by his executor . . ." (italics added). It may of course be argued that the slaves who were executed had personally consented. The words "most faithful and willing" appear to suggest this, but whether they had any real choice in the matter cannot be accurately determined. What sketchy evidence there is points to the contrary. Thus, on the occasion of the death of a chief in 1841, several slaves sought refuge in the vessels of Captain Henry Trotter's expedition, alleging that they had been marked for funeral rites.

Further evidence that Aboh slaves could be treated as chattel is to be found in their use as security for debts, or what in the commercial vocabulary of the time was known as "trust." This was a system of credit developed by European and African traders along the west coast of Africa in order to cope with the growing volume of trade. African traders or "middlemen" were advanced or trusted with manufactured goods by European traders. The middlemen provided no security, the essential element being the confidence reposed in them to deliver the equivalent of the trust in commodities. This enabled the Africans to acquire the capital to trade for commodities in the interior, and they were usually allowed considerable time to liquidate the trust. By the late 1850s, Aboh traders who sought credit were, however, obliged to provide security in the form of slaves or bags of salt. The following is probably typical of these transactions (Cole 1862:63): "Prince Akia [Okeyea] called upon me to solicit an advance of goods to the value of a ton of oil, promising to pay me within a stated period, and furthermore to place a slave in my hands as security." That slaves were considered negotiable and disposable property is suggested by the dialogue that followed:

Cole: But should this slave die, shall I lose my oil?
Okeyea: Oh no. Should he die during my absence, you must cut off one of his
    hands, and retain it until I return, and I would make the amount good by
    the payment of a fresh security.

There is perhaps little doubt that the majority of slaves were shielded from the worst abuses by the fact of their partial assimilation into the Aboh kinship structure, and that strong personal ties often existed between masters and slaves. But the fact remains that freemen were not subjected to the pattern of disciplinary authority noted above. Pawnship (igbamibe), which is similar in many respects to the provision of security in the trust system, was extensively practiced in Aboh, but in neither of these circumstances is there strong evidence that members of umudei class were used.

The overwhelming subordination of the slave to his master's authority, evident in the incidents related above, raises the question of the propensity of slaves to escape. Here again, the evidence is slim, but what little there is suggests that masters of large households were perenially plagued by the problem of runaways. Chief Aje, whom Cole depicted as a particularly harsh man, was reported to have lost a large number of slaves in this manner. On one occasion seven of his slaves escapted on arrival at Idah. Cole reported that Chief Aje's "niggers are running away daily, so much so that Aje is fearful of my possessing charms to aid their escaping for he cannot recover them" (1862:185). While many slaves might have contemplated escaping, most probably resigned themselves to their lot in Aboh; for escape, as many learned from experience, did not necessarily imply freedom. The kings and chiefs of the lower Niger towns in which the runaways sought refuge often enslaved them or at best kept them beyond the pale of society. They were clearly unable to start life anew as "free" citizens in their host country. In the middle of the nineteenth century, for example, a slave from Ndoni, near Aboh, absconded from his master at the Onitsha market. He was caught and taken to the obi of Onitsha, who rejected the master's plea for the repossession of his slave. According to the Reverend Taylor, "If a servant flees from a neighbouring country into his [the obi's] land, he is never delivered up to his former master, nor to be oppressed by a new one, but yet would never be considered a sojourner, but as a fugitive slave" (Crowther and Taylor 1859:329). The very young slaves who had been recruited from distant lands, and for whom the surroundings were clearly unfamiliar, would have been unable to find their original homes; for them, Aboh was their only home. Adult slaves who escaped ran the risk of recapture and sale. In general, of the slaves who escaped, a certain number were recovered by their masters.

It must not, however, be thought that masters resorted to the threat of extreme sanctions as a matter of course. One of the most powerful considerations against maltreating a slave was the dire economic consequence to a master of the loss of his slaves. Certainly, a master stood to lose his valued personnel and the minimum stability needed for successful trading if most of his slaves went about with the fear of death and torture hanging over their heads for the most trivial offenses. For this reason, the more grotesque sanctions must have been applied on a limited scale only.

THE MOBILITY OF SLAVES

The use of slaves in economic production, as in the New World, is frequently associated with chattel slavery and all the negative connotations that the term implies. Paradoxically, the economic use of the Aboh slave did not lead to this kind of social and economic deprivation. There were many opportunities for mobility. While slavery did result in the emergence of a separate social category of slaves, some attained considerable wealth and high status.

Most slaves began their career as crew (*pulla* boys) in the trading and war canoes. Slaves might engage in trading on their own, and the more enterprising would in time accumulate some capital with which they were able to do a respectable amount of business. Admittedly, the slave's mobility depended to a considerable extent upon the status of his master, those in the larger trading households perhaps advancing more rapidly. The opportunity was, however, present and may indeed have induced many slaves to remain in Aboh. In 1832, and again in 1841, Captain William Allen offered to take Ali, a Hausa-born slave of Obi Ossai, with him to England. Ali, however, refused the offer, pointing out that "he was married, and although he . . . was a slave, he had commenced a little trading on his own account, was quite satisfied with his lot and did not wish to leave his country" (Allen and Thomson 1848, 1:252). Allen, who was doubtless impressed, observed that the slaves were induced to stay in

Aboh owing to the practice of "incorporating" them into the society. A considerable number of slaves no doubt made what could be considered a modest living under conditions that were barely distinguishable from the majority of the "free" people. The Reverend Frederick Schön, who was in Aboh in 1841, observed that the surest sign of the increase in the wealth of slaves was the number of wives each one of them had acquired, and some had five or six (Schön and Crowther 1842:231-32). And according to the Reverend Samuel Crowther: "some of the older slaves had themselves become owners of a large property and many slaves, and thus become in a great measure independent of their masters except waiting on them occasionally" (Crowther and Taylor 1859:438).

One of the better-documented cases of the upward mobility of slaves was that of Azaka, an acquaintance of William Cole. Azaka began his meteoric rise as a slave with only one thousand cowries (about the value of 20 cents), which he might have saved from such petty trading as he was able to engage in during missions on his master's behalf. Within two years he had purchased a good canoe, the most important piece of capital equipment, and acquired "a couple of slaves." He later built his own house, and before long was the head of a large compound (ogbe) and trading corporation (Cole 1862:22-24). Azaka was not the only slave to establish a compound; and this, for the Aboh, is the zenith of achievement.

THE SOCIAL STATUS OF SLAVES

In some of the societies described in this volume, slaves do not appear to have crystallized into a clear social category. Aboh presents an entirely different picture. Although mobility in the economic sphere was accelerated by the incorporation of the slave into the kinship structure, there was no equality of access to ritual and political power. This created the somewhat unique situation where individuals who were otherwise kinsmen belonged permanently to different social categories. For the slave and his descendants, membership in the ndichie nta class was permanent. This raises the question of "freedom" or "manumission," two concepts which often intrude into the literature on African institutions of slavery. Slaves are represented as being able to "purchase" their freedom or being "set free" by their owners after a period. Although the concept of freedom is not always precisely defined, there is the implication that the status of slavery was transitory and that, with time, slaves acquired all or most of the rights of free citizens. Freedom in this sense did not exist in Aboh. The three social categories of umudei, ndichie ukwu, and ndichie nta were ranked hierarchically. Furthermore, the line of demarcation was rigid and permanent, and mobility, in the purely political and social sense, was confined within the limits of the slave's own stratum.

According to Simon Jonas, Aboh slaves were "set free" after they established their own households and could no longer be called upon by their
masters to perform the customary tasks. Instead, an annual tribute of
forty yams and some stock was substituted (P.R.O., Trotter 1843). Major
Macdonald, who visited Aboh in 1889, asserted that the slaves treated
their masters on "terms of equality." He went on: "The only way in which
they are to any degree hampered in their movements is that they owe a
kind of feudal obligation to the house of their proprietors, so that they
cannot leave the country or town without his permission, but this is a
restriction more theoretical than practical and which is seldom regarded
by the slaves when they wish to disregard it" (P.R.O., Macdonald 1890).
Both reports overstated the case. Tradition denies the nearly absolute
freedom implied in these reports. A slave who had lived and toiled long
enough to be able to build his own house (still within the confines of his
master's compound) and had a wife and children of his own, naturally
enjoyed a greater degree of freedom than a newly acquired slave was
entitled to. There was, however, no question of equality between the slave
and the freeman. The former's permanent membership in the ndichie nta
necessarily restricted his aspirations and set severe limits on his rights. Put
simply, access to real political power was barred to the slaves. In the
Hausa-Fulani emirates, for instance, a "freed" slave could be appointed
village head and some in Bornu even attained to important governmental
positions. In these examples, the same posts could be held by slave and
free alike. In Aboh, on the other hand, certain offices were reserved
exclusively for slaves and their descendants, and neither the "free"
umudei nor the client ndichie ukwu could hold them. By the same token, a
slave or his descendant cold not aspire to offices reserved for the other
strata. It is not necessary to enter here into a detailed discussion of the
various governmental posts or chieftaincy titles (*nzele*). Suffice it to say
that the ndichie nta titles were the least desirable from the point of view of
political power and social prestige. Indeed, ndichie nta titleholders were
primarily palace officials appointed by the obi to perform certain ritual
and domestic services in the palace. Few of the chiefs had any role in the
actual governance of the kingdom.[3]

Slaves or their descendants were prohibited from holding the title of
okpala (elder) of a ward or ward section (ogbe), except in cases where the
ward section was founded by a person of slave ancestry. In one instance,
the descendant of a Hausa slave, who was clearly the oldest man in the

3. A few of the functions of the ndichie nta titleholders clearly reveal the servile character
of these posts. The *ose*'s task was to carry the obi on his shoulders when he, the obi, made
his rounds of the city, usually at night. The *ashimadei* was the royal drummer, and was
usually appointed from among the obi's slaves, while the *obhe* waited on the senior chiefs.
Others actually prepared food for the obi.

ward, was denied the office of okpala. Thus, the freedom of the Aboh slave that Jonas spoke of was narrow in scope and, at best, a relative matter.

However, membership in the elite *Igbu* society is today open to the descendants of slaves, and was apparently open to the nonfree in the past. The word Igbu is derived from *ogbunmo,* literally, "killer of spirits." In the past, the Igbu was a society for men who had performed such acts of valor as killing a man in battle or killing any ferocious animal. Its origins are obscure but its functions were related to a desire to honor warriors. The natural desire to be recognized must have stimulated many into acts of great valor. Such men were initiated in the Igbu amidst elaborate feasting, and they became entitled to wear the feather of an eagle (*abuba ugo*) in their hats and to drink wine with their left hands at public gatherings. A new feather was added for every additional man or animal killed and it was not unusual to see some of the men with a round of eagle feathers in their hats.

The society underwent drastic changes with the inception of European rule. For example, an initiate was no longer required to produce the head of a victim. Instead, an entry fee ranging from 240 dollars to 400 dollars was collected from any person who desired membership, irrespective of his origin. The Igbu was thus one of the few areas where everyone who met the stringent entry requirement met on more or less equal footing. Although the Igbu was essentially a private club, it was nevertheless of paramount social importance, and the greatest ambition of most Aboh was to attain membership in it. The Aboh idea of success in life was (and remains) wealth, children, and membership in the Igbu society. Most Aboh chiefs, officials, and important men are members of the Igbu society, including the obi, who is the patron.

PROPERTY AND INHERITANCE

In discussing ownership rights in property and inheritance, we must distinguish clearly between theory and practice. The Aboh assert that slavery was a permanent status and that the right of a master and his heirs over his slave was inviolable. Although the system provided the slave with some opportunity to acquire wealth, such property was, in law, held at the pleasure of his master. In practice, however, the slave's right to property was accepted, as was the right of his descendants to inherit. Nevertheless, given the power of a master over his slave, the latter's enjoyment of his property rights was clearly limited. In fact the resources of a slave were at his master's disposal whenever the need arose. Realistically speaking, a slave could not successfully refuse his master's request for men and money. It is clear, therefore, that the slave did not exercise full control over his property.

Although the slave was absorbed into the kinship system, he was not included in the inheritance regulations governing true kinship relations. No property passed to him upon his master's death except at the will of the master's heirs. The only exception was an adopted slave, *ukodei,* on whose behalf the special ritual of *igoya n'obi* ("to admit into the lineage through ritual sacrifice") had been performed. It must be emphasized that the ukodei was not a pseudokinsman but a kinsman in the fullest meaning of the term. The status of ukodei was, however, conferred only in exceptional cases—for example, in the absence of a natural heir who could sacrifice at the shrine of the deceased master.

It is perhaps obvious from what has been said that social status in Aboh was largely a matter of ascription rather than achievement. The umudei status was barred to the offspring of slaves, except in one instance: the child of a "free" (*nwadei*) father and a slave mother could escape the status of the mother if it was decided to perform a special purification ritual, *nmo ime,* during the mother's pregnancy (the same ritual was performed with all nonslave wives of umudei as a matter of course). But even then, the offspring was not fully accepted in the umudei category, for he was still barred from certain high offices. It should also be noted that union between a master and his female slave (apparently common in the past) was, strictly speaking, not marriage. As in many African societies, the proper union of a man and woman involves the transfer of bridewealth. A master who "married" his female slave was in a sense exercising his property rights over her since her real kin were not in a position to demand the bridewealth. The situation is perhaps better described as concubinage, which, if it took place between the free, was looked upon with the greatest disfavor. Disfavor—as well as the need to pay bridewealth—also acted as a definite barrier against legal unions of free females and male slaves.

CONCLUSIONS

If the emerging picture of the Aboh slave is not a simple one, it is because slavery in Aboh was a many-sided phenomenon, the result of a combination of varied factors. The slaves were absorbed into the lineage structure as pseudokinsmen. The treatment they received depended upon several variables, perhaps the most crucial of which was the size of the household. The day-to-day living conditions of the majority of slaves, especially with respect to such things as food, housing, and clothing, were probably not markedly different from those of most of the ordinary people. There was no difference in the economic role of slaves and nonslaves, although the more onerous tasks might be assigned to the former. There is no indication that slaves worked longer hours than freemen. They were also provided with wives by their masters and were generally secure in their family life. Instances of slave families being broken apart and the individuals sold off must have been rare. Slaves were a basic factor in the Aboh economy. They played an extremely valuable role in the kingdom's long-distance trade as agents and canoe crews. They were also important in the military organization, the contingents of the chiefs being composed essentially of slaves. They had almost as much access to the kingdom's economic resources as freemen, and many slaves acquired considerable wealth and slaves of their own.

There was, however, a marked disparity in the pattern of authority exercised over slaves as compared to freemen. The former were completely subordinated to the authority of their masters, who quite often excercised their disciplinary powers in ways which suggest that the slaves were regarded as chattel. But this disparity in the subjection to authority was not permanent. Thus, in examining the interpersonal relations between master and slave, careful distinctions should be drawn among the newly acquired slave, one who had lived in Aboh for a considerable period of time, and a second-generation slave. Only in the case of the last two would the pattern of authority approximate to that exercised over true kinsmen. The first category of slaves and perhaps some of the second were probably viewed as having no independent legal existence and could not hire out their labor to anyone without the master's consent. The older slave, on the other hand, probably had a freer hand. Although slaves could hold property, much of it was at the disposal of their masters. It is also necessary to consider the specific economic and social context of master-slave relations. In very small units, where slaves worked beside their masters, closer personal bonds were more likely to develop. Such slaves were presumably treated like true kinsmen. On the other hand, in the larger households, where upwards of two hundred slaves were employed in military and commercial tasks, a slave was more likely to be regarded as a chattel, the master viewing his slaves largely as anonymous units of labor. It is also clear that slaves constituted a distinct and permanent low-status category with no access to real political power.

GLOSSARY

abuba ugo: eagle feather.
akpe: a female of the upper status group.
ashimadei: a royal drummer.
ebo: ward, one of the four units into which the town of Aboh is divided.
igbamibe: pawnship.
Igbu: an elite society in Aboh.

igoya n'obi: a ritual marking admission of a slave or his descendant into a lineage.

ikenga: god of fortune.

inyama: a special personal shrine at which newly acquired slaves were dedicated.

iyasele: prime minister.

ndichie: a common Aboh term for clients and slaves, but elsewhere in Igboland a title of reverence generally referring to ancestors and holders of senior titles.

ndichie nta: lesser *ndichie;* slaves, the lowest status group.

ndichie ukwu: higher *ndichie;* clients, the middle status group.

nigger: a pidgin word meaning slave.

nmo ime: a purification ritual performed during pregnancy by non-*akpe* wives of *umudei*.

nwadei (pl. *umudei*): a noble, prince; a male descendant of the founder of the Aboh kingdom; an upper-status group member.

nzele: chiefly titles.

obhe: an *ndichie nta* title.

obi: king; the ruler of Aboh.

ogbe: a compound, ward-section; subdivision of the *ebo*.

ogbunmo: one who has killed a human being or wild animal; literally, "killer of spirits."

ohu: slave in most Igbo dialects, but not in Aboh.

okpala: an elder; the oldest man and head of a lineage, ward section, or ward.

olie: one of the four days in the Igbo week. The other days are *afor, nkwo,* and *eke.*

olinzele (sing. and pl.): titleholder, chief.

onigbo: a slave (Igala).

onye igbo (pl. *nd'igbo*): impolite term for a slave in Aboh.

onwa ku se: a term for the process by which an alien immigrant became a client of a *nwadei*.

osu: slave in Aboh dialect.

pulla boy: canoe hand (pidgin).

uko dei: a nonfree individual who, having undergone the ritual of *igoya n'obi,* has been received into full membership of a lineage.

REFERENCES

ORAL SOURCES

Some of the material used in this article is contained in recordings of oral traditions made during fieldwork in Aboh in 1969 and 1970.

UNPUBLISHED SOURCES

N.N.A.: Nigerian National Archives, Ibadan.
   Kwale District 1928. File No. 62, Vol. 1.

P.R.O.: Public Record Office, London.
Captain Trotter to Lord Stanley, C.O. 2/24, Enclosure F. in No. 52, March 15, 1843.
Report of Major C. M. Macdonald, F.O. 84/2109, January 9, 1890.

PUBLISHED SOURCES

Alagoa, E. J. 1970. Long-distance trade and states in the Niger Delta. *J. Afr. Hist.* 11:319-29.

Allen, W., and Thomson, R. T. 1848. *A narrative of the expedition to the River Niger in 1841.* 2 vols. London.

Baikie, W. B. 1856. *Narratives of an exploring voyage.* London.

Cole, W. 1862. *Life on the Niger.* London.

Crowther, S., and Taylor, J. 1859. *The Gospel on the banks of the Niger: journals and notices of the native missionaries accompanying the Niger expedition of 1857-1859.* London.

Dike, K. O. 1956. *Trade and politics in the Niger Delta, 1830-1885: an introduction to the economic and political history of Nigeria.* Oxford.

Horton, R. 1969. From fishing village to city state: a social history of New Calabar. In *Man in Africa,* ed. M. Douglas and P. M. Kaberry. London.

Jones, G. I. 1963. *The trading states of the Oil Rivers: a study of political development in eastern Nigeria.* London.

————. 1967. Olaudah Equiano of the Niger Ibo. In *Africa remembered,* ed. P. D. Curtin. Madison.

Klein, A. N. 1969. West African unfree labor before and after the rise of the Atlantic slave trade. In *Slavery in the New World: a reader in comparative history,* ed. L. Foner and E. D. Genovese. Englewood Cliffs, N. J.

Laird, M., and Oldfield, R. A. K. 1837. *Narrative of an expedition into the interior of Africa, by the River Niger, in the steamvessels Quorra and Alburkah, in 1832, 1833, and 1834.* London.

Leith-Ross, S. 1937. Notes on the Osu system among the Ibo of Owerri Province, Nigeria. *Africa* 10:206-20.

Lloyd, P. C. 1963. The Itsekiri in the nineteenth century: an outline social history. *J. Afr. Hist.* 4:207-31.

Schön, F., and Crowther, S. 1842. *Journals of the Reverend Frederick Schön and Mr. S. Crowther who accompanied the expedition up the Niger in 1841.* London.

6

Slavery and the Evolution of Nineteenth-Century Damagaram

(Zinder, Niger)

Roberta Ann Dunbar

The nineteenth century in West Africa was an era of great political, economic, religious, and social change. Islamic reformers toppled old regimes in scores of localities and proceeded to create new systems of government or to establish modified versions of the old governments. African societies on the coast shifted from trade in slaves to trade in other items. New focuses of production and trade networks evolved, and there emerged a class of people who were accustomed to dealing in the two worlds of Africa and Europe. Trans-Saharan traders continued to move slaves along the ancient desert routes, and they added a range of new Sudanese products in their trade. Kingdoms of the interior competed for their favors, thereby affecting their own development.

Change was not a new phenomenon in West Africa, but its itensity increased in the nineteenth century. The challenge is to define how deeply the structure of any one society was affected. A fundamental change is indicated by the increase in scale of the society brought on by an increase in numbers of people and groups interacting and the resulting shifts in intensity of relations from one level to another (Wilson and Wilson

155

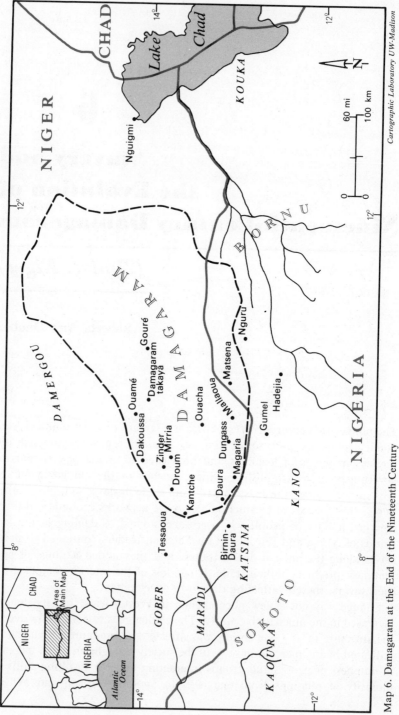

Map 6. Damagaram at the End of the Nineteenth Century

1965:24-25, 44). Social change is not a "change of occupants of existing positions" but rather a change of the positions available for occupancy in society. Larger-scale societies manifest greater specialization, variety, and autonomy among their various elements. As the intensity of wider relations increases, new styles and loyalties replace those of the smaller-scale society (Wilson and Wilson 1965:58-60, 83-86).

The history of Damagaram shows that change can be multidirectional and multileveled. That is, increase in scale at one level, which may intensify and make more complex some relations, is matched by a decrease in intensity and scale at another. Because we wish to focus primarily on one problem:—the effect of domestic slavery on economic, political, and social structures in Damagaram—it will be useful to begin with a brief overview of the history of the kingdom in the nineteeth century.

Bornu was one of the oldest empires in West Africa, encompassing territories to the east and west of Lake Chad. In the early nineteenth century, it faced a major crisis: in the brief space of six years, the Fulani jihad, led by Uthman dan Fodio, consolidated political authority over an enormous extent of territory and created the Sokoto Empire. Sokoto's expansion to the east cost Bornu some of its western provinces and ultimately resulted in the accession of a new Bornu dynasty under Shehu al-Kanemi. Instability and disruption associated with the Bornu-Sokoto wars and with Shehu al-Kanemi's rise to power severely diminished Bornu's control over its northwestern provinces, which lay in the Sudan, just south of the Sahara's edge. Suleiman, the ruler of one of the Kanuri chieftaincies there, had for some years been garnering more and more followers and, in the early years of the century, founded a new capital at Zinder. Although he recognized the suzerainty of Bornu, Suleiman took advantage of the confused situation in the south and of Bornu's weakness, and continued to expand the authority of his new kingdom, Damagaram, over both Kanuri and Hausa-speaking peoples in this ethnic borderland.

Under the leadership of the *sarki* (sultan), Suleiman, and that of his sons, Ibrahim and Tanimu, Damagaram flourished: the protection provided by their armies from the depredations of raiders from the north encouraged the settlement of new groups of peasants. Of overriding importance was Ibrahim's decision to encourage various groups of Aïr Tuareg to trade in his capital and join him in military expeditions. As a result, Zinder became an important commercial center along the trans-Saharan trade route that ran between Kano and Tripoli. Tanimu's reign, from 1854 to 1884, marked the era of greatest economic innovation and prosperity. After an intense series of successful military campaigns, he began to subsidize trading expeditions, plantations, and gardens on behalf of the state. His successors, Suleiman and Ahmadu, threw off all allegiance to Bornu and tried to expand the borders of the kingdom to the south until, by the 1890s, they were in frequent conflict with Kano, one of the most powerful emirates of the Sokoto Empire. Preoccupied with the political affairs of the Central Sudan, Ahmadu and his court were unprepared for the challenge of new arrivals, the French, and quickly succumbed to their authority in 1899.

The relatively brief history of Damagaram provides an excellent chance to focus on different types of change. The various peoples who came to live in Damagaram—mainly Kanuri, Hausa, Tuareg, Tubu, and Fulani—shifted their loyalties from the diffuse sovereignty of Bornu to a new political entity whose demands were far more intense and direct. Even today, the sultans of Damagaram, though bereft of their former power and despite years of humiliation under French colonial rule, still command respect from their former subjects.[1]

Zinder became an important commercial center in the trans-Saharan trade because the new dynasty was able to provide security for caravans passing through it, but also, and more importantly, because it created a new center for the collection and distribution of the natural products of the Sudan long associated with the trade: millet, salt, honey, ostrich feathers, skins, cotton fabrics, medicinal herbs, and slaves. The profits of this trade affected people at all levels of the society and, in particular, enabled the rulers to procure guns and technological assistance, which raised their military strength. Slaves, then, played a key role in the growth of Damagaram: they were a critical export commodity and provided an expanded source of labor for the production of crops and manufactures destined for internal consumption and for export.

Leaving aside the role of slaves as an export commodity, we shall focus here on their role in the internal affairs of Damagaram and try to determine the extent of the changes stimulated by their presence. A description of the general conditions of their lives will be followed by a discussion of the various activities in which they participated. The concluding section will include an examination of some of the comparative evidence for similar trends elsewhere in West Africa during the nineteenth century.

THE CHARACTER OF SLAVERY IN DAMAGARAM

A geographical setting without physical barriers has encouraged not only the exchange of goods among the societies of the interior of West

---

1. Brief histories of Damagaram are included in Urvoy (1949), Abadie (1927), and Tilho (1911); in Tilho the historical section written by M. Landeroin contains the best collection of traditions gathered in the early twentieth century. Two more recent studies are Salifou (1971) and Dunbar (1970).

Africa, but also an exchange of ideas, techniques of government, and social attitudes. Similarities in the practice of domestic slavery (Hausa: *bauta*) in Kanuri and Hausa societies were greater than those of either one with societies in the forest regions. Mary Smith (1954) in her biography of Baba of Karo, M. G. Smith (1954, 1955, 1960), and Polly Hill (1972) have laid the foundations of our knowledge of economy and slavery in Hausa society. Ronald Cohen (1967) has published a brief introduction to Kanuri institutions of slavery. In addition to the Kanuri and Hausa segments of Damagaram's people, there were also the Tuareg, whose slaves were a part, albeit somewhat removed, of the society. Studies must eventually be made to show to what extent particularistic distinctions obtained among the slave systems of the different ethnic groups or to what extent they were transformed by the new center of authority and power in Zinder. In addition, other aspects will have to be examined: the differences between pre-Islamic and Islamic practices, the extent to which each of these dominated, and when.[2] These projects for future research are mentioned here to stress the provisional nature of the material to follow.

Adapting a descriptive framework that has proved useful for the comparative study of New World slave societies (Genovese 1969), we will ask the following questions about slavery in Damagaram: How were slaves recruited? How did their living conditions, including food, shelter, and clothing, compare with those of the nonslave population? What was the quality of their life—what laws, for instance, governed their freedom of movement, religion, marriage? How frequent was manumission and what was the status of the freed slave? How were freed slaves integrated into kinship systems? Wherever possible, we shall distinguish the legal rights and obligations from what was, in effect, the practice.

PROCUREMENT OF SLAVES

Slaves were procured primarily in three different ways: by raiding, kidnapping, and purchase.

Raiding was a constant source of tension in nineteenth-century Hausa and Kanuri society, and Damagaram was not exempt. Heinrich Barth noted that while the practice of domestic slavery was not offensive to the eye, domestic needs were the main cause of slave raiding (Barth 1857/ 1965, 1:xxix, 527). James Richardson, an ardent British abolitionist who spent a month in Zinder in the winter of 1850-51, wrote vehemently about the *razzia,* or raiding procedure. The king mounted military expeditions

2. Greenberg (1946) deals with some of the contrasts by looking at the Maguzawa communities. One method for examining the different stages and forms of slavery would be to compare the characteristics of Hausa, Kanuri, and Tuareg slave systems during four periods: pre-Islamic, post-Islamic, pre-1850, and post-1850.

that employed as many as two thousand horsemen and lasted for several days. Summoned by the drum in the capital city, the raiders would depart. Techniques most often used were surprise assault in the early morning, or siege. The latter was particularly successful if the marauders could control the water supply of the town. Men who resisted were killed. Women, children, and old people were caught as they sought frantically to escape (Richardson 1854, 2:238-39, 264-66; Schön 1885, Hausa text:238-39). If the raid was successful, great jubilation greeted the returning troops. Each man had his captive or captives marching in front of him. Some captives were shared out in the field, others at the capital.[3] Two state officials, *sarkin dawaki* (chief of horses) and *sarkin bayi* (chief of slaves) were in charge of those slaves sent to Zinder (Salifou 1971:172). The sultan retained approximately half, although he normally distributed part of his share as gifts. Individuals who had been mobilized for the raid usually kept half of the slaves they caught.[4]

Significantly, most of the communities raided in the early years of the century formed part of Bornu, and sometimes even of Damagaram itself. Political feuding was often the excuse for a razzia. In Damagaram, this was the rationalization for campaigns against Daura and other smaller chieftaincies such as Kantche, in the western part of the kingdom. While all of these areas were nominally Muslim, they contained pockets of "pagan" peoples variously called *azna* or *anna;* raiding them, Muslim officials explained to Richardson, was always legitimate. It probably also avoided the political risks that raiding of the free, Muslim-protected population of friendly neighbors might carry (Richardson 1854, 2:244-45, 252-53).

Toward the end of the century, because much of its area formerly used for slave-raiding had come under a stronger, more centralized, and consciously Islamic authority, Damagaram's raids were directed to the south. In one campaign in Kano in 1897, seven thousand slaves were captured (Salifou 1971:170).

In addition to "state-authorized" raids, individuals also raided caravans and settlements on their own account, and probably this was the

3. Stories of razzia appear frequently in travelers' accounts of the Central Sudan. See, for instance the works of Barth, who spent much time in Bornu, and Richardson, who spent more time in Zinder. Richardson (1854, 2:223, 226, 269-71) described plans for several raids.

4. Reports vary as to how the slaves were divided. Richardson suggests that a subordinate chief would keep half before sending slaves to Zinder. Half of those captured by a "single undistinguished man" would also go to the sultan (Richardson 1854, 2:31, 274). A twentieth-century survey of the customary law of Zinder states that peasants who had been mobilized rarely kept the slaves they had captured, receiving only *ladan yaki,* booty, but probably not slaves (Veillard 1939:165-66).

source of most kidnappings. An example of this appears in the narrative of Dogo. Born in Damagaram, he was captured as a child while taking potash to Gumel, an important market, in a caravan of fifty-seven people. He subsequently was sold to a Yoruba who took him to Badagri, where, under another master, he worked in the palm oil trade for six years before his escape (Schön 1885, English text:177-78). [5]

Two customs that were related to the procurement of slaves and kidnapping should be mentioned: ransoming and pawning. Normally, agreements were made among kingdoms to the effect that princes or other royal personages would not be captured. There is an account in one nineteenth-century source, however, which suggests that such capture was not unknown and that ransom—*fanshe*—could exceed by two or three times the market price of a slave. The same account states that other individuals pawned themselves—*jingine kansu*—in order to rescue relatives from slavery (Schön 1885, English text:164-65). [6]

In Zinder, slaves could be purchased in the markets of *birni*, the walled city, and in Zengou, the Tuareg settlement to the northwest. Richardson (1854, 2:191, 228) reported seeing numbers of slaves from Damagaram and Maradi there. A note in the diary of Cazemajou (1900:302), a French officer who was assassinated in Zinder in 1898, refers to slaves for sale in the market; later French officials also mention them (Salifou 1971:173). [7] The Zinder and Zengou markets were the most important ones for slaves because they were the export markets. The literature rarely comments on whether there was a distinction in price between slaves sold for export and those to be used in domestic affairs. Late-nineteenth-century estimates of the average prices of slaves in different centers within the kingdom are given by Salifou (1971:175-76). The average price per slave in cowrie shells was 10,000 in "original Damagaram" (Damagaram takaya and environs, the original capital of the kingdom), 15,000 in Mirria, 20,000 in Ouacha, and 45,000 in Zinder. In Mirria, Kantche, and the areas of original Damagaram, the difference in price of a male and female slave was not so great; the males sometimes cost more because they were used primarily for

5. Another excellent if fictional account is contained in the novel *Shaihu Umar* (1955), by Sir Abubakar Tafawa Balewa.

6. It is not clear whether the pawned individual then became a slave under the same restrictions as other captives. The extent of pawning in Hausa-Kanuri society is also unclear as there are no other references in the literature regarding it. This is an aspect of slavery that ought to be studied further.

7. It has been suggested by Hill (1972:320) that the absence of extensive comment on slave markets means they may have been sold in the house trade. It seems likely that this might have been true, especially in smaller centers, but Katsina, Kano, Zinder, and Kukawa certainly had slave markets. For Kukawa at midcentury, see Barth (1857/1965, 2:54).

Table 6.1

Late-Nineteenth-Century Estimates of Average Prices for
Different Categories of Domestic Slaves
in cowrie shells

Category	Zinder	Ouacha	Original Damagaram (Damagaram takaya)
Adult male	60,000	30,000	20,000
Adult female	100,000	40,000	30,000
Young person	25,000	20,000	12,000
K'etara shimge	3,000	2,000	800

Source: Salifou 1971:177.

agriculture. Exorbitant prices were paid for women in Zinder because they were overwhelmingly preferred for the export market. Certain ethnic preferences operated as well: Fulani women, because of their legendary beauty, might cost half again as much as other women; Kanuri slaves were allegedly the most disciplined and hardworking; Fulani in general were seen as shiftless; and people from Kano were considered to be the laziest of all. Only a low price could be gotten for the male slave called *k'etara shimge*—"the one who crosses the fence"—because his great height and strength made him a likely runaway. Such slaves were usually chained and kept under strict surveillance (Salifou 1971:176). A price breakdown by sex within Damagaram illustrates the higher price of slaves sold for the export market, at Zinder, in comparison with those sold at the domestic markets of Ouacha and Damagaram takaya (Table 6.1). The similarity of prices for male and female slaves for domestic use was confirmed by Sarkin Dawaki Muhamman dan Ari (interview: January 17, 1968), an official at the present-day court, who also claimed that prices were the same whether sale was in the market or private.

Slaves were also used as payment for tribute and fines. Theft was often punished by sale of the malefactor into slavery. Slaves who argued with their masters or abused their trust were threatened with sale (Richardson 1854, 2:230-31). In Damagaram, no individual could reduce another to slavery because of debt (Salifou 1971:170).[8]

LIVING CONDITIONS OF THE SLAVES

One of the striking features about domestic slavery in the Central Sudan is that so little comment on it exists in the literature, even though persons writing on the Hausa-Kanuri area in the nineteenth century believed that most slaves captured in razzia were for "internal consumption" (Fisher

8. In Wadai, the threat of enslavement was sometimes applied to traders who defaulted on their debts (Nachtigal 1971:52).

and Fisher 1971:76). Richardson, writing in 1851, said that the bulk of the slaves of the razzia were employed as serfs on the soil or servants in the town (1854, 2:274).[9] The paucity of comment on the condition of domestic slaves is, I believe, a matter of perception: at each level of society the differences in status were camouflaged by similarities in dress, work, food, and shelter. In the rural areas, one could scarcely distinguish the *bayi* (sing. *bawa*), or slaves, from the *talakawa* (sing. *talaka*), or free peasants. Even where entire settlements were slave, their living conditions were scarcely distinct from those of peasant settlements nearby. This is not to say that all lived comfortably; far from it. But they had the same access to goods and services as did free persons in the rural areas. At the court, with the exception of differences of regalia, slave officeholders lived as well as free ones, and at the end of the century some of the powerful slave officials amassed greater quantities of luxury goods than did some of their free colleagues.

Loyalty and diligence were demanded, however, and those who erred or misjudged stood to suffer. Domestic slaves in Zinder, and particularly those of the sultan, were frequently in irons (Richardson 1854, 2:223, 236).[10] There were, too, those men who suffered castration. This ancient practice was forbidden by the Koran and by Muslim tradition alike. The use of eunuchs was widespread in the Muslim world, however; rulers frequently evaded responsibility for the operation by purchasing slaves who had been made eunuchs by Christians or Jews (Mez 1937:353-54).[11] Castration was first introduced to Damagaram on a significant scale during the reign of Ibrahim (1822-46); occasionally, eunuchs were exported in the trans-Saharan trade, but they also were increasingly used at the court. At the end of the century, five of the top officials at the court were eunuchs (interview: Sarkin Dawaki Muhamman, March 5, 1968; Abadie 1927:221; A.A.N., Fremineau 1952:1).

TYPES OF SLAVES AND QUALITY OF LIFE

Slaves who had been captured or purchased were called bayi. They could be physically abused by their masters and could be sold. Persons born into slavery, *cucenawa* (sing. *bacucane*), could not be sold, and it is this group that merged with the talakawa. Although in principle each

9. This is confirmed by Lieutenant Colonel Monteil during his trip through Sudan in the 1890s. His comments refer mostly to Kano, but he cites the use of slaves in agriculture, domestic service, and commerce (Monteil 1894:286-88).

10. Slaves were chained by the neck or the feet when they were "suspect," and all slaves were watched by a person called *mai tsaren bayi* (interview: Liman Mustafa, February 25, 1968).

11. I am indebted to Herbert L. Bodman for his comments and references on this matter.

slave owner had absolute rights over his slaves, only the sultan could authorize the infliction of death (Veillard 1939:165-66; Salifou 1971:173).

No bridewealth was paid in slave marriages in Damagaram. If both slaves belonged to the same master, as was most often the case, the children were the property of the master, and as cucenawa they could not be sold (Salifou 1971:174).[12] Children born of a marriage between two slaves belonging each to a different master were considered to be the property of both masters. In case of divorce, the children became the property of the mother's master. The sultan or any free male could make his female slave a concubine; with the birth of a child, regardless of the sex of the child, the mother became a *kambe,* the Kanuri word designating a free person. She could then either continue as concubine, leave her master, or marry him. Although this change in status suggests a loss to the master, there was no fee of compensation to him; probably this was because the actual relationship rarely changed in substance. And since children of the sultan by a concubine had equal rights to the throne with the sons born of marriages with free women, it may be that the actual birth of the child and subsequent addition to the size of the family was viewed as adequate compensation (Salifou 1971:174).[13]

There were two categories of slaves belonging to the sultan. Those captured very young, and whose parents had been captured, sold, or killed in the course of battle, became part of the royal entourage and recognized the sultan as their father. Such slaves, even though they were first-generation captives, were neither maltreated nor sold. They were in a sense ennobled and came to occupy important state posts. Of those

12. Compare the status of the bacucane with that of the *dimajo* (pl. *dimajai*), persons born in slavery, as described in Zaria by M. G. Smith, cited in Hill (1972:224): He "laboured on the master's farm and received food and housing in return, his marriage was arranged by his master; he was from birth incorporated in the Muhammedan population and addressed his master as father." Dimajai were not customarily sold, though in practice a master hardpressed for money might sell the slaves' children.

13. Fisher and Fisher have summarized Islamic legal norms regarding concubinage and marriage. Slaves may be wives or concubines, but the latter are slaves by definition. In a legal marriage a slave woman generally has rights identical to those of a free woman: for instance, a husband must divide his night visits equally between his slave and free wives. Only a slave woman who is a Muslim may marry a Muslim man. Divorce is somewhat different for a slave wife than for a free one. The slave male is permitted by Maliki law to marry four wives (in contrast to two allowed by some other legal traditions). His wives may be slave or free, though it is prohibited for a Muslim woman to marry her own slave or that of her son. Marriage of a slave man or woman requires consent of the master, an exception being that a slave who travels on his master's behalf may independently acquire a concubine (1971:117-18). Children of free wives and those of concubines are equal in rights and privileges, but historically this was often a source of conflict in political rivalries (1971:124-25).

captured as adults, a certain number were offered by sarkin bayi or sarkin dawaki, as agents of the sultan, to princes, marabouts, and various other individuals, while the majority were the sultan's property. He placed them in the charge of his officials until he wished to reclaim them. Many remained in the capital, where at least two quarters of the city (Ungwal Gwarawa and Ungwal Badawa) were slave quarters under the authority of slave officials entitled *kacella* (interview: Sarkin Dawaki Muhamman, January 17, 1968).[14] Most of the sultan's slaves, however, were settled in several villages around Zinder (Salifou 1971:172)[15] or on his special farms and gardens dispersed throughout the kingdom (interview: Sarkin Dawaki Muhamman, April 25, 1968).[16] Although it is impossible to determine the numbers of slaves owned by the sultans throughout the nineteenth and early twentieth centuries, estimates made by French officials who dismantled the bureaucracy indicated that nearly one thousand people were slaves attached to the throne.[17]

Slaves' rights to inheritance are not yet clearly understood. The estate of a sultan's slave who had resided at the court was claimed by the sultan. He then would decide, at his own discretion, what would be transmitted to the heirs, or in the case of property attached to a title, to the successor to the title. We can at least contrast those circumstances with the inheritance rights of a free peasant, whose entire estate, including movable property, animals, and other goods, could be claimed by the sultan, leaving to the heirs only house and fields (Veillard 1939:154, 156).

MANUMISSION AND THE FREED SLAVE

Masters were encouraged to liberate slaves as an act of piety, and in certain circumstances slaves were able to purchase their freedom. Most enfranchised slaves continued to reside in the same location, though they apparently were free to engage in a broader range of occupations than before, particularly those involving crafts (Salifou 1971:172; interview: Sarkin Dawaki Muhamman, January 17, 1968). Liberated slaves could procure land from their former masters in the same way as other freemen or relatives of the master in his household, in exchange for a portion of the

14. The children of Gwarawa worked in the households of the officials or others designated by the kacella in charge.

15. The villages were Dadin Sarki, Tabkin Kalgo, Ungwal Mandara, Larabawa, Jamburu, Kanya Mau Ruwa (or Kanya Makadari).

16. A distinction is made between a *gandu*, a field where grains were cultivated, and a *garka*, a garden where other plants were grown by use of irrigation or underground springs. Garaka were located in the villages of Albarkaram, Chianza, Ouacha, Dakoussa, Ungwal Auchi, Mirria, Borewa, Gauna, Ifora, Gogo, Dogo.

17. A.N.S., 11G5, No. 207.

crop, or they could purchase land (interview: Liman Mustafa, February 25, 1968).[18] Slaves accumulated the price of their freedom (usually the original purchase price) in a variety of ways: through revenues gained on their own account with skills such as tanning and weaving, which they had possessed when captured, or through sale of extra grain (interview: Sarkin Dawaki Muhamman, January 17, 1968).

Thus, slaves suffered some legal disabilities, but gradual incorporation into the society was feasible, sometimes within the lifetime of the original captive. There were also ways of rising through the ranks to greater prestige and wealth. These ways will be made clearer by examining the various activities in which slaves engaged.

AGRICULTURE

The cultivation of millet was the most widespread agricultural activity in Damagaram, since it was and is the basis of the diet and was, in the nineteenth century, an important export crop. Grown together with millet were peanuts, beans, and manioc. Rice and wheat were also cultivated, but to a lesser extent than the millets. During the dry season potatoes, onions, lemons, peppers, papaya, indigo, cotton, tobacco, and henna were grown in well-irrigated gardens. Certain towns and villages specialized in particular crops.

There were two categories of cultivated land: the heavily fertilized fields, near settlements, where produce was grown every year; and the bush farms, which were periodically left fallow (A.A.N., Brunot 1913; Salifou 1971:146). Ultimate authority over land use lay with the sultan. He and his chiefs granted usufruct rights to land (interview: Sarkin Dawaki Muhamman, January 19, 1968). Once a plot of land was granted to the family head, he and his heirs after him were allowed continual use of it. They lost their rights, however, if they let land lie fallow beyond the normal period, or allowed another farmer to clear the bush after a fallow period (Veillard 1939:149).

Fields could be loaned or rented but, in principle, they could not be sold (Salifou 1971:146). In practice, land may have been sold, but this did not become common until the colonial era, when some plots were sold to *anciens tirailleurs*, foreign African military personnel, who remained in Zinder at the termination of their service in the French colonial army.

18. A full description of an emancipation ceremony in Zaria can be found in *Baba of Karo:* "the *malams* were assembled, a ram was killed, prayers were said and he was given his new name of Usuman. We made porridge and all kinds of food. For two nights there was playing and drumming. . . . Malam Maigari [Baba's husband and the master] gave Usuman a gown and new clothes, Usuman became his son. . . . Everyone brought gifts to Malam—'reinforcements'—some brought two thousand cowries, some brought one thousand, he went to market and bought food and clothes for Usuman—a new gown, trousers, and a blanket" (M. Smith 1954:122).

Liberated slaves may also have been able to purchase land, but it is unclear whether or not this was the case in the precolonial era (Veillard 1939:164; interview: Liman Mustafa, February 25, 1968).

The basic agricultural unit was the farm, which was worked by all members of the household, including women and slaves. Occasionally, the father would give to a son a plot called *gayyamna*, for which the son alone, or with his wife, was responsible. For this, the father would exempt him from work in the communal fields for three afternoons a week (Salifou 1971:146-47).[19] It is difficult to estimate to what extent slaves were employed as agricultural laborers in Damagaram. A variety of sources describing conditions in nearby areas of Bornu and the Sokoto Empire suggest, however, that such utilization of slaves was widespread. Anyone could buy and sell slaves (interview: Liman Mustafa, February 25, 1968). Peasants might not have had many, but there were always some villagers whose wealth or official position made slaves available to them. Whenever possible, men, even as young people, tried to improve their condition by trade and hoped ultimately to procure slaves. The nineteenth-century accounts of two Kano men illustrate this explicitly. They had left their earlier occupations—one as a student in Koranic school, the other as a potter—to seek their fortunes in trade and subsequently as soldiers. Both told of their longing eventually to get fifteen or twenty slaves, go home, marry, and begin farming (Schön 1885, English text: 178-79).

In all likelihood slaves worked together with other members of the family in the communal fields and were assigned certain plots which they worked on their own account.[20] In Damagaram, the fact that liberated slaves who wished to remain in the area could obtain a plot from their

19. Salifou notes that today gayyamna belong exclusively to women, who grow vegetables, cotton, and ground nuts, which they may sell or use for their own food or crafts.

20. We have earlier commented on Richardson's observations at midcentury and those of Monteil in the 1890s. In addition, there is information concerning places in the Sokoto Empire. In Zaria, a slave would be settled with his family in a village or farm belonging to his master. He would work half the day in the master's fields; food for the noon meal would be provided by the master. In the afternoons, the slave and his family worked their own plots (M. Smith 1954: M. G. Smith 1954). In 1827, Clapperton noted that in Sokoto, when slaves were newly sent to a village, the master provided food until the first harvest. After harvest, the slave would receive a bushel of each grain from the master's fields plus the produce from his own fields. Barth observed that in Sokoto slave farms were so numerous, particularly on the lands of important fiefholders, that sufficient produce was raised to free some slaves for other service (Fisher and Fisher 1971:133-34). In 1851, Richardson wrote: "In Kano, a rich man has three or four thousand slaves; these are permitted to work on their own account, and they pay him as their lord and master a certain number of cowries every month: some bring one hundred, some three hundred or six hundred, or as low as fifty cowries a month. On the accumulation of these various monthly payments of the poor slaves the great man subsists, and is rich and powerful in the country" (Richardson 1854, 2:274). See also Cohen (1967:49).

former owner, rather than directly from the sultan (interview: Liman Mustafa, January 25, 1968), suggests that the transition to freedom did not necessarily change in any substantial way the socioeconomic ties established during bondage.

The sultan was the largest owner of fields and gardens, and he and his most prominent courtiers, both slave and free, had whole villages of slaves working at cultivation. Free peasants also were called upon to give their services by tilling, hoeing, and harvesting the crops of the sultan. *Sarkin garka,* slave officials in charge of the sultan's gardens, received part of the harvest as well as produce from their own plot. These state gardens, or *garaka;* were first instituted by Sarki Tanimu, and were worked all year round.[21]

When Sarki Ibrahim encouraged the Aïr Tuareg to come to Zinder, he allocated land to the Tuareg for settlement of their slave cultivators (Hausa: *buzu,* pl. *bugaje)* (A.A.N., Gamory-Dubourdeau; interview: Mohammed Tsoho, January 8, 1968). The sites of these villages are still well known, most of them being located in regions near Zinder.[22] These settlements may not have been completely incorporated into the Damagaram state: for instance, reports about who levied taxes on the bugaje settlements are conflicting. Some say that the bugaje paid the same tax as free peasants plus an additional levy to their Tuareg masters; others that they paid no cowrie taxes but did pay one tenth of their millet harvest to the sultan (interview: Liman Mustafa, February 25, 1968; Gaden 1903:765).[23] The Tuareg, through their official representatives, gave gifts, especially millet and dates, to the sultan. Such presents were not taxes but a symbol of *amana,* which meant among other things trust and friendship (interview: Mohammed Tsoho, January 8, 1968; A.A.N., Gamory-Dubourdeau).[24]

Anyone who wished help in his cultivation could organize a *gayya,* a work party, where friends and neighbors would work in exchange for food and kola nuts. The fact that this custom was widely mentioned by informants indicates that despite the use of slaves, shortages of labor occurred in all peasant households.

21. Dates and barley were grown in Ouacha and Mirria. Wheat, bananas, and papayas were also garka crops. Although cotton plantations were numerous, cotton was not exported (probably because it was utilized in local weaving). A.N.S., 3F11, No. 67.

22. The names of the villages are Gouna, Zermou, Babantapki, Dogo, Droum (interview: Mohammed Tsoho, January 10, 1968).

23. Elsewhere, bugaje paid as much as four fifths of their crops to Tuareg masters (Fisher and Fisher 1971:135).

24. It is not clear whether there were in Damagaram, as elsewhere further west, bugaje villages where people who had escaped their Tuareg masters during the Fulani wars settled down as free peasants, located in communities side-by-side with Hausa ones, on which they depended. Nicholas (1962) has described the relationship between them.

INDUSTRY AND COMMERCE

In Damagaram, as in the Bornu and Sokoto empires, slaves were widely used as specialized artisans: spinners, weavers, butchers, masons, and housebuilders. Others were responsible for less skilled jobs such as herding, caring for horses, exploiting salt works, carrying wood and water, and serving as messengers (Fisher and Fisher 1971:138-40; Schön 1885, English text:18-19). Richardson saw slaves at work in Zinder in the indigo dye pits and manufacturing roofing for houses, an extensive industry under the supervision of three directors who were themselves slaves of the owner of the business (Richardson 1854, 2:227, 242, 274). Slaves were also used in such other economic activities as the tanning of skins, which were an important export at the end of the century.

Domestic slaves were also in common demand as caravan workers and commercial agents, as they were elsewhere in the Central Sudan (Fisher and Fisher 1971:152-77). Descriptions of the commercial operations of Malam Yaro, the wealthiest merchant in Zinder during the last quarter of the nineteenth century, cite his use of slaves as *wakilai* (sing. *wakili*), representatives, in Kano, Hadejia, Nguigmi, and other market centers. These men were in charge of the distribution and sale of goods not only to the merchants but also to retail customers in the towns. The wakili often had several slaves working under his direction (interview: Malam Ali, March 26, 1968[25]). On a much smaller scale, even slave boys were sometimes engaged in petty trading for their masters. Dorugu, a former slave from Damagaram who came into Barth's service, related that he had been asked by his former master to take a horse to Kano to sell it for him. Significantly, he refused, fearing that in such an important slave market as Kano he himself could easily be kidnapped and sold (Schön 1885, English text:20).[26]

SLAVES AND THE STATE

The sultan, and through him the state, was the largest slaveholder. Distinctions between slaves whose responsibilities lay to the sultan per-

25. Malam Ali's father was Malam Yaro, whose real name was Musa ben Abdullahi. Family sources claim descent from a Tripolitan, Musa Abdullahi; Malam Yaro's father, Abdullahi, was born in Ngazargamu but came to Zinder as a merchant in the nineteenth century. Malam Yaro's mother, Karu, was Beriberi. Malam Yaro studied in Agadez as a young man and while there lived with the Kel Tafidet. All other sources claim that Malam Yaro was a member and perhaps a captive of the Kel Tafidet; this version of his background would explain "Malam Yaro," an honorific term for servant.

26. Monteil (1894:288) describes the use of slaves in commerce and stresses the potential for advancement: "the master may give the slave direction of his business interests often in preference to his own sons. As the first recompense, the master gives him a wife, then slaves; soon he himself is a property owner. If he has a family, his fate is definitely fixed: neither he nor his children may be sold."

sonally or to the state were blurred, since the sultan was the key allocator of individuals to official positions and of goods through government channels. Although it is impossible to know the percentage of slaves belonging to the state, we can assume that it was great. Moreover, the positions they occupied often made their influence far exceed their number. We will examine some of the ways in which slaves were used by the state.

There is no precise evidence that slaves were used as colonists in Damagaram, but the creation of slave villages for agricultural purposes and the use of slaves in distant commercial centers would have been a means of extending the sovereign's control. This is particularly so because in Hausa and Kanuri societies prestige and power, in the case of both the individual household head and the sultan, were based not on territory but on the population under one's jurisdiction. The site of Zinder was sparsely settled when the sultanate transferred its capital there. Many of the early population may have "immigrated" as slaves; a number of the quarters of Zinder bear the names of areas, such as Daura and Bede, which experienced heavy raiding under Ibrahim and Tanimu.

The employment of slaves as soldiers is an ancient practice in the Central Sudan and elsewhere. In Fulani areas, slave soldiers were frequently the only ones armed with the new weapons—muskets and, later, rifles. In Damagaram, kacella, junior officers with thirty men under their charge, and grema, with eleven men under them, were slaves. These companies, armed with guns, formed part of the line of march around the sultan. The cavalrymen 'yan lifidi, were under the command of a slave official, sarkin bayi (Fisher and Fisher 1971:154-56; Tilho 1911:524-25; Gaden 1903:756). The size of the army varied with the nature of the campaign. A full-fledged campaign might include five thousand cavalry and thirty thousand archers; by the end of the century, the proportion of cavalry to foot soldiers had increased. Although there was not a standing army based on recruits from all over the kingdom, the kacella, of whom there were about thirty by the end of the century, resided at the capital with the men who were under their command. The rest of the army was made up of courtiers and vassals, some of whom had slaves among their troops. Titled courtiers might command large numbers of men, both slave and free: Sarkin Fulani Aboki, a slave official, fled to Kano in 1900 after the arrival of the French with two hundred horses and about two thousand footmen.[27]

27. N.N.A., Arabic Letterbook, Kadcap Box 43-3, 1900. Two other court officials joined him. This is reminiscent of Lamino, a powerful courtier in Bornu in the 1870s, who had under his command fifteen of the higher-ranking slaves who in turn commanded a force of one thousand horsemen (Fisher and Fisher 1971:159).

The commander-in-chief of the Damagaram army at midcentury was Dan Ciroma, a member of the royal line. By the end of the century, this position had been replaced by the *kaigama,* a position held by a slave, who also exercised political power above and beyond strictly military affairs. At the death of Tanimu's son Suleiman, in 1893, competition between the sons of former Sultan Ibrahim and those of Tanimu threatened to escalate into a war of succession. The kaigama, who had been appointed by Tanimu, informed the notables that he would only accept the accession of one of Tanimu's sons, and he was able to impose this decision upon them (A.A.N., Brunot 1913).

There was the same increased reliance upon slaves in the bureaucracy. It is clear that there was at least one slave official during the reign of the first king of the dynasty in Zinder; thereafter, the appointment of slaves to important titles increased to the point that, by the end of the century, they composed well over one-half of the titled state officials. Such men, including eunuchs, came to occupy positions of responsibility in the maintenance and security of the royal household itself, and they also collected taxes, administered customs duties, and distributed goods and booty for the sultan in his kingdom and to foreign powers. The most important bureaucratic positions held by slaves included *bellama* (a eunuch), provisioner of the royal family; *shetima* (a eunuch), guardian of women; *mustarama* (a eunuch), supervisor of collection of revenue from fines and taxes; grema, an official in the religious hierarchy charged with the division of booty to other religious officials and the distribution of alms; *sarkin kasuwa,* collector of direct taxes levied on goods brought to market and appointer of other *sarakunan kasuwa* throughout the realm; and *sarkin Fulani,* collector of taxes and pasturage fees levied on the Fulani.[28]

The use of slaves as gifts and tribute appears to have been more important symbolically than economically. For instance, tribute was paid to Bornu until 1893, but slaves did not ordinarily form part of the regular tribute, which consisted of cowries or, if they were in short supply of gowns and turbans. After successful raids, the sultan sent some of the slaves to Bornu, but this seems to have been more as a gift than an obligation (interviews: Marusa Mustafa, 1967; Gaden 1903:764; Richardson 1854, 2:243). The sultans also received slaves and other goods as part of the tribute paid to them, or from underlings seeking high office. At its greatest extent, the kingdom contained eighteen vassal chieftaincies, but the number of slaves paid in tribute seems to have been small; horses,

---

28. For a complete discussion of offices and functions in the bureaucracy of Damagaram, see Dunbar (1970, Chs. 5 and 6).

clothing of various types, and foodstuffs formed the bulk of such payments (Tilho 1911:443; interviews conducted in Kantche, May 1, 1968, and in Daura, May 26, 1968). In addition to the payment of large sums in cowries for such services as they might perform prior to military engagements, the titled officials of the religious establishment received from the sultan specified numbers of slaves distributed to them through a slave official, who was also in charge of presents distributed to the poor at feast times (Tilho 1911:536). Finally, the accession of any man to higher office was celebrated by a "gift" of slaves and other trade goods (swords, guns, horses, beef cattle) not only to the sultan but to other officials, higher up, who had interceded on behalf of the new officeholder (Tilho 1911:443; Prietze 1930:139).

CONCLUSIONS

The new state of Damagaram underwent manifold changes in the course of its growth in the nineteenth century. A brief summary will serve to place the developments within the West African context and to comment upon their significance.

As with the development of slavery in some European areas where the shortage of labor was greater than the shortage of land (Domar 1970), African rulers in the boundaryless plains of the Sudan used slavery as a method of intensifying and centralizing control over the labor of people who could otherwise simply move on. Although the demands of external trade were also an important factor at the outset, the sultans of Damagaram, as others before them, realized the potential value of slave labor as a source of greater production and, politically, as an agent of their power.

Critical changes occurred in the organization of the military and bureaucratic structure of the kingdom. The shift away from reliance on nobles to reliance upon slaves in the administration created a loyal and stable bulwark for the sultan's authority. It increased his ability as the years went by to mobilize material goods and human services without fear of frequent rebellion. This development was by no means unique in West Africa, but it marked a considerable change in scale of government for the subjects of the kingdom. It also illustrates a common stage in the political development of many West African states. The reliance upon slaves in the bureaucracy was one instance of the difference made when *new* people filled *old offices*. It was their status, and not who they were or where they came from, that made the difference. Increase in the scale of government, although not exclusively attributable to slaves, was reflected by the increase in functional specialization within the bureaucracy (Dunbar 1970, Chs. 5 and 6, passim).

Slaves were employed in every major economic activity of the kingdom. Their addition to the labor pool meant that enough grain and special food crops were available for export. The availability of more manpower and its greater specialization strengthened the production of crafts and manufactured wares for both internal and external markets: in the place of one man who, with his neighbors, engaged in building housetops, an organized shop of thirty-five workers could be established; or larger quantities of skins could be prepared for sale in the trans-Saharan trade. These changes were characteristic of societies involved in the "interior-trade" circuit of nineteenth-century West Africa, in contrast to the Atlantic coastal trade (Meillassoux 1971:53). The tendency of societies to employ more and more slaves as producers of agricultural and manufactured goods enhanced the trade within the West African Sudan. Because of their numbers and the legal demands of their servitude, slaves began to form a subservient class. Claude Meillassoux has described two types of slavery common in the Sudan: that consisting of "rent in labor," wherein slaves were relatively separate from the distribution system of the master, since they owed him only specified quantities of labor; and that of "rent in kind," wherein slaves working their own plots provided a specified percentage of their crop to the master. In the former system, slave status became hereditary; in the latter, a dependent community was created that avoided a master-slave dichotomy in the society (Meillassoux 1971:63-64).

In Damagaram, these processes did not affect all slaves in the same way; change operated differently at different levels of the social structure. For instance, life for a slave at court was precarious: his was a high-risk, high-gain occupation. The rare references to chained slaves in domestic service pertained to servants of the sultan or of his officials in the capital city. On the other hand, a court slave's hopes of wealth, power, and authority were more likely to be fulfilled than were those of the freeman or slave in rural areas. It seems likely, however, that slaves owned by individual farmers could anticipate losing their slave identity over time. If the accounts of Baba of Karo (M. Smith 1954) and Dorugu, Barth's servant, both observers of nineteenth-century customs, are indicative, conversion to Islam, adoption, enfranchisement, and marriage within the family certainly erased the stigma and eventually the consciousness of slave origin. By contrast, slaves attached to the throne, or to other titled officials, or those who were settled in villages, retained their slave identity over generations.

The slave system was not so highly profitable as to discourage manumission, or so cruel as to breed rebellion or to cause immediate flight by the enfranchised slaves from the site of their enslavement. The absence of rebellion did not, I believe, stem from severe repression or total despair.[29] Freedom of movement, prospects of economic gain, integrity of family, access to education and to positions that challenged their intellectual and administrative ability—all these facilitated the slaves' incorporation into the society. The society as a whole benefited from the leaven of a larger genetic and cultural variety—increased numbers, and a more efficient mobilization of human resources.[30]

The side of the slave system that is the most difficult to assess is the psychic, political and economic cost of raiding. Early in the nineteenth century, so-called "pagan" areas suffered the most. Small communities were disrupted or completely destroyed. A late-nineteenth-century estimate by Hourst for the Mission Démographique du Niger claimed that for each captive taken, nine others probably perished in defense of villages or through abandonment and starvation (Fisher and Fisher, 1971:93-97).[31] Thus, sheer loss of life was one important factor in the cost of the slave system. A second was warfare between rival states, a frequent event in the late nineteenth century, which was always accompanied by raids on the population (Meillassoux 1971:53-54, 73; Hill 1972:132). Third, the very fact that slaves in some social situations tended to be assimilated into the local society created the need to procure more slaves (for further discussion on this point, see Hill 1972:132). Whether slave recruitment was a direct or indirect factor, the threat of resort to violence was always just under the surface. This threat created tensions which could not but be felt at the individual and social levels.

Thus, it was at some cost that the Hausa-Kanuri society in nineteenth-century Damagaram created its new forms. Given the value system and conditions of the day, the significance of that cost was not so glaring to the participants as it is to observers a hundred years later. As the sultans consolidated their rule, overall security, mobility, and access to new and more plentiful goods and services helped to found a new social solidarity. But in the end, we do not know the effects of this new solidarity and these new institutions, nor the effects that the associated internal tensions might

29. The likelihood of rebellion in interracial slave societies is discussed by W. J. Wilson (1973) and Elkins (1968), among others.

30. This idea is also put forth by Hiskett (1968). Estimates of Damagaram's population made in the early years of the twentieth century are misleading: large numbers of people fled to the south; others disguised their allegiance to Damagaram in hopes of avoiding taxes. According to boundary commission reports, the southern cantons contained 170,000 people in 1903 A.N.F.-O.M., Tchad I, 2 bis; A.N.S., 3F11, No. 67). My best estimate for the population of Damagaram as a whole at the end of the nineteenth century would be 400,000 to 500,000.

31. Fisher and Fisher also discuss the loss of slaves in the course of their being transported within the Sokoto Empire.

have had in the long run. The colonial period interrupted the unfolding of these processes, and one can only speculate on what the long-range evolution of Damagaram might have been.

GLOSSARY

amana: friendliness, reliability, trust; usage of the term in diplomatic and court circles implied an understanding, alliance.

anna: variant of *arna*.

arne (pl. *arna*): a term of reference for a non-Muslim.

azna: variant of *arna*.

bacucane (pl. *cucenawa*): a person born into slavery.

bauta: slavery.

bawa (pl. *bayi*): a slave.

birni (pl. *birane*): walled town; capital.

buzu (pl. *bugaje*): a Tuareg serf who frequently settled in one of the farming communities in the borderland between savanna and desert.

dimajo (pl. *dimajai*): a person born into slavery.

fanshe: a form of the verb *fansa,* to redeem, to ransom.

gandu (pl. *gandaye*): a large farm or garden, usually for cultivation of grains.

garka (pl. *garaka*): a fenced garden for cultivation of nongrain crops, usually involving irrigation.

gayya: a communal work party.

gayyamna: a variant of *gayauna* (pl. *gayauni*); in this context, a plot of land given by the household head to a person in the household for his own benefit.

jingine kansu: "pawned themselves," from the verb *jingina*.

kambe: a free person.

k'etara shimge: "the one who crosses the fence"; in this context, a categorical term for slaves likely to escape because of their physical strength.

ladan yaki: "reward of war," i.e., a share of the booty.

liman (pl. *limamai*): an officiating Muslim priest.

mai tsaren bayi: a guard of enchained slaves.

malami (pl. *malamai*): a teacher.

razzia: of Arabic derivation, used by nineteenth-century European writers to mean "raid."

sarki (pl. *sarakuna*): king; village headman.

talaka (pl. *talakawa*): a member of the populace, usually in contrast with *saranta,* "officeholders"; by implication, a subordinate, or person of modest means.

tirailleur: an African soldier in the French army of conquest, frequently serving outside his home area.

wakili (pl. *wakilai*): a representative; a caretaker.

'yan lifidi: cavalrymen.

REFERENCES

ORAL SOURCES

Interviews with informants in Kantche, May 1, 1968.
Interviews with informants in Daura, May 26, 1968.
Liman Mustafa, interviews in Zinder on January 25 and February 25, 1968.
Malam Ali, son of Malam Yaro, interview on March 26, 1968.
Marusa Mustafa, interviews in Zinder in October and November, 1967.
Mohammed Tsoho, interviews in Zengou on January 8 and January 10, 1968.
Sarkin Dawaki Muhamman dan Ari, interviews on January 17, January 19, March 5, and April 25, 1968.

UNPUBLISHED SOURCES

A.A.N.: Archives administratives du Niger, Niamey.
  Brunot, Etude monographique, 1913.
  Frémineau, Notes sur Bellama, 1952.
  Gamory-Dubourdeau, Zinder, 1919-1925.
A.N.F.-O.M.: Archives nationales de France, section Outre-Mer, Paris.
  Tchad 1, 2 bis.
A.N.S.: Archives nationales du Sénégal, Dakar.
  11G5, No. 207; 3F11, No. 67.
Dunbar, R. A. 1970. Damagaram (Zinder, Niger), 1812-1906: the history of a Central Sudanic kingdom. Ph.D. dissertation, Univ. of California, Los Angeles.
N.N.A.: Nigerian National Archives, Kaduna.
  Arabic letterbook, Kadcap Box 43-3, 1900.

PUBLISHED SOURCES

Abadie, M. 1927. *La colonie du Niger*. Paris.
Balewa, A. T. 1955. *Shaihu Umar*. Zaria.
Barth, H. 1857/1965. *Travels and discoveries in North and Central Africa, 1849-1855*. Centenary ed., 3 vols., 1965. London.
Cazemajou, G. C. 1900. Du Niger vers le lac Tchad: journal de route du capitaine Cazemajou. *Bull. Com. Afr. fr.* 10:302-62.
Cohen, R. 1967. Slavery among the Kanuri. *Trans-Action* 4:48-50.
Domar, E. D. 1970. The causes of slavery or serfdom: a hypothesis. *J. econ. Hist.* 30:18-32.
Elkins, S. 1968. *Slavery*. 2d ed. Chicago.
Fisher, A. G. B., and Fisher, H. J. 1971. *Slavery and Muslim society in Africa*. New York.
Gaden, H. 1903. Notice sur la résidence de Zinder. *Revue Troupes colon.* 2:608-56, 740-94.
Genovese, E. D. 1969. The treatment of slaves in different countries: problems in the application of the comparative method. In *Slavery in the New*

World: a reader in comparative history, ed. L. Foner and E. D. Genovese. Englewood Cliffs, N. J.

Greenberg, J. H. 1946. *The influence of Islam on a Sudanese religion.* Monographs of the American Ethnological Society. New York.

Hill, P. 1972. *Rural Hausa: a village and a setting.* Cambridge.

Hiskett, M. 1968. The historical background to Lugard's occupation of northern Nigeria. Critical introduction to *Native races and their rulers,* by C. L. Temple. 2d ed. London.

Meillassoux, C. 1971. Introduction. In *The development of indigenous trade and markets in West Africa,* ed. C. Meillassoux. London.

Mez, A. 1973. *The renaissance of Islam.* Tr. by S. Khuda Bakhsh. Patna.

Monteil, P. L. 1894. *De Saint-Louis à Tripoli par le lac Tchad.* Paris.

Nachtigal, G. 1971. *Sahara and Sudan.* London.

Nicholas, G. 1962. Un village Bouzou du Niger. *Cah. d'outre-mer* 18:147- 54.

Prietze, R. 1930. Bornu-Texte. *Mitteilungen des Seminars für Orientalische Sprachen* 33:111-59.

Richardson, J. 1854. *Narrative of a mission to central Africa.* Vol. 2. London.

Salifou, A. 1971. *Le Damagaram, ou le sultanat de Zinder au XIXe siècle.* Etudes nigériennes, No. 27, Niamey.

Schön, J. F. 1885. *Magana Hausa.* [Hausa and English text.] London.

Smith, M. 1954. *Baba of Karo.* London.

Smith, M. G. 1954. Slavery and emancipation in two societies. *Social econ. Stud.* 3:239-90.

_____. 1955. *The economy of Hausa communities of Zaria.* London.

_____. 1960. *Government in Zazzau, 1800-1950.* London.

Tilho. 1911. *Documents scientifiques de la mission Tilho.* Vol. 2. Paris.

Urvoy, Y. 1949. *Histoire de l'empire de Bornou.* Paris.

Veillard, G. 1939. Coutumier du cercle de Zinder, 1932. In Vol. 3 of *Coutumiers juridiques de l'Afrique occidentale française.* 3 vols. Paris.

Wilson, G., and Wilson, M. 1965. *The analysis of social change.* Cambridge.

Wilson, W. J. 1973. *Power, racism, and privilege.* New York.

Slavery in
the Structure of
Descent Groups

Part IV

7

Wono: Institutionalized Dependency in Sherbro Descent Groups

(Sierra Leone)

Carol P. MacCormack

The Sherbro represent the southern half of the ethnic group known in fifteenth- and sixteenth-century accounts as the Bullom, who then occupied the low-lying coastal region roughly between Cape Verga and Cape Mount (Rodney 1970:9).[1] In the mid-seventeenth century, the Temne, migrating down the Sierra Leone River to the coast, cut the Bullom in half (Fyfe 1962:3) and eventually assimilated them in the area north of the Sierra Leone estuary. The term Sherbro now designates the southern Bullom, who occupy an area that extends about one hundred miles down the coast from Freetown, reaches into the interior about thirty miles, and includes Sherbro, Plantain, and other offshore islands. They number about 73,000 persons.

The Sherbro area is forested and low-lying, drained by several broad rivers. Population in Sherbro chiefdoms has always been sparse, and it now seldom exceeds one hundred persons per square mile (Clark 1966:43). People reside in compounds which contain extended kin and

1. Fieldwork and archival work for this chapter were generously financed by grants from the National Science Foundation and the American Philosophical Society.

Map 7. Sherbro Area

Cartographic Laboratory UW-Madison

clients, and which are clustered into villages. There have been no large
towns in the Sherbro area except for the trading town of Bonthe. The
area's economy is based on shallow-water fishing, hoe cultivation of rice
and cassava, and production of salt and palm oil, which have been
extracted for centuries. Before European contact the Sherbro apparently
were not extensive traders, except perhaps in salt. After contact, ivory,
slaves, timber, palm products, and, most recently, minerals have been the
principal exports.

European trade began in the 1460s with Portuguese ships calling along
the Sherbro coast, exchanging manufactured goods for ivory and slaves.
About 1545 the Mane, a Mande-speaking people, invaded the Sherbro
area from the south (Rodney 1970:46). They were dreaded warriors and
some Sherbro, fleeing from their advance, took refuge on Portuguese
ships, where they were enslaved (Fyfe 1962:2; Kup 1962:131).

As the Mane consolidated their political hegemony, they sold dissidents to traders on waiting ships. Then, responding to a more commercial motive, Mane leaders organized raiding parties to collect captives for sale. During the long reign of Farma, the first Mane overlord, who died in 1606, as many as twenty to thirty ocean-going vessels might lie along the Bullom shore at one time, loading slaves (Rodney 1970:102).

Following the reign of Farma, military domination by the Mane, who were too few in number to colonize, began to wane. In the north they were defeated by Susu and Fula, Muslim people who began to trickle into the Sherbro area to trade in salt, slaves, and other commodities. They sometimes sold their services as warriors to Sherbro leaders, but never attempted armed conquest of Sherbroland.

In the eighteenth century another Mande-speaking group, the Mende, began migrating into the Sherbro area, primarily in response to commercial opportunities on the coast. Oral tradition stresses their rather peaceful accommodation through clientage and marriage. In the nineteenth century, however, armed conflicts occurred with increasing frequency, the situation being exacerbated by the coastal slave trade, which provided a ready market for captives.

The situation was made more complex by the fact that many coastal "Sherbro" leaders in the nineteenth century, some recognized by the British as treaty chiefs, were mulatto descendants of European traders and women of indigenous Sherbro ruling lineages. Bearing the name Domingo, Tucker, Rodgers, or Caulker, the traders had acted as middlemen for a wide range of trade commodities, including slaves.

The history of Sierra Leone as a British colony is marked by abolitionist zeal as much as by zest for trade. The Sierra Leone Colony at Freetown was established in 1787 as a home for repatriated slaves. When slave trading in the British Empire became illegal in 1807, slaves in considerable numbers continued to be exported from the Sherbro coast, immediately south of the Sierra Leone Colony. In 1826 Governor Macaulay estimated that 20,000 slaves were exported annually from the Gallinas area at the southern end of the Sherbro coast (P.R.O., Macaulay 1826). Macaulay's predecessor, Governor Turner, had urged annexation of the Sherbro coast to the colony in 1825, but major annexations did not begin until 1861, when British Sherbro was ceded. British Sherbro consisted of Sherbro Island, small islands in the Sherbro estuary, and an ill-defined area of mainland across the estuary, extending inland about 30 miles (Fyfe 1962:309, 371). By 1881 all the Sherbro ethnic area between British Sherbro and the Freetown peninsula had been ceded (Fyfe 1962:430). The remaining Sherbro ethnic area came under British administration when the protectorate was declared in 1896. The protectorate and the colony, in

1896, together were roughly equivalent to the present Republic of Sierra Leone.

Two years after establishment of the protectorate, a rebellion broke out. Chiefs resented taxation and the diminution of their authority, and they feared that they would be deprived of their domestic slaves (Sierra Leone 1898). The rebellion was put down, and little was done about the relatively benign institution of domestic slavery until it was finally made illegal in 1927. Thus, the Sherbro coast has long been involved in the slave trade, with Mane, Mende, and Sherbro selling captives to Europeans for export. At least since the time of the Mane invasion, Bullom-Sherbro society appears to have been stratified into ruling descent groups and commoner groups (Kalous 1973:111). Regarding a further category, that of domestic slaves, Rodney (1970:108, 290ff.) has concluded from documentary evidence that it did not exist prior to European contact. Sherbro oral tradition strengthens Rodney's conclusions by suggesting great antiquity for a sociopolitical structure in which clients adhered to people of influence but were free to change their allegiance. Not until the eighteenth century do we have a clear picture of domestic slaves as a social category. They were persons owned as heritable property, who resided involuntarily in their masters' households or in nearby villages ruled by the masters' deputies.

SHERBRO SOCIAL AND POLITICAL STRUCTURE

Sherbro society, structured into ranked descent groups, was quite fluid until the late nineteenth century, with descent groups waxing and waning in political influence. In precolonial times a prominent member of an influential group took on executive functions, acting as head, or "chief," of a village or an area of many villages. These leaders' influence derived from birth, marriage alliances, patronage, diplomacy with other groups, trade, and war. Those with most influence were "paramount chiefs" in political and trade matters over those with more localized support.[2] Only after the protectorate was established did the office of chief become formalized; then chiefdom boundaries were drawn and only a limited set of descent groups were recognized by government as having the right to rule. Today the Sherbro reside in about seventeen such chiefdoms along the southern coast, each chiefdom containing some 25,000 people of various ethnicities. Sherbro paramount chiefs rule in nine chiefdoms, but only a small fraction of the residents of a chiefdom are members of the incumbent ruling descent group.

2. Crowder and Ikime (1970:ix-x) note the range of offices designated "chief" in precolonial West Africa, and the lack of a suitable definition for the term. See Finnegan and Murray in the same volume (pp. 407-36) for an account of the changing nature of chieftaincy in Sierra Leone.

Chiefly groups reckon their descent from a named ancestor who moved into an area, often as a hunter of elephant or other large animals. If he established himself at the hunting site with wives, adhering kin, clients, and domestic slaves, and if the area prospered, he and his descendants became local leaders. After death they became revered ancestors, a source of blessings on people and the land. In some cases, the founding ancestor was a conquering warrior or a warrior who was invited to come and provide protection for the local population. He was given, or took, a politically dominant role which his successors inherited. Descendants of such prominent individuals enjoy the status of "owners of the land" and have the right to be considered as candidates for chiefly office. Chiefs were chosen by consensus of the elders in precolonial times, and are now indirectly elected. Another office is that of head of the descent group, be it a chiefly or a commoner group. The office is usually filled by the eldest member of the group, who has ritual functions and who allocates, after consultation with other elders, use of the group's land and other communal resources. There are some commoner groups that may have had considerable influence in the past but have been eclipsed by another group and no longer control access to much farmland or to chiefly offices.

An important sociopolitical category is that of a "stranger" group, which originates when an outsider comes to a person of prominence and attaches himself to that person and his land in a patron-client relationship. If the stranger prospers, his descendants may become quite numerous. In a fluid political system such a group may manage, in time, to muster a kind of legitimacy that would allow it to make a bid for control of land and leadership.

Sherbro descent groups are nonunilineal; an individual's claim to be a member may be made through either a male or female link, although there is a patrilineal preference. The matrilateral connection is usually stressed when the mother's or father's mother's group is of high status. If, for a multitude of reasons, a person is living in an area where land is controlled by a descent group to which he or she has a matrilateral claim, that claim may be invoked. The benefits of affiliation are seen as reciprocal, with the resident contributing to the group as well as using its resources. Today, a person who becomes successful in business, a profession, or politics at the national level is urged by both his father's and his mother's group to take up residence in their local area and to bring with him schools, improved roads, or other benefits of his influence. When a chief is to be chosen, candidates who may have been residing elsewhere return to their ancestral land. Functionally, then, descent groups consist of the resident nonunilineal descendants of an ancestor.

If a male of a nonruling group marries a woman of a chiefly group, the children will likely be absorbed into their mother's kin group. If a male of a chiefly group marries any woman, even a slave, his children will certainly be regarded as "owners of the land" and will have the right to contest for the chieftaincy.[3]

In general, living members of the larger and more important groups—and these may number thousands of members, scattered throughout the country—cannot trace all the genealogical links to their founding ancestor. But these groups are usually divided into politically significant, locally named segments of smaller genealogical depth, where all ancestors are known. In some cases, as in Bumpe and Kagboro chiefdoms, segmentation has resulted in a situation in which paramount chiefs of the same group rule in two adjacent chiefdoms. Even within the genealogically shallower groups, rival candidates from minimal segments stand against each other in chieftaincy elections. During the nineteenth century, this internal competition resulted in warfare and looting and capture of persons, some of whom became domestic slaves while others were sold by their captors to merchants.

Members of named descent groups with local pedigree are *ram de,* ram being the Sherbro word for descent group. Ram de are described as "owners of the land." The title stresses those groups that have had, since colonial times, the exclusive right to put forth candidates for chieftaincy. More loosely, it also includes other ancient groups with lapsed influence, who are technically "commoners." Those who are outside these groups are "strangers." Strangers were either clients or domestic slaves. When a client came to an area seeking to attach himself to an "owner of the land," he approached his desired patron by greeting him with the "shake-hand," a small gift which was perhaps no more than a shilling. The gift symbolized a relationship in which the client initiated the socioeconomic bond and could leave whenever he wished.

A domestic slave was transferred involuntarily into a household through capture, inheritance, gift, or purchase. In the case of purchase, the master paid wealth out for the slave, the payment symbolizing a relationship of bondage in which the slave could not leave his master.

Slave children have been confused with wards in some archival sources. Wards are children sent into nonnatal households for training and any other advantages the household might provide. Most Sherbro have been wards, since parents feel they are too fond of their own children to be able

---

3. One Sherbro paramount chief, Thomas Neale Caulker, who was murdered in 1898, was "looked upon with contempt as the son of a bondswoman" (Caulker 1908, Pt. 2, p. 26). Opposition to his rule stemmed, however, from a number of other causes. This charge may have been used because his enemies felt it would strike a responsive chord with the British colonial government in Freetown, which was concerned with legitimacy of chiefs.

to discipline and guide them properly in the hard realities of life. Wards are transferred within a descent group and between descent groups. Clients may exchange wards among themselves, but prefer to send their children "upward" into households of a ram, usually that of their patron. Children might be adopted into a ram, enjoying the privileges of "owners of the land." All wards are expected to give labor while in the household but are free to leave whenever their parents wish.

THE CONCEPT OF SLAVERY

Domestic slaves are referred to as *wono,* and persons who are not slaves are *mano.* Subsumed under the category of mano are two distinct groups. The highest ranking are ram de, especially those who are patrons to clients and masters to slaves. Below them are their clients. Crosscutting these are wards, persons of temporarily low status because of their youth, who may be children of either ram de or of clients.

There are two Sherbro words for property. *Kuu* is corporate property, which is shared by all in the household, or more broadly, all in the ram; for example, land is kuu and anyone who demonstrates that he is ram de has a usufruct right to the ram's land. *Lok* is heritable property, which belongs to an individual and can be passed on to a specific heir. The term has been broadened to include property transferable by gift or sale.

These terms apply to both things and persons. When a stranger voluntarily attached himself to the head of a household in a patron-client relationship, he was kuu, for he benefited the household or ram by making it grow strong. The expectation that a client would be hardworking, trustworthy, and loyal to those of the ram was implicit. Eventually, he or his children might be incorporated into the ram by marriage or adoption. In contrast to a client, a slave was involuntarily transferred into a household and was lok, property that was acquired by an individual and passed on to his heir. Because he was of such low status, a slave was expected to remain outside the ram, being absorbed neither by adoption nor marriage. Women of the ram should not marry a slave since their children would have their father's low status. Polygynous Sherbro men did have slave wives, but conceptually and functionally they were inferior to wives married with a proper gift or bridewealth, since they could not function to link one kin group with another. Cut loose by slavery from the protection and prestige of their own ram, these women were considered useless in political alliance-making. Only their labor and their procreative abilities were seen as benefits.

Today, as in the past, it is a great insult to address anyone as lok, meaning "you are my slave." Even when slavery was legal, the term lok was not normally used, out of consideration for a slave's feelings. Instead, the term of address was *ta* (son) and *wa* (daughter). A child of the ram would address slave children of his household as *pente* (brother) and *wante* (sister), terms also applied to patrilateral and matrilateral cousins. Reciprocally, slave children referred to children of the ram as pente and wante, and to the head of household as *ba* (father) or, should she be a woman, as *ya* (mother). Ba and ya are terms extended to any respected older person, age-status being carefully observed.

The use of kin terms in addressing slaves both incorporates and sets apart. Today, English-speaking Sherbros say of those who were domestic slaves: "We call them our cousins." The term connotes the familylike relation of the slave to the domestic household. But it is also a polite way of expressing the distance of low status and also the ram's marriage bar against slave men, for he who is "cousin" (pente) is such a close kinsman that to marry him would be incestuous.

RIGHTS AND DUTIES OF DOMESTIC SLAVES

A slave was duty bound to give service to his master during life and after death. When a slave was buried, he was often tied hand and foot, the rope coming out of the grave and tied to sticks stuck in the ground. Today the rope continues as a symbol of slave status. Great offense is taken if a child, in play, ties a rope on another, or even if a man rests his hand on a hamock rope while another lies inside. Before placing a slave in the grave, the master might take a switch and strike the dead body to assert authority over the spirit of the slave, sending him to serve the ancestors of the master's ram. The slave was buried in rags or even naked, since he should not own property.

The slave had no right to present a case in the chief's court. Nor could the slave have a spouse other than the one provided by his master. A slave's children were slaves of his master. Women slaves were either retained as wives of their master or given as wives to his male slaves. In the former case the children would be of the master's ram, and in the latter they would be slaves of the master. In practice, however, there were exceptions to these prescriptions and some slaves transcended their status through full incorporation.

In life as in death, the most onerous deprivation for a slave was to be denied dependents. Without clients, existing as a kind of property (kuu), he had no political supporters; and since his children were the property (lok) of his master, he had no descendants. Without children, he had no way to make his ram live and grow, so that it might remember and revere him as an ancestor.

Slaves did have defined rights. Since human blood spilled in violence defiles the land, no one in the Sherbro area, including slaves, could be punished by death or by a beating that drew blood. The chief, as court judge, and *Poro,* the men's secret society, protected the well-being of the people and the fertility of the land by imposing fines (*kasi*) and cleansing ceremonies upon whoever did violence. Clearly, in the nineteenth century, Poro men, as warriors, raided and killed. With the cessation of hostilities, however, there would often be *Ndolorgbarteh,* a Poro ceremony "to make the country good" (Caulker 1908: Pt. 2, p. 5). Slaves were entitled to protection by the master against outside molestation; but if their master was not adept at diplomacy or lacked enough influence to attract protecting warriors, slaves might by taken as booty in raids. Slaves also had a right to enough land to subsist on, but they were obliged to work in a group and to cultivate plots that produced a surplus for their master. Occasionally they were called upon for heavy tasks such as clearing roads or draining swamps to bring them into swamp-rice production.

Slaves seem to have had a right to considerate treatment and a degree of respect. It is said that if a slave did something irritating and his master, out of vexation, addressed him as wono (slave), the slave would respond by saying: "Is it I whom you call a slave? I will go and weep under that big tree." If the master then went to him in a spirit of reconciliation, the slave would reconfirm his loyalty by saying: "From today, you are my father and mother." If the master refused reconciliation, the slave might go to an influential person and seek his protection. If that person was sympathetic to the slave, or thought attention should be drawn to the shameful behavior of the master, he might agree to "sit near" the slave as his protector. Then the master, to regain his slave, would have to approach a mediating group, usually the chief and other officials of his town, "begging" them to "beg" the slave to return. The officials would then accompany the slave to his master, who would publicly speak well of the slave and offer the officials a kola or other small gift for restoring the slave to him. This procedure is similar to that of a husband retrieving his wife after she had gone to her own people following some domestic difficulty. People say, rather pragmatically, that experience had taught them that this diplomatic way of dealing with slaves was best. If they chased a slave, bound him, brought him back and beat him, he would only run away again at the first opportunity.

Slaves seldom ran away to claim freedom in the colony, although Free-town and, in the latter part of the nineteenth century, British Sherbro were near at hand, Francis F. Pinkett, the administrator-in-chief of British Sherbro, commented to the earl of Derby in 1883: "Domestic slavery in these parts is not what writers paint; the slave lives as well as his master, and sure I am that hundreds of slaves come into Freetown every year and willingly go back with their masters. The native canoes that come from the neighboring territories bringing produce are unquestionably often manned by slaves who come and go without any wish to change their condition" (P.P., Pinkett 1883). Earlier, in 1875, Governor Kortright had remarked to the earl of Carnarvon on the small number of domestic slaves in the Sherbro area who showed any indication of wanting to change their status (P.P., Kortright 1875).

There seem to be three main reasons why slaves seldom ran away. In the first place, one must consider the entire institutional setting of slavery, including its kinshiplike aspects. From infancy, Sherbro are impressed with the need to respect and obey their superiors, however they are defined. If an individual was sold into slavery, his obedience to his new master was defined as analogous to a child's obedience to his parents, or a ward's to his guardians. The terms used to address a slave, ta and wa (son and daughter), reinforced the analogy.

Obedience training is part of initiation into the secret societies, and slaves were universally initiated into Poro, the men's secret society, and Bondo, the women's.[4] Slave children went into the same grove for initiation as the children of their masters; however, especially in Poro initiation, they usually stayed longer, working for the officials of the society. As one Poro man described it: "They learn to be perfectly loyal and obedient. If one were sent to Freetown with a message, he went straight away, finding his own transport, and would never come back without delivering the message and bringing the reply" (interview: Sumner 1970). After initiation, all Poro men, slave and free, had the same basic rights of manhood within Poro, and Poro men I queried said that Poro would not act as a police force to retrieve runaway slaves. However, slaves never rose to become officials in Poro or to command general political influence.[5]

The second reason for the rarity of escape was the practical one for the slave of finding safety and a livelihood. After 1787 he could run away to the colony at Freetown, and after 1861, when parts of the Sherbro coast were annexed, he could go to British Sherbro, where he might obtain wage labor. To appear as a stranger anywhere else, asking for the use of farm-land, he would have had to indentify himself. If, for example, someone presented himself as the son of a particular chief, a messenger would be sent to the chiefdom to verify the fact. If a freeman had misrepresented himself, he might be publicly humiliated by being put in stocks in the place where children play, and women might even pour over him the water in which they had washed fish. If he was a slave, he would be sent back immediately to his master, for to appear to harbor him might incur the wrath of an influential person. A slave who ran away by stealth, intending

4. Known also as Bundu (Krio and Temne) and Sande (Mende). See MacCormack 1975.
5. See Little (1965-66) for political functions of Poro.

never to return, was not treated with the same consideration as a slave who sought reconciliation with his master by asking another influential person to "sit near" him.

A third and probably more important reason why escape was rare was that in the nineteenth century the life of a domestic slave was often better than that of many freemen. A slave was assured enough land to farm and some measure of protection in an era of wars and raids. Everywhere the slave went, he was known to be part of the household of an important person, often a chief, and he usually enjoyed more protection and respect than a freeman of a low-ranking ram or a stranger in a foreign area. In this polygynous society, a young freeman might wait for years before he could hope to accumulate enough wealth and support from elder kin to contract a marriage. Although a slave had no right to demand a wife (or wives) from his master, informants suggest that he obtained one from his rich owner more easily than could an ordinary freeman obtain a wife with wealth from his own relatives. Many women captured as slaves became wives of chiefs and other men of influence, enjoying the security that a wealthy household might provide. In this area of sparse population, labor was a scarce factor of production,[6] and women were especially valued because they were both laborers and procreators.

Since labor was scarce and slaves were costly to obtain through purchase or raiding effort, a master acted in his own self-interest by maintaining his slaves in relative comfort, and encouraging women to reproduce people to insure both the wealth and the continuity of his descent group. Finally, there were avenues for a slave to transcend his status and become a person of consequence himself. Today in the Sherbro area, there are persons of slave families who have become so important that members of higher-ranked families, those who are technically "owners of the land," must go to them for favors and even the use of farmland.

ECONOMIC AND POLITICAL BACKGROUND OF NINETEENTH-CENTURY SHERBRO SLAVERY

Oral traditions about how a ram or its segment arose and took power commonly make reference to the acquisition of slaves as a factor in the rise to prominence. In an example from the southern coast of Sherbro Island, ram Hombai is said to have originated with Hombai, who lived early in the nineteenth century. He killed a large antelope at Belbul; it being too large to carry back, he built a fire and dried it. Then he went to Toma, where he lived, to fetch his wife. Others of his kin also came to Belbul, a place where food was ample, and settled there. Along the river Fama they found

6. Hopkins (1973) discusses the economics of slavery in a wider West African context.

a place to make salt, which they sold on the mainland to Susu traders up the Kagboro River. With the money from the salt, they bought Mende slaves who cleared the forest to make cassava farms and harvest palm fruits.

In a second example, from the mainland, members of ram Ya Kumba were the "owners of the land" in the Kagboro River area for centuries. In the early nineteenth century, Tasso, at the mouth of the Kagboro River, was an important salt-making site. Tasso salt was traded for Mende and Kono slaves, who then made farms for the "owners of the land." Slaves were settled in villages clustered around Tasso. One, Yondu, just up the coast from Tasso, means "slave" in the Kono language; other slave villages were Marthin, Dibia, Pati, and Tisana. Although Tasso is now largely abandoned, it remains the location of the major Poro initiation grove in the lower Kagboro and the burial ground for ram de. The satellite slave villages were headed by a member of the ram, or in some cases by one of the chief's noble-born wives. In this area of villages clustered around Tasso, by the latter half of the nineteenth century slaves and clients together far outnumbered those who were ram de.

These examples serve to illustrate that, in the nineteenth century and no doubt earlier as well, slave populations served two functions. Slaves did the heavy farming, which hunting, fishing, salt-making, and trading people preferred not to do. They also swelled the population of the area, adding greatly to the number of dependents who confirmed the status of a politically important man or woman. One could not become a recognized political leader if one had no clustered population over which to exercise hegemony. According to a proverb, "You cannot sit alone and be a chief."

Creoles from Freetown, the descendants of former slaves repatriated from the New World or taken off ships captured at sea, traded in the Sherbro area. Some may have kept domestic slaves, especially persons pawned by another trader in debt (P.R.O., Bidwell 1860). Portuguese-Sherbro and English-Sherbro mulattoes also traded along the coast, keeping domestic slaves, and clearly acted as middlemen in the Atlantic slave trade as well (S.L.A., Lawson 1877 and 1879). Their domestic slaves were used as porters, in the preparation of palm products, and in farming, but a full-fledged plantation system never developed in the Sherbro area. In the nineteenth century, some of these wealthy and literate traders were recognized by colonial authorities as treaty chiefs and were paid stipends to assist other traders and keep peace so that trade could flourish.

One such trading family were the Caulkers, or ram Ba Kakir (Father Caulker), whose origins go back to 1684, when Thomas Corker, an English agent of the Royal African Company, was sent to the Sherbro coast (Fyfe 1962:10). He married a ranking woman of the chiefly ram Ya

Kumba, and their descendants, keeping the patronymic but stressing matrilateral links to the Ya Kumba, became known as "owners of the land." Thomas Stephen Caulker, a treaty chief who died in 1871, was patron to merchants who came to Bendu, Shenge, and Plantain Island. They would deliver goods to him and he, in the manner of a chief, would distribute them through a network of subchiefs and headmen, guaranteeing repayment in cash or goods through the same network (Caulker 1908: Pt. 1, pp. 1ff.). Rum, gin, tabacco, gunpowder, guns, and cotton goods were exchanged for timber, palm oil, and rice (P.P., Davis, March 12, 1875). Although they were held responsible for keeping the area peaceful, there was considerable rivalry and raiding between trading families as well as within them. Captives in the raids were either kept as domestic slaves or sold into the slave trade (Caulker 1908).

Traders like the Caulkers operated through an extensive kin network, and enjoyed a political advantage in being considered, at least marginally, ram de. Most were Poro men and seemed to have used the men's secret society in prohibiting local people from trading with Creoles from Freetown (P.P., Traders, May 11 and 13, 1882). Muslim traders from the north—Susu, Fula, and Mandingo—were largely outside Poro. They began building kinship networks through marriage with ranking Sherbro and enjoyed some political influence through their ability in magic. These "strangers" built up their retinues of laborers and status-validating dependents by attracting clients and buying or keeping captives from trade wars as domestic slaves. They also sent captives north to their homeland for plantation labor or for export from the area of the Scarcies and Mellacori rivers (P.P., Rowe 1875 and 1876, Havelock 1882).

Nineteenth-century Sherbro slavery was in part an artifact of adjustments between ethnic groups. In addition to those mentioned above, the Mende and the Temne (groups which numerically preponderate in Sierra Leone today) were attracted in great numbers to the Sherbro area by commercial opportunities. Accommodations through clientage were usually peaceful, but there were wars with looting and enslavement as well. According to Paramount Chief Foday Kai (interview: 1974), whose father was a Mende warrior chief, when a chief decided to raid an area, his warriors locked all their valuables, their wives, children, and other non-warrior dependents inside their houses, located within stockaded villages. Each victorious warrior, entering the opponents' village, claimed the goods and persons inside each house he broke into. Later the warriors presented the captives to their chief, who took his pick as tribute; the warriors retained the loot and a majority of the persons as their own domestic slaves. Slaves made warriors free of subsistence tasks, allowing them to pursue mercenary warfare. The rewards were such that aggressive enslavement continued throughout most of the nineteenth century (P.P., Pinkett 1883). The Pax Britannica was not effectively imposed until after the protectorate of 1896 had been established and the ensuing rebellion put down.[7]

These were not ethnic wars, however. Some Sherbro chiefs sent gifts (*konany*) to Mende chiefs, hoping to receive in return warriors to assist them in their own political and economic ventures. For example, in the 1870s, Chief Richard Canray Ba Caulker, in a feud with Caulker kinsmen, allied himself with Gbenje, a Mende warrior in Taiama. Being a coastal trader on the lower Bumpe River, Chief Caulker supplied Gbenje and his warriors with imported weapons, other goods, and, of course, the promise of plunder. To strengthen the alliance, Gbenje gave a daughter, Bora, to Chief Caulker as a wife. When she went to him, she was accompanied by her brother Kong. Caulker built the town of Senehun on the upper Bumpe River for her, settled it with slaves, and placed her in authority as town chief. Other Mende warriors, coming to obtain guns and supplies from Chief Caulker, would stay as guests in Senehun. Some settled there, founding towns around Senehun, which were populated with wives, kin, clients, and slaves. Although these Mende lived there as clients of Richard Canray Ba Caulker, they became so numerous and powerful that the Caulkers eventually lost control of the entire upper Bumpe area. It is now a Mende chiefdom named Kongbora after Bora, Chief Caulker's Mende wife, and her brother Kong (Caulker 1908; Abraham 1971:128-29).

WAYS OF BECOMING A SLAVE IN THE NINETEENTH CENTURY

There were several ways of falling into slavery. Capture, as booty in a raid, was one. Not all who were captured, however, became slaves, some being used only as hostages to ransom captives taken in a previous raid by the other side (P.R.O., Randall 1862; P.P., Davis, July 24, 1875, Gpow 1883).

There are oral accounts of enslavement by trickery. For example, the trading family on Plantain Island allegedly would send word to an inland area they wanted to make a large farm, inviting people to come and feast and dance before they worked. Special foods such as biscuits, tabacco, rum, and other strong spirits would be put out. Some allege that "knock-out" chemicals were put in the food and drink. Hundreds would come to the feast and find themselves in the slave pen the next morning. Those tricked into slavery in such a way were most likely to be loaded on ships in the Atlantic trade. Captives in raids were more likely to be incorporated into the captor's household or settled in satellite villages.

7. On the insurrection, see Denzer (1971).

A fine, paid in rice, palm oil, animals, goods, or money, was proper compensation for all grievous offenses in Sherbro society. In cases of homicide, for example, in order to placate ritually the ancestors following such defilement, as well as to compensate the living, the aggrieved segment of a ram had the right to collect a substantial fine. If the murderer and his kin could not pay it, the chief and other officials of the town might sell the murderer or a designated kinsman to a slave dealer.

Since the ram is a corporate group, the person sold into slavery was not necessarily the specific offender. In some cases, a kinsman might be "pledged," having been turned over as security until the offending group could accumulate the requisite wealth. If the fine was never satisfactorily paid, the pawn remained in the heriditary status of slave. Also, pawns were pledged in return for credit to a trader (P.R.O., Pratt 1830).

Another serious offense was adultery with the wife of a chief or other politically prominent person. If unable to pay the fine, the offender or his kin might be sold into slavery. Informants often talk of people being falsely accused, especially if they were political rivals of the chief. A historical example is the case of Charles Caulker, who was sold into slavery by George Stephen Caulker II, Paramount Chief of Kagboro Chiefdom, for allegedly misbehaving with one of his wives. There had been fractious splits in the Caulker ram to the extent that, in 1881, war broke out when William Caulker challenged the authority of the paramount chief. Although Charles Caulker lived with the latter, his sympathies seem to have been with William Caulker. After being sold to a Susu trader for "woman damage," he was taken to the north rivers (Scarcies and Mellacori) but was later redeemed by his sister (Caulker 1908: Pt. 2, p. 26).

The case serves to illustrate another aspect of becoming a slave. One might be born into a chiefly descent group, but status was not solely a matter of genealogy. One was noble by birth and also by the way one thought and behaved. If the junior kinsman of a chief was blatantly disrespectful and treacherous, he might be socially redefined by the elders of the ram as a slave.

If the fine for a serious offense was beyond the means or the will of the offender's kin group to pay, his fate was not automatically slavery. His status, his past behavior, and his present conciliatory or defiant attitude would have a bearing on the penalty. If he was intractable, even a chief's son might be cast loose, just as a naughty child today is sent from the compound. Selling a person into slavery was a way of driving an incorrigible away—at a profit. Even after arriving in the household of his new master, a person might avoid enslavement and become a client instead. If he presented himself with an air of nobility in his speech and behavior, if he was respectful and humble, and if he convinced his master that he had been unjustly condemned, he might be regarded as a client and near equal.

The status of the new master was also a factor. A chief might regard the young man as a client. In taking him and training him properly, he might effect a politically useful alliance with the young man's ram, similar to that made when a ward or wife was taken. If the master's status was low, however, he would not risk being outranked in his own household and would certainly classify the noble newcomer as wono.

When a person became wono, he was the property (lok) of a single person. He might be transferred by gift, for example, to the master's married daughter, joining her at her husband's residence, or he might be inherited by a son or other specific heir. However, many Sherbro of influence, the people who owned most slaves, were rather mobile, moving up and down the coast to trade, or doing work in Freetown. Since most slaves were settled on the land, farming in satellite villages, they were often left behind under the management of a caretaker. The rule regulating use of land required that specific plots revert to the ram segment should the person using that land stay away for a long time. This principle also applied to slaves. After prolonged absence by a specific owner, slaves served those members of the ram segment left in residence, their services being allocated by consensus, just as the use of land was allocated. Thus, in effect, many slaves ceased to be personal property and became a kind of communal property. It is important to stress, however, that they did not change from lok to kuu, since the marriage barrier was still there and they could not be absorbed into the ram, as clients were.

TRANSCENDING THE SLAVE STATUS

The obvious way of transcending the status of wono was to buy one's freedom, the official cost of redemption in 1896 being two pounds sterling for a child and four pounds for an adult (S.L.A., Native Affairs Department 1896). According to informants, the real redemption price in the late nineteenth century varied, and persons from an important family, caught in a raid, were redeemable at a higher price. Again, it is possible that some captives were regarded as hostages rather than lok (personal property).

Wono had ample opportunity to work for themselves, especially if they were settled in satellite villages. Since a slave should not own any property, he would conceal the accumulating wealth, as today people conceal wealth against the claims of their "fathers" (ba) and other kin. A master might know that his slave was working to free himself, but to be generous was a virtue and a master of good character was not to put obstacles in the slave's way.

When a slave had his redemption money in hand, he took it to a person of influence, usually of his own ethnic group, in another town. That person, calling himself the slave's "cousin" (pente or wante), would offer the money to the master. In this way a slave became mano, transferring himself from his master to his new patron. He was no longer wono (slave) but mano (client), no longer lok but kuu.

If he did not succeed in attaching himself to a benevolent patron, then becoming free might not be a slave's best strategy. Rather than become a vulnerable commoner, with no land and no one to protect him, he might fare better if he remained attached to his master. If he could demonstrate that he was a person of noble character—respectful, loyal, intelligent—there were rewards to be enjoyed in a slave status.

To say that, in principle, mobility could be achieved through "character" takes us into the difficult realm of psychology. One can only speculate about the subtle forces at work within households that shaped the slave child's personality. A man of a ruling ram, who spent his childhood in a household with slave children, tells of his mother portioning out food to the children, all portions kept scrupulously equal, since no overt favoritism was to be shown. But the free boy's portion might include a piece of bone with meat while his slave "brother" was given only meat. The latter quickly ate his, then asked for some from his companion, who was slowly eating the meat from the bone. The freeborn child would then say: "Yes, I will give you some if you will fetch that thing over there for me" thus encouraging the acting out of their respective future roles (interview: Sumner 1970). Discipline was in some respects more lenient with slave children; they were often allowed to go out at night while the freeborn of the household were not. Slave children might not be required to wash as often. If a freeborn child lied, he was punished, but lies were more tolerated in a slave child, the attitude being: "What can you expect?" The above informant recalled being flogged by his mother, who repeated with each lash: "Don't act like a slave."

Whatever the possible effects of these handicaps, some slaves were quite successful. Without formally being given the status of mano (freeman), a slave could become a person of influence. A trusted domestic would sometimes be appointed by his master as a "tutor" in the family, with the authority to punish his young charges as freely as would their father or mother. After long residence in a community, a slave might be given considerable managerial responsibilities by his master, and might even find himself in charge of the household on his master's death. He would look after the affairs of the family, skimming small earnings off for himself. He would conceal those earnings, but as they accumulated over a long period of time, he might become quite wealthy in his own right.

Without actually buying his freedom, a slave could become so widely respected in the community through his authority in his master's household that in some contexts he would no longer be regarded as wono.

Although wono were of such low status that they were "those whom we would not marry," there are cases where, after years of loyal and able service, a trusted slave would be given a woman of his master's ram as a wife. Freeborn children of the household would then address him as *ba mi* (my father). The children of the marriage would not take slave status from their father, as was the usual case, but would be considered ram de, freeborn through their mother. Having achieved this degree of incorporation into the ram, the slave was not, however, entirely secure in his status. If he offended elders of the household, his wife might be "unbedded" and sent away to a different place, plunging him down to a very low status.

A slave child might be adopted into a household in a public ceremony and, at the time of his initiation into Poro, might be given the name of an ancestor of the ram. Such a child could become his master's heir and even successor. He could inherit movable property and the right to share in the control of the ram's communal property. In at least one case, in Kagboro Chiefdom, an adopted "son" of the ram became paramount chief.

There is a distinction to be made between the kind of slaves considered above, who were part of the household of an important person, and those farmed out to satellite villages. The latter simply lived on the land much as freemen would. If their well-being was threatened, however, they looked to the master and his ancestors for amelioration, since they were deprived by slavery of membership in their own corporate ram, with its wise elders and benevolent ancestors. The slave villages being spatially peripheral to the master's household, slaves were often so little supervised that one can give some credence to archival accounts of slaves who kept slaves; a paradox, since slaves could not own property. Some slaves in satellite villages, adept at concealing all kinds of wealth, may indeed have built up a personal group of dependents; or these reports may deal with persons who, though technically slaves, had been given considerable managerial responsibility by their masters. Finally, there is the possibility that European observers may have confused clientage with slavery (P.P., Rowe, January 28, 1876).

In 1855 the United Brethren in Christ, an American Protestant church, began to establish a number of missions and schools in the Sherbro area. They insisted on making education available to all children, slave and free. Although the missionaries occasionally wrote about Poro members carrying "cheeky" slave boys away from school to remind them of their humble and subservient status (Flickinger 1885:184), in general the ram elders encouraged some of their slaves to become well educated so that they might better serve their masters. Some educated slaves became people of influence, and their compounds today show every sign of prosperity. Although there was some mobility in the Sherbro social system, which allowed some slaves to transcend their status through loyal service and intelligence, it was a limited and very selective process. Even today, prosperous wono families remain socially apart as "those whom we would not marry," noble birth being more important than any position derived from visible wealth.

CONCLUSIONS

A chief is spoken of with regard if his chiefdom is "peaceful" or "quiet" —that is, if he is in firm control and the area is not disturbed by famine, disease, or political dissension. For centuries, those who might disturb the peace have been brought under social control by threats of retribution from angry ancestors, by fines, and, in cases of incorrigible behavior, by banishment. After the introduction of large-scale commercial trade and a money economy, following European contact, banishment was accompanied by economic gain: the incorrigible was sold to a dealer as a slave.

Because the ram is a corporate group, and because high social status is confirmed by having many dependents, Sherbro society was in the past and remains today a rather egalitarian system in an economic sense. To be sure, some of the coastal traders lived in European opulence (Wadstrom 1794/1964:99) and some contemporary Sherbro, who are successful in professions and politics, live in obvious comfort in Freetown. But gifts used in diplomacy and claims from kin and other dependents tend to drain disposable wealth away from an economically successful person, spreading it thinly over a wide social field. The first British district commissioner in the Sherbro area, traveling through the hinterland in the late nineteenth century, commented on the chiefs' "very great objection to any ostentatious display" in the Sherbro and Mende country (Alldridge 1901:191). Although he could not identify a chief by his rich gown, he could detect a man of importance by the number of wives and others who attended him. Riches were not so much in things as in persons.

Before European contact, a person obtained adhering dependents through marriage alliances made with bridewealth given in food, native cloth, and other goods. He hoped to obtain many wives and children, who would work his farms and produce surpluses, which could be used to obtain still more wives and descendants. He also attracted clients by his reputation for generosity and his political and ritual skill in keeping them free from disease, famine, and other harm. The reach of a leader's influence was limited by the resources he could give away, the amount of confidence and respect he could command, and by the number of dependents he could acquire by natural increase from his wives and by clientage. With the onset of commercial trade in persons, he could further augment his group of adhering dependents by organizing and financing raids or simply buying domestic slaves.

Since slaves did not come to him through voluntary alliance, as his wives did, nor through voluntary clientage, he was faced with the task of binding them to himself in loyalty and obedience. Rather than resort to coercive force, which was often the New World solution, the Sherbro master tended to use the same blend of considerate treatment and firm authority that "good" parents use with their children and wards. Obedient dependence was encouraged by benevolent paternalism and further insured by denying slaves their own property. They had no wealth for konany, the gift which might induce a chief to protect them with his warriors. They held no commanding offices in Poro, where men were trained in the skills of warfare and bonded into warrior groups. Finally, they could not attract clients as loyal supporters nor could they even have kin organized into a corporate group. Since a slave could not claim his children as descendants to carry on his ram, he would not be remembered with reverence after death as an ancestor. Slaves were not part of their own corporate structure, which provided wise elders and ancestors who smiled with benevolence at one moment and frowned with righteous indignation at another. Instead, slaves could only rely on their master and his ancestors for guidance and protection. The master's political power and authority was maintained inversely with the political initiative of his dependents. In this political context, slaves—children in the legal, ritual, economic, and social sense—were the ideal dependents, providing maximum dependence and minimum challenge.

GLOSSARY

ba: father, or respected older man.
Bondo: women's secret society.
kasi: a fine.
konany: a gift.
kuu: corporate property.
lok: heritable property (could apply to slaves).
mano: a freeman.
Ndolorgbarteh: a *Poro* purification ceremony that took place after raids and
          killings.
pente: brother (or cousin).
Poro: men's secret society.

ram: descent group.
ram de: "owners of the land."
ta: son.
wa: daughter.
wante: sister (or cousin).
wono: a domestic slave.
ya: mother, or respected older woman.

REFERENCES

ORAL SOURCES
Interviews with Foday Kai, Paramount Chief, Telu, Sierra Leone, 1974.
Interviews with D. L. Sumner (of ram Ba Kakir), Shenge, Sierra Leone, 1970.

UNPUBLISHED SOURCES
Abraham, A. 1971. The rise of traditional leadership among the Mende. M.A.
    thesis, Fourah Bay College, University of Sierra Leone.
P.R.O.: Colonial Office Dispatches, Public Record Office, London.
    Macaulay to Bathurst, March 9, 1826. C.O. 267/72.
    Randall to Raffell, September 2, 1826. C.O. 267/73.
    Pratt to Cole, November 19, 1830. C.O. 267/105.
    Bidwell to Police Office, March 20, 1860. C.O. 267/266.
S.L.A.: Sierra Leone Archives, Freetown.
    Government Interpreter's Letter Book, 1876-78: Lawson to Rowe, December
        15, 1877.
    Government Interpreter's Letter Book, 1878-80: Lawson to Rowe, February
        14, 1879.
    Native Affairs Department Letter Book, 1895-96: Native Affairs Department
        to Chiefs. October 21, 1896.

PUBLISHED SOURCES
Alldridge, T. J. 1901. *The Sherbro and its hinterland*. London.
[Caulker.] 1908. Caulker manuscript. *Sierra Leone Stud*. Old ser., nos. 4, 6, 7.
    (Original copy of the manuscript is in the Sierra Leone Archives, Free-
    town.)
Clark, J. I. 1966. *Sierra Leone in maps*. London.
Crowder, M., and Ikime, O., eds. 1970. *West African chiefs: their changing
    status under colonial rule and independence*. Ile-Ife.
Denzer, L. 1971. Sierra Leone-Bai Bureh. In *West African resistance: the mili-
    tary response to colonial occupation*, ed. M. Crowder. London.
Flickinger, D. K. 1885. *Thirty years of missionary life in western Africa*.
    Dayton, Ohio.
Fyfe, C. 1962. *A history of Sierra Leone*. London.

Hopkins, A. G. 1973. *An economic history of West Africa.* London.

Kalous, M. 1973. Some remarks on the Bulom group in Sierra Leone. *Afrika und Übersee* 57:106-14.

Kup, P. 1962. *A history of Sierra Leone, 1400-1787.* Cambridge.

Little, K. 1965, 1966. The political function of the Poro. *Africa* 35:349-65, 62-71.

MacCormack, C. P. 1975. Sande women and political power in Sierra Leone. *W. Afr. J. Sociol. polit. Sci.* 1:42-50.

P.P.: Great Britain, *Parliamentary papers.*

Davis to Kortright, March 12, 1875. In Vol. 52 (*Accounts and papers,* Vol. 11), 1875, p. 807. "Papers relating to Her Majesty's possessions in West Africa; Sierra Leone and the Gold Coast, including Lagos," C. 1343, Pt. I, Enc. 2 in No. 15, p. 17.

Kortright to Carnarvon, June 28, 1875. In Vol. 52 (*Accounts and papers,* Vol. 11), 1875, p. 822. "Papers relating to Her Majesty's possessions in West Africa; Sierra Leone and the Gold Coast, including Lagos," C. 1343, Pt. I, No. 20, p. 37.

Davis to Rowe, July 24, 1875. In Vol. 52 (*Accounts and papers,* Vol. 11), 1876, p. 422. "Papers relating to Her Majesty's possessions in West Africa; Sierra Leone and the Gold Coast, including Lagos," C. 1402, Pt. I., Enc. 13 in No. 2, p. 8.

Rowe to Carnarvon, December 14, 1875. In Vol. 52 (*Accounts and papers,* Vol. 11), 1876, p. 865. "Papers relating to Her Majesty's possessions in West Africa; Sierra Leone and the Gold Coast, including Lagos," C. 1402, Pt. I, No. 42, p. 45.

Rowe to Carnarvon, January 18, 1876. In Vol. 52 (*Accounts and papers,* Vol. 11), 1876, p. 489. "Papers relating to Her Majesty's possessions in West Africa; Sierra Leone and the Gold Coast, including Lagos," C. 1402, Pt. I, No. 53, p. 63.

Rowe to Carnarvon, January 28, 1876. In Vol. 52 (*Accounts and papers,* Vol. 11), 1876, p. 490. "Papers relating to Her Majesty's possessions in West Africa; Sierra Leone and the Gold Coast, including Lagos," C. 1402, Pt. I, No. 55, p. 64.

Traders to Havelock, May 11, 1882. In Vol. 46 (*Accounts and papers,* Vol. 8), 1882, p. 565. "Correspondence respecting the proceedings at the Jong River in May 1882," C. 3420, Enc. 3 in No. 1, p. 13.

Traders to Laborde, May 13, 1882. In Vol. 46 (*Accounts and papers,* Vol. 8), 1882, p. 566. "Correspondence respecting the proceedings at the Jong River in May 1882," C. 3420, Enc. 4 in No. 1, p. 14.

Havelock to Kimberly, June 5, 1882. In Vol. 46 (*Accounts and papers,* Vol. 8), 1882, p. 553. "Correspondence respecting the proceedings at the Jong River in May 1882," C. 3420, No. 1, p. 3.

Gpow to Tucker, March 11, 1883. In Vol. 47 (*Accounts and papers,* Vol. 10), 1883, p. 365. "Correspondence respecting the disturbances in the neighbourhood of British Sherbro in April and May 1883," C. 3765, Enc. 2 in No. 1, p. 9.

Pinkett to Derby, May 16, 1883. In Vol. 47 (*Accounts and papers*, Vol. 10), 1883, p. 371. "Correspondence respecting the disturbances in the neighbourhood of British Sherbro in April and May 1883," C. 3765, No. 4, p. 14.

Rodney, W. 1970. *A history of the upper Guinea coast, 1545-1800.* Oxford.

Sierra Leone. 1898. *Report of Her Majesty's commissioner and correspondence on the subject of the insurrection in the Sierra Leone Protectorate 1898.* Parts 1 and 2. London.

Wadstrom, C. B. 1794/1964. An essay on colonization. Reprinted in *Sierra Leone inheritance,* ed. C. Fyfe, 1964. London.

8

Imbangala
Lineage Slavery

(Angola)

Joseph C. Miller

The Imbangala,[1] one of the KiMbundu-speaking peoples of northwestern Angola, counted many of their number as slaves at the end of the nineteenth century, defining them according to their position on the low end of a continuum that indicated the nature of an individual's affiliation to a lineage, the fundamental group of Imbangala society. Although outsiders have described several types of Imbangala lineage affiliation by analogy to Western slavery, the resemblance of Imbangala slavery to European and American slave systems was limited to its connotation of social inferiority and did not necessarily extend to economic or political disability. Imbangala thought emphasized the fact that slaves had transferred their primary allegiance from their natal lineage to an alien descent group, a notion necessarily absent from conceptualizations of slavery in bilateral societies of European origin. While the term slave may have identified with some precision one category of persons regarded as having originated outside the local descent groups,[2] slaves formed but a single class in a much larger

1. This chapter was written in March 1972 and was subsequently revised. Among the several colleagues who have read and commented on earlier versions, I am especially indebted to Wyatt MacGaffey and John Smail and to the editors of this volume.

2. The definition of slaves as essentially kinless outsiders is hardly original; see, for example, essays by M. I. Finley (1967, 1968, and reprinted in several anthologies).

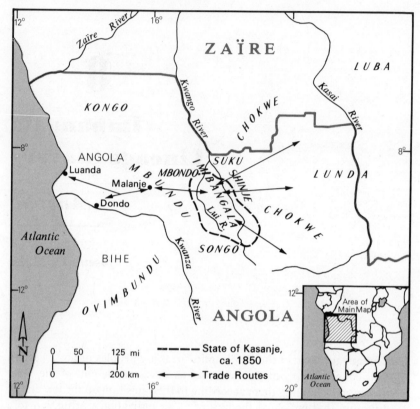

Cartographic Laboratory UW-Madison
Map 8. Mbundu and Neighboring Peoples in the Late Nineteenth Century

field of people who had lost their primary kin-group allegiance. The Imbangala definition of their slaves in terms of their descent groups justifies treating their institutions as examples of what may be termed "lineage slavery."

Imbangala practices during the period from 1870 to 1920 illustrate the range of their modifications of lineage affiliation and the techniques they used to transfer people from one social position to another. My data leave unanswered many questions about Imbangala slavery,[3] especially about

3. The research forming the basis for this chapter concerned political and historical problems rather far removed from the social institutions considered here. Accordingly, social anthropologists will notice the incomplete nature of my ethnographic research. I wish to thank the Foreign Area Fellowship Program of New York for a grant that enabled me to perform fieldwork in Angola during 1969 and 1970. The program bears no responsibility for the conclusions expressed in this chapter nor for the deficiencies in my research.

the empirical workings of a system presently described incompletely and only in an idealized and regularized form. But a number of points based on Imbangala conceptualizations of their social structure help to illuminate their social and political history and thereby demonstrate the value of seeing the world through Imbangala eyes as a preliminary step in the analysis of Imbangala social institutions.

IMBANGALA HISTORY AND SOCIETY

By the late nineteenth and early twentieth centuries, the name Imbangala designated people of varied origins who lived in the broad valley of the Kwango and Lui rivers, just to the east of the then-expanding Portuguese colony of Angola. Most Imbangala matrilineages claimed a tenuous kinship with the belt of matrilineal peoples that stretched over the higher savannas beyond the Kwango, especially those united in a single, segmentary lineage system extending through the Chokwe to the east and the Songo to the south. Other Imbangala matrilineages felt more closely connected to other Mbundu peoples living to the northwest and west, and many Imbangala of slave status would have traced their ancestries as far east as the Lunda and Luba across the Kasai. What united these diverse peoples was their common history as subjects of the once-powerful slave-trading state of Kasanje, whose kings had dominated the Lui-Kwango valley since the first third of the seventeenth century.

Slavery and related methods of modifying lineage affiliation had conditioned Imbangala history since the formation of the Kasanje state. An influx of various peoples from surrounding areas had accompanied the kingdom's growth, and the Kasanje kings had become wealthy and powerful through their monopoly over the sale of people as slaves to European traders. The various means of altering social status had allowed Imbangala to assimilate other aliens into the local society, where they and their descendants accounted for a large proportion of the Imbangala population by the 1870s.

The decades between 1870 and 1920 saw a transition from the slave-trading prime of the Kasanje kings to a period of Portuguese colonial overrule and economic depression. Slave exports from Angola declined after 1850 and the once-unified Kasanje state dissolved into several hostile regional principalities that formed around holders of provincial Kasanje political titles. A Portuguese military column managed to destroy the Kasanje royal emblems in 1911, thus formally ending the kingdom, but effective Portuguese authority did not reach the Imbangala until the 1920s; in the interim the various pretenders were left as independent rulers over sections of the former state. A boom in rubber exports after 1870 had revivified the moribund economy of Angola, and the demand for rubber had given holders of minor Imbangala titles an opportunity to organize and tax long caravans of Imbangala that conveyed small rubber balls from Chokwe east of the Kwango to such Portuguese trading stations as Malanje, Dondo, and Luanda, enriching them and thus contributing to the process of political decentralization. The rubber trade declined after 1900 and left the Imbangala with only a relatively minor commerce in such locally produced items as salt. Final integration of the Imbangala into the Portuguese colonial economy came with the imposition of compulsory cotton cultivation in the 1920s; the distinctly disadvantageous terms of colonial economic policies brought a deep and persistent depression to the region.

With the kingdom of Kasanje well on its way to extinction, Imbangala political thought and action were primarily framed in terms of the exogamous matrilineal descent groups, or *jingundu* (sing. *ngundu*), which formed the oldest and most stable social institutions in the region.[4] Despite the varied ancestries of the Imbangala, all agreed that their jingundu were vital to their lives, allowing contact with important beings in the supernatural world, bestowing the individual's position in society, giving rights to clear land and plant crops and affording means of coercing rainfall, and providing protection from potentially hostile outsiders. In short, the Imbangala placed the ngundu at the very center of human existence, even seeing humanness itself as an attribute of membership in the descent group.[5] If the Imbangala attached an unusual degree of importance to their lineages, their historical experience probably went far to explain why. The earliest Kasanje kings had suppressed many of the crosscutting nonlineage institutions once found in the region (circumcision camps, hunting societies, cults of affliction, and so on), and later rulers entrenched the jingundu descent groups as the major components of the Kasanje state by awarding noble state titles to the lineages as corporate groups. The kings allowed the kin groups to recruit occupants for the noble positions according to their normal matrilineal descent rules (male siblings, dropping to sisters' sons in the succeeding generation), and competition for the royal titles always took place in terms of lineage factions. The rules governing access to political authority in Kasanje thus reinforced the dominance of the jingundu over the lives of most Imbangala and made their lineage affiliation a very important component of their social status.

Imbangala beliefs that have been referred to as "positional succession"

4. My *Kings and Kinsmen: Early States among the Mbundu of Angola* (1976) discusses the evidence for dating the more remote levels of Imbangala lineage genealogies to the sixteenth century or before.

5. Their attitudes resembled those described for the twentieth-century Kongo by Wyatt MacGaffey (1970, esp. Chs. 3 and 4).

defined the ways in which everyone, slave or lineage member, acquired or changed relationship to a descent group. Positional succession[6] relates to the notion that social roles or positions termed "names" by the Imbangala with permanently defined rights and obligations exist independently of actual living persons. Each Imbangala name demanded a human "caretaker," who identified himself with its deceased previous occupants, thus embodying the past in the present and ensuring the continuity of the lineage group that collectively controlled access to each of these positional names. Every Imbangala held one or more positions with their associated rights and privileges (and sometimes disabilities); in the course of a lifetime, they moved from one position to another, seeking to exchange less prestigious statuses for more respected ones. Imbangala children received a succession of names indicating their subordinate positions within the matrilineage (including a birth name, the *jina lya shikaku,* and a name bestowed at puberty, the *jina lya nduku).*[7] The granting of one of a set of adult names owned by their mother's ngundu validated their membership in a lineage at adulthood (interview: Apolo de Matos, October 5, 1969); the adult name established the person's status within the lineage, since all names belonging to an ngundu stood in constant relation to one another and structured the relationships among their holders. This system produced jingundu conceptualized as sets of permanently named positions related to each other by bonds of perpetual kinship and filled through positional succession as the nieces and nephews of adult lineage members assumed names vacated through deaths in their grandparents' generation. In the formal Imbangala view, therefore, jingundu were groupings of perpetual names rather than of particular living individuals.

The Imbangala ranked their named positions according to several hierarchies of prestige within and without the individual lineages. Most named positions brought their holders few rights over the occupants of other positions, but some conferred significant authority over related names within the ngundu, and their holders received elaborately deferential treatment from occupants of positions deemed inferior. In general, names with senior rankings in the perpetual genealogies that linked the

6. I have adopted the terminology of Ian Cunnison (1956). Similar ideas have been widely noted as manifested in political titles in Shaba (among the northern Lunda) and Zambia (Bemba, Mambwe, and the peoples of the Luapula Valley). My research indicates that these notions extend to the social as well as the political institutions of the Mbundu (including the Imbangala) and the Chokwe; Robert Schecter, in a personal communication, has confirmed their presence throughout northwestern Zambia.

7. I have not found a record of the term shikaku among the Mbundu, but Robert Schecter notes that the word occurs in ChiRuund to mean a greeting given upon arrival to a child or younger person; it derives from the verb *kushika,* meaning to arrive. The jina lya nduku apparently is a name taken after a parent or kinsman; see Antonio de Assis, Jr. (n.d.:32).

names to one another merited the respect of holders of junior titles. In addition, each ngundu maintained a few positions with responsibility for the collective welfare of the lineage. One of these titles, the *lemba* (pl. *malemba) dya ngundu* (the "uncle of the matrilineage"), kept alive the name of the alleged founder of the lineage, theoretically a man who had legitimately broken away from some older descent group. The holders of this position had the major responsibility for the survival of the group and for its internal harmony. They discharged these duties by arranging marriages for its nieces and by conducting relations with its ancestors in spirit-possession ceremonies. Holders of other positional names cared for the sacred lineage symbols and interpreted messages received through them from the dead of the lineage. Most Imbangala lineages reserved another set of senior names for their oldest living male members, called *makota* (sing. *kota*), who acted as formal advisers to the lemba dya ngundu and generally attempted to control nominations to most other names in the lineage, including those belonging to a distinct set of political titles. The political titles belonged to the descent groups but were associated with the Kasanje kingdom rather than with the lineages and possessed very different prerogatives and responsibilities from ngundu names. It is important to emphasize the dependence of most Imbangala on the holders of the senior titles, for the senior titleholders' control over access to any social or political position vested them with strong authority and obviated the meaning of personal freedom in Imbangala society.

Fundamental to an understanding of Imbangala slavery is the recognition that individuals routinely exchanged one social status for another by acquiring new positions and their associated rights and obligations. Ambitious Imbangala males tried to work their way through the maze of permanent positions toward titles that brought authority and wealth, often expending large sums along their way. The most successful manipulators of the system held several titles at once, playing with the rights of each to enhance their influence in various social and political contexts. Others moved from their first adult name, usually a lineage position, into the separate hierarchy of political titles of the Kasanje state, aspiring ultimately to reach the position of the king, an office theoretically open to the holder of any political title. Others contented themselves with such influential lineage positions as the lemba dya ngundu, and any male could anticipate an honored old age in one of the makota titles. Kinsmen even temporarily assumed the name and identity of an absent relative on occasions demanding his presence.[8] But less talented people had to

8. Data on positional succession and perpetual kinship among the Imbangala come from a variety of interviews, especially those with Alexandre Vaz and Ngonga a Mbande, September 23, 1969; Apolo de Matos, October 4, 1969; Sousa Calunga, September 10, 1969.

content themselves with positions of little account, and some fell into low-ranking strata that included slaves and others who had lost contact with their own kinsmen.

LINEAGE SLAVERY

The Imbangala defined slaves as persons who had lost the names to which they had a right by birth and had assumed low-status positions affiliated either to other lineages or to one of the Kasanje political titles. These positions for aliens, which Imbangala used to assimilate other strangers of various sorts in addition to slaves, formed a class of names conceptually distinct from the lineage names, just described, that the Imbangala termed *jimbanza* (sing. *mbanza*).[9] The rights and disabilities associated with the alien positions were perceived in relation to the status of the mbanza.

The mbanza—the person eligible to hold an mbanza title by virtue of his or her birth from a female mbanza—possessed the maximum personal autonomy obtainable from membership in an Imbangala matrilineage and had access to any of the ngundu names and titles. The Imbangala regarded mbanza lineage membership as the norm and conceptualized other positions as lying both above and below it; "superior" positions included a number of appointive titles awarded by the Kasanje kings and were described as meriting greater "respect," while inferior positions fell into a variety of categories, including slavery, that denoted less than full integration into the lineage system. The entire hierarchy was defined with regard to lineage affiliation rather than in terms of personal "freedom."

By the late nineteenth century, jimbanza formed a minority of the Imbangala population. Their relatively small numbers resulted from two centuries or more of intensive slave trading in western Angola, which had led to the incorporation of many outsiders in local Imbangala lineages. The influx of outsiders had begun during the seventeenth-century wars that had attended the creation of the Kasanje state; these removed many captives from the security of their native descent groups in the Lui-Kwango valley and in the surrounding regions, integrating them into the formative Imbangala society as direct dependents of holders of Imbangala political titles who settled there at the time. The conquering Imbangala brought with them a sociopolitical system not based on the principles of unilineal descent then prevalent; their main institution was an initiation society called the *kilombo*, which consisted of many followers who had

9. While the word mbanza is well known as referring to a central place, especially a royal compound, in KiKongo and KiMundu, it has the distinct sense of "heir to a perpetual name" among the Imbangala and probably also among the Chokwe and others who live to the southeast of them.

abandoned their lineage affiliation and owed allegiance only to holders of permanent Imbangala political titles.[10] The kilombo type of social organization quickly faded in Kasanje, but left a legacy of people in social positions outside any of the jingundu, affiliated as *abika* (sing. *mubika*)[11] either to one of the resurgent lineages that replaced the kilombo or to one of the Imbangala political titles. Some of the abika who originally regrouped as the dependents of political titles eventually became affiliated to lineages through rules allowing a lineage to inherit the property and dependents of deceased holders of its political titles.

The status referred to as mubika thus designated all people regarded as alien to the local lineages by birth or inheritance of status and defined a category cutting horizontally across the primary social divisions of Imbangala society that delineated its descent groups.[12] During later years, most abika originated as victims of the slave trade outside the boundaries of Kasanje, but some continued to be generated from internal sources. All transferred their affiliation from their natal group to an Imbangala lineage or titleholder by undergoing a *rite de passage.* In the case of the lineages, the lemba dya ngundu first "cleansed" the prospective mubika of all connection with former kinsmen by giving him or her a medicine called *yisaba ya kukuleka*[13] that theoretically eliminated all knowledge of the person's origins. As the Imbangala phrased the matter, they could never "discover the secret of their abika women," that is, the "secret" of the female mubika's natal lineage affiliation, which, if known, might raise doubts about the lineage affiliation of her matrilineal descendants (interview: Mwanya a Shiba, June 14, 1969). This cleansing severed the prospective mubika from his or her original descent group and from the protection of its ancestors and other spirits. It simultaneously relieved the Imbangala lineage of responsibility to the former kinsmen for the mubika's safety, and, as the Imbangala phrased it, "blocked the mubika's

10. A full discussion of the kilombo and evidence supporting this interpretation of it appears in *Kings and Kinsmen* (Ch. 8).

11. Mubika is the standard eastern KiMbundu ("Ambakista") form of a root with reflexes in several neighboring languages; some eastern KiMbundu dialects have *muhika* or *mupika* (Mbondo); Suku has *muhika* as well. Interviews: Apolo de Matos, June 18-19, 1969; Sousa Calunga, August 22, 1969; Sokola, June 12, 1969; Alexandre Vaz and Domingos Vaz, June 26, 1969. See also José Ribeiro da Cruz (1940:66). Ladislaus Magyar (1859:213-14, 288) gave the form -*pika* for nineteenth-century Umbundu (spoken south of the Kwanza River). There seems to have been a different specifically Mbangala form, *mulwe;* see Ribeiro da Cruz (1940:66) and Sigurd von Willer Salazar (n.d., 2:108).

12. Mubika is the word that Europeans have customarily translated as "slave" and have erroneously applied to a number of other distinct positions as defined by the Imbangala.

13. The phrase apparently refers to a bunch of leaves and branches (of an unknown plant or plants), the *yisaba,* used for transferring group affiliation (*kukuleka*). Assis, Jr. (n.d.:140, 198).

desire" to flee back home. The mubika-to-be then entered an extremely precarious stage of the *rite de passage* in which he or she lost the protection of membership in either descent group and became vulnerable to fearsome supernatural forces.

The final phase of the ritual reincorporated the person into his or her new lineage with the formal status of mubika, perhaps best described as an "alien dependent" of the lineage. This part of the ceremony resembled procedures used to award mbanza lineage names to full members of the ngundu but differed in that it assigned one of a relatively limited set of names reserved to abika (interview: Mbondo group).[14] The abika joined the owning lineage with a status subordinate to the full jimbanza and were called *baka a ngundu,* or "people of the lineage," as opposed to the *yihunji* (sing. *kihunji*), the classificatory nieces and nephews of the lemba (interview: Apolo de Matos, June 18-19, 1969). The etiquette of deference required of abika toward the jimbanza varied in detail, but it generally connoted the behavior expected of children toward their parents. It thus fit the model of "child" and "parent" roles that in Imbangala society extended well beyond the narrow biological relationship to apply to such inferior/superior pairs in the sphere of political relations as ruled to rulers, or holders of junior titles to holders of senior titles, or, in the social context, of abika to jimbanza. The abika often clapped their hands as a sign of respect and used an honorific form of address, *mwenyishi* (interview: Mwanya a Shiba, June 14, 1969).[15] Funeral ceremonies likewise underlined the dependence of the abika, since their names, unlike those of the jimbanza, would not remain as permanent fixtures of the lineage structure: Imbangala *intambi* (funerary rituals) preserved the name of each deceased mbanza and thus secured his or her place among the quasi-present ancestors of the ngundu, the deceased holders of the living names. But no such rites attended the death of abika (interview: Sousa Calunga, August 22, 1969), whose names passed unlamented and unremembered from the perpetual universe of Imbangala named positions.

The Imbangala used the term *yijiko* (sing. *kijiko*) to indicate those abika whose primary affiliation lay with one of the Kasanje political titles

14. Cf. Ribeiro da Cruz (1940:67-68), who gave a list of similar abika names in use among Shinje living east of the Imbangala: Nzambi, "kya Kamba" (evidently an incomplete form), Mutombo, Kwata ku Meso, Zambikeje (Nzambi a Keje?), Mwata u Meso, Kambondo (all for males), Kubuku, Tumba, and Ngalula (for females).

15. The title is now a general honorific, although its original and literal meaning seems to have been restricted to titleholders with responsibility for land ownership (*mwene* = lord, *ishi* = a possessed parcel of land). The propriety of this form of address by a slave to his or her owner derived from the fact that the lineages owned the land on which the slaves lived; slaves had no rights of their own to land.

or with an individual lineage name, as opposed to the lineage itself (interview: Apolo de Matos, July 8, 1969; Wensilau Luciano, June 10, 1969).[16] Yijiko had no connection with the *ngola*, the dominant lineage emblem, and were members of groups of dependents called *jijiko* (sing. *jiko*), or "hearths," rather than the lineage itself (interview: Sokola, June 12, 1969). A kijiko's connection with his jiko could, it was said, pass through either the male or female line; in fact, inheritance of kijiko status probably did not violate Imbangala matrilineal preferences but could result from the tendency of owners of yijiko to manipulate their dependents' marriages to maximize the number of descendants under their personal control. Those owners who themselves married their female yijiko had sons who lived with their fathers and were under direct paternal authority (superficially a form of patrifilial descent), but only because the owners' kinless wives had no lineage affiliation to pass on to their children. Owners of male yijiko gave them in marriage to their mbanza sisters or nieces to gain nephews who belonged to their own ngundu by the normal rules of matrilineal descent but who lacked ties to any other (that is, a father's) lineage. The title-holding patron was called a *muku a jiko* (*mukwa jiko*), literally the "owner of the jiko,"[17] in relation to these dependents.

The Imbangala social category of mubika implied no necessary economic deprivation in comparison with non-abika. Among a people who made careers by moving from name to name and role to role, modification of personal status in itself carried no stigma. On the contrary, the abika's distinctive lack of kinsmen other than those of their owner made them valuable lineage or personal retainers in circumstances demanding exclusive loyalty, and patrons rewarded some of their abika accordingly. Influential titleholders found their jimbanza relatives, by contrast, torn between allegiances to a titleholder, duties to their lemba, complex alliances with wives' or fathers' descent groups, and myriad other connections cultivated by most full lineage members. Male abika, for example, were entrusted with trade goods and sent east of the Kwango in large trading caravans to exchange salt, beef, and cloth for Chokwe and Lunda rubber during the late-nineteenth-century boom in rubber exports from

16. Since the kijiko status had no legitimacy under Portuguese legislation abolishing indigenous forms of "slavery," the modern sense of the word designates a dependent lineage segment more or less with the ngundu but closely associated with a titled position; see Assis, Jr. (n.d.:68). Seventeenth-century written sources often used the term for a kind of "slave," and some stated specifically that at that time the yijiko formed part of an individual chief's ("soba's") heritable estate. See António de Oliveira de Cadornega (1972, 1:252).

17. *Muku a* (usually elided to *mukwa*) denotes possession in KiMbundu; see Assis, Jr. (n.d.:304).

Angola.[18] Less-favored abika fit into the normal Mbundu division of labor according to sex, with the men performing tasks requiring use of the heavy long-bladed knife known as a *katana* and the women working with hoes in the fields (interview: Sousa Calunga, September 11, 1969).[19] Wealthy Imbangala jimbanza used other abika as personal servants who cut wood, fetched water, or cultivated lineage lands for their masters (interview: Mbondo group). These occupations hardly distinguished abika from other Imbangala except for the tendency of slaves to be found in sensitive positions requiring great trust. The Imbangala economy included too narrow a range of agricultural and commercial activities to leave room for strong differentiation of abika from jimbanza in terms of economic function.

The political value of abika as loyal and dependable retainers in the highly competitive environment of Kasanje politics occasionally gave them positions superior to those open to lineage members. Nobles appointed nonhereditary deputies to a class of titles called *mavunga* (sing. *vunga*) as means of strengthening their personal power beyond the authority inherent in their own position. Mavunga tended to cluster about the holders of the more important political titles, especially around the Kasanje kings, but any holder of a state title could nominate as many as he wished to support. Because titleholders required unswerving personal loyalty from their vunga holders, they sometimes found it expedient to nominate yijiko to the vunga titles. A documented example from the seventeenth century illustrates the structural factors that strongly encouraged such tactics. Titleholders of that time tried to appoint yijiko to the office of *tandala*, one of the most powerful vunga offices, explicitly to discourage tandala-led revolts against their own authority.[20] These occurred with disturbing frequency when the chief's kinsmen held the position of tandala, since they used the office as a base for organizing the jimbanza factions of the lineage to usurp the chief's power. Yijiko, who had no possibility of becoming chiefs, were not so easily tempted to join such plots.

18. H. Capello and R. Ivens (1882, 1:325). The Bihe (Ovimbundu) kings of the 1840s used abika for delicate positions at their courts, especially ones requiring literacy, a skill that they regarded as involving sensitive and even dangerous knowledge; see Magyar (1859:258).

19. A special term (name?) designated this type of mubika: *kasabe*. MacGaffey (1970: 238) mentions a Kongo slave wife, *matsabi*, with similar duties; the two reflexes (*-sabe* and *-tsabi*) appear to be related.

20. The tandala was an appointed official described as early as 1590 as a "minister of justice and war captain" by P. Francisco Rodrigues (1960:199, 211). The exact duties of the tandala varied from title to title, as each titleholder used his tandala variously for receiving foreigners, bearing messages, commanding armies, and so on.

THE EFFECT OF ABIKA ON RELATIONS BETWEEN THE STATE AND LINEAGES

Before the ending of the Atlantic slave trade, most abika who entered Kasanje were sooner or later sold to foreign traders at a royal marketplace located near the king's capitals. Abika typically moved gradually toward the royal court in a sequence of steps that reflected a fundamental opposition that divided the kings from the descent groups of the kingdom. On the one hand, lineage officials used their authority over many aspects of human existence to demand the exclusive loyalty of their kinsmen, but on the other hand political titleholders—especially the kings—demanded tribute and service that weakened the lineages. Lineages conceded tribute to the kings only grudgingly, and they collectively resisted royal exactions whenever they could. The kings tried to overcome lineage parochialism by sheer power, building up large retinues of yijiko, who had no loyalties other than to them personally and who would execute raids against recalcitrant lineages without hesitation or subversion. The jingundu countered by seeking to augment their own followings of abika relative to those controlled by their rulers. Kings and the jingundu of their kingdom thus competed against one another by recruiting and assimilating these alien supporters.

Under these circumstances, a royal monopoly over sales of slaves to Europeans had been crucial to the Kasanje kings' dominant position before 1850 or so. All slaves sold in Kasanje to foreign buyers came from the kings' central marketplace, where consistently large numbers of them were available until well into the nineteenth century. The plentiful supplies of slaves stemmed in part from captives taken in foreign wars and from slaves brought by royal slave-trading caravans sent beyond the boundaries of the kingdom, but many came from internal Kasanje sources tapped according to the dynamics of the opposition between the lineages and the kings. The steady availability of human labor at the court owed much to contributions (*kulambwita*) of abika sent by the lineages to the kings in token of their nominal subordination to the state. These abika had originated in irregular and small-scale purchases and kidnappings by Imbangala lineages from the Shinje, Songo, Lunda, and others who lived around them. The lineages first incorporated these aliens as abika and held them until the royal court demanded people for sale to foreign buyers at the court. Since refusal to honor such royal requests threatened violent raids from the kings' warriors, lineages normally sent the required complement of people, but they protected their longer-range political interests by drawing them mainly from the ranks of their abika, perhaps supplemented by undesired full ngundu members condemned for such crimes as theft or adultery. Only when faced with demands in excess of available abika would they yield favored nieces and nephews of the lineage itself (interviews: Alexandre Vaz, Domingos Vaz, June 26, 1969; Mwanya a Shiba, June 14, 1969). In this fashion, a floating population of abika enabled the Imbangala jingundu to resist depletion by their kings and in exceptional cases became numerous enough to back lineage challenges to royal authority. At the same time, kings tried to restrain descent groups from growing large enough to threaten them by draining their abika and jimbanza manpower. The abika thus served as the pawns that simultaneously maintained the political balance between kings and lineages in Kasanje and provided the plentiful slave exports for which Kasanje became justifiably infamous.

The numbers of abika living with the lineages in the nineteenth century increased as the Kasanje kings' once-unassailable monopoly on slave exports faltered and then crumbled owing to a decline in European demands for slaves.[21] Exports decreased dramatically with the ending of the Atlantic slave trade after 1850, but hard times at the Kasanje kings' court did not diminish the rate at which Imbangala lineages continued to import strangers. These people remained as abika, affiliated permanently to the descent groups, and as yijiko, who supported the rise of regional political authorities as the dominant forces in Kasanje during the 1870s. The kings fell into poverty and isolation in striking contrast to the thriving lineages and the local titleholders with their large numbers of abika out in the provinces. Continued imports of alien women long after the export trade had ceased enabled many Imbangala to build personal followings large enough to make them men to be reckoned with by buying and marrying four, six, or eight female abika.[22] As the lineages increased their strength by holding more abika, some expanded to the point that they split into sections, as prosperous males hived off to found predominantly patrilineal jiko segments composed of their abika wives and their descendants. Large ngundu settlements dispersed into sets of smaller jiko-based villages scattered about the original landholding of the parent lineage, enabling male jimbanza to found their own villages where they could escape interference from the senior officials of their descent groups, surrounded by yijiko dependents and hoping to attract non-abika kinsmen to their side with offers of slave women as wives. On the ideological plane, the swelling numbers of yijiko allowed individuals to fulfill personal ambitions regardless of the communal pressure to subordinate personal achievement to the welfare of kinsmen in so strongly lineage-oriented a society as that of the Imbangala.

Viewed from a slightly different perspective, female abika among the

21. I summarize evidence for this interpretation in Miller (1973).

22. Henrique Augusto Dias de Carvalho (1890:182-487). Capello and Ivens (1882, 1:324-25). Interview: Mwanya a Shiba, June 14, 1969. Martin A. Klein (1971) surveys the increased volume of the intra-African slave trade even as exports from Africa declined.

Imbangala, as in some other African matrilineal societies, provided one means of avoiding the antagonisms that tended to mark relations between men and their wives' brothers, that is, between the fathers and the maternal uncles of children who lived with the male parent but whose primary loyalties were directed toward maternal kinsmen. Ideally, adult males of each lineage resided together on the lands of their own ngundu in sets of uterine brothers; in large and mature descent groups these brothers might increase their followings by attracting their sisters' adult sons and their dependents. The women and young nephews of each ngundu lived with their husbands and fathers in neighboring villages, with boys normally joining their uncles at puberty or young adulthood. But the return of young men to their own lineage village was by no means certain in practice, since their father's ngundu competed with their own ngundu for the young men's loyalty; even political future ngundu leaders might forsake their kinsmen to remain in their father's village in the hope of receiving a prestigious political title or some other advantage there. But since abika had no matrilineal kinsmen, they experienced few such divided loyalties and ensured a faithful and numerous population in the lineage center even though they could not themselves accede to the main ngundu named positions.

Imbangala political thought saw important similarities between political authorities in Kasanje and their yijiko, since both kings and slaves occupied social positions outside the otherwise all-enveloping descent groups. By equating two groups that appear diametrically opposed as inferior and superior in the usual slave-chief dichotomy of Western analytical categories, the Imbangala perspective accurately emphasized the direct relationships between retainers and political power in a technologically uncomplicated society without elaborate weapons or administrative techniques. Imbangala political authorities owed whatever power they exercised over the lineages to yijiko followers who did not belong to the jingundu and would therefore defend their masters against resisting descent groups. During the years when the Kasanje kings exercised effective power, they had depended on abika and yijiko employed as mercenaries, messengers, farmers, and in other ways as supporters in opposition to the interests of the lineages. The state/lineage dichotomy in Kasanje was therefore also an alliance of outsiders, chiefs and abika or yijiko, against the jimbanza of the lineages.[23]

Relatively little direct evidence reveals the precise patterns of abika circulation among the lineages and titleholders of late nineteenth-century Kasanje. Abika must have flowed between the holders of regional political

---

23. The structural similarities between chiefs and slaves have been noticed many times; see, for example, Edmund Leach (1964).

titles and the lineages as their respective fortunes rose and fell. Both sides sought to convert livestock (primarily oxen and goats) or trade goods into political support in the form of slaves (interview: Mbondo group). Abika, together with livestock, trade cloth, and money, circulated also among the lineages and between Kasanje titleholders as compensation (*milonga*) for such crimes as theft, sorcery, adultery, and so on (interview: Sousa Calunga, August 22, 1969).[24] Imbangala abika had value as sources of social and political strength as well as economic wealth.

Still, the Imbangala continued to sell small numbers of slaves to Europeans in Angola even into the early years of the twentieth century in a desultory trade that contrasted sharply with the highly organized and centralized slaving of the Kasanje kings before 1850. Imbangala trading caravans went east of the Kwango primarily in search of rubber, but if a regular Chokwe business associate needed trade goods and had no rubber to offer in exchange, the Imbangala might accept a mubika in payment. They acquired these slaves with no intent of integrating them into their jijiko and jingundu, kept them bound with ropes around their waists, and did not employ them as bearers or as farmers. When the next Imbangala caravans left to deliver their rubber, wax, and ivory to Portuguese merchants in Angola, these abika would be taken and sold there to planters and businessmen in need of labor. Sugarcane planters near Malanje, who enjoyed a brief boom in locally produced rum in the early twentieth century, were among their more important customers. Local missionaries, who began to build mission stations in and near the Lui-Kwango valley after 1910, would occasionally buy or "liberate" young abika whom they enrolled in their schools and agricultural programs (interviews: Ngandu a Kungu, June 27, 1969; Mbondo group).

ASSIMILATION OF OUTSIDERS AS MAVALA

The high value of abika in the context of Imbangala lineage slavery tended to promote their cultural and social assimilation into Imbangala lineages, and descendants of abika often became almost as closely affiliated to their lineage as its jimbanza. These tendencies operated with particular force in the late nineteenth century, after the ending of slave exports to Europeans. Assimilated descendants of abika outsiders, depending on the status and sex of their parents, might retain the status of abika or could become *mavala* (sing. and pl.), a status intermediate between abika and jimbanza.[25] Because one's primary social standing

---

24. Capello and Ivens (1882, 1:283).

25. The term appears to come from the KiMbundu verb *kuvala*, meaning to give birth; see Assis, Jr. Interviews: Ngonga a Mbande, June 26, 1969; Apolo de Matos, June 18-19, 1969; Sousa Calunga, August 22, 1969. Mavala were also known as *bana ba mubika*, or children of a mubika.

derived from the mother under Imbangala rules of matrilineal descent, the child of a mubika mother (whatever the status of the father) assumed the mubika status. Children of a male mbanza and a mubika woman acquired the status termed mavala. They had close ties to their father and to his kinsmen but no maternal uncles on the side of their kinless mothers; they would not leave their father's village at puberty, as did young jimbanza, to seek adult names in their mothers' jingundu but instead remained with their fathers' descent groups. Mavala status similarly pertained to locally born children of two abika or of two mavala of the same ngundu. From an owner's point of view, mavala were ideal dependents, locally born and therefore culturally Imbangala but without outside kinsmen to compete for their loyalty. They did not provoke the conflicts faced by all jimbanza between one's own matrilineage and that of one's father.

The distinguishing feature of the mavala's status lay in their connection to only one descent group, the lineage of their owner (and often that of their father as well). The hierarchy of social status that ranked mubika below mavala and mavala below mbanza found a reflection in the nature of each group's affiliation to the Imbangala lineages; jimbanza possessed both matrilateral and patrilateral local descent-group connections, from their own kinsmen and their fathers' kinsmen. Mavala had connections to only a single local lineage, either that of their male mbanza parent or the common descent group to which their abika of mavala mother and father were affiliated. Abika could claim no local kinsmen at all other than through relationship of dependency on the lineage of their owner.[26] Yijiko, still more remote from the lineages, were associated at a full remove or more through an individual title that was in turn embedded either in the lineage or in state networks of permanent positions.

The principle of matrilineal descent also governed the variations on the status of children of abika. Descendants of female jimbanza inherited their mothers' full mbanza status regardless of their fathers' positions as abika or mavala (interview: Apolo de Matos, June 18-19, 1969). A male mubika who fathered an mbanza child remained a mubika but acquired a secondary status of *sha mbanza*, "the father of an mbanza," which entitled him to a greater measure of respect from his wife's kinsmen than he might otherwise have received. The quasi-honorific sha mbanza acknowledged the likelihood that his personal stature would rise as his child matured and assumed prominent mbanza positions in the lineage.

26. If the scheme I have presented was consistent, children of mavala from two different lineages should have become either an inferior sort of mbanza (because they had two local groups of kinsmen) or a superior kind of mavala (since true jimbanza in fact had connections to four or more jingundu through their grandparents).

The mbanza child of a sha mbanza in practice had a weaker position than his kinsmen with two mbanza parents, since he or she lacked the potential backing of patrilateral kinsmen outside his own lineage. The progeny of abika from two different lineages became dependents of the ngundu of their mother's owner but retained the abika status of their parents (unlike the mavala who resulted from unions of abika of the same ngundu). Bridewealth (*kilembo*) in such abika marriages followed the same pattern as in mbanza alliances—the male mubika's owner paid to the lineage of the female. But by Imbangala reckoning their children did not acquire the affiliation to a single local descent group that defined the mavala (interview: Apolo de Matos, June 18-19, 1969).

The presence of mavala in a lineage introduced tensions between the jimbanza nephews of ngundu elders who would normally stand to inherit wealth and position under the rules of matrilinearity and the mavala sons of the same men who—under certain circumstances—could acquire their goods and titles. Sons of holders of political titles, including mavala, for instance, received positions called makita (sing. kita) that conferred the right to represent their father's political interests in other lineages. Other mavala sons became successful traders with their initial working capital drawn from their father's wealth, thus ignoring the claims of their matrilineal kinsmen. Although ngundu names and titles remained the exclusive preserve of full jimbanza, some specialized types of lineage office were open to mavala. Mavala, for example, often filled a position called the *mukaji a ngola*, which entailed responsibility for the safekeeping of the lineage emblems, cleaning the hut where they were kept, and hiding them during interregna between the terms of malemba dya ngola, the jimbanza guardians of the insignia.[27] As a lineage affiliate, the mavala had a vested interest in the preservation of such sensitive objects, but from the perspective of the lineage he was well placed to handle them because he could not himself become lemba and therefore had no personal reason to steal them.

The structural tensions between abika, mavala, and jimbanza in Imbangala lineages suggest that late-nineteenth-century Imbangala social history featured a widening gulf between the matrilateral members of the Imbangala descent groups and their patrilaterally affiliated abika and mavala.[28] As long as the intra-African slave trade continued to bring alien women to Kasanje, wealthy male jimbanza married them and built up within their lineages large quasi-patrilateral jiko segments over which they

27. Mukaji was also the term that a man applied to his wife.
28. The remoteness of the period, of course, makes it impossible to conduct the kind of census that alone could prove that these developments occurred in the ways hypothesized here.

exercised a measure of authority not obtainable over jimbanza sons or nephews. Mavala segments emerged as rivals to jimbanza nephews for their elder's (respectively, father's or uncle's) wealth, and the competition between sons and nephews tended to split descent groups, reinforcing the desire of male jimbanza to found independent villages of their own and thus helping to account for the movement toward dispersed-settlement patterns prompted by the buildup of yijiko.[29] It seems reasonable to assume that mbanza men married abika women with increasing frequency during this period, since the decline of the central Kasanje kingship not only allowed jimbanza to count on keeping their abika women and mavala descendants but also reduced the need for lineage cohesiveness to oppose the kings' exactions. Formerly, ngundu officials wishing to avert the lineage fragmentation introduced by the presence of too many mavala heirs could have encouraged marriages among their own abika whose mavala children owed loyalty to no particular individual but to the group as a whole.

OTHER FORMS OF ALTERED LINEAGE AFFILIATION

The fundamental Imbangala idea behind the institution of the mubika, that a person's position within the universe of Imbangala descent groups could be altered, explains other social identities that were closely related to the category of slavery and which ranged from pawnship to marriage. A mubika's transfer of his or her lineage affiliation was total and was intended to be permanent, but exactly the same sort of transfer made on a conditional or temporary basis created a pawn, termed *kuri* (pl. *jikuri*).[30] The kuri, apparently almost always a female, was formally attached to a new ngundu for an agreed period of time but did not lose her own lineage membership. In the ritual that altered her lineage status, the lemba dya ngundu of the acquiring group symbolically washed off a special white

29. Otto Schütt (1881:79), a traveler in Kasanje during the 1870s, remarked that the sons of most chiefs were "slaves" (meaning both abika and mavala) and implicitly contrasted them, as the Imbangala now do, with the titleholders' nephews.

30. The kuri was the Imbangala analogue of the "pawn" described by Mary Douglas (1964). Informants disagreed as to the exact term applied to such a person. I have chosen kuri because a number of extended verbs in KiMbundu relate to the idea of pawning (*kukurika, kukurisa, kukurila;* see Assis, Jr. [n.d.:200], although he has the word itself as *dikuri,* meaning a celibate person, p. 344). Some described such a person as a *kihunji* (pl. *yihunji*), the same term applied to any junior female of a lineage; others used *kipoteko,* evidently an Ambakista borrowing from the Portuguese *hipotecado* or *hipoteca,* a lien or pledge. Interviews: Alexandre Vaz, Domingos Vaz, June 26, 1969; Sousa Calunga, September 11 and August 22, 1969; Sokola, June 12, 1969. Some informants offered the word *kubamukula* for "to offer a relative or dependent in satisfaction of a debt owned in material goods, or to pawn," but I found no similar root with a related meaning in KiMbundu dictionaries available to me.

clay called *pemba* that had been applied by her old lineage and then coated her with the pemba of his ngundu (interview: Sousa Calunga, September 11, 1969).[31] The pemba in each case symbolically embodied the supernatural protection of the lineage and made the pawn subject to the lemba that applied it, to his lineage emblems, and to his ancestors. The ceremony corresponded to the *rite de passage* through which abika entered Imbangala society. Since it did not eliminate the kuri's primary membership in her natal lineage, she continued to receive the respect due a person of her original status—mubika, mavala, or mbanza—in the old descent group. Unlike the person integrated as mubika, she retained her own name "so that her kinsmen would recognize her when they wanted to take her back." The recipient lineage undertook a substantial responsibility in accepting a kuri, since the impermanence of the transfer implied that they would return her safely at the option of her own kinsmen or owners.[32] If an mbanza kuri fell ill, therefore, many lineages quickly removed the pemba and sent her back to her own relatives, since her death away from her own lineage would be considered equivalent to a mubika's in the sense that it could leave her without proper installation among the ancestors of her ngundu (interview: Alexandre Vaz, Domingos Vaz, June 26, 1969).[33]

Lineages generally transferred a kuri as a pledge against a debt owed in the form of material wealth. She remained a kuri until her kinsmen could repay the goods owed; at that time, the lemba dya ngundu of the creditor lineage would return her to her kinsmen and formally absolve himself and his lineage of responsibility for the kuri's welfare, saying: "I send this person on her way, wish her health, let her return to her kinsmen, allow her to go and wish her good forture" (interview: Sousa Calunga, September 11, 1969). This ceremony made it illegal for the kuri's kinsmen to attribute her later sickness or death to the former host lineage, effectively putting the kuri beyond reach of witchcraft or sorcery present within the

31. According to Ribeiro da Cruz (1940:66-67), the neighboring Shinje people gave a cup or mug or plate upon receipt of a kuri. Alternatively, the two parties to the transaction killed and jointly ate a chicken, saving the feathers and bones as evidence of the agreement. There were variations on the dominant type of kuri described in the text. A kuri might be given as a pledge against only a portion of the debt, and the debtor lineage would then pay interest in trade goods on the remainder. No substitution of the pemba of one lineage for that of the other took place in that instance. Interview: Sousa Calunga, September 11, 1969.

32. Informants explained the seriousness with which they took this responsibility by noting that anyone who came as a kuri might one day return to his own lineage and rise even to become king of Kasanje. If a lineage had mistreated such a person, they warned, its prospects would be bleak indeed. Interview: Sousa Calunga, September 11, 1969.

33. No informant specified whether a kuri's death made the debt due immediately or whether a new pawn could be substituted.

debtor ngundu that had apparently extended to her while under the temporary protection of its pemba. The kuri's full release was confirmed when representatives of the two lineages met to slaughter a goat provided by the creditors and consumed it in a joint feast (interview: Apolo de Matos, June 18-19, 1969). If the kuri died with the pemba of the host ngundu still on her body, the creditors forfeited half of the outstanding debt but received some token—perhaps a chicken—from the dead woman's kinsmen in recognition of the remaining balance and of their agreement to pay without providing a living person to replace the dead kuri (interview: Alexandre Vaz, Domingos Vaz, June 26, 1969).

Female jikuri often married men of their creditor jingundu, since offspring of such a union possessed desirable social characteristics. Because a kuri retained her primary affiliation to her own descent group, she could marry into her host lineage without violating the rule of lineage exogamy. Such marriages took place without the sanction of the kuri's kinsmen; but after she was redeemed by her lineage, the husband then had to request recognition of the union from his wife's lemba. Her kinsmen were obliged ultimately to accept the marriage but often demanded a lengthy series of gifts while the groom "familiarized himself with the new ngundu"; the less eager the woman's kinsmen were to accept her husband, the more they prolonged the period of gift-giving and thus raised the value of the gifts (interview: Sousa Calunga, September 11, 1969).[34] Although the acceptance of the first offering ensured eventual receipt of the lemba's blessing, this sort of marriage entailed a significant financial risk for the husband and his kinsmen.

But the marriage of a kuri into the creditor ngundu brought returns in the form of her presence in its village and in rights over her progeny, since children born to a kuri belonged to the creditor lineage. Although many males of the creditor jingundu married jikuri for this reason, a lemba sometimes married off a kuri under his protection outside the lineage, received bridewealth from her spouse, and retained authority over children born while she remained kuri, even if the woman later returned to her own kinsmen. A male kuri who married a woman of his creditor ngundu paid no bridewealth and if redeemed by his own lineage left his wife and children with their kinsmen unless his lemba paid the kilembo (bridewealth); in that case, they would reside with their husband and father in the normal Imbangala fashion. If a pawn-giving lineage enjoying particularly friendly relations with its creditor ransomed a female kuri who had borne children, the creditor lineage sometimes voluntarily returned one child out of three or four delivered by the woman while

34. The informant did not discuss the relationship of these payments to the debt owed by the woman's lineage.

under their care. The debtors could pay a certain amount to reclaim the others if they wished (interview: Alexandre Vaz, Domingos Vaz, June 26, 1969). A hostile lineage could take advantage of such a situation to extract substantial interest on its original investment by allowing the kuri to bear several children and then ransoming the children back to their mother's kinsmen at high prices.

The incidence of transferring jikuri seems to have been high during the last decades of the nineteenth century, owing to economic opportunities connected with the rubber boom. The prospect of making a quick profit prompted lineage officials to offer dependents of all categories as jikuri in exchange for wealthy neighbors' trade goods, which they hoped to sell with sufficient gain to buy their dependents back and end up with their working capital intact as a base from which to mount future ventures. Although some malemba evidently abused their right to pawn abika, mavala, and even nieces and nephews as jikuri,[35] most apparently used the system with some sensitivity to ethical issues and with constructiveness to convert the old forms of wealth (dependents of various sorts, especially slaves) into new forms appropriate to the increasingly commercialized environment of the twentieth century. A man poor in trade goods but rich in nephews or mavala might thus offer them as jikuri in exchange for cloth and metalware owned by an established trader, who in turn could profit from additional manpower employed in his commercial activities. Unsuccessful novices, however, sometimes fell deeper and deeper into debt to wealthy creditors and eventually were forced to offer themselves and all their remaining dependents to their creditors as jikuri or abika (interview: Mwanya a Shiba, June 14, 1969). This sort of arrangement contributed to the rise of a class of new men who used wealth and trading acumen to overcome the disadvantages of relatively humble status and replaced the formerly dominant classes of jimbanza lineage officials and political titleholders. These new men today enjoy considerable local prominence and have now turned their wealth back into older forms of status by buying prestigious titles that would once have been far beyond their grasp.

The Imbangala recognized methods of converting the conditional status of the kuri into its permanent mubika analogue when circumstances forced debtors to acknowledge their inability to redeem jikuri given to creditors. The debtor in such cases confirmed the change by offering his creditor a knife, a hat, and something referred to as *argulha* (perhaps *argola*, Portuguese for a ring). The hat stood for the kuri's head, the knife

35. Stories now circulate of drunkards who pawned their own heirs to buy more wine; although no doubt true in some instances, these tales contain a similarity to melodramatic homilies current in abolitionist or temperance circles in American society that makes their representativeness suspect.

his or her severance from his or her kinsmen, and both together meant that the kuri had "died" socially with regard to his or her former lineage, as did all abika (interview: Sousa Calunga, August 22, 1969). Although the value of a kuri in terms of trade commodities undoubtedly varied according to the individual involved and according to commercial conditions, "six trade cloths (*panos*) and two plates" was reported as a representative value at an undetermined date (interview: Mwanya a Shiba, June 14, 1969).[36]

Offenses or debts involving loss of human life could be repaid through another sort of permanent transfer of a person called a *kamwenyu* (pl. *tumwenyu*).[37] The transfer mechanism (termed *kijiba*[38]) operated between lineages if members of different descent groups were entangled in the dispute, or between members of the same ngundu if individually owned yijiko were concerned. If, for example, someone killed a member of another ngundu, the kinsmen of the dead person could demand kijiba from the murderer's lineage under prevailing rules of corporate lineage responsibility for the acts of its members. One of the political titleholders, or even the Kasanje king in earlier years, usually arbitrated the award of kijiba from one lineage to another. The person transferred, any member or affiliate of the guilty man's descent group, entered the plaintiff lineage as a mubika and received a new name to signify the cutting of all ties with his natal lineage and the permanence of the transfer. Former kinsmen henceforth pretended not to recognize him if they encountered him along a path, and he never returned to visit his home village. The institution of kamwenyu seems to have been part of the formal "wars" recognized by the Kasanje political system, since no such payment resulted from deaths suffered in feuds regulated by the lineage system but not authorized by state officials. Although the malemba of the two jingundu conducted most of the negotiations concerning such a payment, they always worked under the supervision of a delegate of the Kasanje king. Depending on the seriousness of the offense, kijiba payments might range up to ten tumwenyu, ten oxen, and ten guns. Relatively amicable settlements amounted to only a few head of small livestock (interviews: Kiluanje kya Ngonga, September 24, 1969; Sousa Calunga, September 11, 1969; Apolo de Matos, June 18-19, 1969; Alexandre Vaz, Domigos Vaz, June 26, 1969).[39]

---

36. Ribeiro da Cruz (1940:66-67) gave the value of a mubika pledged as a kuri at eight to ten kilograms of gunpowder plus ten to fifteen five-yard pieces of striped cotton trade cloth (*riscado*). This remark applied to an area to the northeast of Kasanje at about the time period described here.

37. Kamwenyu referred to life, as opposed to the *kijiba* (death); see Assis, Jr. (n.d.:93).

38. Kijiba also had the sense of "murder"; see Assis, Jr. (n.d.:120).

39. Cf. Salazar (n.d., 2:108).

The Imbangala undoubtedly recognized several other types of permanent transfer of a person to satisfy one lineage's blood debt to another, but only one appears in my notes. This instance, a fine called *milonga makanga,*[40] arose in cases where a lineage determined that one of its female dependents had died through the neglect or malice of her husband, as when a husband abandoned an ailing wife to seek adulterous liaisons with other women. A milonga makanga would be demanded from the husband's lineage and might include a person, called *shipalu.* Less serious offenses not involving death were usually settled by paying a single ox or six goats (interview: Mwanya a Shiba, June 14, 1969.)[41]

A parallel but more honorable transfer of persons from one lineage to another occurred when men abandoned the names in their own ngundu to take some prestigious position—such as one of the political titles of the Kasanje state—owned by a different descent group. Jingundu normally tried to keep the political titles they controlled for their own jimbanza incumbents (*yihingwa,* sing. *kihingwa*[42]), but if the lineage elders could find no suitable candidate among their own nephews they sometimes selected a nominee from a related lineage. The installation of such an alien incumbent required special ceremonies preceding the normal initiation ritual appropriate to the position in which the lineage owning the position paid the ngundu providing the kihingwa a sum of money to compensate it for what they regarded as the "death" of its kinsmen. The new kihingwa could not return to his old descent group unless converse ceremonies transferred him back to his original status. An amount of money, varying according to the rank and prestige of the position in question, changed hands in these instances (interview: Apolo de Matos, July 7, 1969).

CONCLUSIONS

Imbangala slavery derived from a specific social theory and was embedded in a social framework that identified people in terms of their places in a matrix of unilineal descent groups. The Imbangala perceived modifications of individual social position as the assumption of one or more permanent names or titles that made up their lineages and the state of Kasanje. The closest parallels between Imbangala slavery and other

40. The dictionary meaning of makanga is "judgment," or any sort of extreme (high, low, deep, etc.); see Assis, Jr. (n.d.:341). I suspect that the term may be related to another root, *kanga,* meaning outside or external, as a fine (*milonga*) imposed on one outside the lineage.

41. The circumstances described resemble a case of sorcery, but the informant did not mention the term in this instance.

42. The term comes from the verb *kuhinga,* to enter; the Imbangala see the assumption of one of the perpetual names as "entering" the position, as one enters a house (for protection), or as the guardian of the sacred lineage emblems enters the shrine where they are kept.

slaveries occurred in societies organized primarily in terms of lineages: hence the term "lineage slavery."[43]

Imbangala abika formed a subclass of a more comprehensive category of persons who had lost their natal lineage affiliation, a loss signified by their dropping an old name and undergoing *rites de passage;* as abika, they had been integrated into a new lineage or affiliated to an individual title in a new social status. Transfers of status regarded as complete and permanent included not only abika and yijiko slaves but also tumwenyu and shipalu, paid to satisfy blood debts, and kihingwa, occupants of political titles in nonnatal lineages. Partial and temporary transfers like the kuri (pawn) also existed. Marriage resembled pawnship in that it also temporarily transferred rights to a woman's presence to another lineage, and Westerners unfamiliar with African social institutions have been tempted to see both as forms of "slavery." But in the case of the kuri, the woman's kinsmen exchanged her for substantial wealth and, a crucial point in a matrilineal society, this transfer of goods voided her lineage's right to her children. The amount of wealth that changed hands was comparatively small in the case of marriage, and the rights to the woman's children accordingly remained with their mother's lineage. Pawnship therefore transferred the lineage affiliation of children born during the term of the pledge without affecting their status as jimbanza, mavala, or abika. The women in either instance returned to their lineages after a defined period of time—a kuri when her kinsmen repaid their debt, and a wife at the end of her childbearing years.

The aspect of the Imbangala abika that made them most similar to slaves elsewhere was their position as outsiders integrated into local social and political institutions. They were the residents of Kasanje most removed from what the Imbangala considered the essence of their own society and culture: abika possessed no lineage rights and no kinsmen, while Imbangala jimbanza prided themselves on their lineages and on the security they derived from them. Although few physical differences perceptible to casual European visitors distinguished Imbangala slaves from other Imbangala, many abika had been born outside Kasanje, and local residents readily differentiated insiders from people originating elsewhere; the category of mavala, the locally born and culturally assimilated dependents, recognized the distinction that Imbangala made between people born within and without the confines of their society. Special slave names helped to identify those from outside. The Imbangala preferred slaves who were outsiders in the purely geographical sense as well, since

43. In addition to MacGaffey (1970), see Vansina (1973) and the writings of R. S. Rattray on Asante.

abika brought from far away had only a small chance of escape and brought negligible risks of retaliation from vengeful lineage-mates. They were juridically outsiders as well, since their remoteness from the social and political institutions that protected individuals in Imbangala society largely defined their condition; they were totally subject to the arbitrary will of their masters and could not obtain supernatural intercession through lineage emblems or lineage ancestors or expect state authorities to intervene on their behalf. Some individual—an mbanza, kihingwa, king, or even another mubika—always stood interposed between abika or yijiko and the social and political resources available to full lineage members. The ceremonies that attended the transfer of a locally born kamwenyu or shipalu put these people equally, if artificially, beyond the protection of their natal lineages. The attractiveness of inviting alien yihingwa to hold political titles derived from the impartiality in intralineage affairs that could be expected of outsiders without ties to local factions. Jikuri and wives were also outsiders among the male kinsmen with whom they lived, but their alienness was mitigated by the economic or affinal ties between their kinsmen and the people with whom they lived.

Although Imbangala abika had become slaves against their will, the involuntary origin of their status did not clearly distinguish them from people with other kinds of modified status. Tumwenyu and jikuri, and even women given as wives, had little to say about the positions in which they found themselves. The slave/free dichotomy, familiar to Western heirs of the Enlightenment, would not appear so obvious to the Imbangala, since in Kasanje all status was seen as involuntary and no individual considered himself free in any sense close to Western theoretical notions of freedom. Everyone lived subordinated to the collective needs of his or her lineage, subordinated to the character of the name he or she assumed, subordinated to the ideally absolute authority of the king; the fact that Imbangala often went to their deaths striving for possession of a particular titled position did not alter their philosophical position that incumbents were called to their destinies and that all obediently suffered fates determined for them by the gods. It is, of course, possible to distinguish empirically between the involuntariness of a kidnapped mubika's position and that of the Kasanje kings, but no Imbangala would have cited the involuntary origins of the mubika status as differentiating it from any other status.

Imbangala abika had economic value within a defined exchange sphere that included especially those commodities which, like slaves, were alive or had exotic origins—large livestock, imported trade goods, etc.—and owners of Imbangala slaves astutely maximized their value as field labor, traders, servants, and so on. But no master calculated a slave's value only in economic terms, since slaves were readily convertible from forms of material wealth or labor into sources of social prestige and political power. For that reason, the flow of abika between the Kasanje kings and their provincial lords and the movements of slaves from commoner masters to holders of noble titles revealed much about Imbangala social and political history in the late nineteenth century. Conventional Western distinctions between the social, the political, and the economic fail to define Imbangala slavery, since it possessed features of all three.

Deprivation of wealth or authority did not uniformly distinguish Imbangala abika from jimbanza or even from holders of ranking lineage and political titles. The similarity between chiefs and slaves perceived by Imbangala lineage members in some cases extended to great wealth and political power lodged in the hands of slaves, especially the trusted yijiko, who held prestigious vunga positions; by contrast, incumbents in senior jimbanza titles often had few followers and lived in abject poverty. In practice, of course, most abika lived more humbly than did many jimbanza during the late nineteenth century, but it was a period of improving circumstances for many slaves who succeeded in commerce and themselves became wealthy owners of other slave dependents. Whatever their material circumstances, jimbanza always enjoyed a personal respect denied to all abika.

The disabilities suffered by Imbangala abika resulted from their lack of multiple affiliations with different groups that they might play against one another in their own interest. Jimbanza, by definition, had both matrilateral and patrilateral lineages that they might manipulate, and most full lineage members had other kinship and political resources they could call on in time of need. But abika had no one responsible for their welfare other than a single master who, in turn, was accountable to no social or political authority that might act in their behalf. By definition, slaves lacked the kinsmen who were constantly available to Imbangala jimbanza and mavala for assistance in avenging injustices, borrowing wealth, offering solace, or arranging for a spouse. In the final analysis, most abika had the unenviable position of lineageless dependents in a society based on lineages; they lacked the power to take initiatives with regard to others and possessed only limited means of self-defense because their fortunes hinged on the will of others whom they could influence only marginally and informally, if at all. Slaves lacked the "respect" of other people, except for whatever abika they might themselves own. Ranking at the bottom of a clearly defined hierarchy of prestige that reflected power relations in Imbangala society, they were compelled to observe manners appropriate to children. But slavery was not a unique and discrete condition among the Imbangala. However extensively their dependence impaired their personal autonomy in practice, in theory they shared many qualities and disabilities with others on a continuum of dependent outsiders that ranged from noble titleholders to wives.

GLOSSARY

I have included in this glossary all Bantu terms used in more than one place in the text. Terms used only once and adequately defined in accompanying text or footnotes are not repeated here.

jiko (pl. *jijiko?*): literally "hearth," but here used to indicate a group of slaves affiliated to an individual political or lineage title; a subgroup within the *mubika* classification.

kamwenyu (pl. *tumwenyu*): a person given in satisfaction of a blood debt.

kihingwa (pl. *yihingwa*): an occupant of a perpetual title.

kihunji (pl. *yihunji*): a full lineage member; niece or nephew of lineage head.

kijiba: "death"; the practice of transferring a person in recompense for someone's death.

kijiko (pl. *yijiko*): a lineageless dependent person affiliated to an individual name or title.

kilembo: bridewealth.

kilombo: a seventeenth-century Imbangala warrior initiation society.

kita (pl. *makita*): a subordinate political title.

kota (pl. *makota*): a lineage elder.

kuri (pl. *jikuri*): a pawn.

lemba (pl. *malemba*) *dya ngundu*: "uncle" or headman of a matrilineage.

mavala (sing. and pl.): the assimilated descendant or descendants of a slave (*mubika*).

mbanza (pl. *jimbanza*): a full lineage member.

milonga: compensation; fine.

mubika (pl. *abika*): a slave.

mukaji a ngola: a lineage official, the guardian of sacred emblems.

mwenyishi: a honorific title: owner of the land.

ngundu (pl. *jingundu*): matrilineage.

pemba: sacred white clay, symbolic of lineage well-being.

sha mbanza: "father of an *mbanza*"; an honorific applied to slave fathers of *jimbanza* children.

shipalu: a person paid to satisfy a blood debt.

tandala: an important appointive office; a type of *vunga* title.

vunga (pl. *mavunga*): a class of appointive title.

REFERENCES

ORAL SOURCES

All citations of interviews refer to conversations held with Imbangala informants during 1969. Tapes and notes of these testimonies are in my possession and are open to consultation by qualified scholars.

Sousa Calunga, interviews on August 22, September 10, and September 11, 1969.
Ngandu a Kungu, interview on June 27, 1969.
Sr. Wensilau da Silva Luciano, interview.
Apolo de Matos, interviews on June 18-19, July 7, July 8, October 4, and October 5, 1969.
Ngonga a Mbande, interview on June 26, 1969.
Mbondo group, interview.
Kiluanje kya Ngonga, interview on September 24, 1969.
Mwanya a Shiba, interview on June 14, 1969.
Sokola, interview on June 12, 1969.
Alexandre Vaz and Ngonga a Mbande, interview on September 9, 1969.
Alexandre Vaz and Domingos Vaz, interview on June 26, 1969.

UNPUBLISHED SOURCE

Salazar, S. von W. Undated. Bondos e Bângalas: Subsídios etnográficos sobre as duas tribos, recolhidos na área da Circuñscriçao do Bondo e Bângala, do Distrito de Malanje—Angola. Dissertação para o acto de licenciatura, Instituto Superior de Ciéncias Sociais e Política Ultramarina, Universidade Técnica de Lisboa. 2 vols.

PUBLISHED SOURCES

Assis, Jr., A. de. Undated. *Dicionário Kimbundu-Português*. Luanda.
Cadornega, A. de O. de. 1972. *História geral das guerras angolanas*. Ed. J. M. Delgado. 2d ed., 3 vols. Lisbon.
Capello, H., and Ivens, R. 1882. *From Benguella to the territory of the Yacca*. Tr. by A. Elwes. 2 vols. London.
Dias de Carvalho, H. A. 1890. *Etnographia e história tradicional dos povos da Lunda*. Lisbon.
Cunnison, I. 1956. Perpetual kinship: a political institution of the Luapula peoples. *Rhodes-Livingstone J.* 20:28-48.
Douglas, M. 1964. "Matriliny and Pawnship in central Africa." *Africa* 34: 301-13.
Finley, M. I. 1967. The idea of slavery: critique of David Bryon Davis' *The problem of slavery in Western culture. N.Y. Rev. Bks.* 3:7-10.
_____. 1968. Slavery. *International encyclopedia of the social sciences* 14:307-13. New York.
Klein, M. A. 1971. Slavery, the slave trade, and legitimate commerce in late-nineteenth-century Africa. *Etud. Hist. Afr.* 2:5-28.

Leach, E. 1964. *Political systems of highland Burma*. London.

MacGaffey, W. 1970. *Custom and government in the Lower Congo*. Berkeley.

Magyar, L. 1859. *Reisen in Süd-Afrika*. Pest and Leipzig.

Miller, J. C. 1973. Slaves, slavers, and social change. In *Social change in Angola*, ed. F.-W. Heimer. Munich.

_____. 1976. *Kings and kinsmen: early states among the Mbundu of Angola*. Oxford.

Rattray, R. S. 1923. *Ashanti*. London.

Ribeiro da Cruz, J. 1940. *Notas de etnografia angolana*. Lisbon.

Rodrigues, P. F. 1960. Historia inedita de Angola. *Arqs Angola* 2d ser. 17: 199-211.

Schütt, O. 1881. *Reisen im sudwestlichen Becken des Congo*. Berlin.

Vansina, Jan. 1973. *The Tio kingdom of the Middle Congo, 1880-1892*. London.

9

Economic and Social Dimensions of Kongo Slavery

(Zaïre)

Wyatt MacGaffey

Since slavery is the antithesis of freedom, there are as many different kinds of one as of the other. Since both conditions are heterogeneous, analysis of the structural variables implicit in them is more rewarding than an attempt to classify their variations. We must first distinguish between economic and social relations, although the common usage of the term "slavery" associates the two and implies some sort of necessary link between them (Southall 1970:259-61). Finley, for example, defines slavery as a species of dependent labor, which he distinguishes from others by its social features; his discussion (1968) is restricted to societies in which this particular combination of variables seems to be present, mostly classical Greece and Rome and the New World, and ignores those in which similar social factors are not associated with dependent labor. Conversely, many descriptions of social dependence avoid the use of the term slavery because it inappropriately implies brutal conditions of work, and resort instead to uneasy compromises such as "household slavery" and euphemisms such as "adoption," which are in their way equally misleading. Some clarification of the terminological problem should come from structural analysis,

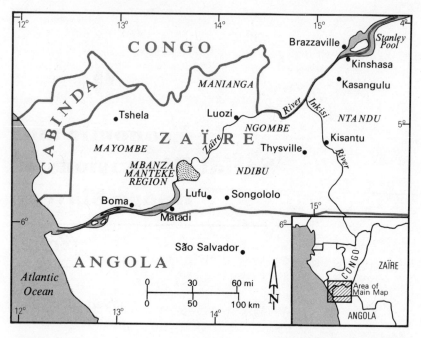

Cartographic Laboratory UW-Madison

Map 9. The Mbanza Manteke Region of Zaïre. Based on map in *Custom and Government in the Lower Congo,* by Wyatt MacGaffey (University of California Press, Berkeley, 1970).

but since particular historical forms of slavery are inevitably the products of unique contingencies, situational vocabularies will probably be more useful than definitions pretending to universality.

In its economic sense, slavery is a form of forced labor to be defined by comparison with other forms of labor in terms of a theoretical paradigm of the relations of production. For Marx and Engels, slavery was "the first form of exploitation, the form peculiar to the ancient world; it is succeeded by serfdom in the Middle Ages, and wage-labor in the more recent period. These are the three great forms of servitude, characteristic of the three great epochs of civilization" (Engels 1942:160). The preceding epoch, that of primitive communism, served Marx and Engels as a residual category embracing the "primitive" societies with which anthropology usually deals. Engels attempted to explore it, using Morgan's stages of barbarism, but his polemical tract can scarcely be taken seriously as an account of primitive modes of production. Since then the primitive world has remained a private park of "ideological" anthropology, closed to historical materialism (Terray 1972:184; Balibar 1971).

Sociologically, slavery is a form of ranked, differential incorporation. As such its relationship to caste and class is commonly recognized, and it is primarily a political phenomenon. Differential incorporation means that control of public resources and policy is reserved for one category of persons to the disadvantage of others (Smith 1969:96). Slavery, class, and caste differ with respect to the rules of categorical recruitment, caste membership being permanently ascribed at birth whereas the manumission of slaves is always a possibility and in the case of term slavery is envisaged from the beginning. Whereas slaves and free commonly share the same basic institutions, castes usually exhibit different institutional sets; members of different classes are distinguished only by secondary factors such as life-style, dialect, and religious denomination. Contrasts of this kind are maintained partly by the rules respecting marriage and the social allocation of children (Smith 1966; Berreman 1967).

Much of the theoretical literature on slavery is taken up with whether the material or the sociological aspect of slavery is the more significant, with the implication that a one-way relationship of cause and effect exists to be discovered. What tends to be lost in the argument is the fact that society and economy are necessarily interdependent. The real issue is not which one matters most, but exactly how they are related in historical communities or communities of a certain type. When we ask economic questions—that is, inquire into the production, distribution, and consumption of goods, particularly of the subsistence goods necessary to maintain the labor force—one kind of system of units emerges. If we ask social questions—that is, inquire into the production and social allocation of the persons necessary to maintain the corporate constituents of a society —a different system of units emerges. The issue is how the two are articulated.

In the present instance my data are taken from the small Kongo community of Mbanza Manteke as it existed in the mid-nineteenth century; or rather, from such evidence as I could elicit from modern traditions and pertinent turn-of-the-century ethnography. Although Mbanza Manteke is central to the Kongo area, it was from the commercial point of view something of a backwater at that time. I also examine what happened to communities of this kind under colonial rule. In the process, a two-dimensional picture of Kongo slavery emerges. The problems of interpreting the principal materials, local political legends, have been discussed in my *Custom and Government in the Lower Congo* (1970; cited hereafter as *CG*). Complementary materials of great interest, referring to the eastern BaKongo, can be found in J. Mertens, *Les Chefs couronnés* (1942); and for the Kunyi in P.-P. Rey (1969).

NINETEENTH CENTURY

LOCAL GROUPS, DESCENT GROUPS AND THEIR MAINTENANCE

A population of about 500 people occupied a group of sites in and around a small valley, in the western part of what is now the Cataracts District, province of Lower Zaïre, Republic of Zaïre. Each such site I call a hamlet, and the group of hamlets a village. According to legend, the village of Mbanza Manteke was founded by immigrants from Mbanza Kongo, the homeland of the BaKongo, in the remote past. These founders belonged to a particular matrilineal clan whose representatives in the Manteke area, the local section of the clan, form an exogamous group. This local clan-section is divided into "houses," each of which collectively owns land. The houses in turn are divided into matrilineages, whose members share certain rights to movable property. Relations between these units, and the position of any individual in his lineage, are given by a genealogy purporting to show descent in the female line from a founding ancestor. Other legends, all more or less controversial, also indicate that the founding clan was followed by other settlers who were dependent upon the founders in one way or another: relatives by marriage, adult children of men of the clan, refugees, purchased slaves, and others. The village therefore came to include representatives of nonfounding clan-sections, each divided into houses and lineages, who were the resident extralineage kin of the founders. Slaves were assimilated to kinship statuses on the principle that the relationship between owner and slave was that of father and son.

The bottom of the valley, where a small stream runs, is filled with forest, and the hamlets, of from ten to thirty houses each, were located on its upper edge. Most of the food consumed—principally manioc and peanuts—was grown by women in small plots on the more fertile slopes and on shallow bottomlands. The women used hoes and usually worked, alone or with the assistance of one or two close relatives, on individually owned clearings. The men's cultivation, also individual, was mostly of tree crops planted in the forest, usually near their habitations. Though its actual nutritional role is not clear, the *nsafu* tree (*Canarium saphu*) was sufficiently important that it remains to this day the symbol of men's crops and the social rights connected with them. Palm trees, like other trees, could be climbed only by men; they were not appropriated unless they had been deliberately planted.

Although the owning house was matrilineal, the children of its men and, in turn, their children—who were members of their own matrilineal clans—were entitled to cultivate plots on the clan's land; they paid no tribute or rent. Moreover, a man, his children, and his grandchildren were entitled to help themselves to the produce of one another's trees. Tradition also speaks of a collective nsafu harvest. There was no shortage of cultivable land in the area as a whole, although the size of villages was partly governed by the accessibility of land suitably divided between forest and bottomlands.

The men of each hamlet ate together in the men's shelter called *mbongi*, but their food was cooked for them individually by their wives. A man's chief contribution to this food—and a legal obligation upon him—was the meat and the salt, obtained by hunting and trade. There were two kinds of hunting (as of fishing), individual and collective, the former practiced at any time of year, the latter only at the end of the dry season, when the entire community, including the women, hunted with the aid of grass fires. The unit of consumption for large game was the village, the chief being entitled, as in other parts of Kongo, to a thigh of each animal. For small game and other foodstuffs, the unit was the hamlet, comprising resident lineage members and their extralineal adherents. Salt was obtained from the coast by trade.

The excess of subsistence production was sold in the markets for currency in the form of brass rods (*makuta*) and strings of glass beads (*kulazi*). The resulting wealth was the joint property of the lineage to the extent that all members shared responsibility for each other's debts; "stealing" within the lineage was not an actionable offense, and the lineage shared the movable property of deceased members. Lineages held exclusive rights of usufruct only in such land as its members were cultivating at the time (ownership of trees did not confer permanent rights over the land on which they stood).

Sovereignty, that is, permanent rights over land of a political and social rather than a directly economic nature, was held by the house and the clan, the estate of the clan consisting of the residual rights of the constituent houses to the land of any one of them, should it die out. Persons, like land, were owned by the house, not the lineage, and could be transferred between houses but not within a house. Compensation for homicide, for example, was payable between houses of the same or different clans but not between lineages of the same house.

Descent groups were not, of course, local groups, but the leading members of a house lived on or near its land. A man might live in the village of his own clan or that of his father's or grandfather's clan, depending on the advantages he saw, and might change his residence several times in the course of his life with changes in his political fortunes. In regulating the affairs of a clan or house, members of other clans who were linked to it through their fathers and were known as its "children and grandchildren" played important and necessary roles (to which slaves were also admitted). As allies, whose own estates and primary political expectations lay elsewhere, "children and grandchildren" could be entrusted with the clan's traditions and insignia and could even represent it during the minority of its hereditary leaders. Accordingly, one of the reasons for living with their fathers was that the children experienced greater social satisfaction there then with their own matrilineal relatives, whose jealousies and intergenerational rivalries might threaten them.

We have seen that production of subsistence goods (largely by female labor in agriculture and male labor in hunting) was carried on in local communities constituted, from the economic point of view, on egalitarian lines: all adults had equal access to the means of production and shared approximately equally in the distribution of produce.

Socially, the population was divided into dispersed matrilineal descent groups, organized internally into a hierarchy of generations. The members married into groups other than their own. In each household, a husband and wife belonging to different clans cooperated in food production and domestic duties, including childrearing. A marriage was contracted and guaranteed by official witnesses, known as the "four chiefs," on each side, consisting of the heads of each spouse's mother's, father's, mother's father's, and father's father's clans. Wedding ceremonies included an exchange of subsistence goods among the parties, typically palm wine, chickens, and plantains. Whether she was married or not, a woman's children belonged to her clan; and a man was socially recognized as the father of his children even when he was not married to their mother. The marriage contract, that is to say, provided for an exchange of domestic services between the spouses, but not of reproductive services.

Together, these relations and processes, economic and social, provided for the physical maintenance of the population and for the continued existence of the localized residential units (which exploited the soil) and the dispersed social units with their estates: clans (with rights over the marriageability of their members); houses (owning tracts of land and the persons of members); and lineages (holding movable property). The structure of this "maintenance sphere" is outlined in Table 9.1.

Table 9.1

Structure of the Maintenance Sphere in the Kongo Economy
of the Nineteenth Century

	Economic Characteristics	Social Characteristics
Groups	local	descent
Product	subsistence goods	domestic services
Distribution	internal	external
Organization	egalitarian	hierarchical

THE PRESTIGE SPHERE

Production and reproduction were not limited to maintenance: there was also a "prestige" or "competitive" sphere, in which distinct kinds of goods (prestige goods) were produced and distributed. These goods, which included slaves, ivory, camwood, guns, gunpowder, and cloth, could not normally be exchanged for subsistence goods, such as plantains or an equivalent value in glass beads. Prestige goods were distributed and consumed in the course of political competition and were the means whereby a kind of social stratification was created and expressed (for analogous "spheres," see Bohannan 1955).

Most of the ivory and of the slaves, and also probably most of the camwood, were obtained from farther inland—from the market area known as Manianga, in the Mpioka Valley, or from as far as Stanley Pool (Vansina 1973). One of the minor trade routes to Mpalabala and thence to the coast ran from Manianga (now the Ngombe plateau) through the Manteke Valley itself. It is clear that chiefs situated along the route demanded passage fees, apparently often paid in gin, but it is not clear that chiefs always or usually organized the armed expeditions by which trade was conducted. With regard to slaves, the rule of *caveat vendor* prevailed: if the slave died within a few months of receipt, it was assumed that his soul had already been the object of a separate, illicit transaction, and the purchaser was entitled to a refund. Since long-distance trade required the use of labor properly organized, equipped, and maintained, I follow Coquery-Vidrovitch (1969) in regarding it as a process of production.

Some prestige goods did not simply pass through Manteke on their way elsewhere, but were retained in the village, distributed, and "consumed," either literally or by endowing them with social significance. And, in the internal distribution system, sovereign rights over land (as distinct from rights to land use) also entered as units exchangeable against, for example, persons, camwood, or guns.

Prestige goods always carry a marked degree of uselessness or redundancy, since their function is social rather than economic. Kongo prestige goods were intended to be used up rather than used, especially at the funerals of the great. Warfare was always more a matter of magical display than bloodshed, and guns were hardly superior to bows and spears for hunting, except in special circumstances. Firearms were most useful in contributing honorific explosions to funeral celebrations, and they could be displayed on graves, as were elephant tusks. Camwood provided a cosmetic necessary for rites of passage, including funerals. Red blankets and other clothes were wrapped in great quantities around the smoke-dried bodies of chiefs. Slaves were buried alive in a chief's grave and others were slaughtered at the inauguration of his successor—the capacity for violence is regarded in local ideology as an essential attribute of chiefship. Important men could send slaves to undergo the poison ordeal for them in witchcraft trials.

Slaves were not usually destroyed, however, and sovereignty over land, a purely abstract right, could never be. Together, slaves, land, and the persons added to the matrilineal house by the normal processes of reproduction constituted the principal elements of its estate. Ownership of land gave a house a visible certificate of its corporate existence and allowed it to extend rights of usufruct to its members, its children and grandchildren, and other dependents whom it might attract. As allies, these dependents supported the house in competition with other houses, whether of the same or different clans. Success in competition might mean that the head of the house could be initiated to a prestigious title (usually referred to in the ethnographic literature as chiefship), which conferred political and magical powers and for which he would have to hand over prestige goods, including slaves, to a superior chief or to existing holders of comparable titles. Failure in competition, on the other hand, might mean that the house would have to pay such goods in compensation for homicide, witchcraft, or offenses against cult rules. Warfare, which elsewhere might have amounted to a form of production of slaves, in Kongo was a kind of ordeal by which disputes were settled. Wars were not fought deliberately to procure slaves; they lasted only for a day or two and were concluded by a negotiated transfer of land or slaves, usually a man and woman, to the winners. Slaves were sometimes kidnapped, but even this method of procuring them was often disguised as compensation for alleged theft.

Four types of transfer were applicable to land and also to persons: they could be lent, given, pawned, or sold between houses. Loans and gifts socially subordinated the recipient and were conditional on his observance of social responsibilities. In practice, creditor-debtor relations, characteristically those created by marriage and the allocation of land to extra-lineage dependents, were maintained primarily between neighboring and co-resident clans, whose members lived mostly in one another's villages. Marriage (the verb "to wed," *sompa*, literally means "to borrow") was a form of loan. On the other hand, pawning and sale implied no necessary or continuing social relationship between the old and new owners (beyond the responsibility of testifying as necessary, later on, to the details of the original transaction). In addition, women, as productive resources, could be held in partnership (*kimbundi*); their offspring would be divided between the owning houses.

Ultimately, land and people were the basic resources, gains in one making it likely that gains would be made in the other. In a patrilineal society, a descent group can hope to expand relative to other groups by increasing the number of wives of its male members and thus the number of their offspring. In matrilineal Kongo, however, a woman's reproductive capacity, not being transferable by marriage, could only be transferred by slavery. By marrying an acquired slave woman, a man and his descent group acquired control over her children (as they did not over a free wife's children, who were recruited by the free wife's descent group). In this way the descent group could recruit children of its male members in addition to the normal recruitment in matrilineal systems of children of female members. The descendants of a female slave became a lineage of slaves incorporated in the house of their owners but not observing with them a rule of exogamy. Slaves also enhanced the importance of their owners, who spoke for them in all social transactions, monopolizing the privileges and responsibilities which, in the case of free men, would be divided among the "four chiefs": the heads of the mother's, father's, father's father's, and mother's father's clans.

In an ideal Kongo success story, the co-resident members of a matrilineal house, assisted by their resident slaves, children, and grandchildren, would convert the surplus of their subsistence production into prestige and social importance by using it to mount trading expeditions. The profits from long-distance trade, together with other prestige items exacted from its neighbors by political means, would eventually increase the house's membership, its landholdings, and its clients, promising bigger trading expeditions in the future.

A slave's living conditions and economic role did not differ sharply from a freeman's. Though a slave would be more likely than a freeman to be chosen for sacrifice or to be handed over in satisfaction of a corporate debt, he might also be chosen, temporarily, to be the head of the house or clan; and slave lineages might well have slaves of their own. In this instance, slavery is a form of social dependence, not of forced or dependent labor. "Slave" translates a variety of KiKongo terms, among them *m'vika*, "owned person," and *muntu wasumbwa*, "bought person." More politely, a slave was known as *mwana*, "child," that is, offspring of a male member of the clan. A pawn was *n'simbi* (from *simba*, meaning "to hold").

SOCIAL MOBILITY

What I have given so far is a description of nineteenth-century Manteke more or less as modern informants would describe it. The distribution and consumption of prestige goods, including slaves, made possible within and between slave-owning clans a greater degree of stratification than could be supported by the subsistence sphere alone.[1] Close study of traditions shows, however, that the reality was more complex.

When speaking of slaves and slavery, informants described a system of caste created by the rule that a slave is a slave forever. Manumission was always possible, providing that the slave's owners and his original clan would cooperate; the standard ritual (verb: *kuula*) required that the slave be marked with chalk as a sign of redemption, and that a pig called "the pig of rubbing with chalk" be transferred to the ex-owners. But the "redeemed" slave was then considered to be the slave of his original clan and could never recover first-class citizenship—that is, access to authority. The same principle was expounded to nineteenth-century ethnographers on the coast, and did in fact stratify the population there, the different castes being distinguished by forms of dress. I have argued elsewhere that the extreme hierarchical idea could only be realized where the circumstances of long-distance trade produced, as on the coast, exceptionally strong chiefs able to resolve by fiat the inherent ambiguities of Kongo status attribution (*CG,* Ch. 10).

In Manteke, stratification was more an ideal than a fact. There was, in practical terms, a series of statuses between slave and free, and movement up or down this scale could happen to anyone. This movement is best discussed in terms of the control exercised by senior members of a descent group, the elders (*bambuta*), over their juniors, the cadets (*baleeke*).

Meillassoux has argued (1960) that in a society with a subsistence econony, in which neither land nor capital can be monopolized as a way of controlling people, elders could control their cadets by controlling access to women, that is, through the system of reproduction. Although a man and a woman might elope, the man's acquisition of his offspring as his dependents, with respect to whose affairs he might himself achieve the social status of elder, was conditional upon their legitimation, that is, the legitimation of a marriage or other contract relating him to them. Such legitimation could be extended only by the elders of his own group, supported by their allies, the elders of other groups. In addition, by a somewhat similar mechanism, elders could monopolize ritual information, such as genealogies and cult secrets; in effect, they would control admission to their own ranks by refusing to credit ritual information put forward by someone they were not prepared to recognize.

The second of these mechanisms, control of ritual information, is

---

1. The main luxury goods (salt, gin, and the cheaper kinds of cloth), though imported from the coast, did not circulate in the prestige sphere; they constituted a special class of luxury goods whose social function was to reinforce the dependence of men on their chiefs through gin, and of wives on their husbands through salt and cloth.

recognized by the BaKongo themselves. The first, control of reproduction, appears at first sight not to apply to a matrilineal society such as this, in which all children accrue automatically to their mother's clan and in which, moreover, the social recognition of paternity does not depend on the father's marriage to the mother. Here, marriage transfers only domestic and not reproductive rights. But reproductive rights, and the subsequent right of the owner to accord domestic rights to himself or to another, *are* transferred by slavery. In addition, as I will explain, such transfers can retroactively affect an entire lineage, which is thereby shifted from the control of one elder to another.

To be an elder is to be recognized by other elders as socially responsible for a group of dependents—one's lineage or one's slaves—in whatever contracts may be entered into. Such responsibility is accorded by traditions of origin, describing the direct descent of free individuals and groups from the earliest ancestors. In the case of slaves, traditions describe the interruption of the line of descent by a sale affecting them or their matrilineal ascendant. Traditions are validated not by written records but by the testimony of approved witnesses, that is, of the elders of other groups, who will testify in their own best interest. Traditions serve as a sign of power rather than, as in Kongo theory, its source.

The position of the head (*nkazi*) of a descent group in relation to its affairs and members is described by the verb *vwa*, "to own" (of which m'vika, "slave," is a derivative), and which applies equally to slaves and free dependents. The social responsibility indicated by the verb is shared, in the case of free dependents, with the other three "chiefs," especially the nkazi of the paternal descent group. When slave sales were still practiced, only a man's own nkazi could sell him, and the man would appeal to the other three "chiefs" to protect him from this fate. If obliged to sell a dependent, the nkazi might sell a free person or a slave, but would probably choose one already in servitude. Decisions in such matters, though announced by and in the name of the nkazi, were in fact reached by the elders of the group he represented, advised by its children and grandchildren.

The essential difference between slave and free can be described as both theoretical (ritual) and practical (political). In theory, not belonging by birth to an autonomous local group, with its own tradition, rights to land, and ancestral graves, the slave was condemned to be a permanent minor and his interests were perpetually given second place. In practice, the slave differed from the freeman in having fewer than the full complement of "four chiefs" to speak for him and defend his interests. In this respect, his position was not, in fact, radically inferior. Anybody's social prospects depended on the number and power of the groups to which he was affiliated and on their willingness to support him.

Examples drawn from tradition show how movement down the social scale might occur. A free woman, whose own nkazi failed to exercise his responsibilities towards her because he lost interest or found it inconvenient, became the responsibility of her husband's nkazi and thus de facto his slave (like the pawn who was never redeemed). Alternatively, her status might change de jure, her original nkazi inviting the other to make a payment transforming the "loan" (marriage) into a sale (*CG*: 76, 218). This kind of "slave by default" was called *mwan'a fundu*. Similarly, an incoming woman's offspring would be given in marriage and eventually buried by their new nkazi, but they could never trace their pedigree through his ancestors; the would remain dependents, and none of them could become a nkazi. Or a freeman could be so much at odds with his own clansmen that he would take up permanent residence with his father, ceasing to participate in his own lineage's affairs and thus in effect volunteering for slavery. Whether or not he was regarded as a slave, he would find himself with less than the full complement of "chiefs," since his father or his father's nkazi would assume the roles of nkazi and "maternal grandfather" in addition to that of "father," and would thus tend to monopolize authority over the newcomer. Individuals, whether slave or free, could also enter into voluntary dependence on the head of a group other than their own by following a set procedure. Voluntary dependence is said to have been an honorable condition, but unless the persons who entered into it, and especially their matrilineal descendants in future generations, were politically successful, they would find their status merged with that of purchased slaves. A refugee was called *mwan'a lufuulu*, "child of house-site."

Freemen might also become slaves—that is, socially dependent upon others—as a result of the political success of the slaves they themselves had acquired. This insecurity was a function of the social structure itself, not merely a consequence of the political adroitness of individuals, and came about as follows. As I have indicated, a free group that acquired slaves as wives also acquired control over these women's progeny (in contrast to the progeny of their free wives) and could thus expand faster than a group that married only free partners. The progeny of such acquired slave wives became slave-branches attached to the free group. Intermarriage between free members and their slaves produced children of whose mother and father both belonged to the group; the children were, therefore, under the undivided authority of the group's nkazi. But this very advantage could have its drawbacks. For the free son of a free woman who had taken as husband a slave of her own clan himself lacked, like a slave, the full complement of "chiefs," having no father's or father's father's clan to which to turn for support if necessary. A like vulnerability might afflict the entire owning group, supposing that they had attempted to be self-sufficient in spouses and thus neglected to ally themselves to other free elders; their slaves, becoming numerous, might be able to put forward traditions showing themselves to be the "true" owners of the group's name and estate, and reduce their erstwhile owners to slavery.[2] This lamentable development is described in a song which says, "E, e, things are growing on the termite hill, alas!"

The promotion of slaves also occurred quietly, without any special efforts on their part, when their owners, seeing their own numbers declining (for whatever reason), decided to co-opt the slaves as a new lineage of the house. The slaves would then be indistinguishable from free members of the clan as far as outsiders were concerned. This promotion was somewhat insecure, however, since the elders of the clan would keep the secret of the ex-slaves' origin for eventual use against them in any dispute. On the other hand, since the "truth" of tradition was ascertained solely by its political viability, even freemen might find that, according to "secrets" only just revealed, they were slaves. In short, the real difference between freemen and slaves was not an absolute condition but a scale of relative political security.[3]

Whereas local social theory, then, delineated a structure of castes or estates, differentiated by direct radial links to Mbanza Kongo or by the lack of them, real communities were very nearly homogeneous, econom-

2. Part of the evidence deployed to justify this "coup d'état" would be genealogical, derived as follows. The slave group (S) and their free owners (F) have regularly provided each other with women in marriage. This situation is known to anthropologists as a type of restricted exchange; it is represented in genealogical form as patrilateral cross-cousin marriage and is conducive to, or at least consistent with, an organization of society into units of small size and egalitarian structure. In Kongo, patrilateral cross-cousin marriage was, in fact, for freemen the preferred form, and was used to ally neighboring clans; but a slave lineage, by definition, was not entitled to arrange the marriages of its own women. Whatever the genealogy showed, group S was therefore permanently in the position of "wife receiver," and could never reciprocate as "wife giver." This situation, structurally equivalent to matrilateral cross-cousin marriage, enables group F to accumulate women (dependents) and is conducive to a degree of social stratification, founded on exploitation of the reproductive capacity of group S. The difference, however, between the two situations lies entirely in the locus of authority (*kinkazi*), which is itself defined politically. The genealogical record of intermarriage between the two groups would be consistent with the location of authority in F, or in S, or equally in both (see Fox 1967, Chs. 7, 8).

3. In economic terms, the assimilation of slaves to free status, or of freemen to slave status, whether done implicitly or explicitly (explicitly, for example, in the sale of a freeman to meet some ritual debt, such as a declaration of witchcraft guilt), represented a conversion between the maintenance and prestige spheres. Successful deployment of labor, adequately fed and equipped, in a trading expedition. partly financed by the sale of surplus foodstuffs (especially peanuts) to the resident population of the trading termini, represented a conversion of resources "upwards," from the maintenance to the prestige sphere. Forced conversion "downwards" apparently occurred at least occasionally, during famines, when people were forced to sell prestige goods, and even persons, in order to acquire foodstuffs.

ically and socially. All of the examples given in preceding paragraphs are drawn from legends relating to the single community of Mbanza Manteke, in which during the nineteenth century a continuous stream of immigrants who entered in different circumstances achieved some degree of assimilation that was described and legitimated by reference to a corporate structure which was, in theory, fixed. Politically successful immigrants were able in time to claim that their ancestors had always lived in the valley. The dominant clan, Nanga, may well have been represented there "since the beginning." But if all the modern legends are true, none of its modern representatives is a genuine matrilineal descendant of the founders of the village.

TWENTIETH CENTURY

In 1879, an English Protestant missionary settled in Mbanza Manteke. In 1883, H. M. Stanley's agents began to appoint officials ("chiefs") responsible for providing porters on the new main route from Matadi to Stanley Pool, which ran through Manteke. Two years later the Congo Free State was officially proclaimed. Within a few years, the new state declared itself the owner of all land not actually in use by the natives, the definition of "use" remaining very vague, and had requisitioned virtually all male labor, channeling it at a stroke into industrial enterprises (Axelson 1970: 17; Dupré and Rey 1969:156). Female labor in agriculture was not directly affected, except that in the next three decades epidemics of sleeping sickness reduced the population of the Lower Congo enormously. "Slavery" was "abolished," but forced and clearly dependent labor was introduced for the first time in the form of military service, contract labor, and porterage on the route to the interior. All trade, except local trade in subsistence goods, was taken over by foreigners, and land transfers under customary law ceased, the official dogma being that there had never been any. Chiefship disappeared, chiefs having been essentially the managers and beneficiaries of the economy of prestige goods.

The people of Mbanza Manteke interpreted their new situation in religious terms, and in 1886 they began to convert to Protestant Christianity. According to my oldest informants, they expected that under the new dispensation of power represented by the missionary, society would begin anew. Slavery and all social distinctions would disappear, as would witchcraft.[4] The hamlets in the valley were abandoned and a new community was built on high ground around the mission station.

4. This chapter isolates the social and economic dimensions of slavery. In indigenous thinking, however, no clear distinction is made between traffic in slaves and witchcraft. Cultic initiations that conferred protection against, or power over, witches were ultimately related to political problems of status definition. To this day nineteenth-century trade with Europeans in ivory and rubber, as well as slaves, is widely apprehended as witchcraft. See MacGaffey (1972).

Although the missionaries understood what was happening in Manteke as conversion, the people thought of it, in the terms provided for them by their culture, as initiation into a new cult which, like other cults, would give them access to powers useful in this world. The missionary was the priest (*nganga*) of this cult. The missionary also bought slaves; or as he saw it, he "liberated" slaves from their masters. Even after the government's official abolition of slavery, however, the conceptual antinomy slave/free, which is a function of the system of matrilineal descent, remained the only basis for social identity. The state did not attempt to abolish descent and the body of customary law relating descent to authority (*kinkazi*, the rights of a nkazi), exogamy, rights in land, inheritance, and succession; on the contrary, under the policy of indirect rule, customary law was endorsed by the government. In customary law, the idea of individual autonomy before the law, which is what the missionary and the state meant by "freedom," does not exist; in customary law, everybody must have his nkazi to speak for him. The missionary's acquisition of slaves therefore merely prepared the way for his own metamorphosis into a chief, according to indigenous rules.

This double process of co-opting the resident missionary into local society on indigenous terms was frustrated by two developments. In the first twenty years of this century, the missionaries began to withdraw from direct contact with local populations, leaving Congolese personnel in charge as catechists and teachers. The parallel withdrawal of administrators, as the practice of indirect rule developed during the same period, left government-appointed "chiefs" in charge. The people were thus expected, in effect, to solve their own local political problems in what Europeans regarded as the traditional way, although local institutions had been deprived of much of the manpower that had formerly sustained them and though the new chiefs had nothing in common with nineteenth-century chiefs and derived such power as they had from the backing of the government.

The people therefore returned to the old criteria of status differentiation, many of them relapsing from Christianity in the process, and began to besiege the government's courts with arguments about land tenure, all turning on questions of tradition and of pedigree—arguments, that is, about who was a slave and who was not. In Manteke, these arguments have had no economic importance (except that court fees constitute an indirect tax) because it is still the case that land is plentiful and anyone who is a land "owner," or child or grandchild of an owner, or spouse of any of these, can obtain what he needs without difficulty. Nor is there any wage labor in the village, except that which is performed by or for outsiders. It seems, rather, that any quarrel turns to slavery on the ground that the offending party "doesn't belong in this community anyway."

The courts took seriously the myth of Mbanza Kongo and the stratification of freemen and slaves. Among freemen, according to the official view of traditional society, hereditary chiefs from the senior line of the senior house of the founding clan governed the community as guardians of sacred ancestral law and tradition. Under European guidance, legends became legal documents, their contradictions to be resolved according to the laws of evidence and the testimony of supporting witnesses. Since such testimony corresponded not to history but to the shifting allegiances of local politics, litigation substituted fairly well for war and trade; cases drag on for decades, and the community remains as unstratified as before. It is organized into a network of ad hoc interlineage committees, such as the "four chiefs," which extends into all the neighboring villages, entirely uncentralized.

A CASE STUDY: MBANZA NTALA

In Manteke, it is probable that the site of the "original" settlement by the Nanga clan was a promontory called Mbanza Ntala, located in the middle of the valley. After the valley had been divided into strips allocated to each of four houses of the clan-section, Mbanza Ntala was regarded as the property of the Mfutu house. Still later, probably after the middle of the nineteenth century, Mfutu moved to a new village on the north side of the valley and left Mbanza Ntala to the Ngoma house of the Ntumba clan. Another Ntumba house, Mvika, claims land on the south side of the valley. The two clans and their adherents constitute the dominant factions of the modern village, and the chief bone of contention between them is the ownership of Mbanza Ntala. Accordingly, the dispute is mentioned repeatedly in my study of Manteke social structure, but it was only in

Table 9.2

Relationship of the Parties to the Dispute over Mbanza Ntala

1. Clan	2. House	3. Lineage	4. Individual
Nanga	Disa		
	Nkuti		Dyasa
	Nsaka		Mbelani
	Mfutu		Hezekaya
	Nzuzi		
Ntumba	Ngoma	Mwema Ngombe	Kyanlasu[a]
	Mvika	Mbuku a Wala	Joel Albert

[a] Allegedly not a legitimate member of this clan but a slave recently acquired from Na Mazinga clan.

1966, after I had left Zaïre, that the ownership of Mbanza Ntala was nominally settled by a court decision. On a second visit to Zaïre, in 1970, I was able to study the transcript of the proceedings and to discuss the case with most of the parties. The testimony they offered, their attitude to the result, and the way the court reached its decision confirm the analysis of Manteke politics in my book and show the critical but ambiguous social role of "slavery" in recent years.

The litigants were Hezekaya, a member of the Mfutu house of Nanga clan, and Kyanlasu, spokesman for Joel Albert, head of the Ngoma house of Ntumba clan (see Table 9.2). In proceedings that extended from October 1965 to July 1966, Hezekaya's arguments challenged the Ntumba position on four sociologically distinct levels:

1. Since Nanga originally founded the settlement, it owns the whole valley. All other clans can only be its clients.

2. The Ngoma house was founded by a woman who married into the Mfutu house. Her descendants, the lineage Mwema Ngombe, became Mfutu slaves and as such were given Mbanza Ntala. The last representative of this lineage, Johnny Matota, died about 1956, and the land therefore has reverted to Mfutu.

3. Joel Albert's lineage, Mbuku a Wala, were "late arrivals," not among the original recipients of the land given by Mfutu but clients of the senior lineage, Mwema Ngombe.

4. Kyanlasu, spokesman for Ngoma and purportedly a member of Mwema Ngombe, has no business in Manteke at all, being merely a slave of the clan Na Mazinga, located in another village, whom Johnny Matota "released from slavery" in 1936 in order to provide himself with a successor.

In the transcript of the case, as is usual in such discussions these levels are merged into a single confused argument, partly because of the absence of a sociologically adequate vocabulary (clan, house, and lineage are all called by the same terms) and partly by the historical perspective in which the witnesses conventionally present themselves as historical actors in the first person singular: "I, Mfutu, married Na Mazele."

Kyanlasu's strategy was to deny Nanga priority and assert that "he" (that is, his ancestors) had originally founded the Mbanza Ntala settlement after being welcomed into the area by Ntambu. Now, the people who call themselves Ntambu are regarded by prevailing opinion as ex-slaves of the Nsaka house of Nanga, manumitted during the 1930s and set up as an independent clan. By appealing to them and a number of other marginal figures to corroborate his testimony, which enhanced their status as well as his own, Kyanlasu hoped to effect a local revolution against the dominant clan, Nanga.

The Manteke court, made up of five natives of the region well versed in Manteke law and familiar with the long history of this dispute, were being asked in effect to decide at what point a long series of immigrants was to be divided into those who had become assimilated ("owned land") and those who remained strangers and clients ("slaves"). Moreover, the decision had to be politically realistic. They decided that Joel Albert of Mbuku a Wala lineage was entitled to succeed Mwema Ngombe lineage in the Ngoma house as owner of Mbanza Ntala because he had "become free" or "become a landowner" (*wayika mfumu*) by exercising responsibility for the funeral of Johnny Matota and thus establishing his autonomy as de facto head of the house. They also threw out the challenge to Kyanlasu's legitimacy by declaring obliquely that "the clan Na Mazinga [to which, according to Hezekaya, Kyanlasu really belonged] is not represented in Mbanza Manteke."

After losing the case, Hezekaya complained bitterly that the court was prejudiced against him; he wrote letters to higher authorities and pulled all the strings he could. He pointed out, for example, that the most influential judge, Damison of Nsundi clan, cultivated Ngoma land as a child of that house; Hezekaya himself is a child of Nsundi, but that clan owns no land locally and could not act as his patron. For that matter, Joel Albert is a grandchild of Mfutu and thus has a personal right to use Mfutu land; people argued that he could get on well with Hezekaya were it not for Kyanlasu, whose own motivation seems to have been that by winning the dispute for Ngoma he would simultaneously secure his own legitimate membership in it.

As a result of Hezekaya's complaints, the authorities convoked a special appeal court of judges drawn from elsewhere in the province, who were thus unbiased but also totally unfamiliar with the complexities of Manteke society. Unable to make much of the substance of the dispute, they turned to neighboring landowners and elders from other villages, none of whom was able to clarify the situation (this development is predictable from the analysis in *CG*). One of them said, "I recognize Nanga as my neighbor, but there are so many Nanga these days." At this point, the late Mbelani Lukeba, of Nsaka house, the appointed government chief of the region (*chef médaillé*), offered testimony conforming to the court's sociological expectations.

In Nanga, he explained, there were five houses, in order of seniority: Disa, Nkuti, Nsaka, Mfutu, Nzuzi. Of these, the representatives of Disa had gone to live in a neighboring village, in circumstances he did not explain. Filling the role of customary chief to perfection, he continued: "I cannot reveal the secrets left to me by my ancestors; they forbade me to, lest it cause the breakup of the clan. If I bring myself to do so, it is only to enlighten the court and to silence those who falsely claim to be original landowners here in Manteke." He proceeded to tell what is in fact the well-known story of how Johnny Matota's ancestress, Na Mazele, had married into Mfutu and later became a slave (mwan'a fundu, slave by default) when her clan failed to accept responsibility for the funerals of her children (*CG:*76).

The court heard this testimony with evident relief and based judgment on it. The judgment reads as follows (my translation).

Whereas the history recited by Mbelani and accepted by all the members of the Nanga clan and the parties in dispute shows that Hezekaya does not belong to the senior branch of the Nanga clan, and

Whereas the sole customary representative of the senior branch is Dyasa of Nkuti, Moanda of Disa being resident in Ndemba village, and

Whereas the dispute between the parties before the court is therefore null and void, and

Whereas there is nevertheless occasion to maintain the peace, the Court *Declares* that Mbanza Ntala belongs to Nanga, of which the senior branch is represented in Manteke by Dyasa, but recognizes the right of members of Ngoma to use the land allotted to them by Nanga.

The court noted that only Nsaka had produced good tradition and fined several neighboring landowners for "false witness," apparently because their testimony did not confirm the officially accepted sociological model.

The court thus in effect accepted, and interpreted to his disadvantage, only the first of Hezekaya's arguments, the one that related to Nanga's rights as the founding clan. Hezekaya was dismayed because he not only lost his quarrel with Kyanlasu but his other quarrels, not directly at issue, with the other houses of Nanga. The irony of the situation is that, in the eyes of Nkuti and Disa, Mbelani's lineage is a group of recent immigrants who have smuggled themselves into the Nsaka house and are therefore quite incompetent to proclaim "the secrets of the ancestors" of Nanga, and that in Nsaka's view, not expressed in court, Disa has been definitively transferred to Ndemba and Nkuti is in pawn to Nsaka, so that both are disqualified permanently from any pretensions to "chiefship." As for Kyanlasu, he has left Manteke, apparently for good.

CONCLUSION

In the nineteenth century, individuals sold into slavery were political losers, like the victims of seventeenth- and eighteenth-century English expropriations and vagrancy laws, rather than criminals. Nor were they debtors, in the European sense, who entered servitude for a fixed term in order to "work off" a debt; this was not, and in the villages still is not, an economy in which labor could be bought. Many of the slaves generated locally, however, as distinct from those acquired inland, were deprived of their freedom as a consequence of accusations of witchcraft, themselves a function of local micropolitics. Monteiro, describing Angola in the 1860s, wrote that witchcraft accusations were the chief source of slaves for shipment, and argued that the reduction of the slave trade had caused the number of executions to rise (1876, 1:61). Although slaves were still being shipped from Cabinda in the 1890s, by the middle of the century, after the decline of the Atlantic slave trade, the principle remaining market was the local one, within a radius of about twenty-five miles.

Under colonial rule, the shell of customary law, artificially preserved after the destruction of its economic base, still commanded great interest among the rural population because it provided the idiom of local politics.

At the level of the territorial courts of appeal where, until 1960, European magistrates supervised the administration of customary law, the contemporary political function of the slavery idiom was not understood; the preamble to one verdict runs: "Whereas, slavery having been abolished, and the ties linking domestic slaves to their owners having become officially nonexistent; and whereas, the former slaves, although officially free, desire the intervention of a judgment, which is the only way for them to establish indisputably in the eyes of the BaKongo their status as freemen . . ." (my translation). In fact, the BaKongo understood that traffic in slaves had been abolished, but could no more readily imagine the abolition of "slavery" than that of "freedom."

After World War II the question of who owned land under customary law acquired a new interest for those who lived near towns such as Matadi or who expected to be paid for timber or mineral concessions to European companies. Not surprisingly, the courts had difficulty establishing customary precedents for some of the problems that arose. Some (Belgian) magistrates, noting that "fathers" and "sons" had jointly exploited the same piece of land, imposed that practice as the rule, ignoring the question of "ownership." Others held that "customary rights" meant rights to subsistence exploitation only, and that even the undisputed owner of a tract must submit to an inquiry to ensure that others would not suffer if the land were withdrawn from "collective exploitation" and used for a banana plantation or for *commercial* firewood gathering, that is, for "exploitation of a European type." By decisions such as this, rural society was restricted to "subsistence" except insofar as its members were willing to leave their artificial enclave and seek wage labor in town.

The rural economy, which provides most of the food consumed by the urban population, including that of Kinshasa, Zaïre's polyglot capital, has come to rest on the labor of women, old men, and the few younger men prepared to struggle with the overwhelming material problems of village life. Hunting is no longer very productive and men now assist their wives in the fields. The only distinctively male crops are fruit trees, whose harvest can be sold in town. Most men of working age live in town, and fewer and fewer of them even think of returning to the village to help their elders prosecute the old feuds. In town, where the people are wage earners and land is distributed by the government to occupants individually, disputes between descent groups do not occur and consequently everyone, no matter how dubious his pedigree, is free to think of himself as "free."

People are no longer sure what the old institutions were and what the old terms meant. Marriage restrictions are rapidly being revised, and some now say that the matrilineal clan was never exogamous, although even now, in my experience, a marriage occurring between two members of the same clan-section is an infallible indication that one or both of their lineages are considered by the elders to be alien. The partners in one such marriage known to me have no idea that this is the case, and the same marriage was pointed out to me by a group of unrelated elders from the neighborhood to "prove" that intraclan marriage sometimes took place, but later they admitted the deceit. As De Sousberghe remarks about the BaPende, the most careful inquiry is necessary in all matters of pedigree (1963:27); they are the main political currency.

Recently the government has nationalized land, thus depriving matrilineal descent of its main functional content. Individuals are now encouraged to acquire title to estates on condition that they develop ranches, plantations, and the like. The new landowners belong to the urban upper class, who alone have the necessary capital, but they often seek out land in their home villages and privately agree to pay a kind of rent to the customary owners. The courts, however, now refuse to hear cases like that of Mbanza Ntala and will not sanction the new rental agreements. The era of indirect rule is over.

Since independence in 1960, the Kongo political party Abako, the government bureaucracy, and in recent years the national Popular Revolutionary Movement have provided alternative political symbols and alternative means of political advancement, especially but not exclusively in urban areas. The new structures dispense illusions less generously than the old and, for the first time, stratify the BaKongo by class.

GLOSSARY

baleeke: juniors, cadets.
bambuta: elders.
chef médaillé: a government chief.
kimbundi: partnership.
kinkazi: authority; from *nkazi,* headman.
kulazi: strings of glass beads.
kuula: to redeem, set free.
makuta: brass rods.
mbongi: men's shelter.
munta wasumbwa: "bought person"; a slave.
m'vika: "owned person"; a slave.
mwana: child; also, a polite term for a slave.
mwan'a fundu: a kind of slave.
mwan'a lufuulu: refugee; literally, "child of house-site."
nganga: priest.
nkazi: chief; the head of a descent group.
nsafu tree: symbol of men's crops and the social rights connected with them.
n'simbi: a pawn.
sompa: to marry (literally, to borrow).
vwa: to own.
wayika mfumu: became a landowner or freeman.

REFERENCES

Axelson, S. 1970. *Culture confrontation in the Lower Congo.* Falkoping, Sweden.
Balibar, E. 1971. The fundamental concepts of historical materialism. In *Reading Capital,* by L. Althusser and E. Balibar. New York.
Berreman, G. D. 1967. Stratification, pluralism and interaction: a comparative analysis of caste. In *Caste and race,* ed. A. de Reuck and J. Knight. Boston.
Bohannan, P. 1955. Some principles of exchange and investment among the Tiv. *Am. Anthrop.* 57:60-70.
Coquery-Vidrovitch, C. 1969. Recherches sur un mode de production africain. *Pensée,* No. 144, pp. 61-78.
De Sousberghe, L. 1963. Les Pende. In *Miscellanea ethnographica,* Musée royal de l'Afrique centrale, Annales, série in 8°, sciences humaines, No. 46. Tervuren, Belgium.
Dupré, G., and Rey, P. P. 1969. Réflexions sur la pertinence d'une théorie de l'histoire des échanges. *Cah. int. Sociol.* New ser. 46:113-62.

Engels, F. 1942. *The origin of the family, private property, and the state.* New York.

Finley, M. I. 1968. Slavery. *International encyclopedia of the social sciences* 14:307-13. New York.

Fox, R. 1967. *Kinship and marriage.* Baltimore.

MacGaffey, W. 1970. *Custom and government in the Lower Congo.* Berkeley.

_____. 1972. The West in Congolese experience. In *Africa and the West,* ed. P. D. Curtin. Madison.

Meillassoux, C. 1960. Essai d'interprétation du phénomène économique dans les sociétés traditionnelles d'auto-subsistance. *Cah. Etud. afr.* 1:38-67.

Mertens, J. 1942. *Les chefs couronnés chez les Bakongo orientaux.* Brussels.

Monteiro, J. J. 1876. *Angola and the River Congo.* 2 vols. London.

Rey, P.-P. 1969. Articulation des modes de dépendance et des modes de reproduction dans deux sociétés lignagères (Punu et Kunyi du Congo-Brazzaville). *Cah. Etud. afri.* 9:415-40.

Smith, M. G. 1966. Pre-industrial stratification systems. In *Social structure and mobility in economic development,* ed. N. J. Smelser and S. M. Lipset. Chicago.

_____. 1969. Pluralism in pre-colonial African societies. In *Pluralism in Africa,* ed. L. Kuper and M. G. Smith. Los Angeles.

Southall, A. W. 1970. Stratification in Africa. In *Essays in comparative social stratification,* ed. L. Plotnicov and A. Tuden. Pittsburgh.

Terray, E. 1972. *Marxism and "primitive" societies.* New York.

Vansina, J. 1973. *The Tio kingdom of the Middle Congo, 1880-1892.* London.

The Historical Dynamics of Slave Systems

Part V

10

Changing Forms of Servitude among the Kerebe of Tanzania

Gerald W. Hartwig

A historical analysis of servitude among the Kerebe, who occupy an island and peninsula in the southeast region of the Victoria Nyanza (Lake Victoria) in modern Tanzania, reveals a complex, altering set of social relationships. Whereas in many of the neighboring interlacustrine societies of East Africa social stratification was often related to the domination of a pastoral minority over an agricultural majority, Kerebe social hierarchy was a product of cultural diversity among different groups of agriculturalists.

The Kerebe offer several advantages for analyzing social stratification. First, the society was basically stratified along cultural lines that could be crossed under certain conditions. Second, each ethnic group in the community was composed of people dependent to varying degrees upon agriculture. Third, the advent of the royal clan in fairly recent times (the seventeenth century) provides oral information that enables the historian approximately to date particular developments. Fourth, the relative wealth of this oral record is ultimately due to a few outstanding persons whose pride in the Kerebe past and whose effort to retain this record permit us to explore the Kerebe heritage.[1]

1. The Kerebe refer to themselves as AbaKerebe and their country as BuKerebe; U-Kerewe and Wa-Kerewe are the Swahili terms for the chiefdom and people. The collection

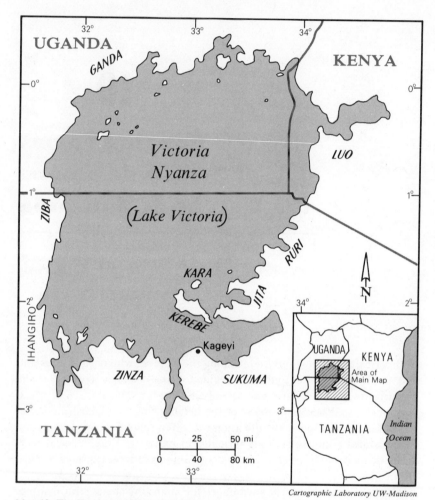

Map 10. The Kerebe and Their Neighbors

Cartographic Laboratory UW-Madison

Unlike the Ganda, on the northwestern shore of the Victoria Nyanza, who gained a considerable part of their servile population by conducting raids on their neighbors during the nineteenth century, the Kerebe were a people who, in the same period, focused their energies on trade. They did not resort to military means to extend their power—probably because of the virtual geographical isolation of BuKerebe from the sparsely populated eastern mainland. Nevertheless, the Kerebe were involved in

of Kerebe oral information in 1968-69 was made possible by a fellowship from the Foreign Area Fellowship Program. The statements and conclusions contained in this chapter, however, are the responsibility of the author.

activities that drew non-Kerebe into their society in a servile role (for an analogous case in East Africa, see Alpers 1967:21 on the Gogo). At the same time, the Kerebe sold relatively few servile persons to coastal traders (Bennett 1970:214).

THE KEREBE POLITY

In the seventeenth century the future royal clan of BuKerebe, the Silanga, and their numerous followers fled from Ihangiro, on the south-western shore of the lake where their clan had ruled as independent chiefs and later, after their conquest by Ruhinda the Great of Karagwe, in the fifteenth or sixteenth century, as subchiefs. The Silanga arrival in BuKerebe produced social stratification on a significant scale. The Silanga-led contingent used force and guile to subdue and subsequently rule the inhabitants of the southeastern lake region. Confronted by language and cultural differences, the victorious migrating band imposed its language and customs upon its subjects, who, over time, generally adopted the new culture. The ruling clan formed the privileged and first rank in the community, and the *omukama* (ruler; pl. *abakama*) was its head. The Sese formed the second major social stratum; they were the descendants of the contingent that had fled from Ihangiro as well as the descendants of the earlier occupants of BuKerebe who had adopted the new customs and language.

By the nineteenth century, the Jita (Kwaya) and Kara (who may possibly have been there at the time of the Silanga arrival in the mid-1600s) are mentioned in oral accounts as distinct ethnic groups living within the chiefdom. The Jita inhabited the southeastern shore of the lake and even in the 1600s were practicing male circumcision, which was anathema to the Sese population. From the small island of BuKara, other immigrants occasionally moved into BuKerebe. Before the arrival of the royal clan, the inhabitants of BuKerebe, BuKara, and BuJita were closely similar in language and most customs. Today many clans identified as Sese in BuKerebe have relatives living in BuKara and BuJita, although their language and customs differ significantly. These kinship ties, bridging ethnic and political units, eased the problem of moving from one district to another as much in 1700 as in 1950.

Geographical factors have historically promoted migration in this region. The Kerebe occupy a district with relatively high, reliable rainfall in contrast to their neighbors along the eastern lakeshore, who suffer periodic drought. Hence, BuKerebe has periodically served as a refuge for those seeking either more favorable agricultural conditions or emergency food supplies. Whereas most servile persons among the Kerebe originated from the eastern lakeshore during the 1800s, from people living north of the Jita, approximately one third of the free Kerebe population in 1900 was classified as Jita. These people, because they were able to take care of their own needs on arrival, had not entered the chiefdom in a servile status but rather as independent nuclear family units or individuals who had requested and received permission to settle and cultivate. It is clear, therefore, that strangers entering the district were not automatically placed in a servile role. In the case of the Jita, their cultural distinctiveness and their numbers provided the basis for a distinct social stratum.

The Sese stratum of the population regarded the Jita as beneath them in rank, and the Kara below the Jita. Descendants of individual Jita and Kara could eventually lose their distinct cultural identity by residing with their Sese fellow clansmen and adopting their language and customs. But the majority did not, and the Jita and Kara remained in the twentieth century as distinct ethnic groups with virtually no intermarriage between them or with the Sese. The only exception was the royal clan, which was above this restriction; its members married representatives of any clan or ethnic group.

Kerebe society was thus divided into social strata involving royalty and ethnicity, with the Silanga clan forming the upper echelon, the Sese clans composing the next rank, the Jita occupying the third, and the Kara the lowest. Allegiance to the omukama bound the community into a single political entity of some forty-five thousand people in 1907 (Hurel 1911:62-65). The approximate proportion of each ethnic group at the turn of the century was Sese, 30 percent; Jita, 35 percent; Kara, 20 percent; others, including the servile population, 15 percent (Hurel 1911:63-65; Baker 1932[?]:4-6).

An understanding of the omukama's authority over his subjects is essential to an understanding of the role of inherited servitude within Kerebe society. Aniceti Kitereza, a recorder of Kerebe customs, described the theoretical powers of the ruler's office thus:

The omukama was greatly respected by his people, as was manifested in greetings and ordinary speech. . . . this respect was essentially paid to him and to no one else in the chiefdom. He was above all and most people feared him. He had power over all things possessed by his subjects—livestock and crops, for example. He could order any death, or the plundering and destruction of any homes he wished. He was expected to be the elder of everyone in the chiefdom and nobody else held these same powers. He was the light, elder, sun, lion, creator, etc. [titles of praise]. When officially greeting him, people took gifts consisting of goats or cattle or millet or hoes or beer. He received presents [tribute] once a year from each home. Headmen and nobles [members of the royal clan] did not contribute to this (Kitereza 1943 [?], tr. by P. T. Magere).

This passage fails to mention that his subjects, particularly the advisors from nonroyal Sese clans, had the right to depose an omukama if they found he did not serve the community satisfactorily. Nonetheless the enormous powers of the omukama suggest that obedience to him was normally in the subjects' best interests. Thus the ruler-subject relationship involved reciprocal rights recognized by both parties. Kerebe oral accounts definitely extol the generous abakama, while those who abused their prerogatives are denounced. The annual tribute to the omukama was regarded as normal, but he was expected to assist his subjects in time of unusual need. This held true for all, regardless of their social position or clan.

SERVITUDE AND THE KEREBE CLANS BEFORE THE NINETEENTH CENTURY

Males with an inherited servile status in Kerebe society were called *aberu* (sing. *omwiru*) and females were called *abazana* (sing. *omuzana*). Both words are from the vocabulary of the interlacustrine peoples, who used them to designate persons of low status. The existence of the words in KiKerebe is specifically linked with the arrival of the royal clan. Servitude thus dates to at least the time when the chiefdom was formed in the mid-1600s. This earlier system was no doubt similar to that which can be traced among the Jita and Kara. Their word approximating the KiKerebe "aberu" and "abazana" is *abagaya*, which refers specifically to the Luo and is definitely related to slaving activities of the nineteenth century. The absence of a word to describe servility (as against a word naming a particular ethnic group enslaved by slavers in recent times) implies the earlier absence of an enduring servile status. This is very likely, for status inequality, except on an age and sex basis, was not a feature of Kara or Jita society. Any dependent individuals would have been adopted into a clan structure and their alien origins readily forgotten. Independent males, on the other hand, could establish themselves without assistance from another clan and could lay the foundations of a new clan.

The clan was the basic social unit among the Kerebe, and the term for it, *oluganda*, encompassed the patrilineal descendants of a known ancestor. Many Kerebe clans were small, often possessing fewer than thirty members, while others, such as the royal clan, counted their numbers in the hundreds. The varying sizes of clans reflected the movements of small groups of people in the eastern lake district in search of better opportunities in a generally dry environment. After settling in BuKerebe, which had favorable geographical conditions, a new clan would slowly increase in numbers over the years. But it was a new clan only in the sense that it represented a new social unit in Kerebe society. Identification and communication were normally retained with kinsmen in neighboring societies, even though the clan members were now established among another ethnic group.

Regardless of the size of the clan, a basic assumption in this community was that an individual's social identity was determined by his membership in a particular clan. For all practical purposes, the clan was the dominant economic, social, ritual, and political unit. Its spiritual, judicial, and economic functions were under the control of the clan elders. This was as true after the royal clan asserted its control as it had been before. With the power of the omukama established, clan elders could petition him for assistance if they felt their powers were inadequate for a given situation. Within a clan, individual property rights scarcely existed, for the clan collectively held recognized property rights over, for example, livestock, land use, and the services of individual members. Thus, at the beginning of the nineteenth century, hoe handles were a scarce commodity, and a man could borrow a handle from a member of another clan without collateral. But if he did not return or replace the handle when requested, the lender could complain to the clan as a unit, and the lending clan could reclaim its property by bringing its case against the borrower's clan before the royal authority.

Clans appear to have been relatively equal in status and economic power before the Silanga conquest, but afterwards competition for status increased, particularly among the Sese. The accumulation of wealth, especially of livestock, before 1800 by the omukama, who distributed some of it to other members of the royal clan as well as to favorites among nonroyal clans, resulted in considerable economic differences and competition for wealth among clans.

Outside the clan structure an individual had no legal identity, no security, and no way of enforcing normal rights. For those persons who, for a number of reasons, were no longer members of a clan, the Kerebe provided an arrangment by which they could be incorporated into a new clan but in a servile status that was inherited by the next generation.

Just as the generous giving of gifts by the omukama represented the most praiseworthy attribute of a great man, so the inability to provide one's own sustenance was the most despised attribute of a poor man. An omwiru was dependent on others and had to place himself in their charge. Whether he was the victim of circumstances, such as a famine, or whether he was a war captive, he was regarded as alone, outside his clan, and therefore totally dependent on strangers. The Kerebe provided a single niche for all such persons: they were given sustenance and thus life in exchange for rights over their services. For, like many other African communities, the Kerebe regarded people as their most precious possession, the "real key to production and prosperity" (Gray and Birmingham 1970: 18).

What of hospitality in Kerebe society? This was accorded to social equals and superiors—equally independent persons with a distinct clan identity. And charity? As practiced among the Kerebe, charity flourished within the clan only. Nonmembers were expected to repay what was borrowed and to reciprocate hospitality. Those dispossessed and without a clan identity could not honor such obligations. The most charitable thing an elder could do, therefore, was to permit them to become his aberu or abazana.

Does this constitute servitude? Recently Tuden and Plotnicov defined slavery as "the legal institutionalization of persons as property" (1970:11-12). This definition does not apply to the type of social relationship that aberu and abazana had with their owners according to Kerebe elders (interviews: Buyanza, Bahitwa, Kaliga, Aniceti Kitereza, Simeo Rubuzi). For the Kerebe, an omwiru or an omuzana can be defined as "a dependent individual outside the pale of his or her own clan who subsequently acquired a socially servile position inheritable by his or her descendants in a different clan." Consequently, the words "slave" and "slavery" will not be used in discussing Kerebe servitude, unless persons were actually traded in the slave trade, in which case the Tuden-Plotnicov definition applies.[2]

THE STATUS OF SERVILE PERSONS

Although servitude among the Kerebe was a clearly defined social status, it was a status characterized by both mobility and covertness. The latter feature explains why informants could only speak with authority about specific aberu or abazana within their own clan. As one of them explained, if one walked into another homestead, "it was very difficult to know who was an omwiru or an omuzana and who was not" (interview: Buyanza). This type of information was a clan affair, not a public one. The Kerebe generally avoided an ostentatious show of all forms of good fortune, whether large herds or numerous children. Only those secure in their social position, such as members of the royal clan, royal advisors, and enfura (friends of the omukama) dared flaunt their wealth and position. As far as could be determined from the oral data, perhaps a third to a fourth of the population actually aspired to accumulate wealth and thereby acquire status, and many of this group were members of the royal clan. It was only within this segment of Kerebe society that men could

2. For a discussion of such variations in African "slavery," see Meillassoux (1971:63-65).

afford to maintain servile persons. Thus a majority of the clans had infrequent association with servile institutions. For clans or segments of clans,
strength meant numerous members. Whether this was achieved through
natural increase or by incorporating outsiders into the clan was relatively
unimportant and certainly not the affair of other clans.

The royal clan was the most absorptive. Numerous clans living in the
chiefdom had rigid restrictions regarding breech births, or the cutting of
upper before lower teeth, or the birth of twins; these children had to be
abandoned. Members of the royal clan had no such restrictions and would
frequently rescue such infants, adopting and raising them as their own.
This same clan also absorbed by far the greatest number of aberu and
abazana. There were some restrictions, however, on their status and that
of their descendants. The fourth omukama, Mihigo I, who probably ruled
in the early 1700s, had an omuzana mother, but this is the only example,
until Mukaka (ruled 1895-1907), of a man with such a heritage becoming
a ruler. And Mukaka's case is special—he was placed in office by the
German authorities. Although sons of an omukama by a former omuzana
could be appointed as *abakungu* (headmen) or otherwise be included in
the privileged princely group (*abahinda*), descendants of ordinary aberu
and abazana who became Silanga (the royal clan) after two or three
generations would not normally be considered for an appointive position.

This same pattern holds true in other clans. If the master married an
omuzana, or another Kerebe redeemed her and then married her, the
offspring were accepted as members of the father's clan with full
inheritance rights. It was when an omwiru married an omuzana, and this
was virtually the only possibility for an omwiru unless he was redeemed,
that the children inherited the servile status, a status that only time and
the social etiquette forbidding open reference to slave origins could
obliterate. The one exception that was mentioned by informants to this
condition of slower mobility for the descendants of aberu arose if an
omwiru married the wife of his deceased master and she bore his children.
He was then accepted as a freeman of his master's clan, with his subsequent offspring legally recognized as members of it.

That Kerebe themselves were often unable to determine without effort
who had a servile status and who had not, suggests that the day-to-day
treatment of servile persons did not vary significantly from that accorded
other members of the homestead. But the major barriers for aberu and
abazana were of a legal nature. Normal inheritance rights enjoyed by clan
members were practically nonexistent for the offspring of aberu or
abazana. Their marriages were arranged by the master. The relative
insecurity of aberu and abazana is most apparent in informants' descriptions of the treatment accorded to persons committing serious crimes. For

example, in sorcery proceedings, a free man or woman could appeal a finding of guilt by an *omufumu* (diviner) to the omukama. The more influential the accused, the longer the appeals could go on. An omwiru or omuzana, who was accused of sorcery by his or her master or other clan members could be executed forthwith. This practice underscores the fundamentally dependent status of servile persons. It was alleged by one informant of probable servile descent that one method of execution of an omwiru or omuzana condemned for serious wrongdoing was to drive a sharpened stake through the top of the head and on through the body. This assertion was vehemently denied by others. While the allegation may not be correct, it is significant that it was mentioned only in relation to servile persons, suggesting that their treatment in extreme instances varied from that of nonservile persons.

Services performed by aberu were usually menial, involved drudgery, and had frequently to do with cultivation. Masters with few aberu might work beside them, while those with many might delegate most of the menial tasks to them. Abazana similarly relieved the master's wife or wives of such chores as cultivation, collection of firewood, and carrying water.

TYPES OF ABERU AND ABAZANA IN
EARLY KEREBE SOCIETY

Servility as an institution in Kerebe society, specifically during the seventeenth and eighteenth centuries, provided the community with a regulated procedure to care for distress cases, to punish wrongdoers, and to incorporate unransomed captives.

In essence, before the nineteenth century aberu and abazana predominantly were persons placed in positions of social dependence because of hardship caused by drought, warfare, or disputes within their formerly secure niche—persons who were in situations in which they were no longer able to claim clan membership or to enjoy its privileges, and who had become dependent upon some other group for sustenance. In exchange for food and shelter, they readily gave up their existence in a clanless limbo. The men who voluntarily sought this dependence from either the omukama or other wealthy Kerebe were called aberu *w'enzara* (of need), and the women were called abazana w'enzara. Persons who came specifically because of hunger were called aberu or abazana *w'engoyelo* (of hunger). It is important to note that only wealthy Kerebe—that is, those who had sufficient food reserves to feed more people—took aberu and abazana.

Some aberu and abazana, then, acquired their status through personal need. Others acquired it through the operation of the omukama's justice. Among the nonroyal clans, for example, if a member of one clan seriously harmed or killed a member of another, the compensation for this deed was most frequently the transference of a person, usually a young girl, from the attacker's clan to the clan of the attacked. The transferred individual was permanently placed in the other clan in a servile status regardless of the social standing of either clan. According to an informant whose clan was politically prominent prior to the establishment of the chiefdom in the seventeenth century, the power of the omukama to arbitrate cases of this nature, and thereby curtail the necessity of blood revenge, was one of the most beneficial results of the chieftaincy (interview: Makene). Similarly, when a fine in livestock was imposed upon individuals for serious infractions and livestock was unavailable, an individual could be given instead.

A third way of acquiring aberu or abazana prior to 1800 was by taking captives in skirmishes with neighbors. Although traditions make little mention of serious military encounters until the latter half of the nineteenth century, it is apparent that endemic hostility existed between the royal Silinga clan and its immediate neighbors and rivals, the Kula, who controlled the southern portion of the peninsula in the 1600s, when the Silanga had entrenched themselves along its northern portion. By intermittent forays, the stronger Silanga gradually forced the Kula from the peninsula onto the island until, by 1850, they occupied only the southwestern corner of the island. Control of strategic land was a factor in these disputes by the 1800s; before that, however, the Silanga wanted to seize cattle from the Kula and their subjects. Occasionally, direct cattle raids occurred, at other times skirmishes ensued, the aim of which was to acquire as many captives as possible, who were then held for ransom in livestock. These captives were called aberu or abazana w'ichumu (of the spear). In one encounter, the Kula ruler was captured and ransomed for significantly more than an ordinary subject.

During these encounters, casualties were minimal and, unlike the pattern in BuGanda in the late 1800s, captives were not solely women and children taken to reward warriors and to increase the servile population (Emin 1888:117; Speke 1864:251). By indicating that male captives were as welcome as females, Kerebe data suggest that the aberu and abazana w'ichumu were essentially hostages to be exchanged for the wealth actually sought, which was cattle. Apparently, spoils were divided among the Kerebe in essentially the same way as they were among the Nyamwezi under Mirambo (L.M.S., Southon 1880). Those warriors who actually captured people were obliged to divide their spoils with the omukama, approximately half going to the latter. But if a successful ransom could be arranged by the omukama, all aberu and abazana would pass through his hands and the successful warriors would receive in return their share of cattle.

REDEMPTION

Regardless of how a person became an omwiru or an omuzana, he or she could be redeemed and thereby removed from servitude. Two options are frequently mentioned in traditions. Individuals from Kerebe clans who became aberu or abazana because of famine or wrongdoing could easily be redeemed by their kin, once compensation was arranged. The price of redemption was based on cattle. An omuzana could be freed with one cow or, if cattle were lacking, with twelve goats, or twelve hoes, or twelve large containers of millet, or any combination of the last three totaling twelve items. For an omwiru, a bull or steer was sufficient or six goats, hoes, or containers of millet. Redemption costs apparently were the same regardless of the age of the individual or how long he had been in the servile state. An additional ritual was added for aberu or abazana from Sese clans seeking redemption. Besides the normal compensation, a hoe or goat was sent to the omukama and the person being released from servility was taken to a crossroads, where his or her head was shaven to symbolize the loss of servility.

The other way of regaining independence was apparently chosen most frequently by those who had migrated into the chiefdom because of famine and had no relatives able or willing to provide the redemption fee. Most of these persons were men (aberu), and, providing they had a good relationship with their master, they could marry and request the use of land to cultivate their own millet and accumulate possessions such as goats. By steadfastly working toward producing a surplus, they could redeem themselves over a period of years by payments to their master. One informant estimated this to be possible in three to five years (interview: Bahitwa). A young, marriageable omuzana could also be redeemed if her master married her and a child was born of the union. Even with these opportunities for redemption, some aberu and abazana remained in a state of servitude, which was then inherited by their offspring, and aberu who pleased their patrons were permitted to marry abazana.

Finally, aberu and abazana had the right to leave a master who unjustifiably ill-treated them and to seek an alternative master in the chiefdom. Their status was unaffected by this action. The original master was not compensated for his loss by the second master. Undoubtedly this procedure was extremely complex, because the omwiru would have to make sure beforehand that another master would accept him, and the move could also provoke ill will between the two masters involved. If a dispute arose in such instances, the omukama had the final word.

Obviously a number of factors could determine whether a man was redeemed by his own clan, or decided to work for his own redemption, or remained in a servile position: his ambition, how close the relationship between himself and his master became, whether he desired to return to his own clan—or whether it wished to have him return—and whether servitude was actually preferable to his previous position. The majority of aberu and abazana belonged to the wealthiest clan, the royal Silanga. The omukama retained sizable numbers for his own court, and also distributed aberu and abazana to his kinsmen as well as to other deserving men from nonroyal clans. Through their abilities, some aberu gained respected positions under the omukama or other powerful elders; consequently they might desire to remain in a servile state, since prestige and power could be attained through it. In general, patrons with obedient, hardworking aberu were anxious to retain their services; and the aberu often found it in their best interests to remain with their patron. Furthermore, aberu were gradually assimilated into their masters' clans. By the third generation the offspring were seldom regarded as aberu or abazana, but were recognized as actual members of the clan.

With these possibilities for redemption or self-improvement in a new clan, it is not difficult to understand the ambiguities that nineteenth-century European observers saw as surrounding slavery in eastern Africa. It is not uncommon to find an explorer such as James A. Grant remarking in the same paragraph that "slavery is the curse of the country and the African races will continue this practice of buying, plundering, and selling slaves to traders as long as the Zanzibar Government . . . supports it," and, on the other hand, that slaves are generally "treated with kindness" and only while they are in the hands of a dealer is their condition "bad" (Grant 1872:250). Robert W. Felkin, a doctor sent to BuGanda by the Church Missionary Society, recorded similar impressions: "slavery has existed in Uganda from time immemorial . . . the number of slaves held varies necessarily with the position and wealth of the owner. They are well treated" (Felkin 1886:746). Toward the end of the nineteenth century, S. Tristram Pruen frankly confessed that slavery in eastern Africa was "a complicated system"; hence it could be described as either "beneficial—or abhorrent," depending on whether the slave trade, with "all its deadly characteristics," was being described, or domestic servitude, which "is only a kind of feudal system" (Pruen 1891:209). What these commentators were commenting upon was a system of servitude that was often a modification of an earlier, benign system, which had been distorted by fundamental changes resulting from long-distance trading, including slave trading, in the nineteenth century.

ECONOMIC AND SOCIAL CHANGES OF THE NINETEENTH CENTURY

So far only four kinds of aberu and abazana have been discussed: war captives, wrongdoers, victims of hunger, and persons who opted for the servile status. Four other distinct types are discernible and, from information provided by Kerebe elders, it is apparent that these became especially important in the nineteenth century. They include persons given to the omukama as gifts from other rulers (aberu and abazana *w'okulungulwa*), persons convicted of sorcery or witchcraft (aberu and abazana *w'ilogo*), persons accused of sorcery or witchcraft, but not convicted, who placed themselves under the protection of the omukama (aberu and abazana *w'ekwitubizya*), and persons who were purchased from inside or outside the chiefdom (aberu and abazana *w'okugula*).

Although these four types cannot be exclusively related to conditions emanating from long-distance trade, it can be safely assumed that they were far more significant in the 1800s than in any previous era. As discussed at greater length elsewhere (Hartwig 1970:535-52), Kerebe oral accounts clearly assert that the chiefdom initially participated in exchanging elephant tusks for imported trade goods during the reign of Mihigo II, whose rule extended from approximately 1780 to around 1820. Furthermore, sorcery—that is, the conscious but secretive effort to harm someone or his property—is claimed by informants to have "begun" shortly after the death of Mihigo II (Hartwig 1971:505-24). Whether or not sorcery actually began at this time or whether it simply increased in extent cannot be determined. But changing social, economic, and political conditions, exacerbated by high mortality rates from diseases such as smallpox and cholera frequently brought by coastal traders, certainly furnished conditions in which belief in sorcery could have flourished. A summary of how extensively trade influenced the Kerebe will provide a background for the increased role that servitude played as the nineteenth century progressed.

Long-distance trade was the exclusive monopoly of the omukama. All ivory exported from BuKerebe was under his control and all imported trade goods were his to distribute as he pleased. His subjects were denied direct participation in this trade which was responsible for introducing luxury goods into Kerebe society. Political instability seems to have been promoted by the trade insofar as there were more successful as well as unsuccessful attempts to depose abakama during the 1800s than previously.

Rivalry within the royal clan for control over the new form of wealth came to the fore in the nineteenth century. A legitimate cause for deposing an incumbent could easily be found by aspiring princes and disgruntled elders; an extended drought could always provide an acceptable basis. But more disruptive was the perceived inability of abakama after Mihigo II to retain satisfactory control over the Kerebe environment. Mihigo is the last omukama in Kerebe oral accounts to be credited with having unimpaired spiritual and secular powers. Whatever occurred in BuKerebe during

Mihigo's reign, whether beneficial or harmful, is always attributed to him in oral accounts: for example, he "brought" both smallpox and cholera into the chiefdom. This type of power is not accorded by informants to any of his successors. This phenomenon has also been noted by Andrew Roberts (1969:58) who generalizes for much of central and western Tanzania when he states that the main change of the nineteenth century "consisted of a shift from religious to military power as a basis for political authority." As succeeding rulers apparently lacked the power to control increasingly difficult conditions, such as those wrought by disease, and as they were increasingly challenged by ambitious kinsmen, they showed a marked tendency to use force to maintain themselves in office.

A concomitant growth in local trade paralleled the development of long-distance trade. As the explorer H. M. Stanley noted in 1875 (Bennett 1970:232), the Kerebe were "an enterprising and commercial people." He noticed their canoes in the far northeastern part of the lake, in the vicinity of Kavirondo Gulf, as well as on the opposite shore north of the present city of Bukoba and along the shore of BuZinza. Any Kerebe with the necessary transportation participated in local trade during the nineteenth century and, to some degree, earlier. For example, hoes were unavailable within the chiefdom and had to be acquired from BuZinza, a dependency from at least the early eighteenth century. Kerebe fishermen and hippopotamus hunters also moved about the southern part of the lake, exchanging some of their dried fish and hippo meat for valued products such as salt, cattle, goats, hoes, hoe handles, and hides. The advent of long-distance trade seems to have intensified the Kerebe desire to accumulate wealth, which in turn was primarily used to counteract the increased insecurity by improving their relationship with the omukama, still the most prestigious and powerful person in the society.

Changes in the amount of millet cultivated illustrates the fundamental shift of values in the Kerebe community. Before the intensification of trade, the usual practice was for a woman to sow enough to provide sustenance for her charges from one planting season to the next. There was little use for an abundant harvest. But by the mid-1800s, ambitious heads of nuclear and extended families were consciously endeavoring to produce an annual millet surplus. This could then be used as barter to supplement the existing exchange goods, which included canoes, oars, dried fish, and hippo flesh. BuKerebe's reliable climatic conditions permitted the inhabitants to use an agricultural product—not a wasting asset such as ivory—to enhance their trading position. Those Kerebe who had a millet surplus then took advantage of any opportunity that presented itself to acquire more valued possessions. Obviously, the best bargains could be obtained when the other party was disadvantaged;

elders note that if drought occurred in BuRuri during a particular year, it was this district that attracted the Kerebe. They would exchange their millet and other products for whatever the famine-stricken population had to offer.

As was not unusual in eastern Africa (Burton 1860:521; Grant 1872: 250; Storms 1888-89:16-17; Becker 1887; 2:339; Burdo 1886:24), Kerebe men limited their participation in agricultural work. Tradition had definitely placed this activity within the sphere of women, although men assisted in breaking ground and were totally responsible for protecting crops from wildlife. With increased agricultural production, there was a need for additional labor to assist the women. By following the example set by the omukama, whose wives were freed from agricultural labor, the aspiring and wealthy Kerebe from royal and nonroyal clans tried to provide laborers to relieve their womenfolk from field work. A distinguishing characteristic of women of high status was their personal ornamentation. They wore heavy metal bracelets, made of iron or copper, which effectively prevented them from using a hoe without considerable discomfort. This marked the wearer as a woman above menial work and reflected well on her husband's ability to relieve her of drudgery. This development naturally increased the desire to obtain additional laborers, thereby affecting the role of the aberu and abazana.

DEMOGRAPHIC CHANGES IN THE NINETEENTH CENTURY

According to the oral data, depopulation within BuKerebe took place on a significant scale once the chiefdom became actively involved in long-distance trade. Informants cite three things to support this assertion. First, Mihigo II, who died about 1820, "brought" disease into the chiefdom and "created" the man/beast Butamile (either a man who "became" a lion, or actually a man-eating lion), who maimed, killed, and generally terrorized the Kerebe, because "there were too many people." Second, during his reign people had to journey to BuZinza to acquire hoe handles, whereas by the mid-nineteenth century this was no longer necessary, for BuKerebe itself could provide a sufficient supply for the diminished population. Third, when the Kerebe expanded into uninhabited areas of the island during the 1920s and 1930s they found grinding stones dispersed in the bush, indicating an eighteenth-century occupation.

There is no feasible method of quantifying this alleged depopulation, but the extent of the mortality caused by smallpox and cholera in other communities, commented upon later in the century by observers, leaves no doubt that any people exposed to these diseases would have suffered significant losses. Wilson, for example, stated that "diseases to which the

Baganda are subject make a formidable list; smallpox is one of the most fatal, coming at intervals in epidemics, and carrying off thousands of victims; few attacked ever recover." (Wilson and Felkin 1882; 1:183). Other observers drew similar conclusions (Cameron 1877:85; Burton 1859:387; L.M.S., Southon 1880). In addition to the disease factor there was the movement of individuals, or even families, from one community to another, seeking refuge following accusations of sorcery or witchcraft.

It is within this milieu that the changing role of the aberu and abazana in nineteenth-century BuKerebe must be understood. Manpower was at a premium, and this altered the role of aberu and abazana and increased the desire to acquire labor for agricultural work both to produce a millet surplus and to gain status by avoidance of field work. Seasonal migrant labor alleviated the manpower shortage only to a degree, particularly during the latter half of the 1800s. These seasonal migrants came from the neighboring island of BuKara, where limited land and dense population combined to encourage men to work as cultivators (*abamilizya*) in BuKerebe in return for a share of the harvest.

POLITICAL CHANGES IN THE NINETEENTH CENTURY

Perhaps the most significant change in Kerebe society in the early nineteenth century was a distinct change in the relations between the omukama and his subjects. Although the ruler's powers were seemingly less effective after 1820, he still occupied the most powerful office in the chiefdom. To be known and trusted by the omukama was the most efficacious way of acquiring a measure of security. As the omukama became increasingly fearful of brothers who might try to depose him, he found it expedient to encourage men with no official advisory capacity to seek his favor. Over a period of time, the omukama developed a cluster of loyal, wealthy men from nonroyal clans to bolster his position. These *enfura* (friends of the omukama) did not completely displace the previous body of official advisers, composed of relatives of the omukama and elders of some Sese clans, but they provided him with an additional source of support and information from the villages. The process of becoming one of the enfura was by no means simple. Anytime a man paid his respects to the omukama (and the more frequently this was done the better acquainted the ruler became with him), a suitable gift was in order. Consequently enfura, and those aspiring to the position, had to be men of considerable means, controlling substantial amounts of prestigious wealth.

The increasing desire by enfura to accumulate wealth in the early nineteenth century was bound up with the desire for a semblance of security, although improved social status was no small additional aspiration. A significant characteristic of information dealing with aspiring enfura is that individuals are described, not clans. Initial evidence from Kerebe accounts indicates that enfura possessed an achieved rather than an ascribed status. These ambitious men, together with those holding a privileged ascribed status, gained materially from their close association with the omukama, who liberally redistributed his trade goods, including cattle and other valued possessions, among them. Ritual security, however, may well have been another, and perhaps ultimate, goal. Participation in long-distance trade, particularly when the Kerebe welcomed coastal caravans to the chiefdom after the death of Mihigo II, occasionally exacted a heavy price in lives by bringing diseases into the community. During Mihigo's reign, the Kerebe attributed all deaths from alien diseases to this ritually strong leader. Succeeding abakama were no longer endowed with equal power, and some deaths were then attributed to sorcerers (fellow kinsmen or close neighbors). Thus, for self-protection enfura sought a close relationship with the omukama, whose ritual power, although reduced, was nonetheless superior to that of his subjects.

Kerebe elders contend that charges of sorcery began in their community during this time, the 1820s and 1830s; whether this is entirely correct or not, the assertion nevertheless suggests that an escalation in accusations must have occurred during this period. The practice of sorcery arises, according to Kerebe theory, from ill-will existing between two parties, frequently within the same clan. In most cases, an aggrieved individual attempts to harm his or her antagonist secretly. The latter is frequently in an enviable position, possessing either abundant livestock or children. The aggrieved, who may feel ill-treated or cheated by the more fortunate person, resorts to sorcery in revenge. An important way for wealthier individuals to defend their position was to seek the protection of the omukama's supernatural power. Seldom were successful men accused of sorcery; if they were, their relationship with the ruler ensured them a sympathetic hearing. They were frequently the aggrieved party, however. In this manner vital social relationships within clans could be adversely affected by increased wealth, by increasing mortality rates, and by individual rather than clan improvement of status.[3]

After the death of Mihigo II, the Kerebe penal system had three options for dealing with a person convicted of sorcery. If the person did not flee BuKerebe, he or she could be fined, or placed into a servitude "of sorcery" (w'ilogo), or executed. In a few instances, nuclear families in a clan or even entire clans were punished in these ways, but they were exceptional cases in that numerous individuals within the clan had been accused or

3. The relationship between witchcraft accusations and conflict is examined by Marwick (1952) and Macfarlane (1970:192-99).

convicted earlier. In common with other East African communities (see, for example, Beidelman 1963:67-68; LeVine 1963:228-29) the Kerebe assumed that sorcery or witchcraft (*obulogi*) was a practice consciously passed on from one generation to the next. By ridding the community of the entire family, they expected that antisocial behavior would cease. Those in authority did not necessarily sentence groups of people in this manner simply to exploit their subjects; it was as likely to be done to cleanse the society of a perceived social malady.

Persons accused or suspected of being sorcerers, but not actually convicted, had the option of fleeing the chiefdom or seeking the protection of the omukama, which meant placing themselves in his service (they were then called aberu or abazana w'ekwitubizya). Oral information does not suggest that redemption procedures for those convicted or merely suspected of sorcery differed from those for other aberu or abazana. In practice, however, some aberu and abazana w'ilogo and w'ekwitubizya would not be redeemed by their clans because these persons had allegedly harmed others within the clan and consequently they were no longer desired by it.

Only the wealthy—especially the enfura (the royal advisers) and men of the royal clan, particularly the sons and grandsons of an omukama—possessed aberu and abazana during the nineteenth century. The vast majority were actually distributed by the omukama to his relatives. The royal village was described in 1877 as a community of some four to five hundred persons (C.M.S., O'Neill 1877) with the number of wives present estimated to have been between twenty and thirty (C.M.S., Wilson 1877). How many aberu and abazana were included in this number is problematical. Each wife had at least one omuzana to serve her, but not all wives lived at the royal residence; a woman about to give birth moved to her father's residence and remained there until the child was weaned. Some of the omukama's messengers (*abazuma*), who also served to protect the village, were aberu, but the majority were freemen. Those aberu at court had specific functions, such as that of gatekeeper. Thus, of the four or five hundred persons in the royal village, an estimated one to two hundred would have been in a servile status.

The homestead of Nansagate, a brother of Omukama Rukonge, offers some insight into the numbers of servile persons attached to an influential member of the royal clan. Nansagate was headman of two strategically located villages and had in the early 1890s eight Luo and ten Kara aberu and abazana in his mother's homestead and approximately an equal number at his own homestead along with two Jita abazana, war captives from an abortive attempt around 1870 to depose Rukonge by one of his other brothers. The homestead of Nansagate was sizable at this time, including twelve wives; hence he was undoubtedly one of the wealthier Silanga princes (interview: Buyanza). All of his aberu and abazana had been supplied by the omukama, which meant that they could also be taken from him if the omukama had a need for them. The aberu at the royal residence had a unique opportunity to become influential and to occupy positions of trust and responsibility. Some of them amassed considerable wealth, in addition to possessing aberu and abazana of their own, and these successful aberu were apparently as plagued by sorcerers as any successful Kerebe.

DIPLOMACY AND SERVILITY

Diplomatic and commercial relations between East African rulers of the nineteenth century were frequently cemented by the giving of persons as gifts (abazana and aberu w'okulungulwa). The Kerebe omukama received numerous women—and fewer men—in this way. We may assume that in these exchanges Kerebe rulers made similar gifts in return. H. M. Stanley (1899; 1:329) noted in 1875 that he participated in one such exchange, between Mutesa of BuGanda and Rukonge of BuKerebe. Mutesa sent Rukonge five tusks of ivory, a "comely virgin of fifteen as wife suitable for a king," trade wire, monkey skins, and a large canoe. Earlier, omukama Machunda (ruled ca. 1835 to ca. 1869) received Namizi, a young omuzana, from a Nyamwezi chief with whom he had commercial relations. Machunda later formally married the girl, who is well remembered by elders for her subsequent part in exacerbating a serious political issue between two Silanga rivals.

Individual abazana or aberu sent by one ruler to another, such as Namizi and the "comely virgin" mentioned by Stanley, tended to be exceptional persons in one respect or another. Undesirables would never be foisted upon a fellow monarch, unless large numbers were involved. In the case of girls, physical attractiveness was a necessary attribute but equally, if not more, important was social sensitivity and a knowledge of etiquette. Relations with persons of the same clan, of different clans, of different ages, and of different social strata (in particular the royal clan) were all rigidly defined. Knowing one's place in the social order and acting accordingly was a fundamental characteristic of a well-behaved individual. Hence, the Kerebe judged their abazana and aberu by their social behavior as well as their work at appointed tasks. Favorites manifested qualities approved by the community. When such persons were expendable, they were the type frequently given as gifts by a ruler. Some aberu acquired by Rukonge from Mutesa of BuGanda, for example, were skilled drum-makers, regarded by the Kerebe as superior to their own craftsmen and consequently assigned the responsibility of producing royal drums

(Hartwig 1969:47). Abazana and aberu, along with ivory, were common items of exchange between rulers in the nineteenth century—both possessed a high value and were easily transported. This exchange was apart from long-distance trade, and the individuals passed along in this manner should not be regarded as items in slave trading. Also, economic motives were attenuated in these exchanges.

Nonetheless, the extent of diplomatic contacts between rulers increased as cooperation became more important, given the intricacies of long-distance trade. Much of the contact, however, dealt with the problem of how to control the unusual or new circumstances that confronted men in authority. They sought, frequently by means of magic, to gain security. When requesting information about how to deal with the situation, the inquiring ruler necessarily sent gifts to the possessor of such knowledge. This same procedure was followed when requesting something more mundane, such as military assistance. Gifts of aberu and abazana facilitated these transactions.

Coastal traders apparently practiced the same custom of giving servile persons as gifts when establishing a formal relationship with a ruler. The Kerebe evidence for this was the presence of a number of Luo aberu and abazana in BuKerebe. Their presence can scarcely be accounted for except by the activities of Songoro, a Swahili trader (Hartwig 1968:211-23). In 1877, Songoro had an establishment in BuKerebe of some eighty persons, which had been started ten to fifteen years earlier. This base enabled Songoro to conduct a twofold operation: to assist Mutesa of BuGanda in moving Ganda ivory across the lake and on to Unyanyembe (Tabora) via Kageyi, and to acquire slaves on his own initiative from the Kavirondo Gulf region (Luo were primarily involved) for shipment southward (Bennett 1970:214). Songoro's alliance with Kerebe rulers enabled him to use their canoes when necessary, as well as their contacts with Ruri elders (Ruri is a generic Kerebe term for various people living north of the Jita), who collaborated with him in obtaining captives from their northern Luo neighbors. The only Kerebe who normally traveled that far north were hippopotamus hunters, essentially men of peace desiring to exchange hippo flesh with the Luo for their excellent salt. Songoro's presence could only have disturbed this relationship and thereby curtailed their activities. Although Songoro exported most of his slaves to the south, he apparently gave many to Rukonge as tribute for his residence on the island. They were aberu and abazana w'okulungulwa (gifts to the omukama) like those given to the Omukama by other rulers. But these Luo aberu and abazana lived under a significantly different set of conditions from that of other servile persons discussed: they were a Nilotic, not Bantu-speaking, people, who were victims of a slave trade and were approximately one hundred miles from their home district. This mean that redemption by their clan was a virtual impossibility. In addition, the language and cultural differences between them and their Kerebe masters were so great that at least the first generation found it more difficult to work for their own redemption than did other servile persons.

ACTIVE ACQUISITION OF ABERU AND ABAZANA

All of the various categories of aberu and abazana mentioned thus far possess one vital characteristic in common: people were not actively sought to fill a servile status but were placed in it in the course of being incorporated as dependent persons into the community. The institution before 1800 was a combined "welfare" and penal system. Refugees, the destitute, sorcerers, and war captives of the 1800s all belonged to the same system. Individuals given as gifts by fellow rulers or coastal traders, however, must be placed in a separate category; they were essentially a by-product of increased communication stimulated by long-distance trade. The appearance of another category of servile person in the nineteenth century reveals major changes in the Kerebe attitude to their servile population. By midcentury, during Machunda's reign, aberu and abazana w'okugula are mentioned in oral accounts. These were individuals purchased outright, from either inside or outside BuKerebe, usually the latter. Paralleling local trading developments, they became the property of well-to-do Kerebe and seldom of the Omukama.

Without exception elders describe these individuals as Ruri. What is clear is that before 1870 the Ruri brought people—almost always children —to BuKerebe to exchange them for millet, particularly during the not infrequent droughts. The Ruri usually attempted to kidnap these youngsters from their neighbors; to exchange their own kin for sustenance would have been an act of desperation. (It is possible that slavers such as Songoro merely exploited this situation.) Also, as already mentioned, people from BuRuri and other areas had drifted into BuKerebe, both on an independent and a dependent basis, as a result of droughts. The southward migration of the Luo by the late eighteenth century may have encouraged such migrations (Ogot 1967:206-10). The acquisition of aberu and abazana w'okugula in the mid-1800s, however, suggests that internecine struggles had begun between people along the eastern lakeshore. As opportunities for trade grew—evidenced in the Kerebe desire for labor—it is likely that the Ruri and Luo engaged in mutually destructive raids for captives and livestock, thus providing a new source of aberu and abazana for the Kerebe.

The purchasing of servile persons implies a measure of selectivity on the purchaser's part, and this in fact occurred. The Kerebe denounced any form of intentional physical mutilation, be it circumcision, piercing of ears, or filing of teeth, all of which were practiced by various people on the eastern side of the Victoria Nyanza. In acquiring aberu and abazana w'okugula, therefore, the Kerebe sought only children who had not been subjected to any physical changes. This desire for unmarked children in itself reveals a significant dimension to Kerebe servitude as it evolved in the nineteenth century. There was little expectation that these particular aberu or abazana would ever be redeemed by their kinsmen. They were virtually destined to remain in lifelong servitude, increasing the numbers of a given homestead, providing manpower to perform menial tasks, and eventually being incorporated into the clan.

The Kerebe became increasingly dependent on this source of aberu and abazana, and by the reign of Rukonge (ca. 1869 to 1895) men left BuKerebe explicitly in search of children to purchase whenever it became apparent that drought had caused famine in BuRuri. The pattern was completely new. Before, the Kerebe had always passively waited for others to approach them. Their dependence upon Songoro for captives may very well have led them to take the initiative after his death in 1877. Nonetheless, the Kerebe seldom raided for aberu or abazana, although some instances of kidnapping are mentioned by informants. They did, however, primarily depend on their climatic advantage that allowed them to exchange their surplus millet for children with neighbors in need of grain.

CONCLUSION

The institution of servitude among the Kerebe altered through time. Aberu and abazana became a feature of Kerebe society when a centralized system of government was introduced and a stratified society developed. The system of servitude was initially a welfare and a penal institution to care for dependent individuals. Redemption was accepted and encouraged, and unredeemed persons after two or three generations became full members of their master's clan. During the nineteenth century, changing social, economic, and religious values and opportunities provided additional sources of servile persons: accused and convicted sorcerers, gifts from other rulers, and purchased individuals. Redemption then became less prevalent because kinsmen frequently lived in distant communities and no longer possessed the same opportunities for redeeming persons as earlier, when local clans were primarily involved. New outlets for millet and the need for labor to cultivate expanded millet plots also served to encourage masters to retain their aberu and abazana. The absorption of descendants of servile persons into the master's clan had always characterized the institution, and in the nineteenth century there was apparently a greater desire or need for it—partly, in fact, because clans sought to offset the effects of depopulation.

Depopulation became an integral part of long-distance trade for the Kerebe. They were spared the worst aspects of slave raiding, but not the fatal diseases that occasionally accompanied trading caravans. Death from this source, combined with the unsettling effects of new luxury trade goods, caused some Kerebe to seek security from the omukama, an endeavor requiring wealth. The wealth was acquired primarily through increased millet production in which the Kerebe utilized the services of the aberu and abazana. Simultaneously, the masters wished to absorb the aberu and abazana into their clans to help overcome the factor of depopulation.

Only a small minority of Kerebe aberu and abazana were exported. The Kerebe had adequate sources of nondepleting agricultural and pastoral produce as well as timber and products from the lake to exchange for trade goods. They did not need to draw upon the servile ranks, which were appreciated as a source both of labor and of future clan members.

The former low status of aberu and abazana is evident today in BuKerebe when one attempts to acquire information from elders. Persons whose ancestry is Sese freely speak of the institution, while descendants of servile persons are unwilling to discuss it except in general terms. Also, only one Kerebe informant (interview: Kaliga) readily supported Stanley's assertion that the Kerebe engaged in the slave trade with coastal traders (Bennett 1970:214). Though this practice is not presently approved by elders, they do not regard the historical institution of servitude as a subject to be concealed; few observers would disagree with their view of it in its original form as a welfare and penal institution. But the evolution of the system in the late 1800s reveals the transition of the earlier form into an institution more closely approximating chattel slavery, although still tempered by mobility and the vital fact that the servile person was not normally regarded as a salable commodity but rather as a valuable addition to the clan.

GLOSSARY

abagaya: the Jita term for servile people.
abahinda: sons and grandsons of *abakama;* "princes."
abakungu: headmen.
abamilizya: nonservile cultivators.
abazuma: messengers of the *omukama*.
enfura: friends of the *omukama*.
obulogi: sorcery or witchcraft.
oluganda: clan.
omufumu: diviner or medicine man.
omukama (pl. *abakama*): ruler, chief.

omuzana (pl. *abazana*): a female of servile status.
omwiru (pl. *aberu*): a male of servile status.
Silanga: Kerebe royal clan.
w'ekwitubizya: (accused) of sorcery or witchcraft.
w'engoyelo: of hunger.
w'enzara: of need.
w'ichumu: of the spear.
w'ilogo: (convicted) of sorcery or witchcraft.
w'okugula: purchased.
w'okulungulwa: given as gifts to the *omukama*.

REFERENCES

ORAL SOURCES

Translated transcriptions of these interviews are deposited in the University of Dar es Salaam Library, Duke University Library, and at the African Studies Association, Center for African Oral Data, Archives of Traditional Music, Indiana University, Bloomington, Indiana.

Bahitwa son of Lugambage, interviews, November 1968 to February 1969.
Buyanza son of Nansagate, interviews, September 1968 to February 1969.
Kaliga son of Lwambali, interviews on December 17 and December 19, 1968.
Aniceti Kitereza, interview on November 5, 1968.
Makene son of Ikongolero, interviews, July to November 1968.
Simeo Rubuzi, interviews, November 1968 to February 1969.

UNPUBLISHED SOURCES

Baker, E. C. 1932(?). Report on administrative and social conditions in the Ukerewe chiefdom. Mimeographed government report. Cory File: No. 9. Univ. of Dar es Salaam Library.
C.M.S.: Church Missionary Archives, London.
  O'Neill, Thomas. Letter to Wright, October 1877. C. A6/0 18.
  Wilson, C. T. Letter to Wright, March 2, 1877. C. A6/0 25.
Kitereza, A. 1943(?). Omwanzuro gw'Abakama ba Bukerebe [History of the chiefs of BuKerebe]. Manuscript at Kagunguli Parish, Ukerewe, Tanzania.
L.M.S.: London Missionary Society Archives, London.
  Southon, E. J. Journal, August 12, 1880.

PUBLISHED SOURCES

Alpers, E. A. 1967. *The East African slave trade.* Nairobi.
Becker, J. 1887. *La vie en Afrique.* 2 vols. Paris.
Beidelman, T. O. 1963. Witchcraft in Ukaguru. In *Witchcraft and sorcery in East Africa,* ed. J. Middleton and E. A. Winter. London.

Bennett, N. R., ed. 1970. *Stanley's despatches to the New York Herald, 1871-1872, 1874-1877.* Boston.

Burdo, A. 1886. *Les Belges dans l'Afrique centrale: de Zanzibar au lac Tanganika.* Brussels.

Burton, R. F. 1859. The lake regions of central equatorial Africa. *Jl. R. geogr. Soc.* 29:1-454.

_____. 1860. *The lake regions of central Africa.* New York.

Cameron, V. L. 1877. *Across Africa.* New York.

Emin Pasha. 1888. *Emin Pasha in central Africa.* Ed. G. Schweinfurth et al. London.

Felkin, R. W. 1886. Notes on the Waganda tribe of central Africa. *Proc. R. Soc. Edinb.* 13:699-770.

Grant, J. A. 1872. Summary of observations . . . of the lake region of equatorial Africa. *Jl. R. geogr. Soc.* 42:243-342.

Gray, R., and Birmingham, D., eds. 1970. *Pre-colonial African trade: essays on trade in central and eastern Africa before 1900.* New York.

Hartwig, G. W. 1968. Bukerebe, the Church Missionary Society, and East African politics, 1877-1878. *Afr. hist. Stud.* 1:211-32.

_____. 1969. The historical and social role of Kerebe music. *Tanzan. Notes Rec.* 70:41-56.

_____. 1970. The Victoria Nyanza as a trade route in the nineteenth century. *J. Afr. Hist.* 11:535-52.

_____. 1971. Long-distance trade and the evolution of sorcery among the Kerebe. *Afr. hist. Stud.* 4:505-24.

Hurel, E. 1911. Religion et vie domestique des Bakerewe. *Anthropos* 6:62-94, 276-301.

LeVine, R. A. 1963. Witchcraft and sorcery in a Gusii community. In *Witchcraft and sorcery in East Africa,* ed. J. Middleton and E. A. Winter. London.

Macfarlane, A. 1970. *Witchcraft in Tudor and Stuart England.* New York.

Marwick, M. 1952. The social context of Cewa witch beliefs. *Africa* 22:120-35.

Meillassoux, C. 1971. Introduction. In *The development of indigenous trade and markets in West Africa,* ed. C. Meillassoux. London.

Ogot, B. A. 1967. *History of the southern Luo.* Nairobi.

Pruen, S. T. 1891. *The Arab and the African.* London.

Roberts, A. 1969. Political change in the nineteenth century. In *A history of Tanzania,* ed. I. N. Kimambo and A. J. Temu. Nairobi.

Speke, J. H. 1864. *Journal of the discovery of the source of the Nile.* New York.

Stanley, H. M. 1899. *Through the Dark Continent.* 2 vols. London.

Storms, Capitaine. 1888-89. L'esclavage entre le Tanganika et la Côte est. *Le mouvement antiesclavagiste* 1:14-18.

Tuden, A., and Plotnicov, L., eds. 1970. *Social stratification in Africa.* New York.

Wilson, C. T., and Felkin, R. W. 1882. *Uganda and the Egyptian Soudan.* 2 vols. London.

11

Slavery and Economic Response among the Vai

(Liberia and Sierra Leone)

Svend E. Holsoe

The Vai are a northern Mande-speaking people, numbering about 50,000 individuals, who today reside in the coastal Gallinas region of southern Sierra Leone and the western area of Liberia. Vai origins can be traced to the savanna region of the present-day republic of Guinea. In about 1500 the Vai began to migrate toward the coast (Holsoe 1974a).

Vai political structure can be considered as a balance between two different bases of power—one located among those individuals who inherited their position through kinship ties, the other among those who achieved their political position. Depending on the circumstances at a particular time, one or the other type of leader emerged and held political control (Holsoe 1974b).

The Vai economic structure was based on swidden agriculture and on trade. After their arrival on the coast, the Vai acted as middlemen between European traders and the peoples of the interior. Although involved in trade, the Vai, like many other societies in this region, defined wealth not in terms of material goods or land but rather by the number of individuals whose services they could control. Thus, the Vai were concerned with acquiring large numbers of wives as one means of increasing the number of dependents. Another method was the employment of

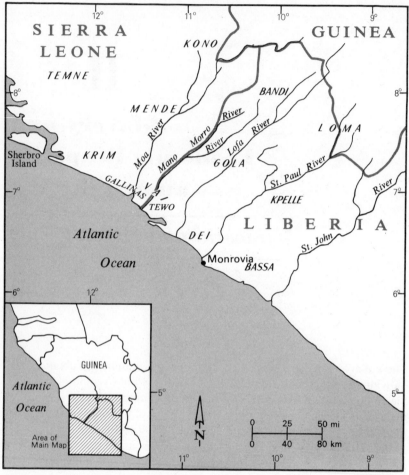

Cartographic Laboratory UW-Madison

Map 11. The Vai and Their Neighbors

mercenaries to capture prisoners. This chapter addresses itself to a study of an additional form of Vai manpower management—namely, those individuals who were considered to be in servitude.[1]

CATEGORIES OF JONNU

The Vai use the generic term *jon* [jɔŋ, pl. jɔŋnu] in opposition to a free-born person, who is a *manja den* [manja deŋ, pl. manja deŋnu] literally, chief's child. The dichotomy implies that jonnu lack full kin status and

1. Much of the information in this chapter came from field research conducted in the Liberian Vai country in 1965-66 under the sponsorship of the Foreign Area Fellowship Program of the Ford Foundation, to which I wish to extend my appreciation.

the rights of manja dennu. There are at least four different categories of jonnu, each of which we will examine here; and we will see how they have changed through time.

Within Vai society, three forms of servitude existed: indentured laborers, pawns, and domestic slaves. Indentured laborers were individuals who had contracted a debt that they were unable to pay. In such cases, the debtor worked for his creditor until the debt was repaid. One of the more frequent ways a man incurred a debt was through an illicit affair with another man's wife. The woman would report him to her husband, who would demand compensation. If the man was unable to pay, he would have to work for the aggrieved husband. The Vai referred to this form of indentured labor as *musu jonja* [musu jɔŋja]—literally, woman servitude. In some cases, the man might be sold as an export slave, particularly in the pre-1850 period, as we shall see. This was not, however, the usual practice.

While the man worked off his debt the creditor, if he had many wives, might offer to give the debtor his paramour as a wife, adding the dowry to the debt. The debtor, now saddled with an additional debt, remained in the compound of his creditor, who gained a new working dependent and with time also had rights to the labor of the debtor's children until the original debt was repaid. The social distance between a manja den and an indentured servant was scarcely noticeable.

The second category of servitude was the result of making individuals pawns, called *seenu* [sɛɛnu, sing. sɛɛ] by the Vai. As the Vai are essentially patrilineal, a maternal uncle had the privilege of pawning his nephews and nieces without complaint from their patrilineage, and might on occasion refer to them as *na jonnu* [na jɔŋnu], my servants. In compensation for this right, nieces and nephews had free access to their maternal uncle's property. Given this special relationship, a man in debt could pawn his sister's children to his creditor until his debt was paid. The resultant servitude sometimes lasted the lifetime of the pawns, who had to work for their master without compensation, the labor being regarded as a form of interest on the original debt. In return, the master had to feed and house them. Depending on the origin of the pawn, his treatment varied from one of scarcely noticeable difference from other members of the household to one of some social distance.

Vai pawns retained their free status as manja dennu even while pawned, and as a consequence they retained their kinship and ritual ties to their families. Given their continued status as manja dennu, pawns might marry into their master's family so long as they remained with his family. Should the pawn not be of Vai origin, however, the social position of the individual easily degenerated into domestic slavery, especially if there was no expectation that the pawn would be redeemed.

Domestic slavery was the third type of servitude.[2] It included individuals who remained within Vai country in permanent servitude. Whereas many of the debtors and pawns in time would be freed or incorporated into their master's family as fellow freeborn members (manja dennu), domestic slaves formed a separate social category.

Domestic slaves were obtained by at least four methods. First, they were captured in wars. Male prisoners who were already slaves remained in servitude. Freeborn captives who were not Vai were enslaved. If they were freeborn Vai, they were either ransomed or killed but were not reduced to slavery. Second, persons became slaves if they committed some grievous crime. This punishment was meted out by the ruler of the area in which the criminal lived. Third, offspring of slaves, or of freemen and slave women, remained slaves. Fourth, on occasion individual slaves might be purchased from neighboring peoples. This was usually the origin of slaves who came from such distant areas as those of the Kpelle and Bassa. In the early twentieth century the Liberian government officially termed this "human pawning," though strictly defined it was obviously not.

Domestic slaves usually were owned by a family head as his personal property. Such slaves were rarely sold, but when sales occurred they usually involved the farm slaves who lived in farm villages rather than those who worked in town for a freeborn family. Geographical distance influenced affection levels. Upon the death of an owner, his slaves and wives were inherited as private property by his next of kin. Usually this was the eldest son, but if he was not of age they went to the man's next eldest brother. A man's head wife also might inherit slaves upon occasion, especially if the woman was strong-willed and her husband had promised them to her.

Although domestic slaves formed a separate social category, their treatment varied depending upon the character and social position of their master, the nature of their work, and the time period in Vai history. Some commentators have stated that at times, if a slave worked hard and was well behaved, he would become part of the household and thus be difficult to differentiate from a manja den. Certainly those male slaves who distinguished themselves in warfare rose in the esteem of their master although their status as jonnu remained unchanged. Farm slaves, however, particularly if many were owned by an individual, often formed separate villages supervised by the master's wife or trusted older slave. Their physical distance led to considerable social distance. Some Vai felt complete contempt for slaves and treated them accordingly. They thought of them as unclean and had no more contact with them than was neces-

2. For further information on this topic see Büttikofer (1890, 2:204-5) and Besolow (1891:33, 64).

sary. Harshness sometimes occurred on the institutional level: slaves were often buried alive at the funeral of an important master, and slave babies were sacrificed in ceremonies when crocodiles, who were believed to be the embodiments of ancestors, were honored.

The slaves themselves recognized their position. Upon occasion, if their masters became too oppressive, they revolted. The Zawo slaves in the Gallinas area raised disturbances in the 1820s and finally fled in the 1850s into the Tewo section of the Vai country, where they were given asylum (Holsoe 1967:143-48).

These were three categories of jonnu within Vai society. There was one other group of jonnu—the export slaves.

During particular periods of Vai history the procurement and sale of export slaves formed an important source of income for Vai rulers. These slaves were obtained in the same way as other jonnu. Some were criminals, some were unredeemed pawns, and many were captives of war. The majority, however, were imported from areas outside the Vai country.

The trading of slaves from the interior to the coast was a practice of long standing. As an example, Bandi peoples living in the far interior were involved and are often mentioned in the oral traditions. Rulers desiring European goods raided neighboring peoples and sent their captives to the coast in exchange for such items as salt, tobacco, and various metals, particularly brass objects (interview: Gawolo 1968). On the basis of the origins of slaves on one vessel, the *Amistad*, which sailed from the Gallinas section of the Vai country in 1838, it is possible to demonstrate that Vai export slaves were drawn from a very wide area. Among the thirty-eight slaves on board, there were Temne, Mende, Kono, Bandi, Loma, and Gola (Barber 1840:9-15).

The nature of servitude categories and the number of individuals in each, as they existed in Vai society during the nineteenth and early twentieth century, reflected specific contemporary conditions; their nature and importance in previous centuries were somewhat different. These changes occurred as the Vai responded to changing opportunities in the coastal trade.

VAI SERVITUDE CATEGORIES THROUGH TIME

The distant past is the most poorly documented, and yet some speculation concerning this period is justified. Our knowledge of Liberian-Sierra Leonean societies prior to European contact in the 1460s is at best fragmentary. Archaeology is in a nascent state, and oral traditions about the Vai during the precontact period refer to an area outside their present-day coastal location. About 1500 the Vai began moving toward the coast, where they came in contact with Portuguese traders (Holsoe 1967, Ch. 2; Holsoe 1974a).

Did slavery exist in 1500 on the coast among the local peoples or among the immigrant Vai? The answer must rely on Portuguese accounts of the general area. These were written at various times during the sixteenth century. Walter Rodney, who has researched this documentation, asserts that it is not possible to establish the presence of slaves among the forest societies (Rodney 1966, and reply by Fage 1969). The sixteenth-century documents mainly refer to the territory around the Sierra Leone peninsula, north and west of the Vai. In addition to that, at least two difficulties can be anticipated with these sources. Would slavery or "social oppression"—the phrase Rodney uses—have been obvious to outsiders? And could an outside observer easily distinguish between forms of service based on kinship links and those that were not? An observer who lived on this coast during the 1840s concluded that "in visiting an African hamlet . . . a stranger would be at a loss to distinguish slaves from free men, or even from their masters" (Lugenbeel 1853:45).

Linguistically, the Vai are Mande-speaking and an offshoot, albeit distant, of the savanna Mande (Welmers 1958:21). It may be assumed that they also brought with them social characteristics, that included concepts of status stratification. Although detailed examination of the viability of savanna Mande social distinctions in an isolated forest setting must for the present be put aside, the variety of forms of servitude that occurred among the Vai suggests that Mande concepts of social stratification were maintained. Nevertheless, it is difficult to establish a base line for the various Vai forms of servitude, and it is not always easy to demonstrate how they manipulated, expanded, or changed to meet the new demands. Some aspects of the process can be suggested, however.

It is possible to divide Vai contact with Europeans into several distinct periods. From about 1500 to 1680, relations between the Vai and Europeans were cordial. Few slaves were exported, other trade items—such as gold, camwood, and ivory—being far more important. Vai society and its rulers were geared to the collection and transport of these items from the interior to the coast. However, as the Dapper account, dated circa 1628, states, servants were an integral part of Vai society and were inherited along with other material goods from father to son. There is little doubt that the servants described were domestic slaves, jonnu. Inheritance of such individuals, which implied social distance, was not possible with other types of people in servitude (Dapper 1670:405-6).

About 1680 relations with Europeans were altered, partly reflecting changes that occurred in Europe. The monopoly of the Royal African Company was broken and trade was opened to many individuals who had no concern about the long-term consequences of their ill-treatment of local African traders, chiefs, and people. Trade patterns began to shift and for the first time trade documents mention the purchase of slaves from the Vai area (Tilleman 1697:18; Gröben 1694:35). As a consequence of mutual suspicion, hostages were exchanged prior to commencing trade —an action unheard of before this time.

From 1680 to 1808 the demand by Europeans for export slaves increased, and when slaves were available the Vai sold them to passing traders. But the Vai country and surrounding regions remained an area of relatively low slave yield when compared to some other parts of West Africa. Curtin cites a survey from the 1770s, according to which individual ports along this coast never exported more than five hundred slaves a year (Curtin 1969:226). Slave traders' account books also indicate that they never obtained large numbers of slaves, no more in fact than ten to fifteen at any one stop. Thus, although there were occasional European residents on the coast as well as Vai traders—some pure Vai, some mulattoes, many of whom were educated in either the West Indies or Europe—none of them established large collecting and storage systems for slaves. Occasionally, when it was known that a European desired a quantity of slaves, an expedition might be made to the interior to obtain them, but this was rare.

As a consequence, slaves continued to compete with other export products that had been sold in earlier periods. Domestic slaves and pawns continued to collect and carry these goods to the coast. Internal Vai social structure still remained basically produce-oriented and all categories of jonnu either grew or collected food, thereby assuring sufficient supplies for the local population and for those individuals involved in the collection and transport of raw materials to the coast.

The year 1807 was a watershed, marking the date that the British outlawed slave trading for their own citizens. Shortly thereafter the British navy, by then in command of the seas, stationed a naval squadron on the West African coast to suppress the trade. Several other nations, however— Portugal, Spain, and Brazil in particular—were slow to respond to Britain's lead.

The effects of these European decisions were felt by coastal slave traders such as the Vai. With the increased danger involved in shipping slaves, the price per slave rose sharply, and it became imperative that waiting slave vessels be loaded with great speed. European slave ships, which in the past sailed leisurely along the coast, collecting small quantities of slaves and storing them in their holds until their cargo was complete, could no longer continue this practice. Now, any vessel discovered with slaves on board was subject to confiscation. The collection and holding of sufficient quantities of slaves to form a complete cargo could only be done safely at a location ashore, if possible one that was out of bounds of the naval squadron. The Vai adjusted their economic priorities and slaving system to meet the new circumstances. What had been a casual system, in which slaves were only one among many products exported, now shifted to a system focusing on the collection of slaves. By 1826 it was estimated that out of a total Vai population of 12,000 to 15,000, three fourths were slaves —no doubt meaning all categories of jonnu (Ashmun 1826).

Drawing upon an internal trading system that had long existed and had serviced the transport of products from the interior to the coast, the Vai adjusted trading ties and networks to supply a greater number of slaves than in the past. A description from the 1820s is illustrative.

The course of trade at Gallinas, as at the other considerable slave markets, is to contract with the King or chief headman, Siaca, for the supply of the total number of slaves wanted and to deliver to him the goods paid in advance for the purchase of them. He makes subordinate contracts with the interior headmen and with slave dealers of the vicinity who undertake to furnish scores or dozens of slaves according to their means of procuring them (P.R.O., Sierra Leone Commissioners 1823).

One consequence of the increased demand for slaves was to stimulate warfare. Numerous accounts exist of wars, including one in Vai country itself, when, by mutual agreement, two slave dealers promoted conflict between the rulers of their respective areas and profited from the whole affair by purchasing prisoners from each party.

During this period, various other means were used to increase the number of slaves available for export. There is evidence that the number of crimes defined as punishable by enslavement for export was increased. Traditional practices were changed, as exemplified by a Vai text written in the Vai script during the late 1830s (C.M.S., Bukara; Holsoe 1976). In the past, it was usual to send a "white thing" as a token to inform a ruler that his wife's father had died. Now, a ruler rejected the token, informing his affines that they must send a slave before he would hear their messenger's news.

Another document of the period provides an example of the manipulation of a traditional method of fining adulterers.

A very common mode of obtaining an extraordinary supply of slaves upon urgent occasion, such as the obligation to complete the delivery of a cargo of slaves by a particular day, is by the collusion of principal chiefs and dealers with their wives. These wives are generally beyond number; the husbands have long ceased to cohabit with the greater part of them. Some they have merely betrothed to them and have not yet commenced cohabitation with them. The women thus separate from their husbands are allowed to go abroad without restraint and to form intrigues with men whom when they entangle, they betray. These men, according to the custom of the country, forfeit ten slaves for the violation of the conjugal rights of the husband. Two of these slaves are for the costs of settling the palaver by the judgment of the chiefs and elders, the remaining eight are for the compensation of the injury alone. The woman is by law liable to punishment if the husband chooses to make a palaver for her, but in cases of this nature they receive presents of cloth and ornaments and other marks of favor instead of being persecuted and punished for their criminal conduct (P.R.O., Sierra Leone Commissioners 1823).

A further example comes from oral tradition intended to illustrate the absolute power of Zolu Duma, who ruled over a part of the Vai country during the first three decades of the nineteenth century. It describes another mode of obtaining slaves.

Zolu Duma's own sister by one mother and father was called Malia. Malia began a Sande [society] bush [school] and many girls came to join it.
   The people who in the past came to buy slaves came to Zolu Duma and told him that they had been purchasing many men, but no women. He heard their complaint and agreed to assist them. Then he called his sister and told her that the white people had come to him to invite all of the members of the Sande bush to come and see their ship. The women received this news with pleasure.
   Zolu Duma then told the white people that the women would come to visit and when a sufficient number of them had come on board their ship, they should fire their cannon. The women went to visit the ship and when a sufficient number of them had boarded the ship, the cannon was shot and the ship sailed (interview: Noa and Kandakai 1965).

It must be assumed that these last two examples did not represent common modes of obtaining slaves, for they would have led to considerable social instability within Vai society. Yet they seem to reflect a situation, not uncommon in the period from 1807 to 1850, when rulers often had to obtain on short notice large numbers of slaves. More commonly, export slaves came from outside the immediate community. They were alienated from their own people, kept separate from local Vai society in barracoons (slave pens), and shipped away as soon as possible. During this period, the numbers of slaves exported rose sharply, estimates being given of 3,000 shipped in 1823 and as many as 15,000 annually during the decade 1840-50—certainly a large number of individuals, given the estimated size of the Vai population (P.R.O., Sierra Leone Commissioners 1823; Denman 1840; Church Missionary Society 1850).

   With the increased emphasis by the Vai on acquiring export slaves, agricultural production was not able to keep pace. Food provided by domestic jonnu, which was normally sufficient for the local Vai population, now had to be supplemented by purchase from interior farmers in return for European trade goods and salt. Observers, particularly in the

Gallinas area, noted that the Vai obtained rice and other foods from the Sherbro and Mende (Hotham 1849). However, if agricultural production, given the nature of the tropical soil, was inadequate to meet the new demands of an increased population during the period of intensive slave exports, the Vai easily adjusted without seriously disrupting the social fabric of their society.

In 1850 the export of slaves from Vai territory was terminated by the British and American naval squadrons and by determined action of the Liberian government (Holsoe 1971-72:174-81). Suddenly the Vai found themselves with large quantities of unsalable export slaves. Interior rulers were upset and turned against coastal rulers, who were not, however, averse to breaking the treaties they had signed with the British prohibiting the export of slaves. Ironically, it was a British firm that in 1853 provided the first opportunity to evade these agreements. The British had established an apprenticeship system to obtain laborers for their Caribbean colonies, particularly British Guiana. Under the terms of their contracts, recruits were to go for a period of two years and would then be returned. The British company agreed to pay Vai chiefs a fixed sum for each apprentice they produced. The chiefs reacted with enthusiasm, and all the old practices of slave procurement were reinstituted. The Liberian government reacted equally swiftly and intervened, stopping the practice and punishing the chiefs involved (Roberts 1853; Huberich 1947:909).

Nevertheless, when the French instituted a similar system in 1857 to obtain laborers for the island of Réunion, Vai chiefs again reacted with great eagerness. For more than a year the Liberian government was unable to control the renewed slave trading, and only with the assistance of the British and American slave squadrons was the practice again terminated (L.G.A., Regina Coeli File). In 1860 one further attempt was made by Spaniards to collect slaves for Cuba, but again the Liberians and the British stopped it (Foley 1965:9-79). The Vai chiefs whenever possible sought to continue the export trade, a lucrative business with which they were familiar.

A British naval captain stated, after the 1857-58 incident with the French, that the Vai chiefs "asked me . . . how they were to live when slave trade and emigration were abolished, for the thing appeared very difficult to them. The way in which they put this question, and their manner, showed me that they considered it an unanswerable reason for their having acted as they had done" (Hunt 1858).

As a consequence of the frustrations that Vai rulers felt in their new situation, internal warfare broke out. The small payments given the chiefs by the British government for upholding their treaty obligations led to squabbles over their distribution and finally to the murder of a principal ruler. Indeed, in the post-1850 period, warfare increased throughout the Liberian and Sierra Leonean area, and there were three major wars between 1860 and 1892, all of them ultimately involving the Vai country (Holsoe 1967, Ch. 5).

These troubles aside, the Vai during this period did manage to adjust to their new circumstances. More emphasis had to be placed upon farming and self-sufficiency, and women and children now became the most prized prisoners of war since they could be put to work in agriculture as domestic slaves. Grown men were usually executed, for the society had no adequate means of dealing with recalcitrant adult male captives, who in the past had been useful only for the export trade (Besolow 1891:64).

In another interesting departure from the past, the ruler of the Tewo area of the Vai welcomed into his area a group of former slaves from the Gallinas area of the Vai country, the Zawo people, who had been in revolt with their masters since the 1820s. In granting these people asylum he located them on the northeastern frontier of Tewo, where they were to act as a military buffer between the Vai and the neighboring Gola. These Zawo, though of slave origin, were granted greater privileges than most previous domestic slaves. The action was politically astute, as the ruler gained the loyalty of militarily tested warriors.

After 1850 the colonial government in Sierra Leone and the independent government in Liberia began to extend their political and economic influence. The Liberians formed a colony on the coast, in Vai country, thereby encouraging their citizens to begin legitimate trade with Vai leaders. Likewise, John Myer Harris, an English trader, moved into the Gallinas area of the Vai country and began business there (Harris 1865:205-6). Palm oil, palm kernels, piassava, and coffee were now sought for export. As in the past, domestic slaves and pawns were used to collect and transport the products to the coastal trading posts. In addition, with the decrease in population and consequently fewer who needed to be fed, the Vai and their domestic servants no longer depended on outside sources of food but were able to produce a sufficient amount within their own area.

Yet when a new opportunity occurred in the 1890s to export Vai laborers, the local freeborn families responded. At that time the Liberian legislature passed laws which permitted, under controlled circumstances, the shipment of laborers down the coast to work in some of the European colonies. Vai took advantage of this new economic possibility and sent their domestic servants, pawns, and individuals of low status. Such workers were employed in agricultural labor on Fernando Póo and in the Gabon; they were engaged to help build the railroad from the coast to what would become Léopoldville, in the Congo; and they assisted the

Germans in their penetration and occupation of the Cameroons (L.G.A., Native African Shipping Bureau 1892-94).[3]

By the late nineteenth century, the Vai had adjusted again to new circumstances. Agriculture and the collection and transport of local produce, which the Europeans now demanded, made it possible to put domestic slaves and pawns to work at these tasks. Vai society remained resilient, and though the Liberian government began to suppress warfare, which had traditionally been a means of gaining slaves, the society continued to absorb newcomers from the interior through what now was called euphemistically the pawning system, though in fact it was no different than the earlier sale of slaves, for the "pawns" never really expected to return home.

The continued maintenance of this system stemmed from new pressures upon interior peoples. As the Liberian central government incorporated more territory and individuals under its administration during the period 1910-30, it also required these people to pay taxes. As most of the products that could be sold for cash to pay the taxes were difficult to transport over very long distances, children remained the one commodity most easily exchanged for money from the coastal peoples such as the Vai. The Vai in turn used these "pawns" for domestic labor or sent them off as workers to the European colonies down the coast.

As before, during the early part of the present century the Vai responded to outside demands and economic opportunities. At the same time they maintained the social differentiation between jonnu and manja dennu. In 1930, however, the Vai, along with others in Liberia, were faced with a new challenge to their social structures, which was to have profound repercussions.

In response to external pressures from the League of Nations and the United States, on September 29, 1930, the president of Liberia, C. D. B. King, officially outlawed the practice of human pawning. Under the terms of the League of Nations' Anti-Slavery Convention, this form of domestic servitude was viewed, not surprisingly, as analogous to slavery (Huberich 1947:906-8).

The consequences of King's proclamation were staggering for many indigenous people in Liberia. For instance:

In sections of the country where it had been a custom for generations for natives to pawn their children away to neighboring tribes, the chiefs declared that their main sources of income had been removed, and they did not see how they are going to

---

3. Elsewhere I have argued the possibility that the Bamum script in East Cameroons was "invented" through the stimulus of the Vai, who were literate in their own script and who were present in the area. See Holsoe (1971:24 n.15).

get the silver to pay their hut taxes if they cannot pawn their children to the tribes nearer the coast (which tribes, in turn, having evidently been getting the silver from the export of coffee, palm kernels, etc.). This is particularly true of the Kpessie [Kpelle] country where the natives are too far from the coast to export palm kernels or piassava and where no coffee has been grown (Travell 1931/1959).

Oral traditions also reflected two basic concerns of the Vai. The first was their ability to muster sufficient labor to maintain agricultural production. For instance, oral testimony states that a woman, Funba Baba, "suffered too much because she didn't have children. She was just dependent on slavery, buying children. She had money, but no children, and all had to go" (interview: Buno 1965). Others shared her problem: "Most of the people, that was the time they were thinking, why I didn't born, . . . because if you didn't have child no one else would work for you" (interview: Buno 1965).

The second concern involved questions of social dislocation—the possible blurring of the distinction between a jon and a manja den, and the consequent reversal of position and rights of the two groups. The Vai manja den saw it as a time when "Your slaves will be leaders and your children will be slaves" (interview: Kiawu 1966). It might be possible, given the government's decision, for a former slave to become a political ruler and thereby dominate freeborn Vai.

For the first time, the Vai social system was shaken. The basis of wealth —namely, access to manpower—had suddenly been removed by the government edict. Many slaves left the Vai country, returning home or moving to urban areas, leaving the Vai to manage for themselves. Not having done much farming in the past, a task that had been left to slaves, they found it difficult. Above all, the changes affected the very core of their self-concept, for farming was not a proper occupation for a manja den (see Davis 1935:284-86). Nevertheless, some manja dennu were able to remain and continue as traders, and some even took up farming, but for most, this was unthinkable. Instead, those who had a craft or skill that was socially approved for their status chose to move to the coastal urban areas, such as Monrovia, where they could adapt and exchange their labor for cash. As a result, and not surprisingly, agricultural production in the Vai area fell sharply. The majority of the individuals who remained behind were either older persons or very young. Even under the new circumstances, however, the Vai continued to maintain their concepts of status differentiation between manja dennu and jonnu, and have done so up to the present day (see Holsoe 1975).

Although the differentiation is less obvious today, it still affects patterns of social behavior. Individuals are no longer referred to as jonnu, but when pressed to compare a freeborn individual with a person of slave origin, they will call the latter *mo* [mɔ], a human being, but never manja den. In addition, during the recent past in Liberia new positions, for example that of town chief, have been granted to individuals of slave origins. Previously this coveted position would have been held by a manja den, and then only by an individual from the founding lineage. Today manja dennu find the task burdensome because it involves distant and time-consuming meetings with Liberian government officials, and therefore many have chosen individuals of low status to represent them. The former slave becomes town chief in name only, however, as power still resides with the eldest member of the founding lineage, and all important decisions must be made by him in conjunction with the manja den elders of the town. Yet viewed from the outside it would seem as if individuals of slave origin have gained an equality and access to political power never allowed before. Such an impression is false; the stratification continues, but now in a less obvious manner.

CONCLUSIONS

The changes that affected Vai society over a period of some four hundred years occurred without imposing great discontinuities on Vai social structure. Even the more encompassing changes imposed by the Liberian government in the recent past have not changed certain basic Vai beliefs. The Vai have maintained their concepts of status differences between individuals who were manja dennu and those who were jonnu, and within the latter category the Vai have manipulated the use of the different forms of servitude in response to changing opportunities. This conclusion contradicts Walter Rodney's thesis that Europeans imposed institutional slavery upon the African societies of the upper Guinea coast.

Possibly more important, the Vai case also challenges current anthropological conclusions about rain-forest societies. For instance, Meillassoux has argued recently that, in the rain-forest setting, with time domestic slaves merged into the dominant lineages (Meillassoux 1971:63). The Vai maintained the distinction between jonnu and manja dennu, and as a consequence domestic slaves were not incorporated into the lineages of the rulers. Likewise, Meillassoux has argued that a consciousness among slaves of similarity of status and their common difference from the ruling class could only occur in the savanna and Sahel in West Africa (Meillassoux 1971:64-65). Again the Vai prove to be an exception. The arguments as normally stated assume that rain-forest societies lack the ability to gain a food surplus and thus are unable to maintain class differences. Yet the Vai, while living in a rain-forest setting, made use of outside economic resources, in this case the European trade, and thereby overcame the limitations of their environment.

GLOSSARY

jon (pl. *jonnu*): an individual held in one of various types of servitude.

manja den (pl. *manja dennu*): literally, a chief's child; the individual who was a freeborn Vai. They were considered full Vai citizens and as such could assume positions of political, economic, and social importance to the society.

mo (pl. *monu*): literally, a human being; sometimes used as a euphemism for *jon*.

musu jonja: literally, woman servitude. A labor arrangement in which an insolvent man who commits adultery is required to pay compensation by working for the aggrieved husband until the debt is paid.

na jon (pl. *na jonnu*): literally, my servant. A phrase used at times by an individual who held a pawn.

see (pl. *seenu*): a person who is placed as a pawn in the hands of another individual by his or her maternal uncle due to the uncle's inability to pay a debt to the receiver of the pawn.

REFERENCES

ORAL SOURCES
The interviews were taped and transcribed by the author. A set of tapes is deposited at the African Studies Association, Center for African Oral Data, Archives of Traditional Music, Indiana University, Bloomington, Indiana.

Buno, clan chief, Lower Mecca clan, Mecca chiefdom, interview on July 18, 1965.

Fasinyen Gawolo, former town chief, Gondolahun, Yawiyazu clan, Bandi chiefdom, interview on July 7, 1968.

Varni Kiawu, elder, Sewulu, Kiawu clan, Tewo chiefdom, interview on June 10, 1966.

Momolu Noa and Zuke Kandakai, elders, Gawula chiefdom, interview on June 3, 1965.

UNPUBLISHED SOURCES
C.M.S.: Church Missionary Society Archives, London.
  Bukara, D. Undated. Translation of the manuscript of Doalu Bukara, the inventor of the Vei-mode of writing. C.A. 1/0135/16B.
Foley, D. M. 1965. British policy in Liberia, 1862-1912. Ph.D. dissertation, Univ. of London.
Holsoe, S. E. 1967. The cassava-leaf people: an ethnohistorical study of the Vai people with particular emphasis on the Tewo chiefdom. Ph.D. dissertation, Boston Univ.

_____. 1974a. The "first" Vai migration. Paper read at the Liberian Research Conference, Univ. of Wisconsin, Madison.

_____. 1975. Vai occupational continuities: traditional to modern. Paper read at the African Studies Association meetings, San Francisco.

L.G.A.: Liberian Government Archives, Monrovia.

Native African Shipping Bureau, 1892-94. Executive Documents.

Regina Coeli File, undated. Executive Documents.

P.R.O.: Public Record Office, London.

Sierra Leone Commissioners, letter to Canning, April 29, 1823. F.O. 84/21, General No. 4.

PUBLISHED SOURCES

Ashmun, J. 1826. Letter to Blumhardt, April 23, 1826. *Afr. Repository* 2 (1827):259.

Barber, J. W. 1840. *A history of the Amistad captives.* New York.

Besolow, T. E. 1891. *From the darkness of Africa to the light of America: the story of an African prince.* Boston.

Büttikofer, J. 1890. *Reisebilder aus Liberia.* 2 vols. Leiden.

Church Missionary Society. 1850. New mission at the Gallinas River 1850. *Church Missionary gleaner.* New ser., No. 9, p. 101.

Curtin, P. D. 1969. *The Atlantic slave trade: a census.* Madison.

Dapper, O. 1670. *Umbständliche und eigentliche Beschreibung von Africa.* Amsterdam.

Davis, T. E. 1935. Letter to J. A. H. Jones, November 19, 1935. In *The economic history of Liberia,* by G. W. Brown. Washington, D.C. 1941.

Denman, J. 1840. Letter, November 28, 1840. In Great Britain, *Parliamentary papers,* Vol. 12, 1842, p. 457. Report from the Select Committee on the West Coast of Africa, Pt. II, Appendix and Index (no. 551), p. 454.

Fage, J. D. 1969. Slavery and the slave trade in the context of West African history. *J. Afr. Hist.,* 10:394-98.

Gröben, O. F. von der. 1694. *Guineische Reise-Beschreibung.* Murjerwerder.

Harris, J. 1865. Testimony before a Parliamentary Select Committee, May 15, 1865. In Great Britain, *Parliamentary papers,* Vol. 5, 1865, p. 206. Report from the Select Committee on Africa (Western Coast) together with the Proceedings of the Committee, Minutes of Evidence, and Appendix (No. 412).

Holsoe, S. E. 1971. A case of stimulus diffusion? (a note on possible connections between the Vai and Cherokee scripts). *Lang. Sci.* No. 15, pp. 22-24.

_____. 1971-72. Theodore Canot at Cape Mount, 1841-1847. *Liber. Stud. J.* 4:163-81.

_____. 1974b. The manipulation of traditional political structures among coastal peoples in western Liberia during the nineteenth century. *Ethnohistory* 21:158-67.

_____. 1976. An early Vai manuscript from Liberia. *Afr. Lang.* Vol. 2.

Hotham, C. 1849. Letter to Secretary of Admiralty, February 13, 1849, and enclosures. In Great Britain, *Parliamentary papers,* Vol. 19, 1849, pp.

157-71. Appendix to First Report from the Select Committee on the Slave Trade, Appendix No. 7.

Huberich, C. H. 1947. *The political and legislative history of Liberia.* New York.

Hunt, J. 1858. Letter to Commodore Wise, November 6, 1858. Great Britain, *British and foreign state papers.* 1858-59. 49:980.

Lugenbeel, J. W. 1853. *Sketches of Liberia.* Washington, D.C.

Meillassoux, C., ed. 1971. *The development of indigenous trade and markets in West Africa.* London.

Roberts, J. J. 1853. Liberia: proclamation, February 26, 1853. *Afr. Repository* 29:184.

Rodney, W. 1966. African slavery and other forms of social oppression on the upper Guinea coast in the context of the Atlantic slave trade. *J. Afr. Hist.* 7:431-43.

Tilleman, E. 1697. *En liden enfoldig Beretning om det landskab Guinea.* Copenhagen.

Travell, W. A. 1931. Letter to Edwin Barclay, November 28, 1931. In *Liberia's past and present,* by N. R. Richardson. 1959. London.

Welmers, W. 1958. *The Mande languages.* Georgetown Univ. Monograph Series, No. 11. Washington, D.C.

12

Slavery among Coastal Middlemen: The Duala of Cameroon

Ralph A. Austen

The Duala of Cameroon are one of those African coastal societies often stereotyped as "slave-trading middlemen." The inferences drawn from this identification have often been grossly misleading and unjust. Nevertheless, it remains true that various forms of slavery did play a critical role in the historical development of the Duala. The traditional Duala view of their own way of life and its relationship to outside groups is intricately bound up with conceptions of servitude. Historical evidence also makes it clear that servile groups constituted important sectors of Duala social, economic, and political organization.

The present chapter will attempt first to define the position of slaves within Duala society at about the middle of the nineteenth century. This will be followed by a somewhat more lengthy examination of the processes that produced this system of stratification and the changes in it from the eighteenth through the twentieth centuries.[1]

1. The material presented here has been assembled in the midst of a more general Duala history project carried on intermittently since 1969 in America, Europe, Nigeria, and Cameroon. I want to thank the Fulbright Foundation, the Rockefeller Foundation, the Social Science Research Council, and the University of Chicago for providing me with travel and research funds. All opinions expressed are, of course, the exclusive responsibility of the author.

305

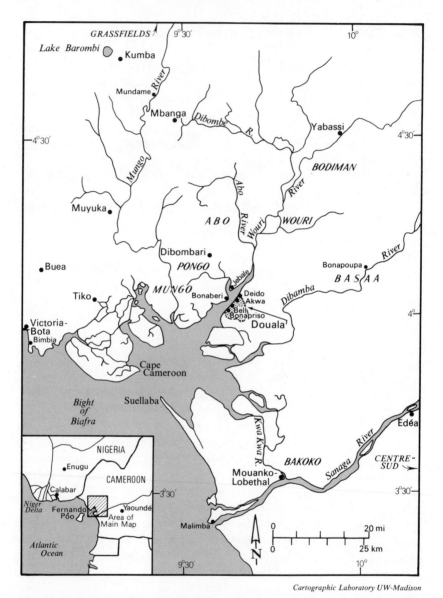

Cartographic Laboratory UW-Madison

Map 12. Northern Part of Cameroon Coast

GEOGRAPHICAL AND POLITICAL BACKGROUND

The Bantu-speaking Duala people have occupied since about the late sixteenth century the site of the present city of Douala, the major seaport of Cameroon.[2] The area is joined to the Atlantic Ocean by an estuary some twelve miles long and is connected to the hinterland by several rivers, most notably the Wouri, the Dibamba, and the Mungo. The Duala proper have numbered, since the end of the nineteenth century, over 20,000. Closely related ethnic groups in the Cameroon coastal region, or littoral, add approximately 30,000 to this population.

Shortly after their settlement on the coast, the Duala entered into trade with Europeans, exporting ivory and slaves from the seventeenth to the early nineteenth centuries, and palm oil, palm kernels, and ivory during the rest of the 1800s. Political authority was divided among the heads of the various settlements making up precolonial Douala. Despite a tendency toward further segmentation of these "towns," during the nineteenth century two competing dynasties were recognized as generally dominant: the Bonadoo of "King" Bell, and the Bonambela or Bonaku of "King" Akwa.

In 1884 the Bell, Akwa, and lesser rulers signed a treaty of protection with the German government, creating the basis for the much larger German territory of Kamerun. Britain and France took Cameroon from Germany in World War I; the eventual division of the colony put the city of Douala and most of the outlying Duala settlements under French rule. Because of their close ties with the British-controlled littoral region west of the Mungo River, the Duala took an active part in the successful movements for reunification, which accompanied Cameroon's post-World War II independence.

DUALA CONCEPTIONS OF SLAVERY

The initially advantageous trading position of the Duala permitted them to play a leading role in Cameroon history. But the nature of their earliest relations with peoples of the interior entirely failed to create any sense of protonationalism or even an effective local imperialism. Instead, the Duala conceived of their ties with other Cameroon peoples in an idiom derived from institutions of slavery.

The importance of slavery for the Duala is attested to by the presence in their language of numerous words that can be translated, in their various contexts, as "slave." Several scholars have attributed more or less precise

2. The most useful general works on the Duala in Cameroon history are E. Ardener (1956); Johnson (1970); Mveng (1963); and Wirz (1972).

meanings to these terms.[3] One must proceed cautiously, however, in any reconstruction, through interviews and etymological reasoning, of a defunct system that was not only quite complex but also remains tied to highly charged ideological issues. In presenting the six major terms listed below, an effort will be made not so much to define them as to place them in their social and ethnogeographical context, which will itself be examined in the rest of the chapter.

1. *Mukom* (pl. *bakom*): the most widely used and broadly applied Duala term for slave. Though etymologically linked to the idea of military capture, it generally refers to slaves purchased commercially and born outside Douala. The peoples of the Cameroon Grassfields, especially the Bamileke, were formerly referred to as *Bakomkom* (sing. *mukomkom*, a pejorative form of mukom). In status, the bakom were generally considered the lowest members of Duala society (the diminutive *ikom* is a term of abuse). They were associated with work unsuitable for free males, especially agriculture.

2. *Mukaki* (pl. *mikaki*): not a very widely used or recognized term, specifying a slave purchased as an adult.

3. *Etumbe* (pl. *betumbe*): a term widely used, even after the decline of other forms of slavery, to denote a mukom purchased as a child. Betumbe were usually brought into the household of their masters, where they performed domestic chores and could participate directly in elite male activities, such as trading.

4. *Mujabedi* (pl. *mijabedi*): another rarely used term (possibly Malimba rather than metropolitan Duala), referring to a slave given as a gift rather than purchased. Dika-Akwa asserts that the mujabedi functioned only as a royal retainer.

5. *Muyabedi* (pl. *miyabedi*): a widely used term, referring to the Douala-born offspring of bakom parents or of slave-free unions. The miyabedi are often referred to as "half-free" because no one maintained property rights over them, but they still suffered from various stigmas attached to their origin.

6. *Mukoma* (pl. *mikoma*): a widely used term to distinguish purchased bakom from war captives, who almost inevitably came from the Duala-related ethnic groups of the littoral. The social status of the *mukoma* was higher than that of the mukom; but precisely because he was difficult to retain in a servile status, he was more likely to be sold overseas or sacrificed.

3. A general picture of the vocabulary and social organization associated with Duala slavery can be drawn from the following works: Bekombo (1963); Bohner (1893); Brutsch (1950); Bureau (1962); Dika-Akwa (1969); Dinckelacker (1914); Helmlinger (1972); Ittman (1953); Reichenow (1873); and Zimmerer (1892).

The general Duala term for a nonslave is *wonja* (pl. *wonja*), meaning a freeborn individual of pure Duala descent. There are also gradations within the wonja grouping that denote wealth and status within free Duala society, but what concerns us most here is the existence of a set of terms providing a continuum from wonja to bakom. Thus, *njan* (pl. *njan*) means a Duala or an outsider who has voluntarily moved from his home area to live in another community. *Tunge* or *dikoti* are people given by one group to another as pawns—i.e., guarantees for debts, usually commercial. *Pu* are people transferred specifically for blood debts. Njan, if of Duala origin, are considered wonja, and no matter what their origins, they usually founded (or retained) autonomous households in their new homes. Tunge, dikoti, and pu, although not considered to be slaves, were always incorporated into the households of their receivers, as were the bakom. Since these first three terms imply regular relations among the groups between which the individuals involved move, they refer almost exclusively to littoral people. The mukom, on the other hand, is considered to derive from so far away that he retains no inherited protection. Duala proverbs often refer to the mukom as a kind of orphan who "has abandoned his household (mboa) in the East" (Hecklinger 1921:145 and passim; see also Ebding 1959).

Despite all the ambiguities, obscurities, and gradations in Duala conceptions of slavery and freedom, it seems useful to present them schematically as sets of linked associations:

mukom	*wonja*
captive	conqueror
orphan	child of a household
stranger	Duala
inland	coastal
female role	male role
agriculture	fishing, trade

This dual list suggests a pattern of binary opposition of the type stressed in the structuralist anthropological work of Lévi-Strauss and his school. At least one scholar has suggested an analysis of Duala culture along these lines (Bureau 1962:33-39; cf. E. Ardener 1972), but there are presently not enough data available to pursue such an inquiry fruitfully. Nevertheless, it should be kept in mind that dualistic associations do govern many of the ways the Duala express and organize their relationship to slaves. Although these conceptions have a historical dimension, they do not always fit the processes of Duala history. But it is precisely the tension between conceptual structure and empirical process that makes this history meaningful.

Most of the substantive issues incorporated into the conceptual scheme outlined above will be discussed under the relevant synchronic and diachronic headings that follow. However, the Duala equation of bakom with "conquered strangers" must be dealt with immediately since it may suggest misleading parallels with castelike slave systems.

The Duala seldom assert any significant cultural or biological distinctions between themselves and the inland peoples whom they classify as bakom. It is as clear to the Duala as to any outsider that, in language, physical characteristics, and probably even origin, they and their neighbors are very close. The peoples who preceded the Duala in the Cameroon estuary—the Basaa and Bakoko—are, like the Duala themselves, Bantu-speakers; other local groups (Abo, Bodiman, Malimba, Mungo, Pongo, and Wuri) speak languages extremely close to Duala and all recognize their common origins. Even the peoples considered as classical bakom— the more eastern Basaa groups and the often non-Bantu populations extending northwest of the navigable Wouri River into the Grassfields— are viewed by the Duala as capable of being individually assimilated into their own society.

The traditional Duala notion of themselves as wonja and other Cameroonians as bakom is ultimately based on the Duala occupation of a geographical area that allowed them to profit from their relations with inland peoples in a number of ways, only one of which was the procurement of slaves and slave services. The conquest dimension of this notion derives from Duala memories of their relatively recent migration. Though this movement was not, even as recounted in most Duala oral traditions, marked by any great military feats, the original Basaa and Bakoko inhabitants of Douala were forced either to move inland or to assume a Duala cultural and political identity.

Most of the slaves acquired by the Duala were not directly captured, as the terminology suggests, but rather purchased from areas farther inland. If the Duala played the role of middlemen in the trade between Europe and Cameroon, the other littoral peoples—especially those on the rivers— were secondary middlemen and developed many of the same servile institutions as the Duala. Well up into the twentieth century, however, the Duala drew far greater advantages from this trade than any other littoral peoples and the mukom-wonja conceptual contrast expresses a concern for maintaining this advantage. The relation of this ideology to historically mutable circumstances will be seen in a later section of this chapter, which examines the way in which mid-twentieth-century political and other pressures have led the Duala to redefine their own "free" ethnic community so as to include virtually all the littoral peoples.

SLAVE STATUS: SUBJUGATION, AUTONOMY, ASSIMILATION

Duala settlement patterns provide both a visual metaphor and a practical application of divisions between bakom and wonja. Within Douala itself, most slaves lived in segregated areas known as *koto* (literally, an enclosure; *mun a koto*—literally, "koto child"—is a euphemism for slave). When the slaves belonged to an important chief, the koto might be a separate, and even relatively distant, village. Within Douala, the koto was always located away from the rivers and coasts, which were reserved for the *mudongo* (literally, a hill, especially one overlooking a river), a term used for the residence of the free Duala. The symbolic and practical point of this arrangement was to reserve for the wonja access to strategic bodies of water and the occupations they represented and to confine the bakom to inland agriculture. At the same time, such a juxtaposition prevented masters from exercising close supervision over their slaves.

Since slaves were, in fact, groups of mixed strangers resettled in or near Douala, their social identity was closely tied to their owner. For marriage purposes, a slave settlement was subject to the same rule of exogamy governing the household of its owner. Masters were responsible for providing their slaves, as they did their sons, with wives. The master held a right to all his slaves' property, exercised parental control over their offspring, and took responsibility for their debts. In reality, most slave communities constituted relatively autonomous units within the larger sociopolitical structure of Douala. Each koto had its own social organization, and the separate villages possessed chiefs who appear sometimes to have been betumbe of the royal households. Apart from services and tributes due to their masters (which do not appear to have been regularly onerous), slaves could sell their labor and products for personal profit. They thus shared in the economic advantages of Douala's geographical position. This situation probably explains why most miyabedi, although technically free, stayed in their places, and few bakom sought to escape even when opportunities were offered.[4]

Female bakom could be brought into free Duala households as concubines. Such women, like koto slaves and legitimate wives, were still responsible for agricultural labor. Purchase of concubines differed from legitimate bridewealth mainly in its lower price (Austen 1974a). The major qualitative distinctions between these two types of union lay in the absence, for the concubine, of recourse to her own lineage, and the lower status of her children. Offspring of concubines were considered miyabedi,

---

4. On an abortive attempt in 1892 by the German explorer Eugen Zintgraff to induce Bali Grassfield slaves to leave their Duala masters, see O.R.S.T.O.M., Zintgraff 1892.

with no rights to inherit their father's social position, although they might effectively succeed to his business affairs. Free Duala children not only enjoyed a favored position in relation to their fathers, but their mothers could also establish linkages between sons and maternal uncles and even found matrilineages subordinate to the predominant patrilineal system. For purposes of household rituals, slaves also enjoyed a special status, but this only emphasized their alien character, since the same roles might be performed by a complete stranger (Bekombo 1963).

Thus, despite a growing influx of slaves into central Duala society on a basis that all outside observers described as emancipated, the stigma of slave origin could never be fully erased. Even in contemporary Duala society, it is generally known which families are descended from slaves though few individuals will themselves admit to such an origin.

Male betumbe, that is, slaves entering Duala society as children, often achieved an even higher status than most miyabedi. Placed as they were in free mudongo households rather than in koto agricultural settlements, they had an opportunity to become important assistants in the most prestigious undertakings of their masters, especially commerce. In fact, because a major trader's betumbe had often begun working with him well before his actual sons reached maturity or were even born, individuals of this status appear among the leading commercial figures in nineteenth-century Douala.

It is particularly the descendants of betumbe who usually claim that their first Duala ancestors were the legitimate sons of the men who, in reality, purchased them. According to contemporary Duala informants, it is usually possible to distinguish between real children and such "adopted" betumbe by means of the special, often slightly bizarre, names that the latter received. Thus the best known case of an etumbe's rise to a high position is that of Mandessi ("irritation") Bell, a Grassfields child who was brought into the household of King Ndumbe Lobe Bell during the 1870s and eventually became the most powerful figure in this dominant clan.

Despite his wealth and prestige, Mandessi's origins definitely prevented him from aspiring to the actual Bell chieftaincy. Such an office could theoretically be acquired by a male mukom or muyabedi if he married a ruler's daughter without paying bridewealth, thus making his children members of her lineage. In practice, this was rare. Most slaves and their descendants could marry free women (which seldom seems to have happened) only if they obtained enough wealth to pay particularly high bridewealth. Slaves usually married other slaves, and their children were miyabedi. In one early nineteenth-century case, however, an Abo (littoral, Duala-related) war captive of some apparent indigenous standing married the daughter of a chiefly wonja and produced, through her line, the ruling family of the major Duala town, Bonebela or Deido. But the subsequent history of Deido is marked by particularly severe conflict with the other Duala towns, culminating in the unprecedented execution of the chief "Charley Dido" (Eyum Ebele) in 1876.[5] Similarly, the long-standing rivalry between the more significant Bell and Akwa political segments is explained by the Bell partisans as having arisen because the Akwa lineage is descended from one of their own ancestors and a male Basaa slave. Certainly, the Bells cultivated a northwestern trade route based on links (including intermarriage) with such Duala-related groups as the Abo and Mungo, while the Akwa strongpoints were more in the east, bringing them into closer touch with the Basaa, from whom slaves were acquired. Thus, to their enemies, Bonaku bakom—"the Akwa are slaves," and ineligible to rule over any Duala. The functional relationship between slavery and Duala political instability will be discussed below, but at a conceptual level it is clear that the free Duala could never fully accept the idea of allowing slaves into their highest social ranks.

SLAVE FUNCTIONS: PRODUCTIVE CAPITAL AND NEGOTIABLE CHATTEL

Insofar as slaves merely aided in the economic activities already carried on by free Duala, their function can be considered one of productive but unspecialized human capital. Their particular value to the Duala arose, however, not from what slaves did but from what could be done with them: they constituted a unique form of chattel for critical economic, political, social, and ritual transactions.

As already noted, one of the principal oppositions in Duala social conceptions is that between servile agriculturalists and free specialists in fishing and commerce; the subjugation of slaves to agricultural functions was the condition allowing others the freedom to engage in more prestigious activities.

From a strictly economic viewpoint, agricultural and nonagricultural occupations in Duala society were more complementary than opposed. Certainly fishing, a dangerous and often unprofitable undertaking, need not be viewed as more attractive than agriculture. But fishing was probably the basis for Duala commerce, as it was for Niger Delta trading

---

5. The very critical situation of Charley Dido in nineteenth-century Douala has been presented in various standard sources according to the dubious preconceptions of their authors. Thus the British consul Thomas Hutchinson saw Charley Dido as an upwardly mobile slave-turned-merchant who was persecuted by the Duala elite. See Hutchinson (1856). Brutsch and others relate Dido's execution to the functioning of a probably mythical general Duala tribunal, the *Ngondo*, discussed later in this chapter.

states, since coastal fish surpluses are readily exchangeable for interior agricultural goods. The peoples resettled as Duala slaves had, in most cases, always been agriculturalists; by moving toward the coast, they actually gained an opportunity to win new kinds of rewards for their cultivation efforts. Slaves, like women, were allowed to gather crustaceans from shallow offshore waters, and to eat and market them. Women were explicitly excluded from the camps in the Wouri estuary, where the most important Duala fishing activities took place, but slaves and children could be brought along for onshore activities; only the free adult males, however, actually went out for deep-water fishing. Miyabedi, considered sufficiently Dualaized to be competent paddlers and swimmers, could take full part in fishing activities.[6]

The complex relationship between Duala ideology and the divisions of status, sex, and labor in their society is embodied in the development of the *Jengu* cult. Jengu (pl. *miengu*) is a water spirit who controls the welfare of fishermen but is sometimes depicted as female and associated, in its oldest forms, with women's rites. During the nineteenth century the Jengu cult came to form the basis for a male secret society which regulated various commercial, political, and even criminal affairs that were beyond the power of the weak and fragmented hereditary Duala rulers. Slaves were specifically excluded from the jengu society and even miyabedi of several generations' standing could enter only its lower ranks. In this same period, other cult societies with similar functions of maintaining order and emphasizing status were developed, partly, according to some accounts, to accommodate the miyabedi and the Akwa, who were not considered pure enough for full participation in Jengu.[7]

Jengu and associated Duala cults are often related in the literature to the *Ekpe* cult of the Efik in nearby Old Calabar (southeastern Nigeria). Contemporary Europeans usually referred to all such cults by the Efik-derived pidgin term *Egbo*. It is true that Ekpe and Jengu played a similar role in the politics and the slave-free relations of their respective societies. There is no evidence, however, that the two cults are related, particularly since their symbolism is so diverse (Ekpe means leopard, an animal associated with neither Jengu nor any major Duala cults). In fact, the use of an aquatic spirit as the object of the most important Duala cult society emphasizes the deliberate isolation of the Duala from inland peoples. By contrast, the Efik Ekpe, which failed to assimilate slaves within Old

6. Most of the information on the social organization of Duala fishing was gathered from interviews in Douala, especially a series carried out in Bonaberi and the Wouri estuary from May 14 to May 18, 1973; see also Makembe (1921).

7. Available literature on Jengu and related cults is highly unsatisfactory, and the subject is difficult to study from the testimony of even the oldest Duala informants. Nevertheless, see Ittman (1957); Hebga (1968:61-84); Wurm (1904); and Rosny (n.d.).

Calabar, did spread from the coast to the interior as the major basis for a trading network far more extensive than anything achieved by the Duala (Ruel 1969:250-58 and passim).

The Duala could afford to limit slave participation in fishing activities and associated cults, since fishing did not offer incentives for major expansion during the nineteenth century. On the other hand, commerce, the basis for wealth and power, required extensive slave manpower. The slave settlements and inland villages established by the Duala assured an independent food supply to a society of noncultivators and also furnished advanced bases for the gathering and processing of ivory and palm products. Duala slaves were also put to more mobile commercial uses. Most formed the crews of trading canoes (despite a Duala proverb comparing the ability of slave canoeists to the effectiveness of a broken rudder—Hecklinger 1921:145). Others, especially betumbe, served as highly responsible commercial agents for their wonja masters and a few eventually rose to great prominence as traders. Some of these successful slaves established themselves as the subchiefs of minor Duala "towns." This was, however, the limit of their upward mobility, for large-scale economic prosperity depended closely upoñ political power (if nothing else, coercion or the threat of it was always needed to collect debts) and political power, at its highest level, required a degree of legitimacy ultimately unobtainable by a slave.

In the course of their commercial and political activities, slaves also participated directly in the petty warfare that characterized much of nineteenth-century Duala history. But it is here that the truly onerous position of Duala slaves as human chattel becomes evident. Slaves were not only the foot soldiers in these minor wars but also the only kind of casualty acceptable to the main combatants. Wars, in fact, often began when a quarrel resulted in the death of a freeman and ended when enough slaves had been expended (either through death in battle or payment as indemnities) to satisfy the aggrieved parties that their honor and their interests had been upheld. On one occasion, in the 1870s, King Ndumbe Lobe Bell was accused of having simulated the results of a military campaign by killing a number of his own slaves and displaying their severed heads as war trophies (Heinersdorff 1880:96; Reichenow 1884:37-39).

Slaves in this context became a kind of political chattel. Their main exploitation as economic chattel came before 1830, when the Duala functioned as minor but steady suppliers to the Atlantic slave trade. The limited data available for this early period make it difficult to determine what, if any, distinctions existed between slaves meant for export and those absorbed into the local system. By the mid-nineteenth century, the greatest threat that hung over slaves was sacrificial execution at funerals or other ritual occasions. There is some evidence in European sources to suggest that the victims on such occasions were always freshly acquired aliens; but this tendency may be explained largely by the ability of resident slaves to appeal to missionaries and consuls for protection against an abuse specifically banned in several Anglo-Duala treaties.

Although no longer sold overseas, slaves still constituted a major commodity in the nineteenth-century trade between Douala and its hinterland. Once acquired by the Duala, they could continue to be transferred via inheritance, gift exchanges, discharge of debts, or loan (under the title of pawns) to guarantee the eventual payment of obligations in some other form of property. Slaves were also a major currency for the payment of various sorts of fines. Here again, as in warfare, the sacrosanct status of free Duala men was emphasized by their freedom to compensate for their own misbehavior through the dispatch of a lesser class of person.

ORIGINS OF DUALA SLAVERY: THE ATLANTIC SLAVE TRADE

The picture given above of Duala slavery during the mid-nineteenth century already contains obvious indications of the degree to which this institution depended upon the interplay of various historical factors. It now remains to examine the development of slavery among the Duala and how, once established, it could be adapted to new situations, including the antislavery policies of the increasingly dominant Europeans.

Unfortunately, given the limits of the documentation available, it is difficult to do more than speculate about pre-nineteenth-century Duala social history. Judging from the Batanga, a related people who had neither important overseas trade nor slaves until the 1850s, we may tentatively assert a local confirmation of the thesis that indigenous African slavery followed rather than preceded European contacts.[8] This seems particularly likely on the Cameroon coast, where low population densities and the very limited contact with other parts of Africa could hardly have fostered the kind of social complexity usually associated with permanent servile institutions. The absence of local slavery may also help explain the reputation for insubordination of slaves purchased in Douala and neighboring ports in the Bight of Biafra during the eighteenth century. Indeed, during the first century and a half of their contact with Europeans, the Duala appear to have specialized in the export of ivory accompanied by only small numbers of slaves (E. Ardener 1968; Austen 1974b).

Intensive Duala participation in the Atlantic slave trade began only during the 1750s. This change must largely be explained by factors outside

8. This idea is suggested in Kouoh-Moukouri and Weber (1971). See Rodney (1966); Richard (1970:17-18).

of Duala society itself; first, the accelerated demand for labor on American plantations (Curtin 1969:150, 154, 221-28) and second, the increased availability of captives following Chamba invasions of the Cameroon Grassfields (Tardits 1971:187-91). For this period we also have some information about human pawning, an institution that may have provided the germ for the development of indigenous Duala servile institutions. The Duala terms for such pawns (tunge, dikoti) and pawning itself (*dumba*) are not etymologically related to words for slavery. Dumba, in both its root and derivative forms, is, however, associated with robbery and plunder, which may suggest the general conflicts that tended to arise between European, Duala, and inland traders concerning debt repayment and/or may refer more specifically to the process through which pawns became enslaved. Early European references to pawning state that it involved free individuals (often the wives and children of debtors) who were left either by inland traders who dealt with Duala middlemen (and vice versa) or by Duala traders who dealt with Europeans. In each case the party giving the pawns had received trade goods without being able immediately to deliver the commodities for which he had contracted. Pawn exchanges between Duala and inland traders involved the ultimate export of ivory. The Duala, however, also gave pawns to Europeans in promise of producing exportable slaves. It was apparently understood that pawns might be sold into slavery overseas if the promised goods were not forthcoming. However, in the series of incidents reported as occurring during 1787, European attempts to sail off with such pawns led to violent reprisals by the Duala traders (Arnold 1789; Robertson 1819).

All that can be made of this information is that the conveyance of persons in connection with commercial transactions could exist among the Duala apart from—or even in contrast to—slavery. Possibly Duala slavery arose during the period of ivory trading from the manipulation of this institution by creditors appropriating pawns from those unable to assert their right to reclaim pawns. But we cannot be sure of such a sequence because the little information we have about early Duala pawn status comes from a period when slavery already existed as a fully developed institution in its own right.

ABOLITION OF THE DUALA OVERSEAS SLAVE TRADE

Although Brazilian and Cuban labor demands helped maintain an active slave trade from many parts of West and West Central Africa up through the 1850s, slaves apparently ceased to be exported in any significant numbers from Douala by the mid-1820s. Some historians have seen in this rapid abolition evidence of moral opposition to slave trading on the part of Duala chiefs (Mveng 1963:141ff.; Webster and Boahen 1967:83-84). Available evidence portrays the Duala as eager enough to sell slaves but unable to attract illicit buyers because of the small cargoes available and the dangers of being trapped inside the estuary by British patrols working from the nearby station of Fernando Póo.[9] Even after the human traffic to the Americas had ended, small numbers of Duala slaves and indentured workers continued to be sent to Portuguese plantations on the islands of Príncipe and São Tomé. The last and most detailed reference to this practice dates from 1877, when the Portuguese, dissatisfied with the results, unilaterally terminated the entire arrangement.[10]

If British pressure rather than abolitionist sentiment led the Duala to abandon the extensive export of slaves, trade in other products (mainly with Britain up to the 1870s) provided alternate uses for slaves. The British consuls, backed by the Royal Navy, imposed a series of anti-slave-trade treaties upon the Duala from 1840 onward while simultaneously attempting to maintain a smooth flow of "legitimate" commerce. In doing so, they continually found it necessary to intervene in debt conflicts between Duala and European traders and ultimately in internal Duala affairs as well. The British insisted (ineffectually, it seems) on abolishing one aspect of internal Duala slavery, the use of slaves as human sacrifices. But their general role as mediators rather than administrators led them to support the property rights of Duala elites over their slaves. An 1844 set of Admiralty instructions specified that "It is not the purpose of these engagements [i.e., anti-slave-trade treaties] to cause any interference in the system of domestic slavery which prevails in the territories of King Bell and King Acqua."[11] In fact, many intra-Duala cases adjudicated by British consuls, either directly or through the Court of Equity that they established at Douala, involved the restoration of slaves to their owners or the payment of slaves as indemnities for various legal obligations.[12]

INTERNAL SLAVE TRADING IN THE NINETEENTH CENTURY

Despite the effective abolition of the overseas slave trade, the manpower demands of nineteenth-century legitimate commerce probably increased

9. On the general considerations governing slave trading in the illegal period, see LeVeen (1971). The regret of Duala kings at giving up slave trading is recorded in Holman (1840:426, 433) and Jackson (1934:101-27).

10. N.N.A., Calabar Provincial Files 4/1, Vol. 6, 1877. There is an echo of this form of slave-trading activity in the prosecution by the German government of several Duala engaged in supply illegal laborers to Fernando Póo; A.N.F.A., Douala District Court transcripts, S1910/106.

11. Great Britain, *Parliamentary Papers,* 1844, Vol. 50 (no. 577), pp. 93-95. For almost complete accounts of the Anglo-Duala antislavery treaties, see Brutsch (1955) and S. G. Ardener (1968:70-83).

12. For records of consular activities in Douala and occasional proceedings of the Court of Equity, see the P.R.O. Foreign Office series, as well as N.N.A., Calabar Provincial Files, Vols. 2-6.

the quantity of slaves arriving in Douala from the interior. These recruits came largely from the Grassfields, where warfare and state-building continued to send out a steady stream of refugees and prisoners (Chilver and Kaberry 1968). As already noted, the Grassfields was probably the most important source for slaves sent overseas from Douala during the earlier periods. In the nineteenth century, when slaves could only be exploited locally, a premium must have been placed on importing them from a remote area. Even today Duala informants distinguish between the loyalty and docility of the mukom, purchased at several removes from a homeland to which he could never return, and the mukoma, captured in wars with the immediate neighbors of the Duala and thus likely both to resent his masters and to escape easily back to his own people.

Even in this period, however, many slaves still came from among the Basaa (Bl.M.S., Copierbuch 1900; Crouch 1889:138) and the still closer littoral peoples. Evidence for the presence of slaves from the littoral within the Douala servile population can be found in the cult societies brought to Douala from closely neighboring areas by slaves and used to defend themselves against persecutions by Jengu and other wonja organizations (discussed in the next section of this chapter).

The actual process of procurring slaves from neighboring societies does not seem to have created great difficulties for the Duala. Conflicts did arise on the special occasions when a major Duala chief died and his successors sought sacrificial victims by making sudden forays into the nearby bush (B.M.S., Clarke 1841, Fuller; P.R.O., Quan 1862). More often, however, slaves seem to have been acquired by mutual agreement; the internal peoples already possessed slaves of their own and sometimes the Duala exported female slaves inland to firm up commercial and political alliances (Zoller 1885:61).

Slave procurement by violence in the littoral during the nineteenth century appears to have occurred more as a by-product of conflicts over other matters than through wars or raids organized specifically to obtain captives. Trading in general, and palm oil commerce in particular, provided plenty of armed quarrels over debt payments, control of routes, etc., and the losers of these conflicts might be enslaved (Nicod 1931:163-66). During the nineteenth century quarreling Duala traders occasionally threatened one another with enslavement; but, apart from temporary seizures (usually resolved by, among other things, payments of slaves) such actions never reduced any wonja to servitude. Possibly during earlier periods, the losers in such encounters could be sent off, safely and profitably, overseas. In the nineteenth century various courts of cult societies, chiefs, or European and African traders might decide that a man had behaved dangerously but they could only seize his property or, in an extreme case such as that of Charley Dido, execute him.

The effect of various historical changes on the Cameroon market for slaves is illuminated, at least to a limited extent, by presently available data on price movements. In the 1790s, at the height of overseas demand, Douala slaves are reported as costing from fifty to ninety dollars, with adult males commanding the highest prices.[13] From the 1860s to the early 1890s, the nominal price for adult males had sunk to a range of twenty-five to fifty dollars, while females and children cost as much as double this amount (Heinersdorff 1880:96; Zoller 1885:61; Zimmerer 1892:517; see fn. 20, below).

This overall price decline must, however, be related to the sharp drop in European production costs (and prices) of the goods sent to Africa (iron, textiles, alcoholic products, etc.) in the course of the industrial revolution (LeVeen 1971:15, 139ff.). The actual quantity of goods exchanged for a slave around Douala had not changed very much in the same period. The relative shift in adult male versus female/child prices reflects the change from New World plantation demands to internal Duala use. Formerly, only adult males were considered fully productive and thus constituted two thirds of most transatlantic cargoes (Curtin 1971:89). For the nonintensive agriculture practiced in Douala, women were about as productive as men. Moreover, female slaves were valued as concubines and fetched high resale prices from slave owners seeking to provide wives for their own male retainers. Children, as already noted, could be incorporated into the masters' own households and thus deployed in a wider range of enterprises than male adult slaves.

SOCIAL TENSIONS AND SLAVERY IN NINETEENTH-CENTURY DUALA SOCIETY

The history of the Duala during the nineteenth century presents an almost uninterrupted succession of violent, if small-scale, conflicts between African and European traders, among rival Duala chiefs, and between Duala and hinterland groups. Contemporary European observers of this unhappy spectacle tended to explain it primarily in terms of tensions arising from changes in the institution of slavery. This view was consistent with the general scorn felt by imperial-minded Europeans for African coastal middlemen who stood in the way of both complete emancipation for their black brethren and full access to African wealth for Western enterprise. The most consistent proponent of this aggressive abolitionist interpretation of Duala society was Thomas Hutchinson, the British consul in the Bight of Biafra in the late 1850s, during which time he witnessed a major civil struggle between slaves and free Duala in the

13. P.R.O., Chancery Masters Exhibit C. 107.

Akwa chiefdom (P.R.O., Hutchinson 1858; Hutchinson 1861:4-6). In 1884, German traders maintained that the main reason the Duala chiefs had signed a protectorate treaty with the kaiser's representative was their inability to control the rising slave class within their domains (Stoecker 1960:88-89). More recently, a school of West African historians has argued that the shift from slave to "legitimate" exports in the overseas trade of the Nigeria-Cameroon coast created a new entrepreneurial class, a proto-"modernizing" elite, of emancipated and semiemancipated slaves who struggled everywhere against the old order of hereditary, slave-trading rulers (Dike 1956:153-59; Webster and Boahen 1967:193-208; cf. Austen 1970).

As already indicated, slavery as such had little to do with the tensions between Duala and European traders in the nineteenth century, although Britain's attacks on the Atlantic slave trade made gunboats and consuls available for intervention in these quarrels. Likewise, the conflicts between Duala and neighboring inland peoples owed relatively little to the actual enslavement of the latter by the former although Duala perceptions of themselves as wonja, versus the inland bakom, undoubtedly added to these antagonisms. An immediate social problem did, however, arise in the midst of Duala society, where individuals of slave status or slave origin came (according to vague but consistent European calculations) to constitute a majority of the population.

The revolt witnessed by Hutchinson in 1858 was attributed to extortions practiced upon slaves by two freeman cult societies, *Mikuka* and *Bongolo* (probably Akwa variants of Jengu). The slaves formed a new society of their own, based on an inland Abo cult. According to Hutchinson, the slave resistance effectively terrorized the Akwa freemen, but his own intervention, justified by threats to British property, led to the dissolution of all the participating cult societies.

Although no slave-freeman conflicts of similar magnitude occurred after 1858,[14] it is doubtful that Hutchinson's actions had the impact he imagined. Cult societies continued to flourish among the Duala and slaves were still excluded from them. Slave cults also survived and may account for the greater security of the servile population. As with the similar uprising in Old Calabar of the slave society called Bloodmen, the Duala "slave revolt" was a fairly brief movement whose leaders seemed satisfied with defending their immediate interests from attack (Latham 1973: 93-96).

There is thus little evidence that the slaves saw themselves as a class more in tune with changing socioeconomic realities than the prevailing

14. A brief and mild later slave uprising in Akwa is reported in the Baptist *Missionary Herald* (1871:10-11).

Duala elite. Indications of the contrary attitude can be seen in the
frustrations of the British Baptist Missionary Society, which had established itself in Douala and neighboring Bimbia and Victoria, beginning in
the 1840s. The Baptists made a very conscious effort to appeal to slaves,
even purchasing a number of them for manumission. Moreover, they
offered training in literacy and artisan skills, as well as a very immediate
kind of European protection, all benefits very much appreciated by the
more dynamic elements within Duala society. Nonetheless, the missionary
demand for a sharp break with indigenous beliefs and institutions
provoked considerable resistance even within the servile community. At
the time of German annexation, in 1884, the various Douala Baptist
churches could claim a membership of only 1 percent of the local population.[15]

A relationship does exist between internal slavery and the extreme
political disorder characterizing nineteenth-century (and possibly earlier)
Duala development. The links are far more complex, however, than
suggested in abolitionist-modernization theory. Some clue to this pattern
may be seen in the comparisons Robin Horton (1969) has drawn between
Kalabari and Efik sociopolitical development. In the Kalabari slave-trading, and later palm-oil-trading, state of Owame or New Calabar, the basic
unit of sociopolitical organization was the *wari,* or canoe house, which
included large numbers of fully assimilated slaves and recognized the
authority of a central monarchy. In contrast, the Efik of Old Calabar and
the Duala trading states were based upon lineage segments that excluded
slaves from full membership and challenged the very principle of a single
political center. The Kalabari may be seen in this comparison as simply at
a more advanced stage of a single development toward functional, and
away from ascribed-status, principles of social organization; Horton
argues however, that this transition was eased for them by the loose,
bilateral kinship structure and multilineal migration and settlement
traditions established during the period when they were merely coastal
fishermen. The Efik, and particularly the Duala, arrived and settled on
the coast as strictly defined patrilineal groups. The most important cult
organization of the Kalabari was the *Ekine,* which held little political
power but provided a means for cultural and thus social assimilation of
slaves. The Ekpe and Jengu societies of the Efik and Duala took the place
of central monarchies in providing some basis for political unity among

15. Information concerning slave proselytization and general membership in the Douala
Baptist churches is given in the *Missionary Herald* (1864:262, 777; 1869:9) and the Baptist
Missionary Society *Annual Report* (1871:75-78), both publications in the Society archives in
London; and in Gwei (1966:121-24).

independent patrilineages, but in doing so they emphasized the divisions between freeborn and slaves.

Slave uprisings did not threaten to overturn Efik or Duala society, but they did manifest the absence of an authority structure attuned to the needs of expanding international commerce. The major wars within Douala during the nineteenth century involved conflicts between the "kings," particularly Bell and Akwa. While this struggle made use of a wonja-mukom idiom, it actually involved slaves on both sides playing the role of political chattel, described earlier in this chapter. The appeals by the Duala kings for British and German protection resulted primarily from these wars and in 1884 were related specifically to the anxieties created by an emerging Bell ascendancy.[16] On the Nigerian coast, New Calabar (along with its similarly structured Ijaw neighbors, Brass and Bonny-Opobo) also experienced considerable political instability; but it is significant that they appeared able to resolve these problems autonomously, while the Efik of Old Calabar felt some necessity, like the Duala, to request European overrule.

SLAVERY IN THE EARLY COLONIAL PERIOD

Whatever the relationship between their arrival and Duala servile institutions, the German rulers of Cameroon not only hesitated to interfere with Duala slavery but for a time unwittingly encouraged its expansion. German policy up to 1902 was officially aimed at undermining slavery by indirect measures (Rudin 1938:389-96). During the first year of their rule (1884), the Germans abolished the Douala Court of Equity, through which British consuls and traders, in partnership with Duala chiefs, had occasionally been forced to sanction slave ownership. The new German administrative court at Douala had no African participation and theoretically granted the same status to all Cameroon "natives," slave or free. In reality, however, the officials of this court were willing to disturb local customs only when they directly affected European interests; they therefore rendered numerous judgments enforcing property in slaves.[17] It was only in 1895 that Theodor Seitz, then Douala Bezirksamtmann (district

16. For a summary of European accounts of the Douala situation at the time of annexation, see S. G. Ardener (1968:19ff.). The Duala oral tradition of these events, which clearly exaggerates the influence of local events upon European policy, has been reported by Doumbe-Moulongo (1972:11-13).

17. For the first four years of the official Douala District Court (1892-95) there are records (in A.N.F.A.) of twenty-one cases concerning the restoration of slaves including one (1895/15) in which the defendant was actually forced to sell a slave for which he had already been paid.

commissioner) and later governor of Cameroon, announced that the government court would no longer entertain appeals for the restoration of slaves.[18] But no such restriction was placed upon the purely African courts of first and second degree, officially established by the Germans from 1892 onward among the Duala and neighboring peoples. Moreover, an 1895 decree outlawing the internal Cameroon slave trade seems to have received little enforcement or even publicity for some years. As late as 1901 Manga Bell, the leading Duala chief, successfully persuaded the government to pardon two convicted slave traders because no natives really understood that such transactions were illegal.[19]

The Germans did not, in fact, believe that legislation could or should be used to effect radical changes in the Duala social order. Instead, they assumed, as Seitz states in his memoirs (1927, 1:64), that "the transformation of the entire native economy . . . must, by itself, bring about the disappearance of slavery."

In reality, the economic situation created by the German presence on the Cameroon coast appears to have stimulated an increased demand for slaves among the Duala. Contemporary missionary critics argued that such a development had taken place, and pointed to a rise in slave prices to support their argument. The limited data available on early colonial slave sales suggest that the demand for slaves may have gone down during the first decade of German rule but rose again at the turn of the century. In particular, the relationship between prices for adult males and for females or children had once again reversed itself. After 1900, for the first time since the abolition of the overseas trade, adult males appear as the most sought-after category of slaves.[20]

This shift in the internal Cameroon slave market coincides with the beginnings of Duala commercial cocoa farming. Ever since their arrival in Cameroon, the Germans had attempted to persuade the Duala to abandon middleman trading for a healthier, more productive, and—for European commercial interests—more agreeable concentration on export agriculture. During the 1890s, efforts by the Duala elite to comply with this policy were frustrated by the difficulty of persuading supposedly

18. A.N.F.A., Douala District Court transcripts, 1895/387. Missionary complaints about the support given a slave buyer earlier in the same year may have influenced this reform: see Bohner (1900:10).

19. A.N.F.A., Bezirksamt 1901, and Douala District Court transcripts, 1901/352 (also S1902/246).

20. For the period 1892-98. Bohner (1893 and 1900), Zimmerer (1892), and some twenty A.N.F.A. court cases give prices for males ranging from twelve to forty dollars and for women and children from fifty to seventy-five dollars; Missionary Lauffer (1901) gives prices at Edéa (ninety kilometers inland from Douala) as thirty to fifty dollars for males and about half this for women and children.

servile cultivators to take the risk of investing their labor in such a novel enterprise as planting cocoa (Seitz 1927, 1:60). Yet from about 1901 onward, the Duala planted a great number of cocoa trees, particularly on lands belonging to the Bell clan along the Mungo River.[21] It can thus be reasonably inferred that the Duala increased their purchases of slaves around 1900 precisely in order to supplement established agricultural laborers with workers more adaptable to the pressures and opportunities of a modernized economy.

The shift in slave exploitation to cash-crop cultivation probably added little abuse to the existing Duala system of servitude. Despite the delayed and somewhat insecure profits from planting cocoa, which apparently dissuaded the first generation of colonial Duala slaves, the work required in cultivating this crop is not particularly arduous. Moreover, had slaves been misused in any unprecedented manner, it is unlikely that such practices would have escaped the attention of the Germans, who later came into severe political conflict with the Duala, and with the Bells in particular.

THE DECLINE OF DUALA SLAVERY

The period during which the Duala flourished as pioneer indigenous cocoa planters proved to be an Indian summer, both for their control of slaves and their general preeminence in the development of Cameroon. The downfall of the Duala cannot be explained primarily in terms of slave institutions, although the fullest recognition by the Duala of their new situation has been expressed in a reversal of their traditional conceptions concerning slavery and ethnic identity.

When, on February 21, 1902, the German colonial authorities finally promulgated an ordinance for the gradual abolition of internal slavery in Cameroon, they presented themselves as virtual spokesmen for Duala institutions. The first two articles stated: (1) "The customary law established among the Duala people, whereby the children of domestic slaves (*mukom*) are regarded as half-free (*mujaberi* [sic]), is to be applied throughout the Protectorate"; (2) "Children born to half-free individuals (*mujaberi*) after the promulgation of this ordinance are free" (*Deutsches Kolonialblatt* 1902, 13:107-8).

As their earlier reports indicated, the Germans were quite aware that the offspring of Duala slaves did not become free in any socially meaning-

---

21. A.N.F.A., Mattner 1911, is a report on a survey of Duala cocoa farms giving age of trees as up to ten years. Wirz (1972:202-22) gives an excellent account of the general German "cash-crop" policy and its results. The movement of slaves to the Mungo in this period is still remembered by the elders of Ngombe, a former Bell slave village on the Wouri (interview in Ngombe, May 15, 1973).

ful sense even after several generations. But the only direct effect the Cameroon government could have upon servile institutions at this point was to hinder the further recruitment of slaves from the hinterland. Some documentary evidence indicates that after 1902 German administrators did in fact increase anti-slave-trade measures, at least in southern Cameroon. In any case, the increasing effectiveness of colonial rule in general must have made procurement of slaves far more difficult.[22] In the immediate post-World War I period, French administrative reports indicate that the only slaves still coming into Douala were young children "adopted" into urban households, where they performed domestic tasks.[23]

From the latter German years up to about 1930, Duala cocoa plantations continued to expand, but used mainly free labor.[24] This development would seem to have vindicated the German (and later French) conviction that slavery was incompatible with economic modernization. In the depression of the 1930s, however, Duala agricultural enterprise experienced a crisis from which it has never really recovered. The key reason for this collapse was precisely that the Duala, faced with falling cocoa prices, could not successfully maintain a paid working force of the size needed for commercial farming. Cocoa cultivation in the main Duala area, the Mungo sphere, as well as in the newer and more important Centre Sud Cameroun region, became concentrated on relatively small-scale farms run by families with only limited needs for outside labor.[25]

Had slavery been allowed to continue into the twentieth century, it is conceivable that Duala planters might have been better able to survive the vicissitudes of international price fluctuations, thus providing Cameroon agriculture with much-needed elements of large-scale indigenous entrepreneurship. Such a suggestion raises questions of economic analysis that cannot be satisfactorily pursued here; at the very least, however, it

22. From 1904 onward there is evidence in the A.N.F.A. court records of both severe punishments (up to five years imprisonment) for convicted slave traders and also many false accusations of slave trading, indicating that the act was now recognized and treated as a serious crime. Cases of sales on the coast were followed up by investigations of slave sources in the Grassfields (e.g., case S1909/760).

23. A.N.F.F., Douala-Edéa correspondence, March-April 1917, and Douala administration to Government, Yaoundé, December 25, 1922.

24. A list of Mungo plantations and their labor force compiled during October 1913 indicates that most of the workers came from traditional bakom groups (Bamileke are even cited as "Bakamkam") but specifically mentions only two workers as slaves (A.N.F.A., Frommhold 1913). Unfortunately, there is no information about the relationship between labor recruitment for European plantations and public enterprises and employment practices of Africans in the two articles on workers in Stoecker (1960:149-286).

25. See reports on Duala cocoa farming and Bamileke colonization in the 1930s administration touring reports from Mbanga (Mungo) district, A.N.F.F., A.P.A. 11634/F, 11796/A, 11797/C, 11798/K; also Tardits (1960:87-91).

challenges the contention that slavery, even in an African context, need necessarily be classified as an institution out of step with economic modernization.[26]

The eclipse of the Duala middleman role in Cameroon history was due not only to a loss of control over commerce and agricultural labor but also to a whole range of political, economic, demographic, and geographical factors, which cannot be elaborated here.[27] To some extent the Duala compensated for their decline in more established occupations by exploiting a head start in Western education so as to occupy a disproportionate place among white-collar professional posts open to Africans. But in their relations with both European colonialists and other Cameroon ethnic groups, the new Duala évolués have often been seen as not very different from their slave-trading and slave-owning ancestors. Thus, when Duala spokesmen took initiatives in pressing for the revision of their country's colonial status, German and particularly French administrators could dismiss them as a selfish, corrupt, and parasitic minority, trying once more to impose themselves upon the loyal, unspoiled, and hardworking majority groups of the interior, such as the Ewondo of Yaounde.[28] A certain degree of spontaneous hostility has also arisen between the Duala and such groups as the Ewondo and Bamileke, former "bakom" (even if the Ewondo were seldom enslaved), now risen to greater power than those who still consider themselves their superiors.

Contemporary Duala leaders are realistic enough not to entertain any hopes of restoring their traditional hegemony. In fact, with the advent of electoral politics after World War II and the resultant need to use ethnicity for mobilizing votes and influence, an attempt was made to define the Duala historical experience on an entirely new basis. For this purpose the Duala chiefs "revived" the *Ngondo,* a supreme political and judicial council that had allegedly flourished in the precolonial period.[29]

26. I hope to follow up this issue in a work now in progress on general African economic history. The view of plantation slavery as economically efficient owes much to my colleague Robert Fogel (Fogel and Engerman 1974) and his students.

27. The best account of Duala political relations with the Germans is that of Adolf Rüger in Stoecker (1968:181-257). For the later politics of the Duala see studies in preparation by Ralph A. Austen; Jonathan Derrick, School of Oriental and African Studies, University of London; and Richard Josephs, Nuffield College, Oxford.

28. See various Duala petitions to the Versailles Peace Conference and the League of Nations, 1919-30; a petition of the Ewondo chiefs and notables protesting against the Duala petitions, April 3, 1931; and a letter, Marchand to Colonial Ministry, 1930, in A.N.F.F., A.P.A. 10890.

29. On the position of the Duala and the Ngondo in modern Cameroon politics, see Johnson (1970:56-58, 154 and passim), Gardinier (1966), and Harter (1968:59-97). Additional information was gathered by the present author while attending the 1970 Ngondo festival. See also Doumbe-Moulongo (1972).

Whatever the Ngondo may or may not have been in the past, its twentieth-century version was designed for a new political situation and consequently embodied major changes in Duala self-perceptions, particularly those related to the mukom/wonja dichotomy. The constituency of the new Ngondo was not restricted to the nuclear chiefdoms of the Douala urban zone—this would be far too small a group to have any effect on Cameroon politics—but extended to all of the littoral peoples, including Duala-related groups, such as the Mungo, Abo, and Pongo, and the ethnically unrelated Basaa.

The central event of the present-day annual Ngondo festival is a ritual involving an exchange of gifts with the Jengu water spirits. Much of the detail of this rite as well as its general notion of propitiating a spirit responsible for local material welfare remains more or less consistent with Duala tradition. What appears to contradict the earlier function of the Jengu cult is its present celebration as a public event to promote unity among all the inhabitants of the coastal zone.

The irony of this development becomes most directly apparent at the high point of the ritual, when the boatmen going out to meet the Jengu are encouraged by mass cries of *"yai assu yai."* When questioned about the meaning of this incantation during the 1970 Ngondo festival, most participants offered the translation "Come *assu,* come" assuming that assu was some alternate name for Jengu. In fact, this word belongs not to normal Duala but to the secret language of the Jengu cult and means essentially the same thing as wonja, i.e., a freeman or aristocrat, as opposed to someone tainted by slavery. Its use at this point in the ritual is designed to tell the Jengu that it may appear because only those acceptable to it are present (an alternative explanation is that the cry was used by Jengu members to summon help during conflicts with slaves). Thus the new Ngondo makes use of a cult originally intended to maintain divisions between free and slave and even encourages the erstwhile bakom to announce themselves as freemen.

CONCLUSIONS

Despite its continuing popularity as a folk festival, the Ngondo did not succeed in restoring a decisive political position to the Duala within contemporary Cameroon. It would indeed be surprising if the Duala could have manipulated their traditional sense of ethnicity in such a sharply reversed manner.

The historical development of Duala society was, after all, intensely identified with concepts and institutions of slavery. Servitude among the Duala did not entail the inhumanity that modern European consciousness has associated with slavery. Duala bakom led, for the most part, lives not very different from those of their wonja masters. Nevertheless, those thousands of slaves sold by the Duala overseas, as well as the hundreds who lost their lives in sacrifices and warfare and the thousands again transferred involuntarily from one master to another, can only be considered to have been treated as chattel, expended in ways that no Duala freeman would tolerate for himself or his fellows.

The mistreatment suffered by Duala slaves can be seen as the price paid for the political and economic development that the Duala contributed to Cameroon history. Because of the intervention in this history by Europeans who were committed ideologically to the abolition of slavery and economically to the elimination of competition from African middlemen, Duala servile institutions were cut off just at the point where they might have been used to their maximum effect. It is beyond the scope of this chapter to judge whether the development patterns introduced into Cameroon under colonialism are preferable to the consequences of a more fully realized Duala system. All that has been attempted is to demonstrate that any serious evaluation of this system requires a careful and dispassionate comprehension of the role played by servitude.

GLOSSARY

etumbe (pl. *betumbe*): a slave purchased as a child and brought directly into the household of the owner.

Jengu (pl. *miengu*): water spirit; the object of a Duala cult society.

koto: literally, an enclosure; used to denote the separate slave sector of a Duala settlement (see *mudongo*).

mudongo: literally, a hill; used to denote the elevated riverside sector of Duala settlement inhabited by free population (see *koto*).

mukom (pl. *bakom*): a general Duala term for slave; more specifically, a slave purchased as an adult.

mukoma (pl. *mikoma*): a war captive.

muyabedi (pl. *miyabedi*): the offspring of a slave and a free parent, or of two slaves, but born in Douala.

wonja (pl. *wonja*): a free Duala, without slave ancestry.

REFERENCES

ORAL SOURCES
Interviews conducted in Bonaberi and the Wouri estuary, May 14-18, 1973.

UNPUBLISHED SOURCES

A.N.F.A.: Archives nationales Fonds allemands, Yaoundé.
Kaiserliche Bezirksamt Duala: Protokolle des summarischen Gerichtsbarkeit (court transcripts), 1892-1910.
Duala Bezirksamt to Governor, Buea, July 20, 1901. File 1501.
Gärtner Mattner, report on a survey of Douala cocoa farms, November 20, 1911. File 1385, pp. 6-8.
Gärtner Frommhold, report of October 23, 1913. File 1385, pp. 64-70.
A.N.F.F.: Archives nationales Fonds français, Yaoundé. Affaires politiques administratives (A.P.A.) series.
Douala-Edéa correspondence, March-April 1917. A.P.A. 12052/M.
Pétitions à la Société des Nations, 1919-31. A.P.A. 10890.
Douala administration to Government, Yaoundé, December 25, 1922. A.P.A. 11282.
Tournées Mbanga, 1931-38. A.P.A. 11634/F, 11796/A, 11797/C, 11798/K.
Austen, R. A. 1974a. Bride price and the changing status of women among the Duala of Cameroon. Paper presented at the Social History Workshop, Newberry Library, Chicago, January 26, 1974.
Bl.M.S.: Basel Missionary Society Archives, Basel.
Kamerun Copierbuch 1900, No. 45, Bruderkonferenz, November 3, 1900. Part 4. Sklaverei.
B.M.S.: Baptist Missionary Society Archives, London.
John Clarke, African Journal, entry of February 1, 1841. Box A2.
Joseph Jackson Fuller, Recollections. Box A5.
Dika-Akwa, B. G. 1969. Les fondements de l'évolution du pouvoir politique chez les Duala du Bas-Cameroun. Typescript mémoire, Diplôme des Etudes supérieures No. 168, Ecole pratique des hautes Etudes, Univ. de Paris.
Gwei, S. N. 1966. A history of the British Baptist Mission in Cameroon. B.D. dissertation, Baptist Theological Seminary, Rüschlikon-Zurich.
Hegba, M. 1968. Le concept de métamorphoses d'hommes en animaux chez les Basa, Douala, Ewondo Bantu du Sud-Cameroun. Dissertation (doctorat du 3e cycle), Univ. de Rennes.
Kouoh-Moukouri, M., and Weber, J. 1971. Le concept de mode de production et l'évolution africaine. Typescript mémoire, Diplôme des Etudes supérieures, Univ. de Paris X (Nanterre).
LeVeen, E. P. 1971. British slave trade suppression policies, 1821-1865: impact and implications. Ph.D. dissertation, Univ. of Chicago.
N.N.A.: Nigerian National Archives, Ibadan.
Calabar Provincial Files 4/1, Vols. 2-6. Correspondence between Portuguese Governor of Sao Tomé and Príncipe and King Bell, February 14, 1876 to March 26, 1877.
O.R.S.T.O.M.: Office de la Recherche scientifique et technique Outre-Mer, Yaoundé.
Zintgraff, v. Steinecker, v. Zimmerer, July 11-18, 1892. German file 51:VI, Vol. 2, Erforschung der Hinterländer durch Reisende: Expedition Zintgraff.

P.R.O.: Public Record Office, London.
  Chancery Masters Exhibit C. 107, unmarked bundle: inset of the Brig "Sarah," Captain John Goodrich, Rogers Papers. (This collection is available on film with accompanying catalog, William P. Perkins Library, Duke Univ.)
  T. J. Hutchinson to Foreign Office, May 26, 1858. F.O. 84/1061.
  William Quan, deposition of May 5, 1862. F.O. 84/1176.
Rosny, E. de. Undated. Papers. Abijan, Ivory Coast. (Some of the papers have been published in *Ndimsi* [Paris, 1975].)

PUBLISHED SOURCES

Ardener, E. 1956. *Coastal Bantu of the Cameroons*. London.
_____. 1968. Documentary and linguistic evidence for the rise of trading polities between Rio del Rey and Cameroons, 1500-1650. In *History and social anthropology*, ed. I. M. Lewis. London.
_____. 1972. Belief and the problem of women. In *The interpretation of ritual*, ed. J. S. La Fontaine. London.
Ardener, S. G. 1968. *Eye-Witnesses to the annexation of Cameroon, 1883-87*. Buea.
Arnold, J. 1789. Testimony of March 28, 1789, in Great Britain, *Parliamentary papers*, Vol. 26 (*Minutes of the evidence . . . to consider the slave trade*, Vol. 1), Reports of the Lords of the Committee of Council, 646A, pp. 50ff.
Austen, R. A. 1970. The abolition of the overseas slave trade: a distorted theme in West African history. *J. hist. Soc. Niger.* 5:257-74.
Austen, R. A., with Jacob, K. 1974b. Dutch trading voyages to Cameroon, 1721-1759: European documents and African history. *Annls Fac. Lettres Sci. hum. Univ. Yaoundé* 6:1-27.
Bekombo, M. 1963. Conflits d'autorité au sein de la société familiale chez les Dwala du Sud-Cameroun. *Cah. Etud. afr.* 14:317-29.
Bohner, H. 1893. Sklaverei und Sklavenhandel in Kamerun. *Evangelisches Mission-Magasin* 37:16-29.
_____. 1900. Die Sklaverei in Kamerun. *Afrika* 7:10.
Brutsch, J.-R. 1950. Les relations de parenté chez les Douala. *Etud. cameroun.* Nos. 31-32, pp. 211-30.
_____. 1955. Les traites camerounaises. *Etud. cameroun.* Nos. 47-48, pp. 1-34.
Bureau, R. 1962. Ethno-sociologie religieuse des Doualas et apparentés. *Rech. Etud. cameroun.* Nos. 7-8, pp. 1-172.
Chilver, E. M., and Kaberry, P. M. 1968. *Traditional Bamenda*. Buea.
Crouch, A. P. 1889. *Glimpses of feverland*. London.
Curtin, P. D. 1969. *The Atlantic slave trade: a census*. Madison.
_____. 1971. The slave trade and the Atlantic basin. In *Key issues in the Afro-American experience*, ed. N. Huggins et al. New York.
Dike, K. O. 1959. *Trade and politics in the Niger Delta, 1830-1855: an introduction to the economic and political history of Nigeria*. Oxford.
Dinckelacker, E. 1914. *Wörterbuch der Dualasprache*. Hamburg.
Doumbe-Moulongo, M. 1972. *Le Ngondo, assemblée traditionnelle du peuple Douala*. Yaoundé.

Ebding, F. 1959. *Duala Sprichwörter.* Anthropos-Institut Micro-Bibliotheca, No. 31. Posieux-Fribourg.

Fogel, R. W., and Engerman, S. L. 1974. *Time on the cross.* 2 vols. Boston.

Gardinier, D. E. 1966. *Political behavior in the community of Douala, Cameroon: reactions of the Duala people to the loss of hegemony, 1944-1955.* Athens, Ohio.

Harter, P. 1968. Le Ngondo. *Bull. Ass. fr. Rech. Etud. cameroun.* 3:59-97.

Hecklinger, P. 1921. Duala Sprichwörter. *Zeitschrift für Eingeborenen-Sprachen* 11:35-70, 125-60, 220-39, 306-15.

Helmlinger, P. 1972. *Dictionnaire Duala-français.* Paris.

Heinersdorff, C., ed. 1880. *Reinhold Bucholz' Reisen in West Afrika.* Leipzig.

Holman, J. 1840. *Travels in Madeira, Sierra Leone, Teneriffe, St. Jago, Cape Coast, Fernando Po, Princes Island, etc., etc.* 2d ed. London.

Horton, R. 1969. From fishing village to city-state: a social history of New Calabar. In *Man in Africa,* ed. M. Douglas and P. M. Kaberry. London.

Hutchinson, T. J. 1856. Report to Foreign Office, June 20, 1856. In Great Britain, *Parliamentary papers,* Vol. 16 (*Accounts and papers,* Vol. 9), Abstracts of Reports on . . . Trade, No. 2201, 1857 session I, p. 441.

――――. 1861. *Ten years wandering among the Ethiopians.* London.

Ittman, J. 1953. *Volkskundliche und religiöse Begriffe im nordlichen Waldland von Kamerun.* Supplement 26 to *Afrika und Übersee.* Berlin.

――――. 1957. Der kultische Geheimbund Jengu an der Kameruner Küste. *Anthropos* 52:135-76.

Jackson, R. M. 1934. *Journal of a voyage to the Bonny River . . . .* Ed. R. Jackson. Letchworth, Eng.

Johnson, W. R. 1970. *The Cameroon federation.* Princeton.

Latham, A. J. H. 1973. *Old Calabar, 1600-1891.* Oxford.

Lauffer [a missionary]. 1901. Sklaverei und Sklavenhandel in Kamerun. *Afrika* 8:132-36.

Makembe, P., with Meinhoff, C. 1921. Duala-Texte. *Zeitschrift für Eingeborenen-Sprachen* 11:161-81.

Mveng, E. 1963. *Histoire du Cameroun.* Paris.

Nicod, H. 1931. *Sur les sentiers de l'Afrique équatoriale.* Paris.

Reichenow, A. 1873. Über die Negervölker am Camerun. In *Verhandlungen der Berliner Gesellschaft für Anthropologie, Ethnologie, und Urgeschichte.* Berlin.

――――. 1884. *Die deutsche Kolonie Kamerun.* Berlin.

Richard, M. 1970. *Histoire, tradition et promotion de la femme chez les Batanga.* Bandundu, Zaïre.

Robertson, G. A. 1819. *Notes on Africa.* London.

Rodney, W. 1966. African slavery and other forms of social oppression on the upper Guinea coast in the context of the Atlantic slave trade. *J. Afr. Hist.* 7:431-43.

Ross, D. 1965. The career of Domingo Martinez in the Bight of Benin, 1833-64. *J. Afr. Hist.* 6:79-90.

———. 1969. The first Chacha of Whydah: Felix Francis De Souza. *Odu.* New ser. 2:19-28.

Rudin, H. R. 1938. *Germans in the Cameroons.* New Haven.

Ruel, M. 1969. *Leopards and leaders.* London.

Rüger, A. 1968. Die Duala und die Kolonialmacht, 1884-1914: eine Studie über die historischen Ursprünge des afrikanischen Antikolonialismus. In *Kamerun unter deutscher Kolonialherrschaft,* ed. H. Stoecker. Vol. 2. East Berlin.

Schwarz, B. 1888. *Kamerun.* Leipzig.

Seitz, T. 1927. *Vom Aufsteig und Niederbruch deutscher Kolonialmacht.* Vol. 1. Karlsruhe.

Stoecker, H., ed. 1960-68. *Kamerun unter deutscher Kolonialherrschaft.* 2 vols. East Berlin.

Tardits, C. 1960. *Les Bamiléké de l'Ouest-Cameroun.* Paris.

———. 1971. Les savanes du Nord: le peuplement du rebord occidental de l'Adamawa. In *Histoire générale de l'Afrique noire,* ed. H. Deschamps. Vol. 2. Paris.

Webster, J. B., and Adu Boahen, A. 1967. *The revolutionary years: West Africa since 1800.* London.

Wirz, A. 1972. *Vom Sklavenhandel zum Kolonialhandel: Wirtschaftsräume und Wirtschaftsformen in Kamerun vor 1914.* Zurich.

Wurm, P. 1904. *Die Religionen der Küsten-Stämme in Kamerun.* Basel.

Zimmerer, E. von. 1892. Report. *Deutsches Kolonialblatt* 3:513-21.

Zoller, H. 1885. *Forschungsereisen in der deutschen Colonie Kamerun.* Vol. 2. Berlin.

13

Servitude among the Wolof and Sereer of Senegambia

Martin A. Klein

The Senegambian area was the first in Black Africa to enter into relations with Portuguese navigators. It was thus the first to become involved in the Atlantic slave trade and was over the years the base of operations for many European enterprises. For the historian, one of the results of this extended contact is that we have written accounts in European languages of Senegambian societies and thus can easily trace into the relatively distant past a variety of social and economic institutions. This chapter seeks to trace the development of servile social relationships. I shall describe these institutions, trace changes in them, and relate the changes to the Atlantic slave trade, to the rise of reformed Islam, to the growth of the peanut trade in the nineteenth century, and to colonial domination.[1]

Unlike the upper Guinea coast described by Walter Rodney (1966 and 1970), Senegambia clearly knew both servile institutions and a long-distance trade in slaves when the Portuguese first made contact with the area.

1. I would like to thank Paul Lovejoy, Judith Irvine, Philip Curtin, Claude Meillassoux, and B. E. N'Jie for their comments on an earlier version of this chapter. Since this article was first written, I have done field research in the Kaymor area of southern Saalum. I am grateful to both the Canada Council and the Social Science Research Council for grants that made this research possible. The translations of quotations from French sources cited in the text are mine unless otherwise noted.

Cartographic Laboratory UW-Madison

Map 13. Precolonial Senegambia, Showing Wolof and Sereer Areas. Based on map in *Islam and Imperialism in Senegal: Sine-Saloum 1847-1914,* by Martin A. Klein (Stanford University Press, Stanford, 1968).

This may help explain the importance of the area in the early years of the transatlantic slave trade. Senegambian societies were used to selling slaves, and they had slaves to sell (Curtin 1969:100-102). This also means that the area participated in the export of slaves over an unusually long period, which makes it more difficult to evaluate the impact of the export trade. Before looking more closely at these questions, we must look briefly at the states involved and at the position of the *jaam,* or slave, in traditional Wolof and Sereer social structures.

The area is open savanna country that receives between 10 and 40 inches of rainfall in most years, the amount increasing farther south. Both groups cultivated millet, though Sereer agriculture was more intensive, they kept more cattle, and their population density was higher. The Wolof and Sereer were divided into six centralized monarchies, probably including from 50,000 to 75,000 people in each. Wolof society was nominally Muslim, but was deeply divided between an orthodox community and a political elite that was frequently lax in its religious observances. The Sereer resisted Islam more strongly than any other people north of the Gambia, though they resemble the Wolof in most ways and participated in a Wolof-dominated "international system" that dates back to an earlier period of political unity under the domination of the Wolof state of Jolof.

SOCIAL STRUCTURE

The Wolof and Sereer recognize four major status groupings (Diagne 1967:61-73, 106-22; Gamble 1957:44-46, 101-2; Labouret 1941:125-37). The first two are *gor*—high status, or "free." The first of these is the *garmi*, which encompasses the members of those lineages who are eligible to provide the rulers. In the two Sereer kingdoms, Siin and Saalum, the *Buur* (ruler) was elected from the *gelwar* matrilineage. In Jolof, eligibility was determined by patrilineal descent from the founder, and in the other three Wolof states (Waalo, Bawol, and Kajoor) by a combination of these principles. There were a number of gradations of status within this group, which need not concern us here. Two things must be understood however. First, the garmi members were highly mobile. Royal power was nominally the result of election, but in fact was usually contested on the field of battle. Losers could and regularly did move to neighboring states, where they were integrated at their social level. In fact, for all status groups except slaves, it was easier to move between ethnic groups than between status groups. Second, and most important, it is these royal lineages that provided the rulers and controlled a large part of the servile population.

The second status group included the *jaambuur*. This term is usually translated as "freemen." In most areas they were the largest single social group and in many, the oldest inhabitants. Local members of the other three status groupings were often descended from immigrants, though immigrants who had been totally assimilated over the course of centuries. The jaambuur played an important role in the political system: a jaambuur chief or a council of jaambuur chiefs generally selected the ruler from among eligible garmi candidates, and an assembly of jaambuur confirmed the new ruler in power. In recent centuries this simply legitimated the rule of the strongest.

The third status group, the *nyenyo*, consisted of artisan and *griot* castes. The artisans were blacksmiths and jewelers, leatherworkers and woodworkers, while the griots were musicians, praise-sayers, and historians. Marriage with non-nyenyo members was not permitted and inter-caste marriage seems to have taken place only between blacksmiths and leatherworkers. While many of the nyenyo were in client relationships to the more powerful chiefs, they cannot strictly speaking be considered servile. They often migrated in search of better opportunities, taking with them their skills and, probably, the institution of caste (Diagne 1967:54). The type of work done by nyenyo was never done by non-nyenyo. The griots were distinctive within this group because they produced nothing. Because of their position at court, they played a crucial role in society, but were at the same time the most strictly circumscribed of the castes. Until recently they were not buried in the ground, but in the hollows of baobab trees (Rousseau 1929:175-81; Silla 1966; Boilat 1853:299-312; Gamble 1957:39).

The jaam, or slaves, composed the fourth group. In listing them last, I am not necessarily putting them at the bottom of the ladder. Western writers tend to see social categories in hierarchical or prestige terms. In fact, a jaam was often better off economically than a jaambuur. A more meaningful way of looking at social stratification would be to contrast those who participated in the exercise of power and those who did not. Those who participated consisted of the nobility, their jaam, and artisans and griots in client relationships to the nobility.[2] According to Yoro Dyao, a nineteenth-century Wolof noble, most slaves actually lived either in chiefly compounds or in villages near one of the capitals (Rousseau 1929: 189-96; Carrère and Holle 1855:53-58). Politically, the most important jaam were the *tyeddo*, slave warriors who did most of the fighting and administering. The jaambuur ranked high on a prestige scale, but the vast majority did not participate in power or its rewards. In fact, the tyeddo increasingly dominated the rulers they served, and the confirmation in office by jaambuur chiefs simply made official what had already been decided by military force.

Few reliable data exist on the number of jaam in the total population or the percentage of jaam who were tyeddo. An early (1892) census from the cercle of Sine-Saloum put the tyeddo at about 30 percent, but it used the term tyeddo for the politico-military elite and thus included garmi and probably griots (Noirot 1892).[3] A 1904 estimate put slaves at one third of the population of Sine-Saloum, with the percentage somewhat higher in Muslim areas (A.N.S., reports of January 26 and May 30, 1904). It is not

2. Judith Irvine's informants listed jaam as nyenyo; they also made no categorical distinction between garmi and jaambuur. These were, however, important historical distinctions (Irvine, pers. comm.; Rousseau 1929:189-96; Carrère and Holle 1855:53-58). My informants made the distinctions.

3. The precise figures were 15,211 tyeddo out of 52,233, with another 559 mysteriously listed as "captifs du Roi." More than half of the villages, including the capital, were listed as tyeddo villages. The jaambuur tended to cluster in much larger villages, probably for security reasons.

clear whether this included tyeddo, for by 1904 the term tyeddo had virtually disappeared from the archives. By way of comparison, two estimates of neighboring Mandinka areas suggest a servile majority. At the beginning of the nineteenth-century, Durand wrote that three fourths of the Mandinka were slaves (Durand 1802:41). This was probably an exaggeration, but in 1894 the first British travelling commis ioner on the North Bank of the Gambia suggested that slaves outnumbered freemen two to one (P.R.O., Ozanne, June 28, 1894). Father Renault cites a figure for the whole of Senegal of 174,245 (Renault 1971). Renault's figure is based on early-twentieth-century estimates. Majhemout Diop thinks that the real figure was higher (Diop 1972). So do I. The precision of this figure can be discounted; censuses were unreliable and these were estimates. Renault's figure would suggest that 15 to 20 percent of the total population was servile. There are several problems with ...ese statistics beyond the unreliability of the data. First, people had good reason not to publicly declare their slaves. Second, the 1890s had seen large-scale flight and redemption. Third, we are never sure exactly what is meant by "slave" at any given time. Turn-of-the-century administrators did not collect data with great precision. They could count, but not define. The data do, however, give us some conception of the range of possibilities.

POLITICAL HISTORY

The Wolof were once united in a loose empire under Jolof, which seems to have been founded in the twelfth or thirteenth century. The Sereer represent a more ambiguous situation. The term Sereer has been used to refer to a number of different peoples. The first, the Sereer-None and Sereer-N'Duut, are very small groups that speak languages unrelated to others called Sereer (Pichl 1966). These people, who have never been studied intensively, will not concern us here. The rest of the Sereer trace their origins to a migration from the north, probably in the same period that saw the creation of the Jolof empire. The bulk of them belonged to two states, Siin and Saalum. Though they were ruled by a matrilineage of Malinke origin, the political history of these states closely associated them to that of the Wolof.

Those Sereer-speakers who did not come under state systems—the Nyominka, the Sereer-N'Dyegem and the Sereer-Safen—preserved rel atively egalitarian and undifferentiated social systems (Lafont 1938). Politically uncentralized, they lacked slaves and did not have castes. Furthermore, even within the Sereer states, there were areas where slavery and castes were either unknown or were late developments. This was especially true of the *tanngann,* the fishing people of coastal villages, but even in the area where Siin, the first Sereer state, was founded, slavery and castes were a late development. Siin traditions trace the kingdom's origins to the village of Mbissel, near the coast. The capital moved north and east in the fifteenth and sixteenth centuries and has long been at Diakhao, which is near the frontier with Bawol, a rival Wolof state. The area around Diakhao had a high percentage of slaves and artisans. Conversely, near Mbissel, it is possible to trace the arrival of various castes to the last two or three generations, that is to say, to the late nineteenth and twentieth centuries. The area seems to have been almost solidly jaambuur (Basse, pers. comm.). The factories established on the coast to supply European slavers were in relatively autonomous trading communities, each of which depended on a distributive system centered on one of the states. Slaves were numerous in these trading communities, but frequently nearby villages had few. For example, there were slaves in Joal, Siin's trade outlet, but on the island fishing village of Fadioute, facing it, there were few. Corre wrote in 1883: "Slavery exists among the Sereer. However, the inhabitants of Fadiouth have only had slaves for very few years and in imitation of what they have seen among the Wolof" (Corre 1883:20).

This suggests that slavery and a more hierarchical social order were extended to the Sereer as a result of their participation in a Wolof political system. The gelwar matrilineage of Mandinka origin, which ruled the two Sereer states, does not seem to have brought in caste organization or slavery. Oral traditions reinforce this impression. Thus, the expansion of the second Sereer kingdom, Saalum, is associated with its third Buur, Latmingé Jélen N'Diaye. Latmingé was of Jolof origins and his kinship link to the gelwar may have been a fiction necessary to legitimate colonization of an area with important salt resources, on the frontier between Wolof and Mandinka domination. Latmingé settled his slaves in the village that now bears his name; the chief of the village is still called *farba,* generally a slave title (interview at Latmingé 1964).

When the first Portuguese explorers visited Senegambia, slavery and the slave trade were well developed. Thus, Cadamosto wrote that the Wolof king, the Buurba Jolof,

has no fixed income save that each year the lords of the country, in order to stand well with him, present him with horses, which are much esteemed owing to their scarcity, forage, beasts such as cows and goats, vegetables, millet and the like. The King supports himself by raids which result in many slaves from his own as well as neighboring countries. He employs these slaves in cultivating the land allotted to him: but he also sells many to the Azanaghi merchants in return for horses and other goods, and also to the Christians, since they have begun to trade with these blacks (Cadamosto 1937:30).

Thus, slaves were already being exported from Senegambia over the Sahara. Jean Boulègue has estimated this trade at about 500 to 1,000 a year. The king's wealth depended on both the slave trade and slave labor

(Boulègue 1968). This trade was important to Jolof because it provided horses, which were eagerly sought throughout the western Sudan. One horse was worth anywhere from six to fifteen slaves (Mauny 1961:285-86).

Equally important in Cadamosto's description are agricultural laborers on royal estates. It may have been from this population that the tyeddo were first recruited. In later centuries, there was no distinction among the royal slaves between those who cultivated and those who fought. With the exception of the chiefs, all farmed and all fought, but war became their major function. We cannot even say at this time whether the tyeddo existed as a distinct status group. Kings had suites of 150 to 200 men, but there is no indication whether these were slaves, retainers, or clients, nor is there any indication of the relation between the ruler and his soldiers. Fernandes also speaks of servile agricultural labor and tells us that slaves owed their masters six days a week, a rather high obligation unless he also fed them (Fernandes 1951:11).

SLAVERY AND THE ATLANTIC SLAVE TRADE

During the sixteenth century, Senegambia was one of the two or three most important sources of the Atlantic slave trade (Curtin 1969:100-101). It declined in relative importance after that, largely because of the availability of better populated areas farther down the coast and the limitations of a lightly settled hinterland. From 1720 on, there was actually a decline in the number of slaves exported (Curtin 1975:164). Nevertheless, the slave trade was a constant, and the Senegambian bases—James Island, Gorée, and St. Louis—provided slaves until the early nineteenth century. No area in Africa was more exposed to the trade over a longer period of time.

The most important question that must be asked about the slave trade is its effect on the participating societies, and in particular, on the development in them of servile institutions. Fifteenth-century Portuguese accounts do not give us many data about social structure, but what they do provide does not sound very different from more recent descriptions. This contrasts with the upper Guinea coast, where Walter Rodney has been able to argue, from the absence of any mention of slavery in early Portuguese accounts, that "social oppression" was clearly related to participation in the transatlantic slave trade (Rodney 1966). The only comparable phenomenon in Senegambia was the extension of servitude among the Sereer. Nevertheless, I believe that we can make further remarks about the effects of participation on the Wolof and Sereer.

First, the state controlled the trade and profited from it. The rulers made war, took prisoners, sentenced wrongdoers to enslavement, or sent warriors to attack dissident villages. Similarly, the same rulers and those who served them received most of the benefits of the trade.

Second, the slave trade probably limited the development of other forms of trade and productive activity both because it involved the export of labor and because it created conditions of insecurity not conducive to economic development (Klein 1972; Barry 1972:109-10). This, however, is difficult to measure. Local trade remained important and the export of gum and hides developed parallel to the trade in slaves (Curtin 1975; Boulègue 1972).

Third, the slave trade contributed to the differentiation of an elite of warriors and nobles from the mass of peasants and led to the emergence of the tyeddo to the point where they controlled crucial political decisions. Boubacar Barry (1972:102-3) links the development of tyeddo power to the tension between the ruler of Waalo and the more powerful hereditary chiefs. Thus, the creation of slave titles and the expansion of a corps of slave warriors increased the royal power. Barry attributes the expansion of tyeddo power to the period after the *tubenan* rising, a Muslim revolt led by a Mauritanian cleric, which was hostile to the slave trade and briefly dominated northern Senegal from 1673 to 1677. The tubenans were defeated by an alliance of the traditional elites, the French and the ruler of Saalum (Barry 1972:135-59; Curtin 1971).

Lucie Colvin (1971:48-54) describes a similar political revolution associated with the *Damel* (the ruler of Kajoor) Lat Sukaabe, the first strong ruler to come to power after the defeat of the toubenans. Lat Sukaabe organized a corps of tyeddo armed with guns purchased from the Europeans. He also created a series of titles to be held only by tyeddo. Slave officials held many court posts. They were the *alkalis,* who collected taxes and represented the damels in those places where trade was conducted with Europeans, and they held key territorial commands in the marginal areas in the northern and southern parts of the kingdom. These slave warriors were expected to loyally serve the royal power. Being essentially kinless, they were presumed to be dependent on those they served, but they developed into an independent corporate group with its own sense of identity and the power to make and unmake rulers. It is likely, therefore, that whatever its origins, the expansion of tyeddo power was a phenomenon of the late seventeenth and the eighteenth centuries.

Lat Sukaabe also created a number of marabout positions, probably in an effort to co-opt a potentially dangerous alternative elite. The new titles involved court offices or territorial commands in the Muslim areas of the northern or southern parts of the kingdom. Ironically, in trying to limit the power of hereditary chiefs, Lat Sukaabe built up the two groups who were to contest for power in the late nineteenth century. The Muslim community gathered around marabout chiefs was more puritanical than the tyeddo and participated much less in the benefits of the slave trade though they later exploited slave labor more systematically. Although not opposed to slavery. Muslim reform leaders were often strongly opposed to the sale of slaves to Europeans. They also opposed the enslavement of Muslims and sought the liberation of anyone who could read the Quran (Barry 1972:142-47, 215-18; Roger 1828, 1:209-10). As the jaambuur were increasingly the victims of tyeddo military activity, they became more and more responsive to the alternative leadership of the marabouts.

TYPES OF SERVILE STATUS

We can say more about jaam during the period of the mature slave trade (late seventeenth century on), largely because our sources are fuller and more detailed. During this period we can speak of three kinds of slaves. First, there were the trade slaves (*jaam sayor* in Wolof, *pad o kob* in Sereer). These were people who had been acquired through war, kidnapping, or purchase. The largest number clearly were taken in war or in raids. In 1738, Francis Moore described the practice in Saalum:

Whenever the King of Barsally wants Goods or Brandy, he sends a messenger to our Governor, at James Fort, to desire he would send a sloop there with a Cargo. . . . Against the arrival of the said Sloop, the King goes and ransacks some of his enemies Towns, seizing the people and selling them for such Commodities as he is in want of, which commonly is Brandy or Rum, Gunpowder, Ball, Guns, Pistols, and Cutlasses, for his Attendants and Soldiers; and Coral and Silver for his Wives and Concubines. In case he is not at war with any neighbouring King, he then falls upon one of his towns, which are numerous, and uses them in the very same manner (Moore 1738:65-66).

It is probable that in most cases tyeddo raided either other kingdoms or chiefs that had been refractory or hostile to the established power (Colvin 1971:41-43).

Three other sources of jaam were famine, kidnapping, and judicial penalties. The sale of children seems to have been an act of desperation during famines and after wars (Ritchie 1968:352). Kidnapping was a more recurrent phenomenon (Curtin 1967:17-59). On the use of the courts, Moore wrote: "Since this Slave Trade has been us'd, all Punishments are changed into Slavery; there being an advantage on such condemnations, they strain for Crimes very hard, in order to get the Benefit of selling the Criminal. Not only Murder, Theft and Adultery, are punished by selling the Criminal for Slave, but every trifling crime is punished in the same manner" (Moore 1738:42). Sorcery also seems to have led to enslavement and deportation (Boilat 1853:315).

The trade slave had no value in the area where he was enslaved (Curtin 1975:155). He also had no social identity until he was integrated into a new social unit. The second group, domestic slaves (*pad bin* in Sereer, *jaam juddu* in Wolof) were those who had been integrated into new social units. Integration was a slow process. For women and boys it could happen during their lifetime. Marriage and the production of offspring tended to tie jaam into new social networks, but the only fully integrated jaam were probably those born in the society (Klein 1975). They could be neither killed nor sold and were essentially members of the family. Their treatment probably reflected their length of time in the community and the personality of both slave and master. An early missionary wrote of them that "their relations with their masters appear very close, they eat almost always from the same calabash and sit on the same mat" (A.C.S.E., Gallais 1849). Domestic slaves were generally not sold except in extreme circumstance, such as famine. Moore, who was in the slaving business, wrote:

And tho' in some Parts of Africa they sell their Slaves born in the Family, yet in the River Gambia they think it a very wicked thing; and I never heard of but one that ever sold a Family-Slave, except for such Crimes as would have made them to be sold had they been free. If there are many Family Slaves and one of them commits a Crime, the Master cannot sell him without the joint Consent of the rest; for if he does, they will all run away, and be protected by the next kingdom, to which they fly (Moore 1738:33; see also Mollien 1820:89-90. Bérenger-Féraud 1879:236).

Third, there were the tyeddo. Theoretically slaves, they suffered none of the disabilities usually associated with servile status. They did the bulk of the fighting, collected taxes, and handled any minor administrative tasks. It was through the tyeddo that royal power expressed itself; as a result, they received much of the revenue of the slave trade and did not pay taxes. This in turn led to their developing certain distinctive characteristics. They drank heavily, wore bright clothes and long hair, and were arrogant (Carrère and Holle 1855:55-63). Though they supplemented their military activities with farming, they were contemptuous of the more industrious Muslims. The conflict between the tyeddo and the puritanical Muslims was very much a conflict between opposing life-styles and value systems (Klein 1969). Only the griots rivaled the tyeddo in their opposition to Islam. One of the effects of tyeddo power was to limit the Islamization of the garmi, whose autonomy and decision-making power was increasingly restricted by the tyeddo. The number of Muslim rulers seems to have declined rather than increased with time.

Many of the tyeddo were directly attached to a royal office. Larger numbers seem to have been attached to various garmi matrilineages. This relationship between the tyeddo and the matrilineages deserves special attention. Every Wolof knows his matrilineage, but it is less important for him than his patrilineage, for inheritance is predominately patrilineal. The exception is the garmi. In three of the four Wolof states, membership in one of the garmi matrilineages was a factor in determining eligibility for royal office. Among the matrilineal Sereer it was the only factor. It is here that the tyeddo became important. A captive could be assigned to either an individual or a matrilineage. Those assigned to individuals became part of the patrilineal inheritance, divided and redivided over time. By contrast, slaves assigned to matrilineages tended to remain as a group. Competition for office kept the competing matrilineal groupings united and encouraged an accumulation by them of large bodies of tyeddo (Rousseau 1929:189-94).[4] Thus, the *geej*, the most powerful matrilineage in Kajoor, had sixteen jaam villages (Monteil 1967:267-68). The cohesion and size of the geej may have been unusual and quite possibly can be attributed to the decision by Lat Sukaabe to attach slaves to the geej matrilineage rather than to the royal office (Colvin, pers. comm.). In Saalum, there was a different situation. The royal office passed within the gelwar matrilineage, but many of the larger provinces were formed by migrations from patrilineal Jolof. In these provinces tyeddo belonged to the ruling patrilineage. Thus, in Kaymor, the *jaam i Kaymor*, the tyeddo of the provincial chief, were part of the Ndiaye patrilineage. There was also a body of *jaam i Kahone* attached to the royal title in Saalum. Thus, depending on the way authority was contested, tyeddo could belong to an office, a matrilineage, or a patrilineage. Jaam attached to the royal office and those belonging to the lineage in power were exempt from taxation. The garmi entourages also included free clients known as *surga*, who accepted a status that seems to have been almost identical to that of the jaam (Diagne 1967:67-71).

The distinction between patrilineal and matrilineal inheritance also existed among the jaam of the jaambuur and the nyenyo. It is not clear from my sources which mode was predominant or why matrilineal inheritance of jaam was important in a society where inheritance was predominantly patrilineal. L. Bernhard Venema, whose research around Kaymor was more extensive than my own, suggests that newly acquired slaves were passed from father to son, but that subsequent generations passed in the matrilineal line. One of my informants suggested that slaves originating in capture passed from father to son, but those acquired through purchase by a woman or given as a gift, for example as bride-wealth, passed in the matrilineal line.

RIGHTS AND OBLIGATIONS

Most sources suggest that the jaam juddu owed his master five days of labor a week, a working day being considered to run from sunrise to about

4. Jaam that passed in the patrilineal line were *jaam i baye*. Those that passed in the matrilineal line were called *jaam i ndèye*.

2:00. This was the same as the obligation of the unmarried male to the head of the compound. Most of my informants, however, of both jaam and jaambuur origin, stressed the differences in obligations. Most important, the slaves were the weavers. Weaving apparently took up much of their time during the dry season. Kaymor, the area where I worked, lay between the Saalum saltworks and the Gambia. It was also in an area well suited to the cultivation of cotton. The cloth woven by slaves was traded for more slaves, for kola, and for other imports. The women spun the cotton and the men wove. During the rainy season, the work of the jaam was not different in kind from that done by the free, but they clearly did more of it.

Some well-born families had many slaves. Francis Moore cites one lineage that counted two hundred members, including wives, children, and slaves (Moore 1738:43). Moore also suggests that within such a unit it was difficult to tell the difference between the two social statuses: "Some people have a good many House-Slaves, which is their greatest Glory, and they live so well and easy, that it is sometimes a very hard Matter to know the Slaves from their Masters and Mistresses; they very often being better clothed, especially the females, who have sometimes Coral, Amber, and Silver about their Hands and Wrists, to the Value of Twenty or Thirty Pounds Sterling" (Moore 1738:110).

The head of the lineage was expected to feed, clothe, and find spouses for his jaam. Essentially, his obligations were the same as they were to his other dependents, though we can only guess how a family head balanced them between his jaam and his own offspring. Like other dependents, the male jaam generally had his own piece of land, and as he grew older, he devoted more of his time to his own plot. According to Ames, a slave was permitted to devote himself fully to his own land only after marrying his second wife (Ames 1953:15). Other sources would suggest otherwise (Rousseau 1929:189-94). Autonomy probably came soon after marriage and certainly after the birth of children. Male slaves could take a second or even a third wife and many did. The only difference is that the master paid the bridewealth for the first wife and the slave for all subsequent wives. If the wife belonged to another master, all children belonged to her master.

The married jaam still had economic and ceremonial obligations. According to Yoro Dyao (Rousseau 1929:189-94), he owed his master twenty measures of millet (thirty-five kilograms) a year. This was called *yène*, literally "burden of the head." This is suspiciously low. In other savanna societies, the slave's obligations usually ran between 250 and 300 kilograms a year, or approximately the amount of grain needed to feed an adult for a year. A jaam could accumulate wealth, and if he had a trusted position within the household he probably lived much like a jaambuur, but he owed deference to the freeborn. Carrère and Holle tell us that he "always owes profound respect to men of free origin. Even if they are rich, which is not rare, they must salute any jaambuur who passes. If the jaambuur insults or mistreats them, they can neither answer nor respond. A man with a slave ancestor can never sit on a chair in the presence of jaambuur; he sits on the ground. No marriage is possible between a former slave or his descendants and the daughter of a jaambuur" (Carrère and Holle 1855:54). Marriages between jaam and non-jaam were probably rare. A female jaam could become a *tara,* or concubine, or she might be freed and taken as a regular wife. A tara who bore a child for her master was automatically free, as was her child, who inherited his or her father's status.

Liberation of the tara seems to have been the most significant form of manumission, though a slave could purchase his freedom. The price was arranged with his master and was often about the price of two new slaves, which probably gives some indication of the difference in value between a newly purchased slave and one integrated into the household. It is probable that only the slave born in the society ever had the possibility of accumulating enough wealth to purchase his freedom, not to mention that of his wife and children. It is also probable that such a freed slave would remain in the village of his former master and maintain a client relationship. If born in the community he had no other home. His own manumission would only give him freedom from dues hitherto paid his master. In order to get control over his children, he would have to purchase his wife's freedom, and probably that of any children already born.

For the jaam who was mistreated or discontented, there were only two options. The first was flight. This was dangerous because the fugitive ran the risk of being reenslaved. Nevertheless, from the French abolition of slavery in 1848 to the conquest by the French, one of the most important sources of correspondence from African rulers was the fear that their slaves would flee to, and be welcomed by, the French. Flight did take place often enough to suggest that this fear was justified. The French actually closed St. Louis and began expelling "vagrants" to prevent the city from becoming a refuge for slaves of friendly chiefs (Renault 1971).

The slave's second option was to cause an injury for which he would himself be the compensation. Thus, he could cut the ear of a man whom he wished to be his master—or better yet, the ear of the man's horse—or he could destroy certain posts laden with amulets in the courtyard of a chief (Rousseau 1929:195-96; Mollien 1820:138-39). In the novel *Keledor,* Baron Roger gives an interesting case of a slave who "wronged" the

Almamy (ruler) of Fuuta Tooro by interrupting a ceremony, claiming the right to become the Almamy's slave and to serve in his invasion of Kajoor (Roger 1828, 1:80-81). He was granted his request.

In spite of the evidence that jaam sought to escape their status, the evidence of mistreatment of jaam juddu is limited. Most of the cases for which there is evidence in the archives involve people from St. Louis and Bathurst, who were forbidden by law to hold slaves. Despite this, many urban dwellers had slave retainers even in the city. Up to 1903 it was common practice in St. Louis to buy children upriver. These children were then officially freed, but the "liberator" became the child's guardian. Other slaves who were recently acquired or received in payment of debts were kept outside the city and thus outside the surveillance of European authorities. The cases of mistreatment involve these people. The city dwellers lived somewhat outside traditional society and were less responsive to its controls.[5]

It is not clear how much influence Islamic law had on slave status. At an early stage, it may have eliminated the institution of human sacrifice, which was reported by a sixteenth-century Portuguese navigator but is mentioned in no later account (Alvares de Almada 1594/1964, 3:266). Islamic law provides for manumission either as a pious act or as a result of mistreatment. At present, however, I do not have any evidence that either was common. This may have been because Muslim villages depended heavily on slave labor as a result of their greater development in trade and in production for market. Their use of slave labor may also have been a factor in their growth. Kaymor village, the residence of the provincial chiefs, had neither slave settlements nor satellite villages. In contrast, with the major Muslim lineages, there was a constant process of spinning off of new villages, which suggests population increase. This in turn probably resulted as much from the assimilation of jaam, especially female jaam, as from new conversions. It is also clear from both jaam and jaambuur informants that the jaam was seen in these Muslim communities primarily as a source of labor.

The difference between the male and female jaam was significant. Females heavily outnumbered males. A significant percentage of them were absorbed into the jaambuur population as wives and concubines. Thus, they could aspire to a status not unlike that of free women. The male slave was marked by what Meillassoux has termed the absence of paternity (Meillassoux 1975:224; see also Riesman 1974:88). This is

5. For several cases that involve beatings and inadquate feeding, see P.R.O., C.O. 87/144, esp. Regina v. James Edwin. Edwin was a Bathurst trader. For similar cases from St. Louis, see A.N.F.-O.M., Senegal XIV 15, esp. the case of N'diack N'diaye, a resident of St. Louis, who owned at least fifteen slaves.

evident in several ways. When first assimilated in the new community, he received a new name and, by implication, a new identity. His children were not his own, but belonged to his wife's master. According to a Wolof proverb, the eggs belong to the hen's master. Finally, on his death, any wealth he had accumulated reverted to his master. If his children received anything, it was due only to the generosity of the master—who in theory owned all of the jaam's property—and this probably happened only when husband and wife were owned by the same master.

In other ways, the jaam participated in the life of the community. With the exception of weaving, he did the same kind of work, though probably more of it. He spoke the same language, took part in family activities, had a special role in many ceremonies, and usually lived within the compound for all or much of his life. He did not always receive a Quranic education, though young jaam were often taught to read the Quran. Even today, most Muslim offices (imam and teacher) are held by jaambuur, and in the Kaymor area the jaambuur tend to be stricter practitioners (Ames 1955:16-18).

THE END OF THE TRANSATLANTIC SLAVE TRADE

The end of the Atlantic slave trade in the early nineteenth century did not radically alter the nature of servile status in Senegambian societies, but it changed the context within which it existed. The abolition of the trade by the British in 1807 and by the French in 1817 was not immediately effective, but by the early 1830s the control of St. Louis, Gorée and Bathurst by anti-slave-trade powers seems to have effectively ended the export of human cargoes. The slave trade continued but was forced to orient itself to local markets. This in turn weakened a politico-military system dependent on the slave trade. The ability of various rulers to control their own military elite declined with the reduction in their revenues, and unruly tyeddo increasingly preyed on traders and on the more industrious peasants, who generally happened to be Muslims. This, of course, increased tension between the tyeddo and the puritanical Muslims.

During the first years after abolition, the energies of the traders went into the Sénégal River gum trade and a petty coastal commerce in items such as hides and wax. Then, from 1841, the export of peanuts regularly and rapidly increased to the point where it soon surpassed in value the income earlier received from the export of slaves. The peanut trade was different from the slave trade. Slaves came mostly from war, raiding, and trade. It was by definition an elite trade, controlled by the state's military elite, who received in exchange weapons and consumption goods such as cloth and alcohol. Peanuts were and still are a peasant crop. While the state received some revenue from peanuts, much of the income went to the peasants, many of them frugal Muslims, who squandered little on drink and in turn bought guns, horses, and slaves, investments that radically changed the balance of power within Senegambian societies and led to a series of Muslim revolts, beginning with that led by Ma Ba Jaxoo in the kingdom of Badibu in 1861.

The wealthy and powerful supplemented the labor of their families with both slaves and free migrant laborers. The earliest mention of migrant laborers is in the annual report of the Gambia for 1848, fifteen years after the first purchase of peanuts:

The Sera Woolies and Tilli-bunkas often visited the countries near the Gambia, frequently coming not less than 500 or 600 miles in the interior, and on paying a small custom to the chief of the country in which they settle, are permitted to cultivate the ground under his protection for one or more years, according to their agreement, to sell the produce to the European merchant or trader. The greater portion of the groundnuts exported, is raised in this manner by parties who have no permanent connection with the soil they cultivate (Gambia 1848).

The Sera Woolies are Soninke or Sarakollé. Tilli-bunka means "people from the east." The 1851 report again remarked on the phenomenon, commenting that the migrants generally came in parties twenty to one hundred strong and stayed for two or three years.

French archives have much less information. The earliest mention I have seen is from 1884 and refers to a request by Gorée-based merchants for a post at Foundiougne, on the Saloum River, to protect both commerce and "the Sarakollé who come to cultivate the fields" (A.N.F.-A.M., Bayol 1884). This labor migration was probably very much limited by the religious wars, which did not stop until the completion of conquest. They were more bitter and brutal than anything that went on before and certainly increased the risks of migration. The 1884 reference, however, is to the height of a period of conflict.

SLAVES AND PRODUCTION FOR MARKET

Slaves were a major by-product of these wars. Early reports frequently talked of massacres and executions. By the 1870s, slave raiding seems to have become at least as important as direct military confrontation. The increasingly dominant Muslim leaders clearly needed revenue to buy horses, guns, and ammunition. In the early years, peanut sales probably provided much of the revenue needed, but within a decade the nature of the Muslim community changed. Before 1860, all British and French observers commented on the industriousness of the Muslim community, which provided most of the area's trade, but by 1869 a British administrator wrote that each Muslim, as soon as he "has been able to purchase a horse and a gun, considers himself a warrior, lives by plunder and works his fields by the slaves he captures in his expeditions, and thinks it beneath his dignity to perform any work whatsoever, which is left to women and children" (A.G., Administrator 1869). The once embattled Muslim community increasingly financed its war against unbelief with proceeds from the labor of prisoners taken in combat or from their sale. In general, these slaves remained in Senegambia, where the expansion of peanut cultivation and commerce created a large market (Klein 1972). There was also a significant importation of slaves from the territories of Sudanese leaders like Samory.

There were several reasons for this increase in slave raiding. First, constant warfare meant a constant demand for guns, horses, and ammunition. These could be obtained by selling slaves, cattle, or peanuts. Thus, a slave could either be traded or used in the fields, where his labor contributed to his owner's wealth and status. Second, the growth of the peanut trade meant that the market for labor increased substantially. In 1882 Senegal's exports went over 83,000 tons; two year later, Gambian exports went over 18,000. Third, the general availability of slaves and their low price encouraged their wide use. The slave was not only an extra hand in the fields, he was an extra retainer, a servant, and, if loyal, a political supporter. As in previous centuries, the accumulation of slaves was the easiest way for a chief, a lineage, or a polity to increase the scale of its economic and political activities. The slave was both an added person and a laborer who freed others for war and politics. There is clearly a process of accumulation here that differs from the situation during the Atlantic slave trade, when this labor was exported and not used within Africa. Thus the income from peanuts provided the revenue that fueled the accumulation of slaves.[6]

6. In commenting on the paragraph, Philip Curtin suggested that I may have reversed cause and effect—that slaves were available because of chronic warfare in the middle decades of the nineteenth century, and not that warfare resulted from the demand for slaves. The question is an important one, but our data do not permit a definitive statement. I cannot say for sure that the existence of a market for slaves induced men to make war. I would argue, however, that the existence of a market for slaves shaped the way in which men made war. Furthermore, late-nineteenth-century leaders were often caught in a price squeeze. Faced with expanding European power and unresolved local conflicts, they sought military modernization. Production could be expanded only if labor was available, and only the slave trade could meet these labor needs. Thus, there was a pressure to take prisoners even though military success simply forced the price of slaves down. In Senegambia the price never reached the derisory level (500 kola nuts) found in the wake of Samory's campaigns (Meillassoux 1964:270). The expansion meant that the market was willing to assimilate those who were offered, but even in Senegambia slaves could be purchased for under one hundred francs (about twenty dollars at the time).

A significant market for slaves existed within both the British and French communities. The French gave slave women as booty to their soldiers and their allies. In some cases they were referred to as wives in official correspondence, but the women seldom had any choice and sometimes were sold by their "husbands" (Renault 1971:46-47; Klein 1968: 166-67; Bouche 1968:80). In addition, there was a market for servants and concubines. Though slavery was illegal wherever the Union Jack or the French tricolor flew, a market existed even among town dwellers, extra women and servants being highly desired.

Above and beyond the services a slave gave, he was a form of capital investment. There were very few ways in which a chief or the head of a lineage could conveniently increase his wealth. The accumulation of slaves and cattle was probably the most important, most other goods being perishable. The only other item that seems to have played a similar role was cloth, which also served as a form of money (Ames 1955). Land was freely available to all and thus was not a scarce good. Labor was more scarce, and as the price of slaves declined, more and more money was invested in accumulating them. Interestingly, in the Gambia, during the decade after British conquest stopped the trade, there were frequent reports of increasingly large herds of cattle.[7] Apparently, cattle speedily took the place of slaves as an investment for capital provided by the peanut trade. Gambian taxes were generally lower than those in neighboring Senegal, and Gambian peasants had more money than peoples farther in the interior. Obviously, the amount invested in cattle was related to the level of taxation and the level of consumer demand for other products.

THE CONTROL OF SLAVERY

Both the French and the British were anxious to restrict the scope of their antislavery legislation, fearing strongly that an antislavery policy would hurt commercial interests with African states. When the 1848 abolition of slavery in French territories drew vigorous protests both from nearby rulers and from the merchants of Senegal, it was speedily watered down, largely by antivagrancy legislation that simply expelled runaway slaves. Only in the 1880s did the courts start enforcing antislavery laws, over the objections of governors and administrators. Even then the fiction of a protectorate was used to shield African chiefs from the effect of these laws. The British had fewer problems because they had no territorial aspirations until the French threatened to deprive them of a hinterland in the late 1880s. The scope of British legislation was limited to the Bathurst area and the upriver post at MacCarthy's Island.

7. See P.R.O., Colonial Office series 87, for the late 1890s.

Events outside Africa forced the colonial powers to act against their considered judgment. Cardinal Lavigerie's antislavery crusade, the Brussels Conference, and the necessity of conciliating humanitarian interests in metropolitan legislatures all forced colonial regimes to act. Treaties with African rulers often provided for an end to the trade, though not to slavery. In 1892, shortly after the Brussels Act was signed, a treaty was concluded with the chiefs of St. Louis that had the following provision: all slaves were to be considered domestic slaves, all slaves received the protection of Muslim law, enslavement was abolished as a criminal penalty, all slaves were given the right to redeem themselves at a fixed rate of five hundred francs, and the sale of slaves was prohibited (Klein 1968:164-70). This treaty was extended to all parts of the colony in the following five years. In 1903 the courts were instructed not to recognize the rights of masters to slaves, and in 1905 slavery itself was explicitly abolished (Renault 1971; Gueye 1965).

Similarly, in the Gambia an 1895 decree provided for gradual emancipation. The slave trade was abolished and mistreatment became grounds for liberation (Gambia Protectorate and Slave Trade Abolition Ordinance, April 25, 1895). Every slave was to be liberated on the death of his master and all children born after that time were to be free. The ordinance was at first applied only in areas west of MacCarthy's Island. A 1906 law tightened this up and provided for stricter sanctions.

It is difficult to evaluate how effectively these laws and decrees were enforced. Only a few administrators corresponded regularly on the slavery question. It is clear that all administrators were willing to turn a blind eye to actions by friendly chiefs. They depended on these chiefs to do most of the work of local administration. Some slave trading continued, mostly of children, who were moved singly or in small groups. An administrator could generally use slave-trading charges to eliminate a chief he disliked and replace him with a protégé. Nevertheless, the situation changed more rapidly than any administrator could have expected. J. H. Ozanne, the first travelling commissioner on the North Bank of the Gambia, nervously wrote Bathurst in 1893 that it was important that local people know that abolition was coming from on high or his life would no longer be safe (A.G., Ozanne 1893). Seven years later, the same administrator was able to report that "the whole fabric of slavery" had collapsed (A.G., Ozanne 1900). In the intervening period, some dramatic changes had taken place.

First, the colonial regimes virtually closed off recruitment of new jaam. Raiding ceased, as did enslavement for crimes; kidnapping and slave trading became isolated phenomena. This meant that the growing labor needs of the expanding peanut crop could not be met by slave labor. Second, flight and redemption radically reduced the number of slaves. A large percentage of the jaam had been taken as prisoners in wars shortly preceding conquest. Families were often able to trace relatives hundreds of miles away. Both colonial regimes facilitated redemptions, but more important than redemption was simply the flight, with an end to inter-necine war, of thousands of slaves to the areas from which they had come. This massively undercut the system. Though administrators were some-times willing to defend the "property rights" of chiefs to slaves,[8] both regimes were reluctant to give slave owners the aid of the colonial courts. Thus, the slave owners had no sanctions to bring to bear against the runaway and were forced to acquiesce. In a few cases, traditional hostilities played their part. The Buur Saalum stopped and liberated a caravan of slaves being moved by his traditional enemies in Muslim Nioro, and much to the annoyance of the administrator in Nioro, his counterpart in Sine-Saloum supported the Buur (A.N.S., Nioro 1895; Administrator Sine-Saloum 1895). Similarly, the Mansa of Badibu gave land to slaves running away from his Muslim Wolof enemies and founded at least one Jola village (A.G., Ozanne 1900). There was seldom any conscious effort to return slaves to their homes. The chief who freed a body of slaves generally gave them land and thus profited from the act of liberation.

Obviously, flight was most attractive to those slaves who remembered their homeland and could return there. There were, however, other options. In Saba, a Muslim Mandinka village in the Gambia, the slaves simply refused to continue working for their masters when British rule was extended into the area. They had heard that Britain did not recognize slavery. The slaves in question were "not newly acquired but the remote descendants of slave successors" (P.R.O., Ozanne, July 31, 1894). The administrator, who was reluctant to extend antislavery legislation, arbi-trated the differences between master and slave with great difficulty, but the long-run tendency was clear.

The Saba case may have been unique. Most of the slaves who fled probably returned to an earlier home. Others cannot be traced. The fact of their flight means that no one remembers them. Some of the refugees joined the army or moved to the growing cities. Many joined the Mourides, a religious order founded by Amadou Bamba early in the colonial period. During the two decades before World War I, the Mourides recruited heavily among former jaam (Cruise O'Brien 1971; Pelissier 1966). Equally interesting, there were important changes among

---

8. For example, French law freed a slave who took refuge in an area of direct admini-stration. This included Foundiougne, in Sine-Saloum, but the administrator was told to return to the Buur Saalum any runaway who did not make it to Foundiougne (A.N.S., Director of Political Affairs 1891).

the jaam who remained. Increasingly, they formed their own households, often in the same village as the former master. In the interwar years, there was a tendency for these households to move out into unclaimed lands. Sometimes they formed scparate villages, though often their new settlements were only a kilometer or two from the village center and are today considered quarters of the original village. The new villages clearly reflect a massive effort by these former slaves to assert their economic independence, though jaam households that remained near their former masters continued to pay a tax called the *assaka.*

NEW LABOR SYSTEMS

The breakdown of the slave labor system had no negative effect on commercial growth. The development of more settled conditions and the decline of the slave labor system encouraged the rapid increase of newer and more efficient forms of labor. In the cities, this meant simply the extension of wage labor. In rural areas, recourse was had to migrants known as *navetanes* (probably from Wolof *nawet,* "rainy season"). The first administrators in both countries found themselves constantly involved with labor migration questions. In 1892, only five years after French conquest, the administrator of Sine-Saloum reported 600 to 700 navetanes (Sénégal, December 3, 1892). A year later, his counterpart on the North Bank of the Gambia reported a thousand (A.G., Ozanne 1894). By 1903, the Gambia was getting almost 6,000 every year (Gambia 1903), and Sine-Saloum generally received from 30,000 to 60,000 a year during the interwar period (Auchapt 1948).

There is a continuity between the position of the jaam and that of the navetane, most notably in the form of tenure. In the most widely noted form of tenure the navetane simply assumed the obligations of a jaam or an unmarried son. The owner gave him a field, a hut, and food. The navetane owed in exchange five days of labor from sunrise to about 2:00 p.m. He worked for himself evenings and on the other two days (Marty 1913:79; Campistron 1939; Fayet 1939; P.R.O., Ozanne 1899). This was gradually reduced. Since World War II, the norm has been four mornings a week, until about noon.

JAAM IN THE TWENTIETH CENTURY

To say that slavery has lost its economic importance is not to say that the associated status no longer exists. Ascribed status is still very important. The fullest description of jaam status in recent years is in David Ames' unpublished dissertation. Ames worked in 1950 and 1951 in two Gambian Wolof villages, one of which had been a slave village. As a resident, he was able to observe social interaction. His description is as follows.

At the present time members of the *jaam* class still give some of the cloth they weave to their masters. They also occasionally work on their master's fields and give them a tithe from their own crops for which they are adequately compensated with farm tools and clothing. A few *jaam* were still observed living in the compounds of their masters, and working for them full-time. *Jaam* continue to perform all their traditional ceremonial duties in return for gifts or clothing, money and food. Also the *jaam* beg for gifts of food and money from their masters.

Jaam are still expected to show deference in the presence of freeborn. However, some of them have taken advantage of the freedom given them by the British and as one elderly freeborn man put it, they "throw their hats as far as they can." *Jaam* still take off their shoes when greeting their masters and respectfully address them as "grandfathers." *Jaam* are thought to have less pride than the freeborn and exhibit this by saying things in public that the freeborn would be ashamed to say, by begging, sometimes wheedling gifts through flattery or entertaining conversation; and by debasing themselves in many other ways. Not all *jaam*, of course, follow these patterns; some of them avoid such behavior to the extent that they are permitted to do so by society (Ames 1953:16).

My own research was in an area not far from where the one that Ames studied, but on the Senegal side of the border and almost twenty-five years later. Around Kaymor, the Wolof jaam no longer weave. Some Tukulor jaam do, but for their own profit. Few jaam live in their master's compounds, but many continue to pay assaka to their former masters. Derived ironically from a Quranic obligation to tithe for the poor, the assaka is neither given to the poor, nor is it a tithe anymore. When asked why they still paid the assaka, former jaam answered simply that it was the custom. I would hypothesize that there are two other factors: the necessity of maintaining face-to-face relations in small communities, and an interest in maintaining clientship ties with more influential families. Jaam also continue to play ceremonial roles at jaambuur functions, and poorer jaam will beg for gifts. This whole relationship is being eroded. The young, the wealthy, the educated, and the independent minded do not pay and do not defer. "My *borom* [master]," one middle-aged jaam proudly asserted, "is Senghor [the president]." He then went on to point to the major highway about a kilometer away. "Do you see those trucks carrying peanuts to market? Most of them belong to jaam." He may have exaggerated, but agricultural officers tend to consider jaam more open to change and some were among the wealthiest members of the community. One was the leader of the local section of the party. Several others were prosperous model peasants. Wealth is today a more important source of power and status than ascribed position.

Even for Ames' jaam the relationship was to some degree a voluntary one. The status remained where the jaam accepted its perpetuation. He had the option of moving or of refusing to play the role assigned to him. The relationship also had limited economic content. Jaam could get cleared land from freeborn families or could clear bush only a half-hour walk from the village. If a jaam cleared bush, he and his descendants preserved rights to that land and, in many cases, were able to "accumulate considerable wealth and thus offset their inferior status" (Ames 1953:18). The economic content of the master-jaam relationship consisted essentially of a form of clientship and of gift exchange, which could operate to the benefit of either side, but was more important symbolically than economically. Both master and jaam could call on the other in moments of need. Thus, jaam status had changed radically from 1890. Ames asked, however, why it persisted:

Several reasons can be posited to explain why the institution of slavery, in spirit, at least, has been retained in so many of its aspects. First of all, it has been noted that *jaam* received adequate compensation for performing their traditional tasks in the ceremonies held by the freeborn. Secondly, they are entitled to beg from their masters anything they need, although they are not always successful. However, the most effective reinforcement of the freeborn-*jaam* relationship today (as probably in the old days also) is religious. Unlike the freeborn, *jaam* are not educated in Koranic schools; all they are expected to know is how to pray. *Jaam* are told that if they work hard for their masters in their fields, present tithes (hassaka), and behave respectfully, they will be blessed and go to heaven (Ames 1953:18).

In Kaymor, too, control of Muslim offices is a factor in continued jaam-buur social domination, but I would argue that two factors are more important. The first is that relations of subordination were deeply engrained in Wolof social structure. The second is that their perpetuation was to some degree in the interest of the jaam.

For Jolof, an area much less well-developed economically, Audiger presented a different picture for the same period:

The caste of the non-free, the *diame*, seems to have disappeared in all villages except Yang-Yang [the former capital], there the former slaves of the court of the Burba still constitute the major part of the population. In general, the slaves of Jolof and Oualo have been sold by their masters to the populations of the valley of the Senegal for millet in periods of scarcity. Many have also profited from seasonal migrations to the city, where a servile tie would pass unnoticed, and have not returned to the village (Audiger 1961:165, tr. from Human Relations Area Files).

Finally, the jaam lost much of their political role. The two-hundred-man suites described by Cadamosto in the fifteenth century had become five-hundred-man forces in the nineteenth century. No Damel or Buur would go to a diplomatic encounter with fewer men. Lesser chiefs, however, had smaller entourages. One of the first tasks of the colonial regimes was to reduce these large and increasingly parasitic tyeddo entourages. In one case, in 1892, chiefs were simply told that they could only come to St. Louis with ten retainers. Every chief needed retainers to carry messages, collect taxes, or represent him in distant corners of his district, but he now needed fewer of them and his ability to support them was less than before. Many in the reduced entourage were still jaam. Ames tells us that chiefs had jaam spokesmen, who made public proclamations for them. Chiefs also maintain griots today, but the vast majority of nyenyo and tyeddo must now support themselves, the former by selling their talents and the latter usually as cultivators. Chiefs, politicians, and marabouts maintain retainers in a "big man" style reminiscent of traditional society, but this reflects various patron-client relationships rather than a continuation of traditional ascriptive roles.

CONCLUSIONS

My description of the history of servitude among Wolof and Sereer is somewhat circumscribed by the data available to me. Every community has its particular characteristics, and there is a good deal of regional variation. On many questions, I have only been able to make qualified statements. On others, I remain ignorant. For example, I have few data on the homogeneously Sereer kingdom of Siin, and yet there are probably some differences between Siin and the Wolof-speaking areas where I did research. Nevertheless, it is clear that servitude as it existed in the nineteenth century was primarily a labor system. In this, my thinking has been very much shaped by H. J. Nieboer's classic ethnographic study, *Slavery as an Industrial System*. Using data available to him at the turn of the century, Nieboer posited that slavery was likely to develop in agricultural societies that met the following conditions: first, a shortage of labor and surplus of land; second, a form of agriculture that did not use expensive capital. Nieboer's conditions certainly existed among the Wolof and Sereer. Several other factors were crucial. Two others were, first, the existence of a market within which slaves could be procured and their products sold, and second, the capacity of the society to integrate jaam.

Servile relationships were a way for elites to assure themselves of goods and services in a society with scarce resources. Once the institution of the jaam came into being, jaam were increasingly called on to meet varying personnel needs of the society. Economic and political functions were intimately related. Power gave wealth and wealth gave power. The jaam in any form were a kind of capital investment. They were also the most efficient way of increasing the scale of various lineages and polities. The individual enslaved could be an extra hand in the fields, an extra warrior in battle, and, if successful, even a chief who would be loyal because he was kinless. From an early date the individual enslaved could also be sold. Trade was a valuable source of both prestige goods and military equipment. Thus, it was also a major source of social differentiation. The war goods—horses, swords, and, from the late seventeenth century on, guns— gave the elites greater control over their own societies. Prestige goods like cloth and alcohol gave them a life-style distinct from that of the majority.

The jaam, whether tyeddo or humble agriculturalist, could either live in a slave village attached to a powerful lineage or title or he could be assimilated into an extended family unit. In neither would the conditions approximate those of the gang-labor systems in early capitalist colonies. Furthermore, domestic slavery within an extended-family system was probably economically rational. The family gained an extra hand, and if it successfully assimilated him, he contributed to its wealth, power, and standing. Given existing forms of social control, a gang-labor system was probably not possible, except as an adjunct of a powerful, centralized monarchy.

Participation in both the slave trade and in "legitimate" commerce tended to strengthen the system and increase the reliance on servile labor. The slave trade created conditions of insecurity that severely limited other possibilities of economic development. Warfare became the major means of accumulating wealth or recruiting personnel. The peanut trade pushed this development even further, for it took place at a time when slaves were cheap, other forms of labor were limited, and insecurity endemic. In the long run, the most radical change came not so much from direct efforts by colonial authorities to regulate slavery as from the incompatibility of slave and wage systems. New forms of land tenure modeled on domestic slavery evolved to cope with the new situations. The result was that servile status became a vestige of the institution that had once played a large role in Wolof and Sereer society.

GLOSSARY

alkali: tax collector.
assaka: a form of tithe paid by slaves to masters, derived from Quranic obligation to give to charity.
borom: master.
Buur: ruler (Wolof).
Damel: title of the ruler in Kajoor.

farba: a title usually used for slave chiefs.

garmi: a status group that included members of certain lineages who could become rulers.

geej: the most powerful matrilineage in Kajoor.

gelwar: a Sereer matrilineage from which rulers were elected.

gor: high status.

griot: a caste made up of musicians, praise-sayers, and historians.

jaam: a slave.

jaam juddu: a domestic slave (Wolof).

jaambuur: a "freeman."

jaam sayor: a trade slave (Wolof).

navetanes: rural migrants who performed tenant labor.

nyenyo: members of the status group that was made up of artisan and *griot* castes.

pad bin: a domestic slave (Sereer).

pad o kob: a trade slave (Sereer).

surga: free clients attached to *garmi*.

tanngann: fishing people of coastal villages.

tara: a slave concubine.

tubenans: converts to Islam.

tyeddo: a slave warrior.

yène: a portion of agricultural production paid by the slave to the master.

REFERENCES

UNPUBLISHED SOURCES

A.C.S.E.: Archives de la Congrégation du Saint-Esprit, Paris.
   Father Gallais to Father Libermann, March 18, 1849. 153 VI.

A.G.: Archives of the Gambia, Bathurst.
   Administrator to Colonial Office, July 26, 1869.
   Administrator to Governor in Chief, Sierra Leone, July 26, 1889.
   Reports by Travelling Commissioner J. H. Ozanne of June 16, 1893, January 6, 1894, and July 14, 1900. (Most of the travelling commissioners' reports are also available in the Public Record Office, London.)

Ames, D. 1953. Plural marriage among the Wolof in the Gambia. Ph.D. dissertation, Northwestern Univ.

A.N.F.-O.M.: Archives nationales de France, section Outre-Mer, Paris.
   Report of Governor Jean Bayol, May 21, 1884, Sénégal IV 104.
   Sénégal XIV 15.

A.N.S.: Archives nationales du Sénégal, Dakar.
   Director of Political Affairs to Administrator Sine-Saloum, July 26, 1891, unclassified.

Administrator Sine-Saloum to Governor-General, October 1895, 13 G 325.
Commandant Nioro to Commandant Supérieur, November 5, 1895, 13 G 322.
Report of Administrator Sine-Saloum, January 26, 1904, K 18.
Report of Police Sergeant at Foundiougne, May 30, 1904, K 18.
Auchapt, M. 1948. L'immigration saisonnière dans le Sine-Saloum. Paper submitted in fulfillment of degree requirements, Ecole nationale de la France d'Outre-Mer.
Boulègue, J. 1968. La Sénégambie au milieu du XVe siècle au début du XVIIe siècle. Thesis presented to the Faculté des Lettres et Sciences humaines, Paris.
Charles, E. 1973. A history of the kingdom of Jolof (Senegal), 1800-1890. Ph.D. dissertation, Boston Univ.
Colvin, L. 1971. Kajor and its diplomatic relations with Saint Louis du Senegal. Ph.D. dissertation, Columbia Univ.
Klein, M. A. 1975. Domestic slavery in the agricultural societies of the Western Sudan. Paper presented to the Mathematical Social Science Board Symposium, Colby College, August 20-22, 1975. (To be published in a forthcoming collection of the Symposium papers, ed. J. Hogendorn and H. Gemery.)
P.R.O.: Public Record Office, London.
Administrator R. B. Llewellyn to Secretary of State for Colonies, June 16, 1894, C.O. 87/146/64.
Reports by Travelling Commissioner J. H. Ozanne: June 28, 1894, in C.O. 87/145/72; July 31, 1894, in C.O. 87/146/84; March 27, 1899, in C.O. 87/158/22.
Cases of mistreatment, in C.O. 87/144.
Note: I am also grateful to J. Irvine of Brandeis University, L. B. Venema of the Agricultural University of Wageningen (Netherlands), and P. Basse of Lycée Gaston Berger in Kaolack for communicating to me the results of unpublished research.

PUBLISHED SOURCES

Alvares de Almada, A. 1594/1964. *Tratado breve dos rios de Guiné do Cabo Verde.* Reprinted 1964, in *Monumenta missionaria africana,* New series, Vol. 3. ed. Padre A. Brasio. Lisbon.
Ames, D. 1955. The use of transitional cloth money token among the Wolof. *Am. Anthrop.* 57:1016-24.
Audiger, J. 1961. Les Ouolofs du Bas Ferlo. *Cah. d'outre-mer* 14:157-81.
Barry, B. 1972. *Le royaume du Waalo, 1659-1859: le Sénégal avant la conquête.* Paris.
Bérenger-Féraud, L. J. B. 1879. *Les peuplades de la Sénégambie.* Paris.
Boilat, Abbé P.-D. 1853. *Esquisses sénégalaises.* Paris.
Bouche, D. 1968. *Les villages de liberté en Afrique noire française, 1887-1910.* Paris.
Boulègue, J. 1972. *Les Luso-Africains de Sénégambie.* Dakar.

Cadamosto, A. da. 1937. *The voyages of Cadamosto.* Tr. by G. R. Crone. London.

Campistron, M. 1939. Coutume Ouolof du Cayor (cercle du Thiès). In Vol. 1 of *Coutumiers juridiques de l'Afrique occidentale française.* 3 vols. Paris.

Carrère, F., and Holle, P. 1855. *De la Sénégambie française.* Paris.

Corre, A. 1883. Les Sérères de Joal et de Portudal. *Revue Ethnogr.* 2:1-20.

Cruise O'Brien, D. B. 1971. *The Mourides of Senegal.* Oxford.

Curtin, P. D. 1969. *The Atlantic slave trade: a census.* Madison.

———. 1971. Jihad in West Africa: early phases and inter-relations in Mauritania and Senegal. *J. Afr. Hist.* 12:11-24.

———. 1975. *Economic change in precolonial Africa: Senegambia in the era of the slave trade.* Madison.

Curtin, P. D., ed. 1967. *Africa remembered.* Madison.

Diagne, P. 1967. *Pouvoir politique traditionnel en Afrique occidentale.* Paris.

Diop, M. 1972. *Histoire des classes sociales dans l'Afrique de l'ouest,* Vol. 2: *Le Sénégal.* Paris.

Durand, J.-B. L. 1802. *Voyage au Sénégal.* Paris.

Fayet, J. C. 1939. Coutume des Ouolofs Musulmans (cercle du Baol). In Vol. 1 of *Coutumiers juridiques de l'Afrique occidentale française.* 3 vols. Paris.

Fernandes, V. 1951. *Description de la Côte occidentale d'Afrique (Sénégal au Cap de Monte, Archipels) par V. Fernandes (1506-1510.).* Ed. T. Monod, A. Texeira da Mota, and R. Mauny. Bissau.

Gambia. 1848, 1851, 1903. *Annual report of the Gambia.*

Gamble, D. 1957. *The Wolof of Senegambia.* Ethnographic Survey of Africa. London.

Gueye, M. 1965. L'Affaire Chautemps (avril 1904) et la suppression de l'esclavage de case au Sénégal. *Bull. Inst. fr. Afr. noire* 27:542-59.

Klein, M. A. 1968. *Islam and imperialism in Senegal: Sine-Saloum 1847-1914.* Stanford.

———. 1969. The Moslem revolution in nineteenth-century Senegambia. In *Boston University papers on Africa,* Vol. 4, *Western African history,* ed. D. McCall, N. Bennett, and J. Butler. Boston.

———. 1972. Social and economic factors in the Muslim revolution in Senegambia. *J. Afr. Hist.* 13:419-41.

Labouret, H. 1941. *Paysans d'Afrique occidentale.* Paris.

Lafont, F. 1938. Le Gandoul et les Niominka. *Bull. Com. Etud. hist. scient. Afr. occid. fr.* 21:358-438.

Marty, P. 1913. *Les Mourides d'Amadou Bamba.* Paris.

Mauny, R. 1961. *Tableau géographique de l'ouest africain au Moyen Age.* Dakar.

Meillassoux, C. 1964. *Anthropologie économique des Gouro de Côte d'Ivoire.* Paris.

Meillassoux, C., ed., 1971. *The development of indigenous trade and markets in West Africa.* London.

———. 1975. *L'esclavage en Afrique précoloniale.* Paris.

Mollien, G. 1820. *Travels in the interior of Africa to the sources of the Senegal and Gambia.* London.

Monteil, V. 1967. The Wolof kingdom of Kayor. In *West African kingdoms in the nineteenth century,* ed. D. Forde and P. M. Kaberry. London.

Moore, F. 1738. *Travels into the inland parts of Africa.* London.

Nieboer, H. J. 1900. *Slavery as an industrial system: ethnological researches.* The Hague.

Noirot, E. 1892. Notice sur le Sine-Saloum. In *Journal officiel du Sénégal,* pp. 7-12.

Pelissier, P. 1966. *Les paysans du Sénégal.* St. Yrieix, France.

Pichl, W. J. 1966. *The Cangin group: a language group in northern Senegal.* Pittsburgh.

Renault, F. 1971. L'abolition de l'esclavage au Sénégal: l'attitude de l'administration française (1848-1905). *Revue fr. Hist. d'outre-mer* 59:5-81.

Riesman, P. 1974. *Societé et liberté chez les peul Djelgôbé de Haute-Volta.* Paris.

Ritchie, C. I. A. 1968. Deux textes sur le Sénégal (1673-1677). *Bull. Inst. fond. Afr. noire* 30:289-353.

Rodney, W. 1966. African slavery and other forms of social oppression on the upper Guinea coast in the context of the Atlantic slave trade. *J. Afr. Hist.* 7:431-43.

———. 1970. *A history of the upper Guinea coast, 1545-1800.* Oxford.

Roger, B. 1828. *Keledor.* 2 vols. Paris.

Rousseau, R. 1929. Le Sénégal d'autrefois: étude sur le'Oualo, cahiers de Yoro Dyao. *Bull. Com. Etud. hist. scient. Afr. occid. fr.* 12:133-211.

Sénégal. 1892. *Journal officiel du Sénégal.*

Silla, O. 1966. Persistance des castes dans la société Wolof contemporaine. *Bull. Inst. fond. Afr. noire* 28:731-70.

The Ecology of Servility in Multi-Ethnic Settings

Part VI

14

Servility and Political Control: Botlhanka among the BaTawana of Northwestern Botswana

ca. 1750-1906

Thomas Tlou

The BaTawana, an offshoot of the BaNgwato, are a Setswana-speaking people who founded a centralized state in Ngamiland, an area in northwestern Botswana, around 1800.[1] As a result of their incorporation of the non-Tawana peoples of Ngamiland, a complex system of social relations developed over the years which featured two distinct systems of dependent relationships—"clientship" and "serfdom" (*botlhanka*). The literature on Ngamiland invariably fails to distinguish between the two, referring to both as slavery, which it describes as widespread. The BaTawana themselves casually refer to both systems—clientship and botlhanka—simply

1. Throughout this essay reference should be made to Map 14 and to Table 14.1. My thanks are due to Ambrose Made of the Geography Department of the University of Botswana, Lesotho and Swaziland for preparing the map. I have not followed the anthropological practice of dropping prefixes before the names of peoples. Rather, I have retained the prefixes because this is how the people refer to themselves, but I have capitalized the radical: thus, BaTawana (sing. MoTawana), and not Tawana. The latter form is reserved for adjectival use.

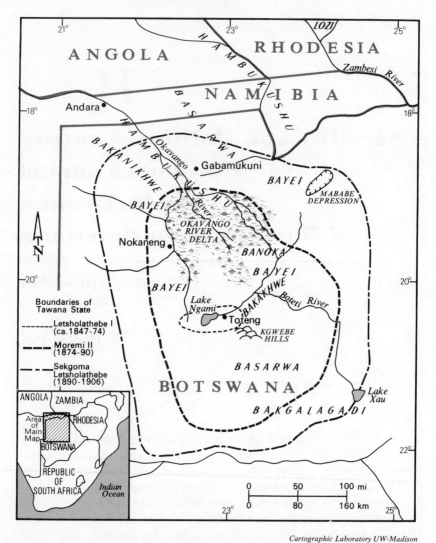

Cartographic Laboratory UW-Madison

Map 14. Tawana Expansion, ca. 1847-1906

as botlhanka. On further questioning, however, they distinguish between those *batlhanka* whom I refer to as clients, and the hereditary serfs, whom they call *batlhanka wa lolwapa* (batlhanka of the household), and they clearly distinguish the different rights they enjoyed.

The aim of this study is to describe these systems and to see to what extent individuals in these categories were deprived of rights. Only then can we decide whether or not these were forms of slavery.

In this chapter, "clientship" is a relationship more or less voluntarily entered into for the mutual benefit of both the client and his patron or master. The client renders service to the patron, who in return gives him protection, food, and other benefits. Clientship is based on wealth. Although the client depends on the patron for livelihood, and may even have been coerced into his position, he formally and legally retains his freedom as a citizen. Botlhanka, on the other hand, is an institution comparable to hereditary serfdom, a person in this status being a *motlhanka* (pl. *batlhanka*). Motlhanka has a range of meanings. A father can proudly refer to his son as motlhanka; here the term emphasizes the connotation not of servitude but of dependence. Similarly, it may refer to a servant and emphasize the connotation of subordination. In this chapter, we shall focus on the meaning that makes motlhanka interchangeable with serf. The main feature of the institution of botlhanka was that those who lived under it lacked certain civic rights, even if, to some extent, their masters accorded them the treatment enjoyed by the masters' own children.

Table 14.1

Population of Ngamiland by Ethnic Groups, 1936 and 1946 (approximate figures)[a]

	1936	1946
BaGcereku	—	1,513
BaHerero	2,933	5,798
BaKalaka	—	728
BaKgalagadi	2,270	1,918
BaRotse (Loze)	—	744
BaSarwa	3,067	3,704
BaSotho	—	42
BaSubiya	—	486
BaTawana	7,072	8,124
BaYei	16,495	13,261
HaMbukushu	5,919	5,286
MaTebele (MaKololo)	—	103
Others	4,402	—
Totals	42,158	41,707

[a] Figures for 1936 are from the 1936 census (Schapera 1959:5); figures for 1946 are from the 1946 census (Schapera 1952:94). Census figures, especially the early ones (before 1960), should be treated with caution because quite often only people in major villages were included. There is also the problem of attempting to differentiate between members of the various ethnic groups. Quite often people failed to distinguish between the BaSarwa and the BaKgalagadi, especially when they led a nomadic life. The BaKgalagadi were sometimes referred to as BaSarwa because they lived by hunting—an activity generally, although not exclusively, associated with the BaSarwa. Censuses before 1936 (e.g., that of 1921) and those since 1946 do not classify the population by ethnic groups.

The study covers the period from about 1750 to 1906, when the British colonial administration deposed the last independent Tawana king, Sekgoma Letsholathebe (reigned 1890-1906). Thus, although botlhanka continued well into the colonial period, I shall examine its functioning in an independent African kingdom.

Ngamiland, the area of this study, lies in the northwestern corner of Botswana.[2] The area is characterized by dry savanna and desert; what makes it habitable on a relatively large scale is the Okavango River Delta —a vast swamp and floodplain area of some 17,000 square kilometers, about half of which is flooded annually (Great Britain 1966:2; Randall 1957:32-36). In historical times, the people on the floodplain and the scrub savanna bordering it have been sedentary pastoralists, whereas those in the more arid parts have been nomads. These divisions were important in the evolution of their social and political relationships.

Ngamiland has an ethnically mixed population (see Table 14.1). The groups that concern us here are those that were in Ngamiland before the twentieth century. (The BaHerero, for example, came in 1904-5 as a result of colonial wars in what was then German Southwest Africa.)

The oldest inhabitants are the BaSarwa, a collective name for several groups of Khoisan-speaking peoples (and therefore related linguistically to the so-called Hottentots and Bushmen). The Sarwa groups I am concerned with are those of the sandbelt, who live by hunting, and those collectively referred to as BaNoka (people of the river), the so-called River Bushmen, who live and fish along rivers and the delta fringes.

The other groups all speak Bantu languages. The origins of the BaKgalagadi are obscure. They speak a Sotho language and, of all the peoples of Ngamiland, they have the closest cultural affinities with the BaTawana, who arrived later.

It is clear from the oral traditions of the various peoples in Ngamiland that the BaSarwa and the BaKgalagadi were the earliest inhabitants of the area. The BaYei, who arrived about the mid-eighteenth century, found them already there. The expansion of Lozi rule to the southern limits of the Barotse plain, around 1750 or later, drove the BaYei and the HaMbukushu from what is now Zambia. Later emigrations were caused by struggles over succession that shook Bulozi in the nineteenth century (Vansina 1968:213-15).

A riverine people and expert canoeists, the BaYei settled on the rivers, islands, and margins of the delta. The HaMbukushu began to appear in northern Ngamiland around 1850, mainly because of the activities of the

2. A geography of Botswana has yet to be written; for description one must therefore, rely on general works—e.g., Pollock (1968:350-56, 390-92); Schapera (1962).

mambari (see Glossary) slave traders at Andara (Schulz and Hammar 1897:245; interview: Kangumbe, April 22, 1970; for a full discussion of the migrations, see Tlou 1972). The ruling Tawana group emerged about 1800 when the Ngwato prince Tawana, as a result of succession disputes, settled with his followers in the Kgwebe Hills in Ngamiland, where he established a state by incorporating the BaSawra, the BaKgalagadi, and the BaYei.

NGAMILAND BEFORE THE BATAWANA

Before incorporation into the Tawana state, early in the nineteenth century, the peoples of Ngamiland were organized into small-scale, stateless societies, and lived in small, independent settlements. In general, the residents of the sandbelt were predominantly hunters and gatherers; those of the floodplain were fishermen and agriculturalists. Agriculture also extended into the savanna that bordered the delta, and hunting dominated the drier scrub savanna.

The BaKgalagadi and the sandbelt BaSarwa relied on game, which roamed the scrub savanna and parts of the sandbelt. In the brief, wet summer, they augmented their meat diet with wild fruit, berries, and roots. Those BaKgalagadi who lived near permanent waterholes also raised goats and grew sorghum on a limited scale. The BaKgalagadi and some BaSarwa were skilled manufacturers of *karosses* (goatskin blankets) and other skin articles. The fact that these two groups were nomadic made it difficult for a sedentary people to impose effective political control over them.

Kinship ties largely defined Sarwa and Kgalagadi social and political organization. The highest level of political organization among the sandbelt BaSarwa was the band, usually consisting of a bilateral descent group of about fifty people, led by a man skilled as a hunter. Most were nomadic, following the seasonal movements of game (Silberbauer 1965: 68-72). Some, however, were fishermen who lived in fairly large villages around permanent pools along the Boteti River. The BaKgalagadi were organized into patrilineages under hereditary chiefs (Kuper 1969:46). Most of them lived a seminomadic life in small villages around waterholes.

The BaNoka and the BaYei were the principal riverine fishermen. The BaNoka, the more ancient inhabitants, do not seem to have had complex, sophisticated fishing techniques, contenting themselves with the use of scoop baskets in shallow waters and the use of poison (interview: Kangumbe, April 24, 1970). Yei immigration introduced a more efficient technology for the exploitation of the riverine environment, most importantly a high-quality net made from a local shrub. A significant technological breakthrough was the introduction of the canoe and the papyrus raft, allowing communication over the otherwise impenetrable maze of the Okavango River system. The BaYei used canoes for trawl fishing. These new techniques enabled the BaYei to increase fish production and made a surplus possible. The BaYei also introduced agriculture to the delta, growing such crops as sorghum, bulrush millets, beans, pumpkins, and watermelons, most of which are still staples today. The efficiency of cropping was raised by using two types of fields, the flood-moisture field and the rainfall field (Chapman 1868:2).

In the past the BaYei were matrilineal (since their contact with the BaTawana, they have been increasingly adopting many Tawana institutions, including a patrilineal organization). The smallest unit of social organization was the extended family, consisting of a man, his wife or wives, his unmarried brothers and sisters, and other dependents. The BaYei paid no bridewealth. At marriage, a young man moved to his bride's family for a period of bride-service; thereafter, he moved in with his matrilineal relatives, his maternal uncles, or his older brothers.

The significant social unit was the matrilineage, which was a corporate, property-holding body. Several matrilineages composed a village, which controlled a territory. The head of the most senior lineage also took the village headmanship, which was thus a hereditary position. The village was the cornerstone of the political structure. Though every village was formally equal to, and independent of, any other, in practice certain lineages and villages had more prestige than others on account of their wealth (Stigand 1923:413). But the BaYei had no age-grades, no centralized authority, no state—facts which, together with their sedentariness, was to facilitate their subjugation by the BaTawana.

SOCIAL RELATIONSHIPS BEFORE 1800

The literature on Ngamiland generally assumes that botlhanka, or hereditary serfdom, developed as soon as the BaTawana established a state in Ngamiland, around 1800. In fact, botlhanka in its most highly developed form began in the reign of King Letsholathebe I (ca. 1847-74), when the Tawana state expanded to incorporate the early inhabitants of Ngamiland. During successive reigns more and more people came under this system as a result of further expansion. It is important, therefore, to understand the social relationships among the various groups before 1800, though paucity of data makes it difficult: one is forced to rely solely on oral data because European travelers visited the area only after 1849.

What, then, were the social relationships among the Ngamilanders between ca. 1750, when the BaYei settled in Ngamiland, and ca. 1847, when Letsholathebe I became king? On the sandbelt, a form of clientship developed in which Sarwa nomadic hunters attached themselves more or less permanently to the comparatively richer sedentary BaKgalagadi, who had goats and raised sorghum. The BaSarwa herded goats and hunted for the BaKgalagadi in return for grain. But before the BaKgalagadi had begun acquiring herds of cattle from the BaTawana, which occurred after 1800, this form of clientship could not have been very widespread or rigidly structured because few, if any, BaKgalagadi commanded the wealth necessary for it. The boundary between clientship and symbiosis was probably not very clear. Nevertheless, the roots of social stratification were present in this early phase: the Kgalagadi masters saw themselves in a higher status than their clients, and the main basis for this was wealth.

In the delta the BaYei intermarried with the BaKakhwe, a subdivision of the Khoisan-speaking BaNoka, whom they today regard as classificatory cousins. Yei traditions indicate that a kind of clientship existed; poorer members of the community attached themselves to richer ones, becoming part of their families. This system was less rigid than that brought by the BaTawana, for in the former intermarriage occurred between the client's and the master's families, a rare practice in Tawana clientship (Tlou 1972: 154). Forced serfdom also existed, aimed at protecting economic rights of various Yei lineages and villages. If members of one village poached on the fishing grounds of another, the headman of the aggrieved village seized the offenders, who not only were deprived of their catch and fishing gear, but also were forcibly incorporated into the village of their captor, where they rendered him service for some time, after which they were allowed to enjoy full citizenship (interview: Seidisa, March 3, 1970).

Before the coming of the BaTawana, therefore, the peoples of Ngamiland coexisted in a fairly peaceful and balanced manner. None of the groups was powerful enough to impose its rule over the others. Hereditary serfdom in its most rigid form was most likely unknown or rare, and what forms of clientship existed appear to have been quite benign.

THE BATAWANA

After seceding from the BaNgwato, the BaTawana established a centralized state at Kgwebe Hills around 1800. A powerful king, backed by a strong army, ruled the new state. The inhabitants of Kgwebe, the BaKgalagadi and the BaSarwa, offered no resistance, probably because they were disunited, stateless societies. The BaTawana brought with them a social structure more complex than that of any of the inhabitants of Ngamiland, and, as they began to incorporate these people into their polity, additional principles of organization were developed.

Tawana social institutions were organized on a patrilineal basis. Not only were property and rank inherited patrilineally, but membership in family and ward, and even nation, was conceived as being by descent through the father. The household, the smallest well-defined social unit, consisted not only of a nucleus of a man, his wife or wives, and.dependent children, but also of the man's married children, siblings, and other relatives and unrelated dependents, some of whom might also have families. The household was a corporate group of one or more families who occupied a homestead and performed their tasks together; the head of the household controlled its property and regulated its social and ritual activities. Several related households living together in the same small area formed a family group. The next unit was the ward, *kgotla,* which represented the transition from the realm of kinship to that of territorial and political organization. The ward united several, usually related, family groups, and was headed by a hereditary headman, *kgosana* (pl. *dikgosana*),[3] who had well-defined administrative and judicial powers and functions. The ward was the highest level of social organization and was also the smallest territorial unit in the adminstration of the nation, in that the king (*kgosi*) delegated some governmental powers to ward heads.

The social and political structure just described existed in both the capital village and the outlying areas. The BaTawana lived in villages or towns whose populations sometimes numbered thousands (nineteenth-century European travelers sometimes cite a figure of 10,000 or more). The core of the state was the capital, which was the largest village, where the king and the provincial governors lived. The country was divided into provinces, each under a governor, who made occasional visits to supervise the affairs of his area. Each province was in turn divided into administrative districts, each headed by a resident senior headman. Throughout the province were scattered villages and hamlets of varying sizes, ruled by village or hamlet headmen assisted by ward heads. Thus, the chain of command extended from the king through provincial governors to the lowest officials, power being delegated from the higher to the lower official at each level of the hierarchy. But ultimately all were responsible to the king.

In all the villages, including the capital, the people were grouped into wards and subwards, each consisting of families, households, and family groups. The wards were arranged more or less concentrically around the main ward (that of the highest official). A ward thus had its own area within the village. The identity of a ward was emphasized by allocating to it a separate piece of arable land. Most of the families belonging to a ward were related to their headman through descent in the male line from a common ancestor. But in almost every ward there were also families or

---

3. Kgosana usually refers to a man of royal birth. In this case it is a dimunitive of Kgosi (king); used with reference to ward heads, it means headman.

individuals unrelated to its original core. These affiliated members might be servants or other dependents, or immigrants placed there by the king because they could not constitute a ward of their own. Tawana political ideas demanded that every person in the nation belong to a ward. This principle was at the basis of citizenship and of the rights of a freeman. Hence, every alien or immigrant family was placed in one of the wards, and within the ward it was attached to one of the family groups. Immigrants who came into the nation in large enough numbers to constitute a ward were allowed to form their own ward with their leader as headman. For example, King Letsholathebe I created the Diphatsa ward for the Kololo refugees of the 1864-65 civil war in Bulozi (interview: Tawana group, April 13, 1970). So important was membership of the ward that transfers from one ward to another had to be sanctioned by the king.

In general, the large social units were endogamous and the smaller ones were exogamous. Thus, the BaTawana expected a man to marry within his ethnic group—BaTawana inside or outside Ngamiland—and, to a lesser extent, within the ward. They looked down upon and discouraged marriage to non-BaTawana. Ethnic endogamy was further fostered by the custom of preferred marriages, those of a man with his mother's brother's daughter and his father's brother's daughter (Schapera 1957:140-42). Thus, endogamy united the BaTawana as a cultural group and tended to separate them from the non-Tawana citizens of the Tawana state. *Bogadi,* bridewealth, was paid in cattle, and any union unaccompanied by bogadi was regarded as concubinage. This represented a further potential social boundary between the cattle-keeping BaTawana and any non-cattle-keeping group they might encounter.

Age-regiments, *mephato* (sing. *mophato*), played a prominent part in the political, social, and economic life of the nation. The king formed them periodically when he initiated all the eligible boys and girls. Every adult in the realm had to belong to a regiment; this was considered his right as a citizen. Like kingship, it was an integrative institution cutting across parochial loyalties of family, ward, or village. The regiments were essentially a labor force and an army; they were called upon from time to time to perform tasks or to fight for the nation and the king.

NEW RELATIONSHIPS IN NGAMILAND AFTER 1800

The relationship of the BaTawana with the other peoples of Ngamiland encompasses two periods: the period of the first Tawana state, destroyed by the MaKololo about 1830; and that of the second and more powerful state, which evolved in the 1840s.

When the BaTawana first arrived in Ngamiland, in the early 1800s, they brought with them concepts and experience of stratification. The

Tawana royals were at the top of the social ladder, followed by Tawana commoners, who were in turn followed by any aliens and their descendants resident among the BaTawana (Schapera 1959:30-34). Within each group, further subdivisions existed. Among commoners, wealthy men enjoyed higher status. The BaTawana were also already familiar with the clientship system that was widely practiced by the BaNgwato, from whom they had seceded. Indeed, at this secession, they had lost most of the Kgalagadi clients they had had in Ngwato territory.

A new form of clientship based on wealth developed between the BaTawana on the one hand, and the BaKgalagadi and the BaSarwa on the other, extending the pattern of clientship that already existed between the BaKgalagadi and the BaSarwa. Not only did the BaTawana possess the necessary wealth in the form of cattle, but they needed herdsmen. All over the Kgwebe area the BaTawana established cattle posts, *meraka*, near permanent water sources, to which they attached Kgalagadi, and sometimes Sarwa, families as herdsmen. In return for service, the herdsmen drank the milk from the cows and received a portion of the meat when the cattle died. The Tawana masters sometimes leased cattle to their trusted herdsmen. These were called *mafisa* (leased cattle). In return, the herdsman gave additional service to the master. If the leased herd multiplied, the herdsman might be rewarded with a cow. Eventually, some of the clients, mainly the BaKgalagadi, came to possess their own herds, established their own cattle posts, and even acquired their own clients (Kuper 1970:106, 155). In this way many seminomadic BaKgalagadi became sedentary pastoralists and practiced agriculture.

These changes affected the BaKgalagadi more than the BaSarwa because the BaKgalagadi, who lived close to the BaTawana, were already semisedentary, rearing small stock such as goats and raising sorghum on a small scale. The BaSarwa, on the other hand, being nomads who lived far from the sedentary population, were less affected.

The social relations between the groups also developed somewhat differently. Tawana men married Kgalagadi women as second or third wives. They could not be senior wives, who were supposed to enhance the prestige of their husbands by their high status, since the BaTawana considered the BaKgalagadi to be of low status. To the BaKgalagadi such marriages brought prestige and bridewealth in cattle. Intermarriage of these two peoples was facilitated by their cultural and linguistic affinities. On the other hand marriage between the BaTawana and the BaSarwa was rare, because the latter were nomadic and were ethnically and culturally different. The BaTawana considered the BaSarwa to be of lower status than the BaKgalagadi.

During the reign of Moremi I (1820-28), the BaTawana moved their capital from Kgwebe to Toteng, on the delta, establishing contact with the BaYei for the first time. But further expansion and innovations in social and political organization were interrupted by the Kololo invasion. The evidence seems to indicate that this first Tawana state had not developed institutions of hereditary serfdom.

Sometime during the late 1820s or early 1830s, the MaKololo, under the leadership of Sebitwane, who had fled from Lesotho because of the disturbances associated with the rise of the Zulu kingdom, attacked the BaTawana, destroyed their state, and took the bulk of the population to Bulozi as captives (Schapera 1954:99-101). In the early 1840s, the BaTawana escaped from captivity and returned to Ngamiland. Mogalakwe, a man of the royal clan, acted as regent until the heir, Letsholathebe I, had attained majority (Moichubedi ca. 1948:35).

The reestablishment of the Tawana state inaugurated a period during which the population of Ngamiland was drawn under Tawana rule. This process eventually led to the development of a new kind of social relationship—botlhanka, or hereditary serfdom—hitherto little known in the area.

The Kololo attack and the long decade of captivity had destroyed the economic base of the Tawana state, for the Kololo had captured Tawana herds. To rebuild the nation (morafe), Mogalakwe invited the BaYei, the BaKgalagadi, and the BaNoka (the Sarwa "people of the river") to join his morafe and to bring their wealth—cattle, sheep, and goats—to the Tawana state. When they refused, he seized their cattle, goats, and sheep. (In 1849 David Livingstone reported that the BaTawana had long-horned, BaYei-type cattle.) By 1853 the BaTawana were again wealthy in sheep, goats, and long-horned cattle (Livingstone 1872:99; Anderson 1855:93; interview: Mosuga, February 10, 1970). Mogalakwe, however, did not incorporate the BaYei, BaKgalagadi, and BaNoka into his state, nor did he set up any form of administration over them. These events would await Letsholathebe I, whom Mogalakwe installed as king in about 1847 (interview: Mosuga, February 10, 1970).

Until Letsholathebe's reign, the BaTawana had no territorial empire; their influence radiated from their main village at Toteng. Letsholathebe extended his direct control beyond Toteng over the area around Lake Ngami. The people who were, until then, outside the Tawana state now became its subjects. The young king divided the state into provinces, each placed under an official called mosemane (pl. basemane; lit. boy or young man). The main duties of these provincial governors were to collect tribute, to act as appeal judges on behalf of the king, and to see to it that the king's laws were carried out.

The Tawana administrative system was superimposed upon already existing systems. In each province the mosemane ruled through hereditary headmen. Thus, the Yei headmen were the link between their communities and the Tawana king through the mosemane, who ran the affairs of the group under him according to the group's own customs and who presided over the local court. But the farther a group was from the Tawana capital, the less it felt the presence of the central government. The riverine environment made regular communications especially difficult, for the BaTawana did not know how to use canoes. The BaSarwa and the BaKgalagadi, separated from the capital by vast sandy stretches, felt the impact of the central government less than the BaYei. This relative political and administrative insufficiency gave room for the development of other systems of social relationships through which Tawana domination was expressed.

CLIENTSHIP

The clientship system that had governed the relations between the BaTawana and the BaKgalagadi at Kgwebe, as described above, was extended to the BaYei and other subject groups. The main feature of clientship, which applied predominantly to the BaKgalagadi, was that even though people initially were forced into clientage by their poverty, once they were clients they continued to enjoy certain basic rights. In the case of the BaKgalagadi, they had their own wards at the capital and in the provincial villages, whereas the BaYei had them only in the provincial villages where populations were predominantly Yei. In villages where BaTawana predominated, the BaYei—like subject peoples other than the BaKgalagadi—had no wards, since they were all attached to the Tawana wards. (Separate Yei wards were not allowed at the capital until 1948, after a political dispute that nearly rent the nation.)[4]

Where independent wards existed the subject peoples settled their disputes according to their own customs, although certain cases, such as murder, were reserved for judgment by the king. They had access to the courts of the land and lived in their own homes. They had the right to own property, and their sons (in the case of the BaKgalagadi) or sororal nephews (in the case of the BaYei) continued to inherit property. They became members of the Tawana regiments, like all freemen in the realm. They had the right to leave their patron if they desired, but they generally did not do so because they were economically dependent. A further limitation was that, although they made political decisions on a local level, they did not sit in the highest councils of state, the preserve of the

4. This does not refer to later immigrants like the MaKololo. Subject peoples here refers to early inhabitants: the BaYei, BaSarwa, and BaKgalagadi.

BaTawana. This was not due so much to their client status as to the fact that they were subject people.

Social status, based simultaneously on both origin and wealth, shaped the clientship system. The BaTawana were mainly the patrons not only because they were wealthy, but also because they were the ruling group. A MoTawana, however poor, was superior in status to any member of the subject groups, just as a Tawana royal was always superior to a Tawana commoner. A MoTawana could never be a client of a subject person. The BaKgalagadi, because of their cultural affinities with the BaTawana, were next in status and could have Kgalagadi, Sarwa, and Yei clients. The BaYei followed the BaKgalagadi and had Yei and Sarwa clients, whereas the BaSarwa came last and could, in theory, have clients only from their own people (Schapera and Van der Merwe 1945:3 interview: Seidisa, March 5, 1970). The relatively higher status of the BaKgalagadi was reflected in the fact that they were the only subject people who had their own wards at the capital, all other subject peoples being attached to Tawana wards.

Discrimination against the BaYei may be attributed in part to their cultural differences with the BaTawana. The two peoples spoke different languages. The BaTawana were patrilineal, the BaYei matrilineal. The cultural difference was reflected in the fact that, whereas the BaTawana and the BaKgalagadi circumcised their youths together, the BaYei did so separately. The BaYei were, and still are, the largest single group in the population, and the BaTawana might have feared that too much political autonomy, including allowing their own wards at the capital, would make them into a dominant political force.

BOTLHANKA

Another system of social relationships between the BaTawana and their subjects was botlhanka, which we have referred to as hereditary serfdom.

It is difficult to gauge how widespread botlhanka was. What is certain is that the number of serfs (batlhanka) was small in relation to the total population. The BaTawana, the second largest group, could not become serfs because they were the ruling group. They could only be clients of other BaTawana. The BaKgalagadi belonged largely to the clientship system. The sandbelt BaSarwa rarely became serfs, because they could easily escape into the Kalahari Desert. Thus, batlhanka were derived largely from the BaYei, the most numerous group, and the BaNoka. Not all the BaYei, however, became serfs; prominent BaYei were specifically exempt from this system, being made into clients instead.

The term batlhanka refers primarily to those individuals who were attached to the households at the capital—hence the name batlhanka wa lolwapa (servants of the household)—and to a few who were attached to the homes of prominent men in the provinces. Not all the residents of the capital owned serfs. Thus, the number of serfs must have been relatively small, since most of the BaYei lived in the provinces, not at the capital, and some of these provincial BaYei were in a clientship relationship with the BaTawana whereas others were freemen.

The economy of the BaTawana did not require intensive labor. They cultivated small fields, which a few serfs together with the members of the family tilled. Cattle herding was done mostly by Kgalagadi clients. Domestic tasks required only a few hands. A man could not own more batlhanka than he actually needed for his tasks because he had to feed, clothe, and house them. The introduction of European trade from the 1850s must have led to an increase in the number of serfs, because they served as porters.

The number of batlhanka increased with the expansion of the state, for only those people who were actually subjects of the Tawana state were made serfs. During Letsholathebe's reign (ca. 1847 to 1874), the number of serfs must have been small because the state was confined to the environs of Lake Ngami, with the capital at Toteng. Then, when Moremi II (reigned 1874-90) expanded the state northwestward, with a new capital at Nokaneng, and northeastward to Gabamukuni, more serfs were acquired. When Sekgoma Letsholathebe (reigned 1890-1906) expanded the state to its greatest extent, embracing the HaMbukushu to the north, just south of Andara, more subjects were added to the state. Sekgoma's expansionism, however, did not add very many serfs. The HaMbukushu never became batlhanka, presumably because by the 1890s Ngamiland had come under British rule. The BaTawana also treated the HaMbukushu with circumspection because they were famous rainmakers; Tawana rulers frequently sent envoys to Andara to ask the Mbukushu king to make rain. It is safe, then, to state that only a relatively small portion of the population of Ngamiland were batlhanka, and most of them were BaYei.

THE ORIGINS OF BOTLHANKA AND ITS RELATION TO CLIENTSHIP

The origins of botlhanka are obscure. What is surprising is that the BaYei, who constituted the main source of hereditary serfs, had not been actively conquered and must have outnumbered the BaTawana about two to one (see Table 14.1, p. 369). David Livingstone attributed the relatively easy subjugation of the BaYei to their peacefulness (Livingstone 1872:74). Like other contemporary European visitors, Livingstone incorrectly assumed that all BaYei were hereditary serfs and suffered the same exploitation, whereas, in fact, Yei heads of clans and lineages and other prominent men were clients who had their own batlhanka. Thus, serfdom did not follow entirely ethnic lines and the benefits of the system extended to a few BaYei as well.

The BaTawana now claim that the BaYei voluntarily attached their children to Tawana households as batlhanka. This explanation appears to be an apology for botlhanka—an attempt by the BaTawana to absolve themselves of holding the BaYei in servitude (interviews: Seidisa, March 5, 1970; Pikinini, May 27, 1970; Ramaeba, May 27, 1970). The BaYei, on the other hand, state that when the BaTawana returned destitute from captivity in Bulozi, they gave them out of kindness their children to perform tasks for them, and they expected the BaTawana to treat them like their own children. This expectation was in keeping with the Yei clientship system in which individuals joining a lineage gradually became full members of the new group. The BaTawana, however, gradually turned these helpers into hereditary serfs, with diminished rights. It seems plausible that, having been dispossessed of their property by the BaTawana, some BaYei, BaKgalagadi, and a few BaSarwa attached themselves as clients to wealthy BaTawana in order to secure a livelihood. As time passed, what began as voluntary service turned into a hereditary one, imposed and perpetuated by the more powerful BaTawana. This did not happen in all cases, however: most clients retained their status. The transformation of voluntary clientship into botlhanka had both economic and political implications. Clients were not easily exploited because they could sue their patrons for abuse, could leave them, and had rights to property. The batlhanka, on the other hand, were a dependable and easily exploitable labor force.

The BaYei, it will be remembered, were a major economic force in Ngamiland. They were expert cultivators of the floodplain, innovative fishermen, and skillful canoeists who, in effect, operated the transportation system of the delta. Thus, access to grain, fish, and transport was through them. The BaTawana were pastoralists whose occupations centered around ownership of cattle; they could nevertheless tap a whole range of additional resources through some control over the BaYei. As we have seen, elaborate adminstrative systems of control over outlying areas were lacking, and here Tawana control and access to resources were to a large degree achieved through the clientship system. But in the core Tawana area, around the capital and in a few provincial centers, a more direct control over labor could be maintained. Here, clientship appears to have been redefined in hereditary terms and finally to have been transformed into serfdom. Eventually, additional serfs for the Tawana home area were recruited in the peripheral areas through the combined channels of political domination and clientship.

Control over the BaYei was facilitated because they were sedentary. The nomadic BaKgalagadi and the BaSarwa could simply disappear into the inaccessible parts of the Kalahari Desert, though the few captured ones became batlhanka. The lack of cultural affinities between the BaYei and the BaTawana did not militate against serfdom. The BaKgalagadi received better treatment and remained predominantly clients.

BATLHANKA RECRUITMENT

The batlhanka were secured in a variety of ways. In addition to the supply of individuals who had voluntarily attached themselves to wealthy families, many batlhanka were supplied by the district governors. They forced subordinate families, especially among the BaYei and the BaNoka, to give up their children. Although some people volunteered their services, the threat of force was always implicit. The Yei headmen and their families were exempt from serfdom, but their retention of their position implied cooperation with governors in obtaining batlhanka; they also benefited from this system because they kept some of the batlhanka for themselves. The governor also kept some of the youths for himself, the rest being taken to the king who distributed them among trusted headmen. The basemane, the group of officials who were the backbone of the king's political power and who were derived from Tawana commoners, received the largest number next to the king, followed by the royals. The batlhanka, therefore, were a currency of political patronage. (Schulz 1897: 323).

Batlhanka were also secured in other ways. A man sometimes attached one of his batlhanka to a friend's household; and childless people were sometimes given batlhanka by either the king or their wealthy relatives. For example, Moremi II gave some goats and two batlhanka to a Tawana woman who had lost her own children in the Tebele war of 1883 (Baldwin 1894:321-22). Letsholathebe I gave his friend, the trader Baldwin, a Sarwa boy (B.N.A., Williams 1901; interview: May 15, 1970). Prisoners of war were often made batlhanka; their numbers must have been small, since the BaTawana did not fight many wars after the Kololo invasion of the 1830s, though many of the BaGcereku captured during the 1893 war were made into batlhanka (Baldwin 1894:321-22; Leyland 1866:181).

Buying and selling batlhanka was not generally practiced. The activities of the mambari slave traders did not extend to Ngamiland, thanks perhaps to the swamps and the malarial environment of the delta, although they operated as far south as Andara. Only in rare instances were youths bartered for certain commodities within Tawana society. For example, some batlhanka came to be named kgomo (cow or ox) or tlhobolo (gun), because they had been exchanged for a cow or a gun. At one time the trader Baldwin exchnged some beads for the motlhanka of Letsholathebe I's uncle. Letsholathebe I and Moremi II sometimes purchased batlhanka from the slave-trading areas to the north, but this was extremely rare (B.N.A., Ellenberger 1926). At times, it seems, what Europeans reported as payment was, in fact, a token of appreciation rather than the actual monetary value of a motlhanka. The virtual absence of buying and selling might also be explained by the fact that batlhanka were needed for the internal economy, and were not regarded as a standard item of export.

THE STATUS OF BATLHANKA

The information about the relationship between the batlhanka and their masters given by nineteenth-century European observers must be handled with caution. Europeans failed to distinguish between voluntary clientship and botlhanka, referring to both systems as slavery and endowing this term with meanings associated in their minds with New World slavery. However, a few observant Europeans, such as the explorer Schulz, showed awareness of the problem: "When talking of slaves amongst natives, the term slave does not bear the same import as to the European mind . . . [the] position between master and slaves is more one of relative domesticity than actual slavery" (Schulz 1897:354).

Assessments by Europeans of botlhanka depended on their particular interests. Missionaries who sought to transform Tawana society by eradicating almost every local custom tended to exaggerate the abuses of the system. Their assessment depended also on whether or not they were friendly to a particular king; if the ruler was a Christian or cooperated with them, they accordingly modified their criticisms of botlhanka. The Reverend James Hepburn, who wanted to involve the London Missionary Society in missionary work in Ngamiland, gave the ending of the "terrible slavery" as the main justification for such an undertaking. When King Moremi II showed interest in church work and even became a Christian, Hepburn sang his praises and toned down criticism of botlhanka. By the 1880s, however, when the king abandoned Christianity, the same Hepburn protested loudly against the cruelty of the BaTawana to the serfs (Hepburn n.d.: 273-80).

The colonial administration was concerned to prevent criticisms of botlhanka by the antislavery groups in England. They therefore took the view that botlhanka was a "modified form of hereditary service recognized by native laws or customs which are not incompatible with the due exercise of Her Majesty's power and jurisdiction" (B.N.A., Stigand 1927). The men at headquarters suppressed critical reports by men-on-the-spot about botlhanka. Francis William Panzera, the resident commissioner, once

warned G. A. Stigand, the resident magistrate who had sent a scathing
report on botlhanka "for goodness' sake not to draw attention to slavery."
The last thing the administration wanted was to have questions about this
raised in Parliament. (B.N.A., Stigand 1927).

The point is made: written sources by themselves are inadequate for a
description of botlhanka. These sources together with oral data, however,
give a fairly clear picture of it.

The most distinctive feature of botlhanka, as contrasted with clientship,
lay in the realm of legal rights. Every freeman had the right to live where
he wished, provided the king allowed him to do so. The batlhanka were
permanently attached to the families of their masters and were inherited
with other property; their children automatically took on their status and
became hereditary serfs of their father's master (we shall say more on
status inheritance presently). A motlhanka could leave his master only if
the king found the latter guilty of cruelty. Even so, the king attached the
aggrieved motlhanka to his own ward or to a new master rather than set
him free, since freeing him would have threatened the system that was a
cornerstone of Tawana economy and polity.

The batlhanka were also denied the right of membership of a ward; they
were attached to Tawana households but did not become ward members.
They did not participate in public assemblies. They could not, therefore,
participate fully in the social, political, and ritual activities of the nation
because participation was through one's ward. This disability had several
serious implications.

Wardlessness meant denial of normal access to the courts of the realm.
Every lawsuit began in a local court within one's ward and was taken to
the king's court only when the local court failed to arrive at a decision. The
local courts were headed by batlhanka owners, who could not be expected
to sit in judgment against themselves, nor could they render justice to their
own batlhanka.

If he had grievances, a motlhanka could flee, but he risked being recaptured and punished. Generally the aggrieved serf fled to the king, to whom
he appealed directly for mercy. But the king's judgment in such cases
depended on his relationship with the accused master. If the master was
his favorite, he merely cautioned him, admonishing him to treat the serf
kindly, and returned the fugitive to him. Masters out of favor with the
king were normally deprived of their serfs and could even be punished.
Moremi II ordered that a MoTawana who had been cruel to his
motlhanka be half-drowned and flogged (Schapera 1959:170, 175). These
cases were settled out of court, unlike those involving freemen, which were
heard at public assemblies. That the king could intervene on behalf of the
batlhanka tended to mitigate abuse. But the system had as much to do

with the king's control over batlhanka owners—he could remove serfs from their households—as with justice for the serfs themselves.

Because they did not belong to wards, the serfs could not own property such as land and cattle, since agricultural and pasture lands were distributed according to wards by the king, who held the land in trust for the morafe. The ward heads then shared out the land among the households and families under their charge. The batlhanka, like dependent children, worked the lands and herded the cattle of the households to which they belonged. They were housed, fed, and clothed by their master, who often referred to them as his children.

How valid is the claim that masters treated the batlhanka like their children? To a limited extent, the analogy holds. A man derived concrete benefits from his children, including their labor, and they in turn had the right to be maintained by him. The nature and extent of parental control varied considerably with individual personalities; some parents were very strict, others were lenient. Children were expected to be obedient to their parents, and disobedience was punishable by lashing (Schapera 1959:170). All the above statements would also apply to the batlhanka. But the similarities between the sons of a man and his batlhanka were in fact superficial because the two did not enjoy the same legal status. Whereas on attaining adulthood one's sons, as a matter of right, could establish their own households and own property, the batlhanka could not. They were, therefore, perpetual dependents who never emerged from the "childhood" status. The laws of inheritance that gave a man's sons the right to inherit his property, succeed to his social status, and enjoy a host of other benefits and privileges did not apply to the batlhanka. The laws of primogeniture applied to Tawana inheritance—only the heir inherited the social position of his father—but the younger sons had a right to a portion of his wealth.

A man generally gave a trusted serf the cattle called *tswaela* or *latswa diatla*,[5] and also a portion of his field for the serf's own use. With respect to inheritance, a better analogy might be to say that the serf was more or less like a man's daughter, who could not inherit his property. Like the serfs, daughters received tswaela cattle from their fathers. But a daughter held these cattle in perpetuity, her children inheriting them after her death, whereas the motlhanka's situation was different. As long as he lived and remained loyal, the motlhanka benefited from this property, using the cattle with the master's permission. When he died, however, the

---

5. *Latswa diatla,* "to lick hands": the meaning is that a child who continually licks his hands has not had enough to eat; the serfs, in other words, never had enough cattle. (They were not, however, entirely without cattle.) *Tswaela,* "to earmark"; the meaning is that the master earmarked some cattle for a trusted serf.

property was not inherited by his children, but reverted to the master together with any property he had earned. Thereafter the master might allow the children of the dead serf to use the property, but again at his discretion and under the same conditions. In essence, then, the serfs were below the Tawana women and even children in status. Children eventually outgrew their childhood. Tawana women belonged to age-regiments, whereas it seems that the batlhanka did not.

Marriage practices are another indication of the subordinate position of the batlhanka. Since the serfs were considered of inferior status, marriage with them was discouraged. Of course, the Tawana system of preferred marriages partly explains why they could not intermarry with the serfs, who were invariably non-BaTawana. That cultural affinities influenced, to some extent, marriage between masters and serfs is demonstrated by the fact that among the BaYei trusted, able, male batlhanka married members of the master's household (daughters, sisters, and other dependents). But these serfs were invariably BaYei or BaKakhwe, whom the BaYei regarded as cousins. The practice, it seems, was for a master to betroth a member of his household to a serf in recognition of meritorious service, and such a motlhanka became free to go and lead a normal freeman's life on contracting the marriage. The children from such a marriage were automatically freemen, unlike the children whose parents were both batlhanka.

In some cases a Tawana master might use a female serf as a concubine, and the sons of such a union were sometimes considered junior sons enjoying the rights of freemen. Sons not so recognized automatically became his batlhanka. Social status influenced concubinage. The BaTawana preferred Kgalagadi to Yei or Sarwa women; the BaKgalagadi preferred members of their own group; and the BaYei preferred other BaYei and BaKakhwe. Occasionally, a master elevated a serf to the status of a wife. In such cases the woman and her children became free.

The above instances were an exception to the general practice, which was for a motlhanka to marry another motlhanka, usually from the same ethnic group. The laws of residence after marriage were adjusted to minimize the loss of serfs through marriage. The male serf moved to the household or ward of his wife's master, and the children from this union became serfs of their mother's master. A motlhanka, therefore, was expected to marry a female serf within his master's household, thus making it possible for the couple to reside at the male serf's household. At whichever household the couple lived, marriage arrangements ensured the integrity of the serf's family. The motlhanka lived with his wife and children in his own house within the master's homestead.

Bridewealth, bogadi, the basis of all marriages between individuals, was not required for batlhanka marriages, presumably because they did not own property. However, when a freeman married a serf—and this was rare—he paid bogadi to her master, who might give part of it to the girl's parents. This woman became free by virtue of marrying a freeman. For both male and female serfs, marriage to the free conferred free status. When bridewealth was paid, the man had a legal right to the children. If bogadi was not paid then the children belonged to the master of the woman, but strictly speaking he did not, when she married, assume the role of father as in normal marriages. The bridewealth was, it seems, a kind of compensation for his loss of the labor of the serf and her offspring.

CONCLUSIONS

The uncritical use of the word "slavery" with reference to the social relationships between the BaTawana and their subject peoples is unacceptable, as the foregoing description of these relationships demonstrates. Nor can it be denied that some form of slavery did exist.

Tawana society clearly was highly stratified on the basis of birth, social status, cultural affinity, and sometimes wealth. Thus a Tawana royal, however poor, always enjoyed higher social status than a wealthy Tawana commoner, and a Kgalagadi commoner held a higher social status in the eyes of the BaTawana than even the Yei headmen, because the BaTawana and the BaKgalagadi had cultural affinities.

Social stratification per se, however, did not necessarily mean that slavery existed. Although the BaKgalagadi were of lower status than the BaTawana, and the Yei headmen lower than the BaKgalagadi, they were not slaves in the strict sense of the word. They belonged to the client class, which enjoyed all the rights of freemen, although they were obviously less privileged than the BaTawana in many respects. However wealthy they were, for example, they invariably wielded less political power than the BaTawana.

This social stratification provided the structure within which clientship operated. Clients enjoyed all the rights of freemen and, in principle, ethnic stratification conditioned, rather than determined, clientship relationships. Clientship operated within each of the ethnic groups; between them, however, it followed the hierarchical order. BaTawana could have BaKgalagadi as clients, and BaKgalagadi could have BaYei as clients, but not the reverse. Also, however wealthy a non-MoTawana was, he never wielded as much political power as a MoTawana, however poor.

Clientship was a system that reinforced political control by the BaTawana. Remaining pastoralists who prized their way of life, the BaTawana could nevertheless benefit from other resources of Ngamiland (such as agricultural, fishing, and transport), which were exploited by the other groups through the system of clientship. This was particularly true for outlying areas, where a more direct control over the other groups would have required a far more elaborate administrative apparatus than the BaTa-wana possessed. In the Tawana home area, on the other hand, more direct control over a labor force was possible, and here clientship became transformed into a kind of hereditary serfdom: botlhanka.

The batlhanka can be cautiously referred to as "slaves" if we consider slaves to be those individuals who were denied the full rights of freemen. They had, for example, no access to the courts of the land, were inherited along with the other property of their masters, and had no title to property. On the other hand, the almost total absence of the exchange of the batlhanka for money makes me hesitate to use the word slaves. Botlhanka's continuity with clientship (which one would certainly not call slavery) is clear—a fact that is crucial both for understanding botlhanka and for defining it.

GLOSSARY

bogadi: bridewealth.
botlhanka: serfdom.
kgosana (pl. *dikgosana*): headman (of a ward).
kgosi: king.
kgotla: public assembly; a place where meetings are held; a ward.
mafisa: leased cattle.
mambari: middlemen traders between the Portuguese on the Angolan coast and the peoples of the interior. They were usually mulattoes.
mophato (pl. *mephato*): age-regiment.
morafe: nation.
Mosemane (pl. *basemane*): provincial governor (literally, boy or young man).
motlhanka (p. *batlhanka*): serf; dependent; servant.
motlhanka (pl. *batlhanka*) *wa lolwapa*: serf of the house.

REFERENCES

ORAL SOURCES
Tapes of these interviews are deposited in the Thomas Tlou Collection at the African Studies Association, Center for African Oral Data, in the Archives of Traditional Music, Indiana University, Bloomington, Indiana; and at the University of Botswana, Lesotho and Swaziland (Botswana Campus) library, Tlou Collection.

Baokuni, interview on May 15, 1970.
Kangumbe, interviews on April 22 and April 24, 1970.
Mosuga, interview on February 10, 1970.
Pheho, interview on April 17, 1970.
Pikinini, interview on May 27, 1970.
Ramaeba, interview on May 27, 1970.
Seidisa, interviews on March 3 and March 5, 1970.
Tawana group, interview on April 13, 1970.

UNPUBLISHED SOURCES

B.N.A.: Botswana National Archives, Gaborone.
Ellenberger, J., to the editor of *The Diamond Fields Advertiser,* January 22, 1926. Secretariat file 43/7.
Stigand to Dutton, March 7, 1927. Secretariat file 43/7.
Williams, A., to Resident Commissioner, September 1901. Resident Commissioner file 6/6.
Moichubedi. ca. 1948. Ditirafalo tsa Merafe ye Batswana. Maun, Botswana [The history of the Batswana nations]. A handwritten manuscript.
Tlou, Thomas. 1972. A political history of northwestern Botswana to 1906. Ph.D. dissertation, Univ. of Wisconsin, Madison.

PUBLISHED SOURCES

Andersson, C. J. 1855. Explorations in South Africa with route from Walfisch Bay to Lake Ngami. *Jl R. geogr. Soc.* 25:79-107.
Baldwin, W. C. 1894. *African hunting and adventure from Natal to the Zambezi, including Lake Ngami, the Kalahari Desert, etc., from 1852 to 1860.* London.
Chapman, J. 1868. *Travels in the interior of South Africa comprising fifteen years' hunting and trading.* London.
Great Britain. 1966. *Botswana, annual report.* London.
Hepburn, J. D. Undated. *Twenty years in Khame's country, and Pioneering among the Batawana of Lake Ngami.* London.
Kuper, A. 1969. The Kgalagadi in the nineteenth century. *Botsw. Notes Rec.* 2: 45-51.
_____. 1970. *Kalahari village politics: an African democracy.* London.
Leyland, J. 1866. *Adventures in the far interior of South Africa, including a journey to Lake Ngami, and rambles in Honduras.* London.
Livingstone, D. 1872. *Missionary travels and researches in South Africa.* New York.
Pollock, N. C. 1968. *Africa.* London.
Randall, D. 1957. *Factors of economic development and the Okavango Delta.* Chicago.
Schapera, I. 1952. *The Ethnic composition of Tswana tribes.* London.
_____. 1954. *Ditirafalo tsa Merafe ya Batswana.* [The history of the Batswana nations]. Cape Town.
_____. 1957. Marriage of near kin among the Tswana. *Africa* 27:139-59.

———. 1959. *A handbook of Tswana law and custom*. London.

———. 1962. *The Tswana: ethnographic survey*. London.

Schapera, I., and Van der Merwe, D. F. 1945. *Notes on the tribal groupings, history and customs of the BaKgalagadi*. Cape Town.

Schulz, A., and Hammar, A. 1897. *The new Africa: a journey up the Chobe and down the Okavango rivers, a record of exploration and sport*. London.

Silverbauer, G. B. 1965. *Report to the government of Bechuanaland on the Bushman survey*. Gaborone.

Stigand, G. A. 1923. Ngamiland. *Geogrl. J.* 62:401-19.

Vansina, J. 1968. *Kingdoms of the savanna*. Madison.

15

The Tuareg
of the Central Sudan

Gradations in Servility at the
Desert Edge (Niger and Nigeria)

Stephen Baier and Paul E. Lovejoy

Tuareg social institutions were characterized by gradations of status. At one end of the scale were slaves with little freedom, and at the other, a class of aristocratic leaders with nearly exclusive control of wealth and power.[1] In the Central Sudan, a term used here to refer to northern Nigeria and much of Niger, the Tuareg were primarily pastoral nomads, but their economy straddled the ecological frontier at the southern edge of the Sahara, and they invested in many aspects of trade and production throughout the region. In order to understand the functions of social stratification in this environment, it is necessary to view the Tuareg network as a whole and to examine the interaction between desert and savanna, an interaction which cut across ethnic boundaries. Expansion and contraction of economy and society at the desert edge were tied to shifts in climate, and to a lesser extent to political disturbances and warfare, both of which disrupted the fragile balance between nature and human activities in the arid lands. By examining the northern, nomadic

1. The authors would like to thank Igor Kopytoff and Suzanne Miers for their comments on an earlier draft.

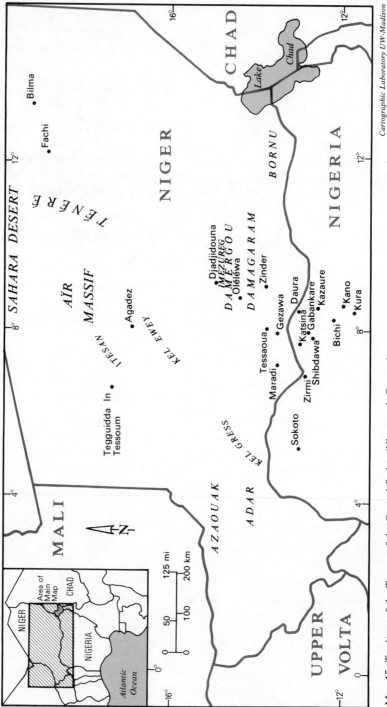

Map 15. Territory of the Tuareg of the Central Sudan (Nineteenth Century)

sector of the desertside economy in the context of the larger economic region of which it was a part, it is possible to isolate some crucial dynamics of this multitiered social system.

RECURRING DROUGHT

The recent Sahelian drought, which began in some places in 1968 and continued until 1973 or 1974, is one of a series of climatic cycles which have effected the Central Sudan over the centuries. Although the historical record is just beginning to be explored, the chronology of major droughts, presented elsewhere in greater detail (Lovejoy and Baier 1975), can be summarized briefly. The chronicles of the Central Sudan mention a seven-year drought in Bornu in the middle of the sixteenth century, an eleven-year famine in Kano at the turn of the seventeenth, and a seven-year famine in Bornu at the turn of the eighteenth. The dates of these events are tentative, since political chronology based on reign lengths remains to be worked out, but the impact on the desert edge was probably dramatic. Information on the eighteenth and nineteenth centuries is more complete. Another seven-year drought hit Bornu between 1690 and 1720, but it is not reported in the Hausa country, although it could have coincided with the famine among the Tuareg in the late 1690s. The major development of the eighteenth century was the drought of the 1740s and early 1750s, which struck all of West Africa and was more severe than any drought until the present one. Another occurred in the 1790s, and although it was not as devastating as the great drought of mid-century, it did force the evacuation of Agadez, caused the depletion of grain stores at Kano, and is probably to be identified with a drought that hit Bornu within the decade after 1793. The nineteenth century is remarkable for the absence of any prolonged droughts, and only one severe drought of a single year's duration, that of 1855, is reported. Years of localized shortages or inadequate rainfall are reported occasionally in the period 1860-90, but severe famine occurred again only after the turn of the century, when a worsening climate culminated in the drought of 1911-14.[2]

These climatic cycles were among the chief determinants of economic fluctuations and population shifts on the desert edge of the Central Sudan.

---

2. The sources for information concerning Central Sudan droughts are the following: "Kano Chronicle," as translated in Palmer (1929; 3:116-30); Diwan of Bornu, in Palmer (1936:94-95); Lavers (n.d.); Urvoy (1949:84-85); Urvoy (1934); Hill (1972:231), who quotes William Gowers, Nigerian National Archives at Kaduna, SNP 17, K2151 (1926). We wish to thank Adell Patton for showing us the original report by Gowers, and Humphrey J. Fisher for sending us a copy of a chronology of African droughts, which is based on substantially the same sources for the Central Sudan. For information on recent droughts, see Grove (1973, 1974), Mortimore (1973), Bernus (1973), and Bernus and Savonnet (1973).

Droughts, especially those lasting several years, set limits on the growth of the desertside sector, which was always more severely affected, since rainfall, even in good years, was marginal. The risks of drought increased the attractiveness of the southern edge of the desert, and this factor helps account for the present distribution of the Tuareg people, over 90 percent of whom are concentrated along the Sahel (Bernus 1966:11n.; Nicolaisen 1962; Lhote 1955:157; Clauzel 1962:24). Since the desert economy could not grow beyond a certain point, the forging of close links between desert and savanna was inevitable. The integration of the desert-edge sector into a larger economy permitted people to survive periodic droughts and to recoup their fortunes in good times.

DESERT-SAVANNA NETWORKS

Desert and savanna were bound together by commerce, for the Tuareg secured a living from the harsh desert environment through specialization in animal husbandry, trade, and transport.[3] Although their mobility and skill in warfare enabled them to dominate the relatively fertile areas of the Sahel, they also relied on trade in their relations with both Sahel and savanna. For the Tuareg of the Aïr Massif, Adar, Azaouak, and Damergou, this meant the areas centering on the Hausa states. These Tuareg could live on milk from their animals for extended periods of time, but they required grain to supplement their diet. Millet consumption averaged as much as 150 kilograms per person per year, a quantity much larger than could be supplied by the scattered and highly unreliable grain production of the Aïr or desert oases (Nicolaisen 1963:209, 213). The concentration of Tuareg along the southern fringes of the desert placed most of them in close proximity to farming villages and savanna markets, where they bought millet, clothing, other manufactures, kola nuts, and tobacco.

The income needed to purchase grain and manufactures was largely derived from the sale of animals (goats, sheep, camels, cattle, and horses), through the provision of services dependent on livestock production, and through involvement in the grain, date, and salt trade (Gadel 1907:361-86; Baier 1974:106-17; Grandin 1951:488-533). The requirements of the herds set limits on Tuareg settlement and economic activity, and the pattern which predominated was one of seasonal transhumance that provided a framework not only for animal husbandry but for trade as well (see Gaden 1903:626-28, 650; Dunbar 1970:203ff.; Barth 1857, 1:279-90, 389-93). During July and August, when some rain fell in the southern desert, herders took their animals to areas with the best pastures. Rainfal

3. The excellent ethnographic studies of Nicolaisen (1963, 1962, 1959, 1957) form the basis for much of the following discussion.

in the Aïr Massif was greater than in the surrounding countryside, so that pastures there held up long enough for a large contingent of the Aïr Tuareg, as well as others from the south and west, to make the annual trek across the arid Ténéré in late October and November to Bilma and Fachi, two oases north of Bornu on the route to North Africa. Here they purchased salt and dates and sold grain. Profits from this trade, together with earnings gained from services given to trans-Saharan commerce, were important supplements to Tuareg income. In December, after the return of the salt caravan, most Aïr Tuareg left for the south, selling salt, dates, and animals along the way, and pasturing the animals they were breeding. The Tuareg of the Adar and Azaouak, areas west of the Aïr Massif, also moved south during the dry season, although they were less involved in the salt trade. Some people moved as far south as Sokoto, Kano, and Katsina, although many others used pastures slightly farther north, just within the territory of the sedentary states along the desert edge. In June, when the rains began again, they left for the north, since the excessive dampness of the savanna at this time of the year endangered the health of the camels, and the return of land to cultivation hindered the free movements of herders.

At the end of the nineteenth century, one of the principal north-south corridors of trade and transhumance extended from Agadez through Damergou and Damagaram, and ended at Kano. The Kel Ewey confederation ("Kel Oui" in most French sources) dominated this route, and its members invested considerable capital in trade and production there. Sections of the Kel Gress confederation dominated the corridor that began at Tegguidda In Tessoum in the Azaouak, extended south through the Adar, and ended in the western Hausa cities (Bonte 1975, 1967:46ff.; Grandin 1951:524; Gaden 1903:626-28; Gadel 1907:374; Djibo Hamane 1975). But not all Tuareg in the Aïr, Azaouak, and Adar were as fully or directly involved in the economy of the savanna. The Kel Ferwan and Kel Fadai, for example, seem to have concentrated almost entirely on animal husbandry and had few direct contacts with their sedentary neighbors. They bought grain and other goods at Agadez and other northern market towns and rarely traveled into the savanna, but their animals were often exported south by livestock dealers from the savanna or Sahel. Such purely nomadic Tuareg, specializing almost entirely in animal husbandry, were less numerous than the Kel Ewey and Kel Gress, and they were less wealthy and less powerful. But even these people had to participate to some extent in the pattern of trade and transhumance described for the Kel Ewey and Kel Gress. Otherwise, they could not have satisfied their requirements for grain and manufactures.

The Tuareg, particularly the Kel Ewey, Kel Gress, and their associates, maintained an elaborate commercial infrastructure in the savanna to handle their business, and they invested heavily in real estate, slave labor, grain production, and such other opportunities as presented themselves (see Lovejoy and Baier 1975; Lovejoy 1973a; Baier 1974). All savanna towns had immigrants from the north who provided accommodation, brokerage, banking, and storage facilities for Tuareg merchants. These communities, which included craftsmen and other immigrants, formed the core of a commercial diaspora similar to other networks in West Africa (see Curtin 1975; Cohen 1971; Lovejoy 1973a, 1973b). Such communities were located not only in the major urban centers of Kano, Katsina, So-koto, and Zinder, but also in lesser towns such as Bichi, twenty miles northwest of Kano, which developed as a commercial center primarily because of its proximity to dry-season campgrounds and pastures. Similar communities existed at Zirmi in the Zamfara emirate, in the Sokoto area, and elsewhere. The town of Kura, twenty miles south of Kano, became a major textile center, largely because it satisfied Tuareg demand for turbans, veils, and other dark blue textiles (Lovejoy and Baier 1975); as in Bichi and other towns, the population of Kura included many northern immigrants (Barth 1857, 1:359, 377, 481, 486). In many instances, Tuareg merchants financed leather workers and other craftsmen by providing the raw materials needed for production.

The Tuareg also invested in farming estates throughout the Katsina and Kano emirates and in the Sahel, including Damagaram, Maradi, southern Adar, and Tessaoua (Lovejoy and Baier 1975; Barth 1857, 1:438, 526; 3:73, 564; Richardson 1853, 2:170, 179, 194; Lovejoy 1973a:93-95). These estates paid tribute in grain, which supplemented millet obtained from trade and other investments. More importantly, the sedentary communities provided a safety valve for nomads in times of scarcity. These dependent communities were bound to accommodate their patrons, and the estates along the north-south corridors of trade and transhumance provided resting places for the wealthy in good times and places of retreat in bad times.

An examination of the Tuareg economy within its wider regional context demonstrates the diversity of Tuareg activity, the complete disregard of ethnic boundaries for investment purposes, and the close integration of Tuareg society and economy with the savanna. The Tuareg protected their ecological niche in the north by maintaining a monopoly of camel transport and by their military might; but from this position on the frontiers of the Central Sudan they became an important source of capital and trained personnel for the region as a whole. This not only contributed to the general prosperity but also offered insurance to the nomads in times of scarcity.

TUAREG SOCIETY

This far-flung system enabled the Tuareg to adjust to changing economic and climatic conditions. When the Sahel received adequate rainfall, income from animal husbandry and trade could support a large population. In good times, the exploitation of the desert economy required the services of many herders, guides to accompany caravans, and farmers to till soil on the desert-edge and savanna estates. Herding in particular was labor intensive, since camels, cattle, sheep, goats, and horses had different pasture and water requirements, and consequently the Tuareg often divided their herds among followers who went in several directions. But when rainfall was inadequate, the large numbers of personnel became superfluous. The desert was suddenly unable to support its population, and competition over resources became acute. During a severe drought of several years, most Tuareg had to flee the desert for the savanna, where the effects of deficient rainfall were less pronounced. However, a hierarchical system of access to resources assured the survival of the system in bad times and its regeneration when climatic conditions improved. Indeed, Tuareg social stratification guaranteed that the power to make economic decisions remained in the hands of a few.

Political power in this desert society was fragmented. At the lowest level was the camp, which consisted of not more than five or six individual families of four or five members each, along with their dependents. There were perhaps half as many dependents as free Tuareg. The next largest grouping was the section, or *tawchit*, which might include as few as two or three or as many as ten or twenty camps. Male household heads of the noble clan of the section chose chiefs from the members of their own clan, but the election was usually confirmed by all the component clans of the section, since the tenure of chiefship depended on the willingness of all free members of the section to pay a small tribute to the chief each year (Briggs 1960:146; Jean 1909:175-76). At the next highest level was the drum group, or confederation, a group of sections recognizing a common leader. At the turn of the century, confederations numbered as many as ten thousand people in the case of the Kel Ewey, or as few as two or three thousand in the case of the Kel Fadai (Jean 1909:102-11; Nicolaisen 1962: 28; Lhote 1955:157). Together the noble clans of the confederations of the Aïr Tuareg elected the *amenokal*, or sultan, of Agadez, but this leader had no control over the people nominally under his command. His chief function was to conduct peaceful relations with outsiders or to lead expeditions against enemies, and in this respect his position resembled that of chiefs of confederations and sections. In this segmentary society, no leader had power over his followers solely by virtue of a position in the political hierarchy.

But wealth was enough to guarantee influence. Nobles (in Tamashek, *amajer,* pl. *imajeren*) in effect acted as managers of large firms and controlled most resources, although they constituted less than 10 percent of the nomadic population. They alone decided on war and peace; from their ranks came the political leaders; and they were the main patrons of Muslim clerics.[4] Indeed, the Tamashek language served as a specialized tongue of this elite and its immediate dependents, so that the nomadic sector of the desert-edge economy was kept distinct from the larger region and maintained its monopoly over resources.

The careers of several important nineteenth-century Tuareg merchants and financiers illustrate the power of the noble class. Two brothers, Annur and Elaiji, dominated Kel Ewey operations in the 1840s and 1850s. Annur was the most influential leader and in effect the titular head of the Kel Ewey confederation, while Elaiji ran the annual caravans to Bilma and Fachi. Between them they controlled thousands of camels, and owned estates at Kazaure, Gezawa, Zinder, Tessaoua, and in Damergou and Aïr. In the 1870s and 1880s, Alhaji Bilhou became preeminent among the Kel Ewey (see Bary 1898:101, 112, 116, 119, 126; Rennell 1926:436, 440); he financed merchants trading to Adamawa, controlled the movements of numerous nomadic dependents, and received tribute from sedentary villages, particularly in Damergou. A distant relative of his, who was a native of Ghāt, in the northern Sahara, acted as his agent in Kano. Another wealthy man was Muhammad Boro from Adar, who received the title Sarkin Turawa in recognition of his importance in the Kel Gress and Itesan caravan trade to Bilma in the 1840s and 1850s; in this capacity, Boro received a percentage of each camel load, a source of capital which financed other investments in the savanna and Sahel. Even deposed sultans of the important market town of Agadez (where political leadership changed frequently in response to shifts in the balance of power among the Tuareg sections) operated extensive commercial networks of their own. One man in the 1850s, for example, maintained commercial outlets in Sokoto, Agadez, Zinder, Kano, and Katsina (Lovejoy and Baier 1975; Lovejoy 1973a:126ff.; H. Barth 1857, 1:321, 323, 338, 343, 370, 3: 129; H. Barth, quoted in Petermann 1851:150). These are but a few of the best-known examples of Tuareg nobles and other important northerners who were involved in stock breeding, transport, trade, grain production on servile estates and villages, craft financing, and commercial brokerage. In other cases, however, individuals did not stand out so prominently, for

4. The discussion of stratification is based on Bernus (1966:12-15), Nicolaisen (1962: 100-107), Rennell (1926:135-40), Clauzel (1962), Richer (1924:3-5), Lhote (1955:191-208), and Nicolas (1939:580-82). The orthography used here for Tamashek words is from Courtade (1967), and the spellings are those given for the Aïr dialect in Clauzel (1962).

many Tuareg sections also acted as corporations, in which investments were managed collectively, though even here wealthy men could emerge (Dunbar 1970:196-98).

Thus, within the north-south corridors of their confederations and spilling over in the savanna, Tuareg nobles, individually and as corporations, controlled large networks of resources and people in varying degrees of servility and dependence. Below the aristocracy were various dependents, including employees, tenant farmers, herders who worked on contract, and slaves. The status of each of these depended on his position in the larger desert-edge system, and each was attached to a specific noble or noble section. They had varying degrees of freedom; they could be attached to a noble camp directly or they could nomadize in separate sections of their own. All these factors influenced the types of servility found among the Tuareg.

THE SERVILE STRATA

The assimilation of outsiders in Tuareg society took several forms. Tuareg took captives when they participated in wars between sedentary states, or during raids on sedentary people. Kel Ewey captives were often exchanged for those of the Kel Gress; by doing this, the Tuareg reduced the necessity of keeping a close watch on newly acquired slaves, who found themselves not only in an unfamiliar environment but also several hundred kilometers from the north-south transhumance corridor that led to their former homes (Gaden 1903:651). Once acquired, slaves became fully assimilated into Tuareg society, and their status began to evolve. Intermarriage between Tuareg men and servile women helped this process. The presence of many darker-skinned Tuareg in all social categories, especially among the Kel Ewey and Kel Gress, confederations with strong ties to the Sudan, suggests the historical importance of recruitment from the people of the savanna.

At the bottom of the status hierarchy were slaves called *iklan* (sing. *akli*); these were the newly purchased or captured people. Some were attached directly to their master and accompanied him on his travels; some were semisedentary; others farmed the estates of the Sahel and savanna. The *iklan-egef* (slaves of the dunes) of Adar, for example, lived in their own camps, and some of them farmed for three or four months of the year and resumed transhumance after the harvest (Bernus 1966:14-16; Lhote 1955:207; Nicolas 1947:113; Mainet 1965; Renard 1922). While farming, they kept their masters' animals and were allowed to keep proceeds from the sale of milk. They owed their masters a fixed annual payment in millet and a portion of the increase in their own herds, and they had to give them additional millet when needed.

In contrast to slaves who lived independently, iklan who were directly
attached to the camps of their masters were integrated into Tuareg society
at the level of the family. Slaves were fictive children and used kinship
terms to address members of the master's real family. The owner assumed
responsibility for bridewealth payments, just as he did for his real
offspring. His behavior toward the wives of his male slaves was similar to
the way he behaved toward real daughters-in-law. A man could marry a
female slave even though she was considered his "daughter"—a practice
that conformed to other situations in which men could marry classificatory
daughters. If a noble married his own slave, their children took on the
father's status; if he married a slave belonging to another man or woman,
he could claim nobility for the children by paying a high bridewealth to the
original owner. These practices followed the injunctions of Islamic law
(Nicolaisen 1962:100-105; Nicolaisen 1957).

In spite of the use of kinship analogies, the position of slaves was very
different from the position of real children. Iklan did most of the hard
work that needed to be done at or near the campsite. Male slaves tended
animals and drew water from wells, while female slaves cooked, brought
firewood to the campsite, and fetched water (Bernus 1973:33-40; Nicolaisen 1959). The standard of living of the slaves was in sharp contrast to
that of the nobles. Nobles wore fine clothing and owned decorated
weapons, and noble women possessed expensive jewelry. Conspicuous
consumption by the aristocracy simply reflected their control of productive
resources—animals and the labor of slaves and other dependents (Bonte
1975:66).

Rights to the ownership of iklan were vested in individuals. Both men
and women could own slaves, although in fact most owners were men. The
ownership of slaves was inherited within matrilineages, and newly acquired slaves were often included in the bridewealth. Once acquired,
slaves were rarely sold, since the main purpose in acquiring them in the
first place was assimilation into the lineage. The relatives of the owner
were considered the relatives of the slave (Nicolaisen 1962:100-106; Nicolaisen 1957; Lhote 1955:194-95; Rennell 1926:140-41).

In contrast to these nomadic and seminomadic slaves in the north and
west, the slaves of Damergou were permanently settled. Damergou,
located just within the limit of rainfall agriculture, about 250 kilometers
south of Agadez, was for centuries the principal granary of the Aïr and the
surrounding desert. Nobles belonging to the most important sections of
the Kel Ewey confederation had estates there and sometimes competed
among themselves for control of sedentary people. Two of the most
powerful factions at the end of the nineteenth century were the Kel Ewey
(whose leader, or *anastafidet,* had several estates near Oléléwa) and the

Imezureg, whose wealth derived from their control of the collection of ostrich feathers for the trans-Saharan trade. Iklan belonging to the anastafidet of the Kel Ewey lived separately in their own villages near Oléléwa; not far away were the estates worked by the iklan of the western Imezureg, whose capital was at Gangara (interviews: Atari Madiguburi, Fokondo Mala, Wuru d'an Tambari Mayaki; Baier 1973; Richardson 1853, 2:164-65).

Most inhabitants of estates farther south, in Damagaram, Kano, Katsina, Tessaoua, and other sedentary states, were apparently *irewelen,* or people of servile ancestry (Gaden 1903:632; Rennell 1926:135-36; Clauzel 1962:143-45; interview: Wuru d'an Tambari Mayaki). Since they were in effect freed slaves, their status was higher than that of iklan, although their daily life and material well-being differed only slightly. Like iklan, these people owed a portion of their harvest to Tuareg nobles, but otherwise they only had to lodge their masters during the dry season or during droughts. The irewelen of Katsina and Kano had a special name in Hausa, *Agalawa.* Over several generations they became fully assimilated into Hausa society, recognizing only a traditional connection with Tuareg lineages. Many of their descendants became successful savanna merchants specializing in importing kola. Their name was derived from the Tamachek term for south, *agali,* and their adoption of a corporate identity, indicated by special facial and body markings, helped maintain a social cohesion that proved useful in business (Lovejoy 1973a: 138-39). Until further research is done, it is not possible to say what proportion of the irewelen on the estates became merchants, or whether this pattern of assimilation was widespread in other areas. But research in Kano, Katsina, and Damagaram suggests that the descendants of northerners were represented in trading networks of the savanna far in excess of their proportion in the population at large (Baier 1974; Lovejoy 1973b).

In a different category were nomadic irewelen, whose life differed radically from that of sedentary Tuareg dependents. They engaged primarily in herding and trade, work involving higher prestige than the domestic tasks or farming assigned to the iklan and sedentary irewelen. They were attached to their former master's camp, but herding and running caravans on their master's account could take them far away for extended periods of time. It is not clear whether or not the passage from the status of iklan to irewelen was marked by a ceremony or other formal recognition, but fragmentary evidence from Zinder suggests that it may have been (interview: Cillo Alassan). In any event, iklan underwent a gradual upward evolution in status, with length of service, reliability, initiative, and other personal qualities playing a critical role in the process. Dependents tended to rise in status almost as soon as they entered the service of a Tuareg family, in part because master and servant increasingly shared common interests.

Intermarriage also affected status. In theory, the offspring of a marriage between free and servile Tuareg inherited the status of their mother, but in practice, children of freemen and servile women were also free (Nicolaisen 1962:105). Offspring of marriages between persons of different servile categories were known as *ibureliten* (sing. *abureli*). Abureli referred not only to a person's personal status, but might also denote membership in a collectivity. Ibureliten sections were transitional groups evolving toward the status of free Tuareg (Clauzel 1962:149-50; Lhote 1955:203-4). Sometimes a servile section, for example, might be granted freedom as a reward for services performed. This happened in the Azaouak in 1898, when a section known as Tamjert received its freedom after a courageous fight against Tuareg enemies from the Ahaggar Mountains (Lhote 1955:208).

A special category of nomadic irewelen and ibureliten were those who had to abandon livestock herding or who chose to take advantage of other opportunities in the savanna and consequently became sedentary savanna inhabitants. In Kano and Katsina, these people adopted a separate identity through the use of common facial markings and a corporate name, *Tokarawa*. Like the Agalawa, they invested in kola importing and over several generations became incorporated into Hausa society. Their previous servile status was indicated by the fact that they continued to call themselves *bugaje* (sing. *buzu*, fem. sing. *buzuwa*), a term the Hausa used for all low-status Tuareg. But, like the Agalawa, they had achieved complete emancipation from all servile obligations and severed all meaningful links with desertside society and economy (Lovejoy 1973a:138-39).

Another category of Tuareg dependents, the *imrad* (sing. *amrid*), can be roughly described as "clients." Most imrad lived in independent nomadic sections, and although their exact origins are not clear, it can be hypothesized that they were Tuareg or other nomads who had submitted to noble sections after losing their herds or suffering defeat in battle (Rennell 1926:136-38; Briggs 1960:136-37; Duveyrier 1864:334-35). Imrad paid tribute to noble sections and in return the nobles were bound to protect their charges from enemies (Lhote 1955:194-95). Unlike the other dependents, imrad participated in political life, though without the full political rights of the nobles. Imrad confirmed the election of the confederation chief, but their participation in the election was optional (Nicolas 1939:580). Apparently, rights to tribute from imrad sections were vested only in groups, not individuals, in contrast to the ownership of iklan by individuals (Nicolas 1939:581; Lhote 1955:194; Duveyrier 1864:

335).[5] The symbolic tribute that imrad paid to nobles was not nearly as important as the services imrad provided. They took charge of surplus animals and in return were entitled to a portion of the increase of the herd. Nobles could reclaim the original loan at any time. Relationships between imrad clients and their noble-section patrons could change in time, people being no more fixed in the imrad status than they were in the other dependent statuses.

Tuareg dependents were not necessarily Tuareg themselves, nor were those people attached to the Tuareg economic network. In Damergou, for example, free farmers lived in villages near Tuareg-owned estates. They were the descendants of Kanuri-speaking people who called themselves Dagera, and of Hausa. Both groups moved north in the late eighteenth and the nineteenth century to exploit frontier regions where game was plentiful and agricultural settlement was sparse. Since unattached sedentary people were in danger of being raided or captured by the Tuareg, they freely submitted to a Tuareg section, agreeing to pay tribute in return for protection (Baier 1973; Salifou 1971; Séré des Rivières 1965:191). In this respect, they were not very different from neighboring iklan. Although, unlike the iklan, they were technically free, they fitted into the same niche in the Sahelian network of trade and production, which spanned ethnic boundaries and extended from the desert far into the savanna.

To the outsider, the Tuareg seemed to make little distinction between their various types of dependents and all seemed to be well treated. All, for instance, shared the same basic diet, and all but those of the lowest status wore similar clothing (Nicolaisen 1962:102). Status was fluid and social distinctions were not always apparent to outsiders. Hausa-speaking people, for example, referred to all Tuareg of low status as bugaje, thus lumping together people of most dependent categories, slave and free, nomad and sedentary. This shows an unfamiliarity with the hierarchical system but accurately reflects their impression that the Tuareg treated most dependents alike. The nineteenth-century scholar Heinrich Barth was struck by the freedom of slaves at the Tessaoua estate of the Kel Ewey leader Annur:

The estate is very extensive, and consists of a great many clusters of huts scattered over the fields, while isolated dum-palms give the whole a peculiar feature. The

5. Ethnographic literature is vague on the nature of the relationships between owners and any of the many categories of dependents. Nor is information available detailing the evolution of these relationships during and after the transition to freedom. Further research is necessary. See Rennell (1926:140-41), Gaden (1903:632), Gamory-Dubourdeau (1924: 241ff.), Nicolas (1939:581), Lhote (1955:194), and interviews with Kelilan Gaja and Fokondo Mala.

people, all followers and mostly domestic slaves of Annur, seemed to live in tolerable ease and comfort, as far as I was able to see, my companion introducing me into several huts. Indeed every candid person, however opposed to slavery he may be, must acknowledge that the Tawarek in general, and particularly the Kel owi, treat their slaves not only humanely, but with the utmost indulgence and affability, and scarcely let them feel their bondage at all. Of course there are exceptions . . . . (Barth 1857, 1:439).

Furthermore, a servile nomad could easily change masters by cutting the ear of a camel belonging to a noble other than his master. Since a master was responsible for the actions of his slave, compensation had to be made for this symbolic transgression—and the slave was handed over to the person who had been "wronged" (Nicolaisen 1962:101-2; Nicolas 1939:582; interview: Cillo Alassan).

Desert life prevented close surveillance of dependents, and such good conditions were closely related to the ease of escape; for, once Tuareg owners left, mistreated individuals could flee south to join existing communities of immigrants from the north. A more important factor, however, was the possibility of drought in the Sahel: people had to be free to emigrate to save themselves. This was true of nomadic and sedentary dependents alike, as well as the free farmers of Damergou and Adar.

THE DROUGHT-TO-RECOVERY CYCLE

The threat of periodic droughts in the Sahel imposed the need to shift population relatively easily within the Tuareg north-south network. Rigid control over dependents would have prevented such movement from the desert to estates in the savanna in bad times, and their return in the opposite direction in good ones. As it was, movement within the network was automatic, assured by the system of priority of access to resources maintained by the stratification of status. The distinctions between different kinds of dependents—which had little importance in prosperous times[6]—came into play in periods of scarcity, when they provided a pattern for sloughing off excess population. The social system offered a clearly delineated blueprint of the order of precedence, from nobles down to iklan.

The operation of hierarchical claims to resources becomes clear through an examination of the drought-to-recovery cycle, when the social organi-

6. Static analysis of Tuareg social stratification led Bourgeot (1972) to the conclusion that status differences had no real meaning for the Tuareg and that the preoccupation of European ethnographers with Tuareg stratification reflects their own ideological bias and a readiness to see class and caste distinctions everywhere. Another observer noted that social stratification no longer had any important political consequences (Murphey 1967).

zation first contracted, then expanded, as the desert economy was able to support a smaller or larger population. Drought in the desert brought about a mass exodus of people trying to save themselves. Among the first to move south were the sedentary people living at the edge of the desert, whose crop failures gave them advance warning of the coming disaster (interview: Haruna Biriam). Servile nomads attached to a noble's camp were affected later, for they were treated as members of the family and were provided for as far as possible. Imrad and irewelen sections were in a worse position, since many of the animals in their herds belonged to nobles, who reclaimed them as soon as the magnitude of a crisis became clear. Consequently, servile nomads whose herds were too small to support them fled the desert to save what they could. If the drought lasted longer than one year, many turned to farming. Evidence from the early twentieth century suggests that the spillover from prolonged droughts was large indeed. As a result of the droughts of 1913 and the revolt of 1916, many immigrants from the north were permanently lost to the pastoral economy through sedentarization.

As their resources shrank, nobles, with their families and retinues, claimed the hospitality of their dependents in the savanna, both in the many Agalawa villages and in the servile villages and farms close to Tuareg grazing camps. Nobles remained at the southern end of their network until the end of the drought, when the herds began to increase. These southern communities in effect acted as a safety valve in times of scarcity. When rainfall returned to normal, nobles called together a few dependents who had been temporarily sedentary and together they returned to the desert.[7] As the herds recovered sufficiently to support a large population, they enlisted more dependents. Surplus animals were distributed from their herds, although the nobles retained ownership of these animals and could claim them again if conditions worsened. New slaves were acquired by purchase or, more commonly, by raiding and through participation in wars in the savanna. Also, farmers and hunters from the south joined the Tuareg in a dependent capacity of their own free will. The repopulation of Damergou by Hausa- and Kanuri-speaking

7. Far more is known about the movement of desert people toward the savanna than the movement in the opposite direction. One reason is that the sedentarization accompanying the drought of 1911-14 was so extensive that it attracted the attention of colonial administrators (see Gamory-Dubourdeau 1924). In addition, the studies that have been made have not been researched from the northern, desert side of the Tuareg regional network. Of Tuareg ethnographers, Nicolaisen (1957, 1962, 1963) gives most emphasis to links between desert and savanna. For a theoretical discussion of movement across ethnic boundaries, see F. Barth (1969).

immigrants in the nineteenth century, when climatic conditions were favorable, is an example of this kind of movement.

THE SOUTHERN EXPANSION OF TUAREG NETWORKS

The establishment of Tuareg-related communities in the savanna eventually resulted in establishment of a permanent population in the south, which, even while providing a certain reservoir for population shifts back toward the desert, became increasingly rooted in the savanna, growing through natural increase and providing a ready niche for individual as well as group movements into the savanna.

It was not only in times of drought that a southward population movement occurred. A constant, if less dramatic flow away from the desert edge took place in prosperous times as well, partly as a result of individual success in the desert. The desertside sector entailed many risks for investors, be they merchants, farmers, hunters, or pastoralists, but its potential profits were sufficient to attract people. In time, those who prospered in the desert would reinvest their accumulated capital in the savanna—to expand their activities, or to withdraw after minor local crop failure or loss of animals, or as an insurance against potential disasters in the riskier desert. In brief, the desert provided profits which could then be invested in safer economic ventures in the savanna. Such movements to the south, in addition to those impelled by droughts, resulted in the existence of whole communities in the savanna that were tied to the Tuareg network and that had been settled by servile people from the north. Each maintained a separate identity that depended upon the pattern of immigration and occupational specialization. Many were merchants, particularly the Adarawa (people from Adar) in Sokoto, the Agadesawa and Asbenawa (people from Agadez and Aïr, respectively), in Katsina and Kano. Others were craftsmen at the Kura textile center, processed dried, spicy meat (*kilishi*) in Kano and Katsina, or were leather workers in Kano and Zinder (Lovejoy and Baier 1975; Lovejoy 1973a: 93-95).

The Agalawa and Tokarawa perhaps provide the most dramatic example of people connected with the Tuareg network who prospered in the savanna (Lovejoy 1973a:131-77). They were so successful as kola traders that their names became synonomous with the kola-importing business, and they accounted for as much as half of the professional class of merchants who dominated the important export-import trade with Asante, the middle Volta basin, and Borgou. The first Agalawa concentrations were near Katsina, the most important eighteenth-century Hausa commercial center, but after 1800 many people left these early settlements for the Kano area, where an economic boom attracted immigrants. There were at least fifty villages in which Agalawa and Tokarawa were to be found, often together, by the last third of the nineteenth century. By the middle of that century, a majority of both groups were in the city of Kano and its environs.

The related villages of Shibdawa and Gabankare, twenty miles southeast of Katsina, were typical of early Agalawa estates. In the 1850s these belonged to Sidi Ghalli al-Hajj Annur, "one of the first men of Agadez" and an influential "war-chief" from Adar, who mediated a dispute between the Kel Ewey and Kel Gress sometime before 1850 (Lovejoy 1973a:145-50; Barth 1857, 1:340, 371, 481). Their inhabitants traded extensively in kola nuts, Bornu salts, and other goods, and many moved to Kano Emirate, where they founded autonomous communities and severed their servile ties. The most prosperous Shibdawa offspring was Tambarin Agalawa Yakubu of Kano City, one of the wealthiest Hausa merchants in the last third of the nineteenth century. He owned many slaves settled in villages around Kano, maintained a business residence that could accommodate 120 dependents, and imported as much as eighty to one hundred donkey loads of kola each year, equivalent to four or five tons. He was related to people in a number of villages in the Kano countryside, including some at Lambu, west of Kano, and others at Zaibanawa, north of the city. Not many Agalawa were as prosperous as Yakubu, least so those who stayed in the villages; but kinship and friendship relations provided the ambitious with useful contacts in business, especially in the formation of caravans. Most Kano communities included settlers from the Katsina area and from farther north who had moved to Agalawa locations, adopted the same corporate name and body markings, and invested in kola, although all Agalawa also farmed in the rainy season.

Despite their nomadic origins, the Tokarawa followed a pattern similar to that of the Agalawa. Many had relatively humble backgrounds and built up modest businesses in kola importing, but in some cases individuals became very wealthy. The fathers of two of the most important nineteenth-century caravan leaders were successful cattle dealers who reinvested in kola. Their sons, Madugu Isa na Zarahu and Madugu K'osai, were among the wealthiest Hausa commoners, operated extensive business establishments in Kano City, and owned large estates of their own in the countryside (Lovejoy 1973a:150-59; Lovejoy and Baier 1975). Within only a couple of generations, these and other Tokarawa and Agalawa transformed their status from one of dependency in Tuareg society to one of prosperity and independence in Hausa society. Their movement suggests a pattern that was probably followed by many other immigrants.

CONCLUSIONS

The gradations in servile status that characterized Tuareg social structure had both a spatial and a temporal dynamic. Temporally, servile institutions altered according to the drought-recovery cycle. Spatially, they operated within the wide region that encompassed the desert edge and included the savanna regions of the Central Sudan. Two main patterns emerge. First, both servile and free people were recruited in the north during good times, merging, in time, into the general population of Tuareg dependents. Second, a reverse emigration, to the south took place in two different ways: the first and most striking was the mass exodus during bad times, which led to poverty and sedentarization, while the second involved a steadier but smaller emigration in good years as a consequence of localized famine or the desire to take advantage of new opportunities in the savanna. This smaller emigration led in most cases to a rise in status within the host Hausa society and the weakening of ties to Tuareg society. The dynamics of both the spatial and temporal gradients were made possible by the existence of a regional economy in the Central Sudan, of which the desert edge was only a part, albeit an important part whose diversification involved the exploitation of opportunities in both the desert and the savanna. The regular movements of people across ecological and ethnic frontiers indicate that the boundaries between Tuareg and Hausa societies reflected their respective regional specializations, and served to enhance the interaction between them rather than to isolate the one from the other. Hence, in order to understand the gradations in servility in Tuareg society, it is necessary to examine them both historically and regionally. Viewed statically, Tuareg society might appear rigidly stratified, but considered in the larger context of the Central Sudan, the stratification emerges as a flexible strategy that assured the continued domination by a small class of aristocratic Tuareg of sectors of a highly competitive regional economy.

GLOSSARY

abureli (pl. *ibureliten*): a descendant of parents of mixed servile categories.
Agalawa: literally, "southerners"; Tuareg who migrated to the savanna.
akli (pl. *iklan*): slave.
amajer (pl. *iklan*): a Tuareg noble.
amenokal: the leader of the Aïr Tuareg elected by the leaders of the Aïr confederations.
amrid (pl. *imrad*): a nomadic client.

anastafidet: the leader of the Kel Ewey confederation.

buzu (fem. sing. *buzuwa,* pl. *bugaje*): the Hausa name for a Tuareg of low social status.

iklan-egef: slaves living in independent sections.

irewelen: descendants of slaves, often living independently and engaged in either
nomadic or sedentary occupations.

kilishi: spiced, dried meat.

tawchit: a section; a grouping of people in the segmentary structure, smaller in
size than the confederation.

Tokarawa: servile Tuareg who migrated to the savanna.

REFERENCES

ORAL SOURCES

Tapes of the interviews are deposited in the Baier Collection at the African Stud-
ies Association, Center for African Oral Data, Archives of Traditional Music,
Indiana University, Bloomington, Indiana. Copies are deposited at the Centre
Régional de Documentation pour la Tradition Orale, Niamey, Niger.

Atari Madiguburi, interview on October 14, 1972.
Cillo Allassan, interview on October 20, 1972.
Fokondo Mála, interview on October 13, 1972.
Haruna Biriam, interview on October 14, 1972.
Kelilan Gaja, interviews on April 18 and April 19, 1972.
Wuru d'an Tambari Mayaki interviews on October 12 and October 14, 1972.

UNPUBLISHED SOURCES

Baier, S. 1973. The trade of the Hausa of Damerghou, 1900-1930. Paper presented at the sixteenth annual meeting of the African Studies Association,
Syracuse, New York.
_____. 1974. African merchants in the colonial period: history of commerce in
Damagaram (central Niger) 1880-1960. Ph.D. dissertation, Univ. of Wis-
consin, Madison.
Djibo Hamane. 1975. Adar, the Tuareg, and Sokoto: relations of Sokoto with
the Hausawa and Tuareg during the nineteenth century. Paper presented to
the Sokoto Seminar, February 1975, Sokoto, Nigeria.
Dunbar, R. A. 1970. Damagaram (Zinder, Niger), 1812-1906: the history of a
Central Sudanic kingdom. Ph.D. dissertation, University of California at
Los Angeles.
Lavers, J. Undated. Preliminary outline, Chapter VI, Nigerian History Project.
Lovejoy, P. E. 1973a. The Hausa kola trade: a commercial system in the con-
tinental exchange of West Africa. Ph.D. dissertation, Univ. of Wisconsin,
Madison.

Salifou, A. 1971. Rivalités tribales et intervention française au Damerghou. Unpublished paper, August 1971.

PUBLISHED SOURCES

Barth, F. 1969. *Ethnic groups and boundaries: the social organization of cultural difference.* Boston.

Barth, H. 1857. *Travels and discoveries in North and Central Africa.* 3 vols. New York.

Bary, Erwin de. 1898. *Le dernier rapport d'un Européen sur Ghât et les Touareg de l'Air (journal de voyage d'Erwin de Bary (1876-1877).* Tr. by H. Schirmer. Paris.

Bernus, E. 1966. Les Touareg du sahel nigérien. *Cah. d'outre-mer* 19:5-34.

——. 1973. Drought in the Niger Republic. *Savanna* 2:129-32.

Bernus, E., and Bernus, S. 1975. L'évolution de la condition servile chez les Touaregs saheliens. In *L'esclavage en Afrique précoloniale,* ed. C. Meillassoux. Paris.

Bernus, E., and Savonnet, G. 1973. Les Problèmes de sécheresse dans l'Afrique de l'Ouest. *Présence afr.* 88:113-38.

Bonte, P. 1967. *L'élevage et le commerce du bétail dans l'Ader Doutchi-Majya.* Etudes nigériennes, No. 23. Niamey.

——. 1975. Esclavage et relations de dépendance chez les Touaregs Kel Gress. In *L'esclavage en Afrique précoloniale,* ed. C. Meillassoux. Paris.

Bourgeot, A. 1972. Idéologie et appelations ethniques: l'exemple twareg. *Cah. Etud. afr.* 48:533-53.

Briggs, L. C. 1960. *Tribes of the Sahara.* Cambridge, Mass.

Clauzel, J. 1962. Les hiérarchies sociales en pays Touareg. *Trav. Inst. Rech. sahar.* 21:120-75.

Cohen, A. 1971. Cultural strategies in the organization of trading diasporas. In *The development of indigenous trade and markets in West Africa,* ed. C. Meillassoux. London.

Courtade, J. M. 1967. *Lexique français-tuareg, dialecte de l'Ahaggar.* Paris.

Curtin, P. D. 1975. *Economic change in precolonial Africa: Senegambia in the era of the slave trade.* Madison.

Duveyrier, H. 1864. *Les Touaregs du nord.* Paris.

Gadel, H. 1907. Notes sur Bilma et les oases environnantes. *Revue colon.* 7: 361-86.

Gaden, H. 1903. Notice sur la résidence de Zinder. *Revue Troupes colon.* 2:608-56, 2:740-94.

Gamory-Dubourdeau, P. 1924. Etude sur la création des cantons de sédentarisation dans le cercle de Zinder, et particulièrement dans la subdivision centrale (arrondissement de Mirria). *Bull. Com. Etud. hist. scient. Afr. occid. fr.* 8:239-58.

Grandin, Capitaine. 1951. Notes sur l'industrie et le commerce du sel au Kawar et en Agram. *Bull. Inst. fr. Afr. noire.* 13:488-533.

Grove, A. T. 1973. A note on the remarkably low rainfall of the Sudan zone in 1913. *Savanna* 2:133-38.

_____. 1974. Desertification in the African environment. *Afr. Affairs* 73:137-51.

Hill, P. 1972. *Rural Hausa: a village and a setting.* Cambridge.

Jean, C.-C. 1909. *Les Touareg du sud-est: leur rôle dans la politique saharienne.* Paris.

Lhote, H. 1955. *Les Touareg du Hoggar.* Paris.

Lovejoy, P. E. 1973b. The Kambarin Beriberi: the formation of a specialized group of Hausa kola traders in the nineteenth century. *J. Afr. Hist.* 14:633-52.

Lovejoy, P. E., and Baier, S. 1975. The desert-side economy of the Central Sudan. *Int. J. Afr. hist. Stud.* 8:551-81.

Mainet, G. 1965. L'Elevage dans la région de Maradi. *Cah. d'outre-mer* 69:32-72.

Mortimore, M. 1973. Famine in Hausaland, 1973. *Savanna* 2:103-7.

Murphey, R. F. 1967. Tuareg kinship. *Am. Anthrop.* 69:163-70.

Nicolaisen, J. 1957. Slaveri hos Tuaregerne i Sahara: Foreløbig analyse af dets struktur. *Kuml.* Pp. 91-113.

_____. 1959. Political systems of the Tuareg of Air and Ahaggar. *Folk* 1:67-131.

_____. 1962. *Structures politiques et sociales des Touaregs de l'Air et de l'Ahaggar.* Etudes nigériennes, No. 7. Paris.

_____. 1963. *Ecology and culture of the pastoral Tuareg of Ayr and Ahaggar.* Copenhagen, Nationalmuseet, Ethnografisk raekke, Vol. 9. Copenhagen.

Nicolas, F. 1939. Notes sur la société et l'état chez les Twareg du Dinnik. *Bull. Inst. fr. Afr. noire* 1:579-86.

_____. 1947. La transhumance chez les Iullemmeden de l'est. *Trav. Inst. Rech. sahar.* 4:111-24.

_____. 1950. *Tamesna: les Ioullemmeden de l'est.* Paris.

Palmer, H. R. 1928. *Sudanese memoirs.* 3 vols. Lagos.

_____. 1936. *Bornu Sahara and Sudan.* London.

Petermann, A. 1851. Progress of the African mission, consisting of Messrs. Richardson, Barth, and Overweg, to central Africa. *Jl R. geogr. Soc.* 21: 130-221.

Renard, J. 1922. Etude sur l'évolution des Kel Geres vers la sédentarisation. *Bull. Com. Etud. hist. scient. Afr. occid. fr.* 2:252-62.

Rennell, of Rodd, F. J. 1926. *People of the veil.* London.

Richardson, J. 1853. *Narrative of a mission to central Africa.* 2 vols. London.

Richer, A. 1924. *Les Touaregs du Niger (région de Tombouctou-Gao): les Oulliminden.* Paris.

Séré des Rivières, E. 1965. *Histoire du Niger.* Paris.

Urvoy, Y. 1934. Chroniques d'Agadès. *J. Soc. Afric., Paris* 4:145-77.

_____. 1949. *Histoire de l'empire de Bornou.* Paris.

Slavery
and Emancipation
under Colonial Rule

Part VII

16

Slavery and Emancipation among the Mende in Sierra Leone

1896-1928

John J. Grace

Slavery was not abolished in the British protectorate of Sierra Leone until 1928. Until then, the institution of slavery had played an important role in the life of the Mende, and it continued to do so afterwards in a variety of thinly disguised forms.

If the origins of the Mende people and their institutions are not at all clear, what is certain is that most British observers were wrong about Mende slavery. Official and unofficial circles argued that slavery dated back to the beginnings of West African social structures. Like Sir Frederic Cardew, governor of Sierra Leone late in the nineteenth century, they believed that slavery had been embedded in the manners and customs of the people there since time immemorial (P.R.O., Cardew 1894). Fox Bourne, secretary of the Aborigines Protection Society, wrote that African slavery had existed since prehistoric times—though he otherwise very rarely agreed with Cardew and other British officials (Fox Bourne 1900:1-5).

Anthropological research indicates that the Mende are a mixture of different peoples (Little 1967:21). The historian Rodney regards them as a

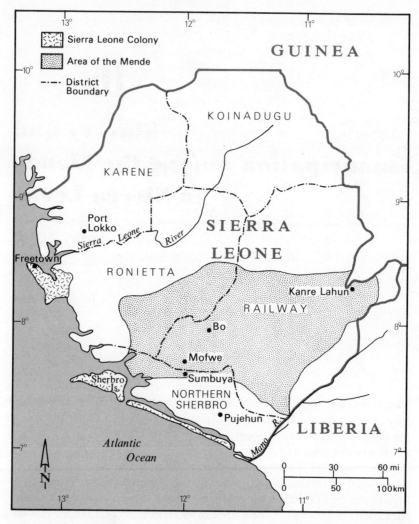

Map 16. Sierra Leone in 1912

Cartographic Laboratory UW-Madison

fusion of Mane invaders with aboriginal Bullom and Kissi peoples in the sixteenth century (Rodney 1967). He also believes that Mende slavery developed when the Mane invaders enslaved the indigenous peoples they conquered; relying too heavily on the evidence of early Portuguese travelers, he concludes that there was no slavery on the upper Guinea coast (which includes Mende territory) during the sixteenth and seventeenth centuries (Rodney 1966).

It cannot be as simple as that. It is probable that the autochthonous peoples had social institutions akin to slavery. The slavery imposed by the Mane cannot have been entirely new to those whom they had conquered. It does seem likely that the Mane introduced a harsher form of servitude or slavery. More important was the impact of the European presence in the area. The demand, first, for slaves to ship across the Atlantic and, subsequently, for legitimate trade in the nineteenth century undoubtedly adversely affected West African slavery. The writings of travelers, traders, missionaries, and officials confirm this; the European presence, both before and after the decline of the transatlantic slave trade, encouraged the growth of a harsher and more extensive type of slavery (Curtin 1964:402, 452; Hargreaves 1965:38-40).

Before 1896, when Britain extended her authority over Mende territory by proclaiming the Sierra Leone Protectorate, Mende slavery probably passed through three stages. First was the comparatively benign form of servitude among the aboriginal inhabitants; second was the harsher form imposed by the Mane conquerors; third was the distortion of the African form of servitude by the impact of the Europeans.

Late in the nineteenth century the political, social, and economic organization of the Mende varied from chiefdom to chiefdom. Despite the varying impact of the Europeans, Mende institutions were still primarily the product of indigenous forces, and it is possible to arrive at a general picture of Mende society. The sources of information are mostly official, but it is possible to obtain a reasonably accurate picture by cross-checking and sifting out obviously unreliable and prejudiced reports. Some protectorate officials were genuinely interested in and concerned with the people there, and used years of experience to collect useful information which was relayed to the governor and to the Colonial Office in their reports.

MENDE SOCIETY

Early in the twentieth century there were about half a million Mende: 557,674, according to the 1921 census (P.P., 1928, Cmd. 3020:45). Most of them lived in the southern part of the protectorate. In 1915, there were fifty Mende chiefdoms, each from forty to four hundred square miles in area;[1] thus, the average population of a chiefdom was about 11,000 people. Mende chiefdoms were less rigidly organized than those of the Temne, the other numerous group of people in the Sierra Leone Protectorate. Chiefdoms and subchiefdoms were ruled by paramount chiefs and subchiefs, with the help of advisers. Sometimes there was a definite line of chiefly succession to the sons or brothers of previous chiefs; in other

1. These estimates are based in information from Clarke (1969); *Parliamentary Papers* (1928, Cmd. 3020); and two P.R.O. documents: C.O. 271/21, XLVI, No. 1536, and C.O. 267/503/16672. The latter is particularly useful.

cases, any important person in the chiefdoms was eligible. A few of the paramount chiefs were women. The heads of families had some voice in electing or confirming the election of chiefs.

After the chiefs, the official advisers or elders ranked second in the chiefdom; these were usually older men, often the heads of the most important families. Then came the ordinary freemen, members of one of the established and recognized families. There was also a second class of freemen, who were strangers to the chiefdom or were descendants of strangers, and were under the protection of an important family. These clients were quasi freemen, usually regarded as freemen but having some form of obligation to their patrons. They or their ancestors might have been strangers who had sought the protection of a powerful person during periods of local warfare or slave raids. In some cases, their ancestors had been slaves and they were unable to leave their former chiefdom with their personal property. The obligations of the clients were usually to help their protectors if they were attacked and to cultivate their protectors' farms.

The pawns, or pledges, ranked below the clients. They were usually treated as slaves, but it was comparatively simple for them to retain their freedom. The system was that a debtor could pawn himself or a member of his household to his creditor as security for the repayment of a debt. The pawn was in bondage to the creditor until the debt was repaid, and his services could almost be regarded as interest payments on the debt.

The slaves were the humblest members of Mende society. It is not easy to give a simple description of Mende slavery. Aspects of the institution changed from year to year and could vary greatly from village to village and even from master to master. Another problem is that observers strongly disagreed as to the nature of domestic slavery, and their opinions about the institution were based more on prejudice and preconceived notions than on facts. Yet another difficulty is that I have had to use official information about areas where the Mende were numerous without being absolutely sure that the writer was specifically referring to Mende. An even greater problem is the lack of reliable statistics about the number of Mende slaves. Late in the nineteenth century they were a large proportion of the population, perhaps about half (P.P., 1899, C. 9391:2730-31, 853). Despite these difficulties, it is possible to do two things: to write about the usual characteristics of Mende slavery, and to point out various examples of it at its most benign and its most severe.

MENDE SLAVERY

The Mende word for slave is *nduwe* (pl. *nduwanga*).[2] Some chiefs argued that "slave" was an inaccurate translation of nduwe, but these

2. Crosby (1937). "A slave" is *nduwe* (pl. *nduwanga*); "the slave" is *nduwei* (pl. *nduweisia*).

attempts seem to have been motivated as much by their awareness of European condemnation of slavery as by their genuine desire to make the situation clear to European observers. It is false to argue, as Roy Lewis (1954:73) has done, that slavery in Sierra Leone was only domestic or feudal servitude. To be sure, chiefs stressed the familial aspect of slavery and masters were in fact addressed as *keke* (father). In one area, chiefs told an official that *ke ma lenga* was a term of relationship as applicable to nduwanga as to brothers, sisters, and cousins.[3] The Creole leader Sir Samuel Lewis testified that slaves were attached to their masters by the "patriarchal idea" and that they occupied the same position as free sons (P.P., 1899, C. 9391:2742). On some occasions, Mende rulers spoke of slaves as their "children" (P.P., 1899, C. 9391:4108-13, 4146, 4208).

It is clear that nduwanga were not like other members of the family. Yet the notion of kinship had much to do with their position in the household, especially if they had been born there and were regarded as slaves of the house. Most second- and third-generation slaves were related to freeborn members of the family—they shared the same father or grandfather—and this meant that they were better treated than the trade slaves and the newly acquired domestic slaves. The trade slaves (there were few of them left after years of British action to suppress slave trading) were badly treated and were looked after only to protect their owner's investment. A newly acquired slave was treated harshly until he or she showed signs of settling down in the new household. After years of faithful service, slaves were usually better treated, but there was little hope of freedom for the first-generation slave.

Even when they were fairly well treated, nduwanga and their descendants had little hope of ever achieving true equality with the free. Even if observers found it hard to distinguish between slave and free, the stigma was a very real one for a number of generations. The nduwanga had a prescribed code of conduct, which made their inferior status clear. After describing how the freeborn greeted each other, T. J. Alldridge, for many years a trader and an official in Mende country, wrote: "Slaves merely cringe up and place their two hands one on each side of their master's hand, and draw them back slowly without the fillip, while the head is bowed" (Alldridge 1901:62-63). He observed that nduwanga were apt to be looked down upon; in a heated discussion, they could be reminded that they were "born in the yard" and were consequently inferior to the others (Alldridge 1910:212). The Reverend W. Vivian, for many years a missionary among the Mende, also noted this stigma of slavery: "Of course, rice is the chosen food; cassada is the food of the poor and the slave. The freeborn will scarcely eat cassada if they can get rice, and to like cassada is

3. P.R.O., Merewether, January 9, 1912, which transmits memorandum by Dr. Maxwell. Further enquiries have failed to show that ke ma lenga is or was an accepted term.

taken as a sign of ill-breeding, it being regarded as a choice sneer for an enemy to tell him that 'he eats cassada like a slave' " (Vivian 1896:15).

Moreover, older nduwanga did not receive the respect normally given to older freemen; even when old, they could still be addressed as "boys" (P.P., 1899, C. 9391:4146). Their status remained inferior, even if they enjoyed some of the privileges of kinship, such as giving their opinions on matters affecting the family. They were minors who would never grow up and who would never receive the respect due a mature adult.

To a limited extent, nduwanga were protected from serious maltreatment by customary law and the traditional authorities. They had no right to sue on their own behalf in the customary courts, but others could act for them. The traditional authorities could intervene on their behalf by ordering their masters to stop ill-treating them or by forbidding the punishment of nduwanga without the consent of the chief. District Commissioner J. S. Fenton, who wrote the very useful *Outline of Native Law in Sierra Leone,* reported in 1924 that: "The slave is not a person; he cannot make a contract; he can have little interest in his work; . . . At any time the master may consider his slave guilty of misbehavior or disobedience and at once depress him to his theoretical condition of duties without rights. The slave becomes simply property" (S.L.A., Bo: Fenton 1924).

Like other forms of property, nduwanga were heritable. They belonged to the family. When the head of the family died, they were part of the estate that was shared out among the heirs; they could also be part of the dowry of their owner's daughter.[4] As late as the 1920s, the death of a master could prove a rude shock to nduwanga who had lost their lenient old master and passed into the possession of an heir who was determined to enforce to the full his rights as a slave owner (S.L.A., Bo: Fenton 1924).

As property themselves, nduwanga could not exercise property rights. Whatever they had belonged to their masters. They were allowed the use of land to feed themselves and their families, and in some cases they were allowed a share in the products of their labor. Yet, at redemption or because of a master's whim, nduwanga could lose everything. Only in exceptional cases could a slave acquire property that was truly at his disposal. For example, a master might have told his slave to plant some land with ginger and promised to reward his industry with one bushel in every ten to dispose of as he thought fit. If the slave sold his share of the ginger and bought a ring with the proceeds, this ring would be regarded as

4. West African Lands Committee, Evidence of Major Fairtlough, November 15, 1912, 6316-19. S.L.A., Pujehun: Out Letter Book, Vol. 2, Northern Sherbro, 1916-17, p. 43, No. 13/1917.

his property; but the burden of proof would be on the slave (S.L.A., Bo: Commissioner 1927).

Generally, nduwanga could not reap the rewards of their initiative and energy. If, for example, one set up as a trader, the whole business would go to the master at the slave's death, if not before. Chief George of Mofwe told the local district commissioner that if his seven nduwanga had survived their service as carriers in the East African campaign during World War I, he would have taken all their pay; out of the thirty-five pounds due them, he would have given each a present of five or ten pounds, according to his esteem for each man (S.L.A., Bo: Stocks 1924). Clearly, slave owners did well out of their property as long as slavery was legal, even after building houses and paying hut tax for their nduwanga. The slave owners were men of substance—usually the leading citizens of a Mende town. Though there were some humble slave owners, most of the slaves, like most of the wives, belonged to a handful of people in each community. Late in the nineteenth century a Creole trader who had had many years of experience in Mende territory testified: "The situation is this, a town is owned by only six or eight Chiefs, and of these Chiefs perhaps each has about six wives and ten slaves, and each slave may have two wives" (P.P., 1899, C. 9391:2984-90). I have found no direct evidence that the average Mende freeman was commonly a slave owner.

Slave owning on a large scale was a privilege usually enjoyed by the rich and powerful—chiefs, subchiefs, and headmen. It gave them large benefits, for they enjoyed the rewards of their slaves' labor. In addition to wealth, slave owning conferred considerable social prestige and even political influence. In some cases nduwanga were more important in the latter context than as a source of labor and income; they added to the numbers in the household, and the size of the household was vital to the power and influence of the head of the family.

Nduwanga did not enjoy the normal rights of husbands, wives, or parents. A "marriage" between two slaves was not at all secure because the man and woman still belonged to their respective owners, or perhaps to the same owner. They could be separated at any time; in traditional law, they were not married but merely cohabiting at the pleasure of their master or masters. Some owners were so afraid of the growth of family feeling among their nduwanga that they forbade a slave woman to have successive children by the same man. The children belonged to the mother's master, who claimed them on the grounds that "Mine is the calf that is born of my cow" (S.L.A., Bo: Stocks 1924). The slave parents could only exercise limited rights of parenthood. Slave children were usually taken away from their parents between the ages of seven and ten. The boys went to work for their masters; the girls were put to work until they were given in marriage, often without even consulting the slave parents. Sometimes the girls were married to freemen; they were usually redeemed first by the groom-to-be, and the owner collected the proceeds of redemption and also the bridewealth. Sometimes a girl became a concubine of the head of the household and might earn her freedom by producing sons. In other cases, girls were given to other nduwanga. The marriages could also be a disguised form of pawning the girl, with the master giving her to a creditor until he could pay the debt.

In extreme cases of hardship, nduwanga did not even enjoy the privileges of adequate food and shelter, and the fact that they were slaves could endanger their lives. Among the Mende in the Northern Sherbro District, human parts were used to make "medicine" for members of cannibal societies. In 1913, the district commissioner there was puzzled by a sudden rush to redeem aged and sickly slaves; he then discovered that their masters were donating these people as sacrifices to the cannibal societies.[5]

I have presented the legal position of nduwanga in the most severe circumstances. In practice, most of them in the twentieth century lived reasonably comfortable and secure lives. The influence of the British authorities in the protectorate, which will be discussed in more detail later, was important. Masters were not allowed to trade, mutilate, or kill nduwanga; and since the government forbade the slave trade, the nduwanga were irreplaceable. More important were the modifications of customary law, which gave them some protection. Sometimes the master would claim his full customary rights as a slave owner and insist on being allowed them, but more usually there was a general acceptance of the idea that the master ought to treat his nduwanga humanely.

In particular, the older slaves and the slaves of the house acquired some generally accepted rights as time passed. Even before the British proclaimed the protectorate, it was considered shameful to trade or pawn a slave of the house. Generally, the amelioration of the lot of the nduwanga continued to depend as much on the affection and enlightened self-interest of the master as on the fear of disapproval by the chiefs and the community. Nduwanga of a good master were often content with their lives and were unwilling to return to their natural families, if they knew of them. A typical example of a good master was described by a British official in 1924: "A Timini captured in war 40 years before had been very happy and contented with his Mende master, a native trader in a fair way of business near Sumbuya, who had great affection for him and had paid a

5. P.R.O., Merewether, October 16, 1914, which transmits the Northern Sherbro District Report for 1913, by Fairtlough.

dowry for four wives for him. On the master's death a younger brother succeeded to the estate and began to treat the aged domestic harshly, whereupon his relatives who had long known his whereabouts promptly redeemed him at his own request. He could have had himself redeemed years before but did not wish it" (S.L.A., Bo: Stocks 1924).

Nduwanga were usually given land to feed themselves and their families; typically, they worked for their masters four days a week and for themselves two days a week. Dr. Maxwell thought that this was not a well-defined rule among the Mende, but that the slaves had certain rights to their own labor as long as they satisfied their masters' requirements first.[6]

Normally it was in the interests of the masters to provide their nduwanga with wives. This maintained the supply of slaves—after 1896 the breeding of slave children was the only way this could be done—and familial ties would presumably bind some men more closely to their masters' households. It was comparatively easy for a single man to escape to freedom but virtually impossible for a runaway to send for his family. The interest of the master in making life reasonably pleasant increased after 1896, when the British presence raised the number of attractive alternatives to a life of slavery.

Both before and during colonial times, the more prosperous masters lightened the lot of nduwanga by settling them in slave villages, or *faki*, under the supervision of slave headmen. These faki could be far from the master's home, and they sometimes progressed to a state of semifreedom. The inhabitants were only obliged to send their master a share of their produce and a number of children to be his servants.[7] This form of servitude may be more accurately described as serfdom than as slavery.

The most effective protection for nduwanga was the fact that they were needed; their labor was essential. They played a vital role at the base of the economic, social, and political life of the Mende. Most worked in agriculture. The male slaves did the heavy work of clearing the ground for the women, both free wives and slaves, to cultivate. They were also needed for the laborious tasks of collecting palm kernels and extracting palm oil from the kernels.

In the more remote areas, the men served as porters, carrying palm products for export and bringing European manufactured goods to the interior of the protectorate. They also provided much of the labor for

6. West African Lands Committee, 1916, Appendix Letter No. 3, Report by Dr. Maxwell on Land Tenure in the Sierra Leone Protectorate.

7. P.R.O., Probyn, February 15, 1908 (encloses report on Sherbro District native laws and customs, by District Commissioner Page, pp. 37-39); Little (1967:38-39); S.L.A., Bo: Fenton 1924; and information from oral sources at Pujehun.

public and communal works, like roads and paths, bridges, and the chiefdom guesthouse. They had to build, maintain, and repair houses for their masters. Women and children worked in the house as well as on the land.

There is no evidence that any special craft or skill was the prerogative of the slaves; theirs was the heavy, the unpleasant, and the unskilled labor. But during the twentieth century, in most Mende chiefdoms the free worked alongside nduwanga (S.L.A., Bo: Stocks 1924). Although they bore a heavier burden of the more menial tasks than freemen, nduwanga generally did much the same sort of work as any other Mende not of chiefly status. Despite their disabilities in customary law, most nduwanga lived in much the same way as the poorer freemen. There was one very important difference: the poorest freeman was entitled to the protection of his kin group and could appeal to the chief against injustice and maltreatment. Nduwanga had no such rights and hence no security.

In some ways, nduwanga were no worse off than their masters' wives. One British official argued that in fact the wife was worse off than the slave (P.P., 1899, C. 9391:269-71). There were close links between the institutions of slavery and polygyny: slave women also served as wives or concubines, and agricultural production depended equally on the work of the wives and the slaves in the household. A man with many nduwanga needed many wives to attend to the ground prepared by the men, and a man with many wives needed many male slaves to clear the ground for the wives to cultivate; it was necessary to maintain the right proportion of wives and nduwanga (Crosby 1937:249-64).

The nduwanga, and especially their descendants, were not condemned to remain slaves forever; they could achieve a higher status, sometimes even that of chief. More often than not, it took three or four generations for those of servile origin to achieve the status of clients. The clients were free members of society, except for some nominal obligations to their protectors; some, unlike the wholly free members of the lineage, were not allowed to leave the chiefdom with their personal property. Eventually the servile origin of these clients was forgotten, especially as they continued to intermarry with the established families in the chiefdom.[8] There were also more rapid ways of achieving freedom. In the nineteenth century, for example, Dawa of Wunde earned his freedom by displaying exceptional valor, and he later became a powerful chief in the east of the Mende territory (Wylie 1969). Under the more settled conditions of the twentieth century, there was less chance of achieving freedom in this way.

There was also provision in customary law for slaves to redeem themselves, provided that their master had allowed them to accumulate the re-

---

8. P.R.O., Probyn, April 25, 1908; *Parliamentary Papers* (1928, Cmd. 3020, Enclosure 5, Despatch 3, Captain Stanley's minute); Little (1967:38-39).

demption payment and that the master agreed. Sometimes slaves were redeemed by their family, with the owner's consent. Late in the nineteenth century, the customary fee was about three pounds, or goods to that value. This was sufficiently accepted for three pounds to be known as "a head of money." There is little evidence concerning the scope of these redemptions, but it is clear that they were not uncommon, that the consent of the master was needed, and that chiefs or headmen might be called upon in disputed cases. The commonest form of customary redemption was that of a slave wife who had borne children for a freeman.

THE EFFECTS OF BRITISH INFLUENCE

By the beginning of the twentieth century, Mende slavery had been greatly affected by the influence of Britain on the Sierra Leone area, both before and after the proclamation of the Sierra Leone Protectorate in 1896. Slavery had been abolished on British soil in 1833, and Britain since then had felt a commitment—not always honored—to bring pressure to bear against slavery, even outside British territory. For most of the nineteenth century, Britain had direct jurisdiction over the comparatively small area of the colony of Sierra Leone, near Freetown. There was no question of allowing slavery in the colony, particularly as Freetown had been founded for freed slaves. But the issue was not so clear-cut in the Sierra Leone hinterland, where Britain gradually extended its influence during the nineteenth century. By the exercise of moral pressure, by gubernatorial tours, by treaties with chiefs, by military expeditions and by cautious annexations, the governments of Britain and Sierra Leone had virtually eradicated the organized slave trade in the Sierra Leone hinterland by 1896. They had also made great progress in preventing the kidnapping of potential slaves and the concluding of private slave deals. But although they spared no effort to suppress the internal slave trade, the governments of Britain and Sierra Leone were prepared to tolerate slavery in the hinterland.

Legislation against slave dealing was an important part of the Protectorate Ordinance of 1896, but as the protectorate was still technically foreign soil the British government was not obliged by the 1833 act to end slavery there (Ordinance No. 20, P.R.O., 1896). [9] Yet it was hoped that the measures against slave dealing and other measures against slavery would weaken the powers of the masters over their slaves and that the institution of slavery would wither away. Anybody bartering, pledging, transferring, or in other ways dealing with slaves would be tried and punished. Slaves brought into the protectorate to be sold were declared free. All transfers

9. This ordinance was amended and reenacted in 1897 and 1901, but the clauses on slavery and slave dealing were scarcely changed.

and bequests of slaves were declared null and void (although this clause about bequests referred to specific bequests and did not exclude normal inheritance of slaves by customary heirs). Slaves were given the right of redemption for a payment of not more than four pounds for an adult and two pounds for a child. No claims in respect of any slave were admissible in law courts. This meant an owner could not go to court to regain or to retain a slave. It was made an offense for "a native" to sit in judgment on slave cases, but this was soon repealed, and during the twentieth century customary courts continued to hear disputes about slaves.

The Colonial Office blamed the wars of 1898 on the resentment of the protectorate people against British rule, provoked by British measures against slavery, slave trading and slave raiding in the protectorate. This made the official policy, which consisted of standing aloof from slavery and waiting for it to die away, seem even more justifiable. For the first quarter of the twentieth century Britain took few measures against slavery and may even have tried to prolong its existence by some of its legislation. This was not caused so much by the fear of rebellion recurring in the protectorate as by two other fears. First, there was the fear that the native chiefs, on whom Britain relied so heavily for the administration of the protectorate, would be antagonized by any action against slavery and would withdraw their cooperation. This would probably have meant a complete breakdown of the administration of the protectorate. Second, there was fear that if slavery was ended, slaves would leave the farms in great numbers and the already shaky economy of the protectorate would be ruined.

The most important legislation with a bearing on domestic slavery during the first quarter of the twentieth century was the Protectorate Native Law Ordinance of 1905 (Ordinance No. 16, P.R.O., 1905). This strengthened the position of the customary authorities by clearly defining their rights and by giving official sanction to such customs as forced labor. Clauses 51, 52, and 53, ostensibly based on custom, restricted the rights of people to leave their chiefdoms. They made it a punishable offense to harbor a person who had left his chiefdom without first obtaining the customary permission of his chief, and they obliged chiefs to ensure the repatriation of those who had left their chiefdoms without leave. These measures applied to freemen as well as slaves, although slaves were not specifically mentioned; but the effects were felt by the slaves who wished to run away. It became much more difficult for a runaway slave to remain at liberty in the protectorate. Three years later, the Vagrancy Ordinance of 1908 similarly limited the rights of a runaway to freedom in the colony (Ordinance No. 17, P.R.O., 1908). It provided for the repatriation of "natives" who had spent three weeks in the colony without employment or means of subsistence.

Equally important in preserving slavery in the protectorate were the numerous decisions made by British officials. Although forbidden by the Protectorate Ordinance to recognize in their judicial capacity any claims in respect of slaves, district commissioners in their administrative and executive capacities dealt with many slave cases. They even settled disputes over the ownership of slaves. A. E. Tuboku Metzger, a Creole member of the Sierra Leone Legislative Council and once an assistant district commissioner, told of the administrators' unpleasant duties of listening to an adjudicating complaints about "domestics," which used to detain them for hours.[10] Official papers confirm that district commissioners spent much time on cases involving slaves, especially runaways, and disputes over redemptions and ownership (S.L.A., Bo: Fenton 1924). In the Mende district of Pujehun in 1919 and 1920, out of 352 cases no less than 82 were concerned with slavery, mostly with runaways and redemptions (S.L.A., Pujehun: Native Affairs Record 1919-20). But these cases, which were those that came to the attention of British officials, give only a hint of true numbers, for many other cases were resolved by the traditional authorities and never recorded, and many slaves who ran away were quietly recaptured by their owners.

Slaves had been given the chance of freedom by redemption in Clause 30 of the Protectorate Ordinance; this compelled a master to accept redemption money for a slave. In 1907, the Sierra Leone government hoped to protect the redeemed slave by instituting a definite form of redemption certificate and by ordering that redemption payments had to be made through district commissioners (P.P. 1928, Cmd. 3020:9). Records of redemptions are far from complete, but remarkably few official redemptions took place, considering that there were at least 200,000 slaves in the protectorate in the 1920s. Captain Stanley worked out that from May 1920 to September 1922 there were 1,950 redemptions recorded by the district commissioners (P.P., 1928, Cmd. 3020:38). This had an almost negligible effect on the total slave population. The low rate of redemption can be explained in a number of ways. Some slaves might have led pleasant enough lives and had no wish to be redeemed. Perhaps many slaves were not aware of their right to redemption or were too frightened of their masters' anger to seek redemption; possibly, traditional rulers prevented approaches to British officials to ask for redemption. Finally, many slaves would have had nowhere to go if they were redeemed.

10. *Sierra Leone Legislative Council Debates*, March 24, 1926.

Many slaves, however, did seek their freedom, but not by redemption. It was cheaper and simpler to run away, even after the legislation of 1905 and 1908 made it more difficult for escaped slaves to remain at liberty. The problem of runaway slaves had bedeviled relations between Britain and West African rulers for many years. In the Sierra Leone Protectorate, the chiefs resented the limitations on their rights to recapture their runaway slaves. They frequently complained about what they saw as British encouragement of runaways and forecast disaster if the protectorate was to be continually depopulated by the increasing exodus of slaves.

The single most important reason for the increasing number of slaves who left their masters was the social and economic impact of the presence of the British in the protectorate. It is a strange irony that at the same time as the colonial government was taking legislative and administrative measures that favored the continuance of slavery, the impact of the British was weakening slavery in the protectorate by creating an increasing number of attractive alternatives to a life of slavery.

The attraction of Freetown and other urban centers tempted slaves away from their masters. Seeing the goods of the traders they wanted to be able to buy them, and they could earn money by enlisting in the West African Frontier Force. Many were very unhappy at the prospect of returning to slavery after serving as carriers in World War I. They could also earn money by laboring on the railways or other public works, or by working for traders or as household servants. Women and girl slaves ran away with policemen, soldiers, court messengers, and other government employees. The post-redemption alternatives in the twentieth century did far more to damage Mende slavery than sermons or official disapproval ever did.

By the 1920s, the number of nduwanga was declining. Captain Stanley estimated that only 15 percent, or 83,000, of the Mende were still enslaved (P.P., 1928, Cmd. 3020:45). This was substantially lower than the 50 percent estimated late in the nineteenth century. Only a small part of this decrease can be attributed to redemptions; rather more can be attributed to the runaways. The most important explanation for the decrease is that the master-slave relationship no longer appeared viable in the changing social circumstances and was being replaced by the master-servant relationship. Since there were no fresh enslavements and since the customary transition to freedom over three or four generations continued, it is not surprising that the slave population fell. Furthermore, many chiefs may have freed their slaves to keep them from running away and lowering the numbers in the chiefdoms.

It is clear that in the 1920s the decrease in number of slaves was most marked in the areas nearest the colony and in centers of British influence and power in the protectorate. The most striking example of this was in the mainly Mende Southern Province, where there was a rough correlation between the percentage of slaves and the distance from Freetown. Southeast of Freetown, the first part of the Southern Province—Sembehun District—had an estimated slave population of 10 percent or less. More distant than Sembehun was Sumbuya, with a slave population of between 25 and 50 percent. The remotest districts were Pujehun and Mano River, where slaves constituted over half of the population in some chiefdoms (S.L.A., Bo: Fenton 1924, Stocks 1924).

Although slavery was decreasing, it was not disappearing; officials in Freetown and Whitehall began to realize just how long they would have to wait for slavery to die a natural death in the protectorate. Slavery seemed more and more of a hindrance to the British ideas of progress, and there was mounting criticism in Britain and even in the League of Nations of the continued toleration of slavery. This criticism led to the antislavery ordinances of 1926 and 1927.

Ordinance 9 of 1926 declared that all people born or brought into the protectorate after the commencement of the ordinance were ipso facto free, and that all slaves would become free on the death of their owners; it repeated that no claim for, or in respect of any slave could be entertained by any court in the protectorate (Ordinance No. 9, P.R.O., 1926). The effect of this ordinance would have been to end slavery in thirty or forty years, as the masters and slaves who were alive in 1926 died. This did not satisfy the campaigners against slavery. In 1927 the Supreme Court, in Freetown, found in favor of slave owners who had used "reasonable" force to recapture runaway slaves—their property, according to the majority judgment of the court. This caused a storm of criticism and led to Ordinance 24 of 1927, which abolished the legal status of slavery from January 1, 1928 (Ordinance No. 24, P.R.O., 1927).

At the beginning of 1928, abolition was accepted by the people of the protectorate with surprisingly few complaints or disturbances. This may have been because it made little difference to the lives of most slaves and masters. An institution that was so much part of the lives of the Mende and the other peoples of the protectorate obviously could not vanish overnight. Other customs linked to slavery continued—polygyny, forced labor, and pawning. As various district commissioners noted, only a small proportion of emancipated slaves left their homes; most of them just "sat down" with their former masters (S.L.A., Bo: Confidential Minute Paper 3). Their lives changed gradually after 1928. Even today, nearly fifty years later, the servile origins of some Mende have not been forgotten.

GLOSSARY

faki: slave villages.
keke: father.
ke ma lenga: kinsmen.
nduwe (pl. *nduwanga*): a slave.
nduwei (pl. *nduweisia*): the slave.

REFERENCES

ORAL SOURCES
Conversations at Pujehun with members of Kaikai family and ex-slaves, March 1971.

UNPUBLISHED SOURCES
P.R.O.: Public Record Office, London.
  Cardew to Colonial Office, June 9, 1894. C.O. 267/409/11019.
  C.O. 271/21, XLVI, No. 1536. April 24, 1915.
  Probyn to Colonial Office, April 25, 1908. C.O. 267/503/16672.
  Merewether to Colonial Office, January 9, 1912. C.O. 267/538/2154.
  Merewether to Colonial Office, October 16, 1914. C.O. 267/560/42361.
  Probyn to Colonial Office, February 15, 1908. C.O. 267/501/8463.
  Probyn to Colonial Office, April 25, 1908. C.O. 267/503/16672.
S.L.A., Bo: Sierra Leone Archives, Bo.
  Commissioner, October 8, 1927.
  Confidential Minute Paper 3.
  Fenton, January 26, 1924.
  Stocks, January 24, 1924, Pr. 5.
S.L.A., Pujehun: Sierra Leone Archives, Pujehun.
  Native Affairs Record, Vol. 2, 1919-20.
  Out Letter Book, Vol. 2, Northern Sherbro, 1916-17. No. 13/1917.
West African Lands Committee. 1916. Evidence, correspondence, and draft report. Print for use of Colonial Office, April 1916.

PUBLISHED SOURCES
Alldridge, T. J. 1901. *The Sherbro and its hinterland.* London.
———. 1910. *A transformed colony.* London.
Clarke, J. I. 1969. *Sierra Leone in maps.* 2d ed. London.
Crosby, K. H. 1937. Polygamy in Mende country. *Africa* 10:249-64.
Curtin, P. D. 1964. *The image of Africa: British ideas and action, 1780-1850.* Madison.

Fenton, J. S. 1948. *The outline of native law in Sierra Leone.* Rev. ed. Sierra Leone.

Fox Bourne, H. R. 1900. *Slavery and its substitutes in Africa.* London.

Hargreaves, J. D. 1965. *Prelude to the partition of West Africa.* London.

Lewis, R. 1954. *Sierra Leone: a modern portrait.* London.

Little, K. L. 1967. *The Mende of Sierra Leone.* Rev. ed. London.

Ordinances, Public Record Office (P.R.O.), London: Ordinance No. 20, 1896, C.O. 269/5; Ordinance No. 16, 1905, C.O. 269/6; Ordinance No. 17, 1908, C.O. 269/7; Ordinance No. 9, 1926, C.O. 269/10; Ordinance No. 24, 1927, C.O. 269/10.

Rodney, W. 1966. African slavery and other forms of social oppression on the upper Guinea coast in the context of the Atlantic slave trade. *J. Afr. Hist.* 7:431-43.

_____. 1967. A reconsideration of the Mane invasions of Sierra Leone. *J. Afr. Hist.* 8:219-46.

P.P.: Great Britain, *Parliamentary papers.*

1899. Report by Her Majesty's Commissioner and correspondence on the subject of the insurrection in the Sierra Leone Protectorate, 1898, Part II, Evidence and Documents. Vol. 60 (*Accounts and papers,* Vol. 10), C. 9391. (Note: The numbers given in text citations in this chapter refer to the number of the question and its answer in the oral testimony.) Part I of this report, C. 9388, contains reports by the commissioner, Sir David Chalmers, by the governor of Sierra Leone, Sir Frederic Cardew, and by the secretary of state for the colonies, Sir Joseph Chamberlain.

1928. Correspondence relating to domestic slavery in the Sierra Leone Protectorate. Vol. 18, Cmd. 3020. Contains extract from dispatch of governor of Sierra Leone to the secretary of state for the colonies; minute by Capt. W. B. Stanley, "Estimate of Number of Slaves in the Protectorate since the Formation of the Protectorate into Provinces (i.e., from 1st of January, 1920 to September, 1922)."

Sierra Leone. *Sierra Leone Legislative Council debates.* Session of 1925-26, No. V, March 24, 1926, p. 58.

Vivian, W. 1896. The Mendi country. *J. Manch. geogr. Soc.* 12:1-28.

Wylie, K. C. 1969. Innovation and change in Mende chieftaincy, 1880-1896. *J. Afr. Hist.* 10:295-308.

Social Psychology in a Servile System: An Exploration

Part VIII

17

Responses to Dependence in a Servile Group: The Machube of Northern Benin

Bernd Baldus

The belief that in the long run, men will not tolerate their own subordination and will rebel against it has long been a part of the non-Marxian tradition of work in sociology and political science. In this view, dependence, whether encountered in informal interaction with others or as institutionalized subordination, will ultimately result in corrective conflict and the restitution of some form of justice.

In spite of its widespread acceptance (see, for instance, Tocqueville 1835/1945:247; Durkheim 1915:3, 420; Tannenbaum 1946:125, 127; Parsons 1951:34, 41; Moore 1963:83; Tumin 1967:99; Etzioni 1968:647; Dahrendorf 1969a:41 and 1969b:224; or Wirth 1970:348) the "corrective-conflict" hypothesis, as it may be called, remains exceedingly vague. The authors cited do neither identify the exact form of dependence and subordination that generates conflict, nor do they make an effort to predict what kind of resistance and conflict they expect. The nature of "justice" that corrective conflict reestablishes remains equally indeterminate. And finally, the corrective-conflict hypothesis has been consistently unclear about the precise causes of conflict. It states unequivocally that conflict will occur, and that resistance is "latently" or manifestly present as soon as dependence arises—for this reason, any notion of "false consciousness" is strongly rejected. But it gives very little indication why resistance

435

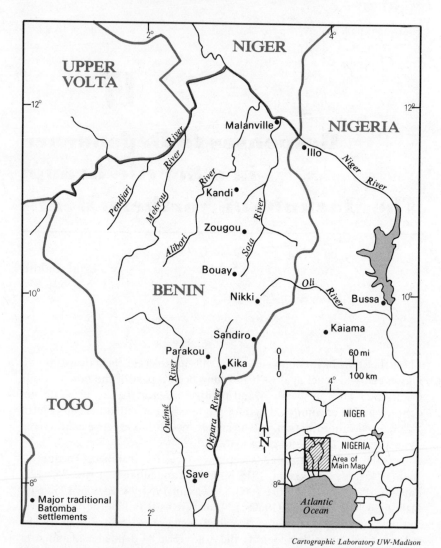

Map 17. Borgou and Northern Benin

develops, except for broad hints at "human nature" or "human needs," which, when stifled, inevitably produce feelings of "alienation" and a desire for retribution (see, for instance, Etzioni, 1968:622-26). It is here that the affinity of the corrective-conflict hypothesis with liberal ideological beliefs of long standing becomes apparent: they share the view that men are rational and intelligent and will not submit to conditions that are not in their favor. The consequence of this is a rather conservative interpretation of any status quo that is uncontested. If it is true that corrective conflict invariably prevails, then existing social conditions that are unopposed must be reasonable and just. The corrective-conflict hypothesis therefore contains ultimately a strong implicit legitimation of social relations that do not give rise to conflict and dissent.

It is interesting to confront this view with Marx and Engels' concept of false consciousness, or their distinction between a "class as such" and a "class for itself." These notions represented an attempt to cope with the empirical variety of reactions to dependence. While Marx provided an explanation for the development of revolutionary consciousness—namely, the growth of structural contradictions in a system of rule—he also identified processes that resulted in interpretations of and reactions to rule, and that left rule unquestioned and contributed to its maintenance over considerable periods of time.

The following is a study of cognitive and behavioral responses to subordination in a contemporary servile society in the Borgou area of northern Benin. Data were collected during eight months of field research in 1968.[1] The Borgou area is inhabited by three main groups: the Batomba, the Fulbe (or Fulani) and the *machube*, a servile group of predominantly Batomba origin. The area was chosen because at the time of the research a substantial part of the servile relationship between machube and Fulbe continued to exist and to function. This relationship has also been very stable and free of conflict.

THE HISTORY OF SLAVERY IN BORGOU

Because of the cultural and geographical isolation of the Borgou area, slavery there had some features not commonly found in other parts of Africa.[2] For many centuries the area was inhabited by the Batomba (sing. Batonu), an agricultural people with stable settlements and a loose political organization divided into several provinces of rule with shifting boundaries.[3] Political and military leadership rested with a hereditary aristocracy, the *wasangari*. Each province was dominated by a single ruler, who distributed his land and his villages, not unlike fiefdoms, to members of his family and to wasangari from other, lesser families. While norms existed that formally regulated access to and distribution of these

1. The research was carried out as part of a project supported by the Deutsche For-schungsgemeinschaft, Federal Republic of Germany.

2. The terms "slavery" and "servitude" are used interchangeably when reference is made to the machube. Slavery implies the possibility to sell or exchange a person in one's service. This possibility disappeared gradually in the Borgou area after slavery was formally abolished.

3. For a detailed account of the political organization of the Batomba, see Lombard (1965).

positions, the internal structure of any particular area was unstable, and alliances between wasangari changed frequently. Conflicts over inheritance of political power caused continuous internal competition and strain.

The relations among the provinces were equally unstable. The people of Borgou distinguished between *wasangariru*, short raids, and *tabu*, longer and well-planned invasions into a neighboring province. Both were led by wasangari with the main object of looting and, most important, capturing as many people as possible. The captives were mainly formerly free Batomba. Captured wasangari seem to have been almost always killed. Only in western Borgou were there raids against neighboring peoples, namely Gurma and Temba. All captives were enslaved. The drop in status and freedom must have been staggering for the individual captive, for free Batomba enjoyed a great deal of independence with respect to the wasangari, whose income was not derived from the free Batomba population but almost entirely from the use of slaves. For all the division and conflict in Borgou, however, there was enough feeling of common identity to suspend hostility for the annual *gani*, a week-long gathering of wasangari and free Batomba from all over Borgou in Nikki, the cultural center of Borgou. Apart from ancestor worship, the competitive display of horsemanship, and entertainment with oral accounts of past feats and achievements, the gani provided an opportunity to affirm old alliances and to form new ones. Above all, however, it maintained the internal cohesion of a politically unstable society.

Captives from raids or warfare were transferred to a camplike slave settlement, called *gando*, near the seat of the wasangari. Subsequent enslavement took three forms. A very small number of slaves became *tkiriku*, personal servants of ruling wasangari. Their position was in many respects the most desirable of the three. Wearing visible symbols of their affiliation, such as particular garments and a partly shaved hairstyle, they performed a variety of tasks including messenger and executive functions. It was always clear, however, that their power was a derived one, and their status was never forgotten. A second category of slaves were the *gando-gibu*, who remained in the gando after their capture, sometimes for an extended transitory stay before they were sold, sometimes permanently. They were, together with looting, the main source of wasangari income. They worked on the land around the gando and turned over part of the produce to the wasangari, his family, and his retinue. Demands on them were particularly heavy before raids or warfare and before the gani, whose festive displays involved heavy costs for the wasangari. In addition, the gandogibu could be sold or exchanged for military assistance either to other wasangari or to free Batomba. Such transactions created a third category of slaves, the *yobu* (sing. *yo*), who worked in the house or on the fields of their free Batomba owners. They could be resold, but were usually integrated into the family of their owner. Even where most visible distinctions between slave and owner disappeared, however, knowledge of their status persisted, and informal but clear rules prevented the men from marrying Batomba women or behaving in any way considered improper for a yo. Debt could also lead to the status of a yo, but compared to capture it was a minor source of servitude in Borgou.

Thus, slavery was already an institution of long standing when the pastoral Fulbe (sing. Pullo) moved into the Borgou area in the eighteenth and early nineteenth century from what is today Niger. The migration of the Fulbe was gradual, and their numbers remained relatively small. Their physique, language, culture, and nomadic pastoralism were all very different from Batomba life. Apart from a somewhat legendary fight near Nikki, which the Fulbe lost, the infiltration was peaceful, for wasangari and other Batomba soon found Fulbe cattle a valuable source of meat, especially for ceremonies and celebrations. A peculiar but stable balance developed, with the Fulbe relying on the wasangari for protection against raids in return for gifts of cattle. Moreover, even though there was no question about the military superiority of the Batomba, both groups developed mutual respect: the Fulbe for the fierceness and military prowess of the Batomba, and the Batomba for the Islamic culture, the cattle, and the elaborate magic of the Fulbe. The Fulbe and their herds became a target for raids and warfare, but the Fulbe were never killed or enslaved, only transferred to the territory of the raiding wasangari. On the other hand, the Fulbe could move on their own initiative whenever they felt badly treated. This gave them a powerful leverage against the wasangari in whose area they lived. Since the Borgou area was never densely settled, and since land was abundant, Fulbe and Batomba settlements remained separated, even though the Fulbe frequently set up their villages not too far from major Batomba settlements to facilitate exchange and keep in contact with the wasangari of the area.

Long before the arrival of the Fulbe, the Batomba believed that a child whose first teeth appeared in the upper jaw would bring disaster, illness, and death to his family, killing "first his brothers and sisters, then his mother and his father." This belief, which exists in other areas of West Africa, was taken especially seriously among the Batomba, where it led to elaborate protective measures. The parents of the child, as well as other members of the family, underwent a purification ritual designed to render the spell of the fateful birth ineffective and to prevent similar calamities in the future. The child itself was killed. In larger settlements, the *gossiko,* whose office was hereditary, took the child and either killed and buried it, or kept it in his household as a slave; the child then had the same status as a yo. Where a gossiko was not available, the child was left in a designated area close to a settlement to die of exposure or hunger.

The Fulbe, who did not share these beliefs, soon began to take up these children and raise them in their own settlements. Eventually, children were directly handed over to them. Such a child was kept in the foster compound, where it learned Fulfulde and adopted most elements of the Fulbe culture including the practice of Islam. Even though the children were fully integrated into the Fulbe family life, there was never any doubt about their identity. When they reached early adolescence, they were required to work. The men herded Fulbe cattle under the supervision of their owner or members of his family. In addition, they engaged in agriculture, which was not done by the Fulbe, and provided the Fulbe with a large part of the produce. The women worked in the ga, the circular arrangement of huts, and assisted Fulbe women in all household tasks.

These men and women formed still another group of slaves in Borgou: the machube (sing. machudo). Although the majority of the machube descended from children whom the Batomba had abandoned, some of them came to the Fulbe as adults. They were former gandogibu or yobu whom the Batomba sold to the Fulbe for cattle. They too adopted the machube culture, though much more slowly. Their children, however, grew up in the Fulbe compounds and were indistinguishable from other machube. Even though the machube remained aware of these differences in their origins, they were treated alike by the Fulbe.

The life of the machube was closely regulated. Held in low regard by both Batomba and Fulbe, they were looked at by the Fulbe primarily as a productive property: they were an inexpensive source of labor that freed Fulbe men and women from some of the more arduous tasks of cattle herding and household work. Expenditures for their work were limited to what was necessary for their physical maintenance and reproduction. Each group of machube was assigned several head of cattle from the herd of its owner for its own use. The machube could also work their own field after they had cultivated a field for their owner, or retain a part of the produce from their agricultural work for the Fulbe. They were not permitted to own cattle. Their daily activities could be curtailed at will by their Fulbe owners, who controlled their movements outside the compound. They could be bequeathed, given, or sold to other Fulbe, though a sale rarely took place. A machube child born to parents from different compounds remained with the mother, and the family was not permitted to live together for fear of disputes over ownership. Sexual relations between machube men and Fulbe women were strictly prohibited, and only rarely did Fulbe men take machube women as second or third wives.

The machube could not participate in important cultural institutions of the Fulbe, such as the age-class system. If they were permitted to imitate Fulbe customs in birth, marriage, and death ceremonies, it was only because the two groups were so clearly and visibly different that the maintenance of cultural boundaries was of no concern to the Fulbe. Of all slave groups in Borgou, with the possible exception of the gandogibu, the machube were most openly exploited as an economic asset. They were charged with the hardest tasks of Fulbe life, going after stray cattle in the heat of the day, working in the fields, carrying water and firewood, and grinding flour for food.

THE STATUS OF THE MACHUBE TODAY

Of the servile groups in Borgou, only the situation of the machube, and in a few instances of the tkiriku, has survived without any major change. Slavery was officially abolished by the French colonial government at the turn of the century. Subsequently, the settlements of the gandogibu became independent of the wasangari. The yobu likewise faced few problems of transition, since they were already relatively well integrated: their new relationship to their previous Batomba owners ranged from a continuing voluntary provision of services to complete separation and an independent life in a different part of the settlement or in another village. The importance of the tkiriku decreased with the rapidly deteriorating social position of the wasangari. The latter, stripped of their major sources of income, had to adopt in most cases a much more modest life style, and this meant independence for the tkiriku, even though many of them decided to stay with their former owners. Only in Nikki is there still a group of tkiriku in an essentially unchanged servile position. Their presence at the seat of the wasangari is of their own choosing. Legally they are regarded as remunerated servants, the remuneration, as in the past, consisting of a chance to farm their own fields and to receive small gifts from the wasangari.

The abolition of slavery had the least effect on the large body of machube. As in the case of the tkiriku, existing arrangements that provided livelihood for the machube, such as the usufructuary right to some of the Fulbe cattle, could be declared a remuneration and thus be legalized. But the Fulbe could not forcefully retain the former slaves or influence the colonial administration to support servitude. Nonetheless, most machube did not leave their former owners. Only small groups of them, mostly descendants of former captives who had not yet fully adopted machube culture, used the possibility to settle in "free" villages offered to them by the administration. It was this group that also participated in violent attacks against some Fulbe in the Nikki area shortly after abolition, and the colonial administration and the Batomba apparently gave them at least a tacit support. These incidents constitute the only attested violent confrontation between machube and Fulbe.

Most of the machube voluntarily remained with their former owners, and machube life today is virtually the same as it was when slavery was widespread in Borgou. Machube status in the eyes of Fulbe and Batomba has not improved. Most important, the Fulbe still claim the surplus product of machube labor. The machube still do the hardest work, freeing the Fulbe for the extensive social contacts, travel, participation in the complex group structures such as the age-class system, and the display of status, which are such an essential part of Fulbe life.

The seemingly voluntary acceptance of servitude by the machube is not a recent phenomenon. With the exception of the incidents referred to earlier, no evidence could be found that the machube ever resisted the Fulbe either individually or collectively. There were reports of flight, which offered a good chance of success unless the runaway machudo was caught by the wasangari of the area. In this case he was returned to his Fulbe owner, even though the wasangari could also keep him or sell him as a yo to the Batomba. Flight thus did not provide an escape from slavery, even though it offered a chance to get away from the Fulbe. But it seems to have occurred rarely and is reported to have involved mostly former captives of war or their descendants. Machube acquiescence in their status is the more striking given the limited means of coercive control available to the Fulbe with their weak collective organization and their territorial dispersion. It can be argued that the Batomba would have intervened in case of large-scale resistance by the machube because of their interest in the supply of cattle from the Fulbe. But no evidence of such an intervention exists. Moreover, the possibility of Batomba intervention in case of a major machube rebellion would not have precluded the success of minor grievances against the Fulbe. Of these, too, there is no record.

Correspondingly, no evidence was found of any formal coercive measures through which the Fulbe could have enforced the subservience of the machube. Interviews with machube and Fulbe revealed that such measures were not needed, and indeed not known. Among the machube, questions relating to the possibility of resistance were frequently not even comprehended until they had been restated several times, and the idea of defying the Fulbe appeared very remote for all of them. The Fulbe, though aware of the possibility of resistance, thought it so unlikely that preventive measures were neither considered nor taken. A high degree of inequality thus coincided with a high measure of internal stability in spite of a complete lack of coercion. It is this stability, or more precisely the behavior of the machube on which it rests, that will now be examined.

COGNITIVE AND BEHAVIORAL RESPONSES TO SERVITUDE: MACHUBE IDEOLOGY

The first and most striking impression one gets from interviewing machube today is their unquestioning acceptance of their subservience to the Fulbe. When asked to rank the three groups, about half (46 percent) of the machube respondents ranked the Fulbe first, and the other half (54 percent) ranked the Batomba first. They ranked themselves lowest, even though in a few cases they placed the Batomba at the bottom. The relative ranking of Fulbe and machube, however, is never in doubt. The machube know and accept their inferior position. The unresisting recognition by the machube of Fulbe superiority pervades their entire relationship. In the account of his life given by the oldest of the machube interviewed, a man of probably seventy years, none of the often far-reaching and arbitrary demands and interventions of the Fulbe is questioned as to its justification. The phases of his life, beginning with his transfer to the Fulbe as an abandoned child, are presented in a well-ordered sequence structured by his "obligations" towards his Fulbe owner. As in other interviews, there is a complete lack of perceived alternatives, or a desire for change, or even an expression of dissatisfaction. The reconciliation with a slave existence is complete:

When I was a child I was taken to the Fulbe. . . . My father was a Batonu. When I was born, the Batomba said that I would kill them. Then I was taken to the Fulbe, and I have lived with them, and I grew up here. When I was taken here I guarded the cattle. When I was older, they found still another machudo. Then I became something like a superior. They have told me to stay here and not to go with the cattle any more. Since that time I have worked for the Fulbe on the field, and now I have constructed my own hut. Even if one lives separately from the Fulbe there is no machube superior. One goes to the Fulbe to settle problems. The Fulbe were the superiors since one can remember. I have been with the Fulbe since my childhood. I have grown up, now I am old, and I am obliged to stay with the Fulbe. That is the reason why one stays with the Fulbe. I have always worked, and even now that I am old and have children I have to stay with the superior. He was my owner, and I do not intend to leave him.

Central to the cognitive images that lead to this acceptance is the knowledge of the reasons for the abandonment of the Batomba children. This appeared in all conversations with machube. The differences among the three groups in the interpretation of the fateful birth accident are striking in the way they reflect the diverse interests of the groups. For both Batomba and Fulbe, the origin of the machube is the basis for their low social evaluation. The low prestige in which the Batomba hold the machube, while connected with some elements of machube culture, is ultimately based on the threat of the child's birth. The child is not a

Batonu any more; it was physically and socially expelled from the community of free Batomba. The Fulbe do not share the belief in the fateful birth. But their knowledge of the origin of the machube reinforces their view of the machube as their property, acquired at little or no expense, and subject to their disposition. Fulbe respondents frequently pointed to the fact that the machube had been "thrown away" by the Batomba, an act which, in a lineage-conscious society, demonstratively indicates a very low regard.

By contrast, the fateful birth serves as a central explanatory and legitimating myth for the machube. It survived as a belief in spite of the general integration of the machube into Fulbe culture and is, in fact, the only element of Batomba beliefs carried over unaltered into machube traditions. It enables the individual machudo to give an acceptable meaning to his situation and it allocates responsibility for it. The myth of the fateful birth makes it possible to link most experiences of servitude to a central cognitive construct that makes them understandable and justifiable—or at least unchangeable. Potential intergroup conflict is prevented because subordination is seen to arise from facts of birth for which neither Fulbe nor Batomba are to blame. Frequently in the conversations, this endows specific aspects of the relationship to the Fulbe with a kind of unquestioned inevitability.

A Pullo ranks higher than a machudo because he has taken over the task of raising the machudo. Their origin is that a Batomba child has its first teeth in the upper jaw. The Batonu can abandon it and the Pullo can take it, or the Batonu can give it to the Pullo as a gift. He cannot keep the child. The Pullo raises it and provides nourishment until the child has reached an age where it is reasonable. One carries out his commands. The machube do everything that the Fulbe demand because they have grown up with the Fulbe, and already their ancestors have always been machube of the Fulbe. The Fulbe own us, therefore one works for them. The machube always carried out the commands, even if it was at night and the Pullo woke them up to ask for something. One carried it out.

The myth also eliminates the possibility of holding the Batomba responsible for the situation of the machube, by exculpating them for their act: abandoning the child appears as unavoidable and beyond any moral reproach.

The machube are the lowest because they come from the Batomba who have given them to the Fulbe. This is how we have found it, and this is what one must follow. I am machudo because my parents were not happy with my birth. When the first teeth of a child appear in the upper jaw the parents are afraid and they bring it to the Fulbe, and from then on it is called machudo. They are afraid because the child brings misfortune. It kills the entire family. I do not know why.

In addition to defining the relationship to the other two groups in a way that exempts them from responsibility for the fate of the machube and, ultimately, from becoming a target of hostility, the myth of the fateful birth instills in many machube respondents feelings of shame and self-blame. Frequently, respondents became hesitant when asked the first questions about the birth incident. Their responses were given with signs of embarrassment, and only after they were informed that the interviewers knew about this aspect of machube origin did information come forth freely.

The stigma of the fateful birth and the shame and self-blame among the machube reinforce the importance of another element of machube ideology: the belief in the partial removal of the stigma through living with the Fulbe. It is perhaps the single most important factor in the relationship of the machube to the Fulbe. The custom of abandoning children is not practiced by the machube, and there is a positive emotional association of the machube with their owner, which sometimes contains visible elements of gratitude. The belief that the stigma is, in effect, partially removed is very likely a generic element of machube culture and was created by the machube themselves. While it is possible that the custom among the machube of abandoning children was discouraged by the Fulbe because of their interest in them as property, there is no indication of any Fulbe rule or intervention to this effect.

Among machube respondents, three versions of the beneficial consequences of being with the Fulbe were found. The first sees the benefit as an integral aspect of machube existence: by living with the Fulbe, the fateful consequences of the appearance of the first teeth in the upper jaw simply vanish, making it possible to disregard the precautions taken in such a case by the Batomba. The second version connects the disappearance of the birth spell with the adoption of Fulbe culture by the machube. Respondents giving this interpretation frequently display a sense of superiority over the animistic Batomba, whose abandonment of children is presented as a sign of an inferior culture. But the most frequent response relates the disappearance of the birth stigma directly to the power of the Fulbe and their cattle, and to their possession of remedial magic (*lekki*), which is relatively highly developed compared to similar cultural elements among other groups in Borgou. Most accounts link the power of the Fulbe to overcome the effects of the fateful birth to the obligation of the machube to stay with their owners.

If a child is born to the Batomba and its first teeth grow in the upper jaw, one believes that it brings disaster. The Fulbe take care of the child and they have the power to make this disaster disappear. It grows up with the Fulbe and considers them its parents. One always carries out the commands of the Fulbe because they have taken care of the machube. Therefore one obeys them. I work for the Pullo because he has taken me as a child from the Batomba. He has raised me, washed me, he has given me milk and everything else I needed until I had grown up. For this reason, as a sign of recognition, one carries out all his commands.

In the evaluation by Fulbe and machube, the same act—the initial adoption of the abandoned child—assumes a completely different meaning. What was for the Fulbe an act of self-interest, free—as far as the evidence indicates—of moral or humanitarian considerations, appears to the individual machudo to demand gratitude and to establish an obligation to stay with and work for his owner. But the two interests meet in a perfect complementary fit: machube gratitude makes an unsolicited contribution to the stability of the servile relationship, which is the primary concern of the Fulbe (on the concept of complementarity, see Baldus 1975, 1976). This gratitude is maintained even where the stigma of being a machudo is clearly felt and resented. The Fulbe are explicitly exempted from any blame. "The machube don't like it if one treats them as machube of the Fulbe. But if it is their owner who tells them that they are machube of the Fulbe they accept it. But if someone else treats them like machube they do not accept it. They do not want it, because that other person had not fed them, they object, they resist him."

Machube notions of "fate," "tradition," and "order," widespread in Borgou, also make servitude stable. The idea of fate appears in two forms: supernatural intervention, associated with Allah; or the more general concept *hoddirore,* signifying unpredictable and unchangeable turns of events. Fate as an explanatory label renders servitude inevitable, and therefore acceptable, thus precluding an interpretation of the reality of servitude that could disrupt the machube-Fulbe relationship. Similarly, the traditionalization of servitude-related experiences, which occurs in stereotyped formulations such as "it has always been that way," "it has been this way since the time of our ancestors," or "we have found it this way from the beginning," keeps the structural features of servitude outside the bounds of doubt and conflict. In an environment full of unpredictable and uncontrollable events, tradition becomes a sign of at least some certainty. Events that are recurrent, or institutions that have lasted, acquire by their very endurance justification or at least an appearance of invariable permanence.

The same function is performed by a set of images that can best be described as a "syndrome of order." The pervasiveness of internalized commitments to order and hierarchies has been noted for the Borgou area by Lombard (1965). Lombard observes that, for the Batomba, "every behavior in daily life tended always to express a social position, and there was no contact between individuals which was not preceded by the recognition by one side of its own subordination—if not dependence—in a social hierarchy" (Lombard 1965:177). A similar awareness of social inequality can be found even among the more individualistic and less hierarchically organized Fulbe (Hopen 1958:105). The substance of the machube view of order does not differ from that of the other groups. Its ideological function derives from the context in which these beliefs occur, and from their contribution to the relationship of dominance and dependence that exists between Fulbe and machube.

The imagery that appears in the order syndrome is typically vague, as evidenced in the following interview sequence: "Men are not equal. Inequality comes from Allah. Even if one looks at our fingers they are not equal. With men it is the same. Some are great, some are in the middle, and some are inferior. This is the reason for the differences. For those who are great like, for instance, the head of the family, this comes from Allah. If you are old then it is you who leads the house. He who is great will occupy himself with everything that needs to be done in the house." Other frequently appearing images refer to the family structure or political structure of local or regional superiors. Once identified in these terms, an event or a state is positively accepted and becomes part of a structure invariably seen as stronger than the individual confronted with it. This is particularly marked where the analogy chosen is the relationship between persons and property. In this case any possibility of independent action is given up. Person-thing relationships symbolize the most extensive form of dependence. They are exclusively determined by the proprietor no matter how arbitrary his disposition over the things he possesses. Asked for the reasons for their obedience, machube respondents explained: "If you have a bag of money, and if you need the money and you want to take it out of the bag, will the bag refuse to give you the money?"; or, "If you have a cock, then you do with the cock what you want, don't you?" Resistance against the Fulbe, and against one's position in the inequality structure, appears as unlikely as the resistance of a thing against the dispositions of its owner. An important part of the experience of social inequality is thus interpreted in a way that makes any idea of change or even a mere objection to the inequality structure appear senseless.

The general acceptance by the machube of their servile position, the acceptance of the belief that led to their original abandonment, the resulting exoneration of Batomba and Fulbe, and the various ways in which the experience of servitude is given a legitimating meaning all facilitate a relationship to the Fulbe characterized by a strong desire to imitate Fulbe culture. Imitative behavior becomes in many cases so intense that it changes to identification and to an attitude of the machube respondent to his Pullo owner and to the Fulbe as a group that contains clearly identifiable affective ties. There were, of course, few if any conceivable alternatives to the adoption of Fulbe culture. The machube children who grew up in the Fulbe compound were immersed in it from the beginning, and for those machube who were bought as adults, some form of assimilation was an instrumental necessity. Isolated, and never together in large numbers, the captives of war could not preserve such basic cultural elements as Batomba language beyond their own lifetime. Their children were completely assimilated, and it can be assumed that such assimilation occurred with the tacit or active encouragement of the Fulbe, who were interested in an uncomplicated handling of the machube.

On the other hand, the responses indicate that the imitation of the Fulbe is more than merely the result of these circumstances. In the self-understanding of the machube, imitative behavior has a symbolic character. It permits a sharing in the prestige of the Fulbe and provides a means of compensating for the low evaluation shown to the machube by all other groups. In fact, the imitation itself gives rise to continuous ridicule of the machube by both Fulbe and Batomba. Derogatory and ridiculing comments by Fulbe or Batomba about the imitative behavior of the machube were encountered very frequently during the research, and were often made in the presence of machube. After my interest in the machube had become known, bystanders would often point to a machudo and make a pejorative statement about his "wanting to look like a Pullo," and surrounding Fulbe or Batomba would join in laughter when the remark was particularly pointed. Such occasions occurred most often during market days or in larger towns such as Nikki, where machube attempted to dress up for the occasion. The physical appearance of the machube, as well as the fact that many of them were known, made their social position unmistakable, and underscored in the eyes of the Batomba and Fulbe the discrepancy between real and pretended status.

While most visible in the manner of dressing, imitation encompasses many other features of Fulbe culture. Among the machube, much of the imitation partially or entirely loses the function that the original behavior has for the Fulbe. Imitation of the complex age-class system of the Fulbe, for instance, is relatively common among machube. For the Fulbe, age-classes provide an important element of cohesion in a nomadic and highly fragmented group. Fulbe adolescents—male and female—enter a particular age-class usually when they are between thirteen and sixteen years old. They remain members in this class for the rest of their lives. Age-classes provide the framework for many social activities on the local level and create important social ties among Fulbe who travel with their herds. A member of a particular age-class can expect hospitality and support from other members no matter where he goes and irrespective of whether they have met before. For the machube, with restricted mobility, these functions are irrelevant. Moreover, the imitation of the age-class system among the machube is imperfect. Incorrect naming of age-classes is frequent, and information about membership is often incorrect. A similar change of function can be observed in the machube imitation of another important Fulbe institution, the flagellation of adolescent males, discussed below.

For the machube the fact that these institutions lose their original forms and functions is of no importance because the imitation of Fulbe customs serves a different purpose. It creates a symbolic proximity that moves the machube out of the isolation between Batomba and Fulbe and compensates for the low social evaluation which they experience. Low self-regard or the threat of being stigmatized seems frequently to give rise to the desire to affiliate with groups or individuals perceived as prestigious (Skolnick 1971; Holmes 1971). Imitation is one way to express this desire. In this respect, it matters little that the imitation does not produce an increase in the esteem in which the other groups hold the machube. Imitation seems to anticipate such an increase, and it is this anticipated prestige that reinforces the imitative behavior. There are many indications, including the self-blame about the birth history discussed earlier, that the stigma of being a machudo is intensely felt by the members of the group. Imitation moves the machube in their own eyes not only closer to the Fulbe, but permits them to see their social distance to other groups in a different light. The view that their own culture, especially the adherence to Islam, is superior to that of other groups in Borgou is widely held among the Fulbe. Sharing in Fulbe culture offers to the machube the chance of a vicarious participation in the Fulbe's aloofness from other groups. The distance from the Batomba can be seen as justified by a difference in culture, in particular since the culture in which one participates appears clearly preferable to that of the animistic Batomba. Even though this does not usually affect the rating of the three groups by the machube, a few machube respondents carry the self-enhancement to its conclusion and rank themselves higher than the Batomba.

Imitation of a superior by an inferior group may eventually lead to the disappearance of group boundaries, unless it is kept within predetermined limits either by external social sanctions or by internalized boundaries that restrict imitation to what is considered "proper." In line with the general absence of coercive control in the relationship between Fulbe and machube, imitative behavior by the machube is not restricted by the threat or the use of punitive interventions other than the ridicule mentioned earlier. The visible differences in build, skin color, and facial appearance contribute of course to the maintenance of the boundaries between the two groups, irrespective of the degree of cultural similarity achieved by imitation. It is equally important, however, that the machube follow internalized standards of permissible behavior. They do not, for instance, wear metal ornaments, or imitate the Fulbe manner of doing their hair. Nor do they herd or acquire cattle, the only imitative behavior that would have threatened the constituent element of the social position of the Fulbe. Machube respondents typically phrase such controls as their own independent decision: the machube "do not like" to imitate Fulbe behavior beyond the internalized limits. "The machube do not like to wear ornaments. The same applies to wearing one's hair. What the machube do, the Fulbe do not do, and what the Fulbe do, the machube do not want to do. One is obligated to this because the Pullo is the superior. There is a difference. They cannot dress like the Fulbe because the Fulbe always stand higher." Coercive control, which may once have existed, has become redundant. Internalized restraints keep machube actions perfectly within the bounds of behavior acceptable to the Fulbe.

The desire to imitate Fulbe behavior—a symbol perceived as enhancing one's own low status—is complemented by a construction of social distance among the machube themselves on the basis of the two different group origins. Little distinction is made by Fulbe or Batomba between the machube who were sold as captives of war and those who were abandoned by the Batomba. Only the Batomba have a separate designation for the latter, *binyobu*, but the term is a general label for a category of machube and is not used for specific individuals. The rapid integration of the two categories into a relatively uniform machube culture quickly obscured any differences between them for Fulbe and Batomba. Irrespective of their origin, the machube shared the same low status, and the Fulbe treated them alike in every respect. It is only among the machube themselves that the distinction survives, and each group tends to downgrade the other.[4] Machube of one group always rank themselves closer to the top of the social scale than members of the other group. As in imitating the Fulbe, this serves to enhance their status by identifying another group as even lower. Descendants of captives of war frequently base their low evaluation of the descendants of binyobu on the latter's stigmatizing appearance of the first teeth in the upper jaw. The positive self-evaluation of the descendants of captives of war may also be associated with the fact that a price was paid for them and that they thus represent a value, whereas the abandoned children were merely "thrown away." "Among the two kinds

4. Current research (Novak and Lerner 1968; Cooper and Jones 1969) indicates that similar pressures among members of stigmatized groups to disaffiliate themselves from others in the same situation occur in other cultural settings. They result frequently in the disorganization and disintegration of the group in question.

of machube the one who has been bought ranks higher because he has a value because of the sale, because he has been bought with something, while the other one whose teeth grow in the upper jaw has no value. He brings misfortune, he is not considered to be a human being. I belong to those who have been bought." Also, captives were once free, and their status was changed by force and not because they brought misfortune to their parents. Conversely, the descendants of abandoned children downgrade former captives of war because they lost their status through a sale or through force.

Frequently it becomes evident in the responses by both groups that the cognitive and affective functions of the mutual distancing and downgrading go beyond the mere compensation for low status and turn into open hostility. In fact, one of the remarkable things about the machube is the extraordinarily high rate of internal disintegration and aggression in the group. Batomba and Fulbe readily volunteer stories about machube proneness for fights and beatings. A good deal of the stigma and the low social esteem in which they are held is associated with violent behavior. They are frequently described as "wild" or as "uncivilized." This view, together with others that make up the social image of the machube as seen by Fulbe and Batomba, is clearly prejudiced. It is applied to every machudo and attributes characteristics to him that are seen as invariable parts of machube nature. But it does reflect an essential aspect of the reality of machube life. Throughout the period of this research, violent conflicts between machube were observed, particularly during market days, when they gathered in large numbers. In only one instance did such a conflict involve a machudo and a Batonu; in all others it was entirely limited to machube. In contrast, violent conflict among Batomba or among Fulbe occurs but rarely, and violence between Batomba and Fulbe is almost completely absent. The norms of mutual respect shared by both groups prevent it. Moreover the machube, even those who left the Fulbe and today live together in independent villages, have no functioning systems of mutual aid, or more than a rudimentary organization based on age or on kinship, both of which are highly developed among Batomba and Fulbe.

Several of the structural conditions under which the machube live may have contributed to their low internal cohesion. Machube did not exist before the arrival of the Fulbe in Borgou, and they appeared in considerable numbers probably only in the late eighteenth or early nineteenth century. Once a child or a captive became a machudo, moreover, his past family history and his previous social connections were completely severed. This has resulted in relatively short lineages among the machube, many of whom are today with the Fulbe only in the second or third generation. The frequent separation of machube families and the occasional transfer or sale of a machudo by his owner further prevented the growth of a stable pattern of internal group relations. Finally, machube settlements, with a few exceptions, were small, since many Fulbe had no stable residence. And even if several Fulbe families lived together, individual compounds were dispersed, offering the machube from one compound few opportunities for interaction with machube who belonged to other familes. Many machube lived a life of relative social isolation. One, two, or three to a Fulbe ga, they rarely had a chance to maintain sustained contact with other machube. Stable interaction and personal ties could develop only among small groups living together or in close proximity. Even nuclear families could frequently not develop because of the overriding interest of the Fulbe in their property.

In addition, among the Fulbe there is a tradition whose imitation provided something of an opportunity for the development of violence among the machube. It was mentioned earlier that the machube took over elements of the age-class system, even though the imitation was incomplete and retained none of the functions it had for the Fulbe. An important part of the age-class experience for the young Pullo was and continues to be flagellation. At irregular intervals, but usually during Muslim holidays, Fulbe of a particular area come together to participate in the activities surrounding it. The flagellation itself involves young male Fulbe between the ages of sixteen and twenty. Its manifest purpose is to display tolerance of pain: two young Fulbe, stripped to the waist, hit each other with a stick, and each partner tries to show as little sign of pain as possible by controlling his facial expression, sometimes with the aid of a mirror. The beating often produces open wounds that later scar over and thus remain visible, an effect that is intended. The functions of the flagellation are complex: it lays an important groundwork for the prestige structure among the adult Fulbe, provides a major chance for communication among Fulbe who often travel to the event over a long distance, and especially gives the young Fulbe of both sexes an opportunity to meet and establish relations that may lead to marriage. Where the machube imitated the age-class system, similar flagellations were organized but were apparently marred by much more violence than the carefully controlled flagellations of the Fulbe. But the existence of flagellation as a Fulbe tradition made violence almost certainly more familiar and acceptable to the machube than it would have been without it.

All these conditions were conducive to disintegration and eventually to a high incidence of violent behavior among the machube. But they did not produce it. Its ultimate cause can be found in the profound mistrust and the absence of internalized controls of violent behavior in the individual machudo. Mistrust is pervasive, covering even close social ties among neighbors, friends, or family members, and preventing the development of systems of mutual aid, which are such a basic element of the social structure of the other groups of Borgou and of African societies in general. Any thought of cooperation and of reliance on others seems inappropriate. It cannot work because it never did, or because one anticipates dissent and conflict.

Three possible causes of this mistrust suggest themselves. Recent research on aggression has shown that it may result from the experience of annoyance (Feshbach 1961; Doob and Wood 1972), from the experience of frustration (Geen 1971; Konecni and Doob 1972), or, under specific circumstances, as self-punitive behavior from the experience of aggression from others (Stone and Hokanson 1969) or of self-blame or guilt (Costanzo 1970). All three sources of aggression may be present among the machube. The most likely one appears to be the experience of annoyance from the frequent and unconcealed expression of contempt, low social esteem, and sometimes the open verbal hostility of the Batomba and Fulbe. Both groups see no reason to hide their low regard of the machube, and make derogatory comments about them, unperturbed by their presence. The view of machube aggression as a result of frustration poses some problems. It is clear that one aspect of the ideological adjustment to-subordination by the machube lies in a severe curtailment of their goals. Where this adjustment is successful, frustration should not appear. Still, opportunities for frustration existed, as in the arbitrary intervention by the Fulbe in machube behavior, in the separation of the parents of a child, or in the transfer of a machudo in the course of inheritance, sale, or gift exchange. Finally, there is the possibility that aggression appeared in the group as a self-punitive act. With the strong self-blame present among the machube and associated with their own view of themselves, there is reason to assume that it may have given rise to a high rate of internal violence in the group.

Irrespective of its origins, high internal aggression seems to coincide with the nonavailability of targets for aggression other than members of one's own group. In the case of the machube, their peculiar ideological construction of the world exculpates both Batomba and Fulbe from the responsibility for their low social position. Moreover, the outlook that leads to the imitation of the Fulbe by the machube precludes deliberate and lasting hostility or resentment against them. Machube aggression has nowhere to go, except against other machube.

The permanent and unpredictable possibility of conflict among the machube demands permanent vigilance and preparedness. Again, the model for the violence that eventually appears among the machube originates with the Fulbe, but it is reinterpreted to make it compatible with the requirements of machube ideology. Two elements of Fulbe culture undergo this change. The first is the Fulbe custom of wearing a stick as an almost permanent part of their attire, a peripheral component of a herding culture. The machube imitate this custom, but the thin stick that is primarily used for directing cattle becomes now a means of violence or of defense against it: on their trips to markets or to towns such as Nikki, and often in larger machube settlements, the machube carry heavy sticks, which are frequently weighted at the end with wire or with metal pieces, or with leather whips into which wire or metal is woven. These easily visible symbols of the "wildness" and "brutality" of the machube are the target of much open derision by the other groups, who know that the machube use the tools of violence only among themselves.

The second means of preparedness against violence among the machube consists of protective magic. Fulbe magic is complex, and their expertise in it is recognized by all other groups in Borgou. Most of it remains inaccessible to the machube. Only two kinds have been imitated and developed extensively: *lekki sauru,* the substance that protects against beating with sticks, and *lekki jamdi,* which protects against iron—that is, against knives. Both are produced by machube, but those acquired from Fulbe or from Hausa traders are generally considered more effective. All machube respondents consider the two substances the most important, and their acquisition often requires considerable expense. And all see it in close relationship to the pervasive threat of conflict: "There is a substance against the stick and against the knife. . . . Everyone here makes it. . . . We make it because a man who walks alone never knows when fate is going to bring him a quarrel with others. If you have this substance in the body . . . and someone beats you, you don't feel anything. And the knife, too, cannot enter your body. One can never know the thoughts of others. Even between man and wife one never knows what is at the basis of thought."

CONCLUSIONS

The ideological system of the machube consists of a number of interrelated beliefs. The most important of them is the acceptance of the myth of the fateful birth among those machube who are descendants of abandoned children. One effect of this is the creation of feelings of shame and self-blame, which indicate at least a partial acceptance of the responsibility for their present fate by the machube themselves. The second and closely related effect is that it exculpates the Batomba from the initial abandonment of their children and the Fulbe from the subsequent enslavement of the machube. The exoneration of the Fulbe is reinforced by the belief that the effects of the birth are eliminated through living with them. The Fulbe thus become the primary reference group for the machube: affiliation with them and imitation of their culture offer a variety of compensations for the stigma and the limitations of machube life. While the elimination of the effects of birth is of interest only to those machube whose ancestors were abandoned by the Batomba, the benefits of affiliation with and imitation of the Fulbe apply to both machube groups. These basic elements of the ideology of the machube are complemented by a number of flexible explanatory concepts that provide a meaningful and acceptable interpretation of both recurrent and unique experiences in the relationship with the Fulbe.

The ideology is completed by the relations among the machube themselves. Mutual distancing and downgrading between the two groups of different origin provide each with enhanced self-esteem. But they also facilitate a high rate of internal conflict. Since both Batomba and Fulbe appear free from blame for the situation of the machube, since the machube attach a strong positive value to the Fulbe, and since they have no social interaction with groups other than Batomba and Fulbe, aggressive behavior remains internal to the group. The machube themselves appear to each other as the only acceptable targets for conflict.

The framework of meaning that the machube apply to their experience guides and limits their behavior in such a way that their inferiority and dependence persist with a minimum of friction. Coercive control is not only absent, it is not even known. The cognitive and behavioral adjustment of the machube to servitude is so perfect that the Fulbe see no need to anticipate resistance and to devise coercive interventions. The thought of resistance does not occur to the individual machudo. And occasionally, the ideological reversal of the world of the machube is complete. Servitude appears as the realm of freedom:

Q: What happened if the orders [of the Fulbe] were not carried out?
A: Nothing happened, because the machube did carry out all orders. They found that already their grandparents carried out orders, and nobody has refused. I am contented to be with the Fulbe because the Pullo does not take my possessions away, and every time I am with the Fulbe they let me make my own fields, and the Fulbe let me weave and make my cloths, and if I make them I make them for their children, too. Being with the Fulbe I feel free. That is why I am satisfied with my life.

Two more general results emerge from the study of machube ideology. Its longevity, its complexity, and its systematic character show, first, that subordination does not necessarily produce self-corrective conflict. The astonishing stability of the relationship between machube and Fulbe and the absence of coercive control demonstrate that even structures of extreme inequality can persist over a long time with little or no opposition. This is, of course, not only the case in Borgou. Even a cursory look at the history of most societies reveals long periods when dependent groups contributed, through their adjustment to the inequality to which they were subjected, to the maintenance of the very structure that suppressed and exploited them.

Second, the study of the ideological beliefs of the machube shows the need to return to empirical research on false consciousness. The concept of false consciousness has been frequently misinterpreted and dismissed as being purely a matter of normative judgment. In its original use by Marx and Engels, the term identifies consciousness that is a causal determinant of the persistence of structures of rule and social inequality over time. Interpreted in this way the concept directs research to the origins, the forms, and the causal effects of false consciousness. Such research has been greatly neglected in the study of social inequality in recent decades. This is particularly evident in the study of slavery. Whereas its structural characteristics have been described relatively frequently, very little is known about the interpretation of their situation by slave or servile groups. This applies to false consciousness of the kind described in this chapter, as well as to reactions to servitude or slavery that lead to resistance and conflict. Only in this way can a better understanding of the complex interaction between the structural and the subjective dimension of servitude be gained.

GLOSSARY

binyobu: slaves who were abandoned as children because of their fateful birth, or who are descendants of such children.
ga: the circular arrangement of huts of a Fulbe family.
gando: a camplike settlement of *gandogibu*, usually in the vicinity of seats of *wasangari*.
gandogibu: a slave group, subordinate to *wasangari* and mainly of Batomba origin.
gani: annual reunion of Batomba in Nikki, centering around ritual worship of ancestors.
gossiko: a Batonu whose office involves the performance of protective and purifying rituals for parents whose child grows its first teeth in the upper jaw. The gossiko may also kill such children or keep them as *yobu*.
hoddirore: a Fulfulde term denoting fate or unpredictable turns of events.
lekki: defensive or aggressive magic of the Fulbe.
lekki jamdi: magic that protects against knife attacks.

lekki sauru: magic that protects against beating with a stick.

machudo (pl. *machube*): member of a slave or servile population in the Borgou area, subordinate to the Fulbe but mainly of Batomba origin.

tabu: longer warfare between *wasangari*.

tkiriku: slave servants of *wasangari*.

wasangari: the Batomba aristocracy.

wasangariru: short raids carried out by *wasangari* into the territory of neighboring *wasangari*.

yo (pl. *yobu*): a slave or servant of a Batomba commoner.

REFERENCES

ORAL SOURCES

The oral sources for this chapter include 198 taped interviews with machube, carried out in 1968 in the area surrounding Nikki in northern Benin. All direct quotations of machube in the text are taken from this material.

UNPUBLISHED SOURCE

Baldus, B. 1972. Social cohesion in liberal systems. An examination of the problem of order in capitalist societies. Mimeographed. Toronto.

Baldus, B. 1976. Social control in capitalist societies. An examination of the problem of order in liberal democracies. Mimeographed. Toronto.

PUBLISHED SOURCES

Baldus, B. 1975. The study of power: Suggestions for an alternative. *Canadian J. Sociol.* 1:179-201.

Cooper, J., and Jones, E. E. 1969. Opinion divergence as a strategy to avoid being mis-cast. *J. Personality soc. Psychol.* 13:23-30.

Costanzo, P. R. 1970. Conformity development as a function of self-blame. *J. Personality soc. Psychol.* 14:366-74.

Dahrendorf, R. 1969a. On the origin of inequality among men. In *Social inequality*, ed. A. Betaille. Harmondsworth, Eng.

———. 1969b. *Class and class conflict in industrial society*. Stanford.

Doob, A. H., and Wood, L. 1972. Catharsis and aggression: the effects of annoyance and retaliation on aggressive behavior. *J. Personality soc. Psychol.* 22:156-62.

Durkheim, E. 1915. *The elementary forms of the religious life*. London.

Etzioni, A. 1968. *The active society*. New York.

Feshbach, S. 1961. The stimulating vs. cathartic effects of vicarious aggressive activity. *J. abnorm. soc. Psychol.* 63:381-85.

Geen, R. G. 1971. Effects of frustration, attack, and prior training in aggressiveness upon aggressive behavior. In *Human social behavior: a contemporary view of experimental research*, ed. R. A. Baron and R. M. Liebert. Homewood, Ill.

Holmes, D. W. 1971. Compensation for ego threat: two experiments. *J. Personality soc. Psychol.* 18:234-37.

Hopen, C. E. 1958. *The pastoral Fulbe in Gwandu*. London.

Konecni, V. J., and Doob, A. H. 1972. Catharsis through displacement of aggression. *J. Personality soc. Psychol.* 23:379-87.

Lombard, J. 1965. *Structures de type "féodal" en Afrique noire*. Paris, The Hague.

Moore, W. E. 1963. *Social change*. Englewood Cliffs, N.J.

Novak, D. W., and Lerner, M. J. 1968. Rejection as a consequence of perceived similarity. *J. Personality soc. Psychol.* 9:147-52.

Parsons, T. 1951. *The social system*. New York.

Skolnick, P. 1971. Reactions to personal evaluations: a failure to replicate. *J. Personality soc. Psychol.* 18:62-67.

Stone, L. J., and Hokanson, J. E. 1969. Arousal reduction via self-punitive behavior. *J. Personality soc. Psychol.* 12:72-79.

Tannenbaum, F. 1946. *Slave and citizen*. New York.

Tocqueville, A. de. 1835/1945. *Democracy in America*. Vintage Book ed., 1945. New York.

Tumin, M. M. 1967. *Social stratification*. Englewood Cliffs, N. J.

Wirth, L. 1970. The problem of minority groups. In *Minority responses*, ed. M. Kurokawa. New York.

Index

Index

DESIGNED BY RON FENDEL
COMPOSED BY FOX VALLEY TYPESETTING, MENASHA, WISCONSIN
MANUFACTURED BY THE MAPLE PRESS COMPANY, YORK, PENNSYLVANIA
TEXT IS SET IN TIMES ROMAN, DISPLAY LINES IN BODONI AND TIMES ROMAN

ധ

Library of Congress Cataloging in Publication Data
Main entry under title:
Slavery in Africa.
Includes bibliographies and index.
1. Slavery in Africa, Sub-Saharan—Addresses, essays, lectures.
I. Miers, Suzanne. II. Kopytoff, Igor.
HT1427.S8S58   301.44'93'0967   76-53653
ISBN 0-299-07330-0